# Contents

*3*

# Educators
## Program

Chair
**Colleen Case**
Schoolcraft College

4

# Conference Abstracts and Applications

**Educators Program**

Colleen Case
Schoolcraft College

**Panels**

Kathryn Saunders
ThinkTech

**Emerging Technologies**

Mk Haley
Walt Disney Imagineering

**Sketches & Applications**

Dena Slothower
Stanford University

Computer Graphics Annual Conference Series, 2001
A Publication of ACM SIGGRAPH

SIGGRAPH 2001 Conference Abstracts and Applications

COMPUTER GRAPHICS
Annual Conference Series, 2001

The Association for Computing Machinery, Inc.
1515 Broadway
New York, New York 10036 USA

ISBN 1-58113-403-7
ISSN 1098-6138
ACM Order No. 435013

Additional copies may be ordered pre-paid from:
ACM Order Department
P.O. Box 12114
Church Street Station
New York, New York 10257 USA

Or, for information on accepted European currencies
and exchange rates, contact:
ACM European Service Center
108 Cowley Road
Oxford OX4 1JF
United Kingdom
+44.1.865.382338
+44.1.865.381338 fax

Credit card orders from U.S. and Canada:
800.342.6626

Credit card orders from the New York
metropolitan area and outside the U.S.:
+1.212.626.0500

Single copy orders placed by fax:
+1.212.944.1318

Credit card orders may also be placed by mail.

Electronic mail inquiries may be directed to:
orders@acm.org

Please include your ACM member number and
the ACM order number with your order.

Background Image Credits
Page 3: Perspective Study of a Chalice, Paolo Uccello, 1430-40.
Page 4, 5, 6, 7: W. S. Burroughs Calculating Machine, Patent document, 1888
Page 56, 57, 58, 59: Planetary Machines, William Pearson, The Cyclopaedea, 1820
Page 110, 111, 112, 113, 137: Multiplying or Dividing Machine, Otto Steiger, Patent document, 1895
Page 138, 139, 140, 141: Calculation Diagram, Vilhelm Bjerknes, Dynamic Meteorology and Hydrography, 1910

# CONTENTS

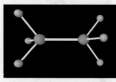

5

*Chair*
COLLEEN CASE
Schoolcraft College

*Committee*
JAMES MOHLER
Purdue University

JACQUELYN FORD MORIE
USC Institute for
Creative Technologies

ART DURINSKI
The Durinski Design Group

STEPHEN WROBLE
Schoolcraft College

MARK HARRIS
Schoolcraft College

MICHAEL MEHALL
Schoolcraft College

SUSAN LUPO
Schoolcraft College

*Administrative Assistant*
MELINDA BUSH
Schoolcraft College

*Jury*
JAMES MOHLER
Purdue University

ART DURINSKI
The Durinski Design Group

JACQUELYN FORD MORIE
USC Institute for
Creative Technologies

STEPHEN WROBLE
Schoolcraft College

MICHAEL MEHALL
Schoolcraft College

*6*

"TELL ME AND I MAY FORGET,
SHOW ME AND I MAY NOT REMEMBER,
INVOLVE ME AND I WILL UNDERSTAND AND LEARN."
– *Native American Saying*

*Rethink what "Education" is.*
*Learning concerns us all.*
*Learn through relevant experience.*
*Think together.*

Like all facets of work and society, education is reinventing itself in response to the growing presence of digital technologies, visual communication, and the expanding universe of knowledge. This year's Educators Program presenters have designed experiences that help attendees discover innovative and creative uses of computer graphics and interactive techniques for learning. They focus on physical and virtual computer-supported, collaborative-learning environments and activities or materials that take advantage of digital resources and engage the learner.

*New!* The SIGGRAPH 2001 Educators Program offered Open Forums where conference participants and presenters joined in a dialogue that encouraged collective observation and thought, enabling groups to think beyond their members' individual limitations.

Forums were designed to cluster the shared interests of SIGGRAPH presenters and attendees. Topics included:

- The Promise of the Web for Learning
- The Emerging Computer Graphics Discipline
- Games and Education
- Explorations in Visual Communications and Meaning
- Studio Views on Demo Tapes
- The Teaching of Computer Graphics in Computer Science Curriculum
- The Teaching of Computer Graphics in Art & Design Cirriculm

We can no longer afford to look at education simply as the transmission of information from an instructor to students. We must focus on the social engineering of multidisciplinary collaborative learning spaces in order to create the next generation of innovative thinkers who utilize new communications and media to meet the challenges of the 21st century.

*Colleen Case*
*Educators Program Chair*

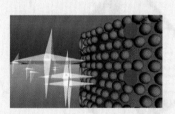

7

# I.R.I.S.: New Models of Communication

*Contact*
Murry Christensen
The Goldman Sachs Group, Inc.
180 Maiden Lane, 21st Floor
New York, New York 10038
USA
+1.212.357.7567
murry.christensen@gs.com

Eli Kuslansky
4D Visual

Goldman Sachs operates in a global digital economy moving at warp speed, where knowledge capital is key. In this environment, Goldman Sachs' knowledge workers must be open thinkers who quickly formulate meaningful patterns from a high volume of information drawn from multiple sources. Informed decision making in financial markets requires new visualization models that are multi-dimensional yet easy to understand. To manage this information, maintain a keen competitive edge, and continue to lead the market, Goldman Sachs' workforce needs to constantly hone the interpretive skills that are fundamental to all of the company's revenue activities.

To set the tone of the 180 Maiden Lane training center as a thought-provoking and engaging learning environment, we created a new aesthetic experience that models the world in which Goldman Sachs does business. The Intelligent Recognition Inference System (I.R.I.S.) is an advanced computer graphic visualization system that simulates and interprets the processes, patterns, and flow of the environment in which a 21st-century knowledge company operates. Using the languages of learning, culture, and science, I.R.I.S. brings into focus the forces that will shape new forms of business.

It is an icon from the future.

On entering the 180 Maiden Lane learning center, a visitor en route to a training session encounters a series of four horizontally mounted flat-panel HDTV monitors that display a series of programs on advanced visualization. The onscreen imagery forms patterns of movement and growth in a simulated universe, illustrating relationships among market data, narrative and fact, cycles and randomness. With I.R.I.S., the visitor is introduced to insights on how time, culture, behavior, and movement influence patterns and relationships within systems.

## An Experiential Walk-Through
### Content
On-screen, the visitor sees a program in a series of discrete but related segments. Each segment runs from 15 to 180 seconds and cycles throughout the program. The segments are presented in a 3D computer-generated synthetic environment that uses live data feeds to reflect the realities of the real world, where things change constantly and chaotically.

The content speaks to the two fundamental ways we gather information: language and images. Complex ideas live in a metascape of language, requiring a slower pace and attention that allows people to think, a metascape that is continuously evolving, not constantly concluding. Each segment is framed with a display of moving text and images that both introduces and completes that segment.

### Image Recognition
For image recognition, I.R.I.S. models the thought process involved in interpreting graphics by boiling it down to its rich and dynamic essences. Like the "smart posters" that one sees while waiting for a train, these images create mental maps of disparate data and the

relationships between them in a short timeframe. The images challenge the assumptions of the visitors and inspire them to think in a new way that is appropriate for acquiring new skills at the learning center.

### Operating in a Created Environment
All real and virtual organisms, like companies and industries, operate in organic and dynamic environments. Sensing your place and direction in these environments is a gateway to knowledge. With a motion-tracking video camera, I.R.I.S. places the visitor in the program, creates a dialogue between the real and virtual environments, and expands the level of interaction and association with the information. The visitor's movement in the room and relative distance from the installation triggers a process that switches data sets and modifies segments of the program. This creates a never-repeating environment in which viewers participate and with which they interact.

## Physical Architecture
The transformation to a digital economy involves merging disparate sciences, from economics to genetics and information technology. New models of communications, integrated financial services, and physical and virtual architectures will evolve. With these sweeping changes in mind, the physical architecture of I.R.I.S. is designed with an advanced mounting system and next-generation, flat-panel, high-definition digital television (HDTV) displays.

The installation is composed of four custom-built stainless-steel poles. Mounted on each wing-shaped pole is a curved and frosted glass panel and a 42-inch HDTV monitor. Ten feet in front of these monitors and embedded in the ceiling is a three-CCD (Charged Coupled Device) color digital video camera connected to a high-speed image processor. This camera tracks the motions and traffic patterns in the training center.

Powering the four HDTV monitors is an SGI Onyx Reality 2 server that sends digital video signals to the monitors in real time. A high-speed Internet connection combines these feeds with a database of parameters and pre-rendered programming and then composites them into a digital video signal. These composite images are processed in the SGI Onyx 2 and sent to the HDTV screens.

View of installation.

Detail of "Roots."

# Internet Studios: Teaching Architectural Design Online in the United States and Latin America

*Contact*
Alfredo Andia
Florida International University
Internet Studio Consortium
236 VH Building
School of Architecture
Miami, Florida 33199 USA
+1.305.348.6703
alfredoandia@yahoo.com

This project is one of the most extreme combinations of computer graphic technology and Internet communication in contemporary architectural education. The findings can be applied to any discipline that consists of a large number of participants within a design setting. Over the past two years, the experiments have allowed more than 130 students and 20 professors from seven schools of architecture, in Miami, Buenos Aires, Caracas, Santiago de Chile, Valparaiso, Mar del Plata, and Santa Fe de Argentina, to work concurrently in a semester-long design studio. Most of the collaboration has been accomplished by using low-bandwidth Internet communication such as Web publishing, Chat, Web3D, RealPlayer, IP videoconferencing, CAD software, and other technologies such as ISDN broadcasting. New grants from Global Crossing, Cisco Systems, and Lucent Technologies support future experimentation with high-bandwidth technologies on the Internet[2] Abilene Network.

## Traditional Architectural Studios

Typically, design studios are at the core of the curriculum in architectural teaching. These studios are usually held in rooms with drafting tables, on which students develop models, sketches, architectural drawings, and perspectives of the projects assigned during the semester. Architectural studios not only simulate the real-time experience of working in an architectural office, but also provide a very intense interpersonal environment for students to learn from each other as they search for design solutions. Knowledge, solution strategies, and design culture are transmitted by what Donald Schon calls a process of "tacit learning."[3] "Tacit learning" cannot be fully explained or fully structured. It is transmitted by examples, gestures, and acts, and developed by investigation of problems as they arise.

Studio reviews, or design juries, are the traditional method of assessing student architectural work. Conventionally, students pin their drawings to a wall behind their physical models and explain their design concepts orally to professors, visiting critics, and students who gather around the pin-up space. After the oral presentation is completed, critics develop oral arguments for or against different aspects of the student's design. After the presentation and the critique are completed, the pin-up spaces are dismantled, and the jury moves on to review the next student.

## The Objectives

The primary question of this study is: How can we use new-media technologies to enrich the learning environment offered in the traditional design studio? This is a very complex question, since most distance-education software design and online teaching experiences support a more structured mode of teaching and learning. Thus, the study's objectives are:

- Exploration of technologies and techniques that support rich interaction among a large number of international participants with methodologies that sustain a variety of learning styles and technological conditions.

- Development of pedagogical strategies for these technologies and techniques with the objective of increasing the "speed" of architectural progress in these design communities.

- To reposition the creative processes of architecture in a highly digital environment by increasing skills and, ultimately, altering the design methodologies, imagination, and ambition in improving urban life.

## Low-Bandwidth Technology: Chat, Web Publishing, and IP Videoconferences

The initial experiments of the Internet Studios initiative explored synchronous and asynchronous collaboration with low-bandwidth technology. This was necessary due to technological conditions in the participating Latin American schools of architecture. The most popular technique for weekly synchronous reviews of student work was a combination of chat and Web publishing that we called Web-chat. Students posted their weekly work on individual Web pages, then professors and visiting critics from all over the world set a time to review the students' pages. Student Web pages contained CAD renderings, process drawings, photographs of physical models, video animations, and Flash animations. Students presented this work via Web pages and chat, and then received instant responses from reviewers.

Weekly synchronous communication was also supported by unstructured IP videoconferences through the low-bandwidth Internet (software: Netmeeting, Vocaltec, and CU-SeeMe). The IP videoconference technology worked well for one-to-one communication among students and/or for professor coordination. However, it was considered too disruptive for online reviews with a large number of participants. Initially, every effort was made to conduct reviews using an IP videoconference format and supported by students' Web-page publication. However, surprisingly, over time, the combination of chat and Web pages became the preferred method for reviews, and videoconferences became unnecessary. The Web-chat technology was universally available (it required only a Java-enabled browser), and it provided instantaneous feedback. IP videoconferencing proved to be useful for developing initial social contacts among the teams.

## Evaluating Studio Reviews: Real Classrooms vs. Online Low-Bandwidth

Several experimental evaluations were conducted to compare real vs. virtual studio reviews. We conducted online and local reviews at the same time and began to compare results from evaluations, record anecdotal references, and document the behavioral differences of participants based on each of the environments. The most important conclusions:

9

### Review Tolerance

Participants in online reviews via Web-chat mode tended to have lower levels of time tolerance. Typically, review teams using Web-chat would spend no more than five minutes with each student project. Teams in traditional real-time settings were willing to spend 15 to 20 minutes per student.

### Oral vs. Written Explanations

Surveys showed that student explanations via chat were more direct, articulate, and memorable to the reviewer than oral explanations.

### Oral vs. Written Response

Reviewers also noted that online comments could be written simultaneously, and reviewers could quickly notice the similarity of their criticism without waiting for everybody to speak.

### Electronic Anonymity

Another important observation refers to the lower level of diplomacy that is sometimes apparent in chat environments, where one can go directly to the point without reacting to a student's facial reaction.

### Synchronous and Asynchronous Review Space

In traditional environments, reviewers can see the student work only during the pin-up time. In the online environment, reviewers usually become familiar with the student Web pages prior to the Web-chat review.

### HIGH-BANDWIDTH TECHNOLOGY:
### ISDN VIDEOCONFERENCE AND INTERNET 2 IP MULTICASTING

Only ISDN videoconference technology was tested in our Internet Studios during 1999 and 2000. Due to cost constraints, we maintain this technology for very structured sessions, which occur only two to three times per semester. During 2000, we obtained grants that provided 40 Gbps connections with major academic networks in the Americas through the Global Crossing inter-oceanic link. The grants support a DS3 connection in every country where the intercontinental network lands in Latin America and the Caribbean. The DS3 connection will link to our POP server in the US, which in turn will connect the universities to Internet 2. In testing this new bandwidth, we began to experiment with node-rooms with wide-IP multicasting technologies such as Access Grid on Internet 2. The Access Grid allows constant videoconference concurrency for a large number of participants. Each video and audio channel is connected at 800kbps, which allows for excellent-quality transmission. The experiment used a system that cost less than $15,000. It included three computers, three projectors, and a specially designed audio-video system.

### EVALUATING STUDIO REVIEWS IN REAL CLASSROOMS VS. ONLINE HIGH-BANDWIDTH ENVIRONMENTS

As stated above, our experience with high-bandwidth technology is very limited. However, our initial evaluation revealed the following:

### Similar Review Culture

Design reviewers in both real-time proximity and high-bandwidth networks tend to follow the diplomacy, time tolerance, and review format of traditional studio jury processes.

### Potential for Distraction

Although time tolerance and review formats are similar, spectators of the multicasting environment are more easily distracted than if they were in real review spaces. Techniques for moderating multicasting events have became elements of design. A very structured program is generally recommended. Our experience also suggests that, for online juries, tolerance lasts one to 1.5 hours, while in real environments they last approximately three hours.

### Potential for Supporting A New Studio Culture Online

Our initial evaluations of IP multicasting technology, such as the Access Grid on Internet 2, have shown that this technology has more value in building social relationships than the more structured reviews. This is a very important factor in the studio experience, and one that needs to be maintained.

### Lack of Spatial Orientation

Most high-bandwidth technologies still resemble human interaction at the level of a television monitor. The evaluators observed that more work remains to be done on physical design and layout to engage audiences with the actions and behaviors that transpire in traditional studios.

### NEW PROPOSALS

Our evaluations and observations will be translated into the following specific projects for the next academic year:

An improved low-bandwidth review space. Two schools of architecture that participate in the Internet Studio consortium are designing and testing a video-chat interface for design review. The video-chat combines three frames in a single web page. In the bottom-right frame, there is a chat area. The bottom-left frame is an embedded RealPlayer video window for live broadcast. And the top frame is a space where students can publish their work.

### WebCam for Low-Bandwidth Social Space

During the Fall of 2001, two schools are incorporating Web cams in their studio spaces, with CU-SeeMe conferencing, to allow more social interaction among students in the studios.

*Synthetic World: iStudio for Low-Bandwidth Interface*
We are also beginning to develop 3D worlds that can structure "community behavior" in virtual systems. We have initiated this work based on critical observations of similar experiments, such as MUS, MOOS, DIVE,[1] MASSIVE,[2] and many other popular versions of virtual worlds. The virtual studio space prototype, iStudio, investigates the software design and human behavior of studio life in digital conditions. The design of the prototype does not attempt to recreate the space of the traditional studio. Instead, it supports community actions in design education. Three large box-rooms appear when one enters the iStudio:

1. The exhibit room, where students virtually pin-up their process during the semester.
2. The review rooms: Four virtual rooms where virtual reviews are held.
3. The forum: A space for building virtual community life. In this space, private meetings are held in secluded rooms, and public meetings, such as exhibitions and lectures, occur.

One of the most important aspects of a virtual world is the need to rebuild the human body. The body helps to develop a sense of scale and a feeling of community. When they enter a world, users can always see the red bodies of the all the avatars that are using the system; one red avatar represents each user.

The eye and the body are attached-but-separate concepts in the iStudio. The body of the avatar only moves horizontally in the planes that users visit. But users can move freely in 3D. The hand and the body are also attached-but-separate concepts in the iStudio. Whenever users touch one of the elements in the 3D space, user movement is triggered. In this way, users can travel quickly among student files, rooms, and boxes.

Communication among users is chat-based. Via local software, the text in the chat is transformed into voice. Icons in the world can also trigger other communication applications to open, such as IP videoconferences, Web-page browsing, etc. Students are required to design their own exhibit spaces and review rooms. Files such as JPEGS, CAD, videos, and audio files are uploaded into the iStudio via a simple Web interface. Each of the virtual walls can be edited remotely by using Java applets in the student Web pages. The iStudio is designed to render different spaces in stages, so users never see the complete world at one time. The goal is to keep the world accessible to users with low-bandwidth technology (less than 1,000 polygons) and a reduced number of texture maps at all times.

*Grants for "Last-Mile" High-Bandwidth Projects*
Although Latin America is currently connecting to the first 40 Gbps inter-oceanic and terrestrial network, additional work is required to connect each university and architectural school to the national nodes of high-speed networks and Internet 2. At the Summit of the American Presidents held in Santiago de Chile in 1998, the "last mile," between the universities and the national nodes, was recognized as the most difficult aspect of networking

in Latin America. The Internet Studio experience demonstrates the usability of the technology. Members of the Internet Studio consortium are working closely with national institutions such as Educ.ar (Argentina) and Reuna (Chile) to develop and promote "last-mile" grants that will support high-bandwidth projects.

*Space Design for High-Bandwidth Video Spaces*
One frequently observed situation when high-bandwidth videoconferences are conducted, is that they engage the participants at the level of a television screen. As architects, some participants are taking the initiative to design new video spaces, that can absorb other senses of the human body. For example one group is working on developing a prototype of an Internet Studio room in which video projectors enlarge human figures to 1:1 scale. The walls on which the images are projected are no longer video walls. They are areas of social interaction in which ad hoc events can occur. Another technique is to project horizontally by using blue-screened table surfaces, where physical models and drawings can be placed, viewed, touched, and acted on remotely.

CONCLUSION
Our experiences with several low-bandwidth Internet technologies indicate that the preferred method for virtual design reviews is the combination of student Web-page publishing and chat. Technologies that we favored initially, such as IP videoconferencing, were found to be useful in one-to-one conversations but did not support large design review sessions. Several differences were found between traditional review procedures and online session. Among online reviewers, time tolerance tends to be smaller, and student explanations and commentaries tend to be more direct, precise, and shielded by electronic anonymity. This is a product of the ability to edit information online and the constant accessibility reviewers have to student material during the semester.

This experience has triggered a set of observations and conclusions for conducting Internet studios in low-bandwidth conditions, and translated into a series of follow-on projects. We are working to develop a better Web-page interface with Web publishing, chat, and IP video broadcasting. We are testing Web-cam technology to support spontaneous multimedia collaboration. And we are developing virtual reality prototypes that support creation of virtual communities.

11

We have more limited experience with high-bandwidth technology and expect to work with it more in 2001, due to a series of grants that allow us to experiment with Internet 2 in Latin America. In our initial observations, we found that there is no significant difference between in studio design reviews and reviews that use high-bandwidth technologies. Similar cultural and behavioral codes are observed on both sides of the virtual experience. Among the slight differences we found were a higher potential for distraction in online audiences and a need to develop better spaces for interaction. These conclusions have prompted a number of initiatives for improving the physical design of interactive spaces. In the future, designs will attempt to enhance engagement of the body and senses of the participants in their meetings.

In the past two years, we have proven that the online design studio experience can be accomplished, and all of the participants acquired an increased appreciation of their ability to communicate, teach, and learn remotely. As we continue to experiment with the technology, we are starting to develop academic agreements and curricula to offer post-graduate degrees in conjunction with the participating US and Latin American universities.

ACKNOWLEDGMENTS
I would like to thank the professors, researchers, students, and the large number of international reviewers who participated in the experience. The names and work of the participants can be found in the studio Web site:

miami00.tripod.com

Figure 1.
Weekly synchronous communication was supported by unstructured IP-video-conferences over regular Internet connections (top). However, the most popular method for weekly synchronous reviews and communication was Web-chat (bottom).

Figure 2.
The virtual studio space prototype, iStudio, investigates the software design and human behavior of studio life in digital conditions. Students and professors interact in the prototype with avatars in two VRML review rooms that are supported with chat and Web page links.

References
1. Carlsson, C. & Hagsand, O. (1993). DIVE: A platform for multi-user virtual environments. *Computer Graphics*, 17 (6), 663-669.
2. Greenhalgh, C. & Benford, S. (1995). MASSIVE: A collaborative virtual environment for teleconferencing. ACM *Transactions on Computer-Human Interaction*, 2 (3), 239-261.
3. Schon, D. (1984). *The reflective practitioner: How professionals think in action*. Basic Books. bn

*12*

# Speeder Reader: An Experiment in the Future of Reading

*Contact*
Maribeth Back
Xerox PARC
3333 Coyote Hill Road
Palo Alto, California 94304 USA
+1.650.812.4726
back@parc.xerox.com

Jonathan Cohen
Rich Gold
Steve Harrison
Scott Minneman
Xerox PARC

Speeder Reader is an interactive reading station built around two primary ideas: dynamic text, especially RSVP (rapid serial visual presentation), and driving as an interface metaphor. As words flash one at a time on a screen, the reader controls the speed of the words with a gas pedal (up to 1,850 words per minute). Text selection is performed with a steering wheel. Thus, one can "drive through a book." Speeder Reader leverages the familiar activity of driving an automobile (or, in the case of children, operating a speed-racing video game) to allow comfortable and intuitive access to the possibly less familiar world of interactive text.

Speeder Reader was designed as part of a six-month museum exhibit at the Tech Museum of Innovation in San Jose. The exhibit, titled "XFR: Experiments in the Future of Reading," was designed and built by the RED (Research in Experimental Documents) group at Xerox PARC. It ran from March to September, 2000 and attracted about 350,000 visitors. In 2001, XFR will begin a three-year tour to other science and technology museums.

The topic RED chose for the exhibition was reading and technology, and in particular how digital technology impacts nearly everything we read. The XFR exhibit presents a series of explorations in new ways of experiencing text, including new genres, new styles of interaction, and unusual media. Because the exhibit took place within the context of a modern technology museum, the XFR exhibits are primarily interactive and hands-on.

## The XFR Exhibits
The XFR exhibits fall roughly into three categories: augmented books, machine reading, and reading and the world.

In augmented books, we expanded on the idea of the personal reader and experimented with different modalities, interfaces, and designs to discover how the reader-author contract can be reinforced to add depth without distraction. Some examples of these different modalities are alternative physical relationships to text, dynamic arrangements of text and images under personal control, and exploration of how an added modality (sound or auditory illustration) might affect the reader-author relationship. The exhibits include a book that users play like an instrument, a drive-through book (Speeder Reader) and a life-size walk-through comic book.

Machine reading showed machines that did the actual reading of documents, through OCR (optical character recognition) or other visual analysis. These machines then interpreted the data they read into some other modality, such as speech or pictures. For example, an OCR-to-speech-synthesis system was installed in the form of a robotic dog, which read aloud whatever was placed in front of it. Reading and the world allows visitors to examine the history of reading, the varieties of its current proliferation, and some experimental art in the world of book arts.

## Analyzing the Audience
The exhbits were designed primarily for teenagers 10 to 14 years old, although we tried to make sure that the exhibit language and presentation would be enjoyable and accessible for everyone, including younger children and adults. Though the topic of the exhibit is reading, many of the exhibits examine reading in conjunction with image or sound, so they provide some content for non-readers. The Tech Museum gets about 700,000 visitors per year. Many mixed-age family groups come through. Every morning and afternoon, waves of schoolchildren are delivered by the busload. After hours, the museum is very often rented by Silicon Valley's high-tech companies for parties and receptions. This offers another interesting demographic: highly educated, technically savvy adults. We designed the exhibits to play on multiple levels, from the 30-second "quick take" to deeper levels for visitors who became intrigued with the ideas and exhibits.

## Museum Visitor as Researcher
The design of the exhibit space aimed to reproduce the feeling of "the research center after dark," so it looked as if scientists were gone for the evening, leaving their experiments running on their workbenches. Visitors were encouraged to take on the role of the scientist-researcher, consider unusual aspects of reading, and develop their own questions about the reading devices. The exhibits were designed to encourage a playful sense of fun and exploration about reading. Signage for each exhibit featured a provocative question and pointed out a few salient points about each reading experience. For example: "What if you had so many ideas they could fill a room?" Or: "What if you could walk right into the pages of a comic book?" For Speeder Reader, the question is: "What is it like to drive through a book?"

## Messages of the XFR Exhibit
Reading continually adapts to technological and cultural change. In some cultures, reading is a social act, primarily performed in public; words are written on walls or in books that are performed publicly. In other cultures, reading can also be a private, personal experience. The nature of that personal experience is always changing as well. Several companies now offer "e-books," hand-held electronic devices with downloadable texts. Cultural observers call this idea "convergence," where all text that one reads winds up being on one single hand-held device like a PDA, e-book, or cell phone. Our observation is that digital technologies, far from limiting the reading available in the world, make reading almost ubiquitous. In addition to books and magazines, we read walls, clothing, and electronic equipment. Even fresh fruit has labels and sometimes advertising on it. Digital technologies also enable the form of the reading device to match the the content of the text. A story about falling into a world of text is told on walls that surround the visitor with words. A story about travel is told on a device that looks like a vehicle. The XFR show is both a comment on the anti-convergent nature of text in the world and an experiment in authoring form along with content.

## Speeder Reader
One major point of the entire XFR exhibit is to associate a sense of excitement, fun, and personal control with the idea of reading. So, for Speeder Reader, we built a speed-racing interface onto

*13*

speed-reading software. The exhibit, placed near the front of the gallery, attracted people (especially children) with its half-familiar, game-like interface and brightly colored dynamic text.

### Rapid Serial Visual Presentation (RSVP)

People read printed words on a page in "saccadic jumps," a series of somewhat erratic eye motions around a page. RSVP is a kind of dynamic typography wherein words or short phrases appear in sequence in one spot on a screen. As the words continually flash in one spot, readers do not have to move their eyes, so they avoid the saccadic jumps and eliminate the time used in moving and refocusing the eyes. With this protocol people have been known to increase their reading speed up to 2000 words per minutes (an average fast reader can read about 400-600 words per minute). RSVP was investigated in the 1980s as a presentation protocol for text[4]. It has been used in several products as a speed reading technology, and is sometimes used as a research tool by neurologists and perceptual psychologists. Other affordances of dynamic typography have been explored by a number of people[3, 5, 6, 7]. In the final design of Speeder Reader, we were primarily interested in enabling the reader's words-per-minute speed. However, we did experiment with some more expressive mappings early on, with the idea that the reader could choose more or less graphically expressive typefaces. This is a promising path, but requires a longer learning period than most museum visitors will have.

### The Driving Metaphor: Navigation

One problem with RSVP text is how to browse it. How does one find different sections of content, play them at an appropriate speed, and replay them at will? Speeder Reader's interface allows personal control over all these parameters. The RSVP text is visible through a rectangular window in a specially designed monitor bezel (Figures 1, 2). Users navigate to different streams ("lanes") of text by turning the steering wheel, which moves the window to a different lane. A foot pedal ("gas" pedal) gives users control over the speed of the text being displayed, up to 1,850 words per minute. These two primary controllers allow users to choose text and control its speed. Several secondary controls allow a finer resolution of control. The stick shift can switch between different sections in the lane of text. A Cue button allows users to skip backward to set points in the text (beginning of last sentence: one button punch; beginning of last paragraph: two punches; preceding paragraphs: any additional punches beyond two). An accompanying Reset button starts the text over from the beginning.

### Visual and Physical Design

Speeder Reader was built in 80/20, a type of aluminum framing often described as "an industrial-strength Erector set." Since we anticipated heavy use from enthusiastic pre-teens for six months straight, Speeder Reader was designed for ruggedness. We gave it a strong, four-legged "workbench" table, with the computer stored in a built-in box underneath and the signage attached along one corner. The game controller hardware was bolted onto one-inch particle board covered with formica and cornered with soft black plastic.

Speeder Reader's visual presentation was multi-layered, in a deliberate attempt to blur the lines between the screen-based graphics and their physical surroundings. The graphics shown in Figure 2 were embedded behind four layers of thin materials with offset edges, to give a sense of depth similar to that in a dashboard.

### Authoring for Speeder Reader

*Authoring Speeder Reader raised several points besides navigation:*

- Rhythm as punctuation: Content-appropriate rhythms can greatly increase both speed and comprehension in RSVP and other dynamic text. For example, titles or subheadings may be given greater temporal weight than normal text.

- Type design: Appropriate typographical choices also aid in comprehension and speed. Characters may possess particular typographical characteristics. For example, san serif fonts are more readily recognizable as they flash past. Serifs seem to confuse the eye at high rates of speed. Or some words and phrases may be given more size or greater color contrast. Proper nouns, unusual words, and numbers are more difficult to recognize at high rates of speed; type differentiation and timing differentiation can address this problem.

- Narrative structure: We tried several different structures for the content. We settled on five lanes of text, with four subchapters in each lane (the four states defined by the gear shift). Each state in this content matrix contained approximately 1,000 words, since we wanted people to be able to remain in each state long enough to get a feel for really reading in RSVP. So the authoring task required a minimum of 20,000 words.

We made a test model that featured dynamic rhythms, fonts, and colors in presentations of several Lewis Carroll poems (Jabberwocky, Father William, The Walrus and the Carpenter, Turtle Soup). We wanted to tie the content of each of the XFR exhibits at least loosely to the physical form of the reading device. Speeder Reader's current content is a fictional account of a young girl's travels throughout the Solar System. As she visits each of five planets, she records salient facts and personal observations about it in her travel journal. Each lane features a different planet; each gear position is a new daily entry in her journal about that planet.

14

## System Design

All the devices, steering wheel, pedal, gearshift, and buttons are connected to an A/D converter, which communicates with the host computer via serial line. A Java 2.0 program reads the serial information and converts it to actions in the program, thus affecting the text in response to user input. We use XML to specify not only the text, but also its size, color, font, and background color.

## Future Work

Speeder Reader runs robustly and is popular with museum visitors. We are continuing our exploration of alternative content and iterations of the interface design. A Web-reader version of Speeder Reader is in development, as are some experiments with smaller, hand-held or embedded-RSVP readers, and RSVP readers as assistive devices.

## Conclusion

Several of the XFR exhibits attracted groups of people as often as they did single individuals. It was not uncommon to find several children piled into one of the Listen Reader armchairs, for example, or to find clusters of children around Listen Reader,[1,2,8] Fluid Fiction,[2,8] or the Reading Eye Dog.[2,8]

All 11 of the XFR reading experiences were designed with the idea that form affects meaning, and in fact is inextricable from it. We found that by authoring the form as conscientiously as the content, we were able to achieve some unusual goals: getting people to read deeply in a museum setting, for example, and getting people to read socially, in groups, often aloud to each other. Interviews with visitors indicate that the exhibit succeeded in its primary mission: causing people to consider the origins of the text they read every day, and to ask themselves how it might be read differently.

## Acknowledgements

The authors gratefully acknowledge the support of our colleagues in the RED group at Xerox PARC: Rich Gold, manager; Maribeth Back, Anne Balsamo, Mark Chow, Matt Gorbet, Steve Harrison, Dale Macdonald, and Scott Minneman. Significant contributions to XFR were made by Jonathan Cohen, Maureen Stone, Mark Meadows, Polle Zellweger, Jock Mackinlay, Bay-Wei Chang, and many others (unfortunately, too many to list here). We also thank Jock Mackinlay of Xerox PARC, for consultation on RSVP, and Terry Murphy of Exhibit Engineering. The XFR Web site is: www.thetech.org/xfr/

Figure 1. Speeder Reader, at the San Jose Tech Museum of Innovation, was one of eleven innovative reading experiences in "XFR: Experiments in the Future of Reading."

Figure 2. Presentation graphics and physical overlay for Speeder Reader. Blue indicates the side-lit lasercut Lexan overlay; red and black, and the background to the text, are all screen display areas; white shows where physical layers of felt and black plastic (under the top-layer Lexan) block the rest of the computer monitor from view.

*References*

1. Back, M., Cohen, J., Gold, R., Harrison, S., & Minneman, S. (2001). Listen Reader: An electronically augmented paper-based book. *Proceedings of CHI 2001,* ACM Press.

2. Back, M., Gold, R., Balsamo, A., Chow, M., Gorbet, M., Harrison, S., MacDonald, D., & Minneman, S. (2001). Reading the future: Designing innovative reading experiences for a museum exhibition. *IEEE Computer, 34,* (1).

3. Boguraev, B.K.B, Wong, Y.Y., Kennedy, C. Bellamy, R.K.E., Brawer, S., & Swartz, J. (1998). Dynamic presentation of document content for rapid on-line skimming. AAAI Spring Symposium on Intelligent Text Summarisation.

4. Chao, C. & Maeda, J. Concrete programming paradigm for kinetic typography. (1997). IEEE Symposium on Visual Languages.

5. Ishizaki, S. (1997). Kinetic typography: Expressive writing beyond the smileys :-). *Vision Plus 3 Conference Monographs,* July, 1997.

6. Potter, M. Rapid serial visual presentation (RSVP): A method for studying language processing. (1984). In ed. Kieras & Just, *New Methods in Reading Comprehension Research.* Erlbaum, Hillsboro, NJ.

7. Wong, Y. Y. (1995). Temporal typography: Characterization of time-varying typographic forms. Master's Thesis, Massachusetts Institute of Technology.

8. www.parc.xerox.com/xfr/

*15*

## 21st Century Literacy: Media and Meaning

*Moderator*
Sarah Feldman
Director of Content Strategy-
Audience Development
Oxygen Media, Inc.
75 West Ninth Avenue, 7th Floor
New York, New York 10011
USA
+1.212.651.5316
+1.212.651.2099 fax
sfeldman@oxygen.com

*Panelists*
Anthony Chapman
Thirteen/WNET

Sarah Feldman
Oxygen Media, Inc.

Faith Rogow, PhD
Insighters Educational
Consulting; Alliance for a Media
Literate America (AMLA)

Elana Rosen
Just Think Foundation

### Media & Meaning: Hypertext, Context, What's Next?
*Sarah Feldman*

Before we can look to effectively creating and using media in education, we must first ask this fundamental question: In the 21st century, what does it mean to be educated? Is it the retention of facts, or is it the ability to locate, convey, analyze, and make meaning out of the "facts" and ideas we encounter? Only when we can define what we aim to do can we explore what we need to do to educate.

Too often our escalating frenzy to create dazzling content overwhelms our capacity to process that content. While discussions surrounding accessing information are important, it is equally valuable to look at the need for assessing information — evaluating media for accuracy, relevance, and quality. But media literacy doesn't stop at honing our ability to analyze images and information. The depth and inherently conjunctive role of hyper-textual environments present whole new possibilities for perceiving, organizing, and communicating ideas. While many traditionally see links as a disassociative interface convention, it is also important to look at their synthetic potential. In other words, where once information was organized in linear outlines and encyclopedic formats, now information is seen through the prism of its connections to other data. Where once we proclaimed "content is king," one could argue that "context is queen." But are digital artists taking full creative advantage of this new way to communicate? Are educators? Savvy interface designers are moving away from the logo-phobia that once plagued them, instead recognizing text's vital role in enhancing and extending content and the users' experience.

This session explores the possibilities that the Web's hyper-textual and video-enhanced interfaces present to students, educators, and other media makers and consumers. The session included the capacity of interfaces to redefine the ways in which we organize, convey, and understand information; their role in a whole new artistic and communication paradigm; and the stylistic and syntactical uses of hypertext. The panelists looks at how new video and Web-converged media may potentially shape the way we make — and make meaning of — media in the 21st century.

Sarah Feldman has more than 15 years' experience as a strategist, presenter, writer, and consultant for a broad spectrum of media and education outlets. She is currently senior producer for Oxygen.com and director of internal content strategy for Oxygen Media, a unique cable television and online network for women. She was previously producer and writer for Oprah Goes Online, a Web site dedicated to helping Web neophytes use the Internet. And as the director of audience development for several sites that serve as portals to Oxygen's multiple suite of online venues, she devised and implemented converged content strategies for Oxygen's wealth of Web-based and video programming. Previously, she served as National Project Director for PBS' Thirteen/WNET. As Director for the National Teacher Training Institute for Math, Science and Technology, she traveled across the country conducting presentations to hundreds of education, television, and online professionals on the strategies and vision needed to integrate technology and media into curricula. In addition to her work as a consultant and "evangelist," she developed content for a variety of broadcast, multimedia, K-12 curriculum, online, and videotape projects. She also conceived and developed numerous educational programs, curricula, and online material. Prior to working for Thirteen/WNET, Sarah wrote for the "MacNeil/Lehrer NewsHour" and taught second grade in Harlem and the South Bronx.

### Using Web-Based Technologies for Education
*Anthony Chapman*

In the burgeoning world of multimedia, PBS' Thirteen/WNET New York has remained ahead of the curve in every facet of electronic production, regularly winning top awards for its Web site and its companion pieces for all the major Thirteen-produced series and specials. From video streaming to online classroom instruction, The Kravis Center for Multimedia Education has yielded top-notch, highly creative projects in this sophisticated and rapidly evolving environment.

Long a pioneer in educational uses of television and technology, Thirteen/WNET is actively involved in the ongoing digital revolution, with The Kravis Center being a vibrant laboratory for research and production of advanced multimedia projects for educational purposes. In addition, Thirteen/WNET's Web site, Thirteen Online, features sophisticated and in-depth online companion pieces to our ongoing national series and original online content to complement Thirteen/WNET's other educational initiatives. Projects as varied as New York: A Documentary Film and NATURE Online allow viewers to interact with our programming in exciting new ways.

### New Media Literacies for a New Century, New Technologies
*Faith Rogow*

America's public school system was created when print was the dominant form of mass communication so, naturally, curricula and teaching methods reflected the need to be literate in that medium. But in the digital world, print is no longer supreme, and it is time for schools to catch up. But what does that mean? What does literacy for the 21st century actually look like? What should it look like? Rogow's presentation shows how media literacy provides a new foundation for teaching and learning, emphasizing a vision of literacy that includes the ability to interpret and communicate with images, sound, and technology along with print.

Called the "Wayne Gretzky of media literacy," Faith Rogow has trained thousands of teachers, students, childcare providers, and parents to understand and harness the power of television in her nearly 20 years as a media educator. She has authored award-winning training and educational outreach materials for "The Puzzle Place," "Teletubbies," "Theodore Tugboat," "Storytime," and "Tots TV," as well as discussion guides for the "P.O.V." Television Race Initiative, and media literacy materials for "Life & Times Tonight" and "Bill Moyers: Close to Home." She has served as a consultant to PBS' Ready to Learn Service, Sesame Workshop, "Frontline," and a variety of instructional television productions. In recognition of her work on outreach for "Sesame Street," she was given the Ralph B. Rogers Award in 1996 by Children's Television Workshop. She is currently owner of Insighters Educational Consulting and national president of the Alliance for a Media Literate America (AMLA).

### From Smoke Signals to 3-D VR: Why Media Education is Fundamental
*Elana Rosen*

Though most of the world's population has access to media produced in America, we are the last developed country to integrate media courses into our primary, secondary, or higher educational systems. Rosen discusses Just Think's work around the globe and examines model programs at home and abroad with a special eye to ensuring that all young people have the access to the media and technology tools critical to lead thoughtful and productive lives.

Elana Rosen has 15 years of experience in the nonprofit and media worlds, working with KQED-TV in the news, current affairs, and cultural departments before joining George Lucas' Educational Foundation. As senior associate, she developed educational interactive prototypes, produced the content for dramatic films on learning environments of the future, and created a national information resource for dissemination on the Internet. Elana has lectured on multimedia, online information, and educational issues at such institutions as Stanford University, Mills College, the California State Department of Health and Human Services, the University of Catamarca, and the White House. In 1995, she produced an interactive exhibition for the 50th anniversary of the United Nations. In March of 1995, she co-founded the Just Think Foundation and has served as its executive director since its inception. She is the co-author of "Changing the World Through Media Education" and received an Emmy nomination for the documentary "Czeslaw Milosz: A Poet Remembers."

*17*

# INTERNET2 APPLICATIONS AND INFRASTRUCTURE

*Contact*
TED HANSS
Internet2
3025 Boardwalk, Suite 100
Ann Arbor, Michigan 48108
USA
+1.734.913.4256
ted@internet2.edu

Internet2 (www.internet2.edu) is a consortium led by over 180 universities working in partnership with industry and government to develop and deploy advanced network applications and technologies, accelerating the creation of tomorrow's Internet. Internet2 is recreating the partnership among academia, industry, and government that fostered today's Internet in its infancy. The primary goals of Internet2 are to create a leading-edge network capability for the national research and education community, enable revolutionary Internet applications, and ensure rapid transfer of new network services and applications to the broader Internet community.

This talk provides examples of the types of applications under development within the Internet2 community in support of research, teaching, and learning. These include streaming video (up to HDTV quality), high-energy physics data mining, digital libraries, virtual reality in health care, and much more. Hauss also discusses examples of advanced services, such as security, directories, quality of service, video frameworks, collaboration tool infrastructures, multicast, etc., and identifies support resources available to application developers.

Internet2 has recently expanded access to its national backbone, Abilene, to include K-20 organizations outside the research universities that make up the core of the membership. We hope this will lead to new collaborations and new applications. In addition, Internet2 has many international partnerships working together to support global education communities.

18

## DESIGNING EXPERIENCE: MODELING ON-LINE COLLABORATIVE LEARNING IN ART & DESIGN

*Moderator*
THECLA SCHIPHORST
Technical University of
British Columbia
Suite 301, 10334 - 152A St
Surrey, British Columbia
V3R 7P8 Canada
+1.604.586.5279
schiphorst@techbc.ca

*Panelists*
STEVE DiPAOLO

SUSAN KOZEL
University of Suvrey

ALICE MANSELL
RON WAKKARY
Technical University
of British Columbia

How do we involve the learner in the individualization and co-construction of the digital learning environment? There is an explicit relationship between building experience and interaction in participatory learning. In this panel, presenters with diverse backgrounds in the art and design field explore new trends in designing experience-based models for learning online. The focus of the panel is the design of learning environments for the new virtual classroom.

Innovations in online learning involve moving beyond a simple desire to make the education process more effective by incorporating networked systems into instruction; they are based on a deeper understanding of the collaborative learning process in a connected environment. Experience- and studio-based methodologies engage visual, aural, and physical activities and practice, and are drawn into online learning environments.

The Designing Experience panelists are actively engaged in online learning and the use of educational technology. They routinely explore how to design experience in online collaborative environments utilizing both synchronous and asynchronous models. Their expertise ranges from user-interface design to curatorial practice, performance, dance and theater, virtual worlds and gaming, narrative and storytelling, painting and visual arts, and instructional design for online collaborative learning environments. The range of experience-based models explored in this panel discussion include responsive spaces, event-based interaction, online virtual communities, problem-based collaborative models, and questions of narrative and staging practice in the virtual classroom. Presenters represent educational design and pedagogy as it is being researched at Stanford University, the Technical University of British Columbia, and The University of Surrey.

### Thecla Schiphorst

Thecla Schiphorst is a computer media artist whose work includes interactive installation, performance, and software design. She is currently assistant professor in interactive arts at the Technical University of British Columbia. She is the recipient of the prestigious 1998 Canada Council PetroCanada Award in New Media granted biennially to a Canadian artist for contributions to new technologies research. Her research includes gestural interface design, computer interactive installation, and kinesthetic systems for collaboration and performance. She has an interdisciplinary MA in computer compositional systems from Simon Fraser University, undergraduate studies in dance and computer science, and a diploma of technology from BCIT in computer programming and systems analysis. She is a member of the original design team that developed Life Forms, the computer compositional tool for animation and choreography. Her computer installation work has toured extensively, and it has been exhibited in numerous international conferences and festivals including SIGGRAPH, SIGCHI, Ars Electronica, ISEA, Interaction '97 in Gifu Japan, Interactive Screen, CyberArts, and others. Schiphorst designed, directed and produced the award-winning multi-media interactive project entitled "immerce," which won three first place festival awards at the International Digital Media Awards Festival

and a Graphex award in design. It was also presented at the ARC awards in Los Angeles. She is the co-director of Then/Else, the Interactivity Research Centre at TechBC and is involved in exploration of collaborative immersion, in which gesture and movement analysis principles are utilized to augment user experience and communication.

### Steve DiPaola

Steve DiPaola has been involved with the cutting edge of the interactive fields of 3D animation and Web-based design since 1984, when he was a senior member of the Computer Animation Research Group at the New York Institute of Technology. At NYIT he conducted research and development in 3D character and facial animation, and produced animation for film, television, and fine art projects. He worked for advertising giant Saatchi and Saatchi, where he founded and co-ran its independent innovation arm, Darwin Digital, in San Francisco. As creative director, he explored state-of-the-art media and interactive projects for major accounts such as Hewlett-Packard and Macromedia.

DiPaola was director of development and design at the OnLive Group of Communities.com, where he led a team of artists, architects, user-interface designers, and musicians in designing and developing 3D voice-based avatars and virtual worlds for such clients as NEC, MTV, ABC, and Universal Studios. Previously, he was at the Advanced Technology Group of Electronic Arts. He directed a group that spearheaded development of advanced techniques in CD-ROM-based interactivity. Considered a pioneer in alternative user interface design, he has spoken at major conferences such as Internet World, SIGGRAPH, SIGCHI, and The Institute for the Future. At these conferences, he has delivered presentations and published papers on interactive characters, advanced Internet design, collaborative virtual environments, and the future of identity. He is currently Vice President of Creative Development at Muse Communications, which is creating a next-generation, broadband platform that integrates multiple technologies such as HTML, rich media, 3D graphics, and multi-user community into a unified, synergistic environment.

### Susan Kozel

Susan Kozel is a performer, choreographer, and researcher specializing in live performance in responsive spaces and development of digitally connected learning environments. She is currently working as a senior research advisor with the Institute for New Media Performance Research at the University

*19*

of Surrey on creation of an online module called "The Extended Body: Gender and New Media Performance," which places particular emphasis on online, real-time visual/audio/text exchange, plus studio experimentation in physical as well as virtual environments. She is now a member of the faculty of Interactive Arts at the Technical University of British Columbia. She is also undertaking a research project into motion capture in theatrical installations with the Institute of Dramaturgy of the Aarhus Universitet.

Kozel has a PhD in phenomenology from the philosophy department of the University of Essex and has experience with a wide range of movement practices. She is a founder, member, and director of Mesh Performance Partnerships, a professional cross-disciplinary artists' organisation specialising in media technologies. Recent Mesh projects include Contours (1999) supported by the Arts Council of England and Figments (1999) supported by the UK National Lottery. Her most recent project is Trajets (2000), co-directed with Gretchen Schiller and co-produced with the Banff Centre for the Arts. She has performed in many countries and is widely published. Her writings can be found in books and journals of performance, architecture, and film from the UK, Australia, the USA, Holland, Sweden, Belgium, Italy, France, and Morocco.

### Alice Mansell

Alice Mansell is vice president, academic at Canada's newest university, the Technical University of British Columbia. TechBC's mandate is to provide advanced education and research in applied and technological fields and to make a significant contribution to the economic development of the province. Its initial program areas include Information Technology, Management and Technology, and Interactive Arts.

At TechBC, Mansell has led development of new programs, integration in defining innovations in pedagogy in the online learning environment, and definition of new research and program directions in Interactive Arts and beyond. She has long advocated exploration of a fusion of arts, science, technology, design, and management, and the opportunities that success in those integrations can bring to the business and cultural arenas. Her current research interests include interactive learning and its relationship to personal narrative in art-based electronic commerce models. She served as president of the Nova Scotia College of Art and Design, where she led collaborations among government, education, and industry partners in development of new-media education and research initiatives. She was professor and chair of the Department of Visual Arts at the University of Western Ontario and a faculty member in the Department of Art at the University of Calgary, where she led development of interdisciplinary studies in gender and the arts in Canada.

Mansell continues to pursue an active studio practice in the visual arts. She enjoys an international reputation as an artist and lecturer in contemporary art theory and art education. She is currently a member of the Board of Directors of CANARIE and serves on its Learning Advisory and Content Committees. She is an active member of the Surrey Public Art Advisory Committee and in 1996 was selected as Women of the Year (Education & Research) in Halifax. She was born in Alberta and holds degrees from the University of Calgary and the University of British Columbia.

### Ron Wakkary

Ron Wakkary is associate professor and dean of academic planning at the Technical University of British Columbia. His research interests include interaction design, network interactivity, and art and technology. Beginning in 1995, as director and cofounder of Stadium in New York, he collaborated on many leading and pioneering projects in art and the Internet with internationally recognized and emerging media artists. Many of these projects have been displayed at ZKM in Karlsruhe, the Whitney Museum of American Art, ARCO in Madrid, and the Museum of Modern Art in New York. He has led Internet projects for the Museum of Modern Art, the Guggenheim Museum, the Dia Center for the Arts, and Electronic Arts Intermix in New York. He is an editorial review panelist for the Leonardo Digital Reviews, an advisory board member of WebLab in New York, and director of Then/Else: Interactivity Centre at TechBC. He was formerly on the digital design faculty at Parsons School of Design of the New School University in New York. He is currently researching a social network game in collaboration with Nokia, in Tampere, Finland.

20

# Webtanks: Tools for Learning by Design

Zann Gill
Research Scientist
Research Institute for
Advanced Computer Science
NASA Ames Research Center
MS 19-39
Moffett Field, California
94035-1000 USA
+1.650.604.4370
sgill@mail.arc.nasa.gov

This paper describes a collaborative Web environment, or Webtank (think tank on the web) to support student learning by design. Targeted for high school students in a newly developed cross-disciplinary science and technology curriculum, it supports students in their design and invention projects. The paper describes results from a pilot test of the curriculum and additional student brainstorming sessions on "designing a Webtank to support design."

The Webtank serves three learning functions, as a:

- Series of prompts to help student designer and inventors generate innovative, integrated design concepts and new inventions. Webtank prompts the thinking of individual students on their projects.

- Framework to facilitate collaboration, where students interact with other students around issues that arise as they design their projects and integrate their individual projects into a larger, collaborative project plan.

- Way to structure archives and resources in order to retrace creative processes that have occurred in this environment. The Webtank provides a vehicle for researchers to observe design and collaborative problem-solving in action.

I use the term Webtank to refer to a Web environment that supports think-tank activities. Webtanks enable distributed collaboration using available Internet technologies and bandwidth. A key question: How can the design of the Webtank be informed by human design and collaborative problem-solving processes, and at the same time provide a way to observe and better understand those processes? This chicken-egg question demands an evolutionary development strategy.

NASA Ames Research Center and the Research Institute for Advanced Computer Science (RIACS) are developing a think tank supported by a Web environment to spur NASA cross-disciplinary collaboration. In order to test some Webtank ideas in a near term application, I began to collaborate with SETI on the last Evolution of Technology module in their cross-disciplinary high school science curriculum (physics, chemistry, biology, and evolution of technology). This paper describes one Webtank application for a high school cross-disciplinary science and technology curriculum and considers what can be learned from that experiment that may be applicable to intranet e-learning in general.

## Application in a Cross-Disciplinary Science Curriculum

The primary objective of the Webtank is to provide an "intelligent framework" to guide and record the thought processes of "students as designers and inventors." Students at the Harker School in San Jose, California are also taking part in hands-on brainstorming sessions on how to design a Webtank to support design. The Voyages Through Time (VTT) pilot test took place in January 2001. Input from this test is being used to redesign the field test, which takes place during the 2001-2002 school year. The VTT Webtank experiment will feed into development of a prototype Webtank for a NASA think tank. So SIGGRAPH 2001 occurs at an ideal time to involve members of the SIGGRAPH community who are interested in questions such as

- How can we design a webtank that is truly interactive, with the capacity to "self-organize" as it scales up, and the potential to expose students to other outstanding student work?

- How can the Webtank become an experimental vehicle to explore how intranets can support various types of networked learning?

This paper demonstrates the intranet architecture for the Webtank, explaining how it serves two complementary functions: providing process support for invention and collaborative problem-solving (active mode) and offering a knowledge-management framework for information resources and project archives (passive mode). Users can click back and forth between active and passive modes. I describe how the TRACE cycle, a cognitive model, enables this complementarity between the active and passive modes.

In the active mode, a Webtank Integration Broker serves a brokerage function for collaborative transactions, enabling students to introduce their project ideas and find other students with whom they can work on a "bigger picture" that combines multiple projects. In the passive mode, completed individual Web entries are evaluated and archived with multiple mechanisms for search and matching by the Webtank integration broker, and a knowledge-management framework to grow the knowledge bank organically. The first SETI implementation focuses not primarily on the technology but on design of the interface and knowledge-management system.

21

THE WEBTANK AS A CURRICULUM DEVELOPMENT TOOL
The Webtank is a tool not only for the students and teachers who use it for design projects, but also for curriculum designers, who can use it to respond to student needs as indicated in Webtank records of their performance. The Webtank is designed to support three approaches to learning:

• Learning by seeking information as needed to develop a plan (project-based learning).

• Peer-to-peer learning through sharing ideas in a collaborative Web environment.

• Learning through synthesis, so that all students understand where their contributions fit, and how can they can be integrated, into a bigger picture.

The Webtank is designed to grow as it supports students to generate novel ideas for their new technology design, and documents their projects as resources for other students.

Edwin Hutchins has advocated creating a synthetic network and observing how consensus is attained in such a network. In contrast, my focus is on how convergence can be achieved in real group problem-solving and how such a process can be supported in a Webtank environment. Yale University professor Irving Janis studied why committees fail by analyzing a number of case studies from public policy. His observations of the dynamics of group process should inform Webtank design. In *Groupthink: A Psychological Study of Policy Decisions and Fiascos*, Janis analyzed a series of major public policy blunders and showed why groups notoriously produce decisions that are more foolish than what their individual members might have produced alone.

Though Janis' case studies preceded the widespread use of Internet and collaborative tools, by highlighting the importance of the individual in collaborative decision making, they provide insight for today's Webtank designers. Janis showed that, because of pressure for consensus, the intelligence and effectiveness of the individuals in the group had little to do with the effectiveness of the group as a whole. If Janis was correct in stressing the importance of each individual's perspective in group process, then a Webtank to support self-directed learning and innovation will require mechanisms to retain individual identity within the larger group process. Drawing an analogy between collaborative problem-solving and evolution supports this position. Having a lot of cells doesn't make an organism complex; it's still just a lot of cells. Differentiation is a prerequisite for complexity and individually motivated learning.

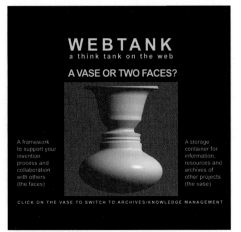

Dual portal to the Webtank's complementary functions: process support for invention and collaboration (active mode: click on the faces) and knowledge-management framework for information resources and project archives (passive mode: click on the vase). Users can click back and forth between active and passive modes.

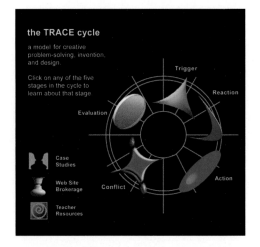

Portal to the five stages of the TRACE model, each of which offers prompts to support and guide student designers and inventors.

## Conclusion

Webtanks can address three prerequisites for shifting the passive delivery paradigm by supporting demand:

- For more student-directed learning by doing.

- To pioneer new ways to use the Web in innovative learning environments.

- For research on collaborative problem solving using the Webtank to gather data.

This third demand uses the Webtank as a petri dish to culture the creative process, so that "invisible observers" can watch how students perform in this environment. Though any theory about the creative process is hard to prove, my premise is that a partial correlation can be drawn between individual creative process (which is unobservable) and group processes of design and concept formation, where the process of invention is open to view. Using the Webtank to support learning by doing raises a range questions:

- How can we pioneer new ways to support self-directed learning?

- How can we support new forms of student collaboration across distance and through time?

- How can we create a growing repository of student projects to inspire future generations of students and address the knowledge-management challenge of "scaling up?"

Webtanks can not only support cross-disciplinary groups as they develop new concepts, but also track these work sessions as case studies in cross-disciplinary learning and innovation.

Zann Gill (MArch Harvard) is a research scientist with the Research Institute for Advanced Computer Science, where she is responsible for program development for the Ames Institute for Advanced Space Concepts (a think tank). Various NASA enterprises have identified the need for more effective methods to promote cross-disciplinary collaboration. Her research focus is on evolutionary models for design and collaborative problem solving. She has collaborated with SETI and the Harker School to test ideas for how a Webtank can be used to promote collaborative problem solving in a learning environment.

Group challenges require students to integrate many components into a coordinated design strategy or plan. Two images of the immersive workbench at NASA Ames Research Center. Virtual Mechano-Synthesis software by Chris Henze allows designers and researchers to simulate and visualize new molecular combinations for drug design. In a simulation, we can see patterns that we did not see in the data alone. So visualization gives us another problem-solving tool. Students are asked to explore how new tools may change our ways of working in the future.

Group challenge to imagine how new visualization tools will change the way we work in the future. Students choose an earth environment (for example: ocean, desert, Arctic, Antarctic) and design an expedition to test methods and technology for a future Mars mission. In an ocean-analog mission, students simulate a mission to Jupiter's moon Europa, using the TRACE model to guide their collaborative problem-solving process. Conflict and Evaluation are two key stages of the five-stage process.

23

# Curricular Modules: 3D and Immersive Visualization Tools for Learning

*Contact*
Andrea Wollensak
Associate Professor of Art
Connecticut College
270 Mohegan Avenue #5641
New London, Connecticut 06320
USA
+1.860.439.2748
ajwol@conncoll.edu

Bridget Baird
Steve Loomis
Connecticut College

Many scientific principles are dynamic in nature but are commonly presented through static two-dimensional media such as textbooks and blackboards, leaving the student to make the connection between the two. In several science courses at Connecticut College, faculty experiment with the use of 3D animations to increase the students' understanding of these concepts.

Curricular Modules: 3D and Immersive Visualization Tools for Learning, a project funded by the National Science Foundation, provides innovative pedagogical tools for subjects in the sciences that have been traditionally challenging for students to master. The 3D and virtual reality tools represent groundbreaking advances in pedagogy in a wide variety of areas of science education.

Six science modules were created by cross-disciplinary teams comprised of faculty (fellows at the Center for Arts and Technology) and students from the science, computer science, and design departments. A benefit of this team approach is the mutual understanding gained from working with individuals with different expertise and backgrounds.

Specific subjects included human physiology, graph theory, introductory physics, organic chemistry and biochemistry, cell biology, and astronomy education. For example, users understand the production and propagation of an action potential through immersion in a 3D environment, experiencing how the ions flow back and forth. A multi-sensory approach is used in which some of the modules include audio and haptics (force feedback).

## Interdisciplinary collaboration

This project represents a collaborative effort among faculty from a wide range of disciplines. The modules were developed by small teams of three students and three faculty members, each representing a different discipline — science, computer science, and design. The team approach provided a rich and focused learning environment, allowing students to collectively understand and solve visualization problems. All participants developed a greater respect both for the collaborating outside disciplines and their own specialties.

Students in the center's certificate program explore the symbiotic relationship between technology and the arts, developing an understanding of the meaning and role of technology within the larger context of the liberal arts. Students who are accepted into the center's certificate program must take an interdisciplinary course in the history of arts and technology as well as courses in the arts and computer science. Furthermore, they must complete a summer internship and subsequently spend two semesters working on an integrative project. Throughout the program, they are exposed to colloquia and symposia, and the students participate in exchanges emphasizing the connections between the arts and technology.

The modules that students worked on were complex and abstract in nature. Initially, all participants met for a discussion of the principle concepts of the modules. Students then began to sketch out the narratives of the scientific principles, brainstorming together to develop visually possible metaphors to describe the principles. The design of the scientific principles was explored on three levels: information design, interaction design, and sensorial design.

The computer science students began to test and modify the sketches, and to build them in different digital environments. At this stage, it was important to maintain clarity and the carefully crafted visual aesthetics. Once the direction and procedure was clear, work on the computers began in earnest. Design students explored components of information design by testing color, form, text, and shape on the computer screen, taking into consideration legibility and clarity of the narrative. The interactive components were also tested and modified, ensuring that links, input systems, and calculators worked effectively. The sensorial component (force feedback) tests involved applying varying stress to visual elements within the chemistry module, which added an enriching detail to the user experience. These design considerations all contributed to a virtual reality space that represented an information—complex-visual form, information source, transmission conditions, users, and their responses.

The technology used to develop each module enabled sophisticated graphics and clear information design through immersion in a virtual reality environment on a PC or UNIX platform and a 3D Web version (either VRML or ActiveX plugins). Most of the modules were developed on a PC/UNIX platform using C++ and Sense8's virtual reality libraries. Some of them used the Sense8 WorldUp software, and others were programmed specifically for the Web. Those that use haptics were programmed using SensAble's C++ Ghost toolkit libraries.

## Examples

The modules examine six different concepts. The first is in human physiology and concerns the molecular events that take place during the production and propagation of an action potential. A second concept is the relationship between molecular configurations and mathematical equations. The third concept is in mathematical graph theory and calculates maximal flow through a network. Another concept, in cell biology, is the continuous flow of membrane during exocytosis. The fifth concept is the electric potential function in physics. The last concept is the idea of a galactic center in astronomy. The concepts were chosen because they are difficult to learn from a textbook situation and would benefit from visualization and interaction. For example, in the chemistry module, reading about the relationship between a mathematical formula and the forces on a molecule is not as clear as watching the relationship dynamically develop. Likewise, being able to walk through a graph algorithm, testing hypotheses along the way, makes the algorithm more vivid and the understanding of the mathematical proof more complete. Several of the modules are described in more detail below.

*Action Potential*

The molecular events that take place during production and propagation of an action potential are important concepts for students in human physiology to understand. The operation of voltage-gated channels with the subsequent flow of ions in and out of the axon is a dynamic process that can best be visualized through animation. This module allows students to see the results of opening and closing the sodium and potassium voltage-gated channels during the production of an action potential. In the design of this module, students chose to emphasize a shape for the sodium ions that matches the shape of the corresponding gate, thus making clear that these gates only allow certain ions to pass through. The animation allows the students to choose the perspective from inside or outside the axon and is accompanied by audio. There are two versions of this module: one runs on the Web in VRML; and one uses a C++ environment and may be viewed in stereo.

*Molecular Conformations*

Another example comes from chemistry. It is very important for students in organic chemistry and biochemistry to understand why molecules adopt their particular geometry. Length, bond angle, dihedral deformations, and a variety of non-bonded interactions are responsible for specific conformations. In molecular mechanics, all of these contributions to the total strain energy are molded by mathematical formulas that are minimized to find the lowest-energy configuration. By using a force-feedback hardware device called the Phantom (from SensAble), this module actually allows students to feel the forces acting on an atom as they simultaneously view the corresponding graph. For example, as a carbon atom in an ethane molecule is moved away from the other carbon atom, the student feels the restoring force. The virtual environment allows students first to choose a particular mathematical equation, then they are able to pull the atom in the molecule, either stretching or compressing the bond, and simultaneously observe the mathematical graph generated. There is an audio explanation of the mathematical equations and how they model the chemical processes. This virtual environment uses a force-feedback device (the Phantom from SensAble), so users can actually feel the increase in forces acting on the atom.

*Maximum Flow in a Network*

Another module, in graph theory, helps users understand how maximum flow through a network is produced. The mathematical justification for this algorithm lies in the relationship between minimum cuts and maximum flow. A cut is produced by dividing the vertices of the graph into two sets and then adding up flows on edges, joining vertices of the two sets. Cuts may be thought of as bottlenecks so, in some sense, the largest flow will be constrained by the narrowest bottleneck. As users pick out cuts and test them, they achieve a better grasp of the mathematics.

*Electric Potential*

Another module deals with the electric potential function in physics. Students enter information (including location) about test charges, and then a 3D landscape is created where the altitude or depth at a location is the value of the electric potential. Values for this function depend on distance from the charges and the magnitude of the charges; these values may be positive or negative. Visualizing this function as a 3D landscape shows these relationships more clearly. By varying the magnitude of the charges, by making them positive or negative, and by changing their locations, users produce different landscapes. A test charge is also incorporated into the landscape, and this test charge moves according to the gradient of the potential. Additional modules deal with concepts in cell biology and astronomy.

EVALUATION AND SUMMARY

The plan for evaluation is simple, but effective. The students exposed to the modules in the classroom were able to immediately evaluate the user experience and respond to the clarity of the information graphics. Tests were conducted this semester and there have not yet been any modifications.

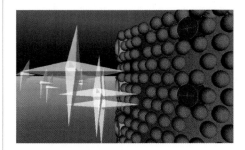

Sodium ions (pink) outside the cell wall (brown), sodium-gated channels (blue), and potassium-gated channels (green).

As the student moves one of the carbon atoms away from or close to the other, the green ball traces the mathematical function.

# Life Drawing and 3D Figure Modeling with MAYA

*Contact*
Gregory P. Garvey
Yale University Digital Media
Center for the Arts
149 York Street
New Haven, Connecticut 06520
USA
+1.203.582.8389
gregory.garvey@yale.edu

This paper discusses development and organization of a workshop on modeling the human figure using Maya 3.0. Held at the Yale University Digital Media Center for the Arts, the workshop covers drawing from life, scanning, importing, setup of reference image planes, and introductory modeling. Topics include: discussion of Nicolaïdes' drawing exercises; an overview of selected examples of figurative art from ancient through contemporary periods; planning appropriate poses; drawing from life; scanning the drawings, file importing, and setup of image planes; using NURB primitives such as circles, cylinders, spheres; lofting and stitching; basic transformations (move, scale, rotate); simple component editing using pick-masking; using Artisan (Sculpt NURBS Surfaces Tool); adding a basic skeleton and skinning; painting weights; simple texturing and using Paint Effects (hair); lighting (key, fill, rim); rendering to image files; and printing. This presentation reviews sample tutorials and student work, and concludes with a discussion of the aesthetic outcomes.

## Motivation

Development of computer graphics has been driven in part by the pursuit of photo-realistic rendering. Many computer graphic artists seek to create images of human beings that are indistinguishable from reality. In contrast to this impulse is a very long history of image making in many different cultures that represents the human form in both a believable and recognizable way. Yet the means of representation (the individual gestural mark made with the paint brush or pencil by the artist) is a celebrated part of the aesthetic. With photo-realistic computer graphics, the means of representation is meant to disappear and not be visible. In the western tradition, the figurative works of Titian, Rembrandt, Degas, Cassatt, Picasso, or Alice Neel would lose their meaning and vitality if the gestural line of drawing was removed.

This paper and workshop pose a series of questions:. Can the "natural way to draw" be preserved in the process of modeling the human figure? Can the photo-realistic impulse be set aside in favor of exploring personal expression and the nature of the medium, to reveal a different truth of representation? Are there alternatives to the dominant modes of representation such as photo-realism, pumped-up superheroes, international anime culture or Disneyesque stylization? How can exploration of alternative approaches be best encouraged and developed? Can 3D modeling provide a pathway to discovery and revelation of aesthetic truths and personal meanings that is similar to the pathways explored in the worldwide history of drawing and painting? Do technical demands, the 3D computer graphics modeling process, and ultimately the marketplace make such concerns obsolete and irrelevant?

More than a millennium ago, using language informed by Taoism and Buddhism, the painter Ching Hao (900-960) wrote: "Resemblance reproduces the formal aspects of things but neglects their spirit. Truth shows the spirit and the essence in its perfection."[1] In his book "The Natural Way to Draw,"[2] Kimon Nicolaïdes aims for something quite similar: "You should draw, not what the thing looks like, not even what it is, but what it is doing." He developed a series of drawing exercises in which the artist focuses alternately upon contour, gesture, weight, modeling, memory, analysis of contrasting curved and straight lines, predominating shapes, and their design within the frame. Through such exercises, Nicolaïdes strives for a deeper understanding and empathy with the subject as the artist learns how to represent it.

For Nicolaïdes, learning to draw is an ongoing process of discovery. Fundamentally it is learning how to observe with not only the eyes but all the senses. It is interesting to note that his approach lays the groundwork for literally breaking out of the frame into multi-media and even installation and performance. A contour drawing made without looking at the paper is about touching the edges of form, of pushing and pulling edges that move forward and backward in space. A gesture drawing is learning how to empathize, identify, and participate with what the model is doing, feeling, and thinking. For Nicolaïdes, this is more than action or attitude: "Gesture describes the compound of all forces acting in and against, and utilized by, the model."

Weight and mass drawings seek to feel the effect of the forces and discover the core motivation of a form. This is similar to some modern dance technique where performers focus on the midpoint of their bodies as the locus of energy from which to initiate movement. Drawings from memory emphasize using one's own muscles to remember the movement of the model. Drawing at right angles requires the artist to draw the model from an imagined perspective 90 degrees to the observed viewpoint. This is a skill that directors and animators use in determining camera angle and placement. In fact, a good animator feels and empathizes with the subject in order to understand how the character acts, moves, and behaves.

Another exercise emphasizes using memory and imagination by consciously relating the direct sensory experience of viewing a model to past experience. This free-association could involve any one of the senses. Like Proust's Madeleine, our conscious life is made up of not only the present, but a flood of memories, thoughts, and sensations that reflect our own unique lives and color our current experience. Drawing becomes a dance between objective observation and subjective, even subconscious reactions and recalled experience, mediated by the marks left on the paper. For Nicolaïdes, "drawing depends on seeing. Seeing depends on knowing. Knowing comes from a constant effort to encompass reality with all of your senses, all that is you."

Recent computer graphic techniques for modeling, rendering, and animation have captured the likeness of the human figure with ever-increasing photo-realism. The digital version of Kevin Bacon in the movie "Hollow Man" or the virtual James Brown created for the Experience Music Project proclaim that we may now be unable to perceive the difference between the "real" and the "virtual." Yet all too often what appears realistic today, within a year or so appears as yesterday's artifice. At the same time, character design for games such as Tomb Raider are often highly stylized. This is influenced in part by storage requirements and display constraints, which require fast polygonal rendering. The international comic book and anime culture also plays an important role in this stylization and simplification of 3D characters.

Successful stylization, even with surreal distortions and exaggerations, requires a command of anatomy, proportion, and form, and a sense of color and design. Creating convincing characters with believable movement requires much more than anatomical correctness. Whether designing a photo-realistic virtual actor or a highly stylized action character for gaming, animators, artists, and designers need to start with observing the human form from multiple perspectives and in motion. A mastery of drawing and understanding of anatomy and proportion lay the groundwork for making believable corrections, enhancements, or distortions to polygonal meshes created from 3D scanning. Even with cartoon-like characters or highly stylized comic book action figures, 3D artists need to quickly realize ideas through 2D sketches that can be used as references in 3D modeling. To bring a polygonal model to life requires reaching beyond the surface and somehow investing the character with a personality, a sense of a lived life. As Nicolaïdes wrote: "To what the eye can see the artist adds feeling and thought. He can, if he wishes, relate for us the adventures of his soul in the midst of life."

How appropriate is such a sentiment to the task of 3D scanning, modeling, motion tracking, rendering, and compositing as used in a typical commercial production? What amount of individual expression contained in a drawing will survive the steps of digitizing, modeling, curve rebuilding, reparameterization, and all the rest throughout the production pipeline? Since the final outcome is the result of many hands, individuality must be suppressed. Characters are created by committee and often shaped directly by market forces and audience feedback. Yet some of the best commercial examples do communicate some of the values to which Nicolaïdes refers, although they may well be subordinated to plotline and qualities dictated by appeal to a mass audience. Nicolaïdes himself considered his drawing exercises as learning tools intended not for exhibition but rather as a by-product of the required mental and physical activity. But these exercises give us a glimpse of a larger and more meaningful experience.

The Natural Way to Draw is really a guide to learning how to observe with all of one's faculties, senses, and intelligence. It is essential training for anyone involved in the arts of visualization, from traditional painting to 3D computer graphics. It is preparation and a foundation that applies to many other disciplines. Mastery of life drawing is but one part of a larger pursuit that contributes to formation of a cultivated, self-aware aesthetic sensibility.

Other questions remain unanswered: Can sophisticated 3D computer graphics ever be more than photo-realistic razzle-dazzle that leaves behind the individual gestural mark and personal vision? Are these merely byproducts of working with pencil, pen, brush, paper, and canvas in an aesthetic whose time has come and

gone? Or is there still territory to be discovered and explored by using 3D computer graphics with a unique and individual vision? A provisional answer: Yes. As in traditional sculpture, there are multiple techniques for modeling the human form. An artist can use NURBS, polygons or subdivision modeling. Approaches include modeling the figure from a series of spheres or cylinders, slicing these geometries into patches, rebuilding surfaces, and stitching together reparameterized surfaces. From such techniques might a more individual exploration take place, one that would make the work of an artist as instantly recognizable as that of Francis Bacon, Peter Paul Rubens, or Alice Neel?

With these questions in mind the workshop was conceived as an update to the traditional life drawing course while being at the same time an introduction to MAYA and 3D modeling. This hands-on approach links the know-how of drawing to that of 3D modeling. In referencing Nicolaïdes' exercises this workshop offers a point of departure for further explorations of the human figure inspired by the legacy of expressionism, cubism, surrealism, and even abstraction. Coupled with the increasing interest in non-photorealistic rendering, 3D computer graphics artists may rediscover the value of the individual gesture and personal mark that informed the artistic vision of previous generations of artists.

From the Paleolithic Venus of Willendorf to the sensational work of Jake and Dinos Chapman, the human figure remains a subject of aesthetic interest and the site of contested narratives. In recent years, the "body" has been exhumed and dissected by extensive theorizing. The purported male gaze has been blind-sided and displaced by competing viewpoints with very different agendas. The territory of human skin and flesh has been colonized as an aesthetic object by artistic visions that were once marginalized.

This workshop, while providing an introduction to using 3D computer graphics to model the human figure, also aims to bring to this process the many different viewpoints and approaches that are found in contemporary artistic practice. It is an introduction to the Maya graphical user interface and to 3D modeling in general. Most students who have enrolled in the workshop had limited experience with 3D modeling. Some from the School of Architecture had experience with AutoCAD. Although the workshop is an introduction to modeling with Maya, the primary motivation and starting point is drawing from life and exploration of the role of the personal mark, gesture, and vision, which has remained a hallmark of artistic expression.

WORKSHOP OUTLINE

*Part I*

An orientation to the Maya GUI. A step-by-step tutorial demonstrates modeling a simple figure using NURB primitives such as cylinders and spheres in a four-panel view (perspective, front, side, top).

*Part II*

A survey of figurative work from art history. Posing the model and selection of viewpoints. Arms, legs, and torsos are drawn in profile and frontal views. Sketches are scanned, imported, and set up as reference-image planes.

*Part III*

Using the drawings displayed on the image planes as references, a series of NURB circles is lofted to create arms, legs, and torso.[3] Basic editing with Move, Scale, Rotate, and pick-masking components. Stitching.

*Part IV*

Polygonal and subdivision modeling is introduced by two examples of modeling the hands. Additional modeling techniques using component editing (vertices, edges, and faces), extrude, and Artisan (Sculpt NURBs Surfaces Tool) are introduced and used for refinements and for making simplified facial features on a sphere.

*Part V*

Demonstrations of adding a basic skeleton and skinning followed by a brief demonstration of deformers and painting weights. Basic texturing and the use of Paint Effects (hair), lighting (key, fill, rim) and final rendering to image files. Participants were able to print final renderings.

*Gregory Garvey*

Gregory Patrick Garvey is currently the visiting fellow in the arts and associate professor at Quinnipiac University and is an associate of the Yale Digital Media Center for the Arts. He has exhibited his digital images and interactive installations in North America and Europe and is a frequent contributor to SIGGRAPH and other conferences and symposia on art, technology, and education. He previously lived in Montréal, where he chaired the Department of Design Art at Concordia University, started the Program in Digital Image and Sound (a double major between computer science and fine arts), and served on the Board of Directors of the Montréal Design Institute. While living in Boston, he taught digital art and design at Mass College of Art, the New England School of Art and Design at Suffolk University, and Northeastern University. From 1982 to 1985, he was a fellow at the Center for Advanced Visual Studies at MIT, where he also received a masters of science in visual studies. He also holds an MFA from the University of Wisconsin-Madison.

*Carol Scully–Director, Digital Media Center for the Arts, Yale University*

The Digital Media Center for the Arts is a multimedia facility created to explore new areas of education and cross-disciplinary interaction that result when traditional art collides with the computer age. The DMCA encourages and enables discovery and creation in electronic media, investigates how new information technologies fit into established educational systems in the arts, and implements new models of arts education.

The center was conceived and designed by Yale's leaders in art, architecture, drama, history of art, film studies, music, the University Art Gallery, the Center for British Art, the Art and Architecture Library, and Information Technology Services, working closely with the Offices of the President and Provost.

*References*
1. Keim, Jean A. (1961). *Chinese art: The five dynasties and Northern Sung.* Tudor Publishing Co. New York, NY.
2. Nicolaïdes, Kimon. (1941). *The natural way to draw,* Houghton Mifflin Company, Boston;
3. This workshop is partly inspired by examples from: Harovas, Perry, John Kundert-Gibbs, and Peter Lee, Mastering MAYA Complete2, SYBEX, Alameda, CA, 2000.

28

# HANDS-ON CLASSICAL ANIMATION WORKSHOP

*Contact*
CLIFFORD COHEN
AnimAction, Inc.
1529 North Cahuenga Boulevard
Hollywood, California 90028
USA
+1.323.464.1181
cliffo@animaction.com

AnimAction was formed in 1989 with a single purpose in mind: to create a unique and innovative environment for young people – one where they could experience the spirit of collaboration, develop new skills, and exercise freedom of expression, all with the ultimate goal of articulating a powerful message through the medium of animation. Since then, AnimAction has trained thousands of students on development and production of classical and computer animation in the United States, Canada, the United Kingdom, and Europe.

AnimActions' methodology is successful because the "language" of animation is universal, and it transcends cultural barriers. AnimAction has worked with children in programs at: The World Animation Celebration USA, COMICON International, 3rd World Summit on Media for Children (Greece), International Ottawa Animation Festival, The Chicago International Children's Film Festival, UNCEF, The Los Angeles Unified School District, LA's BEST After School Enrichment Program, LA Children's Hospital, New York School Board, The Office of Criminal Justice Planning USA, YWCA, YMCA, The Gene Autry Museum, The Federation of Saskatchewan Indian Nations, The Solicitor General of Canada, The Teachers Advisory Council on Alcohol and Drug Education (TACADE) (UK), and The Roy Castle Lung Cancer Foundation (UK).

The graphic arts and animation industries have grown in leaps and bounds since AnimAction was founded. Today more than ever, the animation industry is crying out for artists to work in classical style and computer-generated animation. Now that the Internet is available to the general populace, the world's communication system is becoming easier to traverse, and the need for technicians is growing. Indeed, the whole media production world has opened up to provide more employment opportunities for a variety of careers within the rapidly expanding fields of animation and digital production. However, there seems to be a deep crevasse between the educational world and the industry. Should we teach our kids how to work, live, and breathe computers first, but not seriously take into account a solid foundation in art and use of the pencil and paper? Of course, the animation industry looks primarily for experienced artists who have acquired these artistic skills for a number of reasons. They are interested in working with people who can draw and understand the flow of a line. Animation studios will then train artists in the necessary digital technology.

## WORKSHOP GOALS

- Introduce the classical animation process, stressing how a solid foundation in the art of animation will help in digital production.

- Demonstrate and involve all participants in a hands-on experiential workshop, and give them the opportunity to take home their own product on video.

- To de-mystify classical animation production in the classroom (grades 5-12).

*The Workshop*
- Three-hour workshop for 40 people.

- Ages 8-80.

- Participants are arranged in small production teams. Each team works together throughout the workshop. This introduces and builds teamwork from the very beginning.

- Each team works through every stage of animation production to produce up to 10 seconds of animation on the theme: a whimsical look at a digital animation artist compared to a classical animation artist.

*The Animation Stages*
- Story concept
- Character development
- Timing
- Storyboarding
- Production
- Color
- Filming

*Follow Up Panel Discussion*
After the workshop, a panel of workshop participants and carefully selected industry representatives discussed the importance of a classical foundation and how it is linked to digital animation. The panel showed some of the animations produced in the workshop and critiques.

29

Artwork produced by High School Students, San Diego School of Creative and Performing Arts, San Diego City Schools.

Artwork produced by Middle School Students, Sun Valley Middle School, Los Angeles Unified School District.

## Delivering Effective Web-Based Education: Streamed Audio on the Web at SIGGRAPH

*Contact*
MaryEllen Coleman
IBM Corporation
Department 52QA/P384
2455 South Road
Poughkeepsie, New York 12601
USA
+1.845.435.7426
mea@us.ibm.com

Tracy Bondi
Charles Grange
*IBM Corporation*

Providing effective education outside the traditional classroom is a challenge more education professionals will face in the near future. While many approaches exist for solving this problem, one expedient solution is videotaping traditional stand-and-deliver classes, compressing the video to stream off the Web, synchronizing important visual material to key points in the video, and placing everything in a well-designed and easy-to-use Web site.

Our team created a Web site for educating 5,000 IBM field service personnel worldwide. Traditional classroom instruction could not reach that many students. The instructors were, in real life, product development programmers, who barely had time to organize and present the material once. The expected "shelf life" for the information was three years, and every six months there would be significant updates to the material. Running the presentations as satellite classes was not an option because of the lack of universal access to the necessary facilities. The depth and breadth of the material, along with its volatility, squashed any realistic notion of crafting computer based instruction modules. Those who could not attend the live presentations were stuck with downloading the reading handouts from the presentations, muddling along as best they could.

Delivering education and training on the Web is becoming increasingly popular. It is more cost-efficient to run a class on the Web than it is to run it several times in multiple classrooms and require travel to the class. One class can reach a larger audience, including students who may never have had the opportunity to receive the education in person before. Students can also pace themselves, viewing the instruction they require as often as they like, whenever they can fit it in their schedules. And students who are able to attend a face-to-face class can use a corresponding Web-based class to review material they may have forgotten. In our experience, user acceptance of Web-based education has been good.

This workshop, demonstrates how to produce streaming audio with synchronized slides. It reviews the planning issues, discusses strategies for capturing the information, and asks participants to create the audio and graphic files for the Web. Finally, we knit the files together on a Web page that we can view and play from our workstations.

Hardware and software are used to illustrate the process and make it real for the participants. We hope the hands-on experience is compelling, and that it demystifies the process by providing experience with real audio production tools, making them less intimidating.

Web Education

*30*

# RÉSUMÉS AND DEMO REELS: IF YOURS AREN'T WORKING, NEITHER ARE YOU!

*Contact*
PAMELA THOMPSON
Ideas to Go
PamRecruit@aol.com

What does it take to get a job at a visual effects, computer-animation, or interactive company? This workshop shows how to open the door to interviews, put your life on a one-page résumé, and showcase your talent in a three-minute-or-less demo reel.

The purpose of the résumé, portfolio, and demo reel is to get an interview with someone who makes hiring decisions. Prepare these items with care. Ask others for comments and critiques before you send them.

## RÉSUMÉS

If your resume doesn't work, neither will you. Your résumé should tell who you are: what you know (skills), what you've done (accomplishments), and what you want to do (objective or goal). If you are changing careers, focus your résumé on the job you want rather than the job you have. If your résumé shows a variety of jobs, make sure you have an objective at the top that indicates what job you're seeking.

- Make sure your current, correct contact information is on your résumé. This includes your name, phone number (with current area code), and email address (if you have one). Make sure the contact information is easy to read and easy to find.

- Don't send a URL and expect the employer or recruiter to look for your résumé there. If you want someone to see your résumé, email it as a message not an attachment (Sometimes downloads don't work). If you email a résumé, make sure your name, phone number, and email address are on it. Don't email your résumé as a jpeg attachment (they don't print well).

- Choose a type face that is easy to read. Many companies scan résumés into databases. Select a font where the lower case l and number 1 are different enough that the computer won't confuse the characters.

- List your skills. Be specific. Don't say: "a variety of software packages."

- Avoid huge blocks of type.

- If your résumé is more than one page, put your name, phone number, and email address on each page.

- Use paper that copies well (white or off-white). Don't include graphics or artwork on a gray scale behind the type. It doesn't copy or scan well. It's OK to attach sample art work to a résumé. Always include your contact info on attachments.

- Proofread to eliminate typos and spelling mistakes.

## PORTFOLIOS AND DEMO REELS

If you are an artist, an outstanding portfolio and demo reel are essential. Show your best work, and keep it short. The demo reel and portfolio should be relevant to the job you want. If you want a job as a character animator, show mostly character animation work on your reel.

Your demo reel should contain only your best work, and it should be:

- Representative of your recent work, and it should summarize your skills and talent.

- Of high caliber and quality.

- No longer than three minutes, and it can be much shorter.

- Irresistible.

- Labeled with your name, phone number, and email address. Also include slates on your reel with this information, in case the label falls off.

- A VHS cassette in NTSC format. This is the format almost all companies in North America can view.

Remember: Your audience sees lots of demo reels and portfolios. Keep it moving. Put the very best segment first.

Don't expect your work to be returned. Never send your only copy to a prospective employer, or anyone else.

Include slates or a written breakdown sheet that describe each scene and what you did for that segment. If you did everything, include a note stating that.

A portfolio of life drawing, illustration, photography (if you are interested in lighting), sculpture (if you are interested in modeling), character design, or color design is a big plus. If you have a fine art background, include some of the work with your reel (only your best work).

Whether you submit a demo reel, CD-ROM, portfolio, or all three, remember to always include a résumé and breakdown with it. Before submitting a CD, contact the company to find out if that format is acceptable for submission.

Pamela Kleibrink Thompson is a career coach and recruiter for such clients as FrameStore, Digital Domain and Walt Disney Feature Animation. She speaks at colleges and universities about animation and computer graphics careers. Her production background includes features such as "Bebe's Kids," the Fox television series "The Simpsons," and the original Amazing Stories episode of "Family Dog." She writes for Animation Magazine and Animation World Network on careers and animation.

31

## DESIGNING AND DEVELOPING INTERACTIVE ENTERTAINMENT AT BELL H@BITAT, CANADIAN FILM CENTRE

*Contact*
ANA SERRANO
Bell h@bitat
Canadian Film Centre
2489 Bayview Avenue
Toronto, Ontario M2L 1A8
Canada
+1.416.449.9151 x275
aserrano@cdnfilmcentre.com

JEROME DURLAK
York University

DARRYL WILLIAMS
Ryerson Polytechnic University

There is a need for professional producers who are able to create, plan, execute, market, and sell new-media content and interactive entertainment in Canada for the Web, interactive TV, interactive installations, and newly emerging broadband and wireless applications such as multi-user virtual communities and distributed storytelling systems via instant messaging devices.

The School of New Media at the Canadian Film Centre, currently known as Bell h@bitat, began offering its training in new-media product design and development in September of 1977. The vision of the New Media Design Programme is to drive the evolution of new-media content creation in Canada and elsewhere by training new-media thinkers. The program is now completing its fourth year.

### THE RESIDENTS

The five-month course, offered in the fall and winter, accepts a maximum of 12 students, referred to as residents, per session. Embracing the philosophy that compelling interactive entertainment products are best created with input from a variety of specialities, the New Media Design Programme is both project- and team-based. It brings together people from a variety of countries and disciplines, including writers, graphic designers, programmers, filmmakers, television producers, musicians, lawyers, and others already involved in new-media creation. In addition to several years of professional experience, or a portfolio of non-professional work, applicants must demonstrate an entrepreneurial spirit. The program demands people who can work in a collaborative and self-directed environment, and turns out people whose independence suits them to careers in producing interactive entertainment. About half of the residents return to their former industries and become the new-media experts, and the other half begin their own businesses.

The students work together in self-organizing teams. They spend the first two months in a series of hands-on, project-based exercises that provide the building blocks for developing new-media products. In the second half of the course, each team completes a new-media project. Ranging from treatments and prototypes to finished products, these projects draw on each team member's area of expertise, and they provide a practical context for testing new skills.

When the teams do not have all of the required skills or resources needed to complete a project, team members and faculty use their social and professional networks to find the appropriate human skills (a 3D designer; a cartoonist; a soundscape designer; actors; or a Lingo, Java, or XML programmer, for example) and resources (from cutting-edge generative music software to third-generation wireless phones and WAP or Bluetooth software and technology.)

### THE FACULTY

Throughout the program, participants are guided by leading Canadian and international new-media professionals and academics. The faculty at Bell Canada h@bitat is comprised of a team of new-media educators from major universities in Toronto and new-media professionals from Ontario and Quebec.

All of them are innovators from the areas of storytelling, technology, leadership, team building and collaborative project process, and business and entrepreneurial aspects of new media.

### THE CURRICULUM

The first phase of the program consists of a seminar-based, industry intensive, self-directed learning schedule made up of four separate training modules. The second half of the program consists of a production phase in which residents complete prototypes in a collaborative and real production environment.

*Phase I*

*1. Leadership Development and Team Building (week one)*
The leadership and team-building section of the program is based on the recognition that the new-media industry demands new ways of thinking and interacting. Leadership no longer filters down from the top but emerges throughout an organization in individuals who possess vision, passion, and creative insight. Teams are the fundamental units of interaction in the production and creative realm of new media, and together with wise use of leadership, they ensure that great ideas not only become a reality but also get to market on time and at a reasonable cost. The objectives:

- Learn to apply collaborative skills that enhance both creativity and effectiveness.
- Learn how planning, task clarification, and rapid prototyping ensure on-time completion and satisfying team relationships.

*2. New Media Technology Section (weeks two and three)*
This section provides an examination and comparison of the evolution and influence of new-media technology and tools on the nature of different media. It involves three production exercises using Web, video, and interactive software. Residents prepare for this session by gathering written visual and audio material to tell a story. The story is then told three times, first using a linear "video" model, second using a hypertext or Web model, and third using a hypermedia model. Residents are encouraged to work together in teams to create collaborative stories.

*3. Digital Storytelling (weeks four and five)*
Digital storytelling and interactivity are two of the most overused and least understood terms in the new-media environment. One of the continuous discussions during these two weeks is: What is digital storytelling? Is it storytelling using digital media? Are we witnessing the emergence of a new grammar or a new genre? Or is it hype and hoopla and

nothing more? This section examines digital storytelling through a combination of theoretical inquiry; analysis of concrete storytelling models; case studies of Web sites, interactive installations, CD-ROMs, and interactive television sites; and hands-on explorations. Residents interact with numerous guest speakers (first-nation storytellers, installation artists, virtual environment designers, and game designers) and visit the Canadian Broadcasting Company's New Media Group and a number of leading-edge new-media companies.

Working in teams, residents choose a work that has been translated into more than one form or medium and examine ensuing changes to narrative structures; dramatic structure; and concepts of immersion, absorption, and engagement. They also assess a number of interface designers and address issues of accessibility, functionality, and usability. The interfaces range from telephone message systems to new-media interfaces such as mind maps or immersive environments.

*4. New Media Business Practices (week six)*
This component explores the differences in strategies and methods that new media impose on traditional media processes, from production through distribution.

Many traditional project management methods do not transfer well to new media development. In reality, new-media management shares many similarities with the management of innovation. Anticipation of risk, continuous environmental scanning, and Internet time are important. The faculty examines these issues and challenges with presentations from leaders in the new-media field, seminars, and project management activities.

*Phase II*
At the end of the six-week course modules section, residents are asked to form teams, self-selected based on a series of in-depth brainstorming sessions about projects. These teams range from three- to six-person groups, with projects ranging from interactive documentaries to experimental Web art. For the next 10 weeks, these teams produce prototypes that typically act as proofs of concept for their ideas about what makes for a compelling interactive experience.

Faculty at this stage switch roles, from facilitators to project consultants. Once a week, residents and faculty get together in a fish bowl environment to critique the progress of each team and the direction each project takes.

SOME OF THE PROTOTYPES CREATED AT BELL H@BITAT:
*1953: A Night on Shuter Street*
This prototype invites users into an immersive 3-D storyscape. A darkened stage encourages users to uncover the dramatic events surrounding a 1953 jazz concert at Massey Hall, a performance that some consider the greatest concert ever. Collecting visual clues from an environment filled with music and voices, users build their own version of the past from the stories and memories of the event. Creative team: Alastair Jarvis, Katie MacGuire, Carolina Ostos, and Tamara Rebanks

*esc*
A user-empowered narrative journey filled with digital suspense as five "cyber friends" dare to attempt meeting each other in person. Users direct their experiences of the story by selecting the perspective from which to view the action. They may also interact at certain plot points to push the narrative forward. The plot, however, is time-based and is in constant movement toward its ultimate resolution. The esc experience is startlingly close to that of everyday life. Creative Team: Andrew Brady, Daryl Cloran, Jim Hand-Cukierman, Michael Kasprow, and Rebecca Scott.

*Home*
An example of a dramatic, non-linear narrative that moves away from cyberspace in its creation of a cyberplace. This is an intimate journey through household objects that reveal stories about personal history, memory, and identity. Creative Team: Suzanne Stein, Clementina Koppman, and Alan Wong.

*i matter*
A unique creative resource that takes the notion of career and turns it on its head. This prototype, primarily for teenagers, showcases interviews with professionals who share stories of their life's work, their passions, and their career advice. Creative Team: Aurea Dempsey, Richard Lane, and Sharman Wilson.

*Mako Ads*
Explores the next generation of episodic and story-based collectible Web advertising. The user keeps tabs on the journey of two people who fall in love, then decide to meet. The episodes are delivered via rich, interactive video banner ads that are designed to be collected and traded. It's viral marketing at its best. Creative Team: Maxim Fishman, Yong-Eui Hong, and Aidan Tierney

33

*My name is Elliot B.*

An edgy interactive drama that delves into the soul of an urban loner. As the story unfolds, users apply simple and intuitive navigation to pursue distinct narrative paths that revolve around different use-selected themes. Creative Team: Donald Anderson, John Kalangis, and Maria Rotella.

*Revelation*

An interactive narrative about a man who has lost his memory from "The Great Crash" and begins his search to find it. Revelation creates a user-defined, experiential process for storytelling. The user directly participates in the process of one man's journey to self-discovery. The prototype reveals one possible outcome when society becomes too dependent on "computer systems." Creative Team: Noam Muscovitch, Lisa Santanatos, Ed Wong, and Annabelle Hoffman.

*The Great Canadian Story Engine*

The first-ever interactive and immersive online exploration of Canada, its people and places, past and present. Imagine it as an online time capsule for the millennium that gives Canadians the power to tell their own stories without being filtered through traditional media. The engine has the capacity to connect us from one side of the country to the other. It is a brilliant example of how new technologies will revolutionize human communications. Creative Team: Tessa Sproule, Jason Cliff, Kato Wake, Rena Dempsey, and Rand Ardell.

*The Seen*

A new entertainment genre: A Webshow that combines elements of sitcoms, video games, cartoons, and music videos. To be released episodically over the internet, this is the story of Mark Ryder, his childhood in the digital age, and his quest to get a life. Creative Team: Jeremy Diamond, Denny Silverthorne, and Adrian Carter.

## CONCLUSION

Bell h@bitat is a unique environment that changes with each new programme session. Producing new-media prototypes with teams of highly accomplished and creative people from a variety of disciplines who hardly know each other, in a short period of time, almost seemed too daunting a task to undertake. And with each programme session, we are always amazed by the capacity of talented individuals to produce not just any work but very good work indeed. Part of this success has to do with the talent itself, but part of it has to do with the type of environment we are constantly striving to create in Bell h@bitat: flexible, responsive, supportive, and open.

We have discovered interesting ways to create such an environment and have stumbled upon challenges that make creating such a space difficult. We would like to engage in a discussion with our colleagues at SIGGRAPH 2001 about what makes for a challenging and creative learning environment, and share with them the lessons we have learned and the questions we have yet to answer.

# Adventures in Modeling:
# Building Systems with StarLogo

*Contact*
Eric Klopfer
MIT Teacher
Education Program
77 Massachusetts Avenue
MIT Building 7-337
Cambridge, Massachusetts 02139
USA
+1.617.253.2025
klopfer@mit.edu

Vanessa Colella
Mitchel Resnick
Massachusetts Institute
of Technology

## Introduction

For the past two decades, scientists have been building computer models to help them better understand and explain the systems they study. Biologists build models of protein folding, ecologists build models of habitat fragmentation, economists build models of commodity pricing, and physicists build models of subatomic interactions. Computers also make it easier for novices to build and explore their own models, and learn new scientific ideas in the process.

The Adventures in Modeling Project introduces students and teachers to the process of designing, creating, and analyzing their own models of complex, dynamic systems. Our goal is to engage learners in authentic science practice by giving them the tools and the ability to pose, investigate, and answer their own questions. For the past three years, we have taught secondary school students and teachers to build and explore computer models in StarLogo.[3] Unlike many other modeling tools, StarLogo supports a tangible model-building process that does not require advanced mathematical or programming skills. This characteristic makes it possible for students to focus on the content of the model rather than simply on the technical aspects of model creation. Using StarLogo and a variety of off-computer activities, students learn to create and investigate models and develop a deeper understanding of patterns and processes in the world.

## Workshop Organization

The StarLogo Workshops are designed to introduce participants to the computational and cognitive aspects of modeling complex, dynamic systems. During these workshops, participants work together to design, build, and analyze agent-based computer models. They engage in an iterative process of model creation and scientific investigation as they explore important scientific principles and processes. The workshops foster a playful, cooperative, creative spirit, and provide adequate structure for learning how to build models. To accomplish this balance between structure and exploration, the workshops are organized around a set of open-ended StarLogo design challenges on the computer and a series of off-computer activities in which participants enact and analyze a simulation.

Each challenge is a problem statement that is meant to guide participants' explorations and get their creative juices flowing. For example, one challenge asks participants to build a model in which creatures change their environment and subsequently react to those changes. In response to this challenge, one might create a model of a beaver altering its environment by cutting down trees to build a dam, or termites chewing on a log to create passageways. Every challenge includes sample projects, which teachers are encouraged to explore. The challenges and accompanying sample projects facilitate model design and construction, build familiarity with the StarLogo environment, and introduce the principles of complex systems.

Though on-screen computer modeling is one focus of our workshops, "off-screen" activities provide another way to connect abstract notions of scientific systems to personal experience.[1]

These Activities allow participants to think about concepts like exponential growth, local-versus-global information, and group decision making from a personal perspective. For instance, in one activity, participants "fly" around a parking lot trying to form cohesive "bird flocks" without the assistance of a leader.

## SIGGRAPH 2001 Implementation

Attendees began with a group activity called "27 Blind Mice" to spur thinking about the nature of self-organizing ("emergent") systems and the implications of accessing information locally versus globally. Then, participants further explored these ideas through design and construction of their own StarLogo models. The workshop implemented some of the newly developed software scaffolding in StarLogo that supports rapid prototyping of simulation models. Attendees showed their models, described some of their insights to the group, and learned about sharing models through the online StarLogo Design Discussion Area. The workshop closed with some reflections from other workshops we have held and a discussion of how people from diverse organizations (from junior high schools to Fortune 500 companies) are able to use these tools to think about problems in new ways.

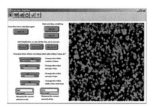

A student-built model of a forest fire.

*References*
1. Colella, V. (2000). Participatory simulations: Building collaborative understanding through immersive dynamic modeling. *Journal of the Learning Sciences.*
2. Colella, V., Klopfer, E., & Resnick, M. (1999). StarLogo community of learners workshop. *Journal of the ISTE Special Interest Group for Logo-Using Educators,* 17 (2).
3. Resnick, M. (1994). *Turtles, termites, and traffic jams: Explorations in massively parallel microworlds.* Cambridge, MA: MIT Press.

Teachers playing 27 Blind Mice.

Teachers working on StarLogo models.

# THE PROCESS BEHIND "RUPERT," A STUDENT PRODUCED 3D ANIMATION

*Contact*
SCOTT PORTER
Brigham Young University
3620 Castano Drive
Camarillo, California 93010 USA
+1.805.383.2766
sap@email.byu.edu

This paper documents the educational experience of collaboratively developing a student-produced animation. It is my hope that these materials will be useful to those planning collaborative artistic endeavors, especially students and educators who are planning computer animations as an educational experience. Video clips and images into the write-up (including the final animation) are included as illustrations in the electronic version of this paper.

I was fortunate to have participated with more than 30 students in creation of the computer-animated cartoon "Rupert," a process that took us about two years. In the beginning, we did not know how to coordinate the efforts of multiple students, so besides learning about animation, we also learned to collaborate on an artistic endeavor (and the different roles that we as individuals could play in this collaborative process). We tried several different approaches to organizing our group during the production of the animation, and though the flow from one form of collaboration to the next was not planned, in retrospect I see a "method to our madness".

Each approach to organizing the group had trade-offs in how well it helped us to effectively distribute work versus how well it helped us to collaborate creatively. In retrospect:

- Different approaches to organization and decision-making were appropriate at different stages of the production.

- The way we organized ourselves in each stage had an effect upon the artistic outcome of our work during that stage of development.

Since it was difficult for us to understand our collaborative experience until after the project was finished, groups organizing other collaborative art projects may be able to use our experience from "Rupert" as a resource.

## THE ARGUMENTATIVE APPROACH TO GOAL MAKING

The project began without an organization per se. We were a large group that was not differentiated into different "jobs." A faculty member arranged for a classroom and a time for a meeting of those who were interested in creating an animation project. We met at the appointed hour and discussed what we wished to accomplish. Initially, decisions were made by group vote. I am not sure if our input was evaluated more by logic, by emotion, or by volume, since all three factors seemed important in getting our point across.

The first progress we made in our discussions was an agreement that we would collectively accomplish "something more difficult" than we had previously been able to do individually or in small groups. We then needed to define "something more difficult." Because working in small groups severely limits the length of the animation you can produce, almost all of our previous student animations had relied on gags or effects to "pull off" something interesting in a short amount of time. Previous student animation projects averaged 10-30 seconds in length. We decided that with more people working together, we could finally do an animation that had an in-depth story and was several minutes in length.

We also discussed the idea that the animation needed to be "worthwhile" to justify the substantial time and resources necessary to complete it. However, it was not easy to define "worthwhile." We decided to define "worthwhile" by the characters and issues addressed in the story. We felt that most of the student computer animations with which we were familiar tried to make up for weak stories by either shocking the viewer with some surprise (visual or narrative), or by showing off the latest and greatest animation technology ("eye candy"). We decided that "worthwhile" for this project meant a story that invited the audience to try to understand the characters and the issues they were dealing with.

Our last requirement was suggested by people who were tired of all the serious talk it took to figure out what "worthwhile" meant for our animation. "Sure it needs to be worthwhile," they said. "But whatever we do, it also should be fun." That was a good idea. We did not want to put in long hours working on our animation unless it was fun.

So, our overall requirements for the animation ended up as follows:

1. Story-driven (rather than being driven by effects or gags).
2. Worthwhile characters and issues.
3. Fun.

Once we had our overall requirements for the animation, we decided on a story. After several stories were suggested and discussed, we voted. First we voted on the top three stories, then the top two, then we took a final vote for the story we would produce. We chose a story that had been written and illustrated as a children's book by Heather Stratton, an illustration student. It follows a little boy named Rupert who heard about microbes for the first time from his older sister. We liked the story, we liked the characters, and the issues that they dealt with, and it seemed that we could have quite a bit of fun exploring Rupert's imagined ideas of microbes.

We now knew what we wanted to do, and we began to decide how to proceed. We already had criteria to help us in making creative decisions, with our three requirements for our story: story-driven, worthwhile characters and issues, and fun. However, we still had to organize ourselves and choose the process by which we would make those decisions (for example should we stick with a simple group vote, and if not, who should decide what, etc?).

Time to proceed; but how to organize or make decisions? Deciding how we would organize ourselves and how we would make decisions was difficult, and we changed our approach several times throughout the project depending upon the needs at the time. Our method of organization progressed from every decision being made by the entire group and competitive bidding to sub-groups whose autonomy increased as the project progressed.

## The large group

The large-group discussion approach was helpful to us during the initial weeks of the project. The creative interchange helped us to develop well-thought-out, worthwhile ideas. If there was a problem with an idea, it was sure to be quickly pointed out in our heated discussions. Ideas would be proposed, rejected, revised, and re-proposed, which helped us to more fully develop our ideas. Also, ideas had to appeal to a large group of people with differing interests. This helped us to avoid story ideas with a narrow appeal.

I did not realize how important it was to have general appeal to the story until later when I came across another story with an extremely narrow appeal. As we began the second year of working on "Rupert," I attended a film market with one of my classes. While there, I saw flyers for a film whose producer was seeking a distributor; I found it humorous that the film was about an oppressed filmmaker whose movies could not get distributed. Although the movie seemed interesting and relevant to the filmmaker, it was not a general-interest film. A comparable mistake for us would have been for us to make an animation about hopeful college age animators, or something to which only computer animators could relate. The large size of the group of people collaborating on the story, some of whom were not even animators, helped us to bring more diverse interests and insights into the creative development of the animation.

Our large-group approach, which allowed everyone to discuss and vote on each issue, held important advantages in helping us to develop our ideas. The problem with the single group approach was our rate of progress. It was slow going. It took more than two weeks just to decide on criteria for the project and pick a story. In order to get more done, we decided that we needed a way to explore more than one idea at once. So we tried a system of competitive bids.

## The competitive bids

We started the competitive bids as we began work on our initial storyboards. There had been several ideas raised in the large-group discussions about possible ways to visualize and sequence the animation. However, the ideas needed further development. We divided our group into three storyboard teams, and each team independently developed the story. Each team made a rough storyboard showing the action and some visual story elements. After all three storyboards were presented to the group, we voted on which version to use as our primary storyboard. The primary storyboard was then re-written and further developed. We fixed problems discovered in the group discussion, and we incorporated some of the better elements from the work by the other two storyboard teams.

There were advantages to the degree of collaboration that we used during this stage of the animation development (as opposed to collaborating either more or less closely). We were far enough into the project that we needed to get more done than we could do in one group. Dividing into smaller groups allowed us to explore multiple creative options simultaneously and helped us accomplish more work because we were not limited to working at the specific times when all 20 individuals' schedules overlapped (usually only during class time). However, it was good that we collaborated closely enough that everyone was able to give story input by helping to develop a storyboard and then by discussing the results. On a project that required enormous amounts of work, this input was important, as it allowed all of us to develop ownership of the project, which helped to keep us going when work on the animation became difficult.

Once again, the collaboration also aided us in producing well-developed ideas. This time it was not simply that we had peer feedback. We also had the advantage of trying several possibilities. When writing a story, this is especially important. Our approach was similar to a technique sometimes used when developing a motion picture script. In this approach, several writers proceed with script development simultaneously. At certain stages, the results are evaluated, and one or more of the writers are asked to continue. This sort of approach is helpful because it is hard, even for experienced writers, to develop a story that "works". The other reason that this method of organization helped us to refine our ideas was that it gave us extra time to work on the ideas. Our smaller groups were able to meet more often than the whole group, so the sub-groups would discuss and develop ideas that they could then share with the whole group.

The obvious disadvantage to collaborating simultaneously in three groups with final decisions saved for the whole group was that progress was still slow. Although we were exploring different options and asking everyone to help create the story, we were also duplicating work. After we finished the storyboards, we realized that at the pace we were progressing, we could not afford to continue to work this way throughout the entire production.

## The beginning of the sub-groups, the dividing of "worlds"

After completing the initial storyboards, we began to write a more detailed storyboard and script based on our rough version. To do this, we decided to break into groups again, but this time we did not duplicate work. We began to use the term "world" for our four groups, because there is the "real world" and the three daydream "worlds" where Rupert's imagination takes him. We used the term "world" inclusively: it was the segment, it was the people working on the segment, it was the location where the story took place. "Battle World is looking good;" "Does Food World have their shot ready?"; and "So, when Rupert first enters Garbage World, what happens?" are all valid statements in Rupert production terminology.

37

Each sub-group (or "world") took their section of the story (which we also called a "world") and fleshed it out into a script by refining the story ideas and by adding dialogue, action, and effects. We also designed the characters, first as sketches, and later in the computer as 3D models. When the entire group met together, we discussed how the segments were meshing. We wanted the segments to play off of each other, but we also wanted each segment to have its own "feel". In order to make the pieces fit together cohesively, we ended up making some pretty dramatic changes. These changes were very important to ensuring that the story was cohesive, that the characters had "depth" (no pun intended), and that the developing story remained fun.

However, although the story was improving, some of the changes that we made for narrative purposes ended up adding enormous amounts of extra work to the production. We had not thought to establish criteria for production decisions such as how long we should extend the production of a segment in order to improve the story. However, if we had established production criteria, such as how long we should continue working on each segment, earlier, it would have been easier for us to know how well we were balancing the creative needs with our production limitations.

FURTHER DEVELOPMENTS IN THE SUBGROUPS

Although the creative work was now being done in several groups working simultaneously on different parts of the animation, the work had not sped up considerably because we still discussed almost every decision with the entire group. Once the story ideas were firmed up, we decided to allow the sub-groups more autonomy as we began to design the characters and the environments of the animation.

These autonomous sub-groups or teams (or "worlds") became the mainstay organization throughout the rest of the production. Although initially these smaller groups were only going to be used during the character and environment design stages, with only occasional changes, we ended up using this same organization throughout the rest of the production. Actually, the groups we used remained fairly close to the groups that began even earlier, during the scriptwriting phase, so these teams worked together for almost the entire process.

These autonomous sub-groups ended up functioning very much like the original large group. The subgroups would usually meet and/or have discussions (via phone and email) several times a week. First, the sub-group discussed the initial ideas for environment design, character design, plot, animation, etc. Next, an individual would be given a particular assignment (for example, designing a character based on the ideas they had discussed). Then the results would be reviewed by the sub-group, feedback would be generated, changes would be made, and more assignments given. When the sub-group was pleased with its progress, it would present it to the entire group for additional feedback. The entire group met either once or twice a week.

Extra autonomy helped in two ways: it allowed us to develop more diverse styles, and it allowed us to get more work done. Although feedback was welcome from the entire group, we did not vote on changes to the sub-groups' work unless it somehow affected the whole animation (for example if segments did not mesh well or if something affected our overall message). Artistically, this let each of the groups develop a unique look and feel for their segment. I do not think that we would have been able to develop such different daydream "worlds" without this autonomy. From a production standpoint, because we were not deciding every detail as a group, we were able to progress more quickly. Because the group only dealt with large-scope issues, individuals were able to spend more time on smaller issues. We were able to focus on the little details that we did not have time or energy to discuss as a group.

Of course, each group did not have as much input from the entire group as we did in the beginning, but we referred to the overall guidelines that we had established, and assistance and advice from either our sub-group or the whole group was readily available.

38

As the project progressed, we continued to develop our organization. Over time, we added a project manager and team leaders in order to ensure that all of the work meshed. The project manager became especially important when schedules became more complicated and acceptable meeting times became increasingly scarce; we needed someone who could track things down, make spot decisions, and coordinate among the groups. The team leaders did similar duty coordinating the members of the group. Due to schedule conflicts, often there would be only one or two members of each team at the meetings of the whole group (hopefully, the team leader was one of them). The individuals at the meeting had to relay their team's input to the group and later relay the group's feedback to their team.

The project managers and team leaders were also important because of the turnover we experienced. We had to acquaint the new students with our creative guidelines and our system of dividing up the work. However, the new students caught on quickly. In fact, one of the new additions to the team became our second project manager and helped push us to completion.

### PULLING IT ALL TOGETHER

Once we started the editing process, it became apparent what had worked and what had not worked in our organizational plan, by what flowed well together and what did not.

Through editing, we were able to see that "Rupert" did indeed work creatively. Although it needed the editing to give the story the right pacing and to tie it all together, the segments meshed, while retaining their own flair, as we had hoped. However, editing also allowed us to see that more rigorous production standards would have been beneficial, because each scene had been completed to a different level of technical rigor (technical issues included lighting, color, realism of motion, etc.). If we had created technical standards, we could have brought each scene to approximately the same technical level, thereby avoiding the necessity of adjoining one scene at 99-percent proficiency with another scene at only 70-percent.

Another issue that became apparent as we began to edit "Rupert" was that we should have been editing all along. We ended up cutting scenes in editing to make the story clearer and to fit within the five-minute limit of the Alias|Wavefront Student Animation Contest (we submitted "Rupert" to the 1999 contest). Editing was frustrating, because the scenes that we had spent extra time perfecting were cut, while scenes that were still rough were left in because they were critical to the story. If we had been editing all along, we would have realized which scenes were critical, and we could have put our extra effort on the scenes that would actually be included. Of course, projects that do not take two years to finish will not have as much trouble with this. We could not even remember who had done the first shots by the end of production, so reworking shots was difficult.

Editing from the beginning would also have helped us creatively. We could have been more sensitive to the story if we had been more aware of how the story would be shaped through editing. We might have made changes to the story in response to the timing and pacing that developed for "Rupert" as part of the editing process.

### LOOKING BACK

All in all, we went through at least four stages in the evolution of our group's organization: the large group, the competitive bids, our initial sub-groups, and the more autonomous sub-groups with a project manager to coordinate; although I am sure that we could further sub-divide our process into additional steps. Each of these stages required a balance between how closely we cooperated, which helped us to develop creative ideas, and how much we separated out the work to improve efficiency. Each different segment of the organization had a place in the development of the animation, and our organization seemed to flow very naturally from one stage to another.

These stages are not only applicable to animation but also to other "creative" group projects. We can summarize the process as follows: a group of people with similar interests meets together to accomplish a creative goal; they decide what it is they want to accomplish and how they think they will accomplish it; decisions and tasks are entrusted to smaller groups, and then to individuals, who report back to receive and act upon feedback. Other creative endeavors could easily fit this model. Closer to everyday life, if we were to plan a social or a party, we might go through many of the same steps to combine our creative ideas while still maintaining a manageable organization. Most artistic or creative endeavors that allow all of the participants to participate creatively will no doubt follow a similar path to ours as the idea progresses from something that is talked about to something that is actively engaged and completed.

Although I think that the way we progressed from one form of organization to another was quite natural and even helpful, there are things that we could have done better. First we could have planned more proactively at the beginning if we had anticipated the kinds of organizational steps to which we would probably progress. This would include establishing guidelines regarding production issues (not just creative issues), clarifying and reinforcing our project guidelines by making them available to everyone in writing, and posting them in meeting rooms.

Also, if we had been more conscious of the process, instead of stumbling upon each succeeding level of organization, we could have maximized the creative potential of each organizational method of each group. For example, when we met as an entire group at the beginning of the project, we could have saved time by discussing only those issues most appropriate for the entire group, realizing that there were certain issues that were best left to smaller groups (even though we did not exactly know the organization that would come later). Similarly, once we organized the sub-groups, we could have waited on small detail-oriented decisions until we could assign an individual to handle them. This kind of awareness of the proper scope of issues to be decided by different segments of the group might have helped us work more efficiently without sacrificing too much of our creative energies.

As I said in the beginning, I feel fortunate to have had the opportunity to participate with so many students in a project that I feel was worthwhile, not simply because of what we learned about animation, but because of how we learned to collaborate on an artistic project. All of us will participate in other creative collaborations (perhaps even on other animations), and our experience on "Rupert" will be a valuable asset. Also, participants in any artistic collaboration will have to deal with the issue of allowing creative collaboration while maintaining a working, flexible organization. Hopefully other groups who are organizing creative collaborations can make use of our experience.

Figure 1. The characters went through several stages of development. Clockwise from bottom left: one of the original illustrations from Heather's story, a storyboard sketch, a shot-breakdown sheet and sketch, and the clay models used to prove that Rupert and Molly worked as 3D characters.

Figure 2. Dividing into teams allowed us to weave four worlds with distinctive looks and feels into the story. Top left: Rupert and Molly in the "Real World." Top right, middle left: Rupert is ready to take on disease microbes in "Battle World." Middle right, Bottom left: In "Food World," Rupert imagines that microbes must test if pickles (or Rupert) are completely fermented. Bottom right: "Trash World" lacks microbes to break down garbage, so trash fills the earth.

## SEEING DRAWING

*Contact*
FARIBA FARSHAD
The London Institute
65 Davies Street
London W1Y 2DA
United Kingdom
+44.0207.514.8052
itrdu@linst.ac.uk

ROBIN BAKER
Ravensbourne College of
Design & Communication

Drawing is central to all that is produced within the broadest spectrum of art and design. It is the core around which the conceptual and intellectual development of students takes place. A number of art and design institutions in the UK are in the process of developing a family of products that address the important subject of drawing. The focus of the project is fundamentally and crucially concerned with the process of developing visual literacy mostly at the undergraduate level. The essential skills of drawing have become marginalised by a series of factors, and effective use of expensive and sophisticated software packages has been constrained by lack of understanding of drawing skills in many art and design applicants. A great deal of costly staff time is needed to retrieve this situation.

Seeing Drawing addressed this problem by producing a resource that will have wide applicability to the subject of art and design, and to other related subjects. The products are readily integrated into teaching and learning practices within higher education, and they will reduce the amount of costly lecturer time presently expended on remedial work.

At the end of this three-year project, the outcome is a set of quality-assured, interactive multi-media DVDs on drawing. The product provides an extremely valuable teaching and learning tool for use throughout education. It enables students to develop as independent learners and provides a much needed, innovative, and cost-effective teaching aid to support hard-pressed teaching staff. In 1998-99, almost six percent of higher education students in the UK were in art and design. If related subjects with a clear interest in drawing such as architecture, engineering, and technology, are included, the total rises to almost 16 percent.

The partners in this government-funded project are:

- The London Institute (lead partner)
- Falmouth College of Arts
- Ravensbourne College of Design & Communication
- University of Ulster Faculty of Art and Design

The University of Glasgow Evaluation Group oversees the process of production, testing, and delivery.

This consortium represents a large part of the total art and design activity in the higher education sector. The expertise available to support the project is formidable. The consortium partners have significant experience in management and delivery of complex publicly funded projects.

### SEEING DRAWING'S SIX SECTIONS

*1. As Exploration*

The section developed by Camberwell College of Arts (The London Institute) enables consideration of "figure and body" and "objective and subjective." It asks us to question how we perceive the world around us and how we "sense" through our own bodies. A three-part approach allows navigation through visuals and text to consider cognition, perception, and the act of drawing by visiting the practice of three well-known artists, and to interact through drawing, in a manner uncharacteristic to computing programs.

*2. As Instrument*

This section, compiled by Ravensbourne College of Design & Communication, represents a survey of the related areas of drawing for design such as architectural, engineering drawing, and drawing with the computer, in both 2D and 3D. Drawing as Instrument does not intend to recreate the drawing environment of either paper and pencil or computer-drawing packages, but instead provides access to the tools, methods, and conventions of drawing processes that support communication and definition of an object or product. The objective is to supply a means whereby students can access central features of measured drawing, enabling them to establish points of reference. Drawing as Instrument works through a number of approaches and levels, providing explicit interaction through which students accomplish key tasks and view examples of drawings, techniques, and conventions.

*3. As Method*

The section developed by the University of Ulster will be used by first-year undergraduates as a reference device. It is intended to reassure those with different levels of drawing ability that experienced designers had the same fears and anxieties in their initial work. It highlights their ways of dealing with the issues. The initial video section introduces the student to the thoughts of a ceramic designer as he selects and draws an object as reference for a later design piece. The approach explains how the designer relates to the drawing process as an informing and selective activity. This is complemented by the work of four other designers who work in product, environment, graphics, and animation. Their thoughts on their work are subdivided into: why draw, approach, application, reference and style. This allows the student to explore in depth how designers integrate and apply drawing to the creative process. The core principles are further illustrated by the sketchbook work of an illustrator who reinforces the similarities and differences in working practice.

This section is a useful touchstone for drawing in an applied context. It complements some of the more personal interactive aspects of the programme, enabling those who wish to undertake design studies to relate to the practice of drawing.

*41*

### 4. As Reflection

In this section, designed by Falmouth College of Arts, students are encouraged to work independently with their peers or with their tutors through creating, selecting, and evaluating. They learn how drawings can be created in response to a variety of contexts. Navigation through the section confronts the user with a number of visual problems that have to be solved to gain access to all four levels. The introduction provides the context. This is followed by a section on Truth, which asks why drawings are created in the first place. Thirdly, the Eye section contains some basic principles of how we might spatially analyse what we see through simple examples of architecture, object, and figure. And finally, in the Beholder section, students view a drawing and ask how can we make objective judgements about it.

### 5. As Understanding

This smaller module, also developed by Falmouth College of Arts, was conceived to support the other modules by introducing propositions about the physical characteristics of how the eye reacts to reflected light to produce sensation. This is followed by a section called the Mind, which interprets user experience to create visual models, and explores the cultural role of the viewer and its impact on interpretation of these models.

### 6. As Fashion

Developed by London College of Fashion (The London Institute), this section shows the importance of drawing for the curriculum. Recent research indicates that drawing can be used not only to develop the ability to see, but also to enhance the individual's capacity for rational thinking generally. Fashion illustration tends to focus upon the technique of drawing and the finished image, thus reinforcing the students' perception of the importance of technique over experimentation and conceptual development.

This section enriches students' drawing experience by showing potential uses in the fashion design process. For the first time, it is possible for fashion students to see the thinking and conceptual development that inform the process of drawing in fashion. They can explore the various functions of drawing in the fashion curriculum from the perspective of practitioners. The content providers rethought the approach and decided to let the excellent examples of work speak for themselves and allow them to dictate the best ways to communicate their message.

The student becomes a much more active participant in working with the material. The sequence of dealing with the material and the speed of learning are determined by the usefulness to the student. Each student's interactive experience with the section is uniquely addressed to and determined by that student's quality and level of interest.

42

### DISSEMINATION

Ownership of these products resides with the consortium partners. Products will be available at marginal cost to all directly funded UK higher education institutions. The consortium partners have sought the widest possible sector involvement in an interactive process of product development, and there has been a sector-wide conference to launch the project.

The Seeing Drawing main menu.

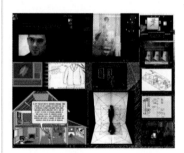

Collage of images from the Seeing Drawing project.

GRAPHICS IN A FLASH:
AN INTRODUCTION TO VECTOR-BASED WEB GRAPHICS

*Contact*
JAMES L. MOHLER
Purdue University
1419 Knoy Hall, Room 363
West Lafayette, Indiana
47907-1419 USA
+1.765.494.9089
+1.765.494.9267 fax
james_mohler@siggraph.org

Due to the inclusion of automatic anti-aliasing, vector graphics are now as much at home on the Web as anywhere else. The added benefits of scaleable images, small file sizes, interactivity, and a range of other features are generating an explosion of vector graphic use on the Web. And Macromedia Flash has been the driving force behind this explosion.

## A NEW HOME FOR VECTOR GRAPHICS

Macromedia Flash is a full-featured package that is quickly becoming the primary delivery vehicle for graphics on the Web. From still images and animated segments to buttons and interface components, it can be used to create objects that were once only deliverable as raster images, and even some that have never been possible on the Web before. With the breadth of content that needs to be pushed over an already busy Internet, Flash presents significant benefits for content developers.

### Anti-Aliasing

Flash-based content provides the ability to display any range of elements, at any size, with anti-aliased (smoothed) edges. Unlike raster graphics, where scaling an image increases file size, these benefits come with no change in file size. Complex blends, minute details, eight-bit transparency, and animated objects, are automatically anti-aliased at any size. Flash also includes a feature that allows users to dynamically zoom graphic content and print Web content with no loss of detail.

### Animation

Typically, animation on the Web is achieved with GIF files, scripting languages such as JavaScript, or programming languages such as Java. Flash provides a completely vector-based environment for creating animations. It supports animations of any size, from full-screen to icon-sized, and it can import raster images, bringing creation and development capabilities full circle.

### Interactivity

Probably the most exciting thing about Flash is that developers now have the ability to create true graphical user interfaces and interactive experiences on the Web. Flash excels at delivering rich graphics for realistic user interfaces, as shown in Figure 1. From buttons and slider bars to complex and original elements, authors can now create a unique user experience without the tremendous overhead typically associated with raster graphics.

Figure 1. Flash enables graphical user interfaces on the Web, making navigation more intuitive and user-friendly.

### Scripting

Internally, Flash offers two scripting options: FlashScript and ActionScript. FlashScript allows Flash movies to communicate with other technologies such as JavaScript, VBScript, Java, C, and Visual Basic. ActionScript, which is closely modeled after the JavaScript Core Language, is an internal programming language that can be used to program things such as interactive games inside Flash, as shown in Figure 2.

Figure 2. Due to Flash's scripting capabilities, Web authors can create unique graphically based experiences.

### Sound

One of the most intriguing things about Flash is its ability to integrate audio. Sound files within authored Flash movies are stored in the SWF file format and can be compressed with one of the newest technologies, MP3, as well as standard ADPCM compression. MP3 offers tremendous compressibility, making it possible to create long-playing animations with voice-overs or music with much smaller files. Moreover, since the audio is stored inside the SWF file, no external references, additional HTML code, plug-ins, or helper applications are required.

### IF YOU CAN DREAM IT

In the past, imaginative Web production was severely limited by raster file sizes. Now, almost anything you can dream up could probably be integrated on the Web. There are some limits to what Flash can do. But it offers a unique alternative and as the volume of Web content increases, Flash movies will continue to play an increasing role in development and delivery of Web-based media.

*43*

# Teaching Computer Animation for Results!

*Contact*

CRAIG CALDWELL
Media Arts Department
University of Arizona,
PO Box 210076
Tucson, Arizona 85721 USA
+1.520.626.9073
craig@u.arizona.edu

KEVIN GEIGER
California Institute of the Arts

JIM MCCAMPBELL
Ringling School of Art & Design

This session presents the teaching of computer animation from three different learning stages: foundation, undergraduate, and graduate. The focus is on demonstrating solid approaches and successful outcomes.

Success in teaching and learning computer animation depends on setting priorities, knowing what to emphasize, and deferring what can be placed on the back burner. Often, teachers and students become distracted by the technology and confuse technique with content. Students prefer to learn the latest 3D animation software tools because they believe this will compensate for any lack of artistic skills. But this isn't realistic because the computer amplifies the students' limitations.

This panel shares examples of successful student animation work from three different levels of computer animation instruction: foundation (University of Arizona), undergraduate (Ringling School of Art & Design), and graduate (California Institute of the Arts). At each stage, the challenges are different. At the foundation level, the challenge is to keep students focused on the basic principles of animation and make the work exciting. At the undergraduate level, the challenge is to keep the animation-production timeline realistic, maintain the focus on quality not quantity, and require students to rework animation as necessary. The point here should not be to impress your audience but to entertain and communicate. At the graduate level, expectations should be very high, yet students still need guidance in balancing their desire to create something completely original and the professional expectation that they will entertain the audience.

Each student embodies a different set of abilities and sensibilities. By recognizing their students' different needs at different stages, instructors do not have to sacrifice long-term goals for more immediate preferences and affinities. This strategy has the added benefit of encouraging students to consider embarking upon a computer-animation career, instead of simply practicing their skills as a hobby.

Craig Caldwell holds an undergraduate degree from Florida Southern University, a MFA from the University of Florida, and a PhD in computer graphics and animation from The Ohio State University. He worked at Walt Disney Feature Animation from 1997-99. His animations have been included in the commercial tapes "Computer Dreams," "Computer Graphics Anthology," and the "SIGGRAPH Interactive Arts and Video Artists" (Issue 40/41). His work has been published in Computer Graphics World, SISEA Proceedings, PIXIM, L'Image numérique à Paris, World Graphic Design Now, the NCGA Conference Proceedings, and IEEE Computer Graphics & Applications. His work has been exhibited at Der Prix Ars Electonica, IMAGINA, and Eurographics.

*Jim McCampbell*

My primary responsibility is to teach upper-level computer animation undergraduates. As the lead instructor for the seniors' final animation project, I approve the work at various stages. So I have witnessed a wide range of varying success in these final projects, from the fair animations that never really take shape to projects that I thought would never succeed but are somehow rescued and projects by students for whom nothing goes wrong. The latter students are always on top of the process, and, in the end, it is really the process at which they excel.

*Kevin Geiger*

I have taught advanced topics in computer graphic animation at CalArts for more than five years. I love it, because it offers me the opportunity to stimulate and motivate the students in original directions. At the same time, I am able to put the entertainment industry in perspective because of my own professional experience. CalArts' is close to Burbank and several Hollywood studios, so the students constantly feel the influence of the industry. This is a seductive reality, but it can also foster significant anti-industry responses. It is my responsibility to channel these reactions into productive creative results. While the responses are diverse, they always challenge the students to create the best work they can.

44

# RICH RESOURCES FOR COMPUTER GRAPHICS EDUCATORS

*Contact*
DALTON R. HUNKINS
Computer Science Department
St. Bonaventure University
St. Bonaventure, New York
14778 USA
+1.716.375.2003
hunkins@cs.sbu.edu

DAVID B. LEVINE
St. Bonaventure University
dlevine@cs.sbu.edu

Demonstration programs have a long and storied history in the field of computer science education. This is particularly true in the area of computer graphics where the displays are often worth more than the proverbial "thousand words." This paper presents a suite of such programs, discusses their pedagogical role within the field of computer graphics education, and places them in context with respect to other such suites currently available.

## INTRODUCTION AND PREVIOUS WORK

Demonstration programs have probably been around as long as computer science has been taught. Examples can be found in essentially every programming language and for virtually every sub-field of computer science. It is now common for the source code to sample programs presented within textbooks to be packaged on CD-ROM or made available through the publisher's Web sites.

Historically, demonstration programs have included both text-based console applications and those using graphical interfaces. Not surprisingly, many of the best examples of the latter illustrate concepts within computer graphics. Whether the output is textual or graphical, a large number of demonstration programs are static. They illustrate their concepts through single runs and/or still images — possibly controlled through initial numerical input.

Within the field of algorithm design, it is not uncommon to see demonstration programs that featured static displays. On the other hand, systems such as BALSA[1] and GAIGS[3] offer students much more. Students are required to interact with the algorithms, and their interactions have noticeable, immediate effect, which, in turn, provide a greater benefit to the students. Studies have established that the increased interaction aids students in learning the concepts presented. Within the field of computer graphics, there are several suites of demonstration programs that are interactive. It would be impossible to list them all here, so only a few representative examples are discussed.

One of the best early examples of interactive programs within the field of computer graphics is Dino's Demos[8]. The demos were written by Dino Schweitzer and are a series of programs that primarily illustrate concepts related to two-dimensional graphics (for example, Bresenham's line drawing algorithm). Dino's programs permit the student to interact with the program, changing parameters dynamically and observing the effect. Variations of some of these demos have been rewritten in Java and are available[4].

Scott Owen's Computer Graphics and Visualization Courseware Repository Web page[6] has links to two suites of interactive demo programs, one of which is Avi Naiman's Interactive Teaching Modules for Computer Graphics[5]. While Naiman's tools also deal primarily with two-dimensional graphics, they are interesting because the package also includes a library of software routines that students (or professors) can use to build their own demonstration programs.

More recently, Rosalie Wolfe[9] has developed TERA (Tool for Exploring Rendering Algorithms). As its name implies, TERA concentrates on rendering algorithms and on how they make objects appear. "With TERA, students can change the appearance of objects in a scene by clicking on a rendering option."[9] One interesting feature of TERA is the opportunity for students to test their understanding of the concepts at hand through the use of built-in quizzes.

Additionally, Nate Robins has produced a suite of demonstration programs to aid in the understanding of OpenGL programming[7]. Of the three suites discussed, Robins' is the closest to the work presented here in that his tutorials cover similar topics and have a similar "look and feel."

## DESIGN GOALS

The suite of programs presented here shares some design goals with each of the previously discussed systems. The primary goal, of course, is to create interactive programs that demonstrate concepts in the field of computer graphics. The other goals are outlined below:

- The programs must allow students to modify parameters of the simulation in a dynamic manner.

- The programs must update the display in real-time in response to student inputs.

- Each user interface must be self-evident.

- The user interfaces must be consistent across the suite.

- The programs should incorporate discussion of the processes being implemented, including the appropriate mathematics.

- The programs should provide an opportunity for informal student assessment.

- The programs should be implemented with reusability in mind so that students or instructors can easily modify and extend the suite to include other concepts.

All of the programs in the suite have similar user interfaces. Upon launching the program, the student is presented with a console window with any instructions specific to that tutorial. Upon dismissing the window, the student sees a split screen. The left-hand side of the screen is dedicated to windows for displaying the model and user controls while the right-hand side is used for discussion of the concept and informal student assessment. The discussion window displays a mix of static text and dynamically updated computations based on user input.

45

## DIFFUSE REFLECTION

The Diffuse Reflection tutorial shows most of the features of the suite. Students interact with this program to see how the perceived color is determined. A simple Phong illumination model is used in this demonstration. A screen snapshot is shown in Figure 1.

The left-hand side of the screen consists of a main viewing window and two control windows. The main viewing window contains a model of two walls meeting at a corner. The student is looking at the corner from the outside. One control window allows the user to control the presence of two omni lights — one on each side of the model — as well as the presence of ambient light. This is accomplished through a radio button interface. The second control window presents a view from above the walls with vectors drawn to show both the vertex normals and the directions from the vertices to the lights. Since the angle between a vertex normal and the direction to a light is important to the diffused reflection computation, the student is allowed to adjust the vertex normals for either wall at their common edge. By selecting a vertex normal and rotating the normal by dragging the mouse, the student can see the effect on the computation and, in turn, the perceived color at the vertex. Each normal may be rotated individually or in concert with the other. The vectors start in their conventional orientation, but the student can experiment with them to learn about particular effects. For instance, when the normals are set for the adjacent edges to point in the same direction, the student will observe that the visible edge between the two surfaces vanishes. No matter what type of manipulation is performed (light changing or normal changing), the model view is updated in real time.

As with other demonstration programs in this suite, the right-hand sub-window contains text designed to support the teaching goals. Discussion of the Phong Illumination Model is given here. At the bottom of this window, the actual computations are shown for the color determination at one of the vertices with the student manipulated normal. The numbers used in these computations are updated in real time and are an accurate reflection of the student's current choice in the control windows.

As the student manipulates the controls (one of the normals, for example) both the input view, in this case the angle used for the illumination computation, and the model view with the resultant color are updated in real-time. Controlling the input helps the student understand the effects of the manipulation, while updating the result helps build connections between the mathematical representation and the visual one.

At any time, the student can ask for a quiz. The form of a quiz question is either multiple choice or true/false. In either case, the student selects an answer from the set of possibilities through mouse input. A hint is available after the student makes at least one attempt to answer the question. Since these programs are envisioned as teaching tools and since there is no control over the testing conditions in any event, no scoring of the quiz is done.

As with all programs within the suite, the quiz questions and the explanation of concepts are stored in separate files in "clear text" format. Thus, an instructor can customize the experience by providing instructions that match particular teaching goals by providing alternate explanations of the process (perhaps to emphasize other aspects of the subject matter), or by providing additional or alternate quiz questions. As a result, it is also a simple task to switch the delivery language for most of the application. One need only change the text files.

## THE REST OF THE SUITE

There are currently eight programs in the suite. The Diffuse Reflection program was described in the previous section. The other seven are:

### Ambient Reflection

This tutorial focuses on the determination of color using the Phong Illumination Model. The student can control the color of an ambient light as it shines on four swatches of material (cyan, yellow, magenta, and white). The color computations for any one material (chosen by the user through a mouse selection) are displayed in the discussion window on the right while the result of the computation is shown in the model window on the left.

### Gouraud Shading

This tutorial shows Gouraud Shading in action. The student is presented with a triangle and can select the colors at each of the vertices. The shading is updated in real time.

### Gouraud Interpolation

This follow-on to the Gouraud Shading program focuses on the computations used to determine the color of "interior" points of a triangle using Gouraud shading. The student is presented with a triangle, whose vertices are red, green, and blue. The student selects a given point of interest within the triangle, and the interpolation computations are then displayed. The student may focus on either the final computation or upon one of the intermediary computations.

46

*Spotlight*

This tutorial demonstrates how changes in the different parameters associated with a spot light effect the image. A simple spotlight is directed at a mesh. The student can control the cutoff angle and the exponent of the light as well as the x-coordinate at which the light points.

*RGB and HSV*

These two tutorials are designed to help students develop intuition about the respective color models. The student is presented with slider values for the parameters of the model as well as a physical representation of the color space (cube or cone). The student can manipulate either the numeric values or the point of interest in the physical space, thereby developing the desired intuition.

*Transparency (See Figure 2)*

This program simply displays a cyan vase on a red and white checkerboard. The student can control the alpha value of the vase, sliding it from opaque to transparent. The blending computations for the selected alpha are displayed in the discussion window.

## CLASSROOM USE

Since the demonstration programs deal with graphics concepts and since the discussion can be easily changed with a switch in a text file, we have used these tutorials with two disparate audiences. At St. Bonaventure University, introduction to computer graphics is taught in two separate courses, Computer Graphics (CS 256) and The Science of Images (CS 126). Computer Graphics is the traditional computer graphics course taught to CS majors. In addition to general concepts in computer graphics, this course concentrates on understanding various algorithms and uses Ada and OpenGL as a teaching vehicle. On the other hand, The Science of Images has no prerequisites and is intended for a general audience. While some CS students do take this course as a university elective, it is primarily intended for students from other disciplines such as the visual arts. Many of the concepts taught in the CS majors' course are also included here. However, since algorithms and implementation are not as important to the non-majors, students in The Science of Images use 3D Studio Max[2] as their vehicle to model and render images.

In The Science of Images, the tutorials are used primarily to build intuition. A powerful tool such as 3D Studio Max may cause distraction when we want to focus on an underlying concept. In this case, the tutorials are presented during lecture to help separate abstract concepts from the manipulative overhead associated with complete image generation. Although there are no formal laboratories involving them, the tutorials are also available for students to use outside of class.

In Computer Graphics, the tutorials are used in three ways:

- The first way is similar to the use in The Science of Images class, but depending on the topic, more emphasis may be placed on the technical computations. (Note, again, that it is easy to craft different text files for display in the explanation window).

- The source-code listings for the tutorials are used as examples of programming with OpenGL. The listings are discussed in class, providing the students with examples of interactive programs and widgets built upon OpenGL and the glut utility library.

- The tutorials themselves are used as a springboard for student assignments. If it is true that we (as teachers) never really learn something until we teach it, then it should follow that the most effective way to teach our students would be to have them teach us. As the students have access to all of the source code and have studied it in class, it is a simple matter to have them construct new tutorials covering other topics. The common user interface and the extensive code reuse throughout the suite enables the student tutorial authors to concentrate on how they wish to present their subject matter, coding of the key concepts, and (gasp!) writing of the explanations and quiz questions. The source code may be given to students for tasks as mundane as changing menu items or as complex as the creation of an entirely new tutorial. In fact, some of the tutorials in this suite were originally conceived and partially developed by Matt Hartloff, one of our students.

## COMPARISON WITH OTHER WORKS

The primary similarity between our work and that of Naiman, other than the subject matter, is that both systems provide libraries for students (or faculty members) to continue to develop more tutorials with the same look and feel. Naiman's suite of programs is a bit larger and more diverse, but as he notes, the tutorials were not written by native English speakers and are therefore a bit difficult for some students to use. Also, since it was developed by a larger group of individuals, there is a greater diversity of user interfaces among them.

47

The largest area of commonality between our suite and the TERA system is in the area of assessment. Both systems can be used either in an exploratory mode or in a mode involving a self-administered quiz. Both have simple user interfaces, but there is a significant difference between them. TERA appears to have all of its images pre-stored on its CD, and the user "controls" the display by making a selection among a small number of discreet display options. TERA's extensive library of images (over 500,000) guarantees that concepts are well covered, but there is a fundamental philosophical difference between the two approaches. TERA shows a number of much richer images, focusing the student's attention on the final image, and provides minimal user control, whereas our suite gives students more control and concentrates their attention on the process.

The suite most similar to ours is Nate Robins'. Like our tutorials, his have a model view and control windows. Whereas our programs focus on the concepts and algorithms used in computer graphics, Robins' programs demonstrate various OpenGL function calls and their effect. In turn, rather than providing user control through manipulation of the model as our suite, Robins provides user control through the varying of the parameters to OpenGL function calls with mouse click-and-drag operations. This is a very nice user interface that is consistent with the intent of being a suite of tutorials on OpenGL. In both suites, three-dimensional scenes are updated in real time, giving the illusion that an interpreter is running the code. There are cosmetic differences between the two suites, namely, explanatory text and quizzes within our suite.

There is no point in attempting to rate the four systems, as they have different intents and design goals. In fact, it is unnecessary to choose amongst them. While the user interfaces are different in each of the four environments, each is so simple to learn that a typical student can master the interface in less than five minutes. Further, it is reasonable for an instructor to use more than one of the suites within the same course, if the choice of topics makes an instructor so inclined. In fact, we have used Robins' tutorials along with ours in our Computer Graphics course for CS majors.

## Further Development
Source code and executables (for Windows) for all of our tutorials can be found at: web.sbu.edu/cs/graphics/

## Conclusions
We have developed and presented a suite of tutorials for use in teaching computer graphics. All of the tutorials permit the user to manipulate a model in a three-dimensional world and see the effects of those manipulations in real time. Each of the tutorials also features a combination of static explanatory text and dynamic displays of the computations being performed. The separation of the explanatory text from the application itself makes it simple to customize each tutorial for different languages or for different courses. The framework also supports the construction of new tutorials with minimal effort.

While other similar work has been presented in various forums, this suite is unique in both the particular concepts addressed and in its presentation of them. In many respects, it combines the best ideas of previous work within one framework. Rather than competing with the previous work, however, it can be integrated with other systems in a mix-and-match style to provide a teacher with the widest possible variety of tools.

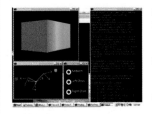

Figure 1. Diffuse Reflection

Figure 2. Transparency

*References*
1. Brown, M. (1987). *Algorithm animation*. MIT Press, Cambridge, MA.
2. discreet, 3d studio max (software package). (2000). URL: www2.discreet.com/products.
3. *GAIG User Manual, Ver. 3.0.* (1994). Lawrence Computing Center Publications.
4. Min, P. (1999). *Computer Graphics Applets*. Online, September 5, 2000, URL: www.cs.princeton.edu/ ~min/cs426/applets.html.
5. Naiman, A. (1996). Interactive teaching modules for computer graphics. *Computer Graphics* 30, 33-35.
6. Owen, S. (2000). Curriculum and instructional materials. Online. September 1, 2000, URL: asec.cs.gsu.edu/asecdl/materials/ C_and_I.htm.
7. Robins, N. (2000). Nate Robins - Open GL - Tutors. Online, September 5, 2000, URL: www.xmission.com/~nate/tutors.html
8. Schweitzer, D. (1992). Designing interactive visualization tools for the Graphics Classroom. *SIGCSE Bulletin*, vol. 24, no. 1, 299-303.
9. Wolfe, R. J. (2000). *3D graphics: A visual approach*. Oxford University Press.

48

# CyberMath: Exploring Open Issues in VR-Based Education

*Contact*
Gustav Taxen
Center for User-Oriented IT Design
The Royal Institute of Technology
Lindstedtsvögen 5
S-100 44 Stockholm, Sweden
+46.8.790.92.77
gustavt@nada.kth.se

Ambjorn Naeve
The Royal Institute of
Technology

Virtual reality (VR) has been shown to be an effective way of teaching difficult concepts to students. However, a number of important questions related to immersion, collaboration, and realism remain to be answered before truly efficient virtual learning environments can be designed. We present CyberMath, an avatar-based shared virtual environment for mathematics education that allows further study of these issues. CyberMath is easily integrated into school environments and can be used to teach a wide range of mathematical subjects.

Virtual Reality systems have the potential to allow students to discover and experience objects and phenomena in ways that they cannot do in real life. Since the early 90s, a large number of educational VR applications have been developed. These include tools for teaching students about physics[6], algebra[1], color science[16], cultural heritage objects[17], and the greenhouse effect[10].

There is convincing evidence that students can learn from educational VR systems[19]. However, a number of unresolved issues regarding the efficiency of such systems still remain. These include:

### Immersive vs. non-immersive VR

Several different authors have shown that immersive VR, where the user is in a CAVE or wears a head-mounted display, can be more efficient for learning than monitor-based desktop VR[4]. However, current immersive VR systems are expensive, fragile, and cumbersome to use. These drawbacks make them hard to integrate into school environments. On the other hand, desktop VR systems can often run on standard PC hardware, equipment that is increasingly common in classrooms today. Also, students using desktop VR systems are less likely to experience motion sickness and fatigue, factors that are known to inhibit learning[7]. It is unclear whether the advantages of desktop VR systems can make up for their lack of immersion.

### Collaboration in educational VR systems

A number of different initial studies suggest that collaboration between students in virtual environments has a positive effect on learning[10, 14, 2, 12]. However, little is known about how the presence of a teacher influences learning in VR applications. It is likely that students will benefit from teacher guidance, but it is also possible that a system that allows the teacher to take a more active role within the virtual environment would have a positive effect.

Avatar-based, multi-user virtual environments often induce the formation of user communities. The increased level of anonymity and "safety" in such communities may encourage users that usually avoid experiential learning situations to participate in educational activities[5]. However, it can be more difficult to avoid digression in discussions when the participants are anonymous than when they are known to each other[11]. There are few available guidelines for handling large-scale participation in educational VR systems.

### Visual realism in educational VR systems

A number of different studies have shown that visual realism in VR applications must be used with care[18]. It is not certain that an increased level of realism will improve learning, since it may distract a student from focusing on the key concepts that are to be learned. However, the motivational value of excessive visual realism is very high, something that the motion picture and computer games industries have been taking advantage of for decades. How to use realism in order to highlight key relations and concepts in educational VR applications is still an open question.

All of these issues can be explored in CyberMath. To our knowledge, no previous educational VR system has all the features necessary for such studies. In addition, CyberMath is built to support the teaching of many mathematical subjects, ranging from elementary school content to post-graduate content. Our system also supports a variety of teaching styles, including teacher lecturing and student-initiated exploration.

## System Description

CyberMath is an avatar-based shared virtual environment that is built on top of DIVE[3]. DIVE has the ability to display interactive three-dimensional graphics as well as to distribute live audio between standard desktop PCs. It also supports a number of other hardware configurations, ranging from head-mounted displays to CAVE environments. It is possible to allow different users to access the same virtual environment from workstations with different hardware configurations. These features make it easy to integrate DIVE applications in schools and also allow us to study how different levels of immersion influence the learning process.

Many students have considerable difficulty appreciating the relevance of mathematics. We believe that an informal and fun milieu aids in motivating such students and also encourages the formation of user communities. Therefore, we have chosen to build CyberMath as an exploratorium that contains a number of exhibition areas (Figure 1). This allows teachers to guide students through the exhibitions, but students can also visit CyberMath at their leisure, alone or together with others. For additional flexibility, we have added a lecture hall where standard PowerPoint presentations can be shown. Furthermore, since DIVE can distribute information across multiple local area networks, users from different physical locations can visit the exploratorium simultaneously.

*49*

Multiple users can simultaneously manipulate an exhibition object in CyberMath. In order to reduce confusion, it is important to make explicit the presence of users in the virtual environment. In addition, we believe that visualizing user presence increases the potential for user-to-user collaboration and interaction. For simplicity, we have chosen to let the standard DIVE avatars represent CyberMath visitors, but we are currently experimenting with alternative avatar designs. The way users control their avatars in CyberMath is similar to many popular computer games. Since many students are familiar with these games, our hope is that this will shorten the time required to master the controls.

When users point to an object in the environment using the computer mouse, their avatars will indicate this through a "laser pointer," a red line from the eye of the avatar through the indicated point on the object. Each avatar also has a sound indicator that is activated when its corresponding user speaks into the computer microphone. Exhibited objects can be rotated and translated by using the computer mouse. Action buttons situated next to inter-active exhibitions control animations and visual representation of the objects in the exhibit.

All objects in CyberMath, including the user avatars, can be visualized at a number of different levels of realism, ranging from uniformly colored surfaces to radiosity lighting. This makes it possible to investigate how realism affects learning in virtual environments.

DIVE supports rapid prototyping through Tcl/Tk scripts. We have complemented this support with a Mathematica-to-DIVE conversion utility that can be used to convert standard three-dimensional Mathematica objects and animations to the DIVE file format. It is then straightforward to add Tcl/Tk code to turn the converted Mathematica objects into interactive CyberMath exhibitions. This makes it possible to support rapid-turnaround teacher-driven development of new CyberMath exhibitions in the same fashion as in the QuickWorlds project[13]. The next step is to develop an exhibition construction tool that will allow teachers without Tcl/Tk knowledge to create their own exhibitions.

It is also possible to associate URLs with CyberMath exhibition objects. When a user clicks on such an object, its URL is opened in a browser. This makes it easy to offer additional information about the exhibited objects (such as mathematical formulae and links to other relevant pages).

DIVE has the ability to log all interactions between avatars and objects. Together with standard audio and video recording equipment, this provides a platform for assessment of learning in CyberMath.

A number of example exhibition areas in the exploratorium have been completed. These include:

### Interactive transformations
In this exhibit, users can explore the effect of any R3-R3 transformation on different mathematical entities such as points, lines, planes, and spheres. Users can interactively manipulate the entities and immediately see the results of the transformation, either in a separate coordinate frame or in the same coordinate frame as the non-transformed surface (Figure 2). This makes it possible to explore transformations in a new way and get an intuitive sense for how a specific transformation works. We believe that this increases the cognitive contact with the mathematical ideas behind the transformation formulae.

### Generalized cylinders
This exhibition illustrates how to increase the number of degrees of freedom in revolution surfaces through the use of differential geometry[15]. In particular, it shows how to construct an orthogonal net across the surfaces for texture mapping. The exhibition includes a number of three-dimensional animations and wall posters. Differential geometry is usually taught at the post-graduate level (if at all). However, our initial usability tests indicate that CyberMath makes it possible to effectively introduce these concepts to undergraduate students.

### Usability Testing
We have completed two initial usability tests: one small test at our lab with three users, and one larger test with 14 users. In both tests, the students were undergraduates at different universities in the Stockholm region. A mathematics teacher from the Royal Institute of Technology (who is familiar with CyberMath) guided the students through the generalized cylinders exhibition hall. The teacher was in a separate physical location, and all students were sitting at different workstations in one room. After the guided tour, the students answered a questionnaire. The questions were divided into four themes:

1. Effectiveness of the human-computer interface (navigation, sound quality, orientation of avatars, etc.);

2. Perceived level of immersion and awareness of other users in the virtual environment;

3. Level of collaboration (teacher-student and student-student);

4. Transfer of content, feasibility of CyberMath as teaching tool.

The average ratings for these themes were 3.23, 3.49, 3.35 and 4.10, respectively. These results are hardly conclusive. Nevertheless, they suggest that even though improvements in user interface and environment design are necessary, CyberMath has the potential of becoming a powerful tool for teaching mathematics.

50

We are planning a larger deployment of CyberMath at the Royal Institute of Technology and a series of new usability tests. These tests will focus on three main areas:

*Immersion*
To what extent do different levels of immersion (desktop monitor, wall projection, head-mounted display, CAVE) influence the long-term retainment of knowledge acquired through virtual environments?

*Collaboration and teaching strategies*
How does the possibility of large-scale participation influence the teaching and learning processes? To what extent must teachers adapt their teaching style in collaborative virtual environments?

*Realism*
Can the increased motivational value of a realistic environment compensate for the lack of immersion in desktop-based systems? Can we produce a set of guidelines for using visual realism in virtual environments for education?

Our hope is that these tests will produce new insights into how to design efficient VR systems for education. We are also planning to build a number of new exhibition areas, including one that presents elementary 3D geometry and one that introduces geometric algebra[8]. We will use results from research on awareness and accommodation in virtual environments to further guide the design of these exhibition areas[9].

Figure 1.

Figure 2.

*References*
1. Bricken, W. (1992). Spatial representation of elementary algebra. In *Proc. IEEE Workshop on Visual Languages* (92), 55-62.
2. Brna, P. & Aspin, R. Collaboration in a Virtual World: Support for conceptual learning? *Proc. Human-Computer Interaction and Educational Tools,* 113-123.
3. Carlsson, C. & Hagsand, O. (1993). DIVE - A multi user virtual reality system. In *Proc. IEEE VRAIS* (93), 394-400.
4. Cronin, P. (1997). Report on the applications of virtual reality technology to education. HRHC, University of Edinburgh, February 1997, URL: www.cogsci.ed.ac.uk/~paulus/vr.html.
5. Dede, C. (1995). The evolution of constructivist learning environments: Immersion in distributed, virtual worlds. In *Educational Technology*, 35 (5), 46-52.
6. Dede, C., Salzman, M. C., & Loftin, R. B. (1996). ScienceSpace: Virtual realities for learning complex and abstract scientific concepts. In *Proc. of IEEE VRAIS* (96), 246-252.
7. Dede, C., Salzman, M., Loftin, R. B., & Ash, K. (1997). Using virtual reality technology to convey abstract scientific concepts. In Jacobson, M. J., Kozma, R. B. (Ed.), *Learning the Sciences of the 21st Century: Research, Design, and Implementing Advanced Technology Learning Environments*. Lawrence Erlbaum.
8. Doran, C., Dorst, L., Hestenes, D., Lasenby, J., Mann, S., Naeve, A., & Rockwood, A. (2000). Geometric algebra: New foundations, new insights, *SIGGRAPH 2000 Course Notes*.
9. Hedman, A. & Lenman, S. (1999). Orientation vs. accommodation - New requirements for the HCI of digital communities. In *Proc. of HCII* (99), 457-461.
10. Jackson, R. L. (1999). Peer collaboration and virtual environments: A preliminary investigation of multi-participant virtual reality applied in science education. In *Proc. of ACM Symposium on Applied Computing* (99), 121-125.
11. Jin, Q. & Yano, Y. (1997). Design issues and experiences from having lessons in text-based social virtual reality environments. In *Proc. of IEEE International Conference on Computational Cybernetics and Simulation* (97), vol. 2, 1418-1423.
12. Johnson, A., Roussos, M., Leigh, J., Vasilakis, C., Barnes, C., & Moher, T. (1998). The NICE project: Learning together in a virtual world. In *Proc. of IEEE VRAIS* (98), 176-183.
13. Johnson, A., Moher, T., Leigh, J., & Lin, Y-J. (2000). QuickWorlds: Teacher-driven VR worlds in an elementary school curriculum. In *Proc. of SIGGRAPH 2000 Educators Program*, 60-63.
14. Moher, T., Johnson, A., Ohlsson, S., & Gillingham, M. (1999). Bridging strategies for VR-based learning. In *Proc. of SIGCHI* (99), 536-543.
15. Naeve, A. & Eklundh, J. O. Representing generalized cylinders. (1995). In *Proc. of Europe China Workshop on Geometric Modeling and Invariants for Computer Vision* (95), 63-70.
16. Stone, P. A., Meier, B. J., Miller, T. S., & Simpson, R. M. (2000). Interaction in an IVR museum of color. In *Proc. of SIGGRAPH 2000 Educators Program*, 42-44.
17. Terashima, N. (1999). Experiment of virtual space distance education system using the objects of cultural heritage. In *Proc. of IEEE International Conference on Multimedia Computing and Systems* (99), vol. 2, 153-157.
18. Wickens, C. D. (1992). Virtual reality and education. In *Proc. of IEEE International Conference on Systems, Man and Cybernetics* (92), vol. 1, 842-847.
19. Winn, W. (1997). The Impact of three-dimensional immersive virtual environments on modern pedagogy. University of Washington, HITL, Report No. R-97-15.

*51*

# From Pixels to Scene Graphs: The Evolution of Computer Graphics Courses

*Contact*
Dennis J Bouvier
University of Houston-Clear Lake
2700 Bay Area Boulevard
Houston, Texas 77058 USA
djb@acm.org

The field of computer graphics is expanding and evolving rapidly. Past computer graphics courses addressed low-level topics such as line-drawing algorithms[13] while the graphics industry has moved toward scene graph representations of three-dimensional scenes. This discrepancy has moved some educators to suggest that graphics courses exclude 2D topics for concentration on 3D. This paper suggests that such a switch is unnecessary and provides a course outline blending old and new topics to provide breadth and relevancy without abandoning the basics.

Since the time of Ivan Sutherland's doctoral work[11] much has changed in computer graphics, and much remains the same. One major change is the pervasiveness of graphics. Computer graphics technology was once reserved for a small number of researchers. Now, with significant computing power available on so many desktops, graphics has become commonplace. So ubiquitous is graphics that we tend to forget that WYSIWYG GUIs are composed of appropriately clipped lines, bit-mapped images, and scalable text. All are produced by some graphic algorithm. These WYSIWYG GUI features are commonly available as part of user interface programming libraries that are not even considered graphics packages.

This ubiquity serves as the impetus for training, or at least introducing, a larger population of students to computer graphics technology. The changing technological landscape provides the motivation to change the content of computer graphics courses. So, once again, the question is "What should be included in the introductory computer graphics course?"

Selecting computing course content presents a design tradeoff between providing technical relevancy and proper intellectual training. Many courses in computer science programs present similar course content design decisions. Often a wide variety of reasonable choices leaves room for a variety of opinions. For example, the selection of the programming language in introductory programming courses is a long-running debate destined not to end. The computer graphics course has a similar choice among graphics APIs.

A more important decision is the relative amount of time devoted to 2D versus 3D topics. This course content issue has been politely debated in a number of publications by a relatively small number of authors[3,4,5,6,10,13]. This paper adds one more voice to the debate and a new point of view.

## From pixels to scene graphs

Recent developments in computer graphics technology have changed the way in which graphics are used and perceived.

Comparing the past and the present situation forms a basis for reasonable discussion for the future. As this paper is focused on the future of teaching computer graphics, the historical look is focused on educational issues more than technology. Each of the recent papers that discusses the content of a computer graphics course provides a summary of technological history[3,4,5,6,10,13]. The reader interested in this history is referred to these sources.

### Computer graphics past

Historically, an introduction to computer graphics course usually started with the definition of a pixel. From the most basic of primitives, the course moved to 2D topics such as line and circle-drawing algorithms[13]. In courses at many institutions, students worked on graphics programming projects using non-standard graphics libraries, or with no library at all. These courses commonly included 3D topics only at the end of the course.

In the computer graphics courses of the 90s, OpenGL was commonly used for programming projects. Scene graph technology is only now becoming common in undergraduate and graduate level courses.

### Computer graphics present

As SIGGRAPH attendees know, computer graphics technology is advancing at a pace that defies description in a few paragraphs. However, it is often easy to experience the results of these changes. Examples of graphics technology are often displayed on movie and television screens, in feature films and commercials. The technological advances are no longer only available to the select few; powerful 3D graphics hardware is available to the consumer. The hardware coupled with graphics application software has turned some average computer users into illustrators and animators. In addition, many computationally expensive graphics algorithms have been moved to the hardware. From MMX extensions in Pentium processors, to the ray tracing hardware (RenderDrive), and consumer 3D graphics rendering cards and chips (GeForce).

What is relevant to this discussion is not so much exactly what the advances are, but what impact these advances should have on computer graphics education.

With changing technology and its availability, an educator must consider the need for updating course content. A number of educators have offered their suggestions for changes. Brief summaries of two published papers appear in the next section.

## Two previous course proposals

Using high-level graphics APIs in programming renders unnecessary detailed knowledge of low-level issues, such as line-drawing algorithms. For this reason, several educators now advocate elimination of the historically basic topics from the "introduction to computer graphics course."

All referenced papers argue that changing technology provides the rationale for a changing graphics course. However, Cunningham takes this a step further, observing that with the growth in graphics availability, through the growing number and variety of applications, there is a large population of computer graphics users to be served in education[5, 6]. In addressing this larger audience, Cunningham proposes that "all course work is done entirely in 3D, with no reference at all to 2D graphics except perhaps in a few specific examples"[6].

Hitchner and Sowizral propose a complete change in course structure and move directly to scene graph based systems[10]. One argument presented for this change is that state-of-the-art implementations of graphics technology do not make use of traditional algorithms, "Scan Line polygon fill is not used in a custom parallel architecture built for rendering speed".[10]

## Proposed Course Content

While the stated positions are valid, other course outlines also address advances in graphics technology without excluding traditional 2D topics. In this proposal, 2D topics are seen as more than just foundation for 3D topics, but relevant and meaningful topics on their own.

Noting technological progress, market changes, and the positions of other educators, the following course content outline is proposed:

### Course Design Considerations

The following course outline is founded upon these tenants:

- Knowledge of lower-level layers provides an understanding of the basic problems, which provides the foundation for reasoning about what is possible and what is not, what is expensive and how to make it less so.

- Although much of the course is focused on 3D graphics, virtually all computer graphics systems use some form of 2D graphics display technology. For this reason, it is appropriate to include 2D topics in an introductory computer graphics course.

- A university course should not train students in a specific software product, but give students the opportunities to learn and explore the possibilities. Specifically, the student is expected to learn the details of commercial software products and/or APIs in programming projects, not lectures.

- The very dynamics of the market are a good reason to avoid radical changes in course content. The technological half-life of the current hot topics is probably shorter than the technology it replaced. Further, some technology becomes attractive after losing popularity. For example, vector graphics has become attractive once again as a way to reproduce graphic art over a network connection. Some Web products (for example, Flash) utilize vector representations to speed graphic descriptions to remote viewers.

### Proposed course outline

The following list of topic areas shows the basic outline of the proposed course.

As the outline shows, the students study graphics topics from pixels to scene graphs.

### Topic 1: Pixels, images, file formats

Virtually all computer graphics work is presented in 2D, and much is stored in files. These topics not only provide foundation for 3D topics to come, but are relevant on their own.

To begin the course, a foundation is laid with 2D fundamentals, including the definition of pixels and image plane. This material includes a few example image-file formats including at least one lossy and one loss-less format. Also discussed are vector vs. raster issues and compression techniques.

### Topic 2: Line drawing, circle drawing

The basic line- and circle-drawing algorithms demonstrate creative ways to improve speed as well as the first occasion to talk about aliasing and anti-aliasing. The line drawing algorithm is used in polygon filling discussions. Line clipping in 2D can be included in this material as well.

Later in the course, it is noted that 3D graphics are projected to a 2D image plane before rendering; therefore, 2D line drawing and polygon filling is used in virtually all 3D graphics systems.

### Topic 3: Color, lighting, shading

Prior to this point, only grayscale images have been discussed. Positive and negative color systems are introduced as well as a variety of color representations such as RGB and CMY. The discussion of color lays a foundation for shading.

53

*Topic 4: 2D transformations*
Two-dimensional translation, rotation, and scaling transforms, their matrix representations, and the use of homogeneous coordinates are presented.

Two-dimensional transformations are used in "paint" applications and in user interfaces, and are worthy of inclusion in the course. However, they are highly valuable in introducing 3D transformations. Two-dimensional images are easily drawn and 2D transformations are easily demonstrated in the class.

*Topic 5: 3D transformations*
Three-dimensional transforms and homogenous coordinates are easily introduced as natural extensions to the corresponding 2D topics. In both 2D and 3D transformations, make the distinction between point and coordinate transformations. At this point it is possible to introduce the OpenGL API.

*Topic 6: Projection*
Having homogenous coordinates as a tool, parallel and perspective projects are presented as matrix multiplication. It is important to explain the view frustum, 3D clipping, and perspective division.

*Topic 7: Introduction to the graphics pipeline*
The flow of data originating from the object vertex through 3D transformations and projection resulting in image plane points brings the course back to 2D line drawing and 2D polygon filling.

*Topic 8: Hidden line and surface removal*
A variety of algorithms is presented for solving occlusion problems. Typically, Painter's Algorithm, Binary Space Partition, Area Subdivision, and Z-Buffer are included in the discussions. Ray tracing is also included as an alternative. The discussion of ray tracing also includes shadows.

*Topic 9: Animation*
Basic animation issues and techniques are discussed. Time constraints usually allow very little detail on the use of key framing and motion capture. The focus is on animation using procedural techniques such as particle systems, motion capture, and inverse kinematics.

*Topic 10: Scene graphs*
Basic concepts of the representation of 3D scenes in a graph-data structure are presented. Programming examples are useful in illustrating the utility of this approach.

*Topic 11: Texture mapping, bump mapping*
Texture mapping and bump mapping are presented as alternatives to detailed 3D geometry.

*Other Topics*
The field of computer graphics is wide, and this course doesn't cover all possible topics. It would be easy to include discussions on transparency and interactivity. Image processing and text rendering are other possible topic areas. Typically, one or more of these topics is introduced at the end of the course, as time permits.

*General comments*
This course is intended for a 15-week semester. Most of the identified topic areas can be covered in about one week. The topic areas that included projection take more time than other topic areas. The timing of each topic area can be adjusted by including more or less detail on specific topics. Usually the discussions of clipping and arbitrary projections are short.

Some reordering of course topics can be done. In particular, the introduction of scene graphs (topic 10) can be moved to topic eight. However, the suggested order of topics allows sufficient time for programming projects as presented below.

*Programming projects*
The course as taught by the author requires a number of student programming projects. The projects reinforce the class material and expose the students to modern APIs such as OpenGL and Java 3D. The APIs are introduced in the lecture, but are learned in the programming projects.

Students are usually excited by the results of their work and quite often will go well beyond the requirements of the programming projects.

*Project 1: Line drawing and file formats*
The first project is completed without the use of any graphics API. The students are given an example program demonstrating how an array is used as an image plane and is written to a simple file format. The students are also provided with a utility for converting the file to other formats.

Students implement a line-drawing algorithm and use it to create a perspective line drawing of a 3D object without knowledge of projection techniques. In this project, students learn the details of line drawing and the difficulty of simulating 3D "by hand."

54

In addition, the students save their images to a file and convert it to a variety of file formats. The students then prepare a report of image file size and note degradation. This experience makes concrete the discussion of aliasing as well as the implications of using lossy file formats.

*Project 2: Simple OpenGL*
Using OpenGL, the students are required to produce a perspective projection of a static 3D scene. Students are given a simple example program that is used as an example and a skeleton.

*Project 3: Simple Java 3D*
Similar to Project 2, but using the Java 3D API to construct the 3D scene.

*Other programming projects*
The three programming projects outlined above also naturally lead to more programming projects. Quite often, the author requires three projects in addition to those described. A fourth is a color version of Project 1. The fifth and sixth are interactive versions of Projects 2 and 3.

*Texts and support material*
While a number of books may be used as the textbook for the course, all have some disadvantages. That is, no existing text covers all of the course topics for the proposed course outline. One possible text is Foley et al[7], or the more compact version[8]. This text requires the instructor to provide additional material on any software used in the course. Alternatives include recently published computer graphics texts that include the OpenGL API such as Angel[1] or Hill[9]. Another possibility is Watt[12] which includes no API and no 2D line drawing.

Missing from all of the suggested texts is information on scene graph software. Probably fewer than 10 books may be easily found that cover any scene graph API. Fortunately there is a free and readily available tutorial on Java 3D[2]. With this tutorial, it is easier for students to use the Java 3D API than Open Inventor for scene graph programming projects.

Also, few texts mention the issues surrounding image file formats. This material is provided to the students by this author.

## SUMMARY
A variety of factors motivate educators to make adjustments in course content. The growth in the number of graphics applications and advances in graphics technology has prompted a variety of educators to publish thoughts on the contents of computer graphics course content. While the views of these authors are valid, this paper provides another perspective.

The proposed course provides the student with sufficient background to read research papers, to enroll in upper level courses such as visualization, and to begin undertaking more complex undertakings in the field.

The proposed outline has been used as the syllabus for a senior-level computer graphics course taught by the author. The course remains popular with students and receives above-average reviews. The students express their interest and satisfaction with the course in a variety of ways, including a low drop rate.

*References*
1. Angel, E. (1997). *Interactive computer graphics, a top-down Approach with OpenGL*, Addison-Wesley.
2. Bouvier, D. *Getting Started with the Java 3D API*, URL: java.sun.com/products/java-media/3d/collateral.
3. Breshingham, J. (1999). Teaching the graphics processing pipeline: Cosmetic and geometric attribute implications. In *Proc. Graphics and Visualization Education* (99).
4. Cunningham, S. (1998). Outside the Box - The changing shape of the computing world, invited editorial. *SIGCSE Bulletin* 30 (4), 4a-7a.
5. Cunningham, S. (2000). Powers of 10: The case for changing the first course in computer graphics. In *Proc. SIGCSE Technical Symposium on Computer Science Education*, 46-49.
6. Cunningham, S. (1999). Re-inventing the introductory computer graphics course: Providing gools for a wider audience. In *Proc. Graphics and Visualization Education* (99).
7. Foley, J. et al. *Computer graphics*. Addison Wesley.
8. Foley, J. et al. (1993). *Introduction to computer graphics*. Addison Wesley.
9. Hill, (2000). *Computer Graphics Using OpenGL*. Prentice Hall.
10. Hitchner, L. & Sowizral, H. (1999). Adapting computer graphics curricula to changes in graphics. *Proc. Graphics and Visualization Education* (99).
11. Sutherland, I.E. (1963). Sketchpad: A man-machine graphical communication System. In SJCC, Spartan Books.
12. Watt, A. (2000). *3D computer graphics*. Addison Wesley.
13. Wolfe, R. (1999). Bringing the introductory computer graphics course into the 21st century. In *Proc. Graphics and Visualization Education* (99).

*55*

# Panels

*Chair*
**Kathryn Saunders**
ThinkTech

# Contents

57

2001

*Chair*
KATHRYN SAUNDERS
ThinkTech

*Panels Jury*
SARA DIAMOND
Banff Centre for the Arts

ISAAC KERLOW
The Walt Disney Company

*Panels Committee*
NAPOLEON BROUSSEAU

BILL KROYER
Rhythm & Hues Studios

STEPHEN BOYD

*Administrative Assistant*
ETTA DiLEO

JILL SMOLIN
Cinesite Visual Effects

CHRIS SHAW
Georgia Institute
of Technology

*58*

"YOU BETTER THINK IT OUT... OUR LUNGS WERE MEANT TO SHOUT.
SAY WHAT YOU FEEL, YELL OUT WHAT'S REAL...
EVEN THOUGH IT MAY NOT BRING MASS APPEAL.
YOUR OPINION IS YOURS, MINE IS MINE...
IF YOU DON'T LIKE WHAT I'M SAYIN' FINE."
– Ice T

SIGGRAPH 2001 Panels were deliberately selected to generate more noise than ever by focusing intense expertise on the most critical questions and controversies in computer graphics and interactive techniques. But the jury's long-range goal extended far beyond the heated debate of the moment. Our hope is that everyone who attended a Panels session, and everyone who reads these panel summaries, will help refine a very broad range of strong opinions and emotional positions into clarity, insight, and provocative visions of the future.

The panelists and the jury are simply facilitators and thought provokers. The Panels sessions and their outcomes belong to all SIGGRAPH 2001 attendees and the entire computer graphics community. It was a great honor, and a fascinating challenge, to help select topics, panelists, and technologies for this extremely diverse field.

In fact, this year's Panels submissions proposed the most extraordinarily diverse range of topics in SIGGRAPH history, from intellectual property rights for digital content to virtual-reality art, video-game design, Internet-

connected appliances, new media and human cultures, reality modeling, non-linear animation, interactive entertainment on instant messaging devices, digital cinema, astronauts as artists, and how computer games affect digital visualization.

We also organized an amazing series of Special Sessions, all of which are documented in this section of the Conference Abstracts & Applications. One explained how Stanley Kubrick's totally analog "2001" inspired today's digital technologies in film and video. A Guided Tour of the New Silicon Senses featured transcontinental control of a robotic arm by a living creature, virtual retinal displays, Web-delivered smells and tastes, and advanced haptics. In Virtual Stars, digital artists revealed how they create digital actors. And in Masters of the Game, the world's leading game producers demonstrated and explained their award-winning work.

SIGGRAPH 2001 Panels and Special Sessions also featured real-time audience interaction via wireless Web access.

I am deeply grateful to the exceptional volunteer members of the Panels Jury, who devoted many, many hours of study, evaluation, research, discussion, debate, decision making, and coordination. Without their dedication and intelligence, SIGGRAPH 2001 Panels would never have been possible. Many thanks also to my wonderful subcommittee members whose perseverance and ingenuity helped produce some spectacular sessions, and to the entire 2001 committee for their support and guidance.

*Kathryn Saunders*
*ThinkTech*
*SIGGRAPH 2001 Panels Chair*

59

2001

# Video Game Play and Design: Procedural Directions

**Moderator**
George Suhayda
Sony Pictures Imageworks
9050 West Washington
Boulevard, Suite 358
Culver City, California 90232
USA
+1.310.840.8411
+1.310.840.8261 fax
geo@imageworks.com

**Panelists**
Tom Hershey
Sony Pictures Imageworks

Dominic Mallinson
Sony Computer Entertainment
America

Janet Murray
Georgia Institute of Technology

Bill Swartout
USC Institute for
Creative Technologies

Procedural simulation is an opportunity to revolutionize the way games are played and produced. Game-play design has relied on traditional models and has been constrained by old hardware design. New consoles will allow for procedural simulation and a "drama-on-the-fly" that no other form of entertainment is capable of. It will allow game consoles to reach their true artistic potential. For the developer, procedural simulation will offer a lighter, more versatile library of assets. The payoff will be twofold: a new, unique art form and a more cost-effective method of recreating intelligence, behavior, physics, and modeled environments.

This panel presents a snapshot of the current state of procedural simulation and the potential that it offers for game play and game design in light of advances in hardware design.

Video and computer games have come a long way from their simple beginnings in the arcades. PacMan, Space Invaders, and Donkey Kong made a fortune on simple colorful game play. As consoles have evolved, game development has become incredibly complex, exceeded only by the consumer's expectations for a higher level of game art and game play. Developers, keenly aware of consumers' expectations and stiff market competition, are spending record amounts of time and money on game development. There is no relief in sight, as manufacturers plan for more highly sophisticated consoles and shorter development times between successive versions.

Despite the pressure, game developers continue to rely on labor-intensive traditional methods (polygonal models, texture maps, and forward kinematics). It's no wonder that the cost of developing new games has risen from $1 million per title to more than $6 million. Production schedules have gone from one year to 2.5 years. Profitability is more uncertain.

The greatest relief for game developers will come in the form of procedural simulation. Creation of rule-based worlds to recreate intelligence, behavior, physics, and modeling could take the place of painstakingly modeled, animated worlds composed of thousands of human-engineered and painted polygons. The greatest advances may come in the type of game play that procedural simulation may allow. So far, game developers have used other art forms, particularly film, as a template for game play. This easy route does not necessarily allow for the computer or console to mature into its own unique art form. Groundbreaking game play development takes time and ingenuity, but it's potentially the greatest windfall for video game and hardware developers. It's already clear that games have piqued consumer interest much more than films. One look at box-office revenues versus game revenues is proof enough. Developers will need to satisfy that interest if they wish to unlock an even larger revenue flow.

## Traditional Notions of Procedural Simulation
Specific areas of traditional procedural simulations include:

### Intelligence
Recreating the inner workings of the human brain has long been a goal of science. Perhaps it's the $8-billion game industry that will lead to the greatest innovations, much like feature film was the catalyst for realistic modeling and simulations.

### Behavior
So far, there is only as much behavior as can be animated using inverse and forward kinematics. The downside to this is that motion and animation are limited to the movement an animator gives a character. What needs to be explored is a universe where the entire range of body motion is written into the character, and intelligent agents within the game choose the proper motions for any given time and situation. The range of possibilities for game play then becomes infinite.

### Speech
Interactive speech is probably the most underdeveloped aspect of gameplay. Pre-canned color commentary gives sports their sense of realism. Introduction of fresh, spontaneous commentary will give gamers a unique experience. Sadly enough, even simple speech communication between players has not been developed, although modems are standard on PCs and the new consoles include ports for broadband access.

### Physics
Some of the greatest advances in procedural simulation are represented by depictions of real physics. Although they do not represent game play, they allow the audience to settle into a real world in which the game play can unfold. Depictions of moving water, collateral damage, and plumes of smoke add to the game's ambience. The consumer has seen what computer graphics are capable of producing with procedural effects in feature film. Their question is simple: "Why can't my console do that?"

### Modeling
A healthy chunk of game production schedules, and the CD on which the game is distributed, is devoted to modeling and models. Modeling of environments, props, and characters is due for a procedural-simulation overhaul. Creation of entire cities and environments using procedural algorithms is potentially the greatest enhancement. The weight of polygons and texture maps is shifted to a lighter combination of lines of code and an infinite number of possibilities.

## Procedural Simulation and Game play
The biggest challenge to researchers in AI is creating fresh, spontaneous gameplay. Hard assets provide limited possibilities in gaming. With procedural simulation, developers could create more malleable assets programmed with a multitude of possibilities, which will allow for more spontaneous game play. Why not create spontaneous drama-on-the-fly? What keeps us from creating a five-act structure on the fly so that games become a roller coaster ride with dips and climaxes like feature films? More importantly, procedural simulation may play its greatest role in creating unique gaming experiences rather than just mimicking other forms of media and storytelling.

*George Suhayda*
A graduate of Clemson University and Yale School of Drama, George Suhayda joined Sony Pictures Imageworks in 1998 and has worked on "Contact," "Snow Falling On Cedars," "Sphere," "City Of Angels," and "What Planet Are You From?" Currently he is visual effects art director on "Stuart Little 2" and working on game development for Sony's PlayStation 2.

*Tom Hershey*

The advent of procedural techniques in videogame design has, and will certainly continue to have, monumental impact on the gaming experience that players enjoy. This impact is multifaceted: ranging from "nuts and bolts" advantages in hardware resource management to influencing the way that game designers approach narrative structure and character/environment interaction.

On a resource management level, procedural approaches optimize storage space and computational capacity, and basically allow more content to be packed into a game. Animations appear more organic than those created by transitioning between pre-calculated, pre-rendered poses, and the computing cycles and storage resources required for procedural-based animation are dramatically lower than those required by traditional methods.

On a higher level, procedure-driven interactions between characters and environments can and will continue to move us toward the realization of our classic vision of AI. To date, players are conditioned to expect a high level of predictability and repeatability in game play. Monsters are triggered to attack when the player enters a room. Guards follow a set search pattern. Shoot a bazooka at a static wall and generally nothing happens. But with a modest amount of procedural "hooks" embedded in the design of the characters and their environments, the game play takes on a radically realistic feel. Adversaries can interact with one another and behave in a more unpredictable, organic way. Environment becomes a major factor: an iron door is harder than a wood one, a stone wall is impervious to a tank, but a brick wall can be broken down. It's clear that in procedural simulation of this type, a little goes a very long way towards fulfilling our perceptions of realism, and we are in the very early stages of what can be achieved.

A graduate of MIT, Tom Hershey worked as a programmer specializing in graphics applications for PCs. In 1988, he joined Columbia Pictures and worked for four years as director of production administration, helping to oversee production of feature films. He now leads Imageworks' movement into content development for Sony's PlayStation 2.

*Dominic Mallinson*

Procedural techniques offer many advantages for interactive computer entertainment. The ability to parametrically describe objects offers a richer variety of graphics and conserves system resources such as memory and memory bandwidth. From a production standpoint, procedural techniques can reduce the amount of manual content creation and consequently offer the possibility of lower development costs. For truly interactive 3D worlds, pre-calculated animations cannot be used. They are too constraining and costly. In these situations, physical simulation must be used to create the best experience. To populate these simulated environments, we need autonomous characters with their own behaviors and decision-making processes.

The state of the art is only just touching the surface of this procedural potential. The latest generation of game consoles such as PS2 enable these technologies, and I am certain that we will see them used with increasing skill to produce more compelling entertainment over the next few years. A glimpse into the future reveals whole worlds described not in terms of polygons, but in terms of their features. Artists may create a terrain by identifying peaks, ridges, rivers, and oceans, and the algorithms will fill in the rich detail of mountains, valleys, and coastlines. When two football players collide, the resulting falls and acrobatics will be different every time and not an inappropriate motion capture. Finally, the most challenging future will be when the player is not sure if the character he is playing against is a human or a computer simulation.

After graduating in computer science from the University of Durham, Dominic Mallinson worked at Microsoft on their first C++ compiler. He returned to the UK to work for Pilkington Glass on CAD and factory automation, then joined Psygnosis and remained there for seven years, during which time Sony acquired the company and launched Sony PlayStation.

*Janet Murray*

Characters provide a good focus for thinking about what can be accomplished in game design using more powerful programming techniques. There is a rich history already of experimentation with characters who have some autonomous or spontaneous behaviors, including most notably, the work of AI researchers such as Joe Bates and Bruce Blumberg; Will Wright's recent game, The Sims; and the success of virtual pets like pf magic's Dogz and Catz series. As broadband technologies bring interactive entertainment into the home, the popularity of such creatures may increase, and they may be used as entry points into complex fictional worlds. One of the clear recent results of this work is the understanding that it is "believability" that is important rather than the elusive goal of actually modeling human (or even doggy) thought. Although researchers, led by Blumberg, have gotten very far with ethology (the science of animal behavior) as a structure for character creation, the range of behaviors that can be produced this way can be less engaging to the interactor than simpler creations if the character cannot dramatize the full richness of its inner life. Similarly, it is possible to create the illusion of a rich inner life with very little modeling underneath. So the problem for designers is one of deciding what is worth modeling.

One way of thinking about this is to start with how the behavior is going to be elicited. For example, the Petz series used "props" like feeding bowls and pet combs and catnip to suggest satisfying dramatic scenarios to the interactor. The more ambitious we make our characters, the more latitude we allow in the virtual worlds, the more complex the design questions of eliciting the characters' behaviors and making them legible and dramatically compelling. The Sims is the most ambitious such undertaking to date, using a dramatic structure much like the 19th century bildungsroman (novel of education) to shape the action. My remarks focus on the challenges of creating expressive characters in a procedural simulation framework and suggest some ways in which designers can think about the problem, drawing in part on the lessons of the earliest work in this genre (long before the days of multimedia): Joe Weizenbaum's classic program, ELIZA.

Janet Murray is the author of *Hamlet on the Holodeck: The Future of Narrative in Cyberspace* and the forthcoming *Inventing the Medium: A Principle-Based Approach to Interactive Design*, both from MIT Press. She is currently serving as a trustee of the American Film Institute and serves as a mentor in AFI's Exhanced TV Workshop. Before coming to the Georgia Institute of Technology in 1999, she led humanities computing projects at MIT, where she remains a distinguished contributing interactive designer in the Center for Educational Computing Initiatives. She holds a PhD in English from Harvard University. Her research has been sponsored by the Annenberg/CPB Project, the National Endowment for the Humanities, the Andrew W. Mellon Foundation, IBM, and Apple Computer. She lectures and consults widely on the future of television, interactive narrative, and curriculum development for interactive design.

*Bill Swartout*

 Procedural simulation holds enormous promise for creating games and simulations that provide much richer and varied experiences than the games we create today. If behaviors are generated dynamically, instead of being pre-recorded, they can respond naturally to situations or circumstances that were not anticipated when a game was originally programmed. In principle, procedural simulation allows us to vary behavior in subtle ways that reflect small differences in circumstances, something that would be very expensive to do if all the behaviors had to be pre-recorded.

But there's a problem. In many cases, procedural approaches can not yet exhibit the required range of behavior in a natural and convincing way. For example, consider machine-generated speech. Most current text-to-speech systems sound very unhumanlike, and even the most natural-sounding are incapable of expressing the range of emotions such as stress, anger, or fear that can be expressed easily by a skilled actor. Thus we seem to be confronted with a dilemma: Either take the procedural approach and use a text-to-speech synthesizer, thereby gaining flexibility but giving up expressiveness; or pre-record a library of a lot of expressive speech fragments with the risk that the right line might not be available in the library when needed.

The way out of this quandary is to borrow from Hollywood, where filmmakers often take a hybrid approach to creating a movie. Recognizing that each technique has its own strengths and weaknesses, Hollywood artists select the most appropriate technique for a each element of an overall scene and then composite the results together to create a unified whole. For example, a single sequence in a film might include live action, models, and computer-generated images, all integrated seamlessly to create a unified view.

In a similar way, procedural simulation techniques can be integrated with conventional approaches if careful thought is given to how the techniques are integrated. Depending on the role they play in a simulation (and the requirements the storyline imposes on that role) some characters might use a procedural approach while the behaviors of others might be pre-specified. In this panel overview, I outline our experiences in using a hybrid approach to integrate procedural simulation into a highly immersive VR simulation we have been creating to train soldiers about decision-making in complex peacekeeping situations. Because no single approach is sufficient for the range of behaviors we wanted to simulate, we found it necessary to integrate multiple approaches.

Formerly director of the intelligent systems division at the University of Southern California's Information Sciences Institutes. Bill Swartout has served as an associate research professor for the past 10 years. He holds a PhD in computer science from MIT. His specific research interests in the area of artificial intelligence include: intelligent agents, knowledge-based systems, knowledge representation and acquisition, and natural language generation. He was elected in 1992 as a Fellow of the American Association of Artificial Intelligence (AAAI). He served as the Conference Committee Chair for the AAAI (1992-1994), as Program Co-Chair at the Third International Conference on Principles and Knowledge Representation and Reasoning (KR-92), and as Program Co-Chair at the National Conference of Artificial Intelligence (AAAI-90).

## Cultural Mediation in New Media Spaces

*Organizer*
GABRIELE BLOME
GMD-Institute for
Media Communication
D-53754 Sankt Augustin,
Germany
+49.2241.14.1557
+49.2241.14.2133 fax
gabriele.blome@gmd.de

*Panelists*
GABRIELE BLOME
MONIKA FLEISCHMANN
WOLFGANG STRAUSS
Institute for Media
Communication

STEVE DIETZ
Walker Art Center

CHARLOTTE PÖCHHACKER
[art.image]

PERTTU RASTAS
Kiasma Museum of
Contemporary Art

WARREN SACK
University of California,
Berkeley

New media technology has given rise to new spaces of communication that require new concepts of culture and art. Some artists and computer scientists are trying to visualize large-scale conversation on the net. Museums, cultural archives, and companies face the challenge of managing their data bases. This requires adapting concepts of knowledge management and semantics.

Artists and gallery curators have adopted the virtual space as a new medium for their work. Art is reaching new audiences. Innovative curatorial concepts try to take into account the special conditions of the Web, such as connectivity and participation. Exhibitions on the Web are part of a communicative process that could define new relationships between artists, curators, and the audience. New forms of culture and creativity emerge through the intersection of real and virtual spaces. In this panel, artists and curators share their projects, such as stages that mix physical presence and virtual spaces.

### Gabriele Blome

netzspannung.org is a next-generation Internet platform that extends the abilities of the art and technology communities, and offers a variety of services and media channels such as infospace, dataspace, and workspace. netzspannung.org members no longer rely on rigid structures of given network architecture, protocols, and data formats. Rather, they are free to set up distributed community engines tailored to their specific needs. Platform architecture supports easy flexibility from the database level to the user interface and enables user-defined forms of interaction. The member-defined modules are spread over the community network or stored on a member's machine, which is seamlessly integrated and becomes a virtual part of netzspannung.org. The distributed community engine enables networked artistic production and offers spaces for presentation, communication, and information within a dynamic context. netzspannung.org was founded by Monika Fleischmann and Wolfgang Strauss at MARS Exploratory Media Lab, Institute for Media Communication

Gabriele Blome was assistant curator at Zentrum für Kunst und Medientechnologie, Karlsruhe, from 1997 to 1999. In 2000, she joined the Exploratory Media Lab, Institute for Media Communication, of the GMD German National Research Center for Information Technology, where she is curator for netzspannung.org.

### Steve Dietz

Even for online or virtual display, strategies acknowledging the convergence of Internet and physical space must be developed. How can the postion of artists, audience, and museums be defined in such hybrid media spaces? What are the new formats and strategies of curatorial work and cultural mediation in networked environments?

Steve Dietz is the founding director of new media initiatives at the Walker Art Center, where he is responsible for information systems as well curating and programming the online Gallery 9. He co-initiated the award-winning ArtsConnectEd collaboration with The Minneapolis Institute of Arts and initiated one of the earliest archive collections of net art: the Walker's Digital Arts Study Collection, including äda'web, Bowling Alley, and DissemiNET.

He has organized and curated new media exhibitions, including Beyond Interface: net art and Art on the Net (1988), Shock of the View: Artists, Audiences, and Museums in the Digital Age (1999), Digital Documentary: The Need to Know and the Urge to Show (1999), Cybermuseology for the Museo de Monterrey (1999), Art Entertainment Network (2000), Outsourcing Control? The Audience As Artist, Open Source Lounge, and the Bureau of Inverse Technology's BangBang for Medi@terra 2000. Telematic Connections: The Virtual Embrace in February 2001.

### Monika Fleischmann and Wolfgang Strauss

Mixed reality means constructing a space by interlinking different layers of reality into a new spatial frequency. Generating this space means staging an experimental field for performative perceptions. The metaphor we use is that of a room filled with data, a space that is performed by networked bodies. The Mixed Reality Stage is an instrument for the human body and vice versa.

Mixed reality requires interfaces to the senses, enabling people to communicate via perceptional channels: hearing, seeing, touching, moving, thinking. It is inhabited by two types of presence: the performers' physical bodies in actual space and virtual bodies in space/time representations. This is illustrated by several examples realized at MARS Exploratory Media Lab: Carry On, i2TV, and Murmuring Fields. In Murmuring Fields, the camera vision system draws traces of human movement in virtual space. Two performers develop a choreographic sequence in a space filled with a virtual sound field: an interactive radio play on stage.

The technical architecture is based on a VRML plugin, the eMUSE (electronic Multi-User Stage Environment) system. eMUSE is a theatrer machine, a multi-user system combined with a camera-tracking system. The eMUSE plugin is available at the netzspannung.org. Monika Fleischmann and Wolfgang Strauss are research artists who studied visual arts, theater,

63

architecture, computer graphics, and visual communication. Since 1992, they have been artistic directors of the Institute for Media Communication, and since 1997, they have directed Media Art and Research Studies (MARS) at GMD, the German National Research Center for Information Technology in Sankt Augusti, Germany.

Their work has been exhibited at the Centre Pompidou and the Museum for Design, and presented at the Museum of Modern Art and conferences such as SIGGRAPH, Imagina, Art Futura, ISEA, and Ars Electronica. In 1992, their Home of the Brain received the Golden Nica for interactive art at Ars Electronica.

### Charlotte Pöchhacker

The ongoing growth of a media/digital culture and the increasingly sophisticated possibilities of the Internet present challenging possibilities for new thought on design and new forms of expression in cultural communication and cultural practice. These new conditions for curating, viewing, and experiencing online content require a profound reconsideration of interdisciplinary collaboration, of the relation of curator, artist, and audience, and of future modes of producing and exhibiting art.

Aganist this background, artimage's Tactical Systems for a New Cultural Practice explores visual, navigational, and technological innovations, and their potential for changing and expanding esthetic experience. The project is a testing ground for concepts that use the discursive and visual space of the Web to flatten distinctions between artist and curator and curator and audiences. Based on the notion that form affects content and comprehension, special attention is devoted to challenging Web design as a new cultural technique. Another important aspect of the project is testing and designing interactive spaces to address and reach different publics (interfaces that allow for individual access and multiple viewpoints: polyperspectivity).

Charlotte Pöchhacker is founding director of artimage and artistic director of the Graz Biennial Media + Architecture (Austria). She has edited several books and catalogues on the interdependency of media, architecture, and society, and conducted extensive curatorial work in the fields of new media art and architecture.

### Perttu Rastas

I want to challenge the notion of virtual space vs. digital space based on my daily work at a new museum, where we have learned that keeping up and running this so called virtual world requires very special and very expensive hardware structure and software knowledge management. Secondly, I want to underline how importnat it is for artists that we have still non-commercial media institutions like museums. Media artists are the most important group and community who can give democratic and humanistic simulation (as a model of possible futures) for the IT-based industrial world. Thirdly, I want to show possibilities for cooperative programs that involve culture institutions and corporations, using the cooperation between Kiasma and Nokia as a sponsorship model.

Perttu Rastas is senior media art curator of Kiasma, Museum of Contemporary Art. He is responsible for Kiasma's information systems and media art collections. He shares responsibility for media art performances and exhibitions and is involved in planning Kiasma's theatrical programming in film and video. He has also worked for KSL's media workshop (1985-1989) as a production editor and as director of operations for the Finnish Media Art Archives, AV-arkki (1989-1994). He has been responsible for planning and coordination of MuuMedia (International Media Art Festival, 1988-1995) and has worked as media art consultant for AVEK (Finnish Audiovisual Support Center).

### Warren Sack

With networked computers, we can begin to imagine the advent of a truly global conversation and meaningful communications among thousands, millions, perhaps even billions of people. But what do these new public spaces look like, and how do they support many-to-many communication? How can we begin to concretely envision these new kinds of connections that link people and media together? I am interested in online public space and public discourse. To better understand and participate in these emergent spaces, I design software to summarize, visualize, and navigate what I call very-large-scale conversations (VLSCs) like those conducted on Usenet and large mailing lists or bulletin boards. In this panel, I demo my Conversation Map system, which can graphically summarize the large volumes of email that constitute most contemporary VLSCs. It is my hope that Conversation Map is a first step toward a set of tools that will provide the means to navigate the social and linguistic connections engendered by the new media spaces of the Internet.

Warren Sack is a software designer and media theorist. Prior to joining the faculty at the University of California, Berkeley in the fall of 2000, he was a research scientist at the MIT Media Laboratory and a member of the Interrogative Design Group at the MIT Center for Advanced Visual Studies. His research interests include computer-mediated communication, online communities, architecture and design for online spaces, social networks, computational linguistics, and media studies. He designs software for navigation, summarization, and visualization of online, public space, and public discourse.

64

# SIZE MATTERS: DIGITAL CINEMA DISTRIBUTION

*Organizers*
KAREN RAZ
Raz Public Relations, LLC
216 Pico Boulevard, Suite 10
Santa Monica, California 90405
USA
+1.310.450.1482
+1.310.450.5896 fax
karen@razpr.com

GENEVIEVE YEE
Past Chair, Los Angeles
SIGGRAPH Chapter

*Moderator*
CHARLES POYNTON

*Panelists*
ALLEN DAVIAU
Cinematographer, ASC

JAMES H. KORRIS
University of Southern California

BOB LAMBERT
The Walt Disney Company

JOSHUA PINES
Industrial Light + Magic

ALLEN WITTERS
WAM!NET

Digital cinema is gaining momentum, and it is becoming a more viable reality. Although there are technical and logistical hurdles to overcome in the implementation of this medium, it will have a profound effect in the way we acquire, create, distribute, and view filmed entertainment. Panelists with varied perspectives on the feasibility of moving digital cinema out to the public outline the status of this film-industry evolution. Society of Motion Picture and Television Engineers Fellow Charles Poynton guides the panelists as they explore topics ranging from how a nationwide digital cinema infrastructure is constructed to whether there is enough bandwidth available to support it. Panelists also speak to the image integrity and film quality issues involved in digital acquisition of filmed entertainment, and how this affects moviegoers.

## Allen Daviau

Allen Daviau has five Oscar nominations and numerous awards to his credit. Raised in Los Angeles, he developed an early interest in photography and lighting, and launched his career during the 1960s shooting pre-MTV music videos for local record companies. From there, he segued into filming commercials and documentaries, and in 1968, he shot "Amblin" for a very young Stephen Spielberg, with whom he eventually reteamed on "E.T. The Extra Terrestrial." He is one of the world's preeminent cinematographers. His work includes "The Color Purple," "Avalon," "Empire of the Sun," and "Bugsy." For "Empire of the Sun," he won a British Academy Award and an ASC Outstanding Achievement Award. In addition to being a prolific traditional cinematographer, Daviau has experience with digital cinema acquisition.

## James H. Korris

James H. Korris currently serves as executive director, CEO of the Entertainment Technology Center (www.etcenter.org) at the University of Southern California. A sponsored research unit of the School of Cinema-Television, the center recently opened its Digital Cinema Laboratory, a permanent testbed in the heart of Hollywood. A neutral forum for development of benchmarks in this emerging technology, ETC is committed to fostering develop-ment of enabling technology for production and distri-bution of all forms of entertainment content. He came to ETC with over 15 years experience in television and film development and production with Imagine Films Entertainment, MCA Television Group, Universal Television, and others. He is a member of the writers, branch of the Academy of Television Arts and Sciences and the Writers Guild of America.

## Bob Lambert

Bob Lambert is corporate senior vice president, new technology and new media at The Walt Disney Company. He leads the group responsible for developing strategy and practice relating to conven-tional and digital production methods across Disney's diverse businesses. Among other initiatives, he was instrumental in the conversion of Disney's animation business to a hybrid of digital and conventional technologies, which won an Academy Sci-Tech award. He has been intimately involved in film, video, and digital techniques for acquisition, production, postproduction, restoration, and exhibition for the past 15 years, including the current deployment of a small number of digital cinema theatres worldwide.

## Joshua Pines

Joshua Pines, digital photography scanning supervisor at Industrial Light + Magic, has overseen the company's film scanning department since 1990 and extensively researched and tested the merits of both traditional and digital cinema. He started his career teaching film courses at Cooper Union in New York City, where he earned his degree in electrical engineering. He started working in visual effects at MAGI in 1982 at the tail end of their work on "Tron". Prior to joining ILM, he also worked at R/Greenberg Associates, where he led the computer graphics division, and at Degraf/Wahrman in the film department. He has always thought that computers could be a useful tool in making better movies, and he still hopes that one day this may come true.

## Allen Witters

Allen Witters, WAM!NET chief technology officer, leads the company's global network and technology operations, including research efforts in digital cinema production and distribution. He has been involved in technical consulting for the computer industry since 1975 and has broad experience in the invention, design, engineering, and implementation of digital media production and distribution networks. He currently operates the world's largest IP network designed specifically for media distribution and is involved in architecting the Navy and Marine Corps intranet, the largest US-government IT project in history. He has spoken extensively about digital cinema and digital distribution.

Monster, Inc
Courtesy of Pixar/Disney

*65*

# Computer Games and Viz: If You Can't Beat Them, Join Them

*Organizer*
Theresa-Marie Rhyne
Independent Consultant
3418 Balfour East
Durham, North Carolina 27713
USA
+1.919-544-1817
rhyne@siggraph.org

*Panelists*
Peter K. Doenges
Evans & Sutherland

Chris Hecker
definition six, inc.

William Hibbard
University of Wisconsin–Madison

Hanspeter Pfister
Mitsubishi Electric
Research Laboratory

Theresa-Marie Rhyne

Nate Robins
Avalanche Software

## Motivation and Key Issues

Historically, the visualization community has been a driving force in high-end computer graphics innovation, fostering new technologies that gradually filtered down to the consumer market. However, in recent years, the financial growth of the computer games market has made it the driving force of consumer graphics. How do trends and advances in computer games impact the scientific and information visualization community? This panel addresses this issue by highlighting the following items:

- How are visualization displays and paradigms influenced by interactive user interfaces and visual metaphors of game design?

- Are 3D visual thinking and visualization hindered or enhanced by 3D computer games?

- To what extent are visualization and visual simulation requirements altered or affected by games-driven enhancements to major application programming interfaces (for example, Direct X and OpenGL)?

- How do short release cycles affect driver stability and completeness of driver implementations?

- Will a computer-games focus produce a lack of advanced rendering features that could stifle visualization research?

- Is there a conflict between acceptable levels of accuracy and quality for artifacts in game development versus scientific and information visualization?

- Will the rapid pace associated with computer-games development be compatible or in conflict with the requirements of the visualization community?

- Will the computer-games arena provide the funding and research to improve graphics performance and price for the computer graphics field in general and visualization specifically?[1]

### Theresa-Marie Rhyne

Fundamentally, computer games are about play, and scientific and information visualizations are about knowledge. It is possible to learn about how communities develop from computer games like SimCity (www.simcity.com) and The Sims (www.thesims.com). It is also possible to find "joyful curiosity" in scientific or information visualization. Could it be said that application of visualization techniques to urban planning is an intellectualized version of SimCity? Perhaps one of the impacts computer games will have on people is to prepare them to use visualization, virtual reality, and visual simulation to examine scientific problems and local community concerns. Artistically, computer game designs are influencing visualization paradigms and facilitating 3D visual thinking. One challenge is to ensure that there is some scientific accuracy in the content of computer games. Given the recent focus on computer gaming consoles, there still needs to be functionality in computer graphics tools to support scientific and information data models. The rapid pace of computer games development needs the calm and quiet zone of scientific and information visualization to allow for steady progress of advanced rendering techniques. Perhaps there is a symbiotic relationship here.

Theresa-Marie Rhyne is an independent consultant in visualization and 3D computer graphics. From 1990 to 2000, she was a government contractor (initially for Unisys Corporation (1990-1992) and then for Lockheed Martin Technical Services (1993-2000)) at the US EPA Scientific Visualization Center, where she was the founding visualization expert. She has organized courses and panels for previous IEEE Visualization and ACM SIGGRAPH conferences. She was IEEE Visualization 1998 and 1999 co-chair and a director-at-large on the ACM SIGGRAPH Executive Committee from 1996 to 2000. Currently, she is the project director of ACM SIGGRAPH's outreach to the computer games community.

### Peter K. Doenges

Rapid development of 3D computer games fuels rampant hardware and software innovation. 3D games are surpassing professional 3D graphics and real-time visual simulation in certain areas. Game 3D technical innovation might benefit scientific and information visualization, but the technology is wired for different objectives. Scientific visualization seeks system understanding and values discovery. It needs flexible interfaces and programming via stable APIs for basic insights into forests of data. It also needs accuracy in multivariate data, data scalability and CPU-graphics bandwidth, and inter-processor communication. 3D games and Vis Sim focus on challenging human performance with fast fixed-function rendering of virtual worlds and landscapes for vital human experiences. Commercial predominance of 3D PCs and consoles could strand scientific visualization without needed features.

Cross-pollination is attractive, but challenges exist for derivative products to serve scientific visualization. Recent 3D game hardware turns to micro-coded pixel shaders, procedural vertex geometry, high micro-polygon densities, animating very large meshes, 2D/3D texture for illumination and reflection, and multi-texturing for pixel pipelines and cascaded separable functions. Developers wonder if PC 3D can scale up in multiple CPUs and 3D boards, if adequate data accuracy, bandwidth relief, viable inter-processor software, and frame-buffer access were available. Such graphics clustering invites balancing system resources and synchronization. It's time to stimulate dialog about what configuring "3D in the small" can do for scientific visualization, and how scientific visualization algorithms could adapt to new architecture. Pertinent lessons emerge from large-scale geographic visual simulation with PC 3D.

Peter K. Doenges earned a BSEE from the Rose-Hulman Institute of Technology and a MSEE from Syracuse University. He is vice president of strategic technology at Evans & Sutherland, where he has been responsible for IG hardware/software, modeling tools, radar/sensor simulation, driving dynamics, early ASIC work, systems engineering, marketing, engineering business, and R&D. He is involved in curved surface and procedural shader R&D and convergence of professional and game 3D technologies with OpenGL and DX. He is member of the IEEE Computer Society, ACM SIGGRAPH, Tau Beta Pi, NSIA/ADPA, Computer Graphics Pioneers, the IMAGE Society Board of Directors, and the RHIT Industrial Advisory Board. He represents Evans & Sutherland with the Web3D/VRML Consortium, participates in the OpenGL ARB, and chaired MPEG-4 Synthetic/Natural Hybrid Coding for streaming 3D. For over 30 years, he has worked in real-time visual simulation and 3D computer graphics. He began with the GE Electronics Laboratory in IG R&D, computer film animation for NASA's Space Shuttle, real-time hardware/software for shuttle simulation, and USAF ASUPT scene generators.

*Chris Hecker*
Since most of the other panelists are coming at this question from the scientific visualization side, I describe the situation from the games side. How does the games community see the scientific visualization community? What are the advanced features that we beg hardware vendors to implement, and how do those features overlap with features needed by the scientific visualization community? And, from a slightly different perspective, how do game developers use scientific visualization techniques during development (or even during the end-user's play experience), and what does this mean for the relationship between the communities?

Chris Hecker is technical director at definition six, inc., a small game development company working on high-end physics and graphics technologies. He has been on the advisory board for the Game Developers Conference for many years and is a regular speaker at the GDC, the annual SIGGRAPH conference, and other conferences. He was co-organizer of the SIGGRAPH 2000 Course on Games Research: The Science of Interactive Entertainment and moderated the SIGGRAPH 99 panel on How SIGGRAPH Research is Utilized in Games. A frequent contributor to Game Developer magazine, he was the technical columnist for the magazine for two years and is currently editor-at-large. He is also on the editorial board of the computer graphics research publication, The Journal of Graphics Tools.

*William Hibbard*
For many years, visualization users bought their graphics hardware from SGI, who built it for them. Now they buy their graphics hardware dirt cheap from NVIDIA and ATI, who build it for people who want to play computer games. So the visualization community has already been revolutionized by computer games.

Since the graphics vendors are building for the gamers, they don't listen to scientific visualization people. But it will work out alright in the long run, since graphics hardware will have to be abstract, programmable, and interoperable in order to serve the needs of gamers. That is, graphics APIs will have to abstract in order to make the wide variety of images that gamers need, so they will be able to make the images that scientific visualization people need. Graphics APIs will need to be programmable to attract a large community of game developers, so they will be programmable by scientific visualization people. And graphics APIs will need to be interoperable, in order to support multi-player games.

Networked computer games will be the medium of the 21st century in the way that movies and TV have been the media of the 20th. So in the short run the graphics market is in turmoil as vendors jockey for a bigger piece of this huge gaming pie, but in the long run the graphics hardware necessary to support gaming will be as stable and cheap as television. The era of special-purpose hardware is being replaced by the era of Toys-R-Us.

William Hibbard is a scientist at the Space Science and Engineering Center of the University of Wisconsin–Madison. He was principal investigator of the NASA grant that supported development of the Vis5D, Cave5D, and VisAD visualization systems. These systems are widely used to visualize numerical simulations of the Earth's atmosphere and oceans. He was an investigator of the Blanca Gigabit Testbed network, studying the use of high-speed wide-area networks for interactive visualization. He has been a member of the Program Committee of the IEEE Visualization Conferences since their inception in 1990. He also writes the VisFiles column in Computer Graphics, the SIGGRAPH newsletter.

*Hanspeter Pfister*
Without question, technical advances in computer graphics are driven by games and entertainment. Computer games are the "killer application" for 3D graphics, and they will play this role for the foreseeable future. Consequently, we have seen an unprecedented rise in graphics performance and features in the PC gaming market. Very soon, you will be able to buy a mid-range PC with a 1GHz CPU and about a gigapixel fillrate. Recent features of commodity graphics cards include multi-texturing, hardware transform and lighting, full-scene anti-aliasing, and bump mapping. Very soon, we will see hardware support for vertex blending, texture transformations, shadow mapping, and 3D textures.

*67*

I think this is great news for the scientific visualization community. However, I dare to raise a word of caution. Let's not forget that many advanced rendering features, such as a wide range of pixel and texture formats, are not available on PCs. Let's not forget that PCs suffer from vastly lower I/O performance and smaller memory capacity than high-end graphics workstations. Let's not forget that the extremely short release cycles of the commodity market lead to unstable and incomplete graphics drivers. And let's not forget that PC games are driving the future development of our graphics APIs. What will happen if OpenGL is not able to compete with Direct3D anymore? Will an API controlled by Microsoft fulfill the needs of high-end visualization? I believe the scientific visualization community has a responsibility to speak out. Microsoft, Intel, and other vendors will listen to a market that is projected to reach $US 13 billion in 2005. Maybe it is time to form an interest group for scientific visualization that addresses these issues.

Hanspeter Pfister is a research scientist at MERL - A Mitsubishi Electric Research Laboratory in Cambridge, Massachusetts. He is the chief architect of VolumePro, Mitsubishi Electric's real-time volume rendering system for PC-class computers. His research interests include computer graphics, scientific visualization, computer architecture, and VLSI design. He received his PhD in computer science in 1996 from the State University of New York at Stony Brook. In his doctoral research, he developed Cube-4, a scalable architecture for real-time volume rendering. He received his Dipl.-Ing. degree in electrical engineering from the Department of Electrical Engineering at the Swiss Federal Institute of Technology in 1991. He is a member of the ACM, IEEE, the IEEE Computer Society, and the Eurographics Association.

*Nate Robins*
Computer games are a powerful driving force in the consumer graphics market. They have brought much of the power from what is normally referred to as the "big iron" down to the consumer desktop. As the computer gaming industry continues to burgeon, more of the capabilities normally associated with high-end graphics hardware will trickle down to the average consumer. This is leading to the possible demise of many of the pioneer graphics vendors, including SGI and Evans & Sutherland. Fundamentally, however, the gaming industry is not an innovator in the graphics arena. It is a consumer. They need the high-end industries, such as visualization, to be the driving force in graphics technology. Because the games industry is driven by a market that has an extremely short product cycle, there isn't much time for innovation beyond proven techniques, many of which are in use (or were invented) by the visualization community today. The visualization community could benefit from watching the games industry and keeping them informed of new innovations that they'd like to see become mainstream. If you invent it, we'll make it popular.

Nate Robins works for Avalanche Software. He is not a very competent video game player, but he really likes the problems involved in making them. He received a bachelors degree from the University of Utah, where he worked with Chris Johnson in the scientific computing and imaging group on the "Big Iron" project. He has also worked for Parametric Technology Corporation, Evans & Sutherland, SGI, and Acclaim Entertainment.

*Reference*
1.  T.-M. Rhyne (2000), Computer games' Influence on scientific and information visualization, IEEE Computer, 33, (12), 154-156.

## THE FUTURE OF COLOR: CREATIVITY AND TECHNOLOGY

*Organizer*
JOSHUA KOLDEN
2860 Exposition #D
Santa Monica, California 90404
USA
+1.310.315.0581
joshua@licenseserver.com
jkdden@ix-netcom.com

*Panelists*
ROGER DEAKINS, ASC

JOSHUA KOLDEN

NEIL ROBINSON
Industrial Light + Magic

BEVERLY WOOD
Deluxe Laboratories

### Roger Deakins

As a cinematographer, Academy Award-nominated Roger Deakins, BSC, ASC, has demonstrated how less is more. His masterful use of color has repeatedly demonstrated the impact of subtle manipulations. Preferring to color with light instead of filters, he creates images that are often dynamic and broad while maintaining a precise emotional impact. Cinematographers such as Deakins work very hard to capture specific emotional details of a story on film. They have a great deal of experience in orchestrating a story using images that are sometimes bold and dramatic, and sometimes extremely subtle. They understand the capacity of their medium, and often test its limits.

It is important for humans to communicate, and technology can be used to further that communication. Skillful cinematography must be supported by equally talented digital artists and tools that are not limiting to either. Furthering understanding of the technology and the art helps everyone communicate better.

Roger Deakins started in still photography and documentaries. He attended the National Film and Television School in England, where he met director Michael Radford ("Il Postino," "1984"). The two worked on documentaries together in school, and when Radford made the transition to drama, Deakins followed. Deakins' first Academy Award nomination came in 1994 with "The Shawshank Redemption." Soon afterward, he won the ASC award. His impressive body of work includes: "Sid and Nancy," "Pascali's Island," "Barton Fink," "Dead Man Walking," "Fargo," "The Hurricane," and last year's "Thirteen Days" and "O Brother, Where Art Thou?"

### Joshua Kolden

A number of new image-representation technologies have surfaced over the last couple of years. In particular, work by Paul Debevec and Greg Larson has shown that images can store incredible amounts of unutilized information. With minimal effort, these data can be extracted and utilized to great effect. Additionally, intelligently increasing the information that is captured can produce remarkably powerful high-dynamic-range images in many areas of computer graphics. High-dynamic-range images were used in the production of the Experience Music Project motion-based attraction to successfully integrate lighting on the world's first CG human face replacement. In addition to remarkably realistic 3D lighting capture, these new image representations illustrate opportunities to store and manipulate images in new ways.

As computer hardware becomes less expensive and digital storage becomes easier to afford, it is becoming possible to address the subtleties of filmmakers' color decisions. It becomes economically feasible not only to maintain the image integrity through the entire digital process, from scan to print, but also to provide new creative tools. This added ability is possible because of the more complete representation of color. In addition, digital artists will need a more discerning "eye" to keep in touch with demanding filmmakers and become familiar with new tools for color manipulation.

Joshua Kolden studied film production at Columbia College, Chicago in the late 1980s. He went on to study computer science at the University of Arkansas at Little Rock. At UALR, he was invited to teach masters-degree courses in computer graphics and help develop the interdisciplinary computer graphics program. Over the last 13 years, he has contributed to innovations in the field of visual effects and computer graphics. Most recently, he supervised groundbreaking effects and animation for the Experience Music Project. This work involved human face animation and high-dynamic-range lighting effects integrated into and indistinguishable from live photography. Currently, Kolden lives in Los Angeles, and consults for leading visual effects facilities.

### Neil Robinson

With the ever-accelerating pace of hardware and software development, it is all but inevitable that digital technology will effect all areas of filmmaking. The development of a digital grading system is just another step toward the full digital cinematic experience. The line between post production and grading is rapidly blurring, and in the process many new creative tools are emerging. Very soon, it will be commonplace for all motion pictures to be finished as a digital master before generation of the required deliverable media. The impact on costs, speed, and creativity should not be underestimated!

There will be "teething" trouble along the way, because the technical challenges are large. Asset management, data storage, transport, and archiving all provide areas ripe for development, as the shear size of the dataset required is astonishingly large! Combining high-dynamic-range image capture, post production, distribution, and projection all in the digital realm, digital grading delivers a realistic end-to-end digital motion picture experience devoid of any photo-chemical processes. The potential enhancements to creative story telling are limited only by the imaginations of their users. As many of us know, this is truly a creative business. After all, telling the story is what it's all about.

Neil Robinson graduated with a bachelor of electrical engineering in 1999 and a master of science in data telecommunications in 1992, and remained at the University of Salford, England until 1997, researching advanced high-speed telecommunication networks. He then applied his skills to the development of the Cineon compositing system as a contract engineer at Cinesite

69

(Europe) Ltd, where he is now senior research engineer. He has been responsible for development of both 2D and 3D image processing tools, and motion picture VFX production pipelines at Cinesite (Europe). Notable career highlights include an award-winning video-to-film tool (now in use in four countries) and development of the image processing work flow for the Cinesite (Europe) Digital Lab. He has been involved with many motion picture and broadcast projects (credits include "Lost in Space" and "Animal Farm").

*Beverly Wood*

Photo-chemical processing techniques have been advancing over the past 20 years. New film stocks and the demand for high-impact images have propelled development of many interesting new technologies, such as Technicolor's ENR process, bleach bypass, and Deluxe's ACE. With the advent of movies such as "Seven," which made use of a sliver-retention process at Deluxe Labs for a few hundred release prints, the demand for these color-manipulation tools has increased.

Digital technology has yet to master even the basic color timing technology used in film laboratories, and yet few digital artists have had the opportunity to learn these techniques or understand their value to filmmakers and the audience. Because of this, there is a great deal of re-invention by talented people who recognize the limitations but do not understand how they have already been solved.

For many years, Beverly Wood has helped directors and cinematographers take advantage of and develop new tools for artistic expression. She is vice president of technical services and client relations at Deluxe Laboratories, where she consults with directors and cinematographers on the lab's high-tech services, including digital, and photo-chemical printing processes. Wood earned her masters degree in analytical chemistry from the University of Georgia. She worked for Kodak from 1980 to 1989 as a technical liaison with film labs, at Metrocolor Laboratories from 1989-1990 when MGM closed that facility, and as an assistant to the director for several made-for-cable movies. For the past eight years, she has been involved with special color-processing needs for such films as "Pleasantville," "Seven," "Sleepy Hollow," and "O Brother, Where Art Thou?"

70

# Visualization, Semantics, and Aesthetics

*Organizer*
Sara Diamond
The Banff Centre for the Arts
Sara_Diamond@BanffCentre.ca

*Panelists*
Sheelagh Carpendale
University of Calgary

Sara Diamond
The Banff Centre for the Arts

Victoria Interrante
University of Minnesota

Jason Lewis
Arts Alliance Laboratories

Joshua Portway
RealWorld

David Sless
Communication Research
Institute of Australia

Sha Xin-Wei
Georgia Institute of Technology

This panel brings together artists, designers, computer scientists, and language theorists whose work integrates different forms of linguistics, such as computational and mathematics, with designing both computational systems and art works.

Visualization represents processes as much as objects, which is contiguous with much of contemporary art. Art and computer code share a basic intent: expression. There is an intense pleasure in putting the unknown and the unknowable into language. And there is tension between computer code and design: code requires precision; art requires abstraction and manipulation.

As images, visualizations are powerful and often beautiful in their own right. Why do some evoke erotic delight, and others a sense of awe? If visualization makes data meaningful to humans, what role does aesthetics play in this process? Where do the aesthetics of visualization act back on current design and art making? Is there a relationship between information: pattern: meaning? Simulations are intended to look like an actual process or natural form. What happens when we abstract simulations and apply them to other semantic systems? If the process behind the visualization itself supplies the "real," then computer science and art share the need to work with structuralist languages, abstraction, and an aesthetics capable of feeling process, rather than representation.

As researchers in the fields of visualization, computational linguistics, simulation, aesthetics, visual arts, and sociology work together, what new forms of language, meaning, and interpretation arise from these collaborations? What language can we use to describe our practice? Topography and topology are two valuable words. Can patterns be recognized in emotional or meaningful ways? What is the gap between recognition and meaning? Can these collaborations bring us beyond aesthetics of space or narrative? In what ways? How can this new knowledge be applied to large-scale systems, such as the Internet, forestry, and astronomy? Can aesthetics make data meaningful to larger publics or user groups?

## Sheelagh Carpendale

In our information-dominated society, the favoured modes of information presentation are shifting away from a primarily verbal emphasis toward incorporation of a variety of visual forms. Rapidly increasing amounts of our communications are visual, and this trend has been accelerating in recent years. A great many advantages have been attributed to the ability to create good visual representations. Card et al. have declared that we should consider the possibility that information visualization can aid thinking processes.[1]

Can we then create visualizations that enhance cognitive abilities? In response to this challenge, there is a growing body of visualization research that strives to create intuitive visualizations through, on the scientific side, incorporation of perceptual and cognitive principles and, on the artistic side, recognition of the importance of emphasis, distinctions, and impact. However, there is another side to this issue: no matter how intuitive these visualizations are, they have to be interpreted by a person.

As a society, we place a great deal of emphasis on educating our children to become verbally literate. With the growing trend toward visual communication, a better understanding of visualization and visual presentation in general is becoming essential. However, to a great extent our education system still ignores this trend. While our children spend approximately 12 years of their lives learning to become verbally literate, comparatively little time is devoted to developing visual literacy.

Sheelagh Carpendale joined the Department of Computer Science at the University of Calgary in October 1999 and is a recipient of the National Science and Engineering Research Council University Faculty Award. Her research focuses on information visualization, where she makes a distinction between creation of visual representations and their presentation. In presentation space, she is exploring the resilient elastic properties available in virtual presentation. In representation space, she is investigating the possibilities of increasing or at least varying the methods that provide people, rather than algorithms, expressive control for creation and manipulation of representations.

## Victoria Interrante

Visualization research is concerned with design and implementation of methods for effectively communicating information through images. The crucial initial step in this effort is conceptualization of the representational methodology: how do we intend to portray a set of data so as to allow the critical information that it contains to be easily, accurately, and intuitively understood? The solution to this problem requires not only a thorough understanding of the needs of the application, in order to choose wisely what aspects or features of the data to show, but also a keen understanding of the processes of visual perception, combined with a healthy dose of creative inspiration, in order to choose wisely how to show it.

A fundamental philosophy that underlies much of my work in visualization design is that there is a science behind the art of effective visual communication that can provide objective reasons why certain pictorial representations of data can be expected to be more effective than others and theoretical guidance for knowing how to create images in which the most important aspects of the information can be most easily and accurately perceived. Although our understanding of the scientific principles that underlie the design of an effective visual representation is still in its infancy, and creating a visualization that works remains largely an art, one of my goals is to make explicit aspects of the intuition that a good designer accumulates from experience and training, and relies upon when translating ideas to images.

*71*

Victoria Interrante is a McKnight Land-Grant Professor in the Department of Computer Science and Engineering at the University of Minnesota and a recipient of the fiscal year 2000 Presidential Early Career Award for Scientists and Engineers. She received her PhD in 1996 from the University of North Carolina at Chapel Hill, where she studied under the joint direction of Henry Fuchs and Stephen Pizer. From 1996 to 1998, she worked as a staff scientist at ICASE, a non-profit research center operated by the Universities Space Research Association at NASA Langley. Her research focuses on application of insights from perceptual psychophysics, art, and illustration to design of more effective techniques for visualizing data.

*Jason Lewis*

First the Dadaists and then the Concrete Poets surfaced the semantics implicit in the aesthetics of written language. Typefaces are not neutral; layout is not simply rational or irrational. Throw text on-screen, give it the ability to move and interact with a user, and the active meaning-making inherent in the visible construction of letterforms becomes impossible to ignore. Now apply that to attempts to visualize large-scale conversations and one quickly finds that the creative and intellectual possibilities are not only infinitely fascinating, but also (potentially) dangerous over-active participants alongside the users themselves.

Jason Lewis brings 10 years' experience in a wide variety of research environments to bear on the question of how to enrich and extend the user's experience of digital media. He is a practicing artist, designer, and technology developer, and recently founded the Arts AllIance Laboratory in San Francisco. His work has appeared at Ars Electronica, ISEA, and the annual SIGGRAPH conference, and he currently has a piece, TextOrgan, on two-year display at the Ars Electronica Center. He has spoken at the Banff Centre for the Arts, the San Francisco Museum of Modern Art , and the UCLA Department of Design, and worked at Interval Research Corporation, the Institute for Research on Learning, Fitch, and USWest Advanced Technologies. He holds a BS and BA degree from Stanford University, and a MPhil from the Royal College of Art, London.

*Joshua Portway*

The RealWorld exhibition will take the form of a darkened room with a domed ceiling upon which a computer display will be projected, like a planetarium. Audiences will be immersed in a world of real-time stock market activity, represented as the night sky, full of stars that glow as trading takes place on particular stocks.

Like the complex visualisation systems used by investors and traders to analyse the market, the system abstracts the information to help us read patterns in the data. Each layer of abstraction distances us further from the actual people that the data represents, until our system comes full circle and a new layer of living creatures emerges within the data itself.

The project links the earliest theories, such as astrology, to the latest scientific visualization systems. It examines the urge to understand our environment; the desire to predict, recognize patterns, and impose structure; and the limits of this ambition. By exploring our desire to abstract and order our environment, the project will act as a focus for debate about how much control is possible over complex systems such as the natural environment or the economy. The project explores an important issue for the 21st century: systems that we have created, such as the economy, the latest computer systems, genetically modified organisms, or even ideas, can generate their own behaviour and eventually transcend their origins, and may already be more powerful than we can control.

Joshua Portway's first video game was published 17 years ago and became a best-seller in Britain. Since then he has produced work as an artist, games designer, and animator. His interactive installation work has been exhibited in the UK, the US, and Denmark, and his animation work (including videos for Peter Gabriel, MTV, and others) has been shown at festivals and on television worldwide. In 1991 he formed Flux Digital, an interactive media and broadcast animation production company, which he left to join RealWorld in 1995. At RealWorld he has been trying to map the strange territories between music and interactive media, and is currently developing some secret and wonderful interactive music technology, to be released "soon." His latest project, Black Shoals, was exhibited at the Tate Gallery, London, in 2001.

*David Sless*

I'm interested in the philosophy of communication: the nature of communication and how we think about it. Approaches to visualisation and aesthetics make assumptions about the nature of communication. Some of these assumptions are built into the programming languages we use. Programming languages have semantic and syntactic properties. The notions of semantics and syntactics derive from communication theory.

I suggest that as these notions are currently applied, they are deeply flawed and impose an unnecessary limitation on programming and other intellectual pursuits. Alongside semantics and syntactics, there is a third category: pragmatics. I have come to the view that syntactics and semantics are subcategories within pragmatics rather than categories in their own right. The implications of this view are far-reaching and may change the way we develop future programming languages. In this panel, I use some of our recent research to illustrate the types of visual aesthetic problems that lie beyond contemporary computing languages but which may be possible if we rethink how such languages are constructed.

David Sless is director of the Communication Research Institute of Australia. He graduated from Leeds University in 1965 with an honours degree in psychology and sociology. Fascinated by communication problems in ordinary life (such things as signage systems that confuse people and labels that people can't understand), he went on to do research into ways of improving communication. In 1975, he was awarded an MSc by Durham University for his research in this field. He was then invited to take up a lectureship at Flinders University in South Australia to continue his research and teaching in communication. The relevance of his research into practical everyday problems of communication has now been widely recognised.

## Sha Xin-Wei

If the power of making a trace comes from fashioning matter in the space of the imaginary, then mathematical drawing, sketching, and tracing have peculiar power. How is it that with a few strokes we create and shape geometries of arbitrary dimension or entities that have infinite extent? The creative power of visualization comes from somewhere in between the topological and the geometric.

What is the geometric? Riemannian geometry, for example, offers enough metric and curvature structure to sustain a kinematic intuition with functional, even computable presentation. But topology sustains ways to work both rigorously and intuitively about notions such as continuity, openness, convergence, and connectedness without binding us to any Cartesian framework. Imagining visualization as a process rather than a static representation, focusing on spaces of mappings rather than particular geometric domains, may bring us to the cusp of meaningful gesture and show us a way into the creation of felt meaning.

Sha Xin-Wei was trained in mathematics at Harvard and Stanford Universities, then worked in the fields of scientific computation, mathematical modeling, and visualization of scientific data and geometric structures. Since 1995, he has extended his work to distributed media authoring systems and media theory, in a three-year workshop on interaction and computational media.

After obtaining an interdisciplinary PhD at Stanford on differential geometric performance and the technologies of writing (in mathematics, computer science, and the history and philosophy of science), he joined the faculty of the School of Literature, Communication, and Culture at the Georgia Institute of Technology. He is currently constructing fusion experiments that materialize as cultural artifacts with colleagues in the TGarden Consortium and the Hubbub urban speech-painting project.

## Sara Diamond

Sara Diamond is artistic director of media and visual art at The Banff Centre for the Arts. She leads all research, residency, exhibition, and training in the field of new media, television, and visual art at this international artistic research and professional development centre. She is also adjunct professor in the Design Media Department at the University of California, Los Angeles. She is currently writer in residence at the University of Surrey.

Her research explores the relationships among performance, role playing, dialogues, and the capacity of technologies, in particular visualization technologies, to provide tools, meanings, and emotional experiences for users. Her own research, Code Zebra, is a multiyear project with collaborators in Brazil, the USA, Canada, the United Kingdom, and Australia, exploring dialogues between artists and scientists using live and virtual tools. She has published extensively and curated exhibitions around the world. She develops new media streams for The Banff Television Festival and other world-renowned events.

*Reference*
1.  Card, S. K., Mackinlay, J. D., & Shneiderman B. (1999). Information visualization: Using vision to think. Morgan Kaufmann, 1999.

*73*

## :-o A CONVERSATION ABOUT INTERACTIVE ENTERTAINMENT EXPERIENCES ON INSTANT MESSAGING DEVICES

*Moderator*
ANA SERRANO
Director
Bell h@bitat
Canadian Film Centre
aserrano@cdnfilmcentre.com
www.cdnfilmcentre.com

*Panelists*
KIM BINSTED
i-Chara Inc.

TOM FREELAND
Cybiko, Inc.

ERIN LEMON
Digital 4Sight

NEIL YOUNG
Electronic Arts Inc.

From mad texting that incites political revolutions to alien-fish swapping games, the usefulness, richness, and whimsy found in the world of instant messaging is often lost on North American audiences. This panel demystifies (and reasserts) the fun everyone is having in Asia, Europe, and, yes, in some pockets of North America with AIM, ICQ, and Messenger, and their cell phones, cybikos, PDAs, and devices that can easily fit into a jean-jacket pocket.

*Ana Serrano*
Ana Serrano is director of Bell h@bitat, the new media training facility at the Canadian Film Centre, a world-renowned film, television, and new media institute established by Norman Jewison. She oversees the strategic planning, programme design, and fiscal development of all of the centre's new media initiatives, including creation of interactive narrative prototypes through the centre's New Media Design Programme. She was formerly the first associate at Digital 4Sight, a think tank and consulting firm founded by Don Tapscott, where she developed new media products and produced the company's first knowledge management toolkit. Featured as one of MacLean Magazine's Top 100 Canadians To Watch in the year 2000, she has recently produced the Great Canadian Story Engine Project, an oral history Web site of personal Canadian stories.

She is a member of the boards of the Canadian Conference on the Arts, Women in Film and Television, the New Media Advisory Committee of the Canadian Film and Television Production Association, and the Muriel Cooper Prize Council at the Design Management Institute. She frequently speaks at new media and film festivals throughout the world about the emerging realm of interactive and networked digital storytelling.

*Erin Lemon*
Erin Lemon is a research analyst at Digital 4Sight, a research and consulting firm specializing in business-model innovation for the digital economy. Her background is in the history and impact of technology adoption, and her areas of expertise include the mobile Internet and telematics. She is currently working on a multi-year research program entitled The Hypernet Revolution: Business Model Innovation in the Mobile Economy, which examines the social and economic impact of pervasive and ubiquitous computing.

*Kim Binsted*
Kim Binsted is one of the leading authorities on artificial intelligence (AI) and human-computer interaction (HCI), particularly as they pertain to character and humour. Her dissertation, Machine Humour: An Implemented Model of Puns, earned her notice in the international media, and she has since been featured in magazines such as Wired and Interview, and on television shows such as the BBC's Tomorrow's World. Her many high-profile appearances include a panel on computational humour at Stanford University with Marvin Minsky, Douglas Hofstadter, and Steve Martin and being the plenary speaker at Computer-Human Interaction 2000.

In Japan, she was a researcher at the Kansai Advanced Research Center and at the Sony Computer Science Laboratories, where she worked on emotionally-responsive HCI. Past projects include BOKE (a Japanese pun generator), Byrne (an expressive talking-head football commentator), HyperMask (a wearable animated face for live performance), and Danger Hamster 2000 (an expressive character in an unpredictable environment). She has a PhD in AI from the University of Edinburgh and a BSc in physics from McGill University.

*Neil Young*
Neil Young, vice president and executive in charge of production at Electronic, is the creator and driving force behind "Majestic," to which he brings more than 10 years of successful interactive entertainment experience and knowledge. He began his career in the interactive entertainment industry in 1988, when he was a programmer and producer at Imagitec, a small British development company, where he worked on platform conversions for games developed by Electronic Arts, ORIGIN Systems, Microprose, and Mindscape. He joined the staff at Probe Software in 1990 as a senior producer, working on a wide variety of titles for Acclaim, Sega, Hudson, USGold, and Virgin Interactive.

In 1992, he moved to the United States and was promoted to vice president for product development at Virgin Interactive. Five years later, he was named vice president and general manager of ORIGIN Systems, a subsidiary of Electronic Arts, where he supervised the launch of the highly successful Ultima Online. In 1999, he assumed his current position at Electronic Arts, where he is currently creating next-generation interactive content for EA.com.

*Tom Freeland*
While studying information technology at the Rochester Institute of Technology, Tom Freeland founded and became president of the Information Student Technology Organization. He also pieced together a virtual reality system and developed multimedia for the hearing impaired. Soon afterward, he brought music to life for the hearing impaired when he created a software package that allows MIDI music to be seen in artful dynamic shapes and colors. He then pursued multimedia design and development, first at Xerox Corporation and then at KLS Studios, where he was the instrumental developer in a team that created a CD-ROM that won an international award from Grafis. As director of game design at Cybiko, Inc., he maintains an unofficial world record of releasing one game every day for the company's wireless computer.

74

# Newton's Nightmare: Reality Meets Faux Physics

*Organizer*
Dinesh K. Pai
University of British Columbia
Department of Computer Science
2366 Main Mall
Vancouver, British Columbia
V6T 1Z4 Canada
+1.604.822.8197
pai@cs.ubc.ca

*Panelists*
Dinesh K. Pai
University of British Columbia

Doug Roble
Digital Domain

Holly Rushmeier
IBM T. J. Watson Research
Center

Richard Szeliski
Microsoft Research

Demetri Terzopoulos
New York University and
University of Toronto

Reality – who needs it? Is computer graphics about building more and more accurate simulations of the real world, down to the last photon? Is computer graphics really hard physics dressed in Hollywood clothing? Or is reality, like, soooooo old fashioned? Is computer graphics now free from its shackles, free to create non-whatever realistic experiences, free to write its own laws, with no relation to reality? This panel sheds some light (real or imagined) on these complex questions.

## Dinesh K. Pai

Computer graphics is indeed about reality, but reality as experienced by humans. We need models of reality but our needs are very different from, say, the needs of physics or engineering. I argue that:

1. New, creative applications in computer graphics need new types of models, but these still need to be rooted in reality, because human perceptual and cognitive systems evolved to cope with it. We need to model not only external physical systems, but also human systems that produce and consume the experience.

2. Traditional models of reality are based on the assumption that measuring the real world is a lot more expensive than simulating it. New and inexpensive sensors have changed the economics of measurement and hence of modeling, making radically different models possible.

3. All models of reality are wrong, but some are more wrong than others for a specific purpose. What matters is to clearly know the metric. Is interactive response more important for perception than accurate motion? Are we trying to convey the details of a real object on an e-commerce Web site, or are we trying to direct attention to the object's most important features?

Dinesh K. Pai, a professor of computer science at the University of British Columbia, received his PhD from Cornell University. His research interests span the areas of robotics, graphics, modeling, and simulation. His current interests are in interactive multimodal simulation of contact (including auditory and haptic displays) and acquiring multimodal models of everyday objects using automated measurement techniques.

## Holly Rushmeier

Design applications where the image is not the end product but a means to predict what a physical design will look like require accurate simulation. Researchers have developed simulations of light transfer to compute the quantity of energy that would pass through each pixel. We can still develop better algorithms, but there are few major problems left in the simulation of light. There is no reason to consider quantum or relativistic effects. Our research challenges are now in psychophysics, understanding what features will have an impact on a human observer.

Many interesting effects have been developed by accident – by setting various parameters and seeing if the resulting image is pleasing. Our knowledge of how to simulate the physics of light gives us the ability to deliberately control rendering to create

consistent, visually rich alternative environments. While talented artists have always done this with effort, we can now facilitate more experimentation. Rather than relying on accident, we should further exploit what we know about light and deliberately change the rules to provide powerful new tools.

Holly Rushmeier received her PhD degree in mechanical engineering from Cornell University and is now a research staff member at the IBM T.J. Watson Research Center. Her research interests include data visualization and realistic image synthesis.

## Doug Roble

In the realm of visual effects, we are always trying to convince people to suspend their disbelief. Of course, there are the big effects (the asteroids and the spaceships and aliens), but audiences know that they aren't real, so digital artists can have fun and get away with non-real effects and graphics. When I reflect on the most gripping visual effects scenes, I think of small effects that fool me utterly: the cow getting hit by the car in "Oh Brother, Where Art Thou?" or Julia Roberts' car accident in "Erin Brockovich." These scenes are devastating in that computer graphics has been used to manipulate and simulate reality so well that you don't have to suspend disbelief. There was never a point where you disbelieved!

So, do we need to simulate reality? Of course! The more accurate the lighting, the fluid dynamics, the surface parameters, the modelling ... the more powerful an artist becomes. Just look at the trends in the effects industry: Years ago, particle systems were all the rage. Now every effects house is developing its own fluid dynamics package. For characters, an IK weighting system controlling a NURBS surface used to be good enough. Now we are all developing physically accurate bone/muscle/skin systems. Visual effects houses have all adopted computer-vision techniques to extract every last bit of information from the real world.

Can we mimic reality without accurately simulating it? Sure! That's what we've been doing for years, and you've seen the results on the movie screens. We need to continue to forge ahead with more detailed and accurate models so that the artists can produce the effects of the future.

Doug Roble is creative director of software at Digital Domain and Sketches and Applications Chair for SIGGRAPH 2002. He has been developing tools and doing research at Digital Domain since 1993. His computer vision system, "track," won a Technical

*75*

Achievement Award from the Academy of Motion Picture Arts and Sciences in 1998. He received his PhD in computer science from The Ohio State University in 1992.

*Richard Szeliski*

"Faux physics or no physics?" For many computer graphics applications, it is often sufficient to simply capture some real-world imagery, and then to manipulate it to get the desired effect. An early example of this was image morphing, where different video streams could be morphed or blended to get compelling transitions between different people or objects. More recently, image-based rendering has suggests that we can often approximate the 3D appearance of an object (and generate novel interactive views) by simply jumping (or interpolating) between different views. Current implementations of the "freeze frame" effect often do just that: jump between a densely spaced set of still images taken with cameras.

Of course, doing computer vision analysis (recovering the geometric side of the "physics") allows us to use fewer cameras or to get better interpolation results. Still images, however, are just a very narrow subset of what we want to synthesize in computer graphics. The temporal analog to image-based rendering is video-based rendering, where sample video clips can be manipulated to achieve novel synthetic video sequences. An early example of this was *video rewrite*, which manipulated (concatenated and blended) digitized lip motions to make a character say new speech. More recently, we have been working on *video textures*, which can synthesize realistic, novel, quasi-periodic motions (waterfalls, flames, swimming fish, talking heads) from sample video footage. Is this "data driven" or "machine learning" ("no-physics") approach the solution to everything? Obviously not.

For many (most?) applications, we will get more mileage by trying to understand (and then simulate) the actual physics (geometry, photometry, dynamics, behavior) of the phenomena we are modeling. For example, recovery of BRDF from multiple images is currently one of the hot areas in image-based modeling. It's just that a complete model is often very hard to achieve, both because of our limited understanding, and because the inverse estimation problems are often ill-posed. Judicious knowledge of when to "fake" aspects of the physics will always remain one of the hallmarks of successful application of computer graphics to complex phenomena.

Richard Szeliski is a senior researcher in the Vision-Based Modeling Group at Microsoft Research, where he is pursuing research in 3D computer vision, video scene analysis, and image-based rendering. His current focus is on constructing photorealistic 3D scene models from multiple images and video. He received a PhD in computer science from Carnegie Mellon University in 1988, and he has been at Microsoft Research since 1995.

*Demetri Terzopoulos*

My holy grail is a "reality emulator" as compelling as the one portrayed in "The Matrix." Although a multisensory computational simulation with such incredible fidelity (never mind

all the exhilarating weirdness!) remains elusive, the trend in computer graphics is clear. With Moore's law on our side, researchers and practitioners alike are eagerly pursuing what might be characterized as the "Taylor series approximation to reality." I, for one, have found it intellectually stimulating to help establish some crucial, low-order terms of this approximation, which now epitomize the prominent physics-based and biology-based (artificial life) paradigms in CG modeling and animation. The endeavor of systematically augmenting the realism of CG models continues to excite me.

However, I also believe that we should explore alternatives to simulation. It behooves us to exploit the special computational structure of the brain, which after all is the client, ideally through a direct brain-machine interface, of our provisionally mythical reality emulator. The brain learns to perceive the raw reality of nature in certain ways and not in others. In this context, recent CG techniques such as the NeuroAnimator (SIGGRAPH 98) are provocative. They suggest that it should be possible to create a new breed of emulation algorithms that, through observation of reality by computational structures analogous to those found in the brain, can learn to mimic a wide variety of natural phenomena (physical dynamics in the case of the NeuroAnimator) with sufficient fidelity to render all residual errors imperceptible.

Demetri Terzopoulos holds the Lucy and Henry Moses Professorship in the Sciences at New York University and is professor of computer science and mathematics at NYU's Courant Institute. He is currently on leave from the University of Toronto, where he is professor of computer science and professor of electrical and computer engineering. He received his PhD degree from the Massachusetts Institute of Technology. He was elected a fellow of the IEEE, a fellow of the Canadian Institute for Advanced Research, a Steacie Fellow of the Natural Sciences and Engineering Research Council of Canada, and a Killam Fellow of the Canada Council for the Arts. Among his many awards are computer graphics honors from Ars Electronica, NICOGRAPH, and the International Digital Media Foundation.

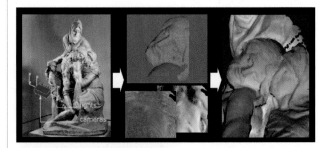

Real…(above)

…or not? (left)

# VIPs: Virtually Invented People

*Organizer*
Kathryn Saunders
ThinkTech
245 Davenport Road, 3rd Floor
Toronto, Ontario
M5R 1K1 Canada
+1.416.200.4316
+1.416.929.8924 fax
kathryn_saunders@siggraph.org

*Panelists*
Andrew Burgess
Ananova

Barbara Hayes-Roth
Extempo Systems, Inc.

R.U.Sirius
Alternating Currents

Thomas Vetter
Universität Freiburg

Keith Waters
LifeFX

Since the early days of computer animation, researchers and artists have been fascinated by the digital grail of creating a life-like resemblance. Recent advances in technology have brought us closer to that reality and toward the possibility of creating credible and plausible digital human forms complete with physical, behavioral, and emotional capabilities.

Building compelling, realistic virtual people is technically challenging, drawing on many disciplines beyond computer graphics. As we move toward a generation of digital characters, we will be presented with new possibilities. Novel forms of personal interaction, as well as human-machine communication, will become viable, and the interactions will be familiar as well as intriguing.

However, what repercussions will they have on our social networks, our basic human needs, our belief systems? This panel presents the exciting new generation of VIPs exlores offer a glimpse into a what the future holds for the next generation of lifelike virtual humans, and discusses the social, entertainment, and psychological challenges that these technologies imply. Ananova, the world's first virtual news anchor (www.ananova. com), combines sophisticated real-time news and information systems with advanced instant animation techniques. The technical challenge for Ananova's creators was to engineer a fully animated virtual character capable of dealing with a vast range of dynamic content. Using XML as a basis for video scripts, the Ananova team gave the character the flexibility to respond differently to any given news item and to behave appropriately in many different situations.

On the Web, Ananova can be seen in the form of streaming video. However, this is only one of many incarnations of the character currently in development. Ananova's vision of the future is one in which users will have access to a fully interactive personal information assistant that can help them find their way through an increasingly information-rich world.

The Ananova service focuses on provision of personalized, real-time breaking news. It alerts users to the information they need to know, the instant it happens. Users tailor the Ananova service to their own interests by choosing subjects from a catalog of over 3,000 topics, which is growing daily. When news breaks in their chosen areas, Ananova contacts the user via the Web, email, SMS, voice, or personal WAP page.

*Andrew Burgess*
Andrew Burgess is responsible for software development, Internet systems and connectivity, Web site construction, and project management for Ananova. He joined PA New Media as head of operations in January 1998 and previously worked for CompuServe UK as technical director during its period of fastest growth. He has also held positions with British Telecom and Knight-Ridder Information Services in a variety of technical and consumer-interfacing roles.

*Barbara Hayes-Roth*
People are social animals. As children, we play with dolls and other anthropomorphic toys. As adults, we enjoy character-based films and stories, as well as the colorful characters who enrich our daily lives. Equally important, whether we are working, learning, or playing, we interact more easily, more effectively, and more happily when our interactive partners are distinctive, interesting, empathetic individuals who communicate with us through natural and familiar social channels. For these reasons, we believe that smart interactive characters will offer a uniquely effective and satisfying interface between people and a variety of electronic experiences.

To fulfill their promise, interactive characters will need to have virtual "minds" that are every bit as expressive as their virtual "bodies." Like great works of art (paintings, photographs, animations, theatrical, and cinematic performances), great interactive characters will create the appearance that personality, thought, feeling, and intention drive meaningful behaviors. However, unlike the players in these traditional art forms, Virtually Invented Persons (VIPs) will not be posed or scripted. Instead, they will be open and dynamic performers, more like improvisational actors or people in their natural interactions. Thus, great VIPs will need expressive graphical bodies capable of generating meaningful but unscripted gestures and facial expressions in real time. And they will need expressive minds to manifest personality, thought, feeling, and intention in real time, in order to drive and coordinate meaningful verbal and non-verbal behaviors.

Barbara Hayes-Roth is the founder and CEO of Extempo Systems, Inc., an innovator in smart interactive characters for online learning, customer relationship management, and interactive entertainment. She led development of Extempo's award-winning technology and products. She holds a patent for the System and Method of Directed Improvisation by Computer Characters and has several other patents pending. Previously, she directed research on interactive characters, intelligent agents, and human cognition at Stanford University, the Rand Corporation, and Bell Laboratories. She has published over 100 research articles and given many invited speeches in the US and abroad. She holds a PhD in cognitive psychology from the University of Michigan, and she is a fellow of the American Association for Artificial Intelligence.

*R.U. Sirius*
From a virtual pop star to a virtual president. William Gibson's "Idoru" is just one among several novels that imagines a world with virtual pop stars. How will virtual celebrities and (eventually) politicians impinge on our social reality and our perceptions of reality? What role does giving synthetic intelligence a face play in preparing us for a human society entertained, entranced, and governed by reasoning machines? And as we move into a world in which even the neighborhood plumber has a persona that's up for periodic reinvention, to what

77

extent will we attempt to virtualize ourselves? Will we get to lead many simultaneous lives? These entertaining and interesting questions have no answers, but they do provide us with abundant opportunity for imagining.

R.U. Sirius was editor-in-chief of the world's first technoculture magazine, Mondo 2000, from 1989-1993. Since then, he has authored several books including *The Cyberpunk Handbook and Design For Dying* (with Timothy Leary), and written hundreds of articles for periodicals including Time, Wired, Esquire, and Salon. He is currently editor-in-chief of Alternating Currents, a quarterly print journal, and chairman of The Revolution, a political party.

*Thomas Vetter*
The challenge of creating virtual persons has always been attractive to humans. With the rapid development of computer graphics, many new forms of synthespians are being developed or discussed. One direction of this research and thought is to create a virtual copy of a real, existing person, a copy that simulates not only visual appearance and voice, but also language, specific knowledge, and behavior.

The focus of research in the computer graphics group at Universität Freiburg is how to create a convincing visual copy of a person's face from a small number of photographs, perhaps even a single image, or from video material. Our goal is to create novel, photo-realistic images and motion sequences that were not part of the original material. The challenge is to understand the minimal requirements necessary to build a convincing computer graphic model of a person's face from images and to understand the perceptual sensitivity of human observers to the variability of an individual face.

Our approach is based on a method that we call a morphable model. It is a general, flexible 3D face model. In an analysis by synthesis loop, a given novel image can be reconstructed by the model. Coded or described in terms of the internal model parameters, a face in an image can be rotated, re-illuminated, and animated. Starting from state-of-the-art image modeling techniques, we explore future directions in automated techniques for manipulation of portraits.

Learning the appearance of faces from other example faces might be a paradigm that could be transferred to simulation of more complex phenomena, such as facial gesture or even behavior and language.

Thomas Vetter is head of the Computer Graphics Group at Universität Freiburg, Germany. He studied mathematics and physics at Universität of Ulm, where he did his PhD on neuronal signal processing. In 1991, he joined a group led by Tomaso Poggio at the Center for Biological and Computational Learning at the Massachusetts Institute of Technology, where he worked on visual object recognition and learning strategies for representations of object classes. In 1993, he joined the Max-Planck-Institute Biologie in Tübingen, Germany, where he started his work on models for analysis and synthesis of face images, which is still his main focus of research.

*Keith Waters*
The human face is the most expressive component of any Virtually Invented Person (VIP) so getting the face "right" is vital. The face has to be believable, especially if we are presented with a representation of a real person. In fact we are "wet wired" to interpret images of faces, which makes the task even harder, because even the subtlest incorrect movements are easily detectable. If it looks like a person, we expect it to behave like a person.

The goal of creating a synthetic representation that is indistinguishable from a real person has been the subject of much investigation over the last decade. Achieving this goal has been technically challenging. Not only does the physical representation of the face have to be accurate, but also the face has to move, talk, and act in a plausible fashion. Progress has been made in some key areas of facial synthesis, while other areas remain relatively unexplored. So what aspects of facial synthesis are easy, and what aspects are hard? What areas of investigation are required to bring life to VIPs? Understanding where some of these technical boundaries exist helps us build new and exciting artifacts.

Keith Waters is currently the senior technical officer of LifeFX. Prior to joining the company, he was a principal member of the technical staff at Compaq Computer Corporation's Cambridge Research Laboratory. While at Compaq, he studied novel forms of human computer interaction, including facial animation synthesis. He is co-author of a standard text in the field, Computer Facial Animation, and he has published numerous papers on the subject. While at Compaq, he was responsible for development of FaceWorks, a Windows-based multimedia authoring tool for synthetic faces. Prior to 1999, he was at Digital Equipment Corporation, where he developed DECface, a real-time synthetic face utilizing DECtalk, a software text-to-speech engine.

*Kathryn Saunders*
Kathryn Saunders is a founding partner of ThinkTech, a consulting firm that designs and develops location-based and e-based experience strategies. She has been actively involved with SIGGRAPH for many years. She is Panels Chair for 2001, and for SIGGRAPH 99, she chaired Emerging Technologies, where she developed and executed the Millennium Motel concept and curated several elements including the entry portal and Route 66.

Trained as an architect, she practiced architecture with two of Canada's leading design firms and has taught architecture at two Canadian universities. Prior to her current post, she was executive director of the Digital Media Institute and creative director, digital media, at the Royal Ontario Museum. At the museum, she developed MYTHICA, an educational entertainment destination that uses a profiling system, wireless technologies, and intelligent autonomous agents to deliver personalized information before, during, and after a visit, based on the visitor's behavior and aspirations. A recipient of many interactive media awards, she has consulted and lectured around the globe from North America to Saudi Arabia and Japan.

# TRADITIONAL SKILLS, NEW TOOLS

*Organizer*
JILL SMOLIN
Cinesite Visual Effects
1017 North Las Palmas
Los Angeles, California 90048
USA
+1.323.468.2102
jill@well.com

*Panelists*
DEREK CHAN
DreamWorks SKG

IVO HORVAT
Sony Pictures Imageworks

STEVEN MARKOWSKI
Cinesite Visual Effects

SANDE SCOREDOS
Sony Pictures Imageworks

TOM SITO
University of Southern California

*Derek Chan*

When I first entered computer science, one of my goals was to create software that "even my mother could use." Now that I've been working at DreamWorks for nearly five years, my goals are more closely aligned with making software that "even a traditional animator could use." In either case, you are looking at a pretty tough road.

In the digital age, the push continues to be for faster and more efficient production pipelines. At DreamWorks, the way we've tried to do this for traditional animation has been through a progression. During the development of ToonShooter, our new Linux-based pencil test system, the goal was to make the current process as quick and painless as possible. We focused a great deal of time on understanding what the traditional animators do and how we could help them do the mundane things faster. This led to a number of new features and enhancements that might not have occurred to us without their involvement. Now that we have gained confidence in providing tools that make their current process as efficient as possible, we are looking at how much faster we could make things if we changed their process. This is where our next stage of development is headed. Can we allow the artists to do what they do best in a way that fits more easily into the digital world? Our development efforts include:

- Digital drawing tools
- CG animation tools geared toward traditional animators
- Remote collaboration
- Integration with other digital departments (editorial and layout)

As we continue to travel down this road of making tools for traditional artists, we're finding it to be an intriguing journey.

Derek Chan has served as a software project manager at DreamWorks on the animated features "The Prince of Egypt" and "The Road to El Dorado." One of the projects Chan helped oversee was setting up the studio's batch queue system, which was used on "The Prince of Egypt" and "The Road to El Dorado," and is currently in use on the forthcoming animated feature "Spirit: Stallion of the Cimarron." Chan has also worked on the studio's new Linux-based pencil test system, ToonShooter, which is now being used for DreamWorks animation projects. In addition, Chan has been involved in pipeline utilities, where he manages and develops software that makes the production pipeline run more efficiently. For Software Operations, he manages a group of six developers who work closely with production to identify and solve development issues.

Prior to joining DreamWorks, he worked at SGI as a member of their SoftWindows development team, where his focus being on multimedia playback. He also worked at IBM on an electronic installation program for Windows and OS/2. He earned a bachelor of science and electrical engineering at the University of California, Los Angeles and studied computer science at Stanford University.

*Ivo Horvat*

It is no secret that computer graphics technology is becoming more accessible everyday to the less technically minded. This has had the effect of shifting the preferred job requirements away from those who have computer science degrees to those who have more developed artistic training. In the past, simply wading through an interface was sometimes a major accomplishment achieved only by the select few. Those few more technically minded specialists were very highly paid and highly regarded, and they had total creative control over the work, because no one with creative skills had enough technical knowledge to confidently direct the work. The result was that the work had a distinct lack of artistic involvement on both sides of the equation: the work that was delivered, and the tools that were conceived to achieve it. The overwhelming attitude at the time seemed to be fear of approaching technological voodoo.

Today however, leaps and bounds have been made in the areas of technological engineering. Even though nothing is quite as intuitive as an analog device, such as a pencil or a paintbrush, technology is bridging the gap, in both hardware and software. The upshot of all of this is that the technological controls are becoming more transparent, and they reveal the artistic shortcomings of their users more quickly.

Ultimately, it is the brain that steers the hand to utilize either brush or stylus. To say that the art is in the medium would be as silly as to say that one artist is more evocative simply because her brushes were treated with a more technologically advanced process. Thousands of years of art history have taught us why this is not so.

Ivo Horvat began his career in the entertainment industry in 1992. After leaving Art Center College of Design, where he was studying transportation design, he quickly secured an agent and began freelancing as a conceptual artist and illustrator. Over the next two years, he did work for clients such as Ridley Scott and Assoc., and Taco Bell. In 1994, he joined the newly formed visual effects facility Sony Pictures Imageworks. Over the next four years, he contributed paintings for the films "Tall Tale," "Speed," "Judge Dredd," "The Cable Guy," "Virtuosity," "Anaconda," "Phenomenon," "The Ghost and the Darkness," "Contact," "Starship Troopers," "The Postman," and "Snow Falling On Cedars."

Utilizing his background in industrial design and illustration, he contributed to the Imageworks art department, creating conceptual artwork for a number of films, including: "James and the Giant Peach," "Harold and the Purple Crayon," "Anaconda," and the first incarnation of "Godzilla." In 1998, joined the matte painting department at Industrial Light + Magic, where he applied his unique talents to "Star Wars:

79

Episode One," "The Mummy," "Wild Wild West," "Galaxy Quest," "The Perfect Storm," "Space Cowboys," "Impostor," "E.T." (15-year anniversary re-release), and "The Mummy Returns." Projects for ILM's commercial division included the Star Wars: Episode One Pepsi campaign and the campaign for First Union Bank, which won an Emmy for Best Visual Effects. In 2001, at the request of Ken Ralston, he re-joined Sony Pictures Imageworks to head the matte painting department. He currently oversees matte painting on: "Spiderman," America's Sweethearts," "Stuart Little 2," and "Harry Potter."

*Steven Markowski*
My attitude when I made the transition from traditional to computer animation was fairly simplistic: "Good animation is good animation. All I need to do is learn the new tool and it's basically the same thing." To a large extent, this is true. The principles of animation remain the same no matter what the medium. But now I think the success of traditional animators attempting to transition to the computer are largely dependent on how they approach their work. Animators who work very intuitively or rely heavily on their strength in drawing can become frustrated by a medium that has only peripheral use for their drawing skills and is too complex to allow excessive intuition. However, those with a more analytical approach to animation, who enjoy honing actions and performances more than drawings, can find it a medium that offers them a greater level of sophistication than they can find in the traditional animation world. There is also a world of creative freedom and exploration that opens up to them when they are given that greatest of gifts that the digital realm has to offer: the "undo" button.

Steven Markowski was born in Brooklyn, New York. Since graduating from the California Institute of the Arts in 1987, he has worked in a variety of traditional animation and story positions for numerous studios, including Disney, Fox, and Turner. By 1996, he had taught himself how to animate on the computer, and he was chosen to supervise the title character for Warner Brothers' "The Iron Giant." He is currently the Animation Director at Cinesite Visual Effects in Los Angeles, where he recently finished supervising the animation for A.M.E.E., the robot star of Warner Brothers' "Red Planet."

*Sande Scoredos*
In recent years, I have seen a tremendous increase in the number of people who enter the computer graphics field with a strong traditional arts background and a good foundation in digital technology. There is no substitute for a good foundation in both traditional and digital skills. Anyone working in animation today would benefit from learning as much as they can about computer tools and traditional art forms. Artist, technicians, and developers gain a better understanding of how to create and use digital tools by working in both the traditional and digital forum.

Sande Scoredos is executive director of technical training and artist development at Sony Pictures Imageworks. She has a background in production tools and methods used in creating computer graphics imagery in the scientific, engineering, gaming, video, and film effects industries. Her technical knowledge includes work in 3D from computer animation techniques to radiosity and volumetric rendering, and she has an extensive background in art education, computer science, and 2D and 3D computer graphics production. Her background in studio art led her to teach at the professional studio and university level. Adding computer science and engineering to her credentials, she began teaching microwave engineering design on 2D UNIX CAD systems. The emergence of UNIX-based 3D computer graphics in the mid-1980s enabled her to combine art and computer technology. As manager of training at Wavefront Technologies for many years, she designed the worldwide training program and curriculum, instructing professionals in the use of 3D computer graphics and animation for broadcast, engineering, gaming, and scientific visualization. She then moved on to Rhythm & Hues, where she again designed a training facility and curriculum, and focused on teaching proprietary software tools and production methods to novice and experienced digital production artists. In 1997, she joined Sony, where she has once again set up a training facility for a production studio. She educates experienced artists to use the tools they need to produce world-class imagery. This training program is also designed to enrich the aesthetic, as well as the technical skills of the artists, and to provide artistic career development.

She is very committed to education. She works with schools to review reels and portfolios for student projects and participates with Sony recruitment at festivals and job fairs. As a UCLA alumna, she is very active in the UCLA Professional Entertainment Studies program and teaches 3D computer graphics courses in the Digital Creation program. She is also chair of the SIGGRAPH 2001 Computer Animation Festival.

*Tom Sito*
Hollywood is a place that frequently like to turn itself upside down over new technologies. But the problem in this mania for change is how to exploit the strengths of the new technologies and still preserve the traditional skills of filmmaking, animation, and story telling. For movies, technology is not an end in itself. The ultimate goal is a good story well told. The time is coming when audiences will stop granting CGI animation a curve because it has not yet reached its potential. The audience demands quality as good or better than the traditional paint and pencil could ever achieve.

Tom Sito is a 26-year veteran of animated film production. His screen credits include the Disney classics "The Little Mermaid," "Beauty & the Beast," "Aladdin," "The Lion King," "Who Framed Roger Rabbit?," "Pocahontas," "Fantasia 2000," and "Dinsosaurs." At DreamWorks SKG, his talents contributed to "The Prince of Egypt," "Antz," "Shrek," "Spirit," and "Paulie." He has just co-directed Warner Brothers' "Osmosis Jones."

He teaches at the University of Southern California and has written numerous articles on animation. He has lectured at New York University, SVA, UCLA, AFI, the annual SIGGRAPH conference, Microsoft, Capilano College, Sheridan College, Ecole du Grand Gobelin, Palma Majorca, and the Yomiuri Forum in Tokyo. He is president of the Motion Picture Screen Cartoonist's Union Local #839, were he is an outspoken advocate for the rights of artists.

# THE CAVE AND BEYOND:
## VR ART IN MUSEUMS AND GALLERIES

*Organizer*
JOSEPHINE ANSTEY
University at Buffalo
248A Center for the Arts
Buffalo, New York 14260 USA
+1.716.645.6902
jranstey@buffalo.edu

*Panelists*
DONNA COX
National Center for
Supercomputing Applications
University of Illinois

HORST HÖRTNER
Ars Electronica Futurelab

DANIEL J. SANDIN
University of Illinois at Chicago

PAUL SERMON
University of Salford

JEFFREY SHAW
Zentrum für Kunst und
Medientechnologie

Immersive, interactive VR systems (CAVEs, domes, etc.) deliver unique artistic, entertainment and educational experiences. Worldwide, there are a growing number of such systems open to the public on a daily basis. This panel examines the historical strengths and weaknesses of using VR in public spaces and the challenges of creating VR experiences for different kinds of audiences. We discuss how the use of VR has expanded; whether the "wow" factor continues to play a stronger role in attracting an audience than the work itself; what has really worked; and what the problems are. We contemplate the directions (aesthetics, content, and technical advancements) for VR as a public display medium.

The motivation for convening this panel is threefold: to discuss VR production and VR installation for public display; to examine the cross-over of the latest technical research into art practice; and to create a forum where the panelists and members of the audience can pool information, learn from each other, and delineate controversial areas.

*Josephine Anstey*
In a typical VR experience, you share the CAVE with a group, flying together across galaxies, watching molecules mate, effecting turbulent gas flows, meeting virtual guides. But what if the guide wants to whisper you a secret? What if you don't want your interactions watched by all the others? I develop virtual fiction experiences. Unlike a novel or film where the audience identifies with the main protagonist, in this fictional form, the user is the main protagonist. For the experience to have the most impact, the user must feel comfortable and confident enough to engage with the piece physically and emotionally. This often means being alone with the piece. The high cost of immersive projection technology (IPT) systems makes them rare in the kind of spaces (museums, galleries, conferences, and festivals) where my VR Fiction shows; their popularity and the economics of throughput make an experience for one user alone unfeasible. Yet I believe that such an intimate setting is crucial for this type of application. The next step is a prototype IPT system that is cheap enough to be widely used for one-on-one experiences in art exhibitions and robust enough for daily wear and tear.

Josephine Anstey is a virtual reality and video artist. Her latest work is an immersive VR fiction, "The Thing Growing." She has collaborated on "Shared Miletus," a networked VR piece, and the "Multi Mega Book in the CAVE," winner of a Multimedia Grand Prix 97 Award from the Multi-Media Content Association of Japan. These VR pieces have shown widely in the US, Europe, and Japan. Since 1983 she has collaborated on a series of videos with video artist Julie Zando, which have shown internationally and won awards including the Best Narrative Video Award (Atlanta Film and Video Festival, 1990) and Best Experimental Video Award (Atlanta Film and Video Festival, 1989). Many of the videos are in the permanent collection of the Museum of Modern Art in New York. She is currently a visiting assistant professor at the University at Buffalo.

*Donna Cox*
In our work with the American Museum of Natural History Hayden Planetarium, my collaborators and I use CAVE technology not only as a display device, but also as a remote production tool. We regularly do Champaign-New York sessions to develop new exhibits using Virtual Director, a choreography tool developed by three artists: Donna Cox, Robert Patterson, and Marcus Thiebaux. The digital dome at the Hayden is like a seven-wall CAVE with edge blending. Projectors throw 70 feet, creating a hemisphere where 440 museum attendees can go on a tour from earth, to the Milky Way, to the Virgo Cluster, and beyond into the large-scale structure of the universe. Our team contributed over four minutes of visualization to the Passport to the Universe digital dome exhibit, and we are currently working on the Big Bang. The digital tours are created from observational and computational data that is artistically choreographed, colored, and rendered. Artists, technologists, and scientists work together to develop content for these large displays. Over two million people have seen Passport to the Universe. The new Big Bang exhibit is scheduled to open 4 July 2001.

Donna Cox is professor in the College of Fine and Applied Arts, University of Illinois, and a research artist/scientist at the National Center for Supercomputing Applications. She is a recognized pioneer in scientific visualization. She was appointed to the editorial board for Leonardo Journal and elected as a voting council member of the Internet2 Strategic Applications Council. She was associate producer for scientific visualization and art director for the Pixar/NCSA segment of "Cosmic Voyage" the IMAX film nominated for an Academy Award in 1997.

*Horst Hörtner*
The City of Linz opened the Ars Electronica Center (AEC) in September 1996 as a Museum of the Future. The museum includes the first CAVE that was open to the public in an institution that is equally dedicated to art and technology. The CAVE environment was specifically designed with the knowledge that it would be heavily used on a daily basis for presentations of all kinds (art, research, industry, architecture, medicine, etc.). To support a CAVE and many changing applications, it is not enough to have specially trained technicians. To create new applications for the Ars Electronica Center's CAVE, the center's development laboratory, Futurelab, is crucial. Its main goals are: to give the computer art community a place to exhibit and work on production (art research); to increase the possibilities for local industry to work with high-end VR equipment on application-based research in VR without incurring immense investments.

*81*

Horst Hörtner is technical director at Ars Electronica Center, where he is responsible for designing and setting up installations, including the CAVE. In 1997, he became director of Ars Electronica FutureLab, where he directs design of virtual environments, concepts for interactive installations, and systems design for Web-based applications. In 1997, he also became a Member of Christian Doppler Laboratorium for software engineering at Johannes Kepler Universität, Linz and associate professor at the Universität, für künstlerische und industrielle Gestaltung, Linz. In 1998, he became a Member of the Multimedia Content And Broadband Expert Group (5th Framework Program, European Commission, DGXIII/E-4).

*Daniel J. Sandin*
A common comment when people first experience the CAVE or even the ImmersaDesk is to say that these devices would have tremendous application in entertainment and museum settings. The chief success of projection-based VR has, however, been in the research community. Deploying CAVEs or CAVE-like systems and even single screen projection-based VR in museum settings has been much less frequent than expected. I think the problem with placing these devices in museums and galleries can be summarized as: they cost too much money, they take up too much space, they have too little throughput, and they have expensive glasses and tethered tracking systems. There are developing technologies that can change this situation. The falling cost of computation, revolutions in projection technology, and the emergence of flat-panel displays provide opportunities to address these issues. I discuss how to apply these technological changes to the design of projection VR installations in a museum context: In particular, two new designs utilizing polarization-based LCD projectors, the Front Projected ElsieDesk and a tripod arrangement of three rear-projected screens.

Daniel J. Sandin is director of the Electronic Visualization Laboratory and professor in the School of Art and Design at the University of Illinois at Chicago. His early interest in real-time computer graphics/video image processing and interactive computing environments motivated his pioneering work in video synthesizers and continues to influence his research interests. He is recognized, along with EVL co-director Tom DeFanti, for conceiving the CAVE virtual reality theater in 1991. Sandin's computer/video art has been exhibited at conferences and museums worldwide. His work is included in the inaugural collection of video art at the Museum of Modern Art in New York. He has received many grants and fellowships from such distinguished organizations as the Rockefeller Foundation, the Guggenheim Foundation, and the National Endowment for the Arts.

*Paul Sermon*
My current research involves the combination of live-action telepresent videoconferencing composited into immersive virtual environments utilising CAVE-based augmented spaces for public exhibitions. The reduction of CAVE-based systems to consumer PC accessibility is making it possible to customize the conventional four-wall CAVE into new interactive museum/gallery exhibits; integrate CAVE-based environments within telepresent installations that necessitate new projection methods for thematic experiences; and explore new architectured projection forms including corridors, alcoves, and staircases. This current research is developing a telepresent CAVE installation of connected rooms that will interface seamlessly with its physical surrounding – an interactive narrative and virtual environment that incorporates the physical installation space directly.

Paul Sermon is guest professor at the Academy of Art and Design in Linz, Austria. He is also reader in creative technology at The University of Salford, Research Centre for Art & Design, Manchester, England. He was awarded the Prix Ars Electronica Golden Nica in the category of interactive art, for the hypermedia installation Think about the People Now, in Linz, Austria, September 1991. He worked as an artist in residence and produced the ISDN video conference installation Telematic Vision at the Zentrums für Kunst und Medientechnologie in Karlsruhe, Germany, from February to November 1993. He received the Sparkey Award from the Interactive Media Festival in Los Angeles for the telepresent video installation Telematic Dreaming in June 1994.

*Jeffrey Shaw*

Many artists are deeply attracted to the unique expressive and experiential possibilities of immersive CG environments such as the CAVE. At the same time, we have to grapple with the related problems of locating and using technologies of this kind for a mass public. I describe four installations that demonstrate innovative technical and artistic solutions enabling public experience and interactivity with such technologies. PLACE is a 360-degree projection environment in which the viewer controls rotation of a large projected image from a motorized platform in the center of a large cylindrical screen. EVE (Extended Virtual Environment) is similar to PLACE in its functionality but uses an inflatable dome and a spherical projection surface so that the projected image can be interactively moved in two axes to create an immersive visualization environment. Room with a View is also a full-dome projection environment, but it uses multiple projectors to completely saturate the dome surface and constitute a fully immersive scene. conFIGURING the CAVE is an application that uses the proprietary CAVE technology but with completely custom software. Attaching cabled interfaces to the viewer was felt to be inappropriate in a museum context, so we developed a unique interface concept: a life-size wooden puppet.

Since the late 1960s, Jeffrey Shaw has pioneered the use of interactivity and virtuality in his many art installations. His works have been exhibited worldwide at major museums and festivals. For many years, he lived in Amsterdam, where he co-founded the Evenstructure Research Group (1969-80). Currently, he is director of the Institute for Visual Media at the Zentrums für Kunst und Medientechnologie in Karlsruhe, Germany. He leads a unique research and production facility where artists and scientists are working together and developing profound artistic applications of the new media technologies. His artworks include: The Legible City, Alice's City, Alice's Rooms, Revolution, the Virtual Museum, Disappearances, EVE, the Golden Calf, PLACE – A User's Manual, conFIGURING the CAVE, The Distributed Legible City, and PLACE – Ruhr.

83

conFIGURING the CAVE.

# Designing, Understanding, and Operating Complex Human-Machine Systems

*Moderator/Organizer*
DAVID ZELTZER
Fraunhofer Center for Research
in Computer Graphics (CRCG)
321 South Main Street
Providence, Rhode Island 02903
USA
+1.401.453.6363 x129
dzeltzer@crcg.edu

*Panelists*
BILL BUXTON
Alias|Wavefront

STEVE CHIEN
Jet Propulsion Laboratory

CHRISTOPHER A. MILLER
SMArt Information Flow
Technologies

ROBERT J. MOLLOY
National Transportation
Safety Board

Many computer-based systems are orders of magnitude more complex than the wireless information appliances that are the current focus of much of the attention of the computer science community. They are often safety-critical systems that have become an important part of the global economy and our daily lives, such as air traffic control, commercial and military aircraft, commercial shipping, municipal rapid transit networks, regional power plants, and oil and natural gas pipelines. This panel calls attention to the problems of interacting with complex, automated systems, describes applications in which appropriate technologies have been successfully applied in the human/machine interface, and points to challenging research issues.

*David Zeltzer*
David Zeltzer is vice president and chief technical officer at the Fraunhofer Center for Research in Computer Graphics (CRCG) in Providence, Rhode Island. He is also adjunct associate professor of computer science at Brown University. In addition to work in virtual environment technology, his research interests include human-machine interface design and knowlege-based visualization systems. He is a senior editor of the MIT Press journal Presence: Teleoperators and Virtual Environments and he is the author or co-author of more than 30 technical publications on virtual environments and human-machine interfaces.

*Bill Buxton*
The three basic rules of real estate (Location! Location! Location!) apply just as well to human-machine interface design. Tell me where a system or device will be used, and I will know an awful lot about its interaction and usability requirements. We can learn a lot from technologies developed by native peoples that allow them to negotiate hostile environments, which would render useless many of our much-touted wireless, GPS-equipped devices. The lesson is that less is more. Throwing technologies at a problem is far less important than understanding well the needs and capabilities of the human users. This applies across a wide range of computer-based systems being deployed today.

Bill Buxton is chief scientist at Alias|Wavefront and its parent company SGI, as well as an associate professor in the Department of Computer Science at the University of Toronto. He is a designer and researcher concerned with human aspects of technology, and his work reflects a particular interest in the use of technology to support creative activities such as design, filmmaking, and music. His research specialties include technologies, techniques and theories of input to computers, technology-mediated human-human collaboration, and ubiquitous computing.

*Christopher A. Miller*
Applying sophisticated, adaptive, and intelligent "information presentation automation" to manage information flow to human consumers in complex systems and domains is not a panacea. At SMArt Information Flow Technologies, our experience includes design of adaptive automation and information systems for multiple "high-end" domains including fighter piloting, attack/scout helicopter piloting, petrochemical refining, and communications resource management for military command and control. Users in such domains are very demanding and critical of automation that does not behave according to their standards and expectations, and it has proven difficult to create systems that are correct enough to achieve user acceptance. Yet we have found that intelligent interfaces and behaviors can be designed so that perfection is not required, but that value is still provided. Such interfaces require detailed consideration and design of the human-automation relationship. A critical mistake is attempting to make the system too autonomous in its behaviors. Instead, the opportunity for explicit and dynamic collaboration about how the system may best serve the human is critical.

The rotorcraft pilot's associate cockpit information manager (RPA) adaptive information management system provides an example. RPA achieved acceptable levels of usability and statistically significant workload reduction compared to an unaided condition in a series of complex and realistic human-in-the-loop mission simulations. It is important to note that these results were obtained in spite of less-than-perfect tracking of the pilot's intent and pilots' reports of having to "now and then" override or correct RPA's behaviors.

One innovation we employed in the RPA cockpit may have influenced these results: a "Crew Coordination and Task Awareness" display that, unlike some previous systems, gave the two human crew members direct insight into, and some control over, RPA's notion of the mission context and main tasks of each crew member. Pilots' acceptance of this display was very high, averaging 4.25 on a scale of 1-5 where 4 corresponded to "Of Considerable Use" and 5 to "Extremely Useful."

The success of this interface innovation has led us to think more seriously about the implications of the associate metaphor for adaptive automation in many domains. Given our experience in working on intelligent information systems, and our familiarity with others in the literature, we have recently drafted a set of "etiquette rules" for adaptive-system behavior. The notion of etiquette rules seems to have an appropriate focusing effect, both placing an emphasis on behavior acceptable to a human supervisor and requiring a degree of anthropomorphic thinking about the system, which seems to be productive. In this panel, these rules are presented, and the general notion of human-machine etiquette is discussed, along with additional examples from RPA concerning the quantification and tradeoff among rules implemented in that program.

Christopher A. Miller is chief scientist of SMArt Information Flow Technologies (SIFTech). He has over 11 years' experience in creating knowledge representations and computational approaches to adaptive user interfaces, automation, and decision aids. Until recently a research fellow at Honeywell Laboratories, he has led intelligent, adaptive information-system design efforts for domains including management of military communication resources, fighter piloting, attack/scout helicopter piloting, oil refinery operations, commercial aviation operations, and ground-based dispatch operations.

References
Banks, S. and Lizza, C. (1991). Pilot's associate; A cooperative knowledge-based system application. IEEE Expert, June. 18-29.

Miller, C., Hannen, M., & Guerlain, S. (1999). The rotorcraft pilot's associate cockpit information manager: Acceptable behavior from a new crew member. In Proceedings of the American Helicopter Society's FORUM 55, Montréal, Québec, May 25-27.

*Robert J. Molloy*
The "pitfalls" of automation in the modern glass cockpit have been a topic of discussion for over 20 years. Concurrent with increased automation in the cockpit, however, has been the increased deployment of automation in surface modes of transportation: transit trains are being operated in fully automated environments, pipeline operations are becoming more centralized and computerized, and maritime operations have seen increases in automation on both the bridge and engine rooms with subsequent reductions in manpower. Visions of the future include single-manned ships operating across the oceans. Even highway transportation is moving to highly automated systems with the development of the intelligent transportation system.

Unfortunately, surface modes seem to be experiencing the same difficulties in the growth of automation that faced the aviation industry in the past. The National Transportation Safety Board's investigation of the grounding of the cruise ship Royal Majesty off the shores of Nantucket came across several deficiencies in automated systems on the bridge. Systems that could have prevented the grounding were turned off due to high false-alarm rates. Systems that controlled the movement of the ship were able to fail in ways unanticipated by the crew. Finally, crew complacency and trust in the system prevented adequate monitoring of the systems. The board's investigation of a pipeline rupture in 1996 near Gramercy indicated that the maritime industry was not alone in its discovery of the "pitfalls" of automated systems. The pipeline controller failed to recognize the significance of an alarm due to the high frequency of alarms in the system. Further, the alarm that signaled a leak was given no higher priority than any other alarm.

Central to these discussions is the danger of moving the operator from direct control to passive monitoring. As the operator becomes less involved in direct control, there is the possibility of losing awareness of the system's state or position in the environment. The National Transportation Safety Board investigated one such occurrence in Cali, Columbia with the crash of American Airlines flight 965.

Accidents such as the Royal Majesty grounding and the Gramercy spill indicate that the problem of poor automation implementation continues to occur in surface modes. As such, more must be done to ensure that we do not revisit each of the "pitfalls" of automation previously discovered in the aviation field.

Rob Molloy joined the National Transportation Safety Board in May 1996 as a transportation research analyst. While at the board, he completed a study of aircraft evacuations and statistical reports on occupant survivability in aircraft accidents, and the relationship between accidents and aircraft age. He is currently co-managing a safety study on supervisory control and data acquisition systems in the pipeline industry. He has also been involved in accident investigations involving automation issues in multiple modes of transportation.

*Steve Chien*
Traditionally, NASA has used robotic spacecraft to explore the far reaches of the solar system by carefully designing spacecraft for the expected environment and controlling the spacecraft using a highly skilled operations team. Next-generation missions involve exploration of rapidly changing environments in situ, such as a lander on the surface of a comet, a submersible in oceans below the ice caps of Europa, and an aerial explorer in the fluctuating atmosphere of Titan. These explorers will need an unprecedented level of autonomy and adaptability to survive, in order to achieve their science goals. Yet other missions propose large numbers of cooperating explorers, such as swarms of rovers, penetrators, and airplanes, to study the climate of Mars.

*85*

These semi-autonomous systems present unique interface and interaction issues for their designers and operators. Designers must be able to determine and envision system performance in a wide range of operating scenarios. Operators must be able to understand the effects of high-level goals now used to command the autonomous explorers. The interaction between humans and space systems becomes a peer-to-peer negotiation, and succinctly summarizing group behavior is critical when tracking large numbers of autonomous entities.

In my presentation, I describe some of the challenges of this mixed-initiative, peer-to-peer model, as well as preliminary work at JPL to address these problems.

Steve Chien is technical group supervisor of the Artificial Intelligence Group and principal computer scientist in the Exploration Systems Autonomy Section at the Jet Propulsion Laboratory, California Institute of Technology. At JPL, he leads efforts in automated planning and scheduling for space exploration. He is the technology community lead for autonomy for JPL. He is also an adjunct associate professor with the Department of Computer Science, University of Southern California.

86

A collection of autonomous rovers and space vehicles that may be part of the scientific exploration of Mars. Jet Propulsion Laboratory, California Institute of Technology

# Non-Linear Animation for Production

*Organizer*
GORDON CAMERON
Softimage
3510 boulevard St-Laurent
Montréal, Québec H2X 2V2
Canada
gocam@netcom.ca
+1.514.845.1636 x3445

*Panelists*
RAF ANZOVIN
Anzovin Studio

MICHAEL ISNER
Softimage

LAURENT LAVIGNE
Pixel Liberation Front

GREG PUNCHATZ
Janimation

SETH ROSENTHAL
Industrial Light + Magic

"Production studios, 3D animators, and vendors of many popular computer graphics packages are increasingly using the term "non-linear animation," which usually describes a way of working with various types of motion data at a higher level where animation sources are abstracted to transportable snippets. Nonlinear tools can be useful in many areas of production, such as previsualization, animation creation, motion editing, retargeting and reuse, choreography, and actor direction. This panel discusses practical and speculative uses of non-linear animation techniques in a production environment."

*Raf Anzovin*
Non-linear animation systems (NLAs) represent the first real improvements on the traditional keyframe animation system. A well-implemented NLA is both an animation editing system, with features analogous to those of nonlinear video editing systems, and an animation-compositing tool that enables the animator to create layers of movement and specify Boolean and other interaction modes among them. These extensions of traditional capabilities are, in my experience, quietly revolutionizing animation practice, and they will have greater impact as NLA tools become more familiar to working animators.

At our production studio, NLA software has become an essential part of the animation process. In fact, it is the indispensable facilitator of everything we produce. NLA tools enable our animators to manipulate their work as a composite of separable but interdependent "actions." Actions can be quickly repurposed for different projects, which is crucial for that segment of our business in which we produce sets of training animations that work variations on a single theme. Moreover, actions are easily shared among animators, which enables those with less experience to quickly build on the work of more experienced artists. The result is a more flexible workflow that is fast, efficient, cost-effective, and well-suited to mass production of commercial and industrial animation, and to hand-crafted works of animation art.

Award-winning filmmaker Raf Anzovin is the co-founder and creative director of Anzovin Studio, a rapidly growing animation company that provides character design and animation for film, video, and interactive media. He is the founding instructor of the advanced character animation courses at the Computer Science Department, University of Massachusetts, Amherst, and runs a yearly animation internship program for five college-area students. From 1999 to 2000, he wrote the monthly animation column for 3D Magazine, and since 1996, he has served as contributing editor for MacAddict magazine.

*Michael Isner*
The main benefits of NLA are:

1. A framework for reducing the complexity of multi-channel animation tasks. This includes blending, layout, cleanup, mirroring, breaking into parts, and assembling. Compounds also speed up manipulation of interdependent channels.

2. Mixing keys, expressions, and constraints open up the opportunity for blends of keys and relations. For example,

"canned animation" and live goal blends are useful for a character that is grabbing onto something (where the something may change position).

3. It brings SRT (scale, rotation, translation) animation into a container that can be used in character setup. Because this container can be weighted and driven in a manner similar to shape animation, many of the character-setup techniques that have evolved from facial animation can be implemented on SRTs. Useful applications range from hand setups to universal facial rigs that are independent from form and features.

4. It's a compositing tool for hybrid motion capture and keyed animation workflows. Moving from pre-viz to a finished shot is generally a transition from raw motion capture to refined animation. This refinement can happen in many different ways, ranging from substitution, extraction (a pipeline to convert mocap into keys), and blending.

Michael Isner works through Softimage Special Projects as a consultant for film and game projects. His experience ranges across modeling, rendering, animation, and character setup and he has written copious custom tools for XSI, ranging from mirroring tools to bone matching heuristics and dynamics. Previously, he was the demo lead in the Softimage Content Group, which put NLA through its first production scenarios. Some of his recent character work can be found at: www.isner.com/new.htm

*Laurent Lavigne*
NLA is an entirely new way to think and deal with motion as an abstraction. The editing paradigm inherent with this abstraction allows the user to focus on events and timing, so it becomes an ideal tool for communication with a director or an editor. Pixel Liberation Front is a company that specializes in pre-visualization for movies and commercials. This is an area where communication with non-technicians is of paramount importance, and one cannot get stuck in the details of animation. NLA was a natural extension of our tool set. It enables pre-viz artists to separate the details of action from the elements of a shot's composition. It eases creation of shots and their deconstruction. It allows, through swapping of motion clips, scaling of the quality of a shot from rough "sliding people" to a fully moving mocaped pre-movie.

Laurent Lavigne is currently working on the pre-visualization of the second "Matrix" movie. In this process he is animating and deconstructing complex stunts and fight sequences. He became part of the pre-viz team at PLF on David Fincher's last

*87*

production, "Panic Room," which (unusually) required pre-viz of the entire movie. Prior to that, he worked for four years in post production, supervising character animation special effects for movies and commercials ("Mortal Kombat," "DnD," Radioshack, Snickers, and others). He started his career in the US working in the gaming industry as a designer and supervisor of animatics. He moved to the US to attend film school at the University of Southern California, where he received an MFA. He also has a master of computer science from Jussieu in Paris, with an emphasis on user interface and L-system fractals.

*Greg Punchatz*
My first reaction to the concept of NLA was the same as the reaction of many other animators. I thought it was a cute software demo, but I probably would never really use it very much. I was wrong. Now I use NLA every day, in ways I never imagined. One of the more interesting things we have done with it was editing a three-minute short film in XSI, where we switched among 35 different cameras using the Animation Mixer. This led me into the whole concept of non-linear film making, in which you could have animators, compositors, and editors on set with the rest of the crew for roughing out effects and edits while scenes are being shot. I really believe this is the future of filmmaking.

Greg Punchatz is director of animation at Janimation. He comes from a background of special makeup effects and animatronics, and he has an artistic family (his father is a well-known illustrator, Don Ivan Punchatz). He attributes his attention to artistic detail to the long hours spent watching his father create his magic through painting. He had an early fascination for fantastic characters, which led to his first career as a special-effects makeup artist. Some of his credits include: the "Robocop" trilogy, "Coming to America," and "Nightmare on Elm Street 2." He has also created stop-motion models for various video games, including the mega-hit Doom.

After seeing Jurassic Park for the first time, he knew that he would have to change his "set of tools" if he wanted to continue creating cutting-edge characters. In 1995, he joined Janimation and traded in his sculpting tools for a mouse. One of Greg's favorite projects to date is a CG turtle for Harrah's Casino, which won the "Big Kahuna" award for commercial animation last year.

*Seth Rosenthal*
Motion-captured animation is a lot like keyframe animation, but it has important characteristics that motivate an emphasis on different editing techniques. In particular, the data are dense and difficult to edit directly. Higher-level editing techniques such as NLA and layer-based editing allow animators to easily manipulate important aspects of motion-capture animation without having to directly edit the original dense data. In addition, the ability of motion capture to generate a large volume of realistic human animation encourages development and use of techniques that can manipulate a library of existing animation as raw material to be formed into new and different performances. NLA and related techniques not only provide artists with better tools for manipulating animations, but they also increase the value of existing collections of animation data.

ILM has used motion capture in shots ranging from dramatic hero performances of the title character in "The Mummy" and "The Mummy Returns" to large crowds in the battle sequence of Star Wars: Episode One "The Phantom Menace" and the intricate three-person dance routine in the Rhythms, Data Dancers commercial. These shots involved complex multi-character performances, elaborate interaction with elements in the live-action plate, and choreography of entire armies. In order to complete this work, we relied on a wide range of animation editing techniques including manual adjustments, animation layering, blending, re-timing, and procedural crowd simulation. In addition, many of our shots made use of secondary simulations of cloth, armor, or flesh, which imposed limits on the physical plausibility of the underlying animation by magnifying editing artifacts such as excessive accelerations. We are working to extend the usefulness of motion capture as a tool for feature film production by exploiting a range of editing techniques that allow us to provide directors with more flexibility in experimenting with and modifying animation and choreography.

Seth Rosenthal joined ILM in 1998 as motion capture supervisor, where he oversees recording and processing of motion-capture data for feature film and commercial productions, and works with the research and development department to develop new technology for integrating motion-capture techniques with ILM's visual effects production pipeline. At ILM, he has supervised motion-capture production for Star Wars: Episode I "The Phantom Menace," "The Mummy," and the Rhythms, Data Dancers commercial. He is currently working on "The Mummy Returns," "Pearl Harbor," and "A.I."

Before joining ILM, he managed production of 3D content for Microsoft's Digital Media Center, where he collaborated with the Human Figure Animation Project at Microsoft Research to adapt their motion-capture processing and animation system for use in production. He earned a bachelor of arts in history from Oberlin College in 1988.

*Gordon Cameron*
Gordon Cameron is development manager for Softimage|XSI. He previously served as project leader for animation and a lead developer on the animation mixer NLA and has worked over the years in other areas such as motion capture, real-time viewing, performance animation, etc. He organized a SIGGRAPH 97 panel on motion capture and character animation and was editor of SIGGRAPH's Computer magazine from 1996 until 2001. He previously worked in the fields of parallel computing, robot vision, and scientific visualization.

# Immersed in Anxiety or a Process to Healing? VR meets Mental Health

*Moderator*
Albert "Skip" Rizzo
Research Assistant Professor
Integrated Media Systems Center
and School of Gerontology
University of Southern California
3715 McClintock Avenue
MC-0191
Los Angeles, California
90089-0191 USA
+1.213.740.9819
arizzo@usc.edu

*Panelists*
Larry F. Hodges
Georgia Institute of Technology
and Virtually Better Inc.

Hunter Hoffman
University of Washington

Dorothy Strickland
North Carolina State University
and Virtual Reality Aids, Inc.

Benjamin Watson
Northwestern University

Albert "Skip" Rizzo
University of Southern California

Maria T. Schultheis
Kessler Medical Rehabilitation
Research and Education Corp.

Brenda K. Wiederhold
VRHealth.com

*Guest "Challenging" Panelist*
Mark Wiederhold
CyberPsychology &
Behavior Journal

Virtual Reality (VR) technology has undergone a transition in the past few years that has taken it out of the realm of "expensive toy" and into that of functional technology. Although media hype may have oversold VR's potential during the early 1990s, computer-based simulation technology is now beginning to emerge as a viable tool for cognitive and behavioral mental health applications.

Virtual reality integrates real-time computer graphics, body tracking devices, visual displays, and other sensory-input devices to immerse a participant in a computer-generated virtual environment (VE) that changes in a natural way with head and body motion. Much like an aircraft simulator serves to test and train piloting ability under a variety of controlled conditions, VEs can be developed to present simulations that can be used to target human behavioral and cognitive processes that are useful for mental health applications. The capacity of VR to create dynamic three-dimensional stimulus environments, within which all behavioral responses can be recorded, offers assessment and intervention options that are not available using traditional methods. In this regard, a growing number of laboratories are developing research programs on the use of VEs for these purposes. As a result, controlled studies reporting encouraging results are now beginning to emerge.

VR applications have shown promise for addressing: fear reduction with phobic clients; pain reduction for burn victims; stress/pain reduction in cancer patients; eating disorders/body image disturbances; spatial navigation training in children with motor impairments; functional skills in persons with developmental disabilities and autism; and assessment and rehabilitation of memory, attention, visuospatial processing, motor skills, and executive cognitive functions in persons with central nervous system dysfunction and the elderly. These therapeutic targets reflect an informed appreciation for the unique assets that are available using virtual technology and provide a foundation of work that is supportive of the further development of VR cognitive behavioral applications. If the associated technology continues to advance in the areas of visual displays, graphics, computing speed/memory storage, 3D audio, wireless tracking, voice recognition, intelligent agents, and VR authoring software, then more powerful and naturalistic VR scenarios will be possible. These advances could result in more readily available desktop-powered VR systems with greater sophistication and responsiveness. This inevitable increase in access will allow for more widespread application of VR technology for clinical assessment and intervention purposes. However, many unanswered questions and issues must be addressed before these types of VR applications can usefully move into mainstream practice.

The panelists have designed and developed VR applications that target a wide spectrum of mental health areas. This group consists of some of the top VR/mental health scientists, who discuss their work using VR to assess and treat persons with phobias, post-traumatic stress disorder, burn and cancer related pain, traumatic brain injury, attention deficit/hyperactivity disorder and learning disabilities, and for specific age-related assessment. The panelists informally present their work in four unified-by-topic groups, less

as a "lecture" and more as a discussion among colleagues on a particular topic. Following these presentations, the guest panelist, Mark Wiederhold, assumes a "devils advocate" role and "challenges" the panelists on topics of concern (ethical/legal, accessibility, digital divide, certification for use, side effects, long-term usage, limitations for use, social ramifications) and on what is needed to advance this technology into the 21st century in a rational manner. The remaining time is devoted to lively panel and audience discussion of the key issues involved in development and implementation of VR applications and where we are heading in the future.

*Skip Rizzo*
Albert "Skip" Rizzo received his PhD in clinical psychology from the State University of New York at Binghamton. He has joint faculty appointments with the University of Southern California Integrated Media Systems Center (IMSC) and the USC School of Gerontology. He is also the director of the IMSC Virtual Environments Lab, which designs, develops, and evaluates the usefulness, feasibility, and efficacy of virtual reality systems targeting assessment and rehabilitation of spatial abilities, attention, and other cognitive functions. Additionally, he is conducting research on 360-degree panoramic video HMD applications for exposure therapy (currently social phobia), computerized facial recognition, and facial avatar animation. He is also designing better human-computer interaction systems for the elderly and persons with disabilities. His other IMSC activities involve provision of human-factors input on IMSC projects in teleimmersion as well as research on integration of immersive audio in virtual environments.

He is the associate editor of the journal CyberPsychology and Behavior and is on the editorial boards of The International Journal of Virtual Reality, Cognitive Technology, and Presence: Teleoperators and Virtual Environments. He is the creator and manager of the Virtual Reality Mental Health Email List server (VRPSYCH). He also chaired the SIGGRAPH 2000 panel on this topic and is an internationally known speaker in this area, presenting at numerous professional events and conferences. Prior to his USC affiliation, he was a cognitive rehabilitation specialist for eight years, developing and implementing cognitive rehabilitation programs for clients with traumatic brain injuries.

89

*Larry F. Hodges*

Larry F. Hodges is associate professor in the College of Computing and head of the Virtual Environments Group at Georgia Institute of Technology. He is also co-founder of Virtually Better, Inc., a company that specializes in virtual reality exposure therapy of anxiety disorders in Atlanta. He received his PhD from North Carolina State University in computer engineering (1988), a MS in computer science from NCSU (1984), a MA in religion from Lancaster Theological Seminary (1978), and a BA with a double major in mathematics and physics from Elon College (1974). His research interests are in software and algorithm development, experimental quantification, and application development for virtual reality systems. He is on the editorial boards of the journals Presence: Teleoperators and Virtual Environments and CyberPsychology and Behavior, and is a member of the Steering Committee for the annual IEEE Virtual Reality Conference.

*Hunter Hoffman*

Hunter Hoffman studied memory at Princeton University and investigated human memory and attention with eyewitness/false-memory expert Elizabeth Loftus. He is a project manager at the University of Washington Human Interface Technology Laboratory and an affiliate faculty of psychology. He studies the use of immersive VR to help reduce pain during wound care in burn patients at Harborview Burn Center. He also conducts controlled laboratory experiments exploring the relationship between the illusion of "presence" in virtual reality and analgesic effectiveness (attempting to maximize analgesic effectiveness). In other projects, he is exploring the use of VR exposure therapy for treating spider phobia, the value of adding tactile cues (position-tracked toy spiders) to increase treatment effectiveness, and using real (mixed reality) chocolate bars to add taste to virtual objects. He has published over 20 peer-reviewed manuscripts, including six in the Journal of Experimental Psychology. He presented at panels on virtual healing at SIGGRAPH 98 and SIGGRAPH 2000, and at the SGI booth at SIGGRAPH 98. He will be giving immersive demos at the MultGen-Paradigm booth at SIGGRAPH 2001.

His research has been covered by CNN, Scientific American Frontiers, the BBC, and the Discovery Channel. He has served as an ad hoc reviewer for JEP:LMC, Psychological Sciences, Presence: Tele-operators and Virtual Environments, SIGGRAPH 99, the Journal of Applied Psychology, and ACM Transactions on Human Computer Interaction. He is also a scientific advisor to VR researchers in Spain and Japan.

*Dorothy Strickland*

Dorothy Strickland is president of Do2Learn, a computer software company developing virtual reality games for children with autism and related learning disabilities. Her present project, funded by the National Institutes of Health, has designed Web-playable virtual reality games that help children with special needs learn safety and social skills. She is also an adjunct faculty member at North Carolina State University and has presented her research at various conferences including SIGGRAPH 96, SIGGRAPH 98, and SIGGRAPH 2000; the new 2001 game conference Entertainment in the Interactive Age sponsored by the Annenberg Center; and VRAIS, the largest international VR conference, where she has been the keynote speaker. She has published her work in numerous journals, including serving as guest editor for the Communications of the ACM special SIGGRAPH 97 edition on "Virtual Reality and Mental Health." Her research has been reported in several news sources worldwide, including an Associated Press feature and a more recent Discovery Channel special aired in 2001.

*Benjamin Watson*

Benjamin Watson is assistant professor in computer science at Northwestern University. He earned his doctoral and masters degrees at Georgia Tech's Graphics, Visualization and Usability Center, and his bachelors degree at the University of California, Irvine. His dissertation focused on user-performance effects of dynamic-level-of-detail management. His other research interests include model simplification, visual fidelity, tangible interfaces, information visualization, computer games, and spatial applications of computer graphics. He is on the conference committee for the IEEE VR 2001 conference, and is program co-chair for the Graphics Interface 2001 conference.

*Maria Schultheis*

My Maria T. Schultheis is a clinical research scientist in the Neuropsychology & Neuroscience Laboratory and an instructor in the Department of Physical Medicine and Rehabilitation at the University of Medicine and Dentistry of New Jersey-New Jersey Medical School. Her clinical and research experience have focused on rehabilitation of cognitively impaired populations, including patients with traumatic brain injury, multiple sclerosis, and stroke. Her expertise is in the area of driving capacity following neurological involvement, focusing on the cognitive demands of driving and the development of new driving assessment protocols. This includes research focusing on application of new technologies such as virtual reality for neuropsychological assessment and treatment. Her research has received funding by such organizations as the National Institutes of Health, the National Multiple Sclerosis Society, and the National Institute for Disability and Rehabilitation Research. She is active in several professional organizations related to neuropsychology and rehabilitation, and currently serves as an editorial consultant to the Journal of Head Trauma Rehabilitation, Rehabilitation Psychology, and the Archives of Physical Medicine & Rehabilitation. She also serves on the Transportation Research Board of the National Research Council.

*90*

*Brenda K. Wiederhold*

Brenda K. Wiederhold serves as director of the Center for Advanced Multimedia Psychotherapy and the Center for Applied Behavioral Services at the California School of Professional Psychology Research and Service Foundation in San Diego. She is a licensed clinical psychologist and has a doctorate in clinical health psychology. She is nationally certified in both biofeedback and neurofeedback by the Biofeedback Certification Institute of America. She serves on the editorial board of CyberPsychology & Behavior and is recognized as a national and international leader in the treatment of anxiety and phobias with virtual reality exposure therapy, having completed over 1,000 VR therapy sessions. CAMP maintains comprehensive programs to treat fear of flying, fear of driving, claustrophobia, panic disorder and agoraphobia, social phobia, fear of heights, fear of public speaking and eating disorders using a combination of cognitive-behavioral techniques, virtual reality exposure therapy, and physiological monitoring. She completed a masters in business administration, has 19 years experience as chief financial officer of an investment firm, and was a former government auditor. She currently is completing her third book and has over 50 publications. She serves as chief executive officer of VRHealth.com, a company that develops virtual environments and conducts clinical research studies using virtual environments and Internet-based worlds.

*Mark Wiederhold*

My interest in virtual Mark D. Wiederhold is a physician executive with a diverse background in academic health, clinical research, and product development. At Science Applications International Corporation, he invented and patented a non-invasive method for cancer diagnosis that is currently in phase II testing at Tripler Army Medical Center, Honolulu. He also developed a PC-based rugged portable diagnostic medical device for the US Navy and Marine Corps that is currently deployed to the Pacific Fleet. This device was approved by the FDA in four months, and was funded by Congress for two years. He has eight years' experience developing telemedicine systems, including wireless data transmission protocols. He was formerly director of clinical research at the Scripps Clinic in La Jolla, California where he has been a staff physician for the past 15 years. He completed an internship and residency in internal medicine and critical care medicine at the Scripps Clinic. He is on the faculty of the University of California, San Diego Medical School and professor of health psychology at the California School of Professional Psychology in San Diego. He is the editor-in-chief of CyberPsychology & Behavior and editor-in-chief of IEEE Transactions in Experimental Biology and Medicine. He serves on several advisory, editorial, and technical boards. He completed an executive MBA program at the University of California, San Diego, and he is a Certified Physician Executive, a Diplomate of the American College of Physician Executives, and a Fellow of the American College of Physicians. He has over 150 scientific publications.

*91*

## Internet Appliances: New Horizons for the Web

*Moderator*
Mickey W. Mantle
Vice President of Development
Gracenote (formerly CDDB)
2141 4th Street
Berkeley, California 94710 USA
+1.510.849.2332
+1.510.849.2366 fax
mmantle@gracenote.com

*Panelists*
Seamus Blackley
Microsoft Corporation

Kent Libbey
Excite@Home

Andrew Luan
Metricom, Inc.

Gregory D. Abowd
Georgia Institute of Technology

This panel provides an overview of emerging Web technologies that are fueling the broad range of internet appliances that are starting to appear. While some of these devices are capable of presenting rich media technologies, many are not even capable of presenting full HTML. Enhanced graphics, sound, and animation may not be feasible on many of these devices. Yet many have much more capabilities than even today's personal computers. Will this drive a "lowest common denominator" approach to these devices, or will other factors influence their capabilities? Will Web-based advertising continue to wane? Will other financial models be needed to fuel content for these devices? Will bandwidth be the driving technology?

*Mickey W. Mantle*
A member of the University of Utah gang, Mickey W. Mantle was a contributor to many early computer graphics products from Evans & Sutherland and Pixar, including Pixar's RenderMan software. He has a degree in computer science from the University of Utah and has been attending SIGGRAPH conferences regularly since 1978. He last chaired a SIGGRAPH Panel in 2000.

After joining Broderbund Software in 1991 as vice president of engineering/chief technical officer, he managed technology initiatives and contributed to development of many successful and award-winning products including Living Books, Myst, Riven, and many more. In 1999, he joined Gracenote (formerly CDDB, Inc.) as vice president of development, where he oversees all development of Gracenote Internet services. This includes software for enabling CD audio player applications such as MusicMatch Jukebox, RealJukeBox, WinAmp, Apple's iTunes, and many others.

*Seamus Blackley*
Connected Internet appliances will make their way into the living room in a big way with the next generation of video game machines. These appliances are multi-purpose devices that play CDs, DVDs, and, of course, video games. Plus they are inherently connected to the Internet, because they are designed for broadband connectivity from the outset. These devices will spawn a new generation of applications for the living room that utilize extremely rich media and expect connectivity and high-bandwidth capabilities. They will also be fun to interact with!

Seamus Blackley oversees advanced technology development for Microsoft's Xbox, a consumer-oriented video game machine capable of advanced 3D graphics, CD and DVD playback, and Internet connectivity. The Xbox is scheduled for launch in the United States in September 2001. Prior to Microsoft, he was the project lead on a major game title at DreamWorks SKG, and before that he applied his PhD in physics at Looking Glass Software, where he developed the highly lauded flight physics for its Flight Unlimited game.

*Kent Libbey*
Among these new devices will be "broadband TV" systems that display directly to television (as the only monitor in most living rooms and other communal spaces in the home – kitchens, bedrooms, etc.) and are connected to broadband networks, either directly or indirectly (for example, through a home area network). User interface design and development for such devices involves a different set of constraints and opportunities than designing content and applications for a PC. Lower resolution, navigation with a remote control (rather and a mouse and keyboard), group viewing, and several other factors need to be considered in this design.

Kent Libbey is responsible for development of advanced TV products for Excite@Home, extending the company's broadband content, applications, services, infrastructure, and operations to the TV and other home entertainment outlets. He oversees a staff of 50 people, including product managers, engineers, and user-interface developers. His work in interactive television began in 1993 as director of product management for Bell Atlantic Video Services, where he established and led a staff of marketing and operations professionals, building and running the world's first all-digital video-on-demand television service trial delivered over DSL. Later, as vice president of operations at Tele-TV, a joint venture of Bell Atlantic, Pacific Telesis, and NYNEX, he was in charge of project management, product strategy, operations, and information management for a 150-channel broadcast digital television service.

After leaving Tele-TV, he established the Broadband Services Group, a Los Angeles-based management consulting firm, which provided strategic and business development advice to communications and media companies seeking to leverage emerging broadband technologies. He has also held positions at MCI Communications and McKinsey & Co. He holds a BA from Harvard College and an MBA from the Stanford University Graduate School of Business.

*Andrew Luan*
The Internet has changed the world, bringing instant access to the incredible amount of information available online whenever you are at your computer. Numerous connected devices are beginning to let you access the Web from an untethered device. The Geode Web Pad brings the full capabilities of a Web browser to a device that is convenient to carry and use wherever you are within its vast service areas. How will internet appliances change the way people interact with the Web, and what new products and services will spring up to cater to those who can utilize information "on the run?" Will medium bandwidth be sufficient or will rich media drive higher connectivity requirements?

As director of business development at Metricom, Andrew Luan identifies and works with strategic partners to create new services and opportunities. Previously, he served in product marketing and market development positions for companies in the e-business and interactive TV/data broadcasting/DTV industries, helping them launch new products and enter new industries. He spent four years as an analyst for the wireless telecommunication industry for RB Webber & Company. His studies included market entry strategies for Sprint, Airtouch, and PCSPrimeco. He received his BSEE from the Massachusetts Institute of Technology.

*Gregory D. Abowd*
There are many tantalizing possibilities associated with the growing adoption of small, networked devices. Indeed, Mark Weiser's decade-old vision of ubiquitous computing is slowly being realized from the device perspective. But his vision for "putting computing back in its place," out of the foreground of our consciousness and into the background of our peripheral awareness, is not necessarily being served by the proliferation of many different devices. I believe there will be no such thing as a "killer app" for ubiquitous computing that will encourage critical mass adoption of a single device for a single purpose.

I am a firm advocate of the pursuit of the "killer existence," in which an effective marriage of device capabilities and human-centered services helps to put computing in its place as a useful aid to our everyday lives. The research conducted by the Future Computing Environments (FCE) Group at Georgia Institute of Technology is aiming to overcome the research challenges to ubiquitous computing applications development. My personal interests lie in general problems of automated capture and access, context-aware computing, and natural-interaction techniques that scale the diverse set of emerging devices. This work requires an effective partnership between the purveyors of new device technologies and the developers of new ubiquitous-computing applications.

Gregory D. Abowd is an associate professor in the College of Computing and GVU Center at Georgia Institute of Technology. His research interests include software engineering for interactive systems, with particular focus on mobile and ubiquitous computing applications. He leads a research group in the College of Computing called the Future Computing Environments Group, which focuses on development of prototype future computing environments that emphasize mobile and ubiquitous computing technology for everyday uses. He received the degrees of MSc and DPhil in Computation from the University of Oxford, which he attended as a Rhodes Scholar. Before moving to Georgia Tech in 1994, he held post-doctoral positions with the Human-Computer Interaction group at the University of York and the Software Engineering Institute and Computer Science Department at Carnegie Mellon University.

*Related Information*

*Wireless Data Access Moves Beyond the Personal:*
*Enabling the Untethered Enterprise*
www.metricom.com/ricochet_advantage/resource_center/Aberdeen.htm

*Internet Appliance Manufacturers, Are You Device Vendors or*
*Service Providers?*
www.devicetop.com/dt/editorial?openArticle=1:26

*Internet Appliance Design Channel*
www.embedded.com/internet/

*Internet Appliance Technology*
internet.about.com/industry/internet/library/weekly/2000/aa051500a.htm

*Future Computing Environments*
www.cc.gatech.edu/fce

*93*

# GAME-STORIES: SIMULATION, NARRATIVE, ADDICTION

*Moderator*
NOAH WARDRIP-FRUIN
Media Research Lab
New York University
719 Broadway, 12th floor
New York, New York 10003
USA
+1.212.998.3475
+1.212.995.4122 fax
noah@mrl.nyu.edu

*Panelists*
J.C. HERZ
Joystick Nation Inc.

HENRY JENKINS
Massachusetts Institute
of Technology

JANET H. MURRAY
Georgia Institute of Technology

CELIA PEARCE
University of Southern California

KEN PERLIN
New York University

ERIC ZIMMERMAN
gameLab

From Monopoly to "The Sims" to improvisational theater, some of the most engaging media experiences ever produced have been described as "game-stories." We may sense that the holding power of the game-story is related to play, simulation, and narrative – but in general we aren't sure how. This panel takes the often vague idea of the game-story and pins it down to concrete examples. The panelists are game theorists, game designers, and game players. They ask if there is a middle ground between game and story, or if game-stories exist in a space of their own. They ask what makes the games we call "interactive narratives" work, and how we can make them work better.

## J.C. Herz

One of the most useful tools for understanding the relationship between game and story is the concept of dimensionality. A cube, for instance, is a 3D object. Reducing its dimensionality yields a square (2D), a line (1D), and finally a point. Reducing the dimensionality of a film yields a still frame. Reducing the dimensionality of urban planning gives you architecture. Reducing the dimensionality of a game, by eliminating all but one of the possible trajectories through the world, yields a story. Essentially, the story is a core sample of the game: one trajectory through the universe of all possible solutions. Outside the system, that story might be dramatic or undramatic, just as the game itself might be satisfying or unsatisfying.

Dimensionality is not a good in and of itself. But the challenge for game designers, as storytellers, is to build a world that's interesting in multiple dimensions: the individual's trajectory through the world, the game as a whole (an overall sense of "gameplay" and dynamics), and the social experience that happens around the game (trading custom skins or levels, fan sites, etc.). Creating a satisfying experience is a more complex task in many dimensions than in fewer dimensions. Herein lies the challenge, for game designers and storytellers alike, as media evolve into more sophisticated, multilayered forms.

J. C. Herz is the author of *Surfing on the Internet: A Nethead's Adventures Online, Little, Brown & Company.* She has written for Rolling Stone, GQ, Wired, and Playboy. A native Texan now living in New York, her first Big Apple hack was crashing the Macy's Parade.

## Henry Jenkins

The false dichotomy frequently drawn between stories and games stems from a too-narrow conception of story. Too often, we value classically constructed narratives over a broader range of storytelling traditions, including accordion-structure narratives (for example, Comedia Del'Arte) that depend on interplay between fixed elements and open improvisation, or spatial stories that focus on exploring or mapping worlds rather than recounting an event chain. Drawing on a comparative media studies perspective, I suggest continuities between games and a broader range of storytelling traditions. My discussion focuses on three recent Electronic Arts releases that demonstrate alternative approaches to integrating story and game: American McGee's "Alice," which draws on the player's preexisting familiarity with Lewis Carroll's universe; Clive Barker's "Undying," which embeds backstory within elements of the story space; and "The Sims," which provides a construction kit for players to create their own stories.

Henry Jenkins, director of the Comparative Media Studies Program at MIT, has spent his career studying media and how people incorporate it into their lives. He has published articles on a diverse range of topics relating to popular culture, including work on "Star Trek," WWF Wrestling, Nintendo games, and Dr. Seuss. He testified last year before the US Senate during the hearings on media violence that followed the Littleton shootings and served as co-chair of Pop!Tech, the 1999 Camden Technology Conference. Jenkins has published six books and more than 50 essays on popular culture. His books include *From Barbie to Mortal Kombat: Gender and Computer Games* (1999), *The Children's Cultural Reader* (1998) *What Made Pistachio Nuts: Early Sound Comedy and the Vaudeville Aesthetic* (1993), *Classical Hollywood Comedy* (1994), *Textual Poachers: Television Fans an Participatory Culture* (1992), and the forthcoming *The Politics and Pleasures of Popular Culture.* Jenkins holds a PhD in communication arts from the University of Wisconsin-Madison and an MA in communication studies from the University of Iowa.

## Janet H. Murray

A compelling design problem for the next generation of story-game environments is creation of an experience for which I would propose the term "dramatic agency." Dramatic agency draws from two domains. First, it involves interactivity, which I have defined in Hamlet on the Holodeck as drawing on the procedural and participatory properties of digital environments. When both the computer's processing and the actions of the interactor are appropriately scripted, the result is the satisfying experience of agency. Secondly, dramatic agency draws on the domain of dramatic form and requires attention to the segmentation and granularity of events. My presentation draws on work done by students in the Information Design and Technology Program at Georgia Tech to demonstrate a range of approaches to dramatic agency.

94

Janet H. Murray is a professor in the School of Literature, Communication, and Culture at Georgia Institute of Technology, and director of the graduate program in Information Design and Technology. She is the author of *Hamlet on the Holodeck: The Future of Narrative in Cyberspace* and the forthcoming *Inventing the Medium: A Principle-Based Approach to Interactive Design*, both from MIT press. She is a trustee of the American Film Institute and serves as a mentor in AFI's Exhanced TV Workshop. Before moving to Georgia Tech in 1999, she led humanities computing projects at MIT, where she remains a distinguished contributing interactive designer in the Center for Educational Computing Initiatives. She holds a PhD in English from Harvard University. Her research has been sponsored by the Annenberg/CPB Project, the National Endowment for the Humanities, the Andrew W. Mellon Foundation, IBM, and Apple Computer. She lectures and consults widely on the future of television, interactive narrative, and curriculum development for interactive design

*Celia Pearce*

The progress of interactive narrative is now in the throes of the evolutionary equivalent of a "small mammal explosion." The "warm-blooded" forms of narrative that are emerging are something halfway between game and story. They are both and yet neither, yielding entirely new forms that merge literature, game, cinema, and improvisational theater. Procedural narrative and collaborative narrative worlds have taken over from their more clunky forebears, such as so called "non-linear" narrative, hypertext, static navigational spaces, and puzzle games. These new experiences are dynamic, participative, and creative. In addition, they redefine notions of authorship as audience members begin to "take things into their own hands" and create, and in some cases trade and sell, their own characters and worlds. These emergent narratives and economies foreshadow a future where the current "narrative hegemony" of Hollywood is called into question by an increasingly interactive audience that has both the desire and skill to creatively partake in its own entertainment and narrative experience.

Celia Pearce is an interactive multimedia designer, artist, researcher, teacher, and author of *The Interactive Book: A Guide to the Interactive Revolution* (Macmillan.) She is a research associate at the University of Southern California's Annenberg Center for Communication and adjunct professor and production track-head of interactive media in the USC School of Cinema-Television. She has 18 years' experience as a designer of interactive attractions, exhibitions, and fine art projects. Past projects include: Iwerks and Evans & Sutherland's award-winning Virtual Adventures: The Loch Ness Expedition, a 24-player virtual reality attraction; the lounge@siggraph and The Virtual Gallery, a VR museum featuring walk-in paintings, both exhibited at SIGGRAPH 95; and Body of Light, an interactive performance piece that has been performed at the Electronic Cafe in Los Angeles and Canada's Banff Centre for the Arts.

*Ken Perlin*

Interactive character animation has focused mainly on animation, physical simulation, and rendering. Traditionally, behavior has been implemented by combining linear animation and motion capture. These techniques work reasonably well for interactive games, where the goal is mainly to explore worlds, gain points, kill enemies, and solve puzzles. But what if we want to go in the direction of interactive narrative – of an online drama or sitcom – of a game-story? In this case, we want to explore the personalities of the characters themselves. Is this possible or even desirable? How do we marry technology and content to find out? For audiences to buy into the believability and psychological presence of an interactive animated character, the whole notion of linear animation needs to be replaced.

Ken Perlin is a professor in the Department of Computer Science and director of the Media Research Laboratory at the Courant Institute of Mathematical Sciences of New York University. He is also director of the NYU Center of Advanced Technology, sponsored by the New York State Science and Technology Foundation. He completed his PhD in 1986 at the New York University Department of Computer Science. His dissertation received the Janet Fabri award for outstanding doctoral dissertation. He received his BA in theoretical mathematics at Harvard University in 1979. His research interests include graphics, animation, and multimedia. In 1991, he was a recipient of a Presidential Young Investigator Award from the National Science Foundation. In 1997, he was a recipient of a Technical Achievement Award from the Academy of Motion Picture Arts and Sciences for his noise and turbulence procedural texturing techniques, which are widely used in feature films and television. He was head of software development at R/Greenberg Associates from 1984 through 1987. Prior to that, from 1979 to 1984, he was the system architect for computer-generated animation at Mathematical Applications Group, Inc.

*95*

*Eric Zimmerman*

One of the difficulties in understanding the relationship between games and "interactive narrative" is that we lack a critical understanding of how they can be designed and deployed. Is every game a narrative? Are all narratives "at play" like a game? Isn't every narrative interactive in some way? If so, what do we mean when we use the term "interactive narrative?" Using plenty of audience participation, this panels looks at some non-digital interactive narratives, such as Choose-Your-Own-Adventure books and surrealist language games, as well as some of my own work, like the interactive paper book *Life in the Garden* and the multiplayer online game SiSSYFiGHT 2000. These examples sketch a taxonomy of narrative and interactivity that can help shed light on the new kinds of narrative experience that digital technology makes possible.

Eric Zimmerman is a game designer, artist, and academic. He is co-founder and CEO of gameLab, a New York-based game developer (www.gmlb.com). gameLab's first titles, BLiX and LOOP, are available on Shockwave.com. His pre-gameLab titles include the critically acclaimed SiSSYFiGHT 2000 (www.sissyfight.com, created with Word.com) and Strain (www.strainlab.com). His non-computer-game projects include the interactive paper book *Life in the Garden* (created with Nancy Nowacek and published in 2000 by RSUB); Organism, a board game published in ArtByte Spring 2000; and game installations in a variety of gallery and museum spaces, including Artists Space NYC. He has taught game design and interactive narrative design at MIT's Comparative Media Studies program, New York University's Interactive Telecommunications Program, and the Digital Design MFA program at Parsons School of Design. He is the director of RE:PLAY, a series of events about game design and game culture sponsored by Eyebeam Atelier. He has published and lectured extensively on the design and culture of play and games, and is currently co-authoring a book with Katie Salen about game design to be published by MIT Press in 2002.

*Noah Wardrip-Fruin*

Noah Wardrip-Fruin is a fiction writer, artist, and research scientist at the New York University Media Research Lab. He is currently the art and performance chair for DAC 2001 and an organizer of the art program for SIGGRAPH 2001, and he is editing *The New Media Reader* (forthcoming from MIT Press) with Nick Montfort and Michael Crumpton. His current fiction projects include a collaboration with a.c. chapman, Brion Moss, and Duane Whitehurst on The Impermanence Agent, a storytelling Web agent that customizes its story of impermanence for each user. This project was featured at SIGGRAPH 2000 and will appear this year in The Iowa Review Web, at a show curated by Harvestworks at The New Museum of Contemporary Art, and at the Brave New Word event at the Guggenheim Museum, New York.

*96*

# BEYOND COPYRIGHT: THE BRAVE NEW WORLD OF DIGITAL RIGHTS MANAGEMENT

*Moderator*
ROBERT ELLIS

DEBORAH NEVILLE
Manatt, Phelps and Phillips

*Panelists*
DAN L. BURK
University of Minnesota

BARBARA SIMONS

SARAH STEIN
North Carolina State University

As more intellectual property (text, music, and images) becomes available in digital formats, there is increasing concern about protection of the material against unauthorized use and the sometimes-conflicting rights of the originators and users of the material. For example, intellectual property (IP) arguments about the use of MP3, the Secure Digital Music Initiative (SDMI), and the DVD Content Scrambling System (CSS) are currently receiving substantial coverage in the technical, business and popular press. Computer graphics professionals are discovering that they must be concerned with not only technical capabilities, but also policy and legal issues.

This panel addresses the following questions:

- Have new national laws (for example, the Digital Millennium Copyright Act) and international treaties (for example, the World Intellectual Property Organization) significantly altered the rights of IP owners and IP users?

- Will the use of digital copy protection systems such as CSS help or hinder acceptance of these devices by consumers?

- Is there a need for digital copy protection in broadcast and distribution of digital video?

- How does the traditional concept of fair use apply to digital forms of IP?

- How do peer-to-peer file-sharing systems such as Napster affect IP rights and fair use?

- Because much intellectual property is created by teams of people rather than a single author, what forms of IP ownership are appropriate?

## Robert Ellis

We have been hearing a lot recently in the technical and popular media about digital rights problems. Unfortunately, we have heard the most from interested parties such as the Motion Picture Association of America (MPAA), the Recording Industry Association of American (RIAA), and the Home Recording Rights Coalition (HRRC). In addition, most of the rhetoric has addressed what can and should be done about accessing and copying digital material, and little has been said about the overall technical and legal issues. I believe it is time to hear from the people who are actually involved with producing and using digital works, academic experts, and practicing attorneys who can take a step back from the heated discussions and offer some practical comments on the problems.

Robert Ellis retired in 1993 as Sun Microsystems' representative on the Technology Policy Committee of the Computer Systems Policy Project (CSPP) and co-manager of Sun's university research program. Previously, he held computer graphics software development and management positions with Sun, GE-Calma, Atari, Boeing, and Washington University, where he received BS and MS degrees in electrical engineering and computer science. He

currently serves as the chair of the Public Policy Program of ACM SIGGRAPH and is a member of ACM's U.S. Technology Policy Committee (USACM). He served as co-chair of SIGGRAPH 80, and he was a member of the SIGGRAPH Executive Committee from 1977 to 1983.

## Dan L. Burk

Over the past decade, courts in the United States have firmly established that standard copyright doctrines such as those regarding fair use or joint authorship apply to digital media. However, the recently enacted anti-circumvention provisions of the Digital Millennium Copyright Act (DMCA) create a new right to control access to copyrighted works, separate from the exclusive rights under copyright. Such rights effectively endow copyright holders with a sweeping new ability to impose terms of access on content users. Consumers who access content without accepting the content owner's terms would be in violation. Even where a particular use would be permissible under copyright law, content owners may be able to exclude or license the use as a condition of access. Moreover, content that Congress is constitutionally forbidden from protecting as intellectual property is swept up into the scope of the DMCA provisions. The breadth of content control granted under these provisions not only far exceeds any treaty obligations that the DMCA was purported to fulfill, but also violates the constitutionally mandated limits on Congressional power to grant intellectual property rights.

Dan L. Burk joined the University of Minnesota faculty in the fall of 2000 as the Vance K. Opperman Research Scholar. He teaches in the areas of copyright, patent, and biotechnology law. His expertise is in the legal and societal impact of new technologies, including scientific misconduct, regulation of biotechnology, and the intellectual property implications of global computer networks. He holds appointments in both the Law School and the Center for Bioethics and currently serves as associate director of the new Joint Degree Program in Law, Health, and the Life Sciences. He has also been closely involved in the development of the new Internet Studies Center. Previously, he taught at Seton Hall University, George Mason University, Cardozo Law School, the Ohio State University Program at Oxford, and Stanford University Law School. He holds a BS in microbiology (1985) from Brigham Young University, an MS in molecular biology and biochemistry (1987) from Northwestern University, a JD cum laude (1990) from Arizona State University, and a JSM (1994) from Stanford University

## Deborah Neville

Digital rights management of the arts is rising to the forefront with lawsuits such as the Motion Picture Association of America (MPAA) versus Scour. It is instructive to look to the music industry, which is embroiled in high-profile disputes over the right of consumers to share their music over the Internet, for a preview of things to come for visual art creators, tool developers, and various other rights holders. Given the inevitability of online

*97*

distribution, the music industry leaders' boycott of grass-roots efforts such as the Future of Music Coalition creates doubt as to the strategy of current rights holders who are ignoring the political voices of creators and technology developers. Provisions in copyright law that criminalize attempts to break through copyright control are viewed as threats to fair use. Will the economics be different in the areas of graphics works, visual arts, and tools? Will the economics encourage content lock-ups? How can creators best position themselves to create freely and derive their constitutionally created rights in the digital era? What will the economics of enforcement really be? Visual artists need to be aware and engaged to keep their freedoms from being eroded piecemeal by a patchwork of ill-conceived so-called protection measures predicated on misrepresented technological capabilities.

Deborah Neville's practice focuses on established and emerging high technology businesses and related intellectual property and business matters. She is senior counsel in the Palo Alto office of Manatt, Phelps and Phillips. Previously, she served as corporate counsel for both Hewlett-Packard Company and Agilent Technologies, Inc. While at HP, she headed the Entertainment Industry Strategic Initiative, creating business opportunities between the company and the media and entertainment industries. Most recently, she was vice president for legal affairs at Applied Science Fiction, a digital imaging company based in Austin. She received her JD from the University of California's Hastings College of Law and her BA in physics and biology from the Catholic University of America.

*Barbara Simons*
With the development of the World Wide Web, futurists predicted that vast libraries and entertainment resources such as movies, music, and games would be accessible from home computers. But much of the technology that makes it possible to access the Library of Congress from your living room also makes it possible to copy and distribute protected information for little or no cost. This fact was not lost on Hollywood and the record industry. Instead of a dream come true, they were experiencing a nightmare. The result of these fears was enactment of the DMCA. Not only does the DMCA threaten user rights of fair use and first sale, but also it does so by criminalizing technologies and technological devices instead of actual infringing behavior. Had such legislation been passed some years earlier, we might have found ourselves with no photocopying machines and no VCRs. In addition to the threat to future technologies posed by the DMCA, the anti-circumvention provisions, if they are taken literally, make many standard computer security techniques illegal. While no one intended to jeopardize our information infrastructure by passing such legislation, this is only one of some very serious potential side effects of the DMCA.

Barbara Simons was ACM President from July 1998 until June 2000. Earlier, she founded and chaired ACM's U.S. Technology Policy Committee (USACM) and chaired the ACM Committee for Scientific Freedom and Human Rights. She was elected Secretary of the Council of Scientific Society Presidents (CSSP) in 1999, and she has been on the CSSP Board from 1998-2000. She is a fellow of

ACM and of the American Association for the Advancement of Science. She earned her PhD in computer science from the University of California, Berkeley, where her dissertation solved a major open problem in scheduling theory. Later, she became a research staff member at IBM's San Jose Research Center (now Almaden), where she did research on scheduling theory, compiler optimization, and fault-tolerant distributed computing.

*Sarah Stein*
Although for educators the notion of "edutainment" evokes an objectionable dumbing down of teaching and learning, there is a useful parallel to be drawn between the entertainment world and higher education. Producing motion pictures and developing computer-based curricula both rely on collaborative interactions between creative and technical teams. The media industry, which encompasses both film and television, has had to create models in which large numbers of personnel, at very different levels of creative input, can be compensated for their work. Thus the motion picture industry's template for compensation (both money and recognition) can provide higher education with a useful model. A more inclusive approach to intellectual property rights, responsive to the integral role of instructional technologists and designers, could benefit creative technical professionals in private industry as well as higher education.

Sarah Stein is assistant professor in the Department of Communication at North Carolina State University and a documentary filmmaker. At North Carolina State, she teaches courses in film, video, and digital production. She has also taught film editing at New York University's Tisch School of the Arts and presented visiting artist lectures at Sarah Lawrence College, Women in Film, Clark University, Hunter College/CUNY, AFI Film Seminars, and Villanova University. Her film work covers topics from social issues to music and art, with productions ranging from Bill Moyers and CBS to public television and independent documentaries. Among her many filmmaking awards are two Academy Awards for documentary editing, the Columbia-DuPont Journalism Award, several Emmy Awards and nominations, and numerous national and international film-festival awards. She has a PhD in media studies from the University of Iowa.

# ART IN SPACE: WHAT FOR?

*Organizer*
LORELEI LISOWSKY
1520 Pershing Drive #E
San Francisco, California 94129
USA
+1.415.516.1861
www.3220.com/zerogravityarts/
index.html
cdm.sfai.edu/mzg
spacegirlin0g@hotmail.com

*Panelists*
TED KRUEGER
University of Arkansas
comp.uark.edu/~tkrueger

MARCO PELJHAN
Projekt Atol
makrolab.ljudmila.org

D.A. SOLOMON

We are standing on the precipice of an emerging art form, Space Art, which is about people from different worlds working together, collaboration between technology and our biological carbon-based forms, finding terrestrial intelligence on earth as well as outside our own orbit, and eliminating the boundaries between art and science.

Should artists, visionary architects, writers, poets, and musicians be working in the space program? The closest artists have come to experiencing space travel is on parabolic flights that create the conditions of nearly zero gravity. Parabolic flights require a specially adapted aircraft and a highly specialized team: flight crew, trained instructors, and physicians. They are undertaken by a handful of space agencies specifically for astronaut training and scientific experiments. During the flights, bodies and objects inside the aircraft float freely for 25-30 seconds. A flight can have between 10 and 40 parabolas. Many people experience severe discomfort and sometimes euphoria in zero gravity.

Emerging artists are realizing that the tools, materials, and activities used by space scientists and astronauts could provide new materials and media for their work. Artists-astronauts in converging spaces are expanding into new realms of art practice by creating socially "holistic" endeavors. An underground movement of American artists has collaborated with the National Aeronautics and Space Administration (NASA) officially and unofficially, for 25 years, and a few artists are now exploring these media. In 1999, the British organization Catalyst Arts and the Slovenian Ministry of Culture provided financial support for theater and dance performances in micro-gravity training aircraft in Russia's Star City. Recently, a team from the San Francisco Art Institute (the only art school in the world to be involved in this type of research) flew the "weightless wonder" as part of NASA's Reduced Gravity Flight Opportunity Program. This has inspired a revival of new space art in California and established a new role for the United States in the "space art race." It has also raised a critical question: Who will be the first artist in space?

Assuming that a real space age finally does arrive, at some point later in the 21st century as new technologies make it cheaper to achieve escape velocity, it will also start to rely heavily on a familiarity on the part of the audience with weightlessness. The more people grow familiar with the radically altered sense of space and time that weightlessness can bring, the more they'll also be ready intuitively to understand the imperatives behind the expanded viewpoints onto reality that the zero gravity arts will create.

> What is the state of weightlessness? In future decades, we'll integrate the presence of inhabited interplanetary stations. This existence of new places will become a new dimension in our cultural consciousness and in our philosophical dimension.
> *Michael Benson (filmmaker who documented the "Noordung" Theatre performance in zero gravity)*

## Ted Krueger

The rigors of high-performance aircraft and space vehicles have led to sophisticated sensing and control technologies, and techniques for imbedding sensors in structural components. A comprehensive biological model for architecture may develop out of research into sensing, active control systems, and interactive materials developed in the aerospace and defense industries during the last decade. The locus of design shifts away from the form to concentrate on the behaviors and the interface that will be required for intelligent and interactive environments. Technology is something independent, on its own developmental trajectory, that could overtake and surpass human development. It may be that we are in a feedback loop with the products of our culture. We experience them within a kind of perceptual Doppler effect. They develop and go out as extensions of our selves and return to us, subtly shifted, as an Other. What could be the consciousness of an architectural artifact modeled on biological phenomena?

The implications of these technological developments are to fundamentally alter our relationship with the products of material culture. Autonomous, adaptive, and interactive environments are no longer physical only, but participants in the social realm as well. This fundamental shift, though founded on technological development, is a cultural operation and points to the need for participation of cultural workers with the technological disciplines.

## Marco Peljhan

Artistic and scientific practices have one common ground: they are both creative behaviors that push and explore unknown territories. Now that the International Space Station is in orbit, it must host not only scientific and commercial components, but also superlative spiritual work. If it does not, there will be a problem for the future of the station and for humankind.

Marko Peljhan set up Makrolab, an art-science autonomous research station resembling the Mir Space Station. It was first shown at Documenta in 1997 and then on the remote Rottnest Island off Australia. He intends eventually to install Makrolab in Antarctica. He founded the arts organization Projekt Atol in 1992 and its technical branch Projekt Atol Communications Technologies (PACT Systems) in 1995. He is the co-founder of the Ljubljana Digital Media Lab (LJUDMILA) and coordinator of the Makrolab and Insular Technologies projects. In 1999 and 2000, PACT worked with the Yuri Gagarin Cosmonaut Training Centre to organize four arts-based parabolic flights, three for the Slovenian Noordung team and one in cooperation with Arts Catalyst for the Franco-British parabolic flight of Kitsou Dubois.

*99*

*D.A. Solomon*

In the past, artists have been excluded from space exploration. During the year 2000, artists and selected individuals gathered to repair this faulty piece of history. They met in a newly installed space at the Stedelijk Museum to design a mission to the International Space Station. The goal of this mission is to optimize conditions for integrating artists into space exploration programs. Current space-program protocols do not provide much room for the creative process that both artists and scientists need to fuel their work. So far, space has been the sole domain of technicians and the military. One of the purposes of the artist-astronaut video document is to issue a strong proposal to NASA and the European Space Agency that shows how a mission can be modified to optimize the creative process and how doing so will be valuable to the scientific process.

*Lorelei Lisowsky*

With the onslaught of our technological age, we continue to be devoured and obsessed with "machinic" transportation and the need to be released from our condition of "gravity." Current trends in social and technological developments speak about the transcendence of our bodies and adjustment of the body in zero gravity. When we enter zero gravity, the first thing that occurs is loss of the brain's logical functions. The second thing is loss of the sense of having a body and awareness of "existence" only (a pure feeling). The body self floats, gravity is gone, and subversion of the vertical gives us a state of being that borders on the divine. This begins the next step of evolution. We cope and explore the greater need, separation, and expansion.

In our experiment on the KC135, we explored human-computer interaction in micro gravity. Through close examination of the data-processed phantasm, movements and flows of the visible and invisible body are given access to visual qualities as well as interpreted in a numerical formula. By interfacing the technological being with the need to escape gravity, transformation of perceived orientation within physical and virtual space can be monitored and scanned to describe multiple dimensional positions and occurrences.

Now is the time to ask the relevant people to explain to the world: why not artists in space?

As a public artist and through her involvement with the Exploding Cinema in London, Lorelei Lisowsky experiences the power and potential of social interaction. Her recent parabolic flight was a life-changing experience.

Noordung performing artists in microgravity aircraft flights.

100

VIRTUAL STARS

*Contact*
DON LEVY
Sony Pictures Imageworks
9050 West Washington Boulevard
Culver City, California 90232
USA
Don_Levy@spe.sony.com

Think of the greatest performances of our time. They are all products of fertile imaginations and great collaborative efforts of many talented individuals. But are their persistent effects "real" or ephemeral? Some of the most enduring characters, the most unforgettable, most indelible performances, live not in real life but in our emotional connections to them

In this Special Session on visual effects, artists from Sony Pictures Imageworks and Rhythm & Hues Studios draw from their repertoire of characters and productions to explore the creative and technical process of bringing characters to life. Their ability to create dynamic digital characters, imbue them with personality and photo-realistic characteristics, and thoroughly and seamlessly integrate them into live-action stories dramatically expands the filmmaker's boundaries. Actors are no longer constrained by the physical limitations of their being. Gravity, strength, and logistics can be defied. Animals can speak. Villains can be unspeakable.

"Stuart Little," "Babe," "Hollow Man," "The Flintstones," and the upcoming productions of "Spider-Man," "Cats & Dogs," "Harry Potter and the Sorcerers Stone," and "Stuart Little 2," display increasingly advanced examples of how digital artists transform the fabric of filmmaking.

Success in creating these performances is a combination of art and science. Mastery comes in the blend of style and technique. In this session, participants explore digital characters through story and character development, art and design, animation and digital production, and technology.

Sony Pictures Imageworks is an award-winning, state-of-the-art visual effects and animation company dedicated to the art and artistry of digital production. It has grown from a small team of artists and producers to a thriving company of over 380 full-time employees in a state-of-the-art facility. It has received three Academy Award (nominations for "Starship Troopers," "Stuart Little," and "Hollow Man") and countless industry merits and awards. Its work has been a major part of numerous features including: "Contact," "Starship Troopers," "Anaconda," "Godzilla," "Patch Adams," "Stuart Little," "What Lies Beneath," "Hollow Man," "Cast Away," and "Charlie's Angels." Current projects include " Harry Potter and the Sorcerers Stone," "Spider-Man," and "Stuart Little 2."

Founded in 1987, Rhythm & Hues Studios is a leading producer of character animation and visual effects for the entertainment industry. In 1995, Rhythm & Hues was honored with the Academy Award for Best Visual Effects for its work on "Babe." Work from the Rhythm & Hues Feature Film Division can be seen in a wide variety of recent films including "Along Came a Spider," "Bedazzled," "How the Grinch Stole Christmas," "Little Nicky," "The 6th Day," "Red Planet," and "Rugrats in Paris." Currently, Rhythm & Hues is in production on "Cats&Dogs," "Dr. Dolittle 2," and "The Sum of All Fears."

*101*

"Babe," Courtesy of Rhythm & Hues

"Cats & Dogs," Courtesy of Rhythm & Hues

"Stuart Little," Courtesy of Sony Pictures Imageworks

"The Flintstones," Courtesy of Rhythm & Hues

"The Flintstones," Courtesy of Rhythm & Hues

"Spiderman," Courtesy of Sony Pictures Imageworks

# MASTERS OF THE GAME

Host
J.C. HERZ
Joystick Nation Inc.

Organizer
KATHRYN SAUNDERS
ThinkTech
245 Davenport Road, 3rd Floor
Toronto, Ontario M5R 1K1
Canada
+1.416.200.4316
+1.416.929.8924 fax
kathryn_saunders@siggraph.org

Winners of the Academy of Interactive Arts and Sciences Interactive Achievement Awards for excellence in: art direction, animation, game play engineering, visual engineering, sound design, musical composition, and character and story development.

Hosted by J.C Herz of Joystick Nation Inc., with an introduction from the president of the academy, Paul Provenzano, Masters of the Game offers a behind-the-scenes look at some of the world's leading games and the people who created them. The award winners will speak about the games, their sources of inspiration, their multi-disciplinary teams, and how they created the magic for which they won the AIAS Interactive Achievement Award.

## OUTSTANDING ACHIEVEMENT IN SOUND DESIGN AND MUSICAL COMPOSITION
*Medal of Honor: Underground (PlayStation)*
*DreamWorks Interactive/Electronic Arts*

Lead Manon from her beginnings in the resistance through her recruitment by the OSS to thwart the German onslaught. Armed with an arsenal of new weapons, you battle tanks, half-tracks, and Gestapo thugs across Europe and North Africa. From the cobblestone streets of Paris to the narrow alleyways of Casablanca, from a doomed Italian monastery to Himmler's dark medieval castle in Germany, you undertake challenging missions to outwit and outgun fierce enemy troops. Procured weapons, expert stealth, and a poised trigger finger – you'll need them all to become a seasoned veteran of the OSS and return home to take part in the liberation of your homeland.

*Speakers*
ERIK KRABER, JACK GRILLO, MICHAEL GIACCHINO

*Erik Kraber, Jack Grillo*
Erik Kraber and Jack Grillo are the lead sound designers for DreamWorks Interactive. Their work on the Medal of Honor series and Clive Barker's Undying has resulted in many accolades, including two AIAS Craft awards for Best Sound Design of the Year. They both began their careers designing sound for films and commercials before joining DreamWorks Interactive.

*Michael Giacchino*
In early 1997, Michael Giacchino was approached by the newly formed DreamWorks Interactive to score their flagship PlayStation video game based on Steven Spielberg's summer box office phenomenon, "The Lost World." The result was the world's first ever completely original orchestral score written for a PlayStation console. Since then, he has composed six additional orchestral scores for DreamWorks Interactive. Last summer, he recorded his score for Medal of Honor: Underground, which garnered him the AIAS craft award for best achievement in musical composition, and in March of this year, he began composing the music for the next chapter in the DreamWorks Interactive Medal of Honor series, which goes before the orchestra in June.

## OUTSTANDING ACHIEVEMENT IN VISUAL ENGINEERING AND GAME PLAY ENGINEERING
*SSX: Snowboarding Super Cross (PlayStation 2)*
*Electronic Arts/Electronic Arts*

Explode out of the gate and launch into the race of your life. Push the boundaries of real physics to dominate the SSX World Circuit. This high-speed arcade racer revolutionizes snowboarding games by taking the sport and tricks of today onto the tracks of tomorrow. Enter mind-blowing worlds with spectacular tracks, while listening to break-beat music that mixes on the fly. Experience full-contact survival-mode racing that keeps you riding the edge between control and chaos.

*Speaker*
MIKE RAYNER, ELECTRONIC ARTS

Mike Rayner has been an active member of the game development community since 1994. He holds both a bachelors of engineering and a bachelors of science from the University of Western Ontario. After distinguishing himself in the R&D group at Gray Matter, he joined Electronic Arts in October 1997. Previously the lead rendering programmer on SSX, he is currently lead platform engineer on the upcoming sequel.

His game credits include: Foes of Ali Boxing (3DO), Perfect Weapon (PSX+PC), The Crow City of Angels (PSX+PC), Manic Marbles (PC), The Condemned (PC), Triple Play 1999 (PSX+PC), Triple Play 2000 (PSX+PC), and SSX (PS2).

Screen Shot from SSX: Snowboarding Super Cross.

## OUTSTANDING ACHIEVEMENT IN GAME DESIGN
*Zelda: Majora's Mask (Nintendo 64)*
*Nintendo Co. Ltd./Nintendo of America*

Thrown into a parallel world by the mischievous actions of a possessed Skull Kid, Link found a land that was in grave danger. The dark power of a relic called Majora's Mask had wreaked havoc on the citizens of Hyrule, but their most urgent problem was a suicidal moon crashing toward the world. Link had only 72 hours to find a way to stop its descent, so he traveled through time and worked ceaselessly until he accomplished his goal.

*Speaker*
KEN LOBB, NINTENDO OF AMERICA INC.

Ken Lobb is director of game evaluation and marketing support for Nintendo of America. Over the years, he has designed and produced games such as Low-G-Man and G.I. Joe for the NES; Rolling Thunder 2, Splatterhouse 3, and Wings 2 for Genesis and Super NES; Killer Instinct, Tetrisphere, Goldeneye, Perfect Dark, and Conker's Bad Fur Day for the arcade and Nintendo 64. Prior to joining Nintendo in 1993, he worked as a product manager for Namco Hometek and Taxan USA and as a product/test Engineer for AMD and Waferscale Integration, Inc. Currently, he is working on projects for the Nintendo GameCube and still loves his job and hobby.

OUTSTANDING ACHIEVEMENT IN
CHARACTER OR STORY DEVELOPMENT
*Baldur's Gate II (PC)*
*Interplay Entertainment, BioWare Corp.*

Every world has conflict. Good and evil. Friend and foe. Safety and danger. In Baldur's Gate II: Shadows of Amn, you find yourself between these factions. This epic sequel immerses you in a world of intrigue, adventure, and fierce combat, where your ability to discern the difference between these sides (with the assistance of steel and spell) determines your fate.

In Baldur's Gate I, you defeated your evil half-brother, Sarevok, and prevented your father, Bhaal, the dead Lord of Murder, from returning to the Forgotten Realms. Now, in Baldur's Gate II: Shadows of Amn, the stakes have become much higher. Will you resist the evil within you and forge a legend of heroic proportions? Or will you embrace your monstrous inner nature, and carve a swath of destruction across the realms?

Your story begins anew in the exotic southern kingdom of Amn, amidst the opulence of the sinister capital city of Athkatla. Journey through the fierce, unforgiving wilderness of Amn and the treacherous caverns of the Underdark in your quest for artifacts of awesome power and treasure of inestimable wealth. Even challenge dragons, if you dare. Such is the life of a legend.

*Speaker*
DAVID HIBBELN, DIRECTOR OF ART, BIOWARE CORP.

Ever since he was a wee lad, David Hibbeln loved to draw, play computer games, and play Dungeons & Dragons, but never dreamed it could be made into a career. As a somewhat older lad, he went to the University of Alberta and graduated with a BA in linguistics and a minor in English. It was there that he learned the finer points of written and oral communication, but his love and passion for art drove him to pursue visual communication. His interest in comic art prompted him to try self-publishing comics. He also did some freelance graphic design work before he was drawn to the beauty and emotion of animation as a visual communication medium. His love of animation and film prompted him to take as many courses and read as many books on animation as he could find.

His first animation work was as assistant animator on a National Film Board of Canada short animation called "Cactus Swing," at Salamander Studios in Edmonton. After that film was complete, he had an opportunity to learn computer animation at a local company. From there, the rare opportunity came to join a new computer-games company: BioWare Corp. He saw this as an opportunity to bring better animation to computer games. As BioWare grew, he formed an animation department at BioWare to specifically meet the challenges of all things moving in a game. Currently, he is director of art for BioWare, where he manages a growing pool of 35 artists. He is also still involved in production, directing the cinematic elements and advising on in-game animation.

*Paul Provenzano*
Paul Provenzano is president and executive director of the Academy of Interactive Arts & Sciences, the professional academy of the $6.1+$ billion interactive entertainment software industry. He is a 10-year veteran in interactive entertainment with 18 years overall in the entertainment industry.

*J.C. Herz*
One of the most useful tools for understanding the relationship between game and story is the concept of dimensionality. A cube, for instance, is a 3D object Reducing its dimensionality yields a square (2D), a line (1D), and finally a point. Reducing the dimensionality of a film yields a still frame. Reducing the dimensionality of urban planning gives you architecture. Reducing the dimensionality of a game, by eliminating all but one of the possible trajectories through the world, yields a story.

Essentially, the story is a core sample of the game, one trajectory through the universe of all possible solutions. Outside the system, that story might be dramatic or undramatic, just as the game itself might be satisfying or unsatisfying. Dimensionality is not a good in and of itself. But the challenge for game designers, as storytellers, is to build a world that's interesting in multiple dimensions: the individual's trajectory through the world, the game as a whole (an overall sense of "gameplay" and dynamics), and the social experience that happens around the game (for example, trading custom skins or levels, fan sites, etc.). Creating a satisfying experience is a more complex task in many dimensions than in fewer dimensions. Herein lies the challenge, for game designers and storytellers alike, as media evolve into more sophisticated, multilayered forms.

103

WEB3D ROUNDUP

TIMOTHY CHILDS
RoundUP Productions and Eyematic

The Web3D RoundUP lives somewhere between classical art and commerce. In the SIGGRAPH context, the RoundUP lives within the nexus between the commercial-oriented Exhibition, the bleeding-edge technology of Emerging Technologies, and the Art Gallery.

Now one of these worlds has dramatically changed the balance. As the swooping pendulum of current market conditions swings toward economic practicality, consolidation and shakeout in the Web3D industry is in process. Now that the installed computer base is actually fast enough for Web3D technologies, major software developers will move into the 3D Web. Pure content "plays" are dead. Just like everyone else, Web3D companies must now seriously start to justify themselves by carving out sustainable ways of staying in operation. Evolve or die! Signs of evolution in Web3D emerge to make real businesses out of creativity, including communications, wireless, and online gaming.

With the emergence of business-based themes that leverage the tools and talents of Web3D, mergers for survival are happening. Quietly, behind the scenes, big software companies have been acquiring enabling technologies, and they are rolling out their solutions at SIGGRAPH 2001. And looming on the horizon is a rapidly growing trend of using easy-to-create avatars (yes the once dreaded "A" word) as a communication medium, representing people across a myriad of networks and devices.

And then there is wireless. (Doesn't everyone have a wireless strategy?) Web3D's role in the emerging wireless field will be bleeding-edge, interesting, and provocative. Unlike bandwidth-clogging video, Web3D is a natural for low-bandwidth wireless networks. Now that 3D-enabled wireless devices are coming to market, depending on where you live, you can soon expect a swarm of 3D characters and applications to be playing on a mobile device near you.

And if there was ever a killer app of Web3D, it would be online gaming. Massive-player online games have revolutionized how content, technology, art (creation and asset management), and financial models are conceived.

The Web3D RoundUP, has been showing the hottest and most bleeding-edge technology for years. We've strived to spur creativity and show you the best of the best. Especially now, the Web 3D RoundUP's goal is make sure that creativity is not lost in this age of business, to help blend technology, creativity, and art in a way that benefits us all in many ways, including financial.

Web3D RoundUP must evolve as well. Prior to SIGGRAPH 2000's boisterous event, we responded to feedback that the "negative sound" devices ("moo canisters") really didn't work that well compared to the happy "wacka wacka" sound devices. So we experimented with the rubber "razzer." It turned out to be much more effective than anticipated. The noisemakers really created a much more raucous feedback session than we had ever seen. So we are on a quest for the perfect noisemaker: not too quiet and not too loud.

ABOUT THE WEB3D ROUNDUP

The Web3D RoundUP is a high-speed shootout that showcases the latest and very greatest interactive 3D content available over the Web. Diplomatically, we describe this as an "interactive event for interactive content." Realistically, it can be a gut-wrenching monster. Have you ever tried doing a cool demo in less than three minutes, with the seconds ticking down on the big screen, in front of thousands of world-class graphics experts, all armed with happy/sad sound effects and ping-pong ball blasters!

Twice a year, at the annual SIGGRAPH conference and Web3D200x, the Web3D RoundUP presents the best the Web3D world has to offer in a cool and entertaining way. The challenge for jurors is to choose two dozen diverse, eye-popping selections from nine dozen submissions. The challenge for presenters is to first finish that killer demo, and then engage the audience in a fun way so that everyone can interactively participate and become part of the event itself. The challenge for the audience is to hold on without blinking during this wild ride, to shake and rattle various "interactive feedback devices" for live comment, and then vote to pick the entry in each category that deserves to receive a coveted "Golden Lasso."

The Web3D RoundUP evolved from the early days of the Virtual Reality Education Foundation (affectionately known as VeRGe), which was created by Timothy Childs, Linda Jacobson and Peter Rothman. Another precursor was the first SIGGRAPH Demo SIG meetings organized by Don Brutzman, where the VRML community kick-started Web-based 3D graphics. It was through those early VeRGe and Demo SIG events that we got our first tastes of technically successful chaos, which morphed into today's Web3D RoundUP. Each year, we continue to grow, adapt, tumble, and evolve as presenters push the limits.

One of the things that gave the Web3D RoundUP its original kick was the oft-occurring computer crash. There seemed to be a direct correlation between a crashing computer and how bleeding-edge the demo was. Now Web3D technology is starting to stabilize (and fewer virtual fire extinguishers are needed). Even so, we're still seeking the bleeding edge.

The Web3D RoundUP became what it is today thanks to great help from all the amazing volunteers at both SIGGRAPH and Web3D conferences, as well as the solid advice and support by many SIGGRAPH chairs, staff, committee members and student volunteers. We're especially grateful and blessed to see some of the same faces return year after year to help out in the days of temporary backstage chaos as we prepare for the event. Thank you all. We are most fortunate to receive sage guidance from the world's greatest audio-visual wizards at (where else!) AVW Audio Visual. Finally, we thank the hardworking technical trapeze artists and content creators, who put in countless hours getting ready for just a few minutes of unforgettably intense glory on stage.

# SENSAPALOOZA: GUIDED TOUR OF THE NEW SILICON SENSES

*Organizers*
KATHRYN SAUNDERS
ThinkTech
245 Davenport Road, 3rd Floor
Toronto, Ontario M5R 1K1
Canada
+1.416.200.4316
panels-s2001@siggraph.org

JAMES GEARY
TIMEeurope.com

*Host*
JAMES GEARY
TIMEeurope.com

*Participants*
FERDINANDO (SANDRO)
MUSSA-IVALDI
Northwestern University

HENRI LUSTIGER-THALER
Aerome USA

THOMAS A. FURNESS III
University of Washington

HIROSHI ISHII
Massachusetts Institute
of Technology
tangible.media.mit.edu/

ELLWOOD IVEY
Trisenx, Inc.

ALEX WAIBEL
Carnegie Mellon University

*Commentators*
ANDREW GLASSNER
Independent Consultant

MONIKA FLEISCHMANN
GMD - Forschungszentrum
Informationstechnik GmbH

ROSALIND W. PICARD
Massachusetts Institute
of Technology

Human beings are embedding computer chips in their bodies to enhance, extend, or repair their senses, while computers are gaining the ability to see, hear, smell, taste, and touch. And once a computer has its own sensorium, it's conceivable that it could at some point learn to think.

This remarkable convergence of body and machine is empowered by merging advanced computing technology with the human nervous system, a combination that holds could restore sight to the blind and help victims of paralysis regain partial use of their limbs. The flexh-chips convergence is also giving individuals bionic senses, such as the ability to see infrared radiation or to feel objects at a distance. Some futurists even suggest that computers will eventually enable extra-sensory perception.

This Special Session is a combination of talk show and television cooking program, with a Greek chorus attached. Six guests (one for each of the five senses and one for the sixth sense, mind) demonstrate leading-edge technologies that show how the human sensorium is being augmented with sophisticated computer chips. During and after the demos, members of the Greek chorus contribute their own observations and comments. The audience participates by entering questions on the Special Session Web site via wireless network connections.

The goal is to provide a compelling and provocative overview of some of the newest technologies that could soon become part of our computers and our bodies.

## SIGHT
Picture this. You are walking down a street in a foreign city, wondering how to find a particular restaurant, where you've arranged to meet an old friend. When you enter a few commands in a small computer attached to your belt, a map of the city appears in the air before you, and you notice that the quickest route to the restaurant is outlined in yellow. When you find the right street, you can't quite make out a sign in the distance. A light touch to your glasses magnifies the image, confirming that this is indeed the restaurant. You enter the restaurant and recognize your friend at a table. And now picture one more thing: You are legally blind. This scenario is far from improbable. In fact, it's already a reality. Visual prosthetics (electronic implants in the eye, the optic nerve, or the brain) are enabling blind people with certain eye diseases to see again, and retinal displays can project virtual images directly into the eye. These technologies are bringing new dimensions to the sense of sight that could provide eyes in the back of your head and the ability to see things beyond the normal visible spectrum.

## HEARING
Voice operation and speech synthesis are increasingly commonplace in mobile phones, automobile navigation systems, and other devices in which portability and ease of use are key. Research is even under way to replace familiar desktop icons with "earcons," audible tones that would alert users to incoming email, changes in stock prices, or important news bulletins.

For mobile devices, this technology would allow users to keep their eyes on the road, the sidewalk, or other travelers instead of casting furtive glances at a computer screen. A travelling day trader could hear the steady murmur of the Dow, for example; when it goes up, perhaps the earcon is a high-pitched squeal of fireworks; when it goes down (who knows?), perhaps the sound of a flushing toilet. The abilities of computers to hear and parse human speech are being put to use in portable devices that provide real-time translations within certain domain-specific subject areas. Other research is dedicated to improving hearing by making the cochlear implant even more like the biological system it emulates. Researchers are finding that the best way to try to match what the senses can do is to study the biology and then replicate key computational concepts in electronics.

## SMELL
Electronic noses, arrays of odor-sensitive electrochemical sensors linked to high-powered computers have been in use for several years, primarily to trace explosive residues, analyze blood alcohol levels, and carry out quality control tests in the food and beverage industries. A new generation of e-noses is beginning to replicate the speed, sensitivity, and discrimination of the human nose. Soon, a digital proboscis will be able to do everything from assist in medical diagnoses to identify leaks of hazardous substances. Thanks to these new engines of olfaction, your family physician may soon be developing a preliminary diagnosis based on information gleaned from an electronic nose in your phone.

Computers can also pass gas. Firms in the US, Europe, and Israel have developed technology that is, in effect, a video player for the nose. When you insert a scent cartridge (a white rectangular box that looks very much like an ordinary video cassette but contains six prefabricated scents) into one of these devices, it releases appropriate aromas in sync with scenes from a video or

*105*

film presentation. These firms claim that they can create any desired fragrance, and that the amount, intensity, and duration of the smells can be precisely controlled. Fragrant Web stes, scented emails, odoriferous interactive games, and aromatic online advertising may be coming soon to a computer screen near you.

## Taste

Companies and research labs are developing electronic tongues that can sample foods, beverages, and even blood. At least one firm plans to deliver fast food over the Internet, which means that die-hard geeks might one day never have to leave their desktops, not even to order pizza. Using technology similar to the scent controller described above, this machine works like a gustatory fax; it transmits a message to the user's computer in response to a click on a taste-enabled Web site. From this message, a miniature kitchen attached to the user's computer then whips up the appropriate flavor. Some researchers imagine the day when miniature taste-sensor technology will be attached to the ends of chopsticks and spoons. Dip your chopsticks into a meal, and they will not only tell you what you are eating, but also list the ingredients and provide you with the recipe. Back home in your Internet-enabled kitchen, just plug the chopsticks into the fridge, and the fridge will call up the recipe on the screen and order any missing ingredients.

## Touch

Technology is getting onto, and under, our skin. Computers are moving off the desktop into everyday objects, and human bodies, putting people "in touch" with technology in an ever-more-intimate embrace. Physicians are implanting electrodes into patients to rehabilitate atrophied muscles, prevent epileptic seizures, and restore motor function lost as a result of paralysis. Engineers are creating hybrid prosthetics such as ankles, legs, and knees in which silicon chips are melded with living tissue. Computer scientists are designing haptic (from the Greek word meaning "to touch") interfaces that allow users to reach out and touch digital information, transforming the plain old graphical user interface into a graspable user interface. By coupling digital information with everyday objects like tabletops, appliances, and coffee cups, the physical world is becoming one enormous interface.

## Mind

Since bodies are essential to the emergence of mind in human beings, it makes sense to assume that artificial creatures need bodies, too, if they are ever to become aware, intelligent, and, perhaps someday, even conscious. The rallying cry for this kind of research might be summarized in a slogan: "No sensation without representation." Computer scientists are providing physical representations for these possible minds by taking Alan Turing's advice: give machines – both virtual ones inside computers and physical ones in the form of robots – the best sense organs that money can buy. Researchers are also growing neurons on silicon chips to create the ultimate man-machine interface, one that could help victims of neurodegenerative brain disorders and empower electronic devices that can be operated by thought alone.

*James Geary–TIMEeurope.com*
James Geary is editor, special projects at TIMEeurope.com. He has written a dozen cover stories on subjects as diverse as language extinction, the neurological basis of memory, and the attempts of European politicians to create a "Third Way." He has edited three Time special issues – "The New Age of Discovery" (1997), "Visions of Europe" (1998), and "Fast Forward Europe" (2000) – as well as special reports on telecommunications, technology, and the Internet in Europe. He won Time Inc.'s President's Award, granted in recognition of excellence in generating ideas and delivering results, for the "Visions of Europe" special issue.

In June 2000, he won the NetMedia 2000 European Online Journalism Award for science with his article "What Is Life?" which explores one man's research in the field of artificial intelligence. In his spare time, he regularly contributes book reviews to the James Joyce Quarterly. He also composed the libretto for the dramatic song cycle, "Broken English," which premiered in Amsterdam in August 1997. His book about computers and the human senses, The Body Electric: An Anatomy of the New Bionic Senses, will be published by Weidenfeld & Nicolson in the fall.

*Kathryn Saunders*
Kathryn Saunders is a founding partner of ThinkTech, a consulting firm that designs and develops location-based and e-based experience strategies. She has been actively involved with SIGGRAPH for many years. She is Panels Chair for 2001, and for SIGGRAPH 99, she chaired Emerging Technologies, where she developed and executed the Millennium Motel concept and curated several elements including the entry portal and Route 66.

Trained as an architect, she practiced architecture with two of Canada's leading design firms and has taught architecture at two Canadian universities. Prior to her current post, she was executive director of the Digital Media Institute and creative director, digital media, at the Royal Ontario Museum. At the museum, she developed MYTHICA, an educational entertainment destination that uses a profiling system, wireless technologies, and intelligent autonomous agents to deliver personalized information before, during, and after a visit, based on the visitor's behavior and aspirations. A recipient of many interactive media awards, she has consulted and lectured around the globe from North America to Saudi Arabia and Japan.

*Ferdinando (Sandro) Mussa-Ivaldi*
Sandro Mussa-Ivaldi is a faculty member at the Medical School of Northwestern University. He holds appointments with the departments of physiology, physical medicine and rehabilitation, biomedical engineering and mechanical engineering.

Originally from Turin, Italy, he received a graduate degree in physics from the University of Turin and a PhD in biomedical engineering from the University of Genova and the Polytechnic of Milan.

His past teaching and research credits include:
- The University of Provence, where he worked with Gabriel Gauthier on coordination of eye and hand movements.
- The department of computer science of the University of Genova as a research fellow, where he worked with Pietro Morasso on computational models of handwriting.
- MIT, where he collaborated with Emilio Bizzi and Neville Hogan on a number of studies aimed at understanding the interplay of neural, mechanical, and computational factors in the control of arm movements.

A significant portion of his research is conducted within the Sensory Motor Performance Program of the Rehabilitation Institute of Chicago. His current studies is the focus on the mechanisms underlying the ability of the central nervous system to learn new movements and to adapt previously learned movements to changes in the body as well as in environmental dynamics. Current knowledge indicates that the brain learns new patterns by establishing long-term modifications in the ability of nerve cells to exchange information with each other. Recently, his research team developed a hybrid system that establishes a bi-directional interaction between living neural tissue and a simple mobile robot. They are trying to exploit the behaviors that emerge from this interaction as a window into the information processing of the brain tissue and, in particular, on the mechanisms of synaptic plasticity.

### Henri Lustiger-Thaler

Henri Lustiger-Thaler has been associated with Aerome Scent Communications since the founding of the Company in 1997. He received his doctorate from Université de Montréal, completed his post-doctorate work at Cambridge University, and has been a visiting fellow at Dartmouth College and the University of Rome at La Sapienza. He has published several books and numerous articles on culture and global communication. He is considered to be the foremost specialist on scent communications in the world today.

### Thomas A. Furness III

Thomas A. Furness III is a pioneer in virtual interface technology and virtual reality. He received a BS in electrical engineering from Duke University and a PhD in engineering and applied science from the University of Southampton. He is currently professor of industrial engineering and adjunct professor of electrical engineering and technical communication at the University of Washington, and is the founding director of the university's Human Interface Technology Laboratory. Prior to joining the University of Washington, he served a combined 23 years as an officer and civilian at the Armstrong Laboratory at Wright-Patterson Air Force Base, where he developed advanced cockpits and virtual interfaces for the US Department of Defense. He is the

author of the Super Cockpit program and served as the chief of visual display systems and Super Cockpit director until he moved to Seattle in 1989.

The overall mission of the Human Interface Technology Laboratory is to empower humans by building better interfaces to advanced machines that will unlock the power of human intelligence and link minds globally. The HIT Lab consists of 120 faculty members, professional staff, students, and visiting scholars. It is supported in part by the Virtual Worlds Consortium, a group of 47 companies that provide funding and in-kind annual contributions to the laboratory's research agenda. The laboratory's work encompasses development of hardware and software technologies, human factors, and applications development associated with advanced interfaces with a focus on virtual reality.

### Hiroshi Ishii

Hiroshi Ishii's research focuses on design of seamless interfaces among humans, digital information, and the physical environment. At the MIT Media Lab, he founded and directs the Tangible Media Group, which is pursuing a new vision of human-computer interaction: Tangible Bits. His team seeks to change the "painted bits" of graphical user interfaces to "tangible bits" by giving physical form to digital information:

From 1988 to 1994, he led a research group at the NTT Human Interface Laboratories, where his team invented Team-WorkStation and ClearBoard. In 1993 and 1994, he was a visiting assistant professor at the University of Toronto. He is actively engaged in research on human-computer interaction and computer-supported cooperative work. He served as associate editor of ACM TOCHI (Transactions on Computer Human Interactions) and ACM TOIS (Transactions on Office Information Systems). He also serves as a program committee member of many international conferences including ACM CHI, CSCW, UIST, SIGGRAPH, Multimedia, Interact, and ECSCW. He received a BE in electronic engineering, and ME and PhD degrees in computer engineering from Hokkaido University.

*107*

### Ellwood Ivey

Ellwood Ivey attended the School of Business at Savannah State College and completed the Sales and Marketing program at Draughons Business College. His many accomplishments include building a 92-member sales team for a major international health food company. He has served as a technology consultant to Hoechst Celenese Corp., a $16 billion conglomerate. In 1991, he founded the D.U.I.E. Project, managed development of its revolutionary technology (hydrocarbon specific sensor), and facilitated its joint venture and licensing deal valued at nearly $10 million. He currently holds four patents, two service marks, two trademarks, numerous copyrights, and other proprietary properties.

### Alex Waibel

Alex Waibel is professor of computer science at Carnegie Mellon University and Universität Karlsruhe. He directs the Interactive Systems Laboratories at both universities, where his research emphasis is in speech recognition, handwriting recognition, language processing, speech translation, machine learning, and multimodal and multimedia interfaces. At Carnegie Mellon, he also serves as associate director of the Language Technology Institute and as director of the Language Technology PhD program. He was one of the founding members of CMU's Human Computer Interaction Institute and serves on its core faculty.

He was one of the founders of C-STAR, the international consortium for speech translation research, and served as its chairman from 1998 to 2000. He also codirected Verbmobil, the German national speech translation initiative. His work on time delay neural networks was awarded the IEEE Best Paper award in 1990, and his work on speech translation systems received the Alcatel SEL Research Prize for Technical Communication in 1994. He received a BS in electrical engineering from the Massachusetts Institute of Technology in 1979, and M. and PhD degrees in computer science from Carnegie Mellon University in 1980 and 1986.

### Andrew Glassner

Andrew Glassner is a novelist, screenwriter, and consultant in computer graphics. He began working in computer graphics in 1978, and has carried out research in the field at the New York Institute of Technology's Computer Graphics Lab, Case Western Reserve University, the IBM T.J. Watson Research Center, the Delft University of Technology, Bell Communications Research, Xerox PARC, and Microsoft Research. A popular writer and speaker, he has published numerous technical papers on topics ranging from digital sound to 3D rendering. His book 3D Computer Graphics: A Handbook for Artists and Designers has taught a generation of artists through two editions and three languages. He created and edited the "Graphics Gems" series and the book An Introduction to Ray Tracing. He wrote the two-volume text Principles of Digital Image Synthesis. His most recent book is Andrew Glassner's Notebook, a collection of the first three years of his regular column by the same name in IEEE Computer Graphics & Applications. He has served as Papers chair for SIGGRAPH 94, founding editor of the Journal of Graphics Tools, and editor-in-chief of ACM Transactions on Graphics. He wrote

and directed the short film "Chicken Crossing," which premiered at the SIGGRAPH 96 Electronic Theater, and designed the highly participatory game "Dead Air" for The Microsoft Network, where he wrote and directed the live-action pilot episode. He is currently at work on his second novel and consulting on computer graphics, storytelling, and story structure for the computer game and online entertainment industry. In his spare time, he paints, plays jazz piano, kayaks, and hikes. He holds a PhD in computer science from the University of North Carolina at Chapel Hill.

### Monika Fleischmann–imk.gmd.de:8081/people/fleischmann.mhtml

Monika Fleischmann studied visual arts, theater, and computer graphics. Since 1992, she has been artistic director of the institute for media communication and since 1997, head of the MARS Exploratory Media Lab at the German National Research Center for Information Technology (GMD) outside Bonn. She also teaches at the Academy of Design in Zurich. Her work, always produced with her partner, Wolfgang Strauss, has been exhibited at the Centre Pompidou, the Museum for Design, the Museum of Modern Art (New York), and events such as the annual SIGGRAPH conference, Imagina, Art Futura, ISEA, and Ars Electronica. In 1992, her Home of the Brain was awarded wih the Golden Nica for interactive art at Ars Electronicaz. Her work ranges among art, science, and technology. In theoretical and practical studies, she explores the creative potential of computer technologies. Her main research topics are human computer interfaces combined with interactive virtual environments and perceptive processes.

### Rosalind W. Picard

Rosalind W. Picard is founder and director of the Affective Computing Research Group at the Massachusetts Institute of Technology Media Laboratory. She holds a bachelors in electrical engineering from the Georgia Institute of Technology and masters and doctorate degrees in electrical engineering and computer science from MIT. The author of over 80 peer-reviewed scientific articles in pattern recognition, multidimensional signal modeling, computer vision, and human-computer interaction, she is internationally known for pioneering research on content-based video retrieval and on giving computers the ability to recognize and respond to human emotional information. She is co-recipient with Tom Minka of a "best paper" award (1998) from the Pattern Recognition Society for their work on interactive machine learning with a society of models. Her award-winning book, Affective Computing (MIT Press, 1997), lays the groundwork for giving machines the skills of emotional intelligence. Her group's research on affective and wearable technologies has been featured in national and international public forums such as The New York Times, The London Independent, Scientific American Frontiers, Time, New Scientist, Vogue, and PBS and BBC specials.

# 2001 IN 2001: HOW A COMPLETELY ANALOG FILM INSPIRED A DIGITAL REVOLUTION

*Panelists*
SYD MEAD
PETER HYAMS
ROBERT ABEL
DENNIS MUREN

*Moderator*
JACQUELYN FORD MORIE

In 1968, Stanley Kubrick transformed Arthur C. Clarke's science-fiction story into an intriguing genre film and, in the process, made history. Awarded the 1969 Academy Award for Achievement in Visual Effects, "2001: A Space Odyssey" defined the future and our place in it. The film created a new perspective of the world and inspired a generation of artists, scientists, and filmmakers to look beyond the limitations of things they know and tools they know how to use.

It has been five decades since humans first left the earth, and just about that long since John Whitney used an analog computer to bring life to ephemeral images. In that time, we have traveled into space and far beyond the reaches of our imaginations to create incredible visions of the distant past and the unimagined future.

This session brings together a stellar group of film industry veterans, historians, and visionaries to discuss Kubrick's "2001: A Space Odyssey." They take us on a stimulating journey through the film and beyond, showing how its influence extends far beyond the reaches of film, space, and time.

*Syd Mead*
Designer and visual futurist of such films as "Tron," "2010," and "Blade Runner."

*Peter Hyams*
Director, writer, and cinematographer, whose work includes "2010," "Timecop," and "End of Days."

*Robert Abel*
Pioneering computer graphicist whose work defined an industry.

*Dennis Muren*
Visual effects creator for "Star Wars," "The Abyss," "Jurassic Park," "The Phantom Menace," and "AI."

*Jacquelyn Ford Morie*
Pioneering computer graphicist and artist who is currently destgning the future at the Institute for Creative Technologies.

*109*

# Emerging Technologies

*Chair*
**Mk Haley**
Walt Disney Imagineering

110

111

*Chair*
MK HALEY

*Program Coordinator*
KATIE RYLANDER

*Committee*
DAVID NEWTON

PRESTON SMITH

CHRIS CARNEY

RALPH LOOS

BRIAN MASHBURN

*A special thanks to
the teams at AVW
and Freeman, and
the SIGGRAPH 2001
Conference Committee
for inspiration
and collaboration,
and a lot of sweat.*

*Jury*
ANDREW GLASSNER
Writer and Consultant

MK HALEY
Walt Disney Imagineering

ISAAC KERLOW
The Walt Disney Company

JOE PARADISO
Massachusetts Institute
of Technology

RANDY PAUSCH
Carnegie Mellon University

SCOTT SENFTEN
SGI

JOSHUA STRICKON
Massachusetts Institute
of Technology

*112*

"IT'S KIND OF FUN TO DO THE IMPOSSIBLE."
*- Walt Disney*

Welcome to Emerging Technologies for SIGGRAPH 2001!

Emerging Technologies is always a dynamic collage of hardware, software, and visions into the world of computer graphics and interactive techniques. This year, we celebrate not only the technology we develop to play, but also the play we all enjoy in exploring the challenge of continually advancing the field, inventing entirely new archetypes, and tackling design issues. From lab prototypes to student research projects and industry beta tests, Emerging Technologies allows you to get your hands on, and your head around, some truly unique visions of the future of technology, as well as some solid examples of the state of the art right now. Everything from display systems to interfaces, robotics, collaboration, simulation, music, and online applications is available for exploration. With submissions from around the world, from a diverse array of fields, I hope that you not only have fun, but that you also see exciting visions of the future that inspire you to think about the effect your work will have in the future of emergent technologies.

*Mk Haley*
*SIGGRAPH 2001 Emerging Technologies Chair*
*Walt Disney Imagineering*

*113*

# α Wolf
*Chair's Prerogative Exhibit*

*Contact*
Bill Tomlinson
Synthetic Characters Group
The Media Lab
Massachusetts Institute
of Technology
20 Ames Street
Cambridge, Massachusetts 02139
USA
+1.617.253.5109
+1.617.253.6215 fax
badger@media.mit.edu

*Collaborators*
Bill Tomlinson
Marc Downie
Matt Berlin
Jesse Gray
Adolph Wong
Robert Burke
Damian Isla
Yuri Ivanov
Michael Patrick Johnson
Derek Lyons
Jennie Cochran
Bryan Yong
Dan Stiehl
Rusmin Soetjipto
Dan Zaharopol
Prof. Bruce Blumberg

AlphaWolf presents a synthetic wolf pack comprised of autonomous and semi-autonomous wolves who interact with each other much as real wolves do, forming dynamic social relationships based on their past experiences. How the wolves interact is determined by their internal state, their social positions in the pack, and their previous experiences with their pack-mates. Each of several participants can affect the emotional state of a wolf by howling, growling, or whimpering into a microphone. In addition, participants can encourage their wolves to interact with specific other wolves in the pack. By letting participants "get inside the mind and body" of a wolf, AlphaWolf provides a compelling opportunity to explore the meaning of social behavior.

This work is informed by the biology and behavior of the gray wolf (*Canis lupus*). In their natural environment, wolves form hierarchical social relationships within their packs. Certain individuals are dominant over other individuals. To demonstrate and maintain these relationships, wolves exhibit stereotypical dominance and submission behaviors toward each other. These social behaviors appear to be derived from other behavioral patterns exhibited by wolves. For example, the two main forms of submission in adult wolves (passive submission and active submission) are quite similar to two forms of pup behavior (reflex urination and food-begging). AlphaWolf explores the connections among social behavior, learning, emotion, and development in virtual wolves to create an entertaining interaction and shed some light on those connections in wild wolf populations.

Since most people interacting with AlphaWolf are novices, it's best to "play" wolf puppies in the beginning. As new additions to the pack, novices, and pups have about the same level of social skills. Just as puppies are tolerated by adult wolves when they behave in ways that are socially inappropriate, novice users should be welcomed into the system despite their limited knowledge of wolf social behavior. Virtual pups should learn at the same rate as the human interactors, so that the two are well matched as they proceed through the social environment together.

AlphaWolf represents the second year of a multi-year project by the Synthetic Characters Group at the MIT Media Lab under the direction of Bruce Blumberg. Through this project, we aim to develop autonomous animated characters whose behavioral complexity, ability to learn and adapt, expressivity, and intentionality rival those of a real dog or wolf. In addition to extending our previous work, AlphaWolf explores the computational representations that must be in place to enable social learning and formation of context-specific emotional memories. The installation showcases the minds and bodies of the wolves themselves and features a suite of supporting technology, including evocative real-time computer graphics, autonomous cinematography, and dynamic scoring and sound design.

*114*

The alpha wolf and his pup howl together.

The pup tries to convince the alpha wolf to play.

The pup submits to the alpha wolf.

## CircleMaze
*Juried Exhibit*

*Contact*
CLIFTON FORLINES
Carnegie Mellon University
630 Clyde Street #202
Pittsburgh, Pennsylvania 15213
USA
+1.412.621.2578
forlines@cs.cmu.edu

*Development Team*
TINA BLAINE
CLIFTON FORLINES
IAN MCCULLOUGH
DONALD ANTONINI
NING HU
RANDY HSIAO

The CircleMaze, developed at Carnegie Mellon University's Entertainment Technology Center, is a multi-user interactive musical game that encourages team building and collaboration. Combining novel input devices with real-time computer graphics on an integrated tabletop surface, the CircleMaze brings together a group of players to participate in group gaming and music-making. Each player has a rotating circular disk that serves as an input device to control audiovisual aspects of the game.

### GOALS

The CircleMaze is a spin-off from the Jam-O-Drum (SIGGRAPH 2000), which was developed at Interval Research between July 1998 and January 1999 under the direction of Tina (Bean) Blaine. The Jam-O-Drum used the metaphor of a digital community drum circle to give novice musicians the experience of ensemble music making in a casual social setting with real-time video and computer graphics. Expanding on this early primarily rhythmic input prototype, we have developed a new interactive gaming experience.

The CircleMaze is a game that furthers communication and collaboration among its players. The task for the players is to guide all of the game's pieces to the middle of the maze. Because the maze is divided into concentric rings, the pieces must pass through each ring in turn to go from the outer edge of the circular table to the center, so all the players must work together to achieve this goal. Movement of the pieces and rings produces changes in the musical score. As players turn their rings, they alter their sonic contribution to the ensemble. Players of the CircleMaze are involved in a goal-oriented game that requires them to work together as collaborative DJ's to affect musical tracks as their disks spin.

No musical experience is required, because any movement of the rings produces a complementary musical effect. It is our hope that people who might ordinarily be inhibited about participating in a public musical activity will approach the CircleMaze simply because of its game-like interaction and engaging appearance. Afterward, participants might realize that they have also been playing an unusual instrument.

### FUTURE POTENTIAL

The CircleMaze is a single step in our continuing research into communal music-making experiences. Several larger research questions remain, such as: How does one encourage spontaneous, non-self-conscious music-making? How does one facilitate real-time collective experiences among strangers? How does one best introduce an inexperienced player to the world of music-making?

We continue to explore interaction designs and input devices that integrate a variety of approaches to combining elements of motion in music and graphics. The CircleMaze is the latest in what we hope is a long series of experiences derived from the Jam-O-Drum.

### EXHIBITION

- The Jam-O-Drum is currently a permanent installation at the Experience Music Project in Seattle.

- The Jam-O-Drum was exhibited at Emerging Technologies, SIGGRAPH 2000.

- In 2001, the CircleMaze is included in a museum-wide exhibit on gaming at the Zeum Youth Art and Technology Center at Yerba Buena Gardens, San Francisco.

# CYLINDRICAL 3D DISPLAY
## OBSERVABLE FROM ALL DIRECTIONS
*Juried Exhibit*

*Contact*
TOMOHIRO ENDO
Advanced 3D
Television Project
Telecommunications
Advancement
Organizationof Japan
6th floor, 1-33-16, Hakusan,
Bunkyo-ku
Tokyo 113-0001 Japan
+81.3.5803.3387
+81.3.5804.7918
yendo@3dpro.tao.go.jp

YOSHIHIRO KAJIKI
Advanced 3D
Television Project
Telecommunications
Advancement
Organization of Japan
www.3dpro.tao.go.jp

TOSHIO HONDA
Chiba University
3D Project

MAKOTO SATO
Tokyo Institute of Technology

This new cylindrical 3D display allows multiple viewers to see 3D images from 360 degrees of arc horizontally without special glasses. The display is based on ray-space and super-multiview concepts, so its images have smooth motion parallax with unlimited viewing distance.

Cylinder-shaped holographic stereograms are widely used for art, advertising, and other applications because they allow multiple viewers to see a 3D image from all directions. But a multiplex-hologram can only show static images. Some displays of volumetric scans can show dynamic images that can be viewed from all directions, but their application is limited because they display "phantom images," in which all of the background objects are translucent. On the other hand, due to resolution limitations and the shape of 2D display devices such as LCD panels, it is difficult to make a multiview display with conventional methods such as lenticular sheets so that the display can be seen from all horizontal directions.

Our technique uses a cylindrical parallax barrier and a one-dimensional light-source array constructed from semiconductor light sources such as LEDs aligned vertically. It is based on the parallax panoramagram. The light source array rotates along the inside of the cylindrical parallax barrier, and the intensity of each light is modulated synchronously with the rotation.

## Enhanced Reality:
## A New Frontier for Computer Entertainment
*Juried Exhibit*

*Contact*
Richard Marks
Sony Computer
Entertainment America
919 East Hillsdale Boulevard
Foster City, California 94404 USA
+1.650.655.5616
richard_marks@playstation.sony.com

*Contributors*
Tanya Scovill
Care Michaud-Wideman
Sony Computer
Entertainment America

Enhanced reality is a new form of computer entertainment that combines live video and computer graphics to produce real-time, movie-like special effects. Because the user is directly involved, enhanced reality can be more personalized and more engaging than traditional computer entertainment (video games). In the enhanced reality demonstrations of this exhibit, participants interact with a virtual character, play with virtual butterflies, interact with virtual crawling spiders, and engage in magic duels.

Enhanced reality is targeted specifically at home computer entertainment, for use in a typical living room or family room environment. When necessary, participants use simple props to enhance the interaction process; this enables a successful user experience despite the unstructured background and widely varying lighting conditions.

The techniques used to achieve enhanced reality fall into two categories:

1. Interpretation, which consists of processing video input to extract information about the participant and the environment, such as the 3D position of special props or a model of the lighting of the scene.

2. Enhancement, which consists of modifying the video image to produce a desired effect, such as rendering synthetic objects that look real.

This work is implemented on PlayStation 2 and displayed on a standard TV set. An inexpensive (<$100) IEEE 1394 Webcam is used for video input. The interaction props are simple plastic and/or foam toys.

Participant plays with a virtual pet.

Participant interacts with a virtual character.

*117*

ENHANCEDDESK
*Juried Exhibit*

*Contact*
YOICHI SATO
Institute of Industrial Science
The University of Tokyo
4-6-1 Komaba, Meguro-ku
Tokyo 153-8505 Japan
+81.3.5452.6278
+81.3.5452.6279 fax
ysato@iis.u-tokyo.ac.jp

HIDEKI KOIKE
The University of
Electro-Communications
Tokyo, Japan

*Collaborators*
TAKAHIRO OKABE
KENJI OKA
IMARI SATO
The University of Tokyo

YASUTO NAKANISHI
TAKASHI FUJII
The University of
Electro-Communications

Experiments with tangible objects, interaction with computer simulations, electronic-media databases, and paper-based materials are common tools for wide varieties of tasks in offices and classrooms. This richness of semi-connected content leaves us with the burden of media synchronization. For example, the overhead of accessing a computer simulation mentioned in a printed book often disrupts the train of thought. A simple dictionary search on the Web while reading a book requires a series of operations that shifts our focus of attention.

This augmented-desk system novel man-machine interfaces based on direct manipulation of both real and projected objects with hands and fingers. The key technical innovations of the EnhancedDesk include fast, accurate tracking of multiple hands and fingers, interactive object registration and recognition of hand gestures, and overlay of interactive functionality.

When this augmented-desk interface system is put to practical use, it will revolutionize the way people use computers in every aspect of their daily lives. For instance, multimedia materials can be used more effectively for study. An enormous amount of information available on the Internet could be more easily combined with physical objects such as paper documents. And EnhancedDesk's intuitive and interactive management of computer applications will provide assistance to many people who would otherwise have problems using a computer.

This work is partially funded by a research grant from Intel Corporation and the Ministry of Education, Culture, Sports, Science, and Technology.

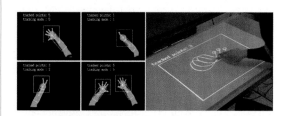

Real-time tracking of multiple hands and fingertips.

Interactive object registration and recognition.

118

EVERYWHERE DISPLAYS
*Juried Exhibit*

*Contact*
CLAUDIO PINHANEZ
IBM T.J. Watson
Research Center
P.O. Box 218
Yorktown Heights, New York 10598 USA
+1.914.945.3251
+1.914.945.4527 fax
pinhanez@us.ibm.com
www.research.ibm.com/people/p/pinhanez

PAUL CHOU
RICK KJELDSEN
ANTHONY LEVAS
IBM T.J. Watson
Research Center

Pervasive computing envisions a world where it is possible to connect anytime and anywhere to all the devices and services that are linked by the Internet. Since most data present in the Internet today are designed to be accessed through a high-resolution graphical interface, to truly pervasively compute we have to carry laptops everywhere, wear computer graphics goggles, or install monitors and displays on the surfaces of spaces and objects and furniture.

Everywhere Displays (ED) explores an alternative approach to providing a graphical interface for pervasive computing. The idea is to couple an LCD projector to a motorized rotating mirror and a computer graphics system that can correct the distortion caused by oblique projection. As the mirror moves, different surfaces become available for displays. The display also uses computer-vision techniques to detect user hand interaction (such as pointing and clicking) with the projected image.

The goal is to develop a projection-based system that creates displays everywhere in an environment by transforming surfaces into projected "touch screens." An Everywhere Displays projector can be installed on the ceiling of a space to provide a generic computer interface to users in an environment. For example, an ED projector in a store can transform pieces of white cardboard attached to shelves into interactive displays for product information. Similarly, an ED projector could be used in a home kitchen to access information, watch TV, read recipes, or simply set and control cooking time.

Everywhere displays propose a shift int he display paradigm where the display ceases to be regarded as a device to be installed in an environment or carried along by a user and becomes a service provided by a space. But like any paradigm shift, ED projectors not only solve a problem but also create a new set of applications. For instance, if information about the location and identity of objects in an environment is known, an ED projector can be used as a device to augment reality, without goggles! It can lead visitors to their destinations in a building by projecting arrows on the floor.

When visitors enter the space, they encounter an incomplete M&M picture and an invitation to interact projected beside the picture. When they touch the projected area to select an M&M color, the projector redirects its projection to point to the bin that contains M&Ms of that color. Visitors go to the bin indicated by the projector, pick up some M&Ms from the bin, and come back to the picture area. The projector points to the precise location where the M&M "pixels" should be placed. As visitors go through the exhibit, the picture emeres from their combined individual work.

A prototype of the Everywhere Displays projector.

An M&M is put in place with the help of the Everywhere Displays projector.

119

## Excerpts from Experiments in the Future of Reading
*Juried Exhibit*

*Contact*
Dale MacDonald
RED - Xerox PARC
3333 Coyote Hill Road
Palo Alto, California 94304 USA
+1.650.812.4914
+1.650.812.4890 fax
macdonal@parc.xerox.com

*RED is:*
Maribeth Back
Anne Balsamo
Mark Chow
Rich Gold
Steve Harrison
Dale MacDonald
Scott Minneman
with assistance from
Jonathan Cohen
Terry Murphy, Folio
Matt Gorbet

XFR: Experiments in the Future of Reading is a museum installation that explores how reading might change in the near future. Featuring 11 interactive exhibits, XFR was designed by researchers in the RED (Research on Experimental Documents) group at Xerox PARC to give museum visitors an opportunity to explore a range of new reading devices.

Reading is intrinsic to how we share knowledge; entertain ourselves; and manage social, political, economic, and educational systems. Reading is also greatly influenced by technologies of various sorts: writing, authoring, presentation, publication, and distribution. XFR presents several speculations on how reading might change with the development of new media and digital technologies.

The physical form of the reading device affects our interpretation of what we read, as does the mode of interactivity. Digital technologies enable design of complex and novel reading technologies, as well as creation of new textual forms and genres. While many people envision a future dominated by hand-held reading devices, RED speculates that the future will include a wide variety of reading technologies.

For SIGGRAPH 2001 Emerging Technologies, RED exhibits three of the 11 XFR experiments:

### Listen Reader
The Listen Reader preserves the tactile pleasure of reading a paper-based book. In this case, books are augmented with digital soundtracks that are activated by the (sensed) position of the reader's hands on a page. Readers conduct the book's soundtrack with hand gestures.

### Speeder Reader
Speed reading combined with speed racing. Using a new speed-reading protocol that presents text one word at a time, this exhibit allows visitors to modulate the speed of presentation. Children are especially excited by the idea of driving through a text. For adults, the familiar driving interface offers readers an intuitive interaction with an unusual mode of text presentation.

### Tilty Tables
Reading is generally thought of as low-energy, static, solitary, and contemplative, engaging the mind more than the body. In designing Tilty Tables, RED wanted visitors to think about how the body can be engaged in the act of reading, especially when reading large documents.

Children reading "The Peace Table."

Speed reading "Podkayne's World."

Reading and listening to "Frank Was A Monster Who Wanted To Dance."

# FEELEX
*Juried Exhibit*

*Contact*
Hiroo Iwata
Institute of Engineering
Mechanics and Systems
University of Tsukuba
Tsukuba 305-8573 Japan
+81.298.53.5362
+81.298.50-3681
iwata@kz.tsukuba.ac.jp

Ryo Kawamura
Fumitaka Nakaizumi
Hiroaki Yanoi

Khoji Abe
University of Tsukuba

In developing and demonstrating haptic interfaces that generate skin and muscle sensation, including sense of touch, weight, and rigidity, we have found that some of them do not convey the presence of virtual objects through haptic sensation. There are two reasons for this phenomenon:

1. Our haptic interfaces allow users to touch virtual objects at a single point or a group of points. This hardware configuration cannot create realistic sensations comparable to hand manipulation in the real world.

2. Visual images are combined with haptic interfaces using conventional CRT or projection screens, so users have to integrate inputs from two different displays.

We designed a new haptic-visual display to overcome these limitations. The device is composed of a flexible screen, an array of actuators, and a projector. The flexible screen is deformed by the actuators to simulate shapes of virtual objects. Images of the virtual objects are projected on the surface of the flexible screen. This configuration enables users to touch the images directly with their bare hands. The actuators are equipped with force sensors to measure force applied by users. The virutal object's hardness is determined by the relationship between the measured force and the position of the actuators.

The newest FEELEX has a high-resolution haptic surface. The distance between the actuator rods is 8 mm. This resolution enables users to hit at least one actuator when they touch any position on the screen. The screen size (50 mm X 50 mm) allows users to touch the surface with three fingers. In order to realize 8 mm resolution, a piston-crank mechanism is employed for the linear actuator.

Since the motor is much larger than 8 mm, the motor should be placed at an offset position from the rod. A piston-crank mechanism can easily achieve this offset position. The flexible screen is made of rubber sponge supported by 23 rods. The rods push the rubber sponge to increase the hardness of virtual objects. This mechanism has an advantage in presentation of soft objects. The user feels a hard object submerged in a soft object. The actuators have force sensors that detect applied force from the user. If the user pushes the hard object, it moves according to the pressure. The device can be applied to a palpation simulator, a haptic touch screen, or virtual clay.

intron.kz.tsukuba.ac.jp

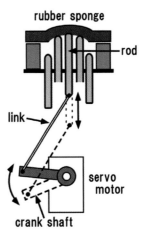

Mechanical configuration of an actuator

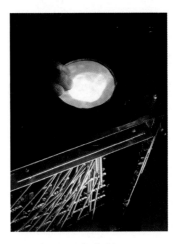

Overall view of the system

Projected image on the flexible screen

121

## I-BALL: INTERACTIVE INFORMATION DISPLAY LIKE A CRYSTAL BALL
*Juried Exhibit*

*Contact*
HIROMI IKEDA
The University of Tokyo
i-ball@hc.t.u-tokyo.ac.jp
www.hc.t.u-toyko.ac.jp/i-ball

*Collaborators*
TAKESHI NAEMURA
HIROSHI HARASHIMA
JUN ISHIKAWA

*Affiliations*
TAKESHI NAEMURA
Stanford University

HIROSHI HARASHIMA
The University of Tokyo

JUN ISHIKAWA
Isikawa Optics &
Arts Corporation

This object-oriented spatial display, i-ball (interactive/information ball), is spherical and transparent, so it looks like a crystal ball and is very attractive and expressive. The system is designed to capture and process images of observers' behavior, which enables not only interactive displays, but also image communication through the transparent ball.

### CHARACTERISTICS
- The images displayed within the transparent ball are slightly distorted by the optical system. This distortion provides the illusion of depth sensation, though it is essentially a 2D display system.

- By capturing viewer behavior, the system can display images interactively.

- When users rotate the ball, the system can display objects for any point of view.

### INTERACTIVE APPLICATION
As the observer's hand moves, a 3D animation is rendered, and the ball is rotated appropriately. For example:

- If you wave your hand to a robot in the ball, he waves back to you.

- If you suddenly stretch your hand toward the ball as if you are punching it, the robot break into pieces.

- If you cover the ball with your hands, the robot objects and shakes his head, and the ball rotates right and left.

- If your hand moves from right to left, the ball rotates and the robot jumps to the surface of the ball.

### VIDEO CONFERENCING APPLICATION
Since i-ball is capable of displaying real images as well as CG, various interactions can be designed for this system. For example, i-ball can be utilized as a video conferencing application. The mirror in the ball does double duty as a reflector for both displaying objects and capturing viewer's behavior, so the optical system can easily recognize gaze awareness. Furthermore, distant particpants can control the direction of the ball, so it appears as if they are turning their heads during the communication.

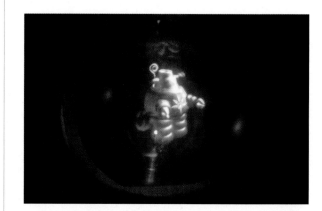

Let's interact with the robot inside the transparent ball.

The i-ball system.

## IllusionHole
*Juried Exhibit*

*Contact*
Yoshifumi Kitamura
Human Interface Engineering
Laboratory
Osaka University
2-1 Yamadaoka, Suita
Osaka 565-0871 Japan
+81.6.6879.7752
kitamura@eie.eng.osaka-u.ac.jp

*Collaborators*
Takashige Konishi
Toppan Printing Co., Ltd.

Fumio Kishino
Toshihiro Masaki
Sumihiko Yamamoto
Osaka University

This interactive display system allows three or more moving observers to simultaneously observe stereoscopic image pairs from their own viewpoints. With a simple configuration, it provides intelligible 3D stereoscopic images free of flicker and distortion. The system consists of a normal display and a display mask, which has a hole in its center. The system tracks the head positions of all the users and generates distortion-free images for each eye of each user. Because the system controls the position of the image-drawing area for each user according to the corresponding user's viewpoint, each user can observe the stereoscopic image pairs shown in an individual area of the display system with shutter glasses.

IllusionHole is useful for applications in which several people work together to perform tasks or enjoy entertainment with a multiplier effect. A complicated set of data that is difficult for a single user to understand becomes a seed of discovery, training, teaching, conferencing, and communicating if it is shared by several people.

Feasible applications include, but are not limited to, engineering or industrial design and evaluation, scientific visualization, medical diagnosis and training, medical analysis, surgery planning, and consumer devices such as 3D TV or games. A paper about IllusionHole is presented in SIGGRAPH 2001 Papers: Interactive Stereoscopic Display for Three or More Users Yoshifumi Kitamura, Takashige Konishi, Sumihiko Yamamoto, and Fumio Kishino.

www-human.eie.eng.osaka-u.ac.jp/IllusionHole

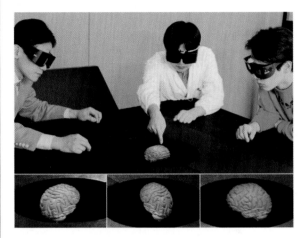

IllusionHole shared by four users. The fourth user's view of human brain analysis. Three brain images at lower column show the views of users standing at left, center, and right, respectively.

123

*Contact*
TOBIAS SKOG
PLAY-Interactive Institute
Box 620
405 30, Göteborg Sweden
+46.31.7735541
+46.31.7735530 fax
tobias.skog@interactiveinstitute.se
www.playresearch.com

*Collaborators*
LARS ERIK HOLMQUIST
LARS HALLNÄS
JOHAN REDSTRÖM

Computers are becoming ubiquitous, but traditional computer graphic displays do not lend themselves well to integration with everyday environments. The computer graphics of the future will need to blend in with the environment, yet at the same time provide opportunities for reflection and stimulation, much like traditional art. This is the motivation behind Informative Art.

Informative Art borrows from the "language" of traditional art (in particular non-figurative painting) to create computer graphic displays that convey some kind of dynamic information. For example, a wall-mounted screen showing geometrical figures reminiscent of the style of the painter Piet Mondrian might in fact be an information display that shows the amount of unread email for each employee in a workplace. In this project, we use several different examples of informative art pieces to show dynamic information from a variety of interrelated sources.

*Reference*
Redström, J., Skog, T., & Hallnäs, L (2000). Informative art: Using amplified artworks as information displays. In: *Proceedings of Designing Augmented Reality Environments* (DARE) 2000, ACM Press.

Dynamic Mondrian projected on a piece of hanging cloth.

Three pieces of informative art.

*124*

# An Interface for Touching the Interface
*Juried Exhibit*

*Contact*
Takuya Nojima
Tachi Laboratory
MEIP Faculty of Engineering
The University of Tokyo
7-3-1 Hong, Bunkyo-ku
Tokyo 113-8656 Japan
+81.3.5841.6917
+81.3.5841.8601 fax
tnojima@star.t.u-tokyo.ac.jp

*Collaborators*
Takuya Nojima
Masahiko Inami
Yoichiro Kawabuchi
Taro Maeda
Kunihiko Mabuchi
Susumu Tachi

The word "haptization" means making it possible to touch. For example, haptic display devices allow users to touch computer-generated images. This process is often called haptization of information. Previous work on haptization is primarily focused on haptization of volume data produced by a CT scanner, a physical simulator, or a similar device. However, these systems haptize static or simulated information and are not effective in a real environment that changes dynamically.

Smart-Tool is a new haptization technology that combines real-time sensing devices with a haptic display. The sensor receives stimuli that change dynamically in a real environment and displays the information to the user through haptic sensation. Therefore, Smart-Tool makes it possible to touch the dynamic information of real environments in real time.

Conventional tools and sensors typically display sensor information visually, requiring the user to constantly monitor the display, interpret information, and take action based on these interpretations, which can be very inaccurate, especially in stressful situations. Redundancy through audio can improve perception, but is still often insufficient because it still relies on the interpretation process. Smart-Tool can assist by sensing the real environment and displaying haptic information. This force is not only a display method that alleviates interpretation of tactile information, but also supports the action of the user.

A quintessential application of this system is surgery. Surgeons use many kinds of tools to incise body tissue, like scalpels, scissors, etc. If the surgeon uses a scalpel enhanced with Smart-Tool technology, the real-time sensor on the scalpel can sense what kind of tissue the edge of the scalpel is touching and inform the user through haptic sensation. When the scalpel is in the proximity of vital tissues such as arteries or a pulsing heart, the Smart-Tool protects them from damage by sensing them and generating a repulsive force that can be naturally interpreted by a surgeon as virtually hard.

At SIGGRAPH 2001, the Smart-Tool system touches the interface between two liquids, which is usually impossible to feel. With Smart-Tool technology, the haptic sensation of the liquid interface is obtained from the tool's sensor and transmitted to the user directly in real time, providing an intuitive way to both analyze and act upon the interface.

Touching the interface.

Marbling.

Marbling II.

125

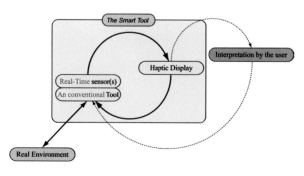

Information flow.

## Just Follow Me: A VR-Based Motion Training System

*Juried Exhibit*

*Contact*
Ungyeon Yang
Virtual Reality Laboratory
Department of Computer Science
and Engineering
Pohang University of Science and
Technology
1 San Hyoja-dong
Pohang 790-784 South Korea
+82.54.279.5664
+82.54.279.5699 fax
uyyang@postech.ac.kr

Euijae Ahn
Seongmin Baek
Gerard Jounghyun Kim
Pohang University of Science
and Technology

Training has been considered one of the most natural application areas of virtual reality (VR). This project demonstrates VR's utility for learning limb-motion profiles required in sports, dance, and the arts (for example, a golf swing, martial arts, calligraphy, etc.) The central concept, called Just Follow Me (JFM), is based on an intuitive interaction method called the "ghost" metaphor (Figure 1). Through the Ghost metaphor, the motion of the trainer is visualized in real time as a ghost (initially superimposed on the trainee) moving out of one's body. The trainee, who sees the motion from different viewpoints, is to "follow" the ghostly master as close as (or as fast as) possible.

The training process can be facilitated by showing other guidance cues (for example, the master's trail, annotations, etc.) and performance feedback (for example, indications of how well the trainee is following), and by adjusting the learning requirements (for example, relaxation of accuracy goals, restricting the motion's degrees of freedom). Evaluation results showed that JFM produced training and transfer effects as good as, and in certain situations better than, the real one. Thus when the system is reinforced and augmented with presence cues, more robust tracking and lighter head-mounted displays, and rich informative graphics and images, VR-based training methods will be attractive alternatives to the traditional "trainer-in-residence" or video-based motor-skill learning method.

The JFM system can be configured in many different ways. For the desktop/arcade version (Figure 2), it is difficult to effectively present the first-person viewpoint. Consequently, the ghost has been modified to what are called "sliding" ghosts; instead of showing continuous movement, discrete freezeframes of next imminent postures from fixed viewpoints (front, back, side) flow toward the dancing character to guide the motion (Figure 3). Another possibility is the "first-person viewpoint" version with the head-mounted display and head tracking, in which the original concept of the Ghost is used (Figure 4). The system uses four cameras mounted on the ceiling to track five highly reflective markers (worn on users' wrists, ankles, and belly). The tracked motion is compared to the reference motion for both online and offline evaluation. As trainees try to follow and imitate the character's dance on the screen, they get a feel for how well they are following the evaluations and corresponding special effects at the key posture frames, and they receive a final score at the end.

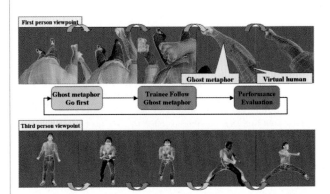

## Meditation Chamber
### *Chair's Prerogative Exhibit*

*Contact*
Diane Gromala
Georgia Institute of Technology
Graphics, Visualization, and
Usability Center
diane.gromala@lcc.gatech.edu

*Supervisors*
Larry Hodges
Diane Gromala
Chris Shaw
Jay Bolter

*Visual Design*
Mirtha Ferrer
A. Fleming Seay
Sue Rinker

*Audio*
Eli Wendkos

*Production*
A. Fleming Seay
Sue Rinker
Eli Wendkos
Robert Todd
Colin Henderson
Chris Campbell

Alternative therapeutic techniques related to relaxation and management of stress are increasingly employed to augment traditional treatment by drug-based, medical therapies. A vast body of results presented in the literature shows that these alternative treatments have great promise and warrant continued use and study. Drug-resistant epilepsy, hypertension, asthma, anxiety disorders, depression, and chronic pain are only a handful of the medical problems that have been successfully addressed through relaxation and meditation techniques.

Though the effects are not fully understood, these relaxation techniques are believed to stimulate production of certain important hormones. It has been demonstrated that experienced practitioners of transcendental meditation create in themselves the same endorphin-release reaction generated by physical exertion in experienced runners, often referred to as the "runner's high." It has also been shown that melatonin, thought to be important in health maintenance and prevention of diseases such as breast and prostate cancer, is found in significantly higher levels in regular meditators.

One roadblock to effective relaxation therapies is the consistency and quality of the experience. Not all formally trained physicians are trained to administer alternative treatments. Also, many people have difficulty with visual imagery and are not good candidates for meditation exercises.

The goal of this research is to design and build an immersive virtual environment that uses visual, audio, and tactile cues to create, guide, and maintain a user's guided relaxation and meditation experience. The virtual environment's design is based on current clinical best-practice techniques used for training and support of clients through a meditation or guided relaxation experience, such as: biofeedback electromyography, progressive muscle relaxation, guided meditation, and mindfulness meditation. We have explored various kinds of visual and audio experiences to evaluate which are most effective in promoting these relaxation techniques.

There are several possible advantages of using a virtual environment to support meditation and guided relaxation. Patients without good imaging skills can benefit from the use of meditation. Clinicians with minimal training in meditation and guided imagery are able to provide a consistent, high-quality relaxation and meditation experience for their clients. And, by providing specific meditation environments, we can guarantee that participants in future studies of the usefulness of meditation and relaxation techniques all receive identical training and treatment.

The collaborators thank the Graphics, Visualization, and Usability Center; the School of Literature, Communication, and Culture; and the College of Computing at the Georgia Institute of Technology for their support of this project.

Lotus position.

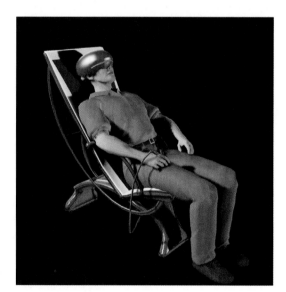

Installation concept.

## MICRO ARCHIVING:
### VIRTUAL ENVIRONMENTS FOR MICRO-PRESENCE WITH
### IMAGE-BASED MODEL ACQUISITION
*Juried Exhibit*

*Contact*
TATSUYA SAITO
Keio University
5322 Endo Fujisawa
Kanagawa 252-8520 Japan
+81.466.47.5000.53665
tatsu@wem.sfc.keio.ac.jp

*Collaborators*
TATSUYA SAITO
SATOSHI KURIHARA
SCOTT S. FISHER
KENJI KOHIYAMA
YUTA NAKAYAMA

This experience allows visitors to visualize and interact with microscopic structures that cannot be seen with the naked eye, but that commonly exist in our everyday surroundings. Through a combination of Micro Archiving and virtual reality technology, it delivers an immersive virtual environment in which participants observe these microscopic structures in a private or collaborative workspace.

Micro-Presence is our term for the ability to experience these hidden realities. There are many terms that describe experiences of presence other than the real world, in which we feel something through our sensory organs directly. For example, Tele-Presence describes the technology that enables people to feel as if they are actually present in a different place or time. Micro-Presence is an environment in which participants feel as if they are tiny and can observe and interact naturally with things in the microcosmic world.

With Micro Archiving technology, it is possible to create high-definition virtual 3D models that are suitable for academic research in fields such as biology and zoology that require real observation of actual things. For educational use, this technology creates a high-definition multimedia space in which visitors can freely participate and interact with the exhibit.

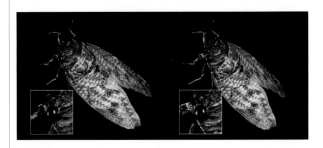

128

## MOBILE AUGMENTED REALITY SYSTEMS
*Juried Exhibit*

*Contact*
STEVEN FEINER
Columbia University
Department of
Computer Science
500 West 120th Street,
450 CS Building
New York, New York 10027
USA
+1.212.939.7083
+1.212.666.0140 fax
feiner@cs.columbia.edu

*Collaborators*
BLAINE BELL
ELIAS GAGAS
SINEM GUVEN
DREXEL HALLAWAY
TOBIAS HOELLERER
SIMON LOK
NAVDEEP TINNA
RYUJI YAMAMOTO
Columbia University

SIMON JULIER
YOHAN BAILLOT
DENNIS BROWN
MARCO LANZAGORTA
Naval Research Laboratory

ANDREAS BUTZ
eyeled GmbH

ERIC FOXLIN
MIKE HARRINGTON
LEONID NAIMARK
DEAN WORMELL
InterSense Inc.

Augmented reality refers to using computers to overlay virtual information on the real world. Mobile Augmented Reality Systems (MARS) uses see-through head-worn displays with backpack-based computers developed by Columbia University and the Naval Research Laboratory, tracking technology developed by InterSense, and an infrared transmitter-based ubiquitous information infrastructure from eyeled GmbH. Our system creates a pervasive 3D information space that documents Emerging Technologies. It demonstrates some of the user interface techniques that we are developing to present information for MARS, including systems that adapt as the user moves between regions with high-precision six-degree-of-freedom tracking, orientation tracking and coarse position tracking, and orientation tracking alone.

As attendees wearing our systems walk around and near our installation, they are tracked by a six-degree-of-freedom tracker. The information they view is situated relative to the 3D coordinate system of the installation area. For example, an installation may be surrounded by virtual representations of associated material. In other parts of the installation area, tracking is accomplished through a combination of inertial head-and-body orientation trackers and a coarse position tracker based on a constellation of infrared transmitters. In those areas, information is situated relative to the 3D coordinate system of the user's body but is sensitive to the user's coarse position. As users move between areas of the installation area where different tracking technologies are in effect, the user interface adapts to use the best one available. Our infrared transmitters will also allow attendees to explore parts of the same information space with their own hand-held devices.

The MARS user interfaces embody three techniques that we are exploring to develop effective augmented-reality user interfaces: information filtering, user interface component design, and view management. Information filtering helps select the most relevant information to present, based on data about the user, the tasks being performed, and the surrounding environment, including the user's location. User interface component design determines the format in which this information should be conveyed, based on the available display resources and tracking accuracy. For example, the absence of high-accuracy position tracking would favor body- or screen-stabilized components over world-stabilized ones that would need to be registered with the physical objects to which they refer. View management attempts to ensure that the virtual objects that are selected for display are arranged appropriately with regard to their projections on the view plane. For example, virtual objects that are not constrained to occupy a specific position in the 3D world should be arranged so they do not obstruct the view of other physical or virtual objects in the scene that are more important.

We believe that user interface techniques of this sort will play a key role in the MARS devices that people will begin to use on an every-day basis over the coming decade.

*Acknowledgments*
MARS research at Columbia University is funded in part by ONR, NSF, and gifts from IBM, Intel, Microsoft, and Mitsubishi. MARS research at NRL is funded in part by ONR.

www.cs.columbia.edu/graphics/projects/siggraph2001-etech/
www.cs.columbia.edu/graphics/projects/mars
ait.nrl.navy.mil/vrlab/projects/BARS/BARS.html
www.eyeled.de
www.isense.com

View management in a collaborative MARS user interface for exploring a virtual campus model imaged through one user's head-worn display. Building labels and documentation surrounding a second user are dynamically arranged to avoid obscuring other buildings and the second user's head.

Mobile augmented reality system with stereo see-through head-worn display. Inset shows user's view after information filtering for route-finding task.

## ORIGAMI DESK
*Chair's Prerogative Exhibit*

With Origami Desk, users learn to fold paper into beautiful shapes. It improves on the inscrutable origami diagrams we all know and love by showing videos that demonstrate what the hands should do, projecting lines onto the paper to indicate where the folds should be, and monitoring the paper folding to give budding origami artists feedback if their folding should go awry.

Origami Desk utilizes projection, electric field sensing, and low-cost radio-frequency identification tags to enable computer users to break free from the CRT-keyboard-mouse interaction paradigm. These technologies allow interactions in the user's space, eliminating the need for metaphoric mapping between the digital world and the physical world. Electric field sensing detects where a user's hands are by measuring capacitance over the work surface. Coupled with the visual interface, this sensor allows dynamic mapping of digital buttons and handles.

Origami Desk breaks new ground in the RF-tagging domain by measuring changes in the resonant frequencies of electromagnetic foil patterns embedded in the origami paper. The coils are coupled to create certain shifts in frequency as the origami paper is folded. These readings in turn allow the computer to infer and provide feedback on whether the user has properly completed the folding step. The projected workspace is delineated into three types of spaces that help choreograph the user's actions and prevent occlusion or inadvertent triggering of commands: interaction areas, display areas, and work areas.

Origami Desk is a powerful embodiment of how real-world graphics, interaction design, and innovative sensing technologies can be pragmatically integrated to create interactive environments centered around the active human user.

*Contact*
WENDY JU
MIT Media Lab
Massachusetts Institute of Technology
20 Ames Street
E15-468b
Cambridge, Massachusetts 02139
USA
+1.617.253.9488
wendyju@media.mit.edu

*Collaborators*
Origami Desk is a joint project between House_n and the Media Lab at MIT.

*Exhibit design*
LEONARDO BONANNI

*RF tag engineering*
RICHARD FLETCHER

*Graphical interface design*
REBECCA HURWITZ
TILKE JUDD
JENN YOON

*Interaction design*
WENDY JU

*Electrical field-sensing engineering*
REHMI POST

*RF engineering*
MATT REYNOLDS

*Our thanks to Neil Gershenfeld, Michael Hawley, and Kent Larson for making this collaboration possible.*

References

Cooperstock, J.R., Fels, S., Buxton, W., & Smith, K. (1997). Reactive environments. *Communications of the ACM*, 40, (9), 65-73.

Omojola, O., Post, E.R., Hancher, M.D., Maguire, Y., Pappu, R., Schoner, B., Russ, P.R., Fletcher, R. & Gershenfeld, N. (2000). An installation of interactive furniture. *IBM systems journal*, 39, 3/4 (Fall 200), 861-879.

Riley, T. (1999). *The un-private house*. Henry N. Abrams, NY.

Underkoffler, J., Ullmer, B., Ishii, H. (1999). Emancipated pixels: Real-world graphics in the luminous room. *Proceedings of SIGGRAPH 99*, ACM Press, 385-392.

Want, R., Fishkin, P., Gujar, A., & Harrison, B. (1999). Bridging physical and virtual worlds with electronic tags. *Proceedings of CHI '99*, ACM Press, 370-377.

Wellner, P. (1993). Interacting with paper on the DigitalDesk. *Communications of the ACM*. 40, (7), 87-96.

*130*

*Contact*
Bryan Loyall
Zoesis Studios
246 Walnut Street, Suite 301
Newton, Massachusetts
02460 USA
+1.617.969.5700
+1.617.969.4472 fax
bryan@zoesis.com

*Collaborators*
Stanton Wood
G. Zachariah White
Peter Weyhrauch
Oliver Strimpel
Mike Shapiro
Liz Schaefer
Paolo Piselli
W. Scott Neal Reilly
Mary McCann
Bryan Loyall
Mark Leone
Russell Lees
Julie Carter
Evan Bernstein
Joseph Bates
Zoesis Studios

OttoAndIris.com is a playful theme park filled with fun activities in a 3D world. The core elements of the park are two interactive characters, Otto and Iris. These characters are constructed using animation, believable agent, and interactive drama technology developed by Zoesis Studios, a spin-off from Carnegie Mellon University's Oz project, which has focused on these research areas since 1987.

Many commentators have speculated about combining Silicon Valley and Hollywood. We believe the most powerful form of this combination will be true interactive stories, where viewers can enter into a world, be substantially free to do whatever they want, and still experience *the* powerful dramatic story that the author intended. We believe this new art form will be extremely popular and will have a full range of forms, from mass market entertainment to conceptual art.

The two core elements of this new art form are interactive characters that seem truly real and story technology that can subtly guide the experience to fulfill the author's intent. OttoAndIris.com was designed to advance the first of these: the art and technology of interactive characters. In the course of its development, advances were also made in interactive story guidance and interactive music.

Participants enter the world using the display and mouse. The display shows a first-person view of the world from the user's current location, and the mouse moves the person's virtual hand in the 3D world. Users also hear music, sound effects, and character voices. As they explore OttoAndIris.com, they can play tag with Otto and Iris, help Otto sing some operas, create costumes with Iris, or participate in several other activities with the characters.

Each character responds immediately to the user's virtual hand, the user beyond the screen, and the other character. This response is appropriate for the character's current situation, limited perception, resource-bounded reasoning, current goals, and current emotions. Every moment-to-moment reaction and self-motivated action is also specific to the personality and individuality of the character as created by their authors.

In the Magic Snowball scene of OttoAndIris.com, a drama management system provides subtle guidance to create a dramatic arc of intensity, while at the same time maximizing how much of Otto's personality is seen by the user during the interaction. An interactive music system in this scene adjusts the music according to the emotions of the characters and position in the dramatic arc.

OttoAndIris.com is deliverable over the Web to machines that were purchased during Christmas 1997 or later. It requires no special software, plugins, or high-speed connections. Using normal modems and Web browsers, participants can simply go to the OttoAndIris.com URL, and start to play.

Helping Otto sing an opera.

131

Playing tag with with Otto and Iris.

## PIRATES!
*Chair's Prerogative Exhibit*

*Contact*
PETER LJUNGSTRAND
PLAY-Interactive Institute
Box 620
40530 Göteborg, Sweden
+46.31.7735543
+46.31.7735330 fax
peter.ljungstrand@
interactiveinstitute.se
www.playresearch.com

*Collaborators*
STAFFAN BJÖRK
JENNICA FALK
REBECCA HANSSON
LARS ERIK HOLMQUIST
PLAY-Interactive Institute

JUSSI HOLOPAINEN
TIMO KOSKINEN
JOUKA MATTILA
EERO RÄSÄNEN
TIMO TOIVONEN
Nokia Research Center

Pirates! is a mobile, multi-user, location-aware computer game that runs on PDAs and is experienced in physical space. The game world is a fantasy archipelago where each player takes the role of a pirate captain. Game objectives include solving missions, making landfall on islands, searching for treasures, trading commodities, and battling other players at sea.

The game is played with proximity-sensing handheld devices that take advantage of, and rely upon, players' mobility as an intrinsic part of the game structure. Each handheld device has a custom short-range radio beacon that identifies when players encounter each other in the physical world. A corresponding encounter is triggered in the virtual world, which enables player-to-player game activities such as battles. Radio beacons distributed throughout the gaming area represent islands that can be explored when approached. Thus walking between different locations in the room becomes equivalent to sailing between islands in the virtual world.

The handheld devices function as thin clients and use a wireless network to connect to a central game server. The server controls the overall game mechanics, such as missions and inventories, and determines the result of the players' actions through the user interface. This allows for dynamic update of the user interface, graphics, sounds, and game rules. The game server also provides an overall game status that is presented on a large public display.

Pirates! was designed to be played in a social setting, encouraging face-to-face interaction between players and non-players alike, and promoting movement and exploration within a defined physical space. Unlike most computer games, playing Pirates! depends just as much on social interaction with people in the real world as on the computer-mediated game play. Rather than continuously gazing at the screen, players have to navigate a social environment to move within the virtual environment and exchange information with other players, or even people not playing the game, to win the game.

On-screen graphics showing Phoenix birds attacking a player at an island.

Two Pirates! players closely engaged in battle.

132

*Contact*
CHRISTA SOMMERER
ATR Media Integration and
Communications Research Lab
2-2 Hikari-dai Seika-cho,
Soraku-gun
Kyoto 619-0288 Japan
+81.774.95.1426
+81.774.95.1408 fax
christa@mic.atr.co.jp

LAURENT MIGNONNEAU
ROBERTO LOPEZ-GULLIVER
ATR Media Integration and
Communications Research Lab

*Interface Design Support*
STEPHEN JONES

Riding the Net presents a novel approach to browsing the Internet in a more intuitive, playful, and entertaining fashion. While two users talk and communicate with each other, keywords of their communication are picked up by the system's speech-recognition engine. These keywords are then used to search and download corresponding images from the Internet. When users, for example, speak about "houses" or "flowers," different images of "houses" or "flowers" are downloaded. As there is usually a vast amount of images available for each keyword, users see new image icons constantly retrieved from the Internet. All images are then collectively displayed in 3D in the system's interactive window and streamed from the respective view of each user. As images come from either the left or right side of the screen, they all stream toward each other before they leave the screen and are replaced by new images derived from new keywords spoken by the two users. The entire image scenario on the window surface constantly changes, since it is a direct interpretation of the users' dialogue and communication with each other.

Both users can also touch the image icons on the screen: this halts the images temporarily so users can look at specific image icons in more detail. When they do this, the exact URLs for these specific image icons can be downloaded onto a separate computer screen, so users can find out where the images came from and what they refer to.

Riding the Net provides an entertaining and playful way to browse the Internet, and users become intensively engaged in the vast amount of visual information available from and presented by the system. Users can control the content of what they are watching through their own decisions, dialogue, and interaction.

*Technical Description*
- Three Pentium III PCs including NVIDIA GeForce2 high-speed graphic cards
- One Internet 100/10baseT hub
- One LCD projection unit: high-resolution LCD projector with true 1280 x 1024 resolution
- One window-detection frame, including IR sensors
- One window-detection interface
- One space construction (approx. 3 x 3 meters), including window glass surface and two chairs
- One graphic software system
- One interface software system
- One speech-recognition and image-retrieval software system

Riding the Net
Christa Sommerer, Laurent Mignonneau, and Roberto Lopez-Gulliver Interactive Web-based image browser developed at ATR MIC Labs. Interface design support: Stephen Jones.

*133*

## RobotPHONE:
## RUI for Interpersonal Communication
*Juried Exhibit*

*Contact*
Dairoku Sekiguchi
Department of Information
Physics and Computing
Graduate School of Information
Science and Technology
The University of Tokyo
7-3-1 Hongo, Bunkyo-ku
Tokyo 113-0033 Japan
+81.3.5841.6917
+81.3.5841.8601 fax
info@robotphone.org

*Collaborators*
Masahiko Inami
Naoki Kawakami
Taro Maeda
Yasuyuki Yanagida
Susumu Tachi

For a long time, robots have been imagined as industrial machines that perform work that humans want to avoid. However, considering the characteristics of their physical embodiment, robots can also be recognized as interfaces for human beings. Using a robot as an interface between the real world and the information world can be referred to as a robotic user interface (RUI). Other good examples include: intelligent robots that act as artificial-intelligence agents and haptic-feedback robot arms used in VR systems.

RobotPHONE is an RUI system for interpersonal exchange that uses robots as shape-sharing agents for physical communication. The shape and motion of remote shape-sharing devices are always synchronized by a symmetric bilateral control method. Robot movements, such as modification of posture or the input of motion, are reflected to the remote end in real time. RobotPHONE users can communicate and interact with each other by exchanging the shape and motion of the robot.

An initial prototype based on the RobotPHONE concept has two snake-like robots for a shape-sharing device. Each snake-like robot has six parallel axes, which form a right angle with the long side of the snake's body. Therefore, range of body movement is limited to the 2D plane, but the body itself represents a shape that can be easily modified by hand.

To make the system more user-friendly for everyone, a second RobotPHONE system that looks like a teddy bear was integrated with a voice-communication system. When users communicate with this system, the teddy bear acts as a physical avatar, so it was very important to give the teddy bear-like robot a shape and a system of degrees of freedom that are very similar to human characteristics. Since users can treat the teddy bear-like robot just like an ordinary teddy bear, this system is very easy to use. If users move the teddy bear's head, hands, or legs, the movements are transmitted to the opposite side. Just as the teddy bear placed in front of the user is an input device, it is also a display device that displays the status of the remote robot. In other words, while each teddy bear acts as an avatar of the user who sits in front of it, it also seamlessly acts as an avatar of the user at the remote side. A mother giving her daughter a stuffed doll to keep her company at night is a form of communication aided by a physical entity. RobotPHONE allows this kind of remote communication not by attempting to transmit users but rather a virtual substitute on their behalf.

134

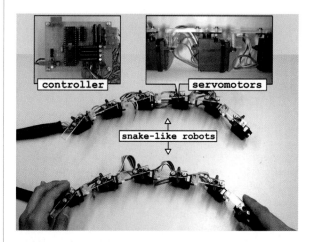

Snake-like robots and controller.

Teddy bear-like robots.

Movements of shape-sharing devices.

*Contact*
HONG Z. TAN
Purdue University
1285 Electrical Engineering
Building
West Lafayette, Indiana
47907-1285 USA
+1.765.494.6416
+1.765.494.6951 fax
hongtan@purdue.edu

*Collaborators*
DAVID S. EBERT
XIAODONG LI
LYNNE A. SLIVOVSKY
NIKOLAI SVAKHINE
ANURADHA VAIDYANATHAN
Purdue University

ALEX P. PENTLAND
Massachusetts Institute
of Technology

STEVE ANDERSON
Electronic Arts, Inc.

The sensingChair introduces a seat that feels its occupant through a layer of "artificial skin." As a new input device, it opens up new opportunities for human-computer interactions. In an automobile, for example, a sensingChair can detect whether the seat is occupied and estimate the weight and size of its occupant. This information can be used to automatically control the car's airbag deployment force. In a teleconference scenario, a sensingChair allows users to zoom in on the remote speaker by leaning forward or pan the remote camera by shifting weight to the left or right. In an office environment, a sensingChair can be a posture coach that monitors the sitting postures of its occupants and detects bad habits such as slouching. For interactive graphic displays, a sensingChair allows one to control certain aspects of a graphic display through body movements.

Pressure sensing in the sensingChair is made possible with a commercially available pressure distribution measurement system. Two sensor sheets, placed inside green protective covers, are surface-mounted on the seat and the back rest of an office chair (Figure 1). The data generated by these sheets, in the form of two 42-by-48 8-bit arrays, can be spliced and visualized as a 2D or 3D pressure-distribution map. For example, Figure 2 is a 3D display of the pressure distribution associated with the posture "sitting upright." The front and back halves of the pressure map correspond to the pressure in the seat and the back rest of the chair, respectively.

THE SENSING CHAIR IS PRESENTED IN THREE SCENARIOS:

1. Visualization of pressure map. As a person moves in the chair, the changing pressure distribution is visualized as terrain with picture, plain terrain profile, and input for a dynamic image.

2. Sitting posture classification. A PCA-based static posture classification system labels an occupant's sitting posture in real time. The output of the classification system is used to select an image that represents someone sitting in a chair with the corresponding posture.

3. Chair-driven computer games. The sensingChair is used as an intuitive interface that allows its user to engage in computer games by leaning and shifting weight in the chair. Information derived from pressure readings (for example, center of force) is used to control several PC Electronic Arts games.

Figure 1. The sensingChair.

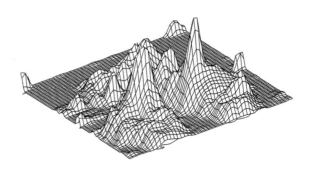

Figure 2. A 3D view of pressure distribution for "sitting upright."

*135*

# Ultra-Bright Ultra-High-Resolution Reality Center
### Chair's Prerogative Exhibit

*Contact*
Andrew Joel
BARCO Simulation Products
(a division of BARCO
Projection Systems)
3240 Town Point Drive
Kennesaw, Georgia 30144 USA
+1.770.218.3278
+1.770.218.3250 fax
andrew.joel@barco.com

*Partner*
SGI

*Collaborators*
Philippe Chiwy
De Pinxi

John Clyne
National Center for
Atmospheric Research

Darrel Fanguy
BARCO Simulation Products

Jeff Smith
NASA Ames Research Center

Vic Spitzer
University of Colorado

David Talaga
Dassault Systems

The Ultra-Bright Ultra-High-Resolution Reality Center demonstrates the latest developments in simulation-based digital light-valve projection technology. The goal is to provide an insight into the future of light-valve projection technologies and their use in high-end, multi-channel projected displays.

Since the first multi-channel, curved-screen Reality Center was installed in Reading, England, in 1994, CRT technology has been utilized almost exclusively as the projection source, primarily because several simulation-based modifications are required for high-end, multi-channel, curved-screen displays, and only CRT projectors have been able to deliver these technologies.

In contrast to the historical norm, this Reality Center installation employs extremely bright high-resolution LCD projectors modified with many of these same simulation-based optimizations that, in the past, have been applied only to CRT projection technology. This high-tech marriage obviates the need to limit ambient light and creates a Reality Center without walls, opening up multi-channel, curved-screen displays to larger audiences and greater collaboration than was previously possible.

Much of the technology demonstrated here represents prototype-stage developments from the R&D department of BARCO Simulation Products. Some of the advancements (such as True Motion Reproduction, Transport Delay Reduction, Color Gamut Matching, and Micro Lens Array options) are available commercially in a mature form. However, several other optimizations that are implemented in this Reality Center (such as the Advanced Geometry Correction and Optical Soft-Edge Matching) represent truly emerging technologies. Each is revealed in its current preliminary version, and each is still in development for eventual commercial applications.

The Advanced Geometry Correction implemented for SIGGRAPH 2001 (called "Warp6" by BARCO Simulation Products) enables electronic generation of complex distortions without any frame delay. Warp6 is implemented within each LCD projector to conform the image data so that the image appears undistorted on a curved screen. Optical Soft-Edge Blending enables this multi-channel display to have a single seamless display between channels. This edge blending is accomplished within the projector's optical path to reduce the black level in the overlap zone while maintaining a full dynamic range.

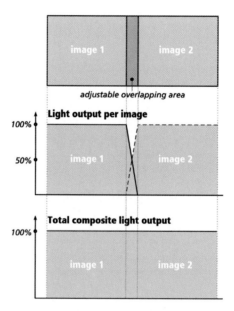

Optical Soft-Edge blending is achieved by modulation of the light output in the overlap zone so that the total light output in that zone equals the light output of the rest of the image.

WARP 6 is a non-linear image mapping processor in SXGA resolution. It is optimized to preserve fine detail in the image and reduce aliasing to an absolute minimum, using bi-cubic interpolation algorithms and a highly advanced processor board.

137

# Sketches & Applications

138

# Contents

*139*

*Chair*
DENA SLOTHOWER
Stanford University

*Program Coordinator*
VICKI CAULFIELD
Sketches & Applications
Program Coordinator

*Committee*
JONATHAN GIBBS
PDI/DreamWorks

DOUG ROBLE
SIGGRAPH 2002
Sketches &
Applications Chair

CHERYL STOCKTON
Studio Firefly
Pratt Institute

GARY TEMPLET
Sandia National
Laboratories

DARIN GRANT
Digital Domain

MARC KESSLER
University of Michigan

JACQUELYN MARTINO
Philips Research, USA

MAUREEN NAPPI
New York University

KATHY NEELY
Fashion Institute of Technology

CARY PHILLIPS
Industrial Light + Magic

GARY PIMENTEL
Evans & Sutherland

*Jury*
SIMON ALLARDICE
Lynda.com

ED ANGEL
University of
New Mexico

CHRIS BAILEY

RONEN BARZEL
Pixar Animation Studios

HISHAM BIZRI
Center for Advanced
Visual Studies

DAVID DeBRY (GRUE)
Industrial Light + Magic

RANDALL FRANK
Lawrence Livermore
National Laboratory

140

"DRAW YOUR CHAIR UP CLOSE TO THE EDGE
OF A PRECIPICE AND I'LL TELL YOU A STORY."
–F. Scott Fitzgerald

SIGGRAPH 2001 Sketches & Applications received close to 300 entries from 23 different countries, and over 130 companies, research facilities, educational institutions, and individuals. The final Sketches & Applications program featured 138 presentations, including emerging work from the technical, education, medical, arts, design, gaming, performing arts, and entertainment communities. Topics ranged from geology, character animation, and psychology to hardware acceleration, traffic patterns, puppetry, and beyond.

Technical sketches demonstrated the variety of disciplines and environments in which computer graphics research and production are developing. Artists and designers described virtual and augmented reality pieces from conception through production. These processes reveal the new and different ways we are choosing to perceive as well as the new ways we are choosing to communicate.

From the museum to the stage, the talks in the Art, Design, and Multimedia area offered fresh visions of the digital landscape and how interaction can occur within these invented spaces. Artists and designers described conception and production of virtual and augmented reality pieces, revealing the new and different ways we are choosing to perceive, while others showed us the new ways we are choosing to communicate.

Animation sketches explained the production process for everything from the cute and cuddly to the loud and scary, and revealed the inner workings of projects both large and small. As a group, the animation sketches demonstrated how confidently the artistry of the animator and the sophistication of the programmer are collaborating to present new and exciting visual experiences.

On behalf of the Sketches & Applications Committee, I would like to thank all of the contributors for giving us a glimpse behind the scenes. Numerous thanks also go to: the committee and jury for their incredibly hard work, SIGGRAPH 2002 committee members Simon Allardice and Doug Roble for pitching in, Lynn Pocock for her support, Tom Appoloni and Scott Senften for letting me follow them around and pick their brains, Vicki Caulfield and Carrie Ewert for making it a breeze to get everything together, and my colleagues in Freshman and Sophmore Programs at Stanford University for their patience and their willingness to give me the time to work on the Sketches & Applications program.

*Dena Slothower*
*SIGGRAPH 2001 Sketches & Applications Chair*
*Stanford University*

141

# "2001: An MR-Space Odyssey:" Applying Mixed-Reality Technology to VFX in Filmmaking

*Contact*
Toshikazu Ohshima
Mixed Reality Systems
Laboratory Inc.
6-145 Hanasaki-cho,
Nishi-ku
Yokohama 220-0022 Japan
ohshima@mr-system.co.jp
www.mr-system.co.jp

Tsuyoshi Kuroki
Toshihiro Kobayashi
Hiroyuki Yamamoto
Hideyuki Tamura
Mixed Reality Systems
Laboratory Inc.

## Introduction

Visual effects (VFX), which composite computer-generated imagery (CGI) onto real scenes in a feature film, usually require a sequence of images that is manually generated in the post-production process. In an alternative approach, mixed reality (MR) merges the real and virtual worlds to achieve real-time interaction between users and MR space[1,2]. In this sense, MR creates real-time VFX seen from an observer's viewpoint. These two fields, which used to be considered independent, will rapidly affect one another. VFX techniques, especially photometric registration, are useful in MR systems. On the other hand, MR technology can be utilized in film production. This sketch introduces the first MR system that is specially implemented for filmmaking.

## Advantages of MR in Filmmaking

The system uses the latest and highest level of MR technology. It calculates depth of objects that move around the real world in real-time so as to realize the dynamic mutual occlusion between the real and virtual objects. The MR system has the following advantages compared to virtual studio systems that are currently used in TV studios:

- No choroma-key technology. Blue or green backgrounds are no longer required. Computer-generated objects are placed not only in front of the real scene but also at any depth in the scene.

- Real-time composition of CGI and the real scene can be observed from an actor's viewpoint with a head mounted display (HMD) and from a cinematographer's viewpoint with a monitor.

These advantages can be applied to filmmaking in two ways:

1. In rehearsal, actors can view virtual characters in HMDs.

2. Depth data acquired in rehearsal can be used in the highly precise post-production process.

## System Configuration

The system is based on a video-see-through MR system as shown in Figure 1.

- Using the Optotrak system, it tracks movements of a video camera and an HMD worn by the actor.

- Zooming is digitally encoded and transferred to a computer.

- Using a computer-vision method, a five-camera depth-detection system dynamically determines the depth of real objects in the scene.

## "2001: An MR-Space Odyssey"

Using this system, we reproduced a few cuts taken from a short film produced by the film director Takashi Yamazaki, in which an actress interacts with a computer-generated creature in our MR studio as shown in Figure 2. Figure 3 shows a frame from the movie, and Figure 4 shows a real-time frame. The director and the audience see the panning and zooming operations of the camera in realtime. The system also allows the actress to change actions and positions as many times as necessary. Through her video-see-through HMD, the actress can see and fight with a virtual creature. This makes trial-and-error experimentation in the movie making much easier, and it allows audiences to see scenes seen from the actress's viewpoint.

## Conclusion

It may take a little while to practically apply this system to actual filmmaking. However, it may soon be utilized as a new type of entertainment in which a viewer can participate as an actor or actress.

*References*
1. Ohta, Y. & Tamura, H., Eds. (1999). *Mixed reality - Merging real and virtual worlds*, Ohm-sha & Springer-Verlag.
2. Feiner S., et al. (1999). Mixed reality: Where real and virtual worlds meet, in *SIGGRAPH 99 Conference Abstracts and Applications*, 156-158.

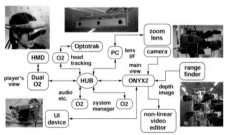

Figure 1. Concept illustration.

Figure 2. Tentative and final composites.

Figure 3. System configuration.

Figure 4.

# 2D Shape Interpolation Using a Hierarchical Approach

*Contact*
Henry Johan
Tomoyuki Nishita
University of Tokyo
henry@is.s.u-tokyo.ac.jp

Shape interpolation has been widely used for modeling and creating visual effects. Recent papers[1,2] have proved that interpolating two shapes taking into account their interiors can greatly improve the quality of the generated intermediate shapes. However, the algorithms are complex and hard to implement. Here, we present an easy and simple method to generate a smooth interpolation between two shapes. Given a vertex correspondence between the boundary of the two shapes, the compatible hierarchical representations of the shapes are constructed. Interpolating these compatible hierarchical representations generates the intermediate shapes. Unlike the previous approaches, our method can be used to interpolate polylines.

## Construction of Compatible Hierarchical Representations

A hierarchical representation of a shape is defined as a set of triangles used to describe the shape with hierarchical relationships defined among the triangles. In the compatible hierarchical representations, each triangle in the source shape has exactly one corresponding triangle in the target shape. The outline of the compatible hierarchical representation construction is as follows:

First, we insert additional vertices into the two shapes: Figure 1(b). Note that we do not insert new vertices into short edges. Then we search for vertices to be removed. A vertex can be removed if its removal does not cause the two shapes to exhibit self-intersection and does not cause a folding problem. After that, we perform the vertex-removal operation and create triangles to represent the removed vertices. Finally, we create the source and the target shapes at the next lower hierarchical level: Figure 1(c). We repeat this operation until the shapes at the next lower level are either triangles or lines. We treat lines as degenerate triangles. We slightly change the algorithm in order to deal with open polylines. We do not remove the vertices at the end points of the polylines and do not perform the folding test.

## Interpolation Between Two Compatible Hierarchical Representations

Our interpolation method proceeds as follows:

First, we interpolate the triangles at the lowest level of the representations: Figure 2(a). Then, we move to the next-higher level, interpolate all the triangles at this level, Figure 2(b), and finally we compute the final shape at this level: Figure 2(c). We perform this operation until we have finished processing the triangles at the highest level of the representations. To compute an intermediate triangle, we determine its ideal shape, its ideal orientation, and the ideal coordinates of its center. We define an ideal transformation between two triangles as a transformation that linearly changes the length of the edges.

## Examples

Figure 3 shows four examples of interpolation between two shapes. In all of the examples, some part of the shapes undergoes rotations. Our method has produced smooth interpolation sequences for all these examples. There is no area deformation and local self-intersection in the intermediate shapes. The compatible

hierarchical representations can be computed in less than 0.2 seconds. The interpolation sequences can be generated in real time. The computation is performed on a machine with Pentium III 800Mhz running Linux.

*References*
1. Shapira, M. & Rappoport, A. (1995). Shape interpolation using the star-skeleton representation. In *IEEE Computer Graphics and Application, 15*, 44-51.
2. Alexa, M., Cohen-Or, D., & Levin, D. (2000). As-rigid-as-possible shape interpolation. *Proceedings of SIGGRAPH 2000*, 157-164.

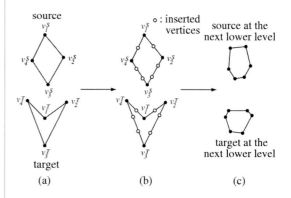

Figure 1. Constructing the compatible hierarchical representations of the source and the target shapes.

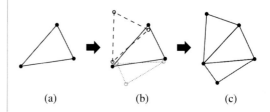

Figure 2. Generating the intermediate shapes.

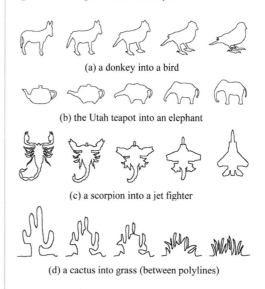

(a) a donkey into a bird

(b) the Utah teapot into an elephant

(c) a scorpion into a jet fighter

(d) a cactus into grass (between polylines)

Figure 3. Interpolation between two shapes.

143

*Contact*
Andre Gueziec
gueziec@computer.org
www.trianglesoftware.com

This sketch presents a system for generating a short narrated animation of highway traffic conditions in a large metropolitan area at a particular moment in time. The task is very challenging: an animated sequence ready for broadcast must be produced within minutes after collecting the most recent traffic data from sensors placed along the roads, police reports, etc.

## An Animated Traffic Report vs. Live Footage

Our animation system incurs significantly lower costs than shooting live footage. Filming traffic from helicopters (which are not as safe as other aircraft) is expensive and may not cover the necessary territory with the required frequency. Fixed cameras provide limited coverage. Despite their popularity among TV audiences, broadcasting real-life accidents or traffic jams is more voyeuristic than informative.

Although this may seem counter-intuitive, live images can misrepresent actual traffic conditions. Traffic experts generally agree that:

- Traffic is significantly random.

- Probably as much as 15 minutes of continuous observation is required to gather reliable traffic flow information for a specific location. Drivers in stop-and-go traffic situations may attest that instantaneous snapshots of speed and density are useless in portraying vehicle flow.

## Data-Driven Visualization in an Animation

Meaningful ways of presenting information on still images (paper) have been carefully studied. But for moving images, there is little published work on how best to visualize information. Further, some visualization scientists turned away from the moving image, arguing that information may be misrepresented in video or film.

At the other end of the spectrum, in artistic animation, animators are faced with a related problem: conveying "information" about what characters feel, think, do, or will do. The elements and tools they have developed to convey this information may have broader applicability. Some of those elements have been applied in this project: appeal, exaggeration and staging. For instance, we found that using realistic vehicle models, despite the effort and strain on the graphics system, provided more appeal to the resulting animations, and thus better served our data visualization goals (Figure 2).

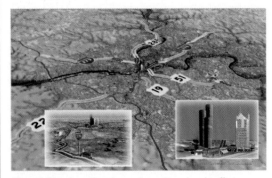

Figure 1. Virtual world used to produce animated road traffic reports for a particular metropolitan area. Colored segments overlaid on major highways indicate traffic conditions.

Figure 2. Using realistically modeled vehicles that are randomly selected from a pool (right) has much more appeal, and is more effective, than repeatedly using the same generic car (left).

## Our System

Our system includes:
1. A modeling environment.
2. A rendering and simulation environment that is tightly coupled with modeling.
3. Interactive movie-making capabilities.

Built on MultiGen tools, our modeling is highly automated. It limits modeler input to artistic and design choices. We use geo-referenced spatial data, and we exaggerate selected elements, to produce minimal and cartoon-like polygonal modeling. The rendering uses Vega and Performer. For interactive movie directing, previewing, and generation of uncompressed video footage, we have engineered our system to render at 30 frames per second on a PC running Windows.

## Some Technical Highlights

*Vehicles.* We opted for visualizing traffic flow using animated vehicles as an intuitive and, we believe, effective solution. We have built a physically based and data-directed vehicle traffic model.

*Timing and exaggeration.* We want to be able to survey a major highway section that is tens of kilometers long in about 10 seconds, by flying a virtual helicopter and observing animated traffic. This requires exaggerating the sizes and speeds of vehicles and simplifying the road network. (In traditional animation, exaggeration is a proven and effective technique.)

*2D map.* To transition smoothly from a 2D map to an animated virtual world, we overlay map-like colored symbols and textures on our virtual world. Placed on the scene graph with proper LODs, they are in turn visible, translucent, or invisible.

*Dynamic scene.* At run time, we regenerate the above polygonal symbols and textures depending upon current traffic data.

## Acknowledgements

From MultiGen-Paradigm, we want to thank Tom Dowgiallo, Mark Ippolito, Nelson Iwai, Paul Levy, Binoy Marvar, Bill Preskar, Steve Thompson, Elizabeth Fox, and John Perser (for a great voice-over of the animation). Jeff Bott and Matt Barlow from Viewpoint have provided superb vehicle models, as well as the Three River Stadium Model. Thanks to Traffic.com. Thanks to Matthias Wloka.

*Reference*
1. Gueziec, A. Architecture of a system for producing animated traffic reports, April 2001.

# ALVIN on the Web: Distributive Mission Rehearsal for a Deep Submersible Vehicle

*Contact*
Jan Jungclaus
Fraunhofer Center for Research
in Computer Graphics, Inc.
Providence, Rhode Island 02903
USA
jjungcla@crcg.edu

L. Miguel Encarnação
Robert J. Barton III
Petar Horvatic
Fraunhofer Center for Research
in Computer Graphics

Dudley Foster
Woods Hole
Oceanographic Institution

## Introduction

The Woods Hole Oceanographic Institution (WHOI) operates the ALVIN Deep Submergence Vehicle (DSV) for scientific research at extreme ocean depths.[1] A key element that determines the length of such dives is the efficiency of the energy budgeting (getting the most out of the two batteries' overall capacity). Energy consumption is mainly determined by the use of outside lights, propulsion tasks, manipulator usage, and the use of experimental devices. Since the ALVIN submersible is a unique research tool that is completely reserved for years in advance, training has been conducted "on the job." To overcome the limited training opportunities, Fraunhofer CRCG constructed the ALVIN Web-based distributive simulator,[2] which will allow scientists to plan and rehearse their dives more efficiently.

## Technical Requirements

In order to implement the ALVIN simulator, Web-interface development had to be pushed into several directions at the same time. One of the main challenges was the requirement to fulfill both scientific and educational tasks. In order to meet this challenge, WHOI and Fraunhofer collaborated to implement:

- Full scientific applicability.
- Distributive operative collaboration.
- Electrical and logical evaluation of experimental and navigational operations.
- Web delivery with state-of-the-art performance.
- Visual feedback for ongoing processes.
- Analog and digital rendering of crucial variables.
- Photo-realistic visual representation.
- 3D look and navigational features.
- Intuitive interaction requiring only basic knowledge of the submarine's functional design.
- Display of impressions from the oceanographic surroundings of the submarine.
- Visual appeal for operational facilitation and to promote educational interest.
- A basic chat tool for supervision and counseling purposes.
- Maintainability of the interface and variables for future design changes and refined power modeling of the submersible.

## Project History

Throughout the duration of the project, the discussion on which approach to take for the distributed ALVIN simulator and training interface was strongly influenced by rapidly changing and improving interface and communication technologies, on the one hand, and slowly maturing virtual reality technologies on the other. These technological developments, in turn, led to a variety of different conceptual designs that exemplify the different approaches to solve these problems from an interface-design point of view.

Initially conceptualized as a distributed collaborative virtual environment (cf. Figure 1, upper left), the immense hardware and software prerequisites for each of the participants prohibited continuation of such a high-realism (but low-accessibility) implementation. Consequently, and supported by professional design expertise and high-performance graphics software for the

Figure 1. Virtual ALVIN mock-up (upper left) and final Web-based simulator interface in Flash.[3]

Web, a 3D-like interface was designed based on photographs taken from the original ALVIN submersible. The interface combines interactivity and visual appeal with a high degree of portability and maintainability (cf. Figure 1, center) and supports (employing Java servlet technology) all the requirements listed above.

*References*
1. Deep submergence vehicle ALVIN. (2000). Woods Hole Oceanographic Institution, URL: http://www.marine.whoi.edu/ships/alvin/alvin.htm
2. ALVIN simulator. (2001). Woods Hole Oceanographic Institution and Fraunhofer CRCG, Inc. URL: http://alvin.crcg.edu
3. Franklin, D. & Patton, B. (2001). *Flash 5! creative Web animation*, Macromedia Press, Berkeley, 2001.

*145*

# ANALYSIS AND SIMULATION OF FACIAL MOVEMENTS IN ELICITED AND POSED EXPRESSIONS USING A HIGH-SPEED CAMERA

*Contact*
TATSUO YOTSUKURA
ATR Media Integration &
Communications Research
Laboratories
Seikei University
2-2-2 Hikaridai, Seika-cho
Soraku-gun
Kyoto 6190288 Japan
yotsu@mic.atr.co.jp

*Contributors*
HIDEKO UCHIDA
San Francisco State Universtiy

HIROSHI YAMADA
Nihon University

NOBUJI TETSUTANI

SHIGERU AKAMATSU
Hosei University/ATR
Integration & Communications
Research Laboratories

SHIGEO MORISHIMA
Seikei University

## INTRODUCTION

The purpose of this research was to examine dynamic aspects of facial movements involving "posed" (intended) facial expressions versus "elicited" (unintended) emotional facial expressions. Participants were shown Gross & Levenson's set of standardized emotional film stimuli1, and their facial expressions were recorded by a high-speed video camera (250 frames/second), which allowed us to analyze facial movements very closely in image sequences. These movements cannot be seen with a regular video camera (30 frames/second). In addition, participants were asked to produce facial expressions of happiness, surprise, and disgust based on the Facial Action Coding System (FACS). The findings suggested that the patterns of facial movements in posed facial expressions and elicited emotional facial expressions are not significantly different, but that there are differences in the intensity of the facial expressiveness.

## METHOD

Twenty-four participants (12 Japanese female, 12 Japanese male) were recorded by a high-speed video camera hidden behind a 21- inch prompter. The film stimuli were adapted from Gross & Levenson's set of standardized emotional film stimuli[1]. The protocol for posed expressions was utilized. We also used Ekman & Friesen's facial action coding system (FACS), an objective method for quantifying facial movements. FACS is an anatomically based coding scheme that codes facial muscular movements in terms of 44 action units (AUs) or action unit combinations (AU combinations). Participants were instructed to perform six basic facial emotional expressions based on combinations of AUs.

## ANALYSIS AND SIMULATION OF FACIAL MOVEMENTS

Images of disgust, happiness, and surprise expressions were analyzed via the high-speed camera. We developed a feature-point tracking tool to analyze the facial movements of emotions. The images were downloaded onto a computer, and 28 dots were manually plotted on the face (four dots for an outline of the eyebrows, four dots for an outline of both eyes, five dots for an outline of the nose, six dots for an outline of the mouth, and one dot at a corner of the jaw) in the initial image. These 28 dots were selected because they were necessary to recreate the movements of basic facial expressions and to design computer graphics programs to simulate natural facial movements.

We examined patterns of facial movements by measuring the movements of the feature points, analyzed the feature points by the facial regions (eyebrows, eyes, and mouth), and computed the mean ratings of each region per emotion for all of the subjects.

Overall, our results indicated that the mean ratings of the eye region were higher than those of the eyebrows and mouth regardless of the emotional category or experimental conditions. Furthermore, we compared the total duration (from neutral to the start of the expression to attainment of peak intensity) between posed and elicited emotion conditions.

Our results demonstrated that the total duration was shorter for the posed expressions for all emotions. Figure 1 shows an example

of the expression of "happiness." We also found differences in the magnitudes of facial movements between posed and elicited emotion conditions. The data showed that the magnitudes of posed expressions were greater than those of elicited emotions in all categories. In addition, the data revealed that the facial movements were nonlinear as a function of time.

We also simulated facial synthesis using Morishima's system.[2] Figure 2 shows a reconstructed facial movement of all frames. The generic facial animation was created through linear animation by morphing. The animation used by our technique is more natural than conventional generic animation.

*References*
1. Gross, J.J. & Levenson, R.W. (1995). Emotion elicitation using films. *Cognition and Emotion*, 9 89-108.
2. Morishima, S. (1996). Modeling of facial expression and emotion for human communication system. *Displays 17,* 15-25, Elsevier.

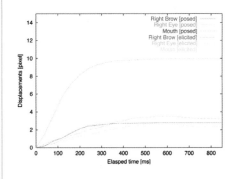

Figure 1. The average number of movements by facial part.

Figure 2. Reconstructed face (expression of "happiness").
(a) Linear animation (30 frames/second).

(b) Nonlinear animation (30 frames/second).

# The Animator-Oriented Motion Generator, Animanium, Based on a Humanoid Robot-Control Algorithm

Contact
Fumio Sumi
Fujitsu SSL
sumi@ssl.fujitsu.co.jp

Hirotaka Imagawa
SEGA Corporation

## Introduction

Currently, 3D computer graphics is the most popular method for making motion pictures, and it is a very powerful tool. But it is still immature compared to the tools of conventional celluloid animation. Some examples:

1. Three-dimensional computer graphics provides few methods for moving shapes. It offers many good modeling tools, but few shape model-handling tools.

2. Poor motion-generation techniques. Motion-capture systems and direct handling of the triple-axis rotation joints are only two methods that provide motion to hierarchical human structures such as hands or the head.

3. Poor operation of CG software tools. Existing CG software has too many functions, and it takes too much time to learn the operation. This is one of the reasons why it is difficult to train staff to use modeling and motion generation.

To solve the above problems (especially 2. and 3.), we developed Animanium, a new animation tool that uses a humanoid robot-control algorithm.

## Implementation

1. Simplification of human-character pose adjustment. The human character is a very complicated link structure, and it has a large degree of freedom. It is difficult to manipulate a whole body at once by the ordinal inverse kinematics method. For this reason, we use the Jacobean matrix of inverse kinematics, which is used to control humanoid robots.

2. We used conventional celluloid animation, a kind of keyframe animation. The process of creating 2D celluloid animation is divided into two phases: making keyframes and creating interpolated frames. Animators make only keyframes, and computers generate interpolating frames.

## System Overview

First, we developed the total motion-generation system based on humanoid robot-control algorithm shown in Figure 1.

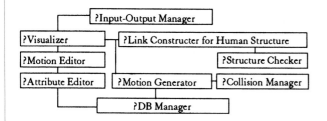

Figure 1. Functional Diagram.

The functions of this system are very useful for an experienced, professional animator. For a less experienced animator, additional steps are helpful functions for generating frames automatically.

## Technology

We developed a new interface method "Pin-and-Drag" for handling the entire body of a human character. This allows the user to drag a link to an arbitrary position with any number of links pinned in the global frame. Inverse and forward kinematics are used for generating and optimizing motion.

We also developed a character-motion adjustment method as a real-time operation, which can correct poses during playback. Using this technique, it is very easy to make create series of derivative motions.

## Result

1. The time and number of steps required to interactively create poses for a human character is greatly decreased compared to other tools.
2. This tool is useful for both skilled and unskilled animators.

## Acknowledgement

This work was supported by the Information Technology Promotion Agency, Japan.

*References*
1. Nakamura, Y. & Hanafusa, H. (1986). Inverse kinematics solutions with singularity robustness for robot manipulator control. *Journal of Dynamic Systems, Measurement and Control.*
2. Nagashima, F. & Nakamura, Y. (1992). Efficient computer scheme for the kinematics and inverse dynamics of a satellite-based manipulator. *Proceedings of IEEE International Conference on Robotics and Automation.*
3. Popovic, Z. (2000). Editing dynamic properties of captured human motion. *Proceedings of IEEE International Conference on Robotics and Automation.*
4. Yamane, K. & Nakamura, Y. (2000). Dynamics filter – concept and implementation of on-line motion generator for human figures. *Proceedings of IEEE International Conference on Robotics and Automation.*

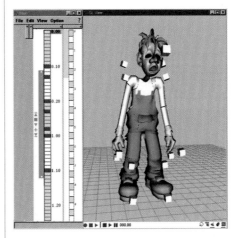

# AntiAliasing Perlin Noise

*Contact*
Ian Stephenson
National Centre for
Computer Animation
Bournemouth University
Poole, Dorset BH12 5BB
United Kingdom

## Introduction

The Perlin Noise function is a key tool in procedural texturing, where it provides the controlled randomness required to create visual interest. However, as with all periodic functions, it is prone to aliasing when sampled at a frequency below the Nyquist frequency. The main approaches used to limit these artifacts are super-sampling, and frequency clamping, at the cost of render time, and shader complexity respectively.

The preferred solution to any aliasing problem is to convolve the continuous signal with a sampling kernel. If we accept a simple box filter, then this reduces to calculating the integral of the signal over the sampling area. However, the random nature of noise, and a lack of understanding of its implementation has led many shader writers to believe that this is not viable.

This sketch demonstrates that integration of noise is relatively simple, provided that lattice gradients are available.

## The 1D Perlin Noise Function

Perlin Noise is a form of gradient lattice noise. A random gradient is generated for each integer lattice point (where the value of the noise is zero), and the gradients are smoothly interpolated between these values.

Interpolation is performed through the use of wavelets. These wavelets are defined to be zero outside the range $\pm 1$, and integrate to zero over that range. When integrating 1D noise, it is therefore only necessary to consider the two wavelets that intersect the sample point. These wavelets are simple polynomials, so they can be trivially integrated. In forming the definite integral, these must be evaluated at each end of the sampling area. Hence, integrated noise is approximately twice as expensive as point sampling.

## The 2D Case

In two dimensions, the wavelets are arranged in a grid. Once again, wavelets fully outside or fully inside the area being integrated over will sum to zero, and may be safely ignored. Those wavelets that intersect the corners of the area may be integrated in a similar fashion to the 1D case (at a total cost approximately four times that of point sampling). However, in the 2D case, we now need to consider those wavelets that intersect the edges of the area (or the faces of the volume in higher dimensional cases). Fortunately, the wavelet functions are of a form that allows integration of an entire edge to be evaluated as a simple summation of gradients, multiplied by a single polynomial. The computational cost of these edge integrals can, therefore, be kept to a minimum.

This approach generalizes to higher dimensions, and though the cost of the boundry evaluation increases with both dimension, and size of the summed area, it does so more slowly than super-sampling.

## Implementation

The integrated noise (Inoise) functions have been implemented, both in a custom renderer and as DSO shadeops for Pixar's PRMan. A naïve implementation of the mathematics is numerically unstable, due to the mixing of floating-point operations with the division of space into lattice cells. However, a stable implementation has been developed and has been shown to accurately reproduce the standard noise function while greatly reducing aliasing artifacts.

Standard noise (left) vs. INoise (right).

# The Attack on Pearl Harbor Battleship Row:
## Everything including the kitchen sink

David Frederic Horsley
Technical Director
Industrial Light + Magic

ILM was given a series of complex scenes for the bombing of Pearl Harbor. As you can imagine, there were numerous actions going on all at one time: explosions, smoke, debris flying through the air, people running every which way to action. In other words: chaos. We had our work cut out for us in trying to determine how to convey that feeling of pandemonium.

We started by going through our extensive library of effects developed for numerous productions that we've done over the years. We then began experimenting with different techniques, in varying combinations, layer upon layer, to obtain just the right look and feel for each sequence. In one instance, we used up to 30 effects elements to complete the final sequence. For example in the FA sequence, the following elements were used to create smoke:

- With the help of Effects Supervisor Ed Hirsh and his team, ILM created numerous practical smoke elements of different scales, under different wind conditions, of different velocities.

- In Baja California, director Michael Bay and his crew created numerous elements to add to our collection of practical smoke elements.

- To achieve correct perspective, computer graphics scientist John Anderson and his software team developed a fluid-dynamic simulation of large plumes of smoke based on our fluid dynamics software. These were rendered as particles.

- In addition to thick smoke plumes, we created lighter, airier plumes to fill the atmosphere around burning battleships.

- Then we added color and variation.

In all, we had 10 different simulations of light smoke and six different simulations of thick plumes.

Maya provided us with more tools to develop different simulations using turbulence plug-ins developed by our production software group. We were also able to emit particles from smoke textures using the same Maya software, to create layers of atmospheric smoke. This method of painting a texture gave us maximum control to create exact shapes.

We pasted smoke simulations on 3D planes that were in turn rendered as smoke elements, like moving images on sprites. Two-dimensional compositing software was used to add smoke-like noise to elements to enhance practical smoke.

The Battleship Row bombing sequence involved the following list of elements and methods:

1. Maya particle simulation of smoke and fire.
2. Proprietary fluid dynamic simulation of gigantic plumes of smoke towering 600 feet into the air.
3. Crowds of particle-animated CG people, running, swimming, and fighting.
4. Accurate depiction of World War II battleships, destroyers, and cruisers.
5. Global illumination rendering of large complex models of battleships.
6. CG water using "Perfect Storm" simulation technology.
7. Global illumination rendering of Japanese planes.
8. Restoration of photographed background plates.
9. Compositing of explosions, fire, and smoke elements shot on stage.
10. Mental Ray and RenderMan for image rendering.
11. "Delayed read archive" RenderMan baked ribs for storage of battleship and airplane geometry and materials, easy access to geometry for efficient loading , and memory allocation.
12. Level of detail for the airplane animation rendering. This was combined with our optimized global illumination method.
13. Baking of ambient occlusion texture maps on our rigid body battleships.
14. Maya particle simulation of water spray and sparks.
15. Rigid-body dynamic simulation engines (proprietary software) for exploding airplanes and debris.
16. Simulated fire and smoke on water.
17. Fluid dynamic simulation torpedo wakes and explosion shock waves on water.
18. Instanced flying debris in air.
19. Splashing of water as debris hits the surface.
20. Boat wakes and bow splashes of moving ships.
21. Painted detailed maps of 10 different battle ships, with color, bump, opacity, rust, scorch, and area maps.
22. Two series of battleships, one before battle in peacetime and one series of destroyed battleships during the attack.
23. The kitchen sink.

# Averaged Area Tables for Texture Filtering

*Contact*
Uwe Behrens
Digital Domain
300 Rose Avenue
Venice, California 90291 USA
ubehrens@d2.com

Attaining high-quality imagery requires that texture samples are properly filtered over the footprint of a pixel in order to reduce aliasing artifacts. Often, accuracy is traded for speed by using a specific kernel to prefilter the texture. At runtime, an approximation of the true filter response is calculated from one or more of the precalculated filter values.

Summed area tables (SAT)[1] are one such prefiltered representation of texture images. They allow for fast calculation of box-filtered texture integrals over axis-aligned rectangular regions. Unlike MIP maps,[2] they do not require the filter region to be square, which reduces blur for filter regions with unequal width and height.

Let $T$ be a 2D texture of integral size $(T_w; T_h)$, and let T(x, y) be the value of $T$ at location $(x, y); x \in [1; T_w]; y \in [1; T_h]$. Let $r$ be a convex region, completely within the bounds of $T$, for which a filtered texture value must be computed. A simple method to approximate the filtered value of $T$ over $r$ uses the smallest, axis-aligned bounding rectangle $R = (x_l; y_l; x_h; y_h)$ of $r$, and computes the average, or *box filtered value* $\mathbf{B}_T(R)$, of $T$ over all points in $R$:

$$\mathbf{B}_T(R) = \frac{1}{\|R\|} \sum_{i=x_l}^{x_h} \sum_{j=y_l}^{y_h} T(i,j)$$

with $\|R\| = (x_h - x_l + 1)(y_h - y_l + 1)$ being the size of $R$ in texture space. $\mathbf{B}_T(R)$ usually gives an acceptable approximation to the integral of $T$ over $r$ in terms of quality, although by no means a perfect result. To calculate $\mathbf{B}_T(R)$ quickly, we precalculate the SAT of $T$, $S_T$ as a texture of the same size as $T$ with:

$$\mathcal{S}_T(x,y) = \sum_{i=1}^{x} \sum_{j=1}^{y} T(i,j)$$

which is the sum of all values in the rectangle (1; 1; x; y). Now, $\mathbf{B}_T(R)$ is simply (with $S_T(x, y) = 0$, if $x \in [1; T_w] \lor y \in [1; T_h]$):

$$\mathbf{B}_T(R) = [\mathcal{S}_T(x_h, y_h) - \mathcal{S}_T(x_h, y_l - 1) - \mathcal{S}_T(x_l - 1, y_h) + \mathcal{S}_T(x_l - 1, y_l - 1)] / \|R\|$$

The major problem with summed area tables is that the values to be stored in $S_T(x, y)$ can become arbitrarily large (cf. Figure 1(b)), so that a SAT for an eight-bit texture must often be stored in floating-point format, requiring 32 or more bits per pixel and time-consuming floating-point operations. This is unacceptable in production environments, where texture sizes of 4,096 x 4,096 pixels are not uncommon. To overcome this, we developed the *averaged area table* (AAT). The AAT of $T$, $A_T$ is defined as a texture of the same size as $T$, but with:

$$\mathcal{A}_T(x,y) = \frac{\mathcal{S}_T(x,y)}{xy} = \frac{1}{xy} \sum_{i=1}^{x} \sum_{j=1}^{y} T(i,j)$$

storing the average, rather than the sum of the values in the rectangle (1; 1; x, y). Clearly, $\forall x; y : A_T(x, y) <= \max(T(x, y))$, hence $A_T$ can be stored in the same amount of memory, and with the same precision as $T$. Rounding errors on the order of 1/max $(T(x, y))$ will be introduced, but since $R$ is already an approximation of the real filter support $r$, in most cases the additional error is negligible. In the example figure, only one entry (marked as *) was rounded from the true value 62.5 to 63. Calculating $\mathbf{B}_T$ is only slightly more complicated from the AAT than from the SAT[1]:

$$\mathbf{B}_T(R) = [x_h y_h \mathcal{A}_T(x_h, y_h) - x_h(y_l - 1) \mathcal{A}_T(x_h, y_l - 1) - (x_l - 1)y_h \mathcal{A}_T(x_l - 1, y_h) + (x_l - 1)(y_l - 1) \mathcal{A}_T(x_l - 1, y_l - 1)] / \|R\|$$

The AAT allows efficient calculation of the filtered value of a rectangular region in texture space. Unlike the SAT, the AAT does not require any additional memory, surmounting even the 33-percent memory overhead of MIP maps. Also, the AAT, like the SAT, avoids the strong blur of MIP maps, which is caused by the limitation to square filter regions. In addition, the SAT/AAT requires only four texture lookups per computation, as compared to eight lookups needed for typical trilinear MIP map interpolation.

Figure 1 (a) shows a simple 6 x 6 checkerboard texture, and its corresponding SAT (b), and AAT (c).

*References*
1. Crow, F.C. (1984). Summed-area tables for texture mapping. In *Proceedings of SIGGRAPH '84, 18* (3), 207-212.
2. Williams, L. (1983). Pyramidal parametrics. In *Proceedings of SIGGRAPH '83, Computer Graphics 17* (3), 1-11.

| 100 | 100 | 100 | 0 | 0 | 0 |
|---|---|---|---|---|---|
| 100 | 100 | 100 | 0 | 0 | 0 |
| 100 | 100 | 100 | 0 | 0 | 0 |
| 0 | 0 | 0 | 100 | 100 | 100 |
| 0 | 0 | 0 | 100 | 100 | 100 |
| 0 | 0 | 0 | 100 | 100 | 100 |

(a)

| 100 | 200 | 300 | 300 | 300 | 300 |
|---|---|---|---|---|---|
| 200 | 400 | 600 | 600 | 600 | 600 |
| 300 | 600 | 900 | 900 | 900 | 900 |
| 300 | 600 | 900 | 1000 | 1100 | 1200 |
| 300 | 600 | 900 | 1100 | 1300 | 1500 |
| 300 | 600 | 900 | 1200 | 1500 | 1800 |

(b)

| 100 | 100 | 100 | 75 | 60 | 50 |
|---|---|---|---|---|---|
| 100 | 100 | 100 | 75 | 60 | 50 |
| 100 | 100 | 100 | 75 | 60 | 50 |
| 75 | 75 | 75 | 63* | 55 | 50 |
| 60 | 60 | 60 | 55 | 52 | 50 |
| 50 | 50 | 50 | 50 | 50 | 50 |

(c)

Figure 1. From texture (a) to summed area table (b) to averaged area able (c).

BRINGING PHOTOREALISM TO FANTASY: THE HYBRID
APPROACH OF A DIGITAL MATTE ARTIST

PAUL HUSTON
Senior Digital Matte Artist
Industrial Light + Magic

The discipline of matte painting has survived, and thrived, in the digital age because filmmakers still need ways to expand the scope of their films without proportionately expanding their budgets. Matte artists are called upon to create images that are grand, glorious, and fantastic, and at the same time completely convincing. These demands have caused matte artists to develop techniques that combine the strengths of various approaches in order to deliver highly complex photorealistic scenes within ever-shrinking production schedules.

This overview of these techniques follows the development of digital matte painting from the early 1990s.

### 2D IMAGE EDITING

With the advent of 2D image-editing software, it became possible to shortcut many of the tedious methods of traditional matte painting. This is done by sampling colors directly from scanned film using cut and paste, levels controls, alpha channels, direct painting, and other approaches to manipulate and combine scanned images for creating and blending additions to pre-photographed scenes. These additions are combined with live-action footage using post-production compositing systems, a direct transition from the traditional method of using photo-reference transferred onto panels using projectors, painting by hand and brush, and compositing with photo-chemical processes.

### EARLY EXAMPLES: "BABY'S DAY OUT" AND THE YOUNG INDIANA JONES ADVENTURES

#### Location and Miniature Photography

The ease of using photographs as a base for creating paintings led to use of location photography and miniature photography. Before and after examples show how miniatures and location photographs were combined to create images for "101 Dalmatians" and "Star Wars Special Edition." One "Star Wars Special Edition" shot is shown as storyboard, concept painting, rough computer model, miniature, live-action elements and final to illustrate the planning process and progressive refinement of the image.

#### 2.5D

The combination of photography-based paintings, simple geometry, and 3D animation led to what was known colloquially as 2.5D and more technically as image-based rendering, which was used in shots for "Mission Impossible" and "Star Wars Special Edition." When the illusion of 3D space created by camera movement and simple image planes placed in depth in the 3D environment was merged with the visual subtleties inherent in photographs, it produced an impressive combination of great realism and low set-up and render times. The approach has its precedents in "multi-plane" camera set-ups developed in earlier matte painting photography and in films using cell animation such as Disney's "Pinnochio" and others. This technique was used to good advantage in creating backgrounds for the Pod race in "Star Wars: The Phantom Menace." It was an extremely efficient technique given the unique conditions for that sequence, which featured point-of-view shots of extremely fast-moving vehicles through an entirely imaginary landscape.

#### 3D CG and Image-Based Rendering

Many matte shots require extensive architecture, and in some cases computer models and shading become the solution of choice. Mechanical and architectural subjects can be rendered synthetically and then animated with image-based techniques (using painting to create complex detail and atmospheric effects). Image-based rendering was used to create geometry and shading as a basis for a painting in shots showing Mos Eiseley for "Star Wars Special Edition" and the princesses palace in "Star Wars: The Phantom Menace."

### CONCLUSION: "SPACE COWBOYS" HM040

As shots become more complex, variations and combinations of techniques are combined to create the desired effect. The closing shot for "Space Cowboys" combines 3D Phong-shaded imagery, image-based rendering of moon surfaces based on NASA photos, image maps created using height fields and shading, and image hulls created from painted depth maps mapped with live-action photography to bring the viewer from moon orbit down into the face-plate of astronaut Hawk.

### STAR WARS SPECIAL EDITION

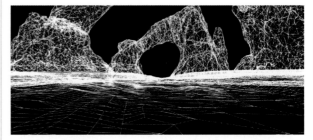

Wireframes of digitized physical models and height map groundplane.

Frame from final comp with motion blue, showing complexity of photographed models.

Storyboard sketch for street scene (left).
Initial round modeling layout (middle).
Frame from final comp (right).

151

Leandro Estebecorena
Lead Technical Director
Industrial Light + Magic

Jonathan C. Lyons
Animator
Industrial Light + Magic

During October 2000, Budweiser asked the Computer Graphic Commercials department of Industrial Light + Magic to produce a new commercial. Several different cutting-edge and traditional techniques were combined to achieve the final images of a huge, totally CG stadium filled with aliens.

The director, Rick Schulze, wanted a sea below the stadium, and various techniques involving displacement maps and particles in Maya were used for this. He also wanted rocks surrounding the view to the ocean, and a fractal system was used to generate CG rocks at the bottom of the stadium. Caustics were implemented to light those rocks with a simulated reflection of the water.

According to the artwork provided by art director Randy Gaul, the stadium was supposed to be filled with a blue fog. Shaders were written to simulate the mist, and CG rigs were set up to support practical smoke elements on top of the stadium torches. Also, volumetric light-and-shadow tools were developed in order to integrate the aliens into the misty stadium. The stadium had to be crowded with aliens, and a special pipeline involving particles and different cycles in three different levels of resolution was set up by technical director Doug Sutton to solve this problem.

The biggest challenge for Carlos Huante, ILM art director and designer of the aliens, was to invent a creature that would be scary at the beginning of the spot but likeable by the end. Reference material included a small maquette, which is seldom done for commercial work. The maquette was quite valuable to ILM modeller Izzy Acar, who modeled the alien using Softimage and ILM proprietary sculpting tools.

Primary animation controls were built by CG commericals artist Todd Krish, using Softimage's inverse kinematics (IK). The alien's legs had three joints, so standard IK solving had a snakelike action. A second IK chain of two joints was added to control the bending, and this provided a more natural motion.

The alien's head design included six "wattles" hanging below the chin. Initially these were to be animated using hair simulation, but the alien's anatomy proved uncooperative, so joint chains were added and keyframed by hand. In pre-production, Paul Griffin, animation director for the show, was also developing animatics for the main establishing shots and setting up a battery of shapes that would later help to implement better alien performance.

Animators gathered for two meetings prior to beginning animation. The first was around a conference table to generate ideas for the behavior of the creatures. The animation was also expected to emphasize the creatures' transition from frightening to friendly. The second meeting was a videotape session using props and interactive lighting, in which animators took turns acting the scenes From these tapes, the director chose takes that were edited into a rough cut of the spot for reference. The reference also included shots of the "Wassup" actors from the original spot.

After extensive pre-production and development, the remaining production time was a scant three weeks. The production team decided to bring on additional animators to maintain quality. Each of the seven animators was asked to animate six different cycles for the alien crowd in the stadium in one day, three of quiet action and three of broad cheering that would be used at the climax. The clients were extremely pleased with the animation in this production.

Using ILM proprietary tools, paint artists Richard Moore and Rebecca Heskes generated the maps and textures for the alien skin, and added details for each shot's camera. Painter Drew Klausner was assigned the task of painting all the details in the spaceship, while technical director Dean Foster was responsible for painting all the architectural details in the stadium (modeled by Larry Tan).

We started to receive plates by the beginning of December 2000. The plates from the set (shot under the supervision of VFX supervisor Kevin Rafferty) were promptly match-moved by Luke Longin and Ingrid Overgard using Softimage and ILM proprietary software.

Once production started, the 12 CGC technical directors assigned to the show faced, and solved, a host of problems to light the crowded stadium and render those believable aliens (for example: volumetric shadow generation, defining the look of the eyes in the middle of production, changes in choreography, modification of caustic light patterns, etc.). To explore different possibilities for the appearance of the alien's eyes, an interactive setup in our compositing tools was developed in the middle of production.

Scripts were set up by assistant TD Michael Muir to generate proof sheets for color continuity evaluation among all the spot's shots on a daily basis. Additional problems (for example, interaction between live elements and CG elements in the "beheading" shot) were solved using Sabre (an ILM high-speed compositing system that incorporates Discreet's inferno-flame software).

The spot started production in December 2000 and required only three weeks of production. It was completed on 16 January, just in time for the Superbowl telecast, 28 January 2001.

152

# CALIBRATION-FREE, EASY 3D MODELING FROM TURNTABLE IMAGE SEQUENCES

*Contact*
SUMIT GUPTA
National University of Singapore
10 Kent Ridge Crescent,
Singapore 119260
eleks@nus.edu.sg

KUNTAL SENGUPTA
National University of Singapore

## INTRODUCTION

Image-based 3D modeling techniques are gaining popularity in computer graphics and virtual reality applications. However, most existing techniques require precise camera calibration, which restricts their application to special environments and can only be performed by experts. We propose a new 3D modeling technique using silhouette-based volume intersection with the following features:

1. The method works without the need of camera calibration.
2. It uses a simple and effective intersection test.
3. It is computationally very efficient because it reduces the number of calculations required to compute the projection from 3D to 2D and requires no additional hardware.
4. Because it is silhouette-based, there is no need to compute dense point matches across views.

Using our technique, designers and modelers who are not experts in the field of computer vision can easily acquire 3D models from multiple views of an object undergoing rotational motion.

## THEORETICAL FOUNDATIONS

In silhouette-based volume intersection techniques, multiple views of an object are captured by a camera, and then silhouettes are extracted for each view. If the positions of the cameras are known, we can estimate the conic volumes that encompass the objects. The volume model that best represents each object is computed by intersecting all these cones. Accurate calibration of the cameras, which is required by all volume-intersection techniques, is a specialized task. Also, each time the setup is changed, the arduous calibration task must be repeated. Hence, these techniques have not gained much popularity outside the computer vision community.

Our contribution to this volume-intersection technique has been in the development of the special calibration matrix P of the form shown below, after an extensive analytical and experimental study:

$$P = \begin{bmatrix} c & 0 & u_0 & cu_0 \\ 0 & c & v_0 & cv_0 \\ 0 & 0 & 1 & c \end{bmatrix}$$

The parameters c and v0 only influence the relative size and the position of the estimated 3D model, respectively. Hence, they can be chosen arbitrarily. Also, u0 is determined from the images directly. Hence, there is no need to perform camera calibration. Our method has been tested successfully on a wide range of objects such as shoes, video cameras, torsos, cups, toys, etc. Some of the estimated models are shown in Figures 1 and 2.

See also: www.ece.nus.edu.sg/stfpage/eleks/silo.htm

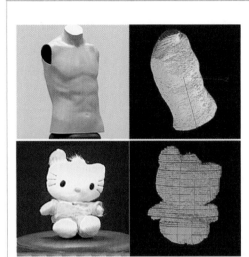

Figure 1. Original objects and the estimated models of a torso and a toy.

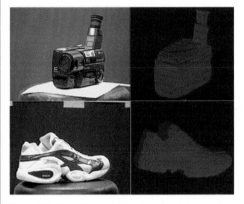

Figure 2. Original objects and the estimated models of a video camera and a shoe.

*153*

# Change Blindness with Varying Rendering Fidelity: Looking but Not Seeing

*Contact*
Kirsten Cater
University of Bristol
cater@cs.bris.ac.uk

Alan Chalmers
Colin Dalton
University of Bristol

A major challenge in virtual reality is to achieve realistic images at interactive rates. However, the computation time required for realistic image synthesis is significant, which precludes such realism in real time. One possible way of producing perceptually high-fidelity images in reasonable times is to exploit the "flaws" in the human eye, for although the human eye is good, it isn't perfect! This sketch shows how the concept of "change blindness" may be exploited to produce realistic images of complex scenes in real time for use on an Explorer/1 motion platform.

Change blindness is the inability of the human eye to detect what should be obvious changes in a scene. Humans can miss large changes in their fields of view when they occur simultaneously with brief visual disruptions, such as an eye saccade, a flicker, or a blink. This concept has long been used by stunt-doubles in film.

We have used the onset of a blank field, mudsplashes, or masking blocks each time an image is changed to create the visual disruption. This swamps the user's local motion signals caused by a change, short-circuiting the automatic system that normally draws attention to its location. Without automatic control, attention is controlled entirely by slower, higher-level mechanisms in the visual system, which search the scene, object by object, until attention finally focuses on the object that is changing. Once attention has latched onto the appropriate object, the change is easy to see, but this occurs only after exhaustive serial inspection of the scene.

The experiment involved 45 images rendered in Radiance.[4] We asked a group of six "judges" to give a short description of the scenes. Their descriptions enabled us to define, for each scene, several aspects that are termed "Central Interest" aspects:[2] those aspects that were mentioned by at least three of the judges. Central interest aspects tended to concern what one would be tempted to call the main theme of the scene. Similarly, we noted several aspects that are termed "Marginal Interest" aspects:[2] those aspects that were mentioned by none of the judges. In the experiment, by manipulating changes in Central or Marginal Interest aspects, we controlled the degree of attention that our subjects would be expected to pay to the changes.

Figure 1 shows an example of the experiments we have conducted with 20 subjects. Figure 1(a) shows a scene rendered in Radiance to a high level of realism, while 1(c) is the same scene rendered with less fidelity for some objects and at significantly reduced computational cost. Figure 1(b) shows the same image as 1(c), but with the mudsplashes.[3] Each original image is displayed under strictly controlled lighting conditions for approximately 400 milliseconds, followed by the mud-splashed image for 60 milliseconds, and finally the modified image for a further 400 milliseconds. This sequence is continually repeated until the user has spotted the change. If no change was observed after 60 seconds, the experiment was stopped. Similar experiments were carried out with the flicker and masking-blocks paradigms.

The results showed that a significant amount of time was required for the user to spot the differences in the images. Future work will involve developing these techniques to dynamic scenes for eventual incorporation on the motion platform.

*References*
1. May, J. (2000). Perceptual principles and computer graphics. *Computer Graphics Forum, 19* (4).
2. O'Regan, J.K., Deubel, H., Clark, J.J., & Rensink, R.A. (1999). Picture changes during blinks: Looking without seeing and seeing without looking. *Visual Cognition*
3. O'Regan, J.K., Rensink, R.A., & Clark J.J. (1999). Change blindness as a result of mudsplashes. *Nature*, 398.
4. Ward Larson, G.(1998). *Rendering with RADIANCE: The art and science of lighting simulation*. San Francisco: Morgan Kauffman.

Figure 1. (a) High-quality image;

(b) low-quality imagewith mud-splashes;

(c) low-quality image.

154

# Character Setup and Animation for "3-2-1 Penguins!"

*Contact*
Michael B. Comet
Big Idea Productions
206 Yorktown Center
Lombard, Illinois 60187 USA
michael.comet@bigidea.com

This animation sketch presents how the Penguins animation team at Big Idea Productions dealt with cartoon-style rigging and animation issues for their new 3D series: "3-2-1 Penguins!" The video blends the traditional quality of animated films, such as exaggeration and cartoon-style action, with a 3D universe.

### Technology

All characters for "3-2-1 Penguins!" were rigged with typical inverse kinematics (IK) setups that included blending for FK and IK arms. In addition, custom controls were written to allow squash and stretch for the limbs and body. Custom MEL scripts were developed to create an easy user interface for the animators that included the ability to select and animate one part of the character while different controls displayed keyframe information on the timeline.

Jason and Michelle, stranded at Granmum's for the summer, explore the attic.

Characters were also set up with a custom "light rig" that illuminated each character individually. A custom light user interface allowed animators to quickly and easily adjust the lighting for all characters at once or to tweak lights independently. The rim light for each character was controlled by a custom plug-in. The plug-in automatically adjusted the rim-lights position and intensity based on the camera and character positions. The characters were also shaded with a variation of the default shader to yield a more traditionally animated appearance. The shader itself integrated into the lighting user interface and controls.

Other utilities included tools to automatically adjust spline curve interpolation to remove unwanted peaks, tools to automatically allow characters to grab and let go of props, and a way to save and reload vertex skin weighting among models with different vertex counts.

Zidgel, Midgel, Fidgel, and Kevin, the wackiest space penguins ever!

### Style

In addition to technical hurdles, the animation team faced the challenge of creating an exaggerated style of animation on a tight deadline. The Penguins team departed from the traditional department approach used in most larger studios and used a smaller "do-it-all" artist workflow and "team-approach" process. The animation process was researched and developed to include a rough "pop-through" stage, which allowed the animators and director to review the blocking quickly and in a way that was geared toward snappy cartoon animation.

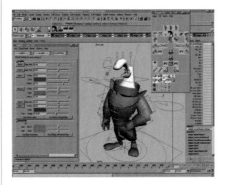

The character rig for Zidgel, showing control curves, the character UI, and the lighting UI.

### Penguins Core Animation Team

*Producer*
Jon Gadsby

*Director*
Ron Smith

*Artists*
Mark Behm
Michael Comet
Jeff Croke
Rob Dollase
Everett Downing
Aaron Hartline
Bill Jacoby

Keith Lango
Tim Lannon
Michael Laubach
Joe Shaw

*Production Assistants*
Katie Carnes
Melody Chesney
Amanda Fragale

*Production Coordinator*
Matt Garbera

*Contact*
John Dingliana
Trinity College Dublin
John.Dingliana@cs.tcd.ie

Carol O'Sullivan
Gareth Bradshaw
Trinity College Dublin

Collision detection, contact modeling, and collision response are vital but inherently expensive features of a physically based animation system. As scene complexity increases, collision handling quickly becomes a major bottleneck in the simulation process. A trade-off between speed and accuracy is often required in order to achieve interactive frame-rates[1]. Our goal in ReACT (Real-time Adaptive Collision Toolkit) is to optimize this trade-off by making simplifications as invisible as possible to the viewer.

Many applications simply address the frame-rate problem through pre-emptive simplification, reducing the complexity of the simulation to a pre-determined "safe" level. However, when complexity changes often over the course of a simulation, such an approach suffers from one of two problems: over simplification of the whole for the sake of relatively few snapshots of high complexity, or a drop in frame rate when the computational workload has been underestimated. We can avoid this through adaptive and interactive simplification of the simulation as it evolves. A popular approach to reducing workload in interactive animation is visibility-based culling, where parts of the scene not inside the visible volume are excluded from normal processing[2]. This is taken a step further in ReACT by applying varying levels of simplification over different regions within the viewable area. Such steps are an improvement, but they do not implicitly guarantee target frame rates if static rules are used to determine the levels of detail for different regions. If, for instance, the higher-priority regions should ever encounter computationally complex situations themselves, then problems similar to those in the pre-emptive simplification approach arise.

Target frame rates can be guaranteed by using time-critical mechanisms for computationally expensive parts of the simulation process. A time-critical (or interruptible) mechanism is halted when a scheduler decides that enough time has been spent on any particular task. For such an approach to work, however, we must ensure that some result is obtained and that some degree of correctness is maintained in the system, regardless of when processing is interrupted. This is achieved by using incremental mechanisms, which generate results of increasing accuracy as more time is spent on processing[3]. One example of this is Hubbard's sphere-tree collision detection system, which is extended in ReACT to return increasingly accurate approximations of contact data for collision response calculations (see Figure 1).

Although an interruptible system may guarantee target frame rates, it does not in itself ensure that the trade-off between accuracy and processing time is optimized. For this, we must incorporate some form of prioritization within the process. Certain events or specific parts of the scene are categorized as being more important and, as a result, given more processing time. Prioritization of the scene is based upon factors related to visibility and perceptibility of approximations within different parts of the scene. In ReACT, for instance, priority can be based on a weighted combination of factors such as eccentricity, occlusion, or projected distance from the user's fixation point determined interactively with the use of an eye-tracker (Figure 2).

*References*
1. Hubbard, P. M. (1995). Real-time collision detection and time-critical computing. *In Proceedings of the First ACM Workshop on Simulation and Interaction in Virtual Environments,* July 1995, 92-96.
2. Chenny, S. & Forsyth, D. (1997). View-dependent culling of dynamic systems in virtual environments. In *Proceedings 1997 Symposium on Interactive 3D Graphics,* 55-58.
3. Dingliana, J. & O'Sullivan, C. (2000). Graceful degradation of collision handling in physically based animation. In *Computer Graphics Forum,* 19 (3), 239-247.

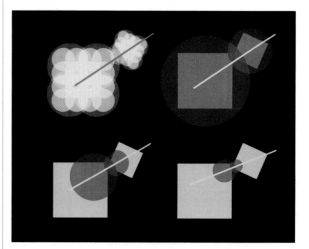

Figure 1. A sphere-tree-based collision-processing system. Shown are the full sphere trees of two objects and the process halted at three different stages. Better approximations of the collision points directly affect the computed response as seen by the direction of the impulse vector in yellow. Red spheres are colliding nodes.

Figure 2. The screenshot shows a projected region on the screen around the user's fixation point, which is given a higher priority, and objects within the region are processed at a higher level of detail.

# Colored-Paper Mosaic Rendering

*Contact*
Sanghyun Seo
Chung-Ang University
ddipdduk@cglab.cse.cau.ac.kr

Youngsup Park
Kyunghyun Yoon
Chung-Ang University

Sungye Kim
Electronics and
Telecommunications
Research Institute

Various features must be considered to produce mosaic effects in colored paper, including paper texture, how the paper is attached by hand, the irregular lines of torn paper, and a white section that shows a cutting plane (see Figure 1).

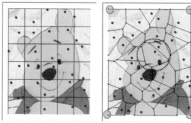

Figure 1. Features of the mosaic work.

## Paper Texture and Shape of Attached Paper

Perlin's noise function is used to get the texture of the paper. This function utilizes an image-coordinate value and the noise function value at each coordinate to create the normal vector. Light vector is used on a random spot of the surface to generate the texture. The Voronoi diagram is used to generate the shape of an attached paper. The input image is divided into even grid sizes to generate the Voronoi polygon. Random points are generated in each divided area. After creating a Voronoi diagram using these input points, the Voronoi polygons are passed to the next stage.

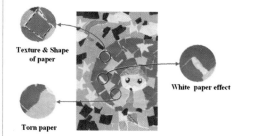

**(a) Grid and random point**     **(b) Voronoi polygon**

Figure 2. Determination of attached paper shape.

## Torn Paper

The random mid-point displacement algorithm is used to generate a more natural torn-paper effect. This method continually adds a random height to the center point between the two points that form the edge of the paper, which is repeatedly applied to generate the resulting random line (Figure 3a).

## White Paper Effect

A piece of colored paper consists of many different layers of fiber. Therefore, when torn, it exhibts a rough white surface. For the purposes of this sketch, we assume that a piece of colored paper consists of two different layers. The top layer is the colored layer, and the bottom layer is the white paper. The sizes and shapes of each paper layer (using the random midpoint displacement algorithm) are different. As random pieces of paper are applied, eventually the white layer is larger than the colored layer, which is the method used to express the white-paper effect of the torn paper (Figure 3b).

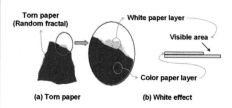

Figure 3. Irregular torn paper and white effect.

## Conclusion and Future Work

The colored-paper mosaic-rendering algorithm proposed in this sketch enables creation of a hand-made mosaic work by using texture as well as the torn-paper effect. The resulting mosaic image is more natural than any other image generated by conventional software. However, the colored-paper mosaic effect uses polygons of the same scale, which reduces thickness and spatiality of the mosaic work. In future work, an adaptive-space (image region) subdivision technique that considers features of input image should be considered to resolve the problem. See also: cglab.cse.cau.ac.kr/npr

*References*
1.  Non-photorealistic rendering. In SIGGRAPH 99 Course #17, 1999.
2.  Barnsley, M.F. (1993). *Fractals Everywhere*, 2nd Edition, AP Professional.
3.  de Berg, M., Kerveld, M. V., Overmars, M., & Schwarzkopf, O. (1997). *Computational Geometry Algorithms and Applications*, Springer.

*157*

Figure 4. Images of colored-paper mosaic rendering.

# ComicDiary: Representing Individual Experiences in Comics Style

*Contact*
Ryuuki Sakamoto
ATR Media Integration &
Communications Research
Laboratories
Japan Advanced Institute of
Science and Technology
skmt@jaist.ac.jp

Yasuyuki Sumi
CREST, Japan Science and
Technology Corporation
ATR Media Intergration &
Communications Research
Laboratories

Keiko Nakao
Kenji Mase
ATR Media Integration &
Communications Research
Laboratories

This sketch describes ComicDiary, a system that automatically creates a personal diary in a comics style. ComicDiary is built as a sub-system of our ongoing project (C-MAP) to develop a personal guidance system for touring museums, trade shows, academic conferences, cities, etc.[1] The aim of the C-MAP system is to provide users with personalized guidance in temporal and spatial situations, as well as for individual interests. We intend that ComicDiary will be used as a casual tool for augmenting each individual user's memory and encouraging users to exchange personal memories.

## ComicDiary: What and Why

The goal of ComicDiary is to allegorize individual experiences by creating comics from users' touring records. Exhibitions are visited by people of all generations. A comics-style representation of personal diaries drawn with amiable expressions[2] is appropriate for such places. The comic, composed of 12 frames, is automatically generated as a diary. Users can view their diaries at information kiosks. They can also choose to print the information at the exit of the exhibition and/or access the information as an online service.

The figure is an example of a comic created by ComicDiary. It shows a user's personal diary during a Japanese academic conference. The comic describes where the conference was held, which presentation was the most interesting, what events the user attended, and so on.

The advantages of using comics for representation of diaries are as follows:

• Comics are a casual medium for exchanging personal experiences among users as well as for personal use.

• Comics make it easy to grasp the entire structure of sequential events.[3]

• Comics enable the use of powerful expressions for emphasizing important episodes.

## The Technique

The user's activities and interest data (generated by a PalmGuide device, information kiosks, and an infrared badge) are stored in the central user database as the user explores an exhibition site equipped with the C-MAP system. The central database also includes an exhibition database, which stores exhibition data such as abstracts of exhibits and timetables of specific events. ComicDiary exploits these stored databases as story sources. ComicDiary generates a comic in three phases:

1. When it receives a user query via CGI, the generative engine in the server-side module considers the user's actual history of exploring the exhibition site from user-database logs involving other C-MAP services.

2. The engine determines the type of user by examining personal data and chooses an adequate story in the comic knowledge base, which contains generative rules for comics. For example, if the user is a child, comic expressions and structure are created to be simple and easily understood.

3. The server-side module sends the user's illustration data, which is drawn in advance, to the client-side module, which lays out the illustration data according to the story.

For the prototype, we have chosen Macromedia Flash 5.0 as the platform for publishing the comic on the client side because it can handle vector data, and it operates on popular Web browsers. Users can view their comics at information kiosks and at home.

## Future Work

This prototype uses only a quadrilateral frame. However, conventional comics provide descriptions with a large variety of frame shapes to provide dynamic effects. To overcome this limitation, we plan to analyze the frame structure of several published comics. We also plan to evaluate the effectiveness of the system in order to redesign the story and structure of each comic. Automatic story generation and frame composition for arbitrary comics rendering are other remaining issues.

*References*
1. Sumi, Y. & Mase, K. (2000) Communityware situated in real-world contexts: Knowledge media augmented by context-aware personal agents. In *Proceedings of PAAM 2000,* 311-326.
2. McCloud, S. (1994). *Understanding Comic,* Kitchen Sink Press.
3. Kurlander, D., Skelly, T., & Salesin, D.H. (1996). Comic chat. In *Proceedings of the 23rd Annual Conference on SIGGRAPH 96 Computer Graphics,* 225-236.

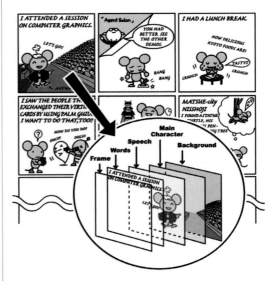

This is a horizontal half-page of a sample comic and the layer structure of the first frame. The main character is the guide agent used in the C-MAP system.

# COMPRESSING LARGE POLYGONAL MODELS

*Contact*
JEFFREY HO
Beckman Institute
University of Illinois
at Urbana-Champaign
Urbana, Illinois 61801 USA
j-ho1@dizzy.ai.uiuc.edu

KUANG-CHIH LEE
DAVID KRIEGMAN
Beckman Institute
University of Illinois
at Urbana-Champaign

With the recent and rapid advances in digital acquisition technology, meshes with millions if not billions of vertices are becoming increasingly common. Existing mesh compression/decompression algorithms are only effective if a representation of the mesh's entire topological and geometric structures (and other attributes) is small enough to fit in memory. Yet for a mesh with a few million vertices, one faces the possibility that there is insufficient memory on a regular desktop computer for the entire model. Our approach to compressing these large models is to automatically partition the mesh into submeshes of smaller size, depending on available local memory, and then compress them separately.

The main purpose of the mesh partitioning is to divide the input mesh into submeshes of roughly equal sizes ( i.e., the partition should be balanced). However, from the compression standpoint, it is also desirable that each region of the partition is "localized" somewhere in the model, and the boundary of each region is as simple as possible. Straightforward mesh partitions using x; y; z coordinate axes or the level sets of some other linear functions generally do not satisfy these requirements (see Figure 1). Instead, we propose a simple partitioning scheme based on a simplified mesh. Using vertex clustering,[1] we obtained a simplified mesh that is typically 100 to 200 times smaller than the original. Each vertex of the simplified mesh has a weight that is the number of corresponding vertices in the original mesh that cluster to the given vertex, and each edge carries a weight giving the number of collapsed triangles that form the edge. The simplified mesh can be partitioned as a weighted graph to obtain a balanced partition that minimizes the edge cuts. The partition of the simplified mesh then induces a balanced partition of the original mesh that usually satisfies the two requirements above. Therefore, we have an in-core representation of a simplified mesh which is used as a kind of blueprint for partitioning and compressing the original mesh.

Armed with this partitioning scheme, we have experimented with two similar methods for compressing large polygonal meshes. One ignores the boundary identifications, while the other compresses the connectivity losslessly.

For the first method, we simply partition the mesh and compress each submesh separately without regard to how different cut boundaries should be identified. By cut boundary, we mean the non-empty intersection between two neighboring regions of the partition. The advantage of this approach is that it is easy to implement and can be built immediately on top of existing mesh compression software.[2,3] The vertices belonging to the cut boundaries are encoded twice; hence, depending on the way the mesh is partitioned and the number of regions in the partition, the number of duplicated vertices can range from as few as one percent of all the vertices to as high as 20 percent; in the worst case, it is possible that more than half of the vertices will be encoded twice. This clearly illustrates the peril of using an arbitrary partition. Using a simplified mesh as a guide, our partitioning scheme will almost never produce the worst-case partitions. It has to be noted, however, that minimizing the number of vertices on the cut boundary does not necessarily guarantee smaller size for the compressed code. Nevertheless, we have observed through our experiments that

the compressed output produced by our partition scheme ranges from two percent to eight percent with an average of four percent less than the compressed output from a "bad" partition.

For the second method, we developed an efficient approach to encoding (and decoding) cut boundaries based on identifying their connected components. The main idea is to use run-length encodings for the regular vertices of the cut boundaries, while for the singular vertices, we simply encode them directly. For meshes with mostly smooth cut boundaries, this part of the compressed code is generally negligible for very fragmented and complex cut boundaries.

Currently, we have only used the connectivity of the simplified mesh. Future research will be focused on how to utilize the geometry of the simplified mesh to define non-linear prediction rules for more efficient geometry compression.

Table 1 shows that a lossless compression ratio greater than 15 to 1 can be achieved on the meshes shown in Figure 2.

*References*
1. Rossignac, J. & Borrel, P. (1993). Multi-resolution 3d approximations for rendering complex scenes. *Modeling in Computer Graphics*, 455-465.
2. Rossignac, J. (1999). Edgebreaker: Connectivity compression for triangle meshes. *IEEE Transaction on Visualization and Computer Graphics, 5* (1).
3. Touma, C. & Gotsman, C. (1998). Triangle mesh compression. *Proceedings of Graphics Interface '98*, 26-34.

| Model | Original File Size | Compressed File Size | Ratio | Bits/ Vertex |
|-------|--------------------|----------------------|-------|--------------|
| David | 173 MB | 10.1 MB | 17 | 19.4 |
| Lucy | 533 MB | 35.6MB | 15.2 | 20.3 |

Table 1: Compression Results: 16-bit coordinate quantization used for David and Lucy. All compressions were done on a Sparc workstation with 58MB of RAM. Each submesh is compressed using Edgebreaker[2] and Parallelogram Prediction.[3]

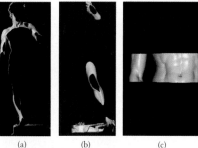

(a)       (b)       (c)

Figure 1. (a) This partition is induced from a simplified mesh; (b, c) partitions using z and y axes, respectively.

(a)       (b)

Figure 2. Two of our test models: (a) Lucy from Stanford 3D Scanning Repository. 28055742 triangles and 14027872 vertices. (b) David from the Digital Michelangelo Project. 8254152 triangles and 4129614 vertices.

# A Computationally Efficient Framework for Modeling Soft Body Impact

Sarah F. Frisken
Ronald N. Perry
MERL

## Introduction

While there has been significant progress in simulating collisions between rigid bodies,[1] much remains to be done for modeling interactions between soft bodies. Graphical techniques for representing and deforming soft bodies range from non-physical (e.g., control point-based) to physically plausible (e.g., FFD) to physically realistic (e.g., FEM).[2] All of these techniques require three operations to model interactions between soft bodies: Detecting collisions between deforming bodies, computing impact forces when bodies collide, and determining deformation forces or contact deformation of the bodies to initialize a deformation technique. In this sketch, we propose a new framework that performs all three operations quickly, with efficient use of memory, and more accurately than previous methods. The results of these operations can be used in any of the deformation techniques mentioned above.

## Utilizing ADFs for Modeling Soft Body Impacts

We recently proposed adaptively sampled distance fields (ADFs) as a new shape representation and suggested that they might be useful for collision detection.[3] ADFs adaptively sample the signed distance field of an object and store the sample values in a spatial hierarchy (e.g., an octree) for fast processing. ADFs have several advantages for modeling impacts between soft bodies including: Compact representations of complex surfaces, trivial inside/outside and proximity tests, fast localization of potential contact regions, more accurate representation of the overlap region, and simple methods for computing material-dependent contact deformation.

## Detecting Collisions, Penetration, and Proximity

The sign of the distance reconstructed from the ADF at any point in space provides a trivial inside/outside test. When detecting collisions between two ADFs, their spatial data structures can be exploited to quickly localize potential regions of overlap. Within these regions, a new ADF of the shape defined by the intersection of the two ADFs is locally generated as illustrated in Figure 1(a). (The intersection is a simple *min()* operation on the distance fields of the two ADFs.) If the intersection ADF is non-empty, a collision is detected and the region is further processed. To test for proximity rather than collisions, an ADF defined by the intersection of offset surfaces can be generated as illustrated in Figure 1(b).

## Computing Impact Forces

There are a number of methods for computing impact forces between two interacting bodies.[4] Penalty-based methods compute impact forces based on how far objects penetrate each other during a discrete time step. Distance fields have been used[5,6] to determine penetration depth at sample points along the penetrating surface as well as to compute contact forces. From Figure 1(c), the total force vector, $\mathbf{F}_V$, acting on V due to penetration of U by V is approximated by the sum of forces $\mathbf{f}_{Vi} = k_U(\mathbf{x}_i)\mathrm{dist}_U(\mathbf{x}_i)\mathbf{g}(\mathbf{x}_i)$, where $k_U(\mathbf{x})$ is the material stiffness of U at $\mathbf{x}$, $\mathrm{dist}_U(\mathbf{x})$ is the closest distance from $\mathbf{x}$ to the surface of U, and $\mathbf{g}(\mathbf{x})$ is the normalized gradient vector of U's distance field at $\mathbf{x}$.

The intersection ADF represents the *volumetric* overlap region to high precision. Previous penalty methods compute $\mathbf{F}_V$ from a small number of points *restricted* to the penetrating surface. Using ADFs, penetration forces can be computed over the surface or the volume of the overlap region. Forces can be computed at an arbitrary number of well-spaced sample points seeded on the surface or throughout the volume, and we are investigating methods to analytically interpolate forces throughout the overlap region. These advantages of ADFs provide the opportunity to compute impact forces more accurately than previous methods.

## Determining Contact Deformation

When using ADFs, there are two methods for determining the initial contact deformation. The first follows common practice and uses the impact forces computed above together with a deformation technique. The second uses the implicit nature of distance fields to compute contact deformation by combining the distance fields within the overlap region. Various methods can be used to combine the fields and achieve material dependent deformation[7,8] (see Figure 2). Figure 3 shows a simulation for the impact of two soft bodies.

*References*
See www.merl.com/reports/TR2001-11

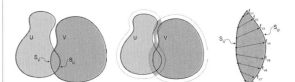

Figure 1. (a) The overlap region (in blue) of shapes U and V is determined by local generation of the intersection of U and V; (b) the overlap region of the offset surfaces of U and V can also be easily generated for determining proximity information; (c) forces acting on $S_V$ in the overlap region of (a).

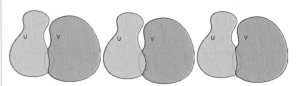

Figure 2. Contact deformation of the objects of Figure 1 with (a) similar material densities; (b) V softer than U; and (c) volume preserving deformation.[7,8]

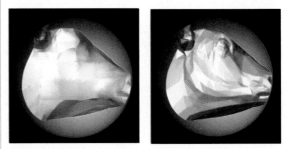

Figure 3. Indentation of a sphere after impact with an ADF of a complex cow model. Contact deformation of the sphere after impact with a soft cow (a) and a hard cow (b).

# Computing 3D Geometry Directly from Range Images

Sarah F. Frisken
Ronald N. Perry
MERL

## Introduction

Several techniques have been developed in research and industry for computing 3D geometry from sets of aligned range images.[1] Recent work has shown that volumetric methods are robust to scanner noise and alignment uncertainty and provide good quality, water-tight models.[2,3,4] However, these methods suffer from limited resolution, large memory requirements, and long processing times, and they produce excessively large triangle models.

Volumetric methods[2,3,4] construct range surfaces for each aligned range image and fill a (fixed-resolution) volumetric representation with signed distances from the range surfaces. The methods use various approaches to reduce the time required to fill and access this volume data, including run-length encoding of the distance values, binary encoding of regions outside a bounded region of the surface, and a three-color octree representation of the volume. The distance values from multiple scans are combined probabilistically using order-independent or incremental updating. Finally, these methods build a triangle model of the iso-surface of the distance volume using Marching Cubes.

In this sketch, we propose a new volumetric method for computing geometry from range data that:

- Computes distances directly from range images rather than from range surfaces.
- Generates an adaptively sampled distance field (ADF) rather than a distance volume or a three-color octree, resulting in a significant savings in memory and distance computations.
- Provides an intuitive interface for manually correcting the generated ADF.
- Generates optimal triangle models (with fewer triangles in flat regions and more triangles where needed to represent surface detail) from the generated ADF octree using a fast new triangulation method.[6]

## Corrected, Projected Distance Images

Constructing 3D range surfaces and computing distances from these surfaces contribute significantly to the computational requirements of volumetric methods.[2,3,4] If, instead, the distance field could be generated directly from 2D range images, model generation times could be reduced. However, range images do not provide true distance data. In the simplest case, a range image records the perpendicular projected distance from the object surface to the image plane. The projected distance field is the same as the true distance field in two circumstances: Throughout the field for a planar surface parallel to the image plane, and at the surface (where both distances are zero) for any surface. Except for the first case, the projected distance field differs from the true distance field for points off the surface, resulting in artifacts when combining projected distance fields from different viewpoints.

For a planar surface, it can be shown mathematically that the difference between the true distance and the projected distance at a location **x** is inversely proportional to the magnitude of the distance field gradient at **x** when the gradient is computed using central differences. Here we propose to *correct* the 3D projected distance field by dividing sampled distances by the local gradient magnitude. This results in a better approximation of the true distance field near the surface, yielding better results when combining projected distance fields. Computing the local 3D gradient to make this correction could be prohibitive (it requires six additional distance computations). Instead, we derive the 3D gradient from a 2D gradient image generated once during preprocessing, resulting in significantly faster generation.

## Adaptively Sampled Distance Fields

We recently proposed ADFs as a new representation for shape.[5] ADFs adaptively sample the signed distance field of an object and store the sample values in a spatial hierarchy (e.g., an octree) for fast processing. ADFs are memory-efficient and detail-directed, so that distance values are computed from the range images only where needed (mostly near highly detailed regions of the surface). Even in 2D, ADFs have been found to require 20 times fewer distance computations than a comparable three-color quadtree representation.[5] Finally, ADFs can be interactively edited via a sculpting interface[6] so that holes and other surface anomalies from occlusions and sensor noise can be easily corrected.

The ADF is generated from sequential or order-independent range images using a tiled generator.[6] Currently, distance values from the range images are combined as though carving the shape from a solid cube of material using a Boolean differencing operator; we have also begun experimenting with adding probabilistic combining functions[2,3,4] for robustness to sensor noise.

*References*
See www.merl.com/reports/TR2001-10

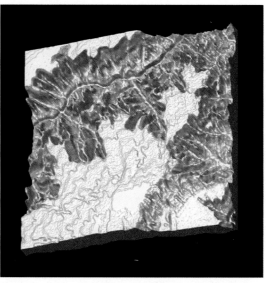

Figure 1. An ADF generated from an 800 x 800 elevation image of the Grand Canyon (data courtesy of USGS). Generation time (from range image to rendered model): 15 seconds.

# COMPUTING NEARLY EXACT VISIBLE SETS WITHIN A SHAFT WITH 4D HIERARCHICAL Z-BUFFERING

*Contact*
NED GREENE
NVIDIA
ned@ngreene.com

We introduce a method for determining visibility within a shaft that exploits nearly all available occluder fusion and culls nearly all occluded primitives, failing to cull only when an occluded primitive is within a user-specified distance epsilon of being visible. Typically, the resulting epsilon-visible set of primitives only slightly overestimates the true visible set, culling more effectively than other practical methods. One important application is determining nearly minimal sets of primitives that are visible from a viewing volume. The method produces a 4D z-pyramid that can later be used for efficient on-the-fly visibility queries.

Within a shaft having quadrilateral endcaps, a primitive P is visible if there is a ray originating on the viewing endcap and piercing the other endcap (a "shaft ray") that intersects P before intersecting any other primitive. We will say that a primitive is epsilon-visible if there is a shaft ray connecting it to the viewing endcap, and occlusion of this ray by other primitives, if any, could be eliminated by moving each of them a distance of epsilon or less.

We construct an epsilon-visible set by subdividing a shaft until its subshafts are occluded by individual primitives, permitting deeper primitives to be culled, as illustrated for a 2D shaft in Figure 1. In this example, subshafts A-C and A-D are occluded by P1, subshaft B-C is occluded by P2, and additional subdivision would establish that shaft B-D is occluded by P2 and P3, and that the red primitives are occluded. Similar hierarchical methods have been applied to radiosity computations (e.g., Teller & Hanrahan, Global Visibility Algorithms for Illumination Computations, SIGGRAPH 93).

The recursive subdivision procedure that computes an epsilon-visible set takes as input the shaft's endcaps and a depth-sorted list of primitives, which it steps through in near-to-far order, testing each to see if it occludes the entire shaft. If so, a farthest depth value for the shaft is established, and any primitive whose nearest depth is deeper is occluded and therefore culled from the primitive list. The nearest primitive within the shaft and the nearest primitives on each of the shaft's "edge rays" are marked visible. After processing all primitives on the list, if not all have been culled or marked visible, the shaft is subdivided into the 16 subshafts formed by connecting all combinations of the four sub-quadrilaterals of one endcap with those of the other. This same procedure is then called with each subshaft's endcaps and the primitives on the current list that intersect that subshaft. Depth-first subdivision proceeds until all remaining primitives within a shaft have been culled or marked visible, or until the shaft width falls below the user-specified distance epsilon, whereupon primitives that have not already been marked visible are marked ambiguous. When the procedure finishes, the visible and ambiguous primitives are the epsilon-visible set, and all other primitives are known to be occluded.

This procedure could be accelerated with graphics hardware by using the method of Durand et al. to detect occlusion of shafts by collections of primitives (Conservative Visibility Preprocessing using Extended Projections, SIGGRAPH 2000). Efficiency could also be enhanced by processing in multiple passes, where the level of subdivision increases from pass to pass, and by organizing the

scene in nested bounding boxes and testing boxes for visibility before testing the primitives that they contain.

In the example of Figure 2, epsilon corresponds to seven levels of subdivision, and our procedure established that 50 polygons were visible (blue/green), one was ambiguous, and 64 were occluded (red). Down to subdivision level five, we saved farthest depth values of shafts in the 4D z-pyramid of Figure 3 (simultaneous 2D subdivision of endcaps produces a 4D image).

Saving a z-pyramid enables fast on-the-fly conservative culling later of other objects within the shaft, using a visibility-query procedure analogous to conventional 2D hierarchical z-buffering (Greene, Kass, & Miller, Hierarchical Z-Buffer Visibility, SIGGRAPH 93). Just the coarsest levels of the pyramid provide a compact occlusion image, which we used to determine that square S was occluded in Figure 2.

In conclusion, our method is essentially 4D hierarchical z-buffering that finds visible geometry by adaptive subdivision, doing only as much work as necessary to establish visibility within a specified tolerance. We have found this approach to be a practical way to compute nearly exact visible sets within shafts containing many thousands of polygons.

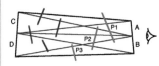

Figure 1. First level of subdivision of a 2D shaft, which established that primitives P1 and P2 occlude sub-shafts A-C, A-D, and B-C.

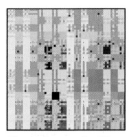

Figure 3. Corresponding "4D z-pyramid" encodes depth of occlusion within shafts.

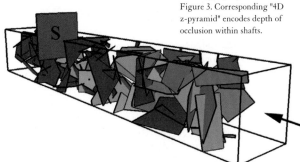

Figure 2. Blue-green polygons are visible and red polygons are occluded with respect to the set of rays originating on the near endcap and ending on the far endcap.

# CONTIGRA: A High-Level XML-Based Approach to Interactive 3D Components

*Contact*
Raimund Dachselt
Dresden University of Techbnology
dachselt@inf.tu-dresden.de

## Motivation

This sketch reports on a new approach to facilitating construction of interactive 3D graphics applications for the Web and introduces the component architecture and underlying high-level languages.

Three-dimensional Web graphics technology is used in an increasing number of application areas such as product presentations, teaching, or 3D navigation (see Figure 1). Considering the huge improvements in graphics hardware and the fast-evolving Internet technologies, it seems surprising that 3D applications are still not widely used. One problem is dependence on proprietary 3D formats or the less successful VRML standard. Even with its promising successor, X3D[1], the wide variety of Web 3D formats will persist. The second major problem is lack of design standards, authoring tools, and concepts of reuse. This is why building 3D applications is still time-consuming and heavily dependent on programming skills. However, interdisciplinary development of 3D solutions (for example, for entertainment or shopping) using building blocks or 3D components is inevitably necessary.

The few existing component approaches like 3D-Beans[2] or i4D[3] have the disadvantage of 3D format dependency or dependence on proprietary technologies. Also, component technologies like JavaBeans are inherently code-centered and thus difficult for non-programmers to use. This sketch addresses these problems and proposes a flexible solution.

## The CONTIGRA Approach

The acronym stands for Component OrieNted Three-Dimensional Interactive GRaphical Applications. The approach introduces a 3D component concept that is largely independent of implementation issues and allows easy, declarative, and interdisciplinary authoring of 3D applications. It is based on structured documents describing the component implementation, their interfaces, and assembly and configuration. The core of the architecture consists of markup languages based on XML, allowing consistent, declarative description of complex 3D scenes. XML has the advantages of hierarchical descriptions matching scene graph concepts, powerful transformation capabilities using DOM or XSLT, and interoperability with other Web technologies. The three multi-layered CONTIGRA markup languages are coded with XML schema.

## CONTIGRA SceneGraph

As an extension to X3D, this schema allows implementation of a 3D component in terms of geometry and behavior, which are described separately. The set of scene graph nodes is extensible. Using XLST or DOM, the documents can be translated to any 3D scene graph format. In addition to the SceneGraph component implementation, there are resource files (sounds, textures, scripts, etc.), all referenced in a homogeneous way (see Figure 2).

## CONTIGRA SceneComponent

This component-description language is used to define component interfaces separated from their SceneGraph implementations. It is well suited for distribution, search, and deployment. Different sections of an interface document allow a rich component description, from offered functionality and configurable parts up to deployment and authoring information. As an abstraction to implementation details, high-level parameters hide scene graph fields. Other components can be encapsulated. Pointers to SceneGraph documents and available editors are included.

## CONTIGRA Scene

This is a high-level configuration language for component integration. Documents coded with this schema represent a declarative description of interactive 3D virtual environments. They contain a hierarchical assembly of configured component instances, component connections, and general scene parameters like cameras, lights, etc. How are these grammars applied? People with knowledge of scene graph concepts implement and describe 3D components using the SceneGraph and SceneComponent level. After distribution, the components can be independently deployed and configured with an intuitive 3D user-interface builder that is now under development. For this tool, CONTIGRA Scene documents also serve as an exchange format. All the documents are finally transformed into a running 3D application, either at configuration time or on the fly in a Web browser, adapted to the configuration of the client.

The declarative high-level languages and the run-time framework are still works in progress. Our preliminary results already show the flexibility and feasibility of the component-based approach to authoring 3D applications. Its major achievements are platform independence, abstraction to specific 3D formats, componentization, and a declarative approach that is well suited for visual tool support.

*References*
1. Extensible 3D (X3D). URL: www.web3d.org/x3d.html
2. Doerner, R. & Grimm, P. (2000). Three-dimensional beans - creating Web content using 3D components in a 3D authoring environment. Web3D/ VRML 2000.
3. Geiger, C., Paelke, V., Reimann, C., & Rosenbach, W. (2000). A framework for the structured design of VR/AR content. VRST 2000.

Figure 1. A 3D representation of a site map allows fast navigation among Web pages.

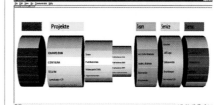

Figure 2. The multi-level Contigra XML suite and related component and application documents.

SCOTT BENZA
Lead Animator

JIM HOURIHAN
Principalz Engineer
Industrial Light + Magic

Aircraft destruction in "Pearl Harbor" was made possible by taking an alternative approach to rigid body systems. This presentation demonstrates ILM's technique for creating realistic dynamic simulations for the film.

Problem: How do you animate destruction of a semi-rigid airplane as it collides with one or more other objects? The plane model may be over-constrained; it may be composed of more than 200 separate objects; and simulation compute time must be reasonable on a desktop workstation.

Solution: A number of algorithmic developments allowed us to achieve the required performance:

- Addition of "clustered" rigid body systems to maximize simulation speed and animation control. This allowed the animators to bypass the more traditional approach to crash simulations, which involve multiple simulation passes to achieve a performance. Clustering gave animators the control and speed they needed to set up an entire crash in a single simulation.

- Optimization of an existing simulation engine (SW1) to handle larger numbers of bodies.

- A robust animation framework.

We also developed a number of external physical force fields, including a pseudo-fluid air field and water field for floating objects. With air and water fields applied to the simulations, objects would flip and tumble through the air naturally, or float and sink once they hit the water.

Finally, a very tight connection was required to make data transfer between the external simulator and Maya as simple as possible. These connection tools gave animators copy/paste functionality directly between the software packages, which condensed an elaborate translation of huge amounts of data to a single mouse click.

# CREATING TOOLS FOR PLAYSTATION2 GAME DEVELOPMENT

*Contact*
KEVIN ROSE
Sony Computer
Entertainment Europe
Cambridge, United Kingdom
kevin_rose@scee.sony.co.uk

SIMON BROWN
The Moving Picture Company
simon.brown@physics.org

## INTRODUCTION

The tools department at Sony Computer Entertainment Europe Cambridge (SCEE Cambridge) created many tools needed for game creation during pre-production of our initial PlayStation2 game. The tools were built while programmers were working on the game engine and artists were creating concept art. The work is currently being used in production of our PS2 titles.

The required tools included a level editor with exporters, miscellaneous art tools, a pipeline, and a data-management system. We wanted to use off-the-shelf software wherever possible. We decided to use Alias|Wavefront's Maya for our editor, as it offers a proven platform with scripting facilities and an open API, and we used Microsoft's Visual SourceSafe for version control. These formed the foundation upon which our tools were built.

## GAME OBJECT SPECIFICATION

Game-play mechanics are built in the level editor using game objects. These objects describe collision areas, how characters behave and navigate, interactive lighting, etc.

In previous projects, writing changes to exporters and creating project specific tools was time-consuming, costly, and error-prone. To avoid these problems, we needed game objects that were customisable and extensible. We classified the many different types of game objects from previous games into six base types and created a scripting system to extend these specialised versions. Using object-oriented design principles, we considered special-case game objects to be derivations of the base types. This allowed us to focus on writing tools for a limited set of base objects, and new derived map-object types no longer required exporter or tool changes.

Our base object types are an extension of Maya DAG-nodes and utilise the MEL script language for adding parameters that describe the object. A limited set of parameters for deriving objects was defined. These described information such as floats, position, file resources, and storage requirements. Using our simple scripts, programmers can derive new game objects. Maya reads these scripts, and our tools automatically generate the appropriate GUI. The exporters, using the fundamental set of base objects and the allowable parameter types, build the new object-data structures.

## PIPELINES

Disparity between the code and art resource management and a lack of reliable version control for art resources caused problems on previous projects. We wanted a simple system with a minimum amount of custom coding for PS2 projects, so we chose Microsoft's Visual SourceSafe, as it is simple to use and maintain. The level editing is done in Maya using custom plug-ins and scripts. Code, game-object scripts, and resources are read into Maya from SourceSafe as required, ensuring that everything is up to date.

Many copies of each landscape are kept, some for artwork, and some for game objects, allowing game play and artwork to be edited concurrently by many people. Our exporters then combine all the exported data for use in the game. Using Maya's scripting system, the exporters also add exported data to SourceSafe, carry out "behind-the-scenes" housekeeping, and start up the game with the exported data. This pipeline is transparent to the user and has been kept relatively simple.

## ART TOOLS

Many art tools have been created, ranging from tools to allow "vertex" colouring on NURBS surfaces to tools that check how suitable a given mesh is for game use.

One particularly useful tool is the plant tool. Placing geometry accurately on a surface can be time-consuming, so a plug-in was written to "plant" a selected object where the user clicks on another surface. Variations on this approach allowed us to directly plant instances and duplicates of objects.

Custom GUIs were created with MEL scripting to present the artist with palettes of textures, geometry, and game objects. Our GUIs connect directly to SourceSafe, so they always retrieve the most recent files.

## ACKNOWLEDGEMENTS

We would like to acknowledge Guillaume Raffy, Andrew Ostler and Adam Garman who worked with us to create these systems and tools.

*165*

Maya showing part of a level with game objects and the game-object browser.

Maya screen grab showing the same part of level, but working on the artwork with geometry and texture browsers.

PlayStation2 screen grabs. Real-time views from two games currently in development. Three of the images are from the same viewpoints shown in the Maya screen grab.

Maya screen grab showing three views of a level.

## CREATIVE APPROACHES TO THE INTEGRATION OF CGI WITH TRADITIONAL ANIMATION IN DISNEY'S "ATLANTIS: THE LOST EMPIRE"

*Contact*
KIRAN JOSHI
Walt Disney Feature Animation
kiran.joshi@disney.com

MARCUS HOBBS
Walt Disney Feature Animation

Over the years, we have seen the advantages of CGI as a tool to artistically embellish and execute scenes that would be cost-prohibitive if done with traditional methods. The task of animating an action adventure feature of epic proportions, as in Disney's first action-adventure animated feature, "Atlantis: The Lost Empire," was only feasible by utilizing CGI. However, the challenges of when, how, and how much CG to use became a matter of creative, technical, and production balance. This sketch provides an overview of artistic and technical approaches to blending the two worlds.

Disney has always sought to enmesh the worlds of 2D and 3D to retain the company's traditional feel while at the same time taking advantage of the wonderful opportunities provided by computer graphics. For "Atlantis," the blend of techniques had to be seamless, or the comic book art direction would not work cohesively. We were embarking on a rather dramatic change in style, genre, and, ultimately, technique. Categorically, it would have not been possible to complete the movie without digital techniques.

The highly stylized, bold posterized look of the film had to be mastered by both the digital artists and the traditional artists in their rendering. The look and the animation style had to be resolved for each scene so the CG elements could be successfully integrated. Therefore, CG elements had to be developed with the same level of flexibility as hand-drawn elements. The details of a CG element were not baked into one level. Creation of many levels of artwork for a CG element provided the flexibility to blend its look to match hand-drawn artwork from scene to scene.

Due to the sheer volume of scenes, it was very clear that we would be required to animate elements both ways, so the method had to be transparent to viewers. Acknowledging the strength and weaknesses of digital mathematical perfection and the natural imperfections of traditional animation was the key to successfully blending of these worlds. Techniques were chosen for their appropriateness to the shot and subject.

To help the traditional animators animate their elements and register hand-drawn artwork to CG-rendered artwork, a custom tracking software was enhanced to utilize the plots of the rendered artwork. This allowed the animators to draw to a fixed, scaled image reference without having to worry about size and motion. The hand-drawn animation was tracked to the CG-animated element's motion path.

With a variety of video clips, this sketch illustrates how we integrated CGI to the creative process in each step of the production. We discuss the creative and technical integration challenges from visual development to production pipelines.

A scene from the Leviathan Attack sequence in Disney's "Atlantis: The Lost Empire."

A scene demonstrating the close registration of 2D traditional character animation with 3D elements in "Atlantis: The Lost Empire."

166

# Death Valley Flyby: A Simulation Comparing Fault-Controlled Alluvial Fans Along the Black Mountain Range

*Contact*
Carlos Seligo
Stanford University
423 Sweet Hall
590 Escondido Mall
Stanford, California 94305-3091
USA
+1.650.736.1432
moth@stanford.edu

Charley Weiland
Academic Technology Specialists
Stanford University

This animation sketch presents how public US Geological Survey (USGS) data can be used to simulate complex geological phenomena for an undergraduate seminar. Our simulated flyby over Death Valley was sufficiently accurate and detailed to represent not only major fault-controlled deformations, but even the sparse vegetation along alluvial fans and evidence of recent seismic activity that was not yet eroded by flash flooding. Finding and downloading data of sufficient resolution, correctly registering 2D images on 3D elevations, and stitching together the quadrangles covered in the flight path proved challenging in a computing environment that was not dedicated to this task. Nonetheless, now that we have solved these problems, we hope the procedure might be more generally applied to rendering geological formations of any site for which similar data are available.

## Technical Problems Rendering 3D Simulations From Public Data

In November 2000, a professor contacted us for technical support of a class on Death Valley. Half-jokingly, she requested an airplane to shoot the fault along the Black Mountain Range, which was beyond the budget of an undergraduate seminar, but we guessed that it would be possible to simulate such a flight from public data. Ten years ago, rendering a photographically realistic and geologically accurate flyby of a fault would have been a piece of experimental computer science that only the military or NASA could afford. Today, the major technical problems have all been solved, but applying these technical solutions in support of a seminar was not a trivial task.

The USGS no longer offers most of its public data for free, but we were able to find nine contiguous 7.5-arc-minute digital elevation models (DEMs) of Death Valley at 30-meter resolution. We downloaded the aerial photographs, or digital ortho quads (DOQs), that corresponded to each DEM from the Digital Alexandria Project. At one-meter resolution, four DOQs make one DEM, and stitched together, these image files were 170 megabytes each before compression. These proved cumbersome to match in brightness and contrast, and because we lacked the geographical tools to adjust them to the curvature of the earth's surface, the registration marks in the 2D images did not automatically correspond with the corners of the 3D models. Nonetheless, we were able to produce simulations that were scientifically accurate enough for our educational purpose using off-the-shelf software: World Construction Set, Lightwave, Photoshop, and Media Cleaner Pro.

## How Simulations May be Applied More Generally to Serve a Wide Variety of Pedagogical Goals

Finally, we would like to suggest how these simulations might be applied more generally to serve the pedagogical aims of educators. For a price, the National Elevation Dataset will burn CDs of comparable data for anywhere in the contiguous United States. GIS Data Depot also provides file-format translators and an uneven selection of free models from all over the world. Not only geologists can benefit from accurate simulations of a landscape. If architects used these tools to preview the views from the windows of the buildings they design, an art historian could reconstruct Cezanne's "Mountains Seen from l'Estaque!"

*Contact*
J. P. Lewis
OHP
501 Glenoaks Boulevard
Suite 656
Glendale, California 91202 USA

This sketch describes some preliminary work on decomposing animated motion into a set of localized "blendshapes" (also called morph targets and shape interpolation) that can be combined to produce that motion. In computer animation, information traditionally flows in the opposite direction. Predefined blendshapes or other primitives are combined to produce the animated movement. To motivate blendshape decomposition (BSD), we note that several computer-vision techniques allow model streams to be acquired from cameras, and these techniques may become routine in the future. The form of the captured data (a stream of unlabeled meshes, often without frame-to-frame registration) does not lend itself to post-capture editing, however. This leads to the frequent comment that motion capture does not reduce the animator's workload. Some post-capture editing of the data is presumed necessary, but this requires constructing an animator-friendly model (often using blendshapes) and then animating this model to mimic the captured performance. Motion capture can obviously drive an animator-friendly model through some automated process, but producing this model remains an issue. Our work is motivated by this issue.

Viewed abstractly, BSD can be seen as looking for a decomposition
$$A = BW \quad (1)$$
where for each of $N_p$ frames of performance the model containing $N_m$ control points is unrolled into a column of A ($N_m \times N_p$), columns of B ($N_m \times N_b$) are the basis being sought, and columns of W ($N_b \times N_p$) are the weights (encoding) for corresponding frames of A; the rank of A is assumed to be $N_b$, so the blendshapes can be regarded as compressing the performance.

Decomposition techniques such as principle component analysis (PCA) and independent component analysis (ICA) provide a starting point for consideration of the BSD problem. The PCA of A is easily obtained from its SVD, $A = UDV^T$; the U matrix is the desired basis. PCA has well known characteristics that make it unsuitable for our purpose, however. The basis shapes are orthogonal, not localized, and usually have no intuitive interpretation, whereas an animator-friendly BSD needs bases with intuitive and preferably local control, such as "smile" or "raise right eyebrow." In other fields, such considerations (especially the lack of locality) has led to the search for alternative decompositions. ICA produces a decomposition in which the basis shapes are not required to be orthogonal, and locality has been demonstrated. On the other hand, ICA is formulated as the solution of the blind source-separation problem in which independently moving sources are added in an unknown combination. Although the BSD problem might be put in this form, at the outset the characterization of individual shapes as completely independent (and an additional requirement that they have non-Gaussian densities) seems unnatural and restrictive. Consideration of other recent literature suggests that this restriction can be avoided.

Two techniques provided inspiration for this work: the Atomizer basis pursuit system and positive matrix decomposition techniques. In Atomizer,[1] a large, overcomplete set of basis functions is generated prior to examining the data. A particular data set is represented by finding weights that minimize the 1-norm rather than the usual 2-norm. The authors observe that the 2-norm disproportionately penalizes large weights, resulting in many small weights that are roughly the same size. In BSD, as in Atomizer, we desire a sparse coding whereby a local deformation is preferably produced with a single (or few) delta shape(s) rather than an overlapping combination of many shapes. Unlike Atomizer, we want a tight rather than overcomplete basis, and we want to derive the bases functions rather than selecting from a large predefined set.

Several numerical techniques (LININPOS, PMF) provide a factorization of the form (1) when A,B,W are all restricted to be positive; software for the PMF algorithm is available commercially.[2] Discussion of these techniques yields a second useful observation: restricting the weights and bases to be positive encourages locality. When weights are unrestricted, a localized shape can be explained with broad bases combined in a cancelling fashion with positive and negative weights. Unlike PMF techniques, we will require both positive and negative excursions in the basis shapes, however.

BSD prototypes that explore locality principles, including those mentioned, above have been implemented. The algorithms perform gradient descent minimization of $tr(A - BW)^T (A - BW)$ starting from random $B$ and $W$ and reprojecting B on the subspace $U$ during the descent iteration. Evaluations of these approaches are not complete, but many one-dimensional and a few three-dimensional simulations have been performed. In these simulations a synthetic dataset was created by randomly combining blendshapes, and the simulation then tries to recover similar local basis shapes without knowing the originals (Figure 1).

*References*
1. Chen, S. & Donoho, D. L. (1995). Atomic decomposition by basis pursuit. Stanford Dept. Statistics TR 479, May 1995.
2. Paatero, P. (1997). Least squares formulation of robust non-negative factor analysis. *Chemometrics and Intelligent Laboratory Systems 37*, 23-35.

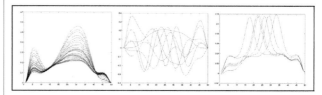

Figure 1. Left: 1D dataset; center: orthogonal basis is complex and not local; right: evolved local basis.

Figure 2. Superimposed original target and recovered delta shape. Note that this is a relatively easy result since most of the geometry here is obtained by keeping the solution $B$ close to a subspace defined by only three shapes.

# Destroying a Dam Without Getting Wet: Rule-Based Dynamic Simulation for "Wave of Death"

*Contact*
Stephan Trojansky
CA Scanline Production
Bavariafilmplatz 7
82031 München, Germany
+49.89.6498470
+49.89.64984711 fax
troja@scanline.de

*Digital Artists*
Stephan Trojansky
Florian Hu
Roland Langschwert
Fritz Beck
Sebastian Küchmeister
Albrecht Steinmetz
CA Scanline Production

The shots presented in this sketch show the breaching of a huge dam. Each shot has been completely computer generated, including the environment, the dam, chunks of concrete, fragments, dust, water, and mist. The work was done by using a rule-based dynamic simulation technology that provides a new technique for digital creation of natural phenomena or catastrophes.

### The Challenge
The film "Wave of Death" revolves around a huge dam that is blown up by terrorists at the end of the story. The destruction of the dam was supposed to be shown in a two-minute effects sequence consisting of 17 shots, with people running on the dam while it slowly disintegrates under their feet.

Since the Scanline team is always looking for new challenges, the thought of a "dry" digital solution, where only the close-ups of the actors are live action, made our eyes sparkle. That alone would have been challenge enough, but after a close look at the very limited budget, we had the feeling of being flooded ourselves. We had a production schedule of six weeks and a team of six animators to get this job done. Our main concern at that point was finding a way to realize this project without getting more than "wet feet."

### The Approach
To achieve extraordinary results in such a short span of time, we had to automate as much as possible, to free the animators from doing work that could be done just as well by a software tool. At the same time, we didn't want to be at the mercy of a mathematical simulation. We wanted to keep the creative direction of the action in our hands. The fact that Scanline is working with proprietary animation software helped a lot. We were able to combine our know-how with the rule-based simulation idea of Cebas Computer, a well-known German software-development team.

### The Solution
The tool we developed provides an efficient and at the same time flexible way of creating dynamic simulations. In contrast to conventional keyframe animation or pure dynamic simulation, rule-based dynamic simulation allows complete control of the dynamic reactions and interactions of all particles involved, without the necessity to determine each one of them separately.

Once we had set up a rule for the "behaviors" of one element (for example, chunks, fragments, dust, water, mist), we were able to apply it to all the other elements of the same kind. By using this strategy, our dam breaching sequence, consisting of a few hundred thousand varying parts, could be controlled by alterations of only a few parameters.

www.scanline.de/WaveOfDeath

169

# The Development of the Virtual Human Abdomen: Algorithms and Methodologies

*Contact*
**Kevin Chugh**
Virtual Reality Lab
State University of
New York at Buffalo
Amherst, New York 14260 USA

**T. Kesavadas**
Virtual Reality Lab
State University of
New York at Buffalo

**James Mayrose**
Department of
Emergency Medicine
State University of
New York at Buffalo

Simulating soft tissue in haptic virtual reality applications presents two difficult obstacles:

1. The ability to compute force-displacement calculations in real time. There are two issues that contribute to this hurdle. The first is that for continuous haptic sensations, an output rate of 1000 Hz or better is required. Second, traditional methodologies for computing force-displacement relationships employ polynomially growing algorithms.

2. The need for physical realism dictates that actual tissue parameters be extracted from tissue and then used in the simulation.

At the Virtual Reality Lab, we have developed a virtual human abdomen that simulates soft tissue for a virtual palpation exam. The simulation overcomes both of these obstacles and, at the same time, provides a realistic and physically accurate model.

## Methodology

To overcome the first obstacle (real-time performance), we have developed a force-displacement computation algorithm/methodology called the Atomic Unit Method.[1] In this methodology, each discrete volume is modeled as an atomic unit, and each atomic unit has its own behavior. Forces are handed off from atomic unit to atomic unit, and the global behavior of the tissue model is computed by aggregating the atomic unit behaviors. Figure 1 depicts a portion of the human abdomen modeled as a set of atomic units before and after palpation.

## Data Collection

Creation of a physically accurate simulation requires tissue parameters. In order to non-invasively collect material properties on human organs, we created a data glove[2] that allows the user to collect information about a palpation exam (the 3D position of the finger as it displaces the tissue, as well as the force used to cause that displacement). This information was used to calculate the stiffness and viscoelastic properties of human soft tissue within the loading ranges of palpation. These viscoelastic properties were then fed into the haptic simulation.

## The Virtual Human Abdomen

Combining the real-time haptic calculation methodology with the data collection device allowed for development of the Virtual Human Abdomen. This is a real-time, physically accurate abdominal palpation simulation that uses real human anatomical images and real human tissue parameters. Figure 2 shows the simulation.

## Presentation

This sketch describes three facets of the development of the Virtual Human Abdomen:

1. The real-time algorithms, their development and implementation, and their asymptotic qualities.
2. The functionality of the data collection device and its supporting algorithms.
3. Validation results. These experiments involved physicians performing palpations on the Virtual Human Abdomen.

*References*
1. Chugh, K., Mayrose, J., & Kesavadas, T. (2000). The atomic unit method: A physically based volumetric model for interactive tissue simulation. World Congress on Medical Physics and Biomedical Engineering, 2000. Chicago.
2. Mayrose, J., Chugh, K., & Kesavadas, T. (2000). A non-invasive tool for quantitative measurement of soft tissue properties. World Congress on Medical Physics and Biomedical Engineering, Chicago, 2000.

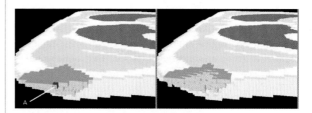

Figure 1. Before and after a palpation.

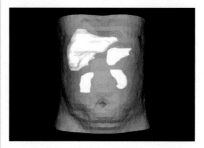

Figure 2. Surfaces are rendered for the Virtual Human Abdomen.

*Contact*
DANIEL PIROFSKY
pirofskyd@pdx.edu

## CONCEPT

These interactive animations are playful meditations on algorithmically discovered, non-objective images. Source animations are mapped to spatial grids, providing non-linear access to frames in any continuous or discontinuous sequence. Viewers can meditate on frames, play strands of continuous motion, or generate unique, spontaneous animations.

## APPLICATION

Photographic virtual reality is a popular medium for interactions with panoramic or three-dimensional images. QuickTime VR panoramas present a screen-based immersive experience that places the user in the center of a scene. QuickTime VR object movies present a three-dimensional object in front of the user that is rotated to display alternative views. In panoramas, the viewer is the center of the universe; with objects, the user is on the periphery looking into and around the center.

Absolute object movies are an alternative, two-dimensional method of organizing multiple images in a non-linear format. Instead of rendering frames as multiple views from positions around the object, an absolute object movie positions images in a grid structure, allowing the user to click on any position to display a frame. This allows interactive access to multiple views and sequences of 2D or 3D images. In this framework, there is no center or circumference: space generates time as the matrix of frames is explored.

Exploiting this feature of QuickTime VR provides an interactive animation experience. Current work presents 12 interactive animations, each composed of 2,700 frames, the equivalent of three minutes of linear animation, mapped across a grid of 25 rows and 108 columns. When an animation loads, a short selection of looped animation plays to preview the imagery contained in the object. Clicking the mouse button down within the object stops the animation to display a single frame from a unique location in the grid. Dragging the mouse button down plays a sequence of frames. Moving horizontally across the grid isolates a single strand from among the 25 rows of 108 frames. Moving vertically down the grid selects frames from a variety of different strands. Stroking the animation in a series of interactions generates unique versions of the animation by displaying a series of continuous or discontinuous frames. Speed of the mouse motion controls the speed of the animation. This simple interaction in visual-temporal space can be intriguing, hypnotic, relaxing, or exciting as images appear, connect, and disappear. Across the limitless spectrum of algorithmically generated, non-objective imagery, traveling through these unique structures of visual space begins to trigger contemplative experience and insight.

## PROCESS

This project began by exploring the graphics technology of Artmatic software, which renders visual images from mathematical structures generated through a combinatorial algorithmic process. I was amazed at the richness of this natural visual order as I discovered, mutated, and rendered images, searching for novel and beautiful structures. From these structures, I rendered animations of sufficient length to explore these visual regions more deeply and

systematically. Playing these animations, I stopped to gaze at key images that captured my imagination. Contemplation of their natural beauty led me to connect these frozen moments back to their original flow by replaying the animation. I meditated on these regions of visual space by first scrubbing across the timeline in an arbitrary, spontaneous, exploratory process, then interacting with specific locations to generate new sequences, revealing unique, tunable insights. This led to recomposing the linear animations into QuickTime VR absolute objects that offer a non-linear format to explore image sequences within the totality of visual space presented.

This enables free play with images and sequences, fast or slow, getting a feel for the totality of the animation and permutations of its structure. Temporal flow of images is presented in a spatial context. Time becomes a non-simultaneous experience of the totality of this visual space. Horizontal motion invokes continuity; vertical motion leaps to connect discontinuous location. The two-dimensional surface becomes an enjoyable play, and in that flow arises a meditation that is aesthetic and insightful in its reconfiguration of temporal into spatial media.

Figure 1. Representative frames from "horizons of unborn insight."

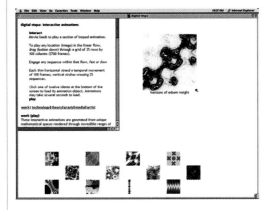

Figure 2. Screen image of digital stupa Web interface.

171

# Digital Tricks for Japanese Cel Animation

*Contact*
Akio Kazumi
OLM Digital, Inc.
kazumi@ilm.co.jp

Megumi Kondo
Katsuaki Hiramitsu
Ken Anjyo
OLM Digital, Inc.

Yoshinori Dobashi
Hokkaido University

This sketch illustrates our unique and original uses of digital technology in creating Japanese cel animation. First we discuss cases that focus on merging 3D CG with cel-animated characters. Then we consider implicit the use of 3D techniques for making 2D painted, cel-based scenes more visually 3D and fantastic.

### Merging a 3D Scene with 2D(Cel-Animated) Characters

In principle, the Western production pipeline is constructed to produce an exact realization of the storyboard of an animation piece. Each process in the pipeline is explicitly distinguished from other processes. This also means that the role of the creators is accurately prescribed. In other words, this production pipeline might be called "top-down," and it is an efficient way to achieve a desired result.

On the other hand, in many cases, Japanese animation is created from rough keyframes based on the storyboard, and then the keyframes are repeatedly arranged by checking test sequence rendering. So the Japanese pipeline is "bottom-up." For example, in the brand-new Pokémon movie, entitled "CELEBI A Timeless Encounter," many cuts are made with the bottom-up approach, where cel-animated characters are placed into a 3D background (see Figure 1). The bottom-up pipeline may force traditional cel animators to adopt a rather strict 3D sense, which represents an alternative way to get the desired result.

Fast rendering tools are indispensable in production work. This is very crucial for Japanese cel animation, because it must be produced on a tight schedule (as short as one year, even for a cel-animated film). In making "CELEBI", a custom fast volume renderer was developed for depicting shafts of light. This renderer is a non-photorealistic version of the fast volume renderer developed by Dobashi et al.[2] This tool is unique in the sense that it allows fine parameter tuning for non-photorealistic effects, such as decay of shafts, consistent with fast processing at high resolution rates.

### Making 2D Painted Images More Visually 3D

In Japanese cel animation, implicit use of 3D techniques for cel-based 2D scenes is often preferable to explicit use of the cel-shaded 3D scene.[1] Camera projection mapping is a good digital technique for providing "visually 3D" effects: inputting a 2D-painted image of the scene to be animated. In the camera projection process, a pseudo-3D structure is constructed from the input 2D image, and then the resultant pseudo-3D model is animated with camera control restricted. An advanced use of this technique is illustrated in Figure 2, where a 3D blobby model is added to the pseudo-3D model of the painted bridge. Then mask animation of the pseudo-3D model is used to describe crystallization of the bridge.

Additional examples of our implicit uses of 3D techniques for cel animation include particles with patch-grid geometry for splash and wave expressions.

*References*
1. Anjyo, K., Arias, M., Horry, Y., & Momose, Y. (2000). Digital cel animation in Japan. *SIGGRAPH 2000 Conference Abstracts & Applications*, 115-117.
2. Dobashi, Y., Kaneda, K., Yamashita, H., Okita, T., & Nishita, T. (2000). A simple, efficient method for realistic animation of clouds. *Proceedings SIGGRAPH 2000*, 19-28.

Figure 1. Frame from "CELEBI A Timeless Encounter."

Figure 2. Frame from a promotional reel of "Lord of the Unknown Tower" (bottom) and 3D blobby hull of the bridge model (top).

172

# Dynamic Flesh and Muscle Simulation: "Jurassic Park III"

Dennis Turner
Technical Animation Supervisor
Industrial Light + Magic

Sebastian Marino
CG Software Engineer
Industrial Light + Magic

## Problem

At first glance, creation of digital dinosaurs for "Jurassic Park III" was a problem with which ILM was well acquainted. Indeed, our digital creature pipeline is still based on the principles and techniques learned on the original "Jurassic Park" and honed on its sequel, "The Lost World." Beneath the surface, however, technological development and aesthetic expectation has increased unabated. ILM's work on projects such as "The Mummy" and "The Phantom Menace," and work from other studios, such as Disney's "Dinosaur," raised the bar that defines believable organic digital creatures.

## Solution

We met the higher expectations for digital creatures by increasing the level of detail. Our performance criteria for the dinosaurs as actors remained the same. What changed was our expectation for how their bodies should react to the performance. In effect, the number of things that happen on the screen when the tyrannosaurus rex lunges forward after human prey increased exponentially.

Flesh simulation techniques developed for "The Mummy" were converted for use on dinosaurs. This allowed us to procedurally create the dynamic, or ballistic, effect of large organic bodies moving under the dinosaur effects of gravity and inertia. Within the dinosaur, we modeled and rigged objects, which represent muscles and bones. These objects make "guest appearances" in shots by providing the effect of masses moving under the skin.

Distinguishing physical differences of the dinosaurs were enhanced by the manner in which flesh simulations were employed. For corpulent creatures, such as the brachiosaurus, muscles and bones were rarely seen, if at all. The effect of dynamics applied to these bodies was nearly pure follow through with overlapping action. In contrast, the muscles and bones on lean creatures, such as the velociraptors, truly defined the form of the models as they moved. These two features were combined to full effect for the heavyweight prize fighter bodies of the tyrannosaurus rex and spinosaurus.

## Artist Application

Additional detail was layered into ILM's existing creature-development and shot-production pipeline. The dinosaurs were modeled with additional surface detail and internal structures as needed, but otherwise were consistent with our standard methods for employing parametric surfaces. The models were then rigged with primary animation controls and enveloping. Additional muscle rigging and enveloping were developed in model sets that could cleanly replace the primary animation models at any time during shot production.

As we identified shots for which flesh simulation would provide perceivable effects, the simulation models replaced the primary animation model set. This was done only in a subsection of the shot pipeline, leaving the performance animation, lighting, and render procedures unencumbered.

*173*

# Dynamic Meshing Using Adaptively Sampled Distance Fields

Jackson Pope
Sarah F. Frisken
Ronald N. Perry
MERL

Many models used in real-time graphics applications are generated automatically using techniques such as laser-range scanning. The resultant meshes typically contain one or more orders of magnitude more polygons than can be displayed by today's graphics hardware. Numerous methods have been proposed for automatically creating level-of-detail (LOD) meshes from large input meshes.[2] These techniques typically generate either one or more *static* LOD meshes, pre-computed before use in the application, or a *dynamic* mesh, where the LOD of the mesh adapts to frame rate requirements. We present a new dynamic LOD technique ideal for applications such as games and physical simulations based upon adaptively sampled distance fields (ADFs).[1] ADFs also provide fast collision detection as required by these applications.

## Previous Work

Existing dynamic meshing algorithms such as view-dependent progressive meshes (VDPM)[3] and hierarchical dynamic simplification (HDS)[4] generate a hierarchy to efficiently process refinement and decimation operations. The hierarchy in VDPM is formed by creating a new parent vertex for every pair of vertices combined by an edge collapse operation. The HDS hierarchy is formed by spatially subdividing the scene into cells and grouping vertices in each cell into a single representative vertex. In both, the screen space error and normal cones (to detect back-facing and silhouette triangles) are used to determine when to refine and decimate the mesh. We present a new method that utilizes a spatial subdivision hierarchy, enables fast collision detection, and uses the distance field to position mesh vertices to optimize mesh shape.

## Generating Meshes from ADFs

ADFs are a new shape representation that adaptively samples the signed distance field of an object and store the distance values in a spatial hierarchy (we use an octree).[1] We utilize a fast, new triangulation method that generates topologically consistent (orientable and closed) triangle meshes from the ADF structure.[5] Cells in the ADF octree that contain the object surface (where the distance field changes sign) are connected to their neighbors by triangles. The technique exploits the hierarchical nature of the octree to produce detail-directed triangles.

## Algorithm

Our method creates a triangle mesh from the ADF, associating triangles with ADF cells, and then adapts the mesh in real time to viewing parameters to optimize visual quality (by using a high level of detail in visually important regions), while meeting user-defined frame rate criteria.

The algorithm is composed of two stages: a pre-processing stage and a real-time stage. The real-time stage is performed every frame or every few frames as required. The pre-processing stage initializes the data required for the real-time stage and creates an initial view-independent active cell list from which a triangle mesh is derived. Each active cell is associated with one ADF cell. Data initialization includes determining and storing normal cones in each boundary ADF cell; these cones bound the normal cones of all the cell's children. The hierarchical ADF structure enables fast view frustum and back-face culling using normal cones.

The real-time stage consists of adapting and optimizing the existing active cell list and corresponding triangle mesh for current viewing conditions. During each adaptation, the active cells are considered to see if they contribute too many or too few triangles to the mesh according to view-dependent cell weights. If the number of triangles is appropriate, the cell is left alone. If the cell contributes too many triangles, triangles associated with the cell and its siblings are deleted from the mesh, the cell's parent is added to the active cell list, and triangles associated with the cell's parent are generated and added to the mesh. If the cell contributes too few triangles, the cell is added to an ordered list of such cells. To ensure that frame rate requirements are met, this cell list is processed in order only while there is frame time available. When processed, triangles associated with cells in the ordered list are deleted from the mesh, the cell's boundary child cells are added to the active cell list, and triangles associated with the cell's boundary child cells are generated and added to the mesh. The different treatment of cells with too many and too few triangles prevents the mesh from growing in size beyond the rendering capabilities of the graphics hardware.

Each cell is assigned a weight based on its contribution to the view. Currently, a cell is assigned a high weight if it is on the object's silhouette, and zero weight if it is back-facing or outside the view frustum. Other parameters could be considered, such as the projected screen size of the cell or whether the cell contains a specular highlight. In addition, our method uses the in-place cell error of the ADF as an indicator of surface roughness and curvature in the cell, and modulates the weight by this error.

## Results

The technique produces detail-directed triangle meshes of high visual quality as viewed from the camera, while minimizing the number of triangles in non-visible portions of the object. It meets frame-rate criteria (currently, at 30 FPS it maintains ~25K triangles), even during viewpoint changes that lead to large differences in the visible portion of the object.

*References*
See www.merl.com/reports/TR2001-13

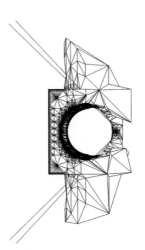

Figure 1. CSG object showing view frustrum (20364 triangle, 41 FPS). Note how areas outside the view frustrum are culled.

# Efficient Update of Geometric Constraints in the Tapestry Evolving Mesh Representation

Maryann Simmons
Sara McMains
Carlo Séquin
University of California,
Berkeley

This sketch describes the use of motion bounds to optimize the evolving mesh representation used by the Tapestry[1] interactive rendering system. The tapestry dynamic display mesh is constrained to be a "spherical depth mesh" (i.e., its projection onto a sphere centered at the viewpoint has no overlapping elements). The mesh vertices are projected onto a sphere centered at the viewpoint to determine the mesh topology during incremental insertion of new points. This makes the insertion more efficient by reducing the problem to 2D. A Delaunay condition is maintained on the projected mesh to produce a good-quality image reconstruction. In addition to the depth mesh and Delaunay properties, minimum projected edge length and minimum projected vertex-edge separation constraints are maintained on the mesh to support a robust implementation. Here, we describe an efficient method for enforcing these constraints during view motion.

## Calculating Conservative Motion Bounds

The mesh is constructed relative to an initial viewpoint. The geometric constraints are enforced by construction for this viewpoint. When the viewpoint changes, we want to retain as much of the 3D mesh as possible, while guaranteeing that all of the constraints are still satisfied. Since it is inefficient to test each triangle in every frame to make sure that its projected topology remains consistent, we assign conservative motion bounds to each triangle, stating how far the user can move before any constraints are invalidated.

For the depth-mesh constraint, this means that all triangles that will become back-facing in the new view need to be removed. We use the distance from the viewer to the plane of the triangle as a conservative bound $d_b$ indicating how far the viewpoint could move before the triangle could be back-facing (see Figure a).

For minimum projected edge length, we note that in the plane, all points for which the angular extent of an oriented edge (a,b) relative to a viewpoint is greater than some minimum epsilon are contained in the circle that has (a,b) as a chord, and an interior angle of epsilon (Figure b). The same construction holds in 3D for the epsilon surface, which can be visualized by sweeping the circle about the edge in the half-space above the plane of the triangle to form a half torus with negative interior radius (Figure c). To determine the motion bounds for edge length, we calculate the minimum distance $d_e$ to the perimeter of this surface.

For minimum edge-vertex separation, the same calculations described in the previous paragraph are performed, but the perpendicular $e_p$ dropped from the vertex to edge (a,b) is used as input instead of edge (a,b) (Figure d).

## Results

We have utilized this update technique to evolve a fully dynamic display mesh used as a front end for ray-tracing.[2] We further optimize the identification of non-conforming triangles by binning the mesh triangles based on the conservative motion bounds. In this way, only a small number of triangles need to be examined each frame, and an even smaller number tested. During an interactive session with a moving observer, and a mesh with approximately 22K triangles, on average only nine percent of the triangles had to be examined, and of those only four percent needed to be removed. The end result is that on average over 99 percent of the mesh could be re-used across view motions, while still maintaining the depth-mesh and minimum feature size constraints.

To ensure a robust mesh and good-quality image reconstruction, the Delaunay condition relative to the new view must also be re-asserted for each triangle. This requires that each sample be re-projected relative to the new viewpoint. As these operations are expensive, in this application we have relaxed the Delaunay constraint for efficiency. Instead, samples are re-projected, and the Delaunay condition tested, only when triangles are encountered in some subsequent mesh operation. The derivation of a similar motion bound for triangles based on the Delaunay condition would greatly improve the performance and mesh quality after motion.

*References*
1. Simmons, M. & Séquin, C. H. (1999). Tapestry: A dynamic mesh-based display representation for interactive rendering. *Proceedings of Eurographics Rendering Workshop*, 1999.
2. Simmons, M. (2001). Tapestry: An efficient mesh-based display representation for interactive rendering. PhD thesis. University of California, Berkeley, May 2001.

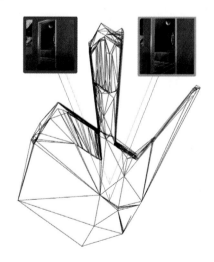

Tapestry Evolving Mesh: A top-down view showing the mesh. The current view frustum is drawn in blue and the next desired view frustum in green. The red mesh edges show the triangles that would invalidate the constraints in the new view. The corresponding views (at higher resolution) for the blue and green frusta are shown on the above left and right, respectively.

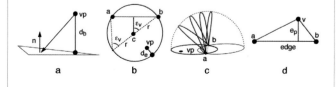

175

# Elastic Object Manipulation Using Coarse-to-Fine Representation of Mass-Spring Models

*Contact*
Hirofumi Kawai
Nara Institute of Science
and Technology
(Presently with Network &
Software Technology Center,
SONY Corporation)
kawai@arch.sony.co.jp

Masatoshi Matsumiya
Naokazu Yokoya
Nara Institute of Science and
Technology

Haruo Takemura
Nara Institute of Science
and Technology
(Presently with Cybermedia
Center, Osaka University)

This sketch describes an efficient method for elastic-object deformation using mass-spring models with coarse-to-fine representation based on the degree of deformation. One of the key technologies for creating realistic virtual environments is real-time manipulation of elastic objects with force feedback. Mass-spring models are widely used for representing elastic objects in virtual environments because they can be applied to both geometrical and topological deformation of objects in real time.[1] However, the increased number of mass points and springs representing more complex deformation usually makes it difficult to simulate the deformation in real time. The proposed method aims to reduce the computational cost for simulating such a complex deformation with mass-spring models.

## Coarse-to-Fine Representation of Mass-Spring Models in Manipulation

The key idea of our method is based on the dynamic combination of different levels of mass-spring models according to the magnitude of object deformation in order to reduce the number of mass points and springs used for calculation. As shown in Figure 1, a largely deformed part of an object is represented and calculated by a fine mass-spring model. The other part is calculated using a coarse model. The velocity and position of mass points are calculated from these dynamic mass-spring models.

The proposed method requires building "hierarchical mass-spring models" as described in Figure 1. In this step, multiple mass-spring models are constructed with different numbers of cells. Note that a cell is composed of $2^3$ connected mass points.

In interactive manipulation, the simulation is carried out as follows. First, a set of mass points for the calculation is chosen with the following criteria. When a manipulator contacts a mass point, the cell including the point is subdivided as in octree subdivision. When a diagonal spring of a cell stretches more than a certain threshold, a finer model is applied to the cell. By these steps, we get a minimum set of mass points and the level of these points in hierarchical mass-spring models. Secondly, we choose the springs connected to those points from hierarchical mass-spring models. Then the velocity and position of those points are calculated by using the chosen springs. Finally, the velocity and position of mass points that are not updated yet in each cell are calculated by linear interpolation of known values. In terms of topological deformation, a conventional method of deleting a spring that is stretched over a certain threshold in the finest mass-spring models is used.[2]

## Results

In order to evaluate the effectiveness of the method, a simple elastic object manipulation system is developed with a force-feedback device on a SGI Octane (MIPS R10000 195MHz.). Figure 2 shows the results of elastic-object deformation. Figure 2 (b) and (c) illustrate coarse-to-fine models of a cubic object. Figure 2 (d) and (e) show examples of geometrical and topological deformations, respectively. Table 1 summarizes the number of springs and the time used for calculation of the models Figure 2 (b)-(e). The computation time is reduced 33.6-64.0 percent of conventional mass-spring models.

*References*
1. Miyazaki, S., Ueno, J., Yasuda, T., Yokoi, S., & Toriwaki, J. (1995). A study of virtual manipulation of elastic objects with destruction. IEEE Int. Workshop on Robot and Human Communication,.26-31.
2. Norton, A., Turk, G., Bacon, B., Gert, J., & Sweeney, P. (1991). Animation of fracture by physical modeling. *Visual Computer 7*, 210-219.

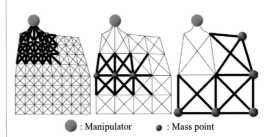

● : Manipulator    ● : Mass point

Figure 1. 2D illustration of coarse-to-fine representation of a mass-spring model.

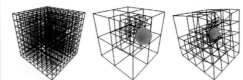

(a) Original mass-spring model    (b) Example of coarse-to-fine representation (1)    (c) Example of coarse-to-fine representation (2)

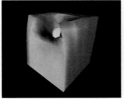
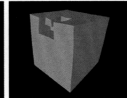

(d) Geometrical Deformation    (e) Topological Deformation

Figure 2. Elastic object deformations.

| | | Fig.2 (b) | Fig.2 (c) | Fig.2 (d) | Fig.2 (e) |
|---|---|---|---|---|---|
| Proposed Method | No. Springs | 937 | 1753 | 1168 | 1170 |
| | Time [msec] | 4.5 | 8.3 | 5.3 | 5.5 |
| Conventional Method | No. Springs | 7448 | | | |
| | Time [msec] | 12.5 | | | |

Table 1. Computation time comparison with conventional method.

# ELMO: A Head-Mounted Display for Real-Time Image Synthesis

*Contact*
Kiyoshi Kiyokawa
Communications Research
Laboratory
kiyo@crl.go.jp
www.crl.go.jp/jt/a114/kiyo

Hiroyuki Ohno
Communications Research
Laboratory

Yoshinori Kurata
Topcon Co

Display devices for mixed-reality systems are expected to produce synthesized images of high quality in real time. We have been developing displays that correct occlusion phenomena between real and virtual images, which is important to make synthesized images convincing.

In see-through optical displays, it is hard to represent mutual occlusion phenomena since virtual objects become transparent due to a half mirror, and the real image is always visible through the virtual image (ghost problem). However, we chose an optical approach because it preserves the intrinsic quality of real images, while the video see-through approach inevitably degrades the spatial and temporal resolution of real images.

We attacked the ghost problem with a novel optical system that has two convex lenses of the same focal length and an erecting prism, thereby making a kind of telescope of one magnification.[1] Then, by locating an LCD panel between the lenses, any portion of the real image can be blocked without defocus by closing respective pixels on the panel. We named the display ELMO (an Enhanced optical see-through display using an LCD panel for Mutual Occlusion).

## Design and Features of ELMO

The latest prototype display, ELMO-3 (shown in Figure 1), is stereoscopic with folded optical paths and a real-time depth-sensing mechanism. We chose a camera-based passive approach[2] to retain two of ELMO's advantages: it does not affect the real environment, and it does not rely on any environmental presumptions.

Five cameras are used for image capturing with a focal length of 6mm and a baseline of 79mm. A high-speed FZ930 stereovision board from Komatsu Co. is used for disparity calculation, which produces 30 depth maps of 280x200 pixels per second with up to 30 disparities. For instance, if the number of disparities to be calculated are set from 0 to 29 pixels, detectable distance is from 831mm to infinity. At the minimum detectable distance, depth resolution is 5.5mm. Captured depth maps are then rendered three dimensionally and transparently to overwrite Z-buffer, from the left and right eyes' positions, to match the respective viewpoints' real images.

ELMO-3 has both an LCD panel for mask pattern and display modules for color virtual images in its body. Their images are optically combined by beam-splitters, whose transparencies are adjusted so that the real scene is bright.

## Examples

Figure 2 shows four images made by and seen through ELMO-3. Conventional optical see-through displays present a combined image like Figure 2(A). By using the light blocking mechanism, virtual objects are made opaque, as in Figure 2(B). By not partially rendering virtual objects by using depth information of real objects, real objects are seen as if they occlude virtual objects: Figure 2(C). Yet virtual objects remain semitransparent. ELMO-3 can show an image like Figure 2(D) in real time, with mutual occlusion phenomena correctly processed and presented within unknown or dynamic environments.

## Conclusion and Future Work

Our latest optical see-through HMD, ELMO-3, can present mixed-reality environments with correct mutual occlusion phenomena without any setups such as lighting conditions and trackers for real objects. Though the current display has a few problems (bulky body, slow response, and low resolution of the LCD panel) many of them can be improved with better LCD modules that have recently become commercially available.

*References*
1. Kiyokawa, K., Kurata, Y., & Ohno, H. (2000). An optical see-through display for mixed reality. *SIGGRAPH 2000 Conference Abstracts and Applications*, 241.
2. Kanade, T., Yoshida, A., Oda, K., Kano, H. & Tanaka, M. (1996). A stereo machine for video-rate dense depth mapping and its new applications. *Proceedings of the IEEE Computer Vision and Pattern Recognition (CVPR) 1996*, 196-202.

Figure 1. ELMO-3 with arm support.

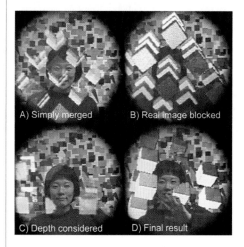

Figure 2. Four images seen through ELMO-3.

*177*

# Elmo's World:
## Digital Puppetry on "Sesame Street"

*Contact*
Emre Yilmaz
PO Box 460022
San Francisco, California 94146
USA
emre@digitalpuppetry.com

*Collaborators*
Dave Satin
Les Rudner
SMA Video

Eric Gregory
Protozoa

Sesame Workshop

Recently, we received an unusual but exciting request: to make a drawer bark like a dog, to make a TV set cry like a baby, and to do it all live on set with Elmo.

Elmo's World is a daily 15-minute show-within-a-show on "Sesame Street." In his imaginary world, the popular red Muppet monster learns about a new concept each day (for instance, dogs, babies, or bananas). Among Elmo's friends in this world are four pieces of furniture. We bring these furniture creatures to life using real-time computer animation, or "digital puppetry." Specifically, we use an experimental motion-capture method.

### The Need

As we worked live on set, our furniture characters were improvising their performances alongside the real puppets. Sesame Street Executive Producer Arlene Sherman further requested that the furniture not only be able to do basic functions, like opening and closing a drawer, but also act like living, thinking beings with personalities and quirks. The idea is that Elmo has drawn these creatures, but they have come to life, and they are not always cooperative. The window shade may be more interested in tickling Elmo than in opening up for him. The TV set may try to come to Elmo, but waddle and fall over like a baby unsuccessfully taking its first steps.

### Digital Puppetry

The models were relatively easy to make, but finding a suitable performance method was difficult. We decided to try an experimental method for puppeteering the characters, using foam rubber blocks outfitted with magnetic motion-capture sensors. If a puppeteer twisted one foam rubber block, the table would twist. If they hopped the foam up and down across the floor, the door character would hop up and down across Elmo's floor. We can't use the captured motion quite straight; we do a lot of real-time modifications on the data to fit the character's proportions and position in the room. In addition to the foam rubber blocks and motion sensors, we provided foot pedals, joysticks, and sliders so the puppeteers could augment the performances. For instance, one foot pedal opened and closed the drawer. That way, one puppeteer could both make the drawer walk around and make its "mouth" open and close.

We felt this would be a very puppeteer-friendly approach, because it allows intuitive control and a great range of motion. The puppeteers could actually grab and manipulate the drawer, the TV set, and the door directly, just as if they were real puppets, watching the live video feedback to see how their characters were moving.

### Production

During taping, the digital puppeteers watch their characters interacting live onscreen with Elmo. The camera sees Elmo in front of the real set, and a quick live composite allows the puppeteers and the director to see how the furniture will look in this shot. What they are seeing is very close to the final result. The puppeteering performance data are captured from the foam rubber blocks and other devices for later playback. Keeping the motion data, and waiting till post-production to commit it to videotape, allowed fixes as necessary.

Three of Sesame Street's regular Muppet performers enact the puppet furniture. The real Muppet performers are highly accomplished at bringing character to inanimate objects. They are also very experienced at interacting with Elmo! Many of the best interactions are improvised live on set. We wanted to enable them to bring all their experience and talent, including improvisation, to the digital characters as seamlessly as possible.

# The Empathic Visualisation Algorithm: Chernoff Faces Revisited

*Contact*
**Andreas Loizides**
Department of Computer Science
University College London
A.Loizides@cs.ucl.ac.uk

**Mel Slater**
Department of Computer Science
University College London

These four pictures of faces represent the financial state of four different companies. In which one would you invest? Without knowing any details of what the facial expressions represent, it is very likely that you would choose the company represented by the bottom-right face as a good investment. In fact, more information can be gleaned from the faces by knowing that the degree of happiness represents profitability, the degree of fear represents liquidity, and so on.

The empathic visualization algorithm (EVA) is a fundamental extension of the type of data visualisation first introduced b y Chernoff,[1] who exploited the idea that people are hardwired to understand faces, and therefore can very quickly understand information encoded into facial features. In particular, it is very easy to cluster Chernoff faces into groups that represent similarities in the underlying data they represent.

Given an nxk data matrix of n observations on k variables, the original Chernoff method assigned each variable to correspond to a particular facial feature like shape of the nose or shape of the eyes. The mapping from data to visual structure was arbitrary, and the resulting face had no correspondence to the underlying semantics of the data. Such faces are good for understanding pattern, but any individual face seen in isolation does not readily convey anything about the data without knowledge of the specific mapping used.

EVA provides an automatic mapping from semantically important features of the data to emotionally or perceptually significant features of the corresponding visual structure, such as a face. In other words, a single glance at the visual structure informs the observer of the global state of the data, since the visual structure has an emotional impact on the observer that is designed to correspond to the impact that would have been generated had the observer been able to analyse the underlying data itself. Finer details concerning interpretation of the visual structure are then available through knowledge of the relationships between semantically important features of the data and emotionally significant aspects of the visual structure.

## The Method

It is assumed that an nxk data matrix is to be represented by a visual structure, ideally one that is naturalistic, in the sense that humans can immediately and transparently interpret the meaning of this structure at a high level. A human face is our paradigmatic example, and we will stay with this example from now on. There are a number of global characteristics that can be used to describe the emotional expressions of a face, such as its degree of happiness, sadness, calmness, fear, or anger. There are also a number of features of a face, such as muscle tensions, that have been used in the Park and Waters model[2] to determine the overall facial expression.

Correspondingly, there will be a number of important global characteristics that are of importance to the consumer of the data. For example, the magnitude of a particular combination of variables (representing, for example, company performance), the difference between a variable and a threshold value, and so on. These global characteristics of the data correspond to the global characteristics of the visual structure. Finally, features of the data (particular combinations of the variables) will determine the features of the visual structure. Thus, if all these features of the data were known, all the features of the visual structure would be known, and the visual structure could be rendered. The global characteristics of such a rendered visual structure could then be measured.

A genetic program is used to determine features of the data so as to minimise a fitness function, which measures the difference between the global characteristics of the data and the corresponding global characteristics of the rendered visual structure. The goal is to minimise the difference, so that the ideal visual structure is one in which its global characteristics correspond exactly to the global characteristics of the underlying data. This can easily be achieved by choosing random functions over the set of k variables to form the first generation of features from the data. Successive generations are formed in the usual way by measuring the fitness of each rendered face and then selecting feature functions with probability proportional to fitness. In our experience, the genetic program typically converges after 75 generations. Initial experiments have shown that even non-expert users can use our technique to quickly interpret the significance of the data.

## Summary

We have introduced a new method for constructing an automatic mapping from data to visual structure, which enforces a homomorphism between important characteristics of the data and the emotional or perceptual impact of the visual structure. Such visual structures are informative "at a glance" but can also reveal important detailed information about the data.

*References*
1. Chernoff, H. (1971). The use of faces to represent points in n-dimensional space graphically. RN NR-042-993, Department of Statistics, Stanford University, December 1971.
2. Waters, K. & Parke, F. (1987). A muscle model for animating 3-dimensional facial expression. *SIGGRAPH 87 Conference Proceedings, Computer Graphics, 21* (4), 17-24.

# Enhanced Reality:
## A New Frontier for Computer Entertainment

*Contact*
Richard Marks
Sony Computer
Entertainment America
richard_marks@playstation.sony.com

This sketch presents techniques for implementing enhanced reality, in which live video and computer graphics are combined to produce real-time, movie-like special effects in the home. The range of achievable effects is limitless, anywhere from something as simple as causing a participant's eyes to glow to something as complex as enabling interaction with an artificial character (for example, Stuart Little). The ability to create such effects enables a new form of computer entertainment that is both more personalized and more engaging than traditional computer entertainment (video games).

### Related Work
Other researchers have considered the interactive modification of video with graphics; this topic of research is commonly referred to as augmented reality. Our work is targeted specifically at home computer entertainment, for use in a typical living room or family room. Whereas many other researchers have chosen to control the environment to achieve a desired visual effect (such as the Mandala system), we have instead chosen to equip the participant with simple props when necessary. By designing the props appropriately, we are able to deal with widely varying lighting conditions and unstructured backgrounds.

### Techniques
The techniques used to achieve enhanced reality fall into two categories: interpretation and enhancement. Interpretation consists of processing the video input to extract information about the participants and their environment. The type of information that is extracted depends entirely upon the particular application. We use several techniques to obtain the following information: a per-pixel labeling that distinguishes users from their environment, a quantitative measure of the visual motion in the video stream, the camera-relative 3D location of special props, an estimated equation for the ground plane, and a model of the lighting of the scene.

Enhancement consists of modifying the video image to include the desired effect. Several rendering and compositing techniques make use of the information acquired via interpretation. These include: rendering to the z-buffer to assign depth cues to parts of the video stream, rendering synthetic objects using the dynamically obtained lighting model of the environment, and rendering synthetic objects to an off-screen buffer and alpha-feathering the edges.

We present several examples of effective ways that information obtained from interpretation can be used effectively for enhancement. We also describe many other possibilities of what may be achievable in the near future.

### Implementation
We have implemented our work on a PlayStation 2 connected to a standard NTSC television set for display and an inexpensive (<$100) IEEE 1394 Webcam for video input. The props are plastic and/or foam toys.

Participants interact with a virtual character...or a virtual pet.

180

# Explicit Control of Topological Evolution in 3D Mesh Morphing

*Contact*
Shigeo Takahashi
Department of Graphics
and Computer Science
Graduate School of
Arts and Sciences
University of Tokyo
3-8-1 Komaba, Meguro-ku
Tokyo 153-8902 Japan
takahashis@acm.org

Kokojima Yoshiyuki
Toshiba Corp.

Ryutarou Ohbuchi
Yamanashi University

Existing 3D mesh-morphing techniques are often limited to cases in which 3D source meshes to be morphed are topologically equivalent. Previously, we published a 3D mesh-morphing scheme based on interpolation of 3D source meshes by using a 4D tetrahedral mesh.[1] While the algorithm could potentially morph source meshes of different topological types, it lacked an effective way to explicitly control evolution of topology. This sketch presents a new approach to explicitly specifying a path of topological evolution while morphing 3D meshes of different topological types. The formalism we employed, while concise, is expressive enough to precisely specify all the possible topological changes that could occur during such topology-altering mesh morphing.

## The Formalism

Our shape-morphing algorithm directly interpolates 3D meshes by using a 4D tetrahedral mesh (a discretized version of 4D hyper-surface), which is embedded in 4D space spanned by x, y, z and t(time)-axis.[1] If a topological evolution occurs during a morph, it occurs at a critical point of the 4D hyper-surface that interpolates the source 3D surfaces. According to Fomenko, et al.,[2] any such topological evolution can be invoked by attaching one of four types of topological handles, listed in Figure 1, to the 3D surfaces involved. In the figure, the shaded part of each handle is "glued" to an existing surface and then eliminated. Careful examination of 4D hyper-surface (and their embedding in 3D space) shows that all the possible transitions in topological evolution are listed in Figure 2.

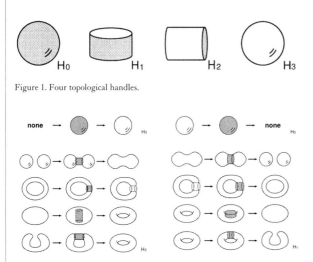

Figure 1. Four topological handles.

Figure 2. List of possible topological transitions.

## The Mechanism

To explicitly specify a topological transition, we insert a topological "keyframe," a concrete version of one of the topological transitions above. A keyframe is a special mesh that consists of two meshes that are geometrically identical but topologically different. Two topologically different meshes in a keyframe relate 3D source meshes of different topological types. Obviously, it is not possible to prepare an infinite number of keyframes for every combination of complex source meshes and topological transitions. Instead, we prepare keyframes in their simplest forms.

As stated above, our algorithm morphs 3D source meshes by interpolating them with a 4D tetrahedral mesh.[1] To simplify the task of creating the interpolator 4D tetrahedral mesh, our algorithm starts from a set of simplified source meshes to create a coarse tetrahedral mesh. The tetrahedral mesh and source meshes are then refined so that the original details are regained in the source meshes. Taking advantage of this framework, we prepare and insert the key frames only at the coarsest of the resolution levels.

As an example, Figure 3 shows creation of two "faces" of a keyframe that relates a simplified torus and a simplified sphere. In the top figure, the hole of a torus is shrunk to a single critical point to make one "face" of a keyframe topologically equivalent to a torus. In the bottom figure, another "face" of the key frame, a mesh topologically equivalent to a sphere, is created by plugging the hole with a topological handle H_1.

Interpolating the keyframe with a pair of (simplified) source meshes of different topological types creates a 4D tetrahedral mesh as shown in Figure 4. Mesh refinement and 3D shape extraction create smooth shape-morphing sequences as shown in Figure 5.

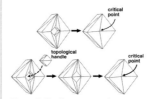

Figure 3. Keyframe generation.

Figure 4. Tetrahedral mesh. (The t and x axes are overlaid.)

Figure 5. Results.

*References*
1. Ohbuchi, R., Kokojima, Y., & Takahashi, S. (2001). Blending shapes by using subdivision surfaces. *Computers and Graphics, 25* (1), 41-58.
2. Fomenko, A.T. & Kunii, T. L. (1997). *Topological modeling for visualization.* Springer-Verlag, 105-125.

*181*

# Fair and Robust Curve Interpolation on the Sphere

Carlo H. Séquin
Jane Yen
EECS, CS Science Division
University of California,
Berkeley

In this sketch, we present a fair and robust interpolating scheme for curves on the sphere. This work was motivated by the desire to create fair curves on the sphere through a sparse set of data points, as might be used in smooth camera motions around an object of interest or in artistic designs. Ideally, the curves should exhibit fairness properties similar to the MVC[1] but would be generated without the need for costly optimization loops. We attempt to obtain such results with a generalization of the classical local four-point subdivision scheme.[2] In order to avoid sharp hairpin turns and cusps, and to obtain a more loopy characteristic of the curves, we forego affine invariance and aim for circular arcs wherever they are compatible with the given data points. Thus, rather than using the traditional cubic polynomial to calculate the position of the new subdivision point, we use a blend of circular arcs (as in Szilvasi-Nagy and Vendel[3]). These circle-splines or C-splines also yield pleasing interpolating curves in the plane and in 3-space.

## Construction

We first describe the C-spline construction in the plane, which extends to the sphere. Given four consecutive data points A-B-C-D, a new subdivision point S halfway between B and C is computed. If A-B-C-D lie on a circle, S is placed onto the same circle at the appropriate intersection with the perpendicular bisector between points B and C. Otherwise, we construct two separate circles through A-B-C and B-C-D, respectively, and blend the two subdivision-points SL and SR proposed by the two arcs (Figure 1a). However, rather than linearly interpolating between SL and SR, we determine S by averaging the turning angles ?L and ?R generated at the points SL and SR (Figure 1b). This interpolating scheme is suggested by a local application of a discrete MVC functional, which aims at averaging the turning angles at consecutive vertices of a piecewise linear curve. To adapt this idea to the sphere, we bisect the angle between the planes through B, C, SL' and through B, C, SR', where SL' and SR', are projections of the arc midpoints onto a concentric sphere enlarged by d/2 = (B-C)/2. With this construct, we achieve that, as the distance BC becomes small compared to the radius of the sphere, the spherical construction transitions seamlessly into the planar construction.

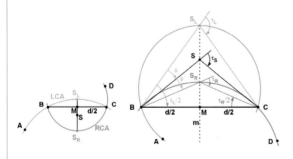

Figure 1. Subdivision of non-cocircular points by linear averaging (left) and by averaging turning angles (right).

Figure 2. Circle splines on the sphere (left). Sculpture model (FDM) made with a sweep along a spherical C-spline (right).

## Properties of C-Splines

The resulting curves have local support and exhibit linear and circular precision by construction. They preserve all symmetries exhibited by the original set of points. The curve is not dependent on evaluation order (unlike quaternion splines[3]), and it thus exhibits "front-to-back" symmetry.

Our construction averages the turning angles at subsequent points, so, on a local scale, it tries to minimize variations in curvature. This property gives it the desired similarity with the MVC. The globally optimized MVC has the undesirable property that it runs away to infinity when constrained by too few points. In our context, dynamic run-away is not a problem, since every subdivision point, once it has been placed, will stay there forever.

## Discussion

The construction on the sphere also gives us an implicit technique to generate C-splines in 3D space. For each set of four consecutive points, an interpolating sphere is calculated, and the above construction is used to find the new subdivision point. The continuity properties for these curves are not yet fully understood. However, in many experiments with a variety of tricky test cases, C-splines have produced fair-looking, seemingly G2-continuous curves. C-splines on the sphere have been used to generate artistic designs that can be enjoyed in virtual form, and which also have been made real through rapid prototyping on a fused deposition modeling (FDM) machine (Figure 2b).

*References*
1. Moreton, H.P. & Séquin, C.H. (1992). Functional optimization for fair surface design. *Proceedings ACM SIGGRAPH 92*, 167-176.
2. Dyn, N., Gregory, J., & Levin, D. (1987). A four-point interpolatory subdivision scheme for curve design. *CAGD 4*, 257-268.
3. Szilvasi-Nagy, M. & Vendel, T.P. (2000). Generating curves and swept surfaces by blended circles. *CAGD 17*, 197-206.
4. Kim, M.J., Kim, M.S., & Shin, S.Y. (1995). A general construction scheme for unit quaternion curves with simple high order derivatives. *Proceedings ACM SIGGRAPH 95*, 369-376.

# A Fast Simulating System for Realistic Motion and Realistic Appearance of Fluids

*Contact*

Yukio Watanabe
System LSI R&D Center
Toshiba Corporation
580-1 Horikawa-cho
Saiwai-ku
Kawasaki 212-8520 Japan
watanabe@sdel.toshiba.co.jp

Atsushi Kunimatsu
Takahiro Saito
Kazuhiro Hiwada
System LSI R&D Center
Toshiba Corporation

Hiroko Fujii
Tsunemi Takahashi
Corporate R&D Center
Toshiba Corporation

Heihachi Ueki
CAE Technology Department
Toshiba CAE Systems Inc.

This sketch presents a system for fast generation of animations that include realistic motion of fluids that obey physical laws and feature shadow and caustics due to the refraction of light at the water's surface. With this system, we can generate fluid animations easily and quickly.

## Fluid Modeling System

Modeling of a scene that includes fluids, and simulation and rendering of the scene, are combined in one system, and they can be controlled through a GUI. In the modeling section, fluids, fluid inlets and outlets, and solid objects are placed. Each object can have its own initial velocity and other parameters, and this information affects the entire simulation. Though fluid simulation and its visualization are very time-consuming processes,[1] since our system can change the LODs of the simulation and the rendering easily by changing the number of grids of the simulation space and changing the level of division of the water surface polygons, the outline of the simulation and the visualization result can be checked very fast. Then we can move to detailed simulation and visualization. Also, we can change the lighting and the viewpoint for each frame while the simulation is running.

## Fast Simulation for Realistic Motion

For realistic motion of fluids, including union and separation, 3D, time-dependent full Navier-Stokes equations have to be solved. To achieve a fast fluid simulation, we adopted two strategies:

1. Use a simulator which itself is fast. For this purpose, we have adopted the Eularian method with a uniform mesh structure. Since this method uses a fixed grid, the calculation efficiency is high. In addition, uniform mesh can speed up the process of solving the Poisson equation for pressure, which requires most of the computation power.

2. Reduce the size of the simulation space by using a low-resolution mesh. However, this also reduces the realism of the motion and appearance of the fluid. Hence, we have adopted the cubic interpolated propagation (CIP) method,[2] which has third-order precision for the fluid transportation problem. In addition, since the CIP method uses the information gradient of volume of fluid (VOF) values, we can reuse the information for the purpose of generating the iso-surfaces, which leads to a smoother surface. Moreover, to generate much smoother surfaces, the Catmull-Clark method[3] was used as a surface subdivision algorithm.

## Fast Rendering for Realistic Appearance

Refractions of light on the water surface yield an aesthetically pleasing pattern of caustics, and refractions of eye vectors create effects such that objects appear to be dancing in the water. These effects are very impressive and important for realistic appearance of fluids. To calculate caustics patterns, two-pass algorithms are often used. In the first pass, distribution of the rays from the light sources is calculated. Then, in the second pass, the scene including caustics is rendered using the distribution information. In earlier methods, these calculations do not match existing rendering hardware and are time-consuming if implemented by software. Hence, we have developed a new rendering method that can utilize the existing polygon rendering hardware. For this purpose, the distribution of the rays is stored as textures (caustics textures) of each object in the scene. First of all, memory for the caustics textures is prepared and cleared to zero. For each water surface polygon, refraction of each vertex is calculated, and then the refracted polygon is drawn to the appropriate caustics texture region by using the alpha-blending function of the rendering hardware. When the water surface is rendered, by calculating the refractions of eye vectors and texture coordinates of objects, refracted eye vector intersections are given. The ordinary texture and the caustics texture of the objects are drawn on the water surface by using the multi-texture function of rendering hardware or the multi-pass approach.

## Example and Evaluation

The figure shows one frame of an animation generated by our system. A fountain was designed with the modeler, and the scene was divided into 40x40x18 mesh for the simulation. Interactions between the fluid and solids are also calculated in the simulator. The caustics pattern due to the refraction of light can be seen on the bottom of the fountain. Even though the simulation space is relatively low, the resulting water surfaces are very smooth and highly realistic. Due to the strategies described above, the beginning 50 frame average simulation and rendering times were only 2.64 and 11.9 seconds, respectively, on a 933MHz PentiumIII PC with 512MB of memory and GeForce2 GTS DDR SGRAM.

*References*
1. Turner, J. A. & Mazzone, A.C. (1999). Multifluid finite volume Navier-Stokes solutions for realistic fluid animation. *SIGGRAPH 99 Conference Abstracts and Applications*, 259.
2. Yabe, T. (1997). Universal solver CIP for solid, liquid and gas. *Computational Fluid Dynamics Review 1997*. Eds. M. M. Hafez and K. Oshima. John Wiley & Sons, New York.
3. Catmull, E. & Clark, J. (1978). Recursively generated B-spline surfaces on arbitrary topological meshes. *Computer-Aided Design, 10* (6), 350-355.

*183*

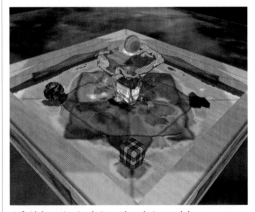

A fluid dynamics simulation and rendering result by our system.

# Fast-moving Water in DreamWorks' "Spirit"

*Contact*

Saty Raghavachary
DreamWorks Feature Animation
1000 Flower Street
Glendale, California 91214 USA
saty@anim.dreamworks.com

Yancy Lindquist
DreamWorks Feature Animation

Contemporary animated feature films often employ a mixture of hand-drawn and 3D computer-generated elements to synthesize water imagery. DreamWorks Feature Animation's first two features, "The Prince of Egypt" and "The Road to El Dorado," both contain ocean water scenes created in this manner. The surfaces were generated procedurally using time-varying turbulence functions with appropriate controls for wave shapes and sizes.[1] In "El Dorado," a program called Spryticle layered foam shapes and handdrawn splashes to add visual complexity and integrate the elements with the rest of the scenes.[2]

For our third feature, "Spirit: Stallion of the Cimarron," a different kind of water surface is called for. Three-dimensional Effects Supervisor Wendy Rogers became responsible for designing the look of water flowing down a hill, rushing past piles of rocks. It was clear to us that the usual wave-based approach would not work in this situation.

## Technique

First, we tried a rather novel technique based on scattered interpolation in two dimensions. A Maya plug-in, *SurfIt*, would interpolate the heights of a set of Maya particles along a regular grid and use the results to deform a NURBS surface whose projection lies on the grid. This did not give us enough control over the look of our surface, so we switched to an alternative technique:

A NURBS surface is sculpted to serve as a "snapshot" of the water surface. At a given frame at each CV of the NURBS surface, another deformer plug-in, *Pokemagnet*, converts the distance to each particle to a "strength," which is then used to find a "pull" on the CV. The pull can be positive or negative, depending on whether the particle is above or below the CV. The largest positive pull and largest negative pull are found by iterating through all the particles. These two values are finally combined with their own user-specified scale factors into a single resultant height offset which is then applied to the CV. This technique yields very precise control over the water surface.

We also came up with an efficient technique to animate particles (for foam and spray) along the generated surface. We sample the surface uniformly along its parametric u and v directions, and store the world-space position, normal, tangentU and tangentV values in custom attributes in a particle "cage." Now, using a particle system, we simply need to search this cage for the sampled surface point closest to each particle. At the first frame, the entire cage needs to be searched for each particle's closest neighbor. Once identified, the cage indices of each closest neighbor are stored in the particle itself, in additional channels. For subsequent frames, we start our search at the previously close neighbor and search only a small neighborhood in u and v, as specified by the user. By using a sampled version of the surface and further restricting the search to a small neighborhood on it, we are able to tackle rather complex surfaces and a large number of particles. The statistics about the closest surface neighbors are written back into the particle object in additional (user-defined) attributes, making it possible for the animator to utilize them in particle expressions to generate arbitrarily complex effects involving particle motion with respect to the surface.

The generated surfaces are environment mapped and rendered with appropriate RenderMan shaders (for example, refraction) to provide the necessary look. Additional foam and splash elements are generated with Spryticle. These elements work to further enhance the look and help blend the result with the rest of the imagery.

*References*

1. Yates, G. & Raghavachary, S. dwNoise and dwNoiseOffset, Houdini & Maya plug-ins, DreamWorks Feature Animation.
2. Ikeler, D. (2000). The use of Spryticle in the visual FX for "The Road to El Dorado." *SIGGRAPH 2000 Conference Abstracts and Applications*.

# FEATURE-BASED TOPOLOGICAL MESH METAMORPHOSIS

*Contact*
SEUNGYONG LEE
Department of Computer
Science and Engineering
Pohang University of Science
and Technology
leesy@postech.ac.kr
www.postech.ac.kr/~leesy

MINSU AHN
Department of Computer
Science and Engineering
Pohang University of Science
and Technology

Metamorphosis, commonly referred to as morphing, deals with fluid transformation from one object to another. Three-dimensional mesh morphing handles two input polyhedral objects and generates an animation in which the source mesh gradually changes to the target through the in-between meshes.

Previous polygonal mesh-morphing techniques consist of two steps: correspondence establishment and geometry interpolation. In the first step, the vertices and edges of the source and target meshes are embedded onto a common domain, such as a sphere, a 2D polygon, and a base mesh. Next, a metamesh is created, where the vertex set contains the source and target mesh vertices, and the intersection points of the edges from the source and target meshes. In the interpolation step, an in-between mesh is generated by interpolating the vertices in the metamesh between the source and target positions.

The basic and common idea of previous mesh-morphing techniques can be summarized as the construction and interpolation of a metamesh. However, this approach has fundamental limitations. First, the metamesh usually has a more complicated structure than the source and target meshes. That is, the number of vertices, edges, and faces in the metamesh are much larger (usually five to 10 times) than those of the source and target meshes. Second, in a metamorphosis of two objects, we expect that all the attributes of the objects will be gradually transformed from one to the other. Hence, in mesh morphing, the topology and geometry of input meshes should change at the same time. However, a metamesh-based approach does not interpolate the topology of input meshes at all. The topology of an in-between mesh is always the same as that of the metamesh. Only the vertex positions are transformed from the source to target meshes.

This sketch presents a novel approach for 3D mesh morphing that is not based on a metamesh and overcomes the limitations of previous work. The approach simultaneously interpolates the topology and geometry of input meshes. With our approach, an in-between mesh contains only the vertices from the source and target meshes. Since no additional vertices are introduced, the number of vertices in an in-between mesh does not exceed the sum of those in the input meshes. Hence, the in-between meshes are much simpler than those generated by previous techniques.

The contributions of this sketch can be specified as follows:

### Topological Mesh Transformation Algorithm
We present an algorithm that transforms the topology of a mesh into that of the other when two homeomorphic meshes are given. Hoppe et al. mentioned that two homeomorphic meshes can be transformed to each other by applying a sequence of three edge transformations: edge collapse, edge split, and edge swap.[1] However, they did not provide an algorithm to derive the sequence of edge transformations that realizes the topological transformation. This sketch presents the required algorithm, in which edge transformations are applied to create or remove edges in the process of establishing one-to-one mapping between the edges of two meshes.

### Feature-Based Hierarchical Algorithm
To control the shape of in-between meshes, a user is allowed to specify the corresponding feature vertices on the source and target meshes. Then the vertex correspondences should be preserved in the topology transformation from the source to target mesh. Further, the topology transformation should uniformly happen in the regions between the feature vertices. We present a hierarchical algorithm based on mesh simplification for uniform topology transformation that reflects the feature vertex correspondences.

### Topology and Geometry Interpolation Algorithm
Once the edge transformation sequence from the source to target mesh has been obtained, we can derive an animation by applying geomorphs[2] to the edge transformations. However, in this case, the topology and geometry do not change uniformly all over an in-between mesh, but only near the transformed edges. We present an algorithm that produces uniform topology and geometry changes over an in-between mesh. The algorithm rearranges the edge transformations into groups and performs the transformations in each group at the same time.

Figures 1 and 2 show morphing examples from our preliminary implementation of the proposed algorithms. In each example, an in-between mesh simultaneously interpolates the topology and geometry of input meshes by using edge transformations and geomorphs. Note that no additional vertices, other than from the source and target meshes, are included in an in-between mesh because the proposed approach does not construct a metamesh.

*References*
1. Hoppe, H., DeRose, T., Duchamp, T., McDonald, J., & Stuetzle, W. (1993). Mesh optimization. *Proceedings of SIGGRAPH 93*, 19-26.
2. Hoppe, H. (1996). Progressive meshes. *Proceedings of SIGGRAPH 96*, 99-108.

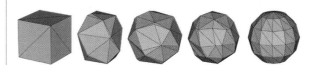

Figure 1. Morph from a cube to a sphere.

Figure 2. Morph from a cube to a triceratop.

*185*

# A FLEXIBLE APPROACH TO 3D RECONSTRUCTION FROM SINGLE IMAGES

*Contact*
S.F. EL-HAKIM
Visual Information Technology
National Research Council
Ottawa, Ontario K1A 0R6
Canada
www.vit.iit.nrc.ca/elhakim/
3dmodels.html

*References*
1. Debevec, P.E., Taylor, C.J., & Malik, J. (1996). Modeling and rendering architecture from photographs: A hybrid geometry and image-based approach. *Proceedings of SIGGRAPH 96*, 11-20.
2. Criminisi, A. & Zisserman, A. (2000). Single view metrology. *I.JCV2000, 40* (2), 123-148.

Traditional image-based 3D reconstruction methods use multiple images to extract 3D geometry. However, it is not always possible to obtain such images – for example, when reconstructing destroyed structures using existing photographs or paintings with proper perspective (Figure 1) and reconstructing objects without actually visiting the site, using images from the Web or postcards (Figure 2). Even when multiple images are possible, parts of the scene appear in only one image due to occlusions and/or lack of features that match between images. Methods for 3D reconstruction from a single image do exist.[1,2] We present a new more accurate, more flexible method that can model a wider variety of sites and structures than existing methods. Using this approach, we reconstructed in 3D many destroyed structures using old photographs and paintings. Sites all over world have been reconstructed from tourist pictures, Web pages, and postcards.

The approach does not need models of the objects nor known internal camera calibration.[1] It also does not use vanishing lines or vanishing points,[2] which may be unavailable or hard to extract. We use several types of constraints: point/coordinate constraints, surface constraints, and topological constraints. We solve first for internal and external camera parameters using one set of constraints, then use additional constraints to obtain 3D coordinates for reconstruction. The camera parameters and 3D coordinates are computed from photogrammetric bundle adjustment: a simultaneous triangulation of all data. Each point p, extracted from an image i, has two image coordinates, xp and yp and contributes two equations (representing the condition that the projection center, image point, and object point all fall on a straight line):

$$x_p = F_x(f_c, x_o, y_o, X_p, Y_p, Z_p, X_i, Y_i, Z_i, pitch_i, yaw_i, roll_i)$$

$$y_p = F_y(f_c, x_o, y_o, X_p, Y_p, Z_p, X_i, Y_i, Z_i, pitch_i, yaw_i, roll_i)$$

The parameters are the internal camera parameters (focal length $f_o$, and principal point $x_o, y_o$), 3D object coordinates of point p (Xp, Yp, , and the camera position and orientation. Those six camera parameters are the same for all points measured in the same image. However, each point adds three unknown XYZ coordinates. The image coordinates xp and yp may include parameters for distortion. In the calibration phase, certain constraints are used. Points with the same X coordinates, points with the same Y coordinates, points with the same Z coordinates, one point with zero coordinates to define the origin of the object coordinate system, and one point with a zero Y and Z to define the orientation. Arbitrary distance is assigned between two points to define an arbitrary scale. When sufficient constraint equations are combined with equations,[1] solution of the internal and external camera parameters is possible. In the econstruction phase, more constraints are combined with equations.[1] These include shapes such as planes, cylinders, quadrics, spheres, and circles in addition to topological relationships such as perpendicularity, parallelism, and symmetry.

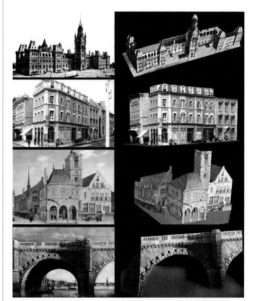

Figure 1. 3D Reconstruction from old photos and paintings.

Figure 2. Examples of 3D reconstruction from tourist pictures.

*Contact*
KEN PERLIN
New York University
www.mrl.nyu.edu

FABRICE NEYRET
IMAGIS

Flow textures defined with shaders that use Perlin Noise can look great, but they don't "flow" right, because they lack the swirling and advection of real flow. We extend Perlin Noise so that shaders that use it can be animated over time to produce flow textures with a "swirling"quality. We also show how to visually approximate advected flow within shaders.

### ROTATING GRADIENTS

The classic Perlin Noise function[1] can be described as a sum of overlapping pseudo-random "wiggle" functions. Each wiggle, centered at a different integer lattice point $(i; j; k)$, consists of a product of a weight kernel K and a linear function $(a; b; c)i;j;k$. K smoothly drops off away from $(i,j,k)$, reaching 0 in both value and gradient at unit distance. Each $(a; b; c)i;j;k = a(x_i)+b(y_j)+ c(z\_j)$ that has a value of 0 at $(i,j,k)$. The result of summing all these overlapping wiggle functions: noise has a characteristic random yet smooth appearance.

Our modification is to rotate all the linear vectors $(a; b; c)i;j;k$ over time, which causes each wiggle function to rotate in place. Because all the $(a; b; c)$ vectors were uncorrelated before the rotation, they will remain uncorrelated after the rotation, so at every moment the result will look like Perlin Noise. Yet over time, the result will impart a "swirling" quality to flow. When multiple scales of noise are summed together, we make the rotation proportional to spatial frequency (finer noise is rotated faster), which visually models real flow.

### PSEUDO-ADVECTION

Beyond swirling, fluids also contain advection of small features by larger ones, such as ripples on waves. This effect tends to stretch persistent features (for example, foam), but not newly created ones (for example, billowing), to varying degrees, according to their rate of regeneration, or structure memory M.

Traditional Perlin Turbulence is an independent sum of scaled noise, where the scaled noise is $bi(x) = noise(2ix)=2i$, and the turbulence is $tN(x) =PN i=0 bi(x)$. This can define a displacement texture $color(x) = C(x + ItN(x))$, where C is a color table and I controls amplitude. Our pseudo-advection displaces features at scale $i + 1$ and location x0 in the noise domain to $x1 = x0 + k ti(x0)$, where k is the amplitude of the displacement (see below). For small displacements, this can be approximated by $x1\_k ti(x1)$, so displacement k is proportional to an amplitude I specified by the user. We can scale this by desired structure memory M, since passive structures are totally advected, when M = 1, while very active structures are instantaneously generated, thus unstretched, when M = 0. Our advected turbulence function is defined by modifying the scaled noise to: $bi(x) = b(2i(x\_IM ti\_1(x)))=2i$ and using this to construct the sum $tN(x) = PN i=0 bi(x)$.

### RESULTS

Many flow textures can be created; some can be viewed at mrl.nyu.edu/flownoise/

*Reference*
1. Ebert, D. et al. (1998). *Texture and modeling*. Morgan Kaufmann Publishers, July 1998.

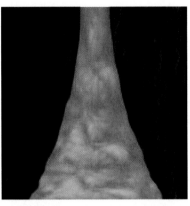

Figure 1. Lava flow.

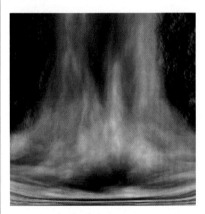

Figure 2. Waterfall.

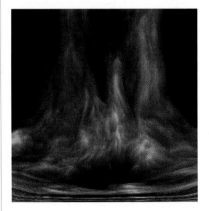

Figure 3. Waterfall with lava-flow texture.

*187*

# FRENCH SURFACE:
## A NEW TECHNIQUE FOR SURFACE DESIGN

*Contact*
ZITA CHENG
Human Communications
Technology Laboratory
Electrical and Computer
Engineering
University of British Columbia
zitast@math.ubc.ca

SIDNEY FELS
Human Communications
Technology Laboratory
Electrical and Computer
Engineering
University of British Columbia

We present a new user-friendly interface for surface design. The goal is to overcome limitations associated with traditional methods: dependence on freehand controling and rigid mathematical structures. Our solution is motivated by the drafter's tool called French curves, which are used as templates for tracing curves.

Digital French curves are, for example, investigated by Singh.[2] Our project considers its analogue in one higher dimension, namely 3D surfaces. A predrawn set of surfaces, called French surfaces, is given to the user. The selected surfaces are then connected together to form the final model. The advantage of this approach is that the only input from users is their artistic expression, not their mathematical skills. Initial testing shows that the system is easy to learn and can be quickly used to construct models. Examples using our technique are shown in Figure 1.

## GENERAL SCHEME
Models are contructed using a stepwise refinement process. In each step, users select a surface from the initial set of French surfaces on the control panel as a starting point for their search. Then they find the exact one they want by adjusting scale bars and action buttons. For example, users can stretch or crop a cone, extend the ring of a torus, tilt the angle of a wedge, or bend a cylinder. The selected surface is then positioned over the ongoing model and blending may be applied.

## THE SET OF FRENCH SURFACES
The set of French surfaces must be large enough to give any shape, but not too large, to allow for easy searching. We have come up with a minimal set of primitive surfaces (for some examples, see Figure 2) ranging from those with a rounded base to those with an elongated base, and from those with a smooth top to those with a pointed top. The set also runs through surfaces of different scale, tilt, and extent. Theoretically, this set, together with the powerful blending technique, is enough to generate any surface. Our system is different from methods in which users manipulate or draw surfaces, such as Welch's approach.[3] In our system, users navigate surfaces rather than manipulate control or surface points to get the surface they want.

## BLENDING SURFACES
Blending is vital to our system. The blend between our triangle tesselated shapes is formed by a family of Bézier curves. This is similar to Welch's method.[3] except the degree of blending is user-adjustable. Rays from the rim serve as a blending guide (Figure 2). In our system, blending preserves the original shape of both the surface and the model.

## WHAT'S NEXT?
Our project suggests a new direction for surface modelling. We have developed a set of French surfaces that can be blended to create any surface features. The idea of using predefined, modifiable surfaces leverages the advantages of the French curves. Our technique applies to applications such as creating predefined libraries of shapes for CSG, spline models, or even freeform shapes for Teddy.[1] Future research includes improvements to the blending algorithm, more user testing, integration of our technique with various surface

modelling packages, support for creating personalized libraries, and use of AI techniques to learn commonly used surfaces for easy access.

*References*
1. Igarashi, T., Matsuoka, S., & Tanaka, H. (1999). Teddy: A sketching interface for 3D freeform design. *Proceedings of SIGGRAPH 99*, 409-416.
2. Singh, K. (1999). Interactive curve design using digital French curves. 1999 Symposium on Interactive 3D Graphics, 23-30.
3. Welch, W. & Witkin, A. (1994). Free-form shape design using triangulated surfaces. *Proceedings of SIGGRAPH 94*, 247-256.

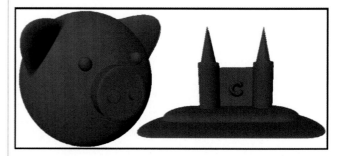

Figure 1. Models created using French Surface: the piggy and the castle.

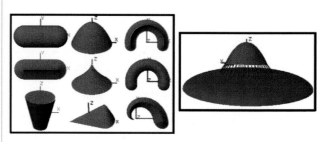

Figure 2. Examples of primitive surfaces and the blending technique.

188

# genieBottles:
## An Interactive Narrative in Bottles

*Contact*
ALI MAZALEK
Massachusetts Institute
of Technology
mazalek@media.mit.edu

ALI WOOD
HIROSHI ISHII
Media Laboratory
Massachusetts Institute
of Technology

The genieBottles system presents a story that is told by three genies who live in glass bottles. When a bottle is opened, the genie contained inside is released and begins to talk to the user. If several genies are released at once, they converse with each other. The physical bottles can be seen as graspable "containers" and "controls" for the digital story information, and wireless tag sensing technology is used to determine their open and closed states. This interface was first used in the musicBottles project, in which sets of glass bottles were filled with musical trios.[1] The genieBottles project explores the application of the bottle interface to the interactive storytelling.

## THE APPLICATION

Storytelling is an important part of human culture, both in entertainment and in education. We find great pleasure in experiencing good stories, and they enable us to learn about our society and history. By creating stories, we structure our perceptions and understandings of the world in a form that can be passed on to others. Over the past 20 years, the increasing accessibility and stability of digital technology has enabled new computational approaches to storytelling. We felt that by applying a tangible interface to the field of interactive narratives, we could provide stories with a means of escaping from the computer box and into our physical environment. Our genieBottles provide an engaging interactive story experience in which the audience can go beyond the visual and auditory senses, and make better use of their sense of touch.

## STORY CONTENT AND NARRATIVE MODEL

The genieBottles story is based on the lives of three genies (Junar, Opo, and Seala). Each has a distinct personality and background that defines the way they talk and interact with other genies. When users interact with the system, they captures the genies at a particular moment in time, during which they talk about their state of being in bottles, about their pasts, and about their expectations or desires for the future. Depending on which genie they listen to most, users will get a slightly different story tailored to that genie's particular history, desires, and beliefs.

The genieBottles use a simple state transition model for interactive storytelling, in which the system plays back the appropriate segment of audio depending on the state it is in, as well as the appropriate segment(s) of audio to transition from one state to another. State changes are caused by user interactions. For instance, if a user opens a bottle, a new genie is brought into the conversation, while if a user closes a bottle, that genie leaves the conversation. The story is organized into many short segments of text ordered according to a narrative progression. Transitioning into a new system state causes the first unused story segment for that state to be played back. This ensures that a new portion of the story will be played back even if the same sequence of interactions is repeated multiple times, allowing the story to maintain a continuous narrative progression.

## FUTURE EXTENSIONS

The genieBottles system gives a concrete example of how the use of glass bottles as an interface for digital information can be applied to interactive storytelling. In the future, we plan to explore alternative narrative models for the bottle interface. We would also like to extend the current narrative model to support different types of story content that could be used for educational purposes. For instance, a set of bottles containing important historical or political figures might be used to teach children about how peace treaties are made. Or perhaps children could fill the bottles with their own stories in order to help them learn different ways of structuring conversation-based narratives.

## ACKNOWLEDGEMENTS

We would like to acknowledge the Tangible Media Group, the Responsive Environments Group, and the Physics and Media Group at the MIT Media Lab. We would also like to thank storytellers Kevin Brooks, Laura Packer, and Raelinda Woad.

*Reference*
1. Ishii, H., Mazalek, A., & Lee, J. (2001). Bottles as a minimal interface to access digital information. In *CHI 2001 Extended Abstracts*, ACM Press.

Figure 1. The three genie bottles (Junar on the left, Seala in the center, and Opo on the right).

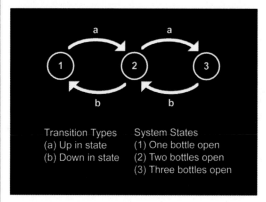

Figure 2. The two types of state transition in the genieBottles system.

*Contact*
IVAN NEULANDER
Rhythm & Hues Studios
ivan@rhythm.com

PEDRO HUANG
HANS RIJPKEMA
Rhythm & Hues Studios

The digital fur in "Cats and Dogs" requires fully CG animals to be seamlessly intercut with their live-action cat, dog, and mouse counterparts. Realistically groomed, animated, and rendered fur is essential to achieving this effect for various types of fur coats. The ninja cats have short sleek hair closely matted against the skin. In contrast, the villainous Mr. Tinkles is a Persian with long and fluffy plumes. Not only must these animals talk, but the furry cast must also perform martial arts and operate tools and machinery such as drills, guns, and log-loaders.

## GROOMING

We begin with a partition of the polygonal skin geometry. The "element normal" and "uv" parameters define a spatially and temporally consistent field of coordinate systems providing for precise local positioning and grooming control. Spline-based control hairs are rooted onto the skin surface through density maps or modified through direct modeling. An interactive 3D fur grooming tool sculpts and grooms the control hair geometry based on global and texture-based parameters such as length, scruffiness, and curvature. The same tool is used to control additional attributes of the instantiated fur. Noise controls generate the irregularity necessary for a natural appearance. Efficient clumping is achieved by correlating the hundreds of thousands of hairs using a clump-control image. Hairs are assigned to various coats such as a thick, dark undercoat, or a sparse set of specular hairs.

## ANIMATION

As geometry, the control hairs can fully utilize the transformation tools in our proprietary animation program. For example, blend shapes target specific emotions. Control is added to constrain the hairs to the surface of the deforming skin. Specialized dynamics modules are written to support concepts such as cohesion and collision using the hair root and tip connectivity.

## RENDERING

Each hair strand is converted by the renderer into a polygonal ribbon representing a generalized cylinder traveling along a Catmull-Rom spline. The ribbon, automatically oriented to squarely face the camera, consists of trapezoidal segments whose density depends on hair length and curvature, as well as camera distance. This arrangement minimizes the hair's polygon count while maintaining frame-to-frame coherence.

The true geometric normals of a hair ribbon are useless for shading. Instead, we use the hair's tangent vectors, which are easily obtained from its spline path. We chose the cylinder-based shading model originally presented by Kajiya and Kay. It produces realistic shading that is free of aliasing and correctly handles backlighting, the phenomenon where edge hair lights up when placed between the light and camera.

The gradual self-shadowing by layers of semi-transparent hair is essential to a photo-realistic render. To capture this, we compute a normal vector and depth value for each hair control point. These define an imaginary sphere that encloses the control point. The distance along any direction from this point to the sphere surface represents the amount of hair material that shadows the control point.

To obtain the self-shadowing normals and depth values, all hair control points are inserted into a voxel grid. A ray-marcher then determines, in each voxel, the ray that escapes the point cloud while encountering the fewest points along the way. We specially mark voxels containing skin polygons, so as to prevent rays from escaping through the skin. After computing the normal and depth values at each voxel, we interpolate them over all the control points. The resulting self-shadowing accurately portrays hair clumping and bald spots.

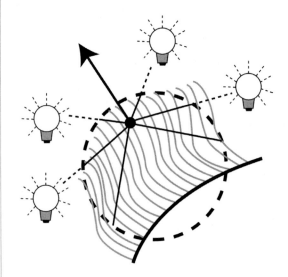

Hair self-shadowing model.

*Contact*
GABRIELE GORLA
gorlik@acm.org

VICTORIA INTERRANTE
GUILLERMO SAPIRO
University of Minnesota

## INTRODUCTION

Adding texture to the surface of a polygonal model can profoundly enhance its visual richness. Given a texture pattern and a surface model, the historical challenge has been to determine how to apply the pattern to the surface in an appropriate manner, minimizing the visual impact of seams and projective distortion while orienting the pattern so that it flows over the shape in a desirable way.

In this sketch, we address the problem of how to seamlessly, and without repetition cover the artifacts or visible projective distortion cover the surface of a polygonally defined model with a texture pattern derived from an acquired 2D image so that the dominant orientation of the pattern will everywhere follow the surface shape in an aesthetically pleasing way. Specifically, we propose an efficient, automatic method for synthesizing, from a small sample swatch, patches of perceptually similar texture in which the pattern orientation may locally follow a specified vector field, such as the principal directions of curvature, at a per-pixel level, and in which the continuity of large and small-scale features of the pattern is generally preserved across adjacent patches

## PROPOSED METHOD

The method that we propose has the advantages of being essentially automatic (requiring no manual intervention), reasonably efficient, fairly straightforward to implement, and applicable across a wide variety of texture types and models. In addition, the resulting textured objects can be easily displayed at interactive frame rates using a conventional renderer on a standard PC with texture mapping hardware.

Our technique consists of the following main steps:

- Partition the polygons of the model into contiguous patches, as nearly planar as reasonably possible.
- Compute a vector field over the object or read a pre-defined field from a file.
- Synthesize the texture pattern over each patch, using an efficient, orientation-adaptive variation of the non-parametric sampling method proposed by Efros and Leung.[1]

The constant direction field used for Figure 1 produces good results in most obvious cases. Of greater intrinsic interest to our ongoing research is the possibility of applying an oriented texture pattern to the surface of an object so that it is everywhere aligned with the principal directions of curvature. Recent results in vision research support the idea that the principal directions play an important role in surface shape understanding.

## APPLICATIONS AND FUTURE WORK

There are many promising applications for this system and many directions for future work. One of the most interesting is multi-texturing. On a per-pixel basis it is possible to change not only the direction of the synthesized texture, but also the texture itself according to any arbitrary function. This multi-texturing method has the potential to be useful for important applications in scientific visualization. Other direction fields, such as gradient descent, hold promise for different applications, such as non-photorealistic

rendering of terrain models. The methods that we have proposed can also be used for visualization of scientifically computed vector fields over surfaces.

*Reference*
1. Efros, A. & Leung, T. (1999).Texture synthesis by non-parametric sampling. *Proceedings International Conference on Computer Vision, 2*, 1033 -1038.

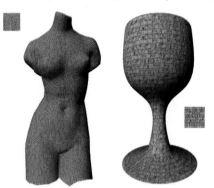

Figure 1. Examples of synthesized surface texture produced by our method. No manual intervention of any kind was employed. The textures were grown following a vector field locally defined by the projection of (0,1,0) onto the tangent plane at each point. The entire process required 12 minutes for the Venus and 20 minutes for the goblet.

Figure 2. The orientation of a directed pattern over a curved surface can influence our perception of the surface's 3D shape. On the left, the bricks are oriented in the direction of least signed normal curvature, and on the right they are oriented in the same constant "up" direction used for the models in Figure 1.

Figure 3. Multiple textures, indexed by illumination, applied to an automatically defined smooth vector field approximating the first principal directions over the Stanford bunny.

# HAND-HELD TORQUE FEEDBACK DEVICE

*Contact*
YUKIO FUKUI
SEIICHI NISHIHARA
University of Tsukuba
fukui@is.tsukuba.ac.jp

KENTARO NAKATA
NEC corporation

NORIO NAKAMURA
JULI YAMASHITA
National Institute of Advanced
Industrial Science and
Technology (AIST)

## BACKGROUND AND PROBLEM

Portable-virtual-environment technology is a recent trend for extending and merging the virtual world into real space. The downsizing of computers and their interface devices has spurred this portability. Portable force feedback devices, in principle, must have some basis to support the reactive force. Conventional techniques in reactive force support utilize some part of the user's body such as the back or upper arm. These methods leave the sensation felt by the user incomplete or unsatisfactory because of the closed force loop.

## TECHNICAL DESCRIPTION OF PROPOSED SYSTEM

The proposed technique requires no support to display force to the user. The key is using the angular momentum transition of rotating wheels. Changing the speed of the wheel generates torque toward the outer housing due to the law of action and reaction. Three motor-driven wheels whose axes are orthogonal to each other generate three momentum components that compound into a single momentum of arbitrary direction and magnitude. Figure 1 shows the composition of momentum and the configuration of the system implemented by the proposed technique. Figure 2 shows the developed torque feedback device: the Gyro-Cube. The table shows the correct ratio of direction that subjects felt as output torque varied by magnitude and duration. The colored region (relatively high score) shows that human sensation of torque is not always proportional to the magnitude of the stimulus.

## FUTURE DIRECTIONS

We will upgrade the device by making it smaller and lighter, and implementing position sensors. It will then be applied to navigation tools for the visually handicapped or products for outdoor games.

*Reference*
Burdea, G. C. (1996). *Force and touch feedback for virtual reality*. John Wiley & Sons, New York.

192

Figure 2. Hand-held torque feedback device.

| Correct answer ratio | | Duration time (sec.) | | | |
|---|---|---|---|---|---|
| | | 0.05 | 0.10 | 0.20 | 0.40 |
| Output | 720 | 91.4 | 95.7 | 95.7 | 98.6 |
| Torque | 504 | 72.9 | 90.0 | 87.1 | 94.3 |
| (gf.cm) | 360 | 65.7 | 85.7 | 84.3 | 75.7 |
| | 252 | 50.0 | 71.4 | 55.7 | 51.4 |

Result of psychophysical experiments.

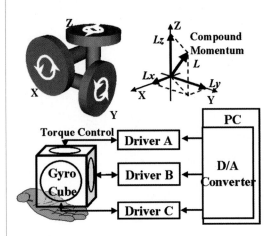

Figure 1. Torque generation of arbitrary direction.

# Hardware Acceleration for Physical Modeling of Deformable Objects

*Contact*
Benjamin Bishop
Department of Computer Science
University of Georgia
Athens, Georgia 30602 USA
bishop@cs.uga.eud

Thomas P. Kelliher
Department of Mathematics and
Computer Science
Goucher College

Recently, there has been a great deal of interest in interactive physical modeling. Most current work has focused on rigid body simulation, since it is typically much faster than simulation of deformable objects. Interactive simulation of scenes containing complex deformable objects on consumer-grade PCs appears to be several years away if we wait for Moore's Law.

## Our Work

We believe that it is possible to use specialized hardware to bring complex interactive physical modeling to the consumer in the very near future, similar to what has happened with the specialized consumer 3D card market. In order to prove this idea, we built a proof-of-concept system that involves a high-density FPGA on a custom board connected to a host machine via parallel cable. It implements forward Euler integration of the spring equations and only simple collision detection in two dimensions. It is non-pipelined and uses reduced precision functional units. An image of the board is shown in Figure 1. The architecture that was implemented in the FPGA is outlined in Figure 2.

Figure 1. Custom circuit board with FPGA.

These simplifications were necessary in order to deal with the area restrictions in the FPGA. The final FPGA utilization was 79 percent of the 250K gates. The high utilization was caused by the lack of interconnect available on the FPGA, and the fact that barrel shifting in floating-point operations quickly consumes interconnect. It is well known that forward Euler integration suffers from stability problems. We chose this scheme only for its simplicity. For later generations, a more suitable (stable and simple) integration technique must be found. This scheme should operate on local data, since global dependencies significantly complicate the hardware design.

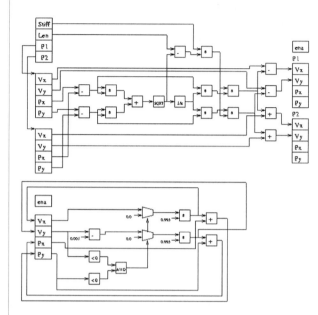

Figure 2. Architecture implemented in the FPGA. Spring solver at top, simple collision detection at bottom.

## Results

Figure 3 shows an animation sequence that was generated on the board. It is a simple four-point, six-spring cube. In comparison with our host machine, we estimated the performance improvement (assuming pipelining and equal clock rates, which would be easily attainable in an ASIC) to be 92 times, so the potential gain from hardware acceleration is clear.

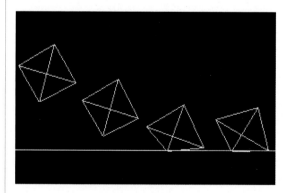

Figure 3. Animation generated in hardware.

# Hardware-Accelerated High-Quality Filtering of Solid Textures

*Contact*
Markus Hadwiger
Helwig Hauser
VRVis Research Center, Vienna
msh@vrvis.at

Thomas Theußl
Eduard Gröller
Institute of Computer
Graphics and Algorithms
Vienna University of Technology

Recent consumer graphics hardware is able to texture 2D surfaces via lookups into a 3D texture domain. This can be used for texturing a polygonal object with a solid texture,[2] for instance. However, the filtering performed by current hardware is constrained to tri-linear interpolation within the texture volume. In order to achieve high-quality reconstruction, filter kernels of higher order have to be used.[3,4]

We describe a hardware-accelerated approach for high-quality texturing of polygonal objects with a solid texture. Several passes with 3D texture mapping and multi-texturing are accumulated to yield the final result. Conceptually, arbitrary filter kernels are possible. On hardware supporting multi-texturing with 3D textures, interactive speeds can be achieved.

### Hardware-Accelerated Higher-Order Filtering

The basic idea of our approach is to reorder evaluation of the filter convolution sum. Instead of calculating each output sample at a point x in its entirety, we instead distribute the contribution of a single input sample to all output sample points simultaneously. We do this for all contributing input samples, accumulating their contribution over multiple passes.

That is, instead of using

FOR ALL output samples $x_i$ DO

  FOR ALL deltas $r_j$ of contributing neighbors DO

    $g(x_i) \mathrel{+}= f[\ trunc(x_i) + r_j\ ] * h(\ frac(x_i) - r_j\ );$

where f[] is the input signal, h() the filter kernel, g() the output signal, the $x_i$ are the output samples at fractional locations, input samples are at the integers, and $r_j$ is an integer in [-m+1, m], with m being half the filter width, we do

FOR ALL deltas $r_j$ of contributing neighbors DO

  PAR ALL output samples $x_i$ DO

    $g(x_i) \mathrel{+}= shift_j(f)[\ trunc(x_i)\ ] * h_j(\ frac(x_i)\ );$

The inner loop is performed in parallel for all output samples (pixels) by the hardware in a single rendering pass. The outer loop is achieved through multiple passes. For the multiplication in the inner loop, we use texture mapping hardware that is capable of multi-texturing. One texture contains the current filter tile (an integer section of the filter kernel, e.g., [-1, 0], [0, 1], etc.), denoted as $h_j()$. The other contains the input texture using appropriately offset texture coordinates to provide the corresponding input values, the offset operation denoted by $shift_j()$.

Figure 1 shows this method for the simplest example of a tent filter, using two passes in order to achieve linear interpolation. Note that the filter shape is not required to be linear at all.

We subdivide the filter kernel into its integer tiles and download each discretized tile as a separate texture. Exactly one tile will be used in a single pass, replicated over the entire output polygon.

This approach immediately generalizes to two and three dimensions. Conceptually, it is entirely independent of both the actual shape of the filter kernel used and its width. A greater width increases the number of passes necessary but does not change the algorithm.

There are as many rendering passes with two-texture multi-texturing as the number of input samples contributing to a single output sample. That is, a cubic kernel requires four passes in one dimension, 16 passes in two dimensions, and 64 passes in three dimensions, respectively.

### Results

Figure 2 shows the vase mapped with a solid marble texture from the ATI RadeonVolumeTexture example,[1] where we have integrated our filtering approach. The cubic B-spline filter clearly exhibits significantly less interpolation artifacts than simple tri-linear interpolation.

For further information regarding hardware-accelerated filtering with arbitrary filter kernels, see:
www.vrvis.at/vis/research/hq-hw-reco/

*References*
1. ATI Radeon SDK. URL: www.ati.com/
2. Ebert, D., Musgrave, F., Peachey, D., Worley, S., & Perlin, K. (2000). *Texturing and modeling: A procedural approach.* Academic Press, 2000.
3. Möller, T., Machiraju, R., Müller, K., & Yagel, R. (1997). Evaluation and design of filters using a Taylor series expansion. *IEEE Transactions on Visualization and Computer Graphics, 3* (2), 184-199.
4. Theußl, T., Hauser, H., & Gröller, E. (2000). Mastering Windows: Improving reconstruction. In *Proceedings of IEEE Symposium on Volume Visualization,* 101-108.

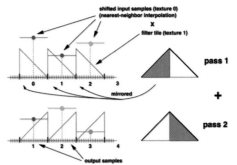

Figure 1. Both filter tiles of a tent filter replicated separately over the output sample grid for two passes. Adding up the two passes yields the final result.

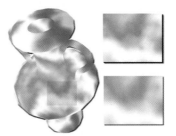

Figure 2. Vase textured with solid marble texture. The shaded area is shown magnified on the right; tri-linear interpolation on top, cubic B-spline at the bottom.

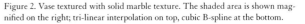

HDR Shop

*Contact*
CHRIS TCHOU
USC Institute for
Creative Technologies
tchou@ict.usc.edu

PAUL DEBEVEC
USC Institute for
Creative Technologies

HDR Shop is a computer application (currently under development) designed to view and edit high-dynamic-range (HDR)[1] images: pictures that can capture a much greater range of light intensities than standard photographs or computer images. This approach is very useful for image-based lighting and post-render processing.

Photographs from traditional cameras do not record the amount of light over a certain level. All the bright points in a photo are white, which makes it impossible to detect any difference in intensity. The standard technique to acquire HDR images that capture this missing information is to take several photographs at different exposures (making each photo progressively darker, without moving the camera), until the bright lights no longer saturate. The sequence of photographs can then be analyzed to derive the light intensity of each point in the scene.

Whereas traditional image editors work with 8- or 16-bit images, HDR Shop is built from the ground up to work correctly with HDR images. All operations are done with linear floating-point numbers. In many cases, this simplifies the code, as well as providing more correct output.

For the purpose of real-time display, however, it is important to quickly convert linear floating-point images to 8-bit RGB with the appropriate gamma curve. The standard gamma formula involves an exponentiation, which is slow. In the interest of speed, we have found it useful to approximate this calculation by constructing a lookup table indexed by the most significant bits of the floating-point values. For common gamma values of 1.4 ~ 2.2, it suffices to use 16 bits (eight exponent bits and eight mantissa bits) to reduce the error below rounding error.

In addition to resampling, cropping, and mathematical operations, HDR Shop also supports transformations among most common panoramic formats, facilitating the use of HDR panoramas in image-based lighting[2]. HDR Shop can also automatically export a low-dynamic-range (LDR) copy of any image to an external image editor. Changes to the LDR image are then incorporated into the HDR image, so existing tools can be used to modify HDR images.

See also: www.debevec.org/HDRShop

*References*
1. Debevec, P. & Malik, J. (1997). Recovering high dynamic range radiance maps from photographs. *Proceedings of SIGGRAPH 97.*
2. Debevec, P. (1998). Rendering synthetic objects into real scenes: Bridging traditional and image-based graphics with global illumination and high dynamic range photography. *Proceedings of SIGGRAPH 98.*

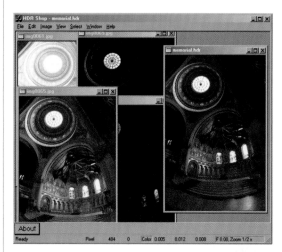

Figure 1. In HDR Shop, a sequence of low-dynamic-range images (left) can be compiled into a single high-dynamic-range image (right).

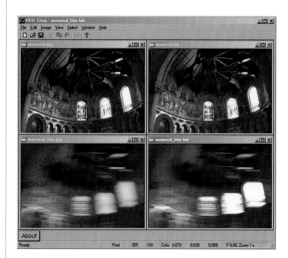

Figure 2. Comparison of HDR Shop's horizontal motion blur on a low-dynamic-range image (left) vs. a high-dynamic-range image (right).

Figure 3. St. Paul's Cathedral panorama, originally in cube-map format (left), converted in HDR Shop to latitude-longitude (upper right), mirrored ball, and light probe formats (lower right).

*195*

# A Head-Mounted Projective Display and its Applications in Interactive Augmented Environments

*Contact*
Hong Hua
Beckman Institute
University of Illinois
at Urbana-Champaign
Urbana, Illinois 61801 USA
Honghua@uiuc.edu

*Contributors*
Hong Hua
Leonard D. Brown
Chunyu Gao
Narendra Ahuja
Beckman Institute
University of Illinois
at Urbana-Champaign

Jannick P. Rolland
School of Optics/CREOL
University of Central Florida

Frank Biocca
Michigan State University

## Technology

The concept of projective displays using retro-reflective material was initially patented by Fergason in 1997, and head-mounted projective displays (HMPDs) were proposed as an alternative to conventional eyepiece-type head-mounted displays and stereo projection systems for 3D visualization.[1] An HMPD consists of a pair of miniature projection lenses, beam splitters, and displays mounted on the head, and a supple and non-distorting retro-reflective sheeting material placed strategically in the environment.[1]

Figure 1. HMPD prototype.

The use of projection lenses and replacement of a diffusing projection screen with a retro-reflective screen distinguish HMPDs from conventional head-mounted displays (HMDs) and stereoscopic projection-based displays. In addition to direct see-through capability, HMPD technology intrinsically provides correct occlusion of computer-generated objects by physical objects and creates ubiquitous display environments in which a retro-reflective material can be applied to any location in space and can be tailored to any shape without introducing additional distortion to the virtual images. Such a design also allows for larger field of view (FOV) and higher optical performance than eyepiece-based HMDs.[2] In multi-user collaborative environments, the retro-reflective screen makes it possible to generate unique perspectives for each user without introducing crosstalk from other participants.[2] We present our recent design of a compact head-mounted prototype implementing ultra-light custom lenses.[2] The prototype (Figure 1) achieved 50 degrees FOV and 3.96 arcmin/pixel visual resolution at a total weight of less than 700 grams.

## Application in Interactive Augmented Environments

To demonstrate the various capabilities of this technology, we present two applications:

1. Play-augmented "GO" chess game with a remote opponent: In Figure 2(a), a computer-generated 3D "GO" chessboard is projected through an HMPD onto a tabletop retro-reflective screen. The local player (1), wearing the HMPD, perceives the virtual chessboard as if it were a real object on the tabletop and manipulates his real chess pieces on the virtual board. A vision-based tracking setup detects the locations of his pieces on the virtual board and transmits this information via network to the remote player. The remote player (2) uses a PC-based game interface in which all game components are visualized on a PC monitor and chess-piece manipulation is achieved via a standard mouse. When the remote player adds a piece to the board, a corresponding computer-generated piece is projected onto the HMPD user's virtual chessboard. Therefore, the HMPD player perceives the virtual chessboard, the real pieces, which correctly occlude the virtual chessboard, and the virtual pieces in a seamless augmented environment. A head-tracking system is used to maintain the correct registration of the real and virtual elements. The virtual and direct views of both players are shown in Figure 2 (b) through (d) respectively.

2. Interactive simulation of fluid flow over a simple terrain: We are also developing an augmented tool for simulation of fluid flow over simple terrain.[3] With this tool, virtual fluid is animated through physical-trough models coated in retro-reflective material. Users can dynamically alter or obstruct the flow with a variety of physical objects, which are tracked via a vision-based algorithm.

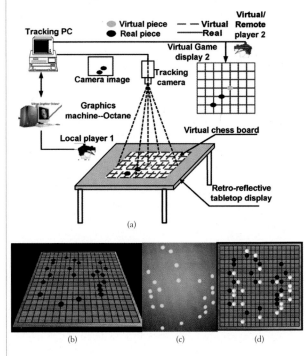

Figure 2. Playing a "GO" chess game with a remote opponent:
(a) setup illustration; (b) HMPD player's virtual view;
(c) HMPD player's direct real view; (d) remote player's PC-based interface.

*References*
1. Hua, H., Girardot, A., Gao, C., & Rolland, J. P. (2000). Engineering of head-mounted projective displays. *Applied Optics, 39* (22), 3814-3824.
2. Hua, H., Gao, C., Biocca, F., & Rolland, J.P. (2001). An ultra-light and compact design and implementation of head-mounted projective displays. *Proceedings of the IEEE Virtual Reality Annual International Symposium 2001* (In press).
3. Chen, J.X. & Da Vitoria Lobo, N. (1995). Toward interactive-rate simulation of fluids with moving obstacles using Navier-stokes equations. *Graphical Models and Image Processing, 57* (2), 107-116.

196

# High-Dynamic-Range Photography, Global Illumination, and Mental Ray on a Commercial Budget and Timeline

*Contact*
Brian Goldberg
Digital Domain
300 Rose Avenue
Venice, California 90291 USA
bgold@d2.com

Dan Lemmon
Digital Domain

This sketch presents a detailed look into the application of high-dynamic-range (HDR) image-based lighting techniques and new features in rendering technology on a high-profile commercial. Two technical directors had two months to build a complete image-based lighting and global illumination pipeline into the current workflow and methodology at Digital Domain. The commercial featured detailed, synthetic characters rendered into live-action scenes using HDR lighting information and global illumination rendering. The final result is an excellent example of how these technologies came together to produce highly believable characters integrated seamlessly into a live-action environment.

## Goals

The illumination pipeline was to use HDR imagery and HDR mapped, reconstructed set geometry as scene lighting information in a global illumination render. Custom software and shaders, controlled by a simple configuration methodology, enabled an easy (as seen by the user) transition from a Maya scene to a GI-rendered sequence through Mental Ray.

## The Approach

The main focus of the project was to use real-world, HDR lighting information in our global illumination renders. To obtain accurate lighting data, we were required to photograph both incident lighting information and the more subtle inter-reflection effects from the live-action set. The complexity of the lighting and shadows on set dictated that we photograph each different lighting setup from multiple positions in order to capture all of the light sources directly.

Far from a point-and-shoot solution, the process of transitioning from camera image to HDR dataset involved shooting a precise range of exposures at calculated set locations. Instead of the traditional "chrome sphere" approach used in obtaining wide field-of-view environment images, we chose to use a 180-degree fish-eye lens attached to a Nikon D1 digital SLR. This enhanced the efficiency of the process, but a great deal of work was done to transform the component images into a "light probe" (a unified, HDR, 360-degree-by-360-degree view of the environment in angular map coordinate space. This work included coordinate space conversion, image stitching, and compilation of HDR images. In some cases, we altered reality by "painting" onto the HDR light probe images, which helped achieve visually appealing results.

Our CG characters were required to interact with the set and to run in and out of light and shadow – the field of view, so to speak, of different light probes. We were faced with the problems of CG characters interacting with a live action set in an image-based lighting environment. Special attention had to be paid to characters that moved from the "field of view" of one light probe to another. We used the HDR information we obtained on set not only to simulate the traditional light fixtures on set, but also to texture map our CG set, in high-dynamic range, in order to accurately capture complex inter-reflection effects from the set pieces onto the characters.

An efficient storage and retrieval mechanism for these data was required. Our HDR data had to be accessible from a multitude of custom and third-party packages, most of which were not designed to handle this sort of data. We eventually settled on a four-channel, eight-bit encoding of the floating-point HDR data, based on the radiance file format. We built the file format around the RGB file structure and called it "rgbe" to emphasize the inclusion of mantissa/exponent information. The resulting data representation allowed us to store HDR lighting data in a compact and highly versatile format.

Bringing Monte Carlo radiosity simulation to character animation work was not trivial. This technique has produced impressive results in situations like architectural lighting simulation. In these applications, surfaces are largely flat and lighting changes fairly smoothly; so sparse samples can be interpolated well. Our situation was quite different. In this project, our out-of-this-world characters were highly organic and had very detailed, bumpy, porous skin. This presented additional technical challenges, as results could not be interpolated smoothly across the surface.

In order to maintain the integrity of our floating-point HDR data through the color and lighting pipeline, we designed a Mental Ray output shader to render the characters in our custom "rgbe" file format. This enabled an enormous amount of freedom for our compositing team. To create a realistic "film look," our compositors matched the characteristic "toe-and-shoulder" response curve that is characteristic of film stock. Using a response-flitting system designed in Nuke, our in-house compositor, they selected a low-dynamic-range "slice" of the HDR image. By using a synthetic "photographic response curve," we were able to generate images that matched the plate photography with unprecedented accuracy.

# How Changes in Technology Change the Use of Computer Animation at Walt Disney Feature Animation

*Contact*
STEVE GOLDBERG
Walt Disney Feature Animation
steve.goldberg@disney.com

This sketch explores how advances in software and hardware have influenced changes in not only our films' aesthetics, but also our artists' attitudes towards the use of computer animation at Walt Disney Feature Animation over the last decade. As the tools get faster and more intuitive for traditionally trained artists, and the gap between "computer people" and "artists" closes, big changes are in store for the animated film medium, both in 2D and 3D. This discussion covers uses of computer animation in the departments of layout, character animation, effects animation, and background painting .

Video progression sequences from "Dinosaur," "Fantasia 2000," "Tarzan," "Hunchback of Notre Dame," "The Lion King," "Aladdin," "Beauty and the Beast," and "The Rescuers Down Under" illustrate how changes in technology have helped to change how our films are made and how they look.

198

"How the Grinch Stole Christmas:"
The Who Construction Kit

*Contact*
Darren Hendler
Digital Domain
darren@d2.com

Dan Lemmon
Digital Domain

## Background

Early on in our involvement with "How the Grinch Stole Christmas," we realized that we were going to be creating many, many characters. The scope of the work dictated both large-scale digital crowds and detailed foreground character animation. Traditionally at Digital Domain, all characters had been modeled, set up, enveloped, and textured on an individual basis, an approach that, while efficient for a few characters, becomes impossible for hundreds of characters. Our solution was to create a system that would enable us to manage a large volume of characters without sacrificing the unique variations of each Who.

## The Who Construction Kit

The challenge was to create a system that would allow designers, animators, and art directors to create characters without any prior technical or even 3D experience. The turnaround time for generation of these characters had to be very short. The newly created characters had to be instantly animatable, fully rigged and weighted, and linked to valid shaders and textures. The system had to be scalable and allow for changes to rigging, weighting, character design, scale, and resolution throughout the production process. It also had to be robust enough to function on its own without constant support from technical directors. This system became known as the Who Construction Kit, and it was used in the creation of each and every Who, from the lowest-detail background characters to high-detail foreground characters.

Because the Who Construction Kit would be used to populate an entire village of Whos, it would have to provide an almost infinite number of character combinations created from a finite set of body sizes, face shapes, textures, and items of clothing. To accomplish this, each item of clothing had to be usable on any character irrespective of shape or size. So, in effect, as the user modified the body of the character, each item of clothing would have to be capable of automatically adjusting and deforming to the correct shape and size of the character underneath. Another difficult issue was the process of automatic character setup: rigging and weighting a character of arbitrary body shape and size with all attached clothing, collision models, and facial setup without any user input. As we began receiving footage, we realized that different sequences would require different clothing schemes. We catalogued our databases of Whos based on sequence, apparel, gender, and other factors.

Character replacement was another problem early on in the project. The more involved the director and art department became in the character-creation process, the more control they required. In the final stages of some shots, we were asked to change the clothing or weight of a particular character. The Who Construction Kit allowed us to import any given character and alter the character's size, weight, age, etc., all within the kit's interface. Once the character had been modified, it could be regenerated and substituted back into the scene within a matter of minutes.

The interface of the Who Construction Kit had to be user-friendly and intuitive so that non-technical users could generate characters quickly. As users created Whos, the construction kit updated the database Web pages with a preview-render and the name of each character. Animators could then peruse the Web pages and choose appropriate Whos for their shots from the catalogue of available characters. The kit interfaced directly with our kinematic and animation tools, allowing animators the ability to import any catalogued character at any point in the animation process. If animators could not find a character to their liking in the catalogue, they could easily create a new one. By keeping the system fast, flexible, and user-friendly, we were able to populate Whoville with hundreds of unique characters while minimizing our technical labor.

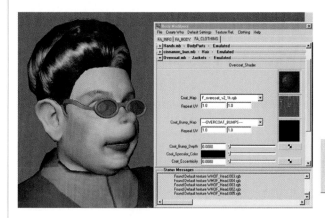

Figure 1. GUI of the Who Construction Kit.

Figure 2. One of the scenes from the movie, in which the character creation kit was used to create the crowd scenes.

*199*

# Human Motion Signatures for Character Animation

*Contact*
M. Alex O. Vasilescu
Department of Computer Science
University of Toronto
10 King's College Road
Toronto, Ontario M5S 3G4
Canada
alexv@cs.toronto.edu

Given motion-capture samples of Charlie Chaplin's walk, is it possible to synthesize other motions (say, ascending or descending stairs) in his distinctive style? More generally, in analogy with handwritten signatures, do people have characteristic motion signatures that individualize their movements? If so, can these signatures be extracted from example motions?

Human motion is the composite consequence of multiple elements – most importantly, the action performed and a motion signature. The *action* captures the person-invariant essence of an activity or movement. The *motion signature* captures the distinctive pattern of movement of any particular individual. In this sketch, we introduce an algorithm that separates these elemental effects and recombines them in novel ways for animation of graphical characters. For example, given a corpus of walking, stair-ascending, and stair-descending motion data collected over a group of subjects, plus a sample walking motion for a new subject, our algorithm can synthesize never-before-seen ascending and descending motions in the distinctive style of this new individual.

Our algorithm first decomposes a corpus of motion data into motion signatures and action components. Next, given an incomplete set of motion data for a new subject, the algorithm extracts a motion signature for this individual from the available data and the corresponding action components obtained previously. The remaining action components can then be recombined with this motion signature to synthesize a complete set of motions in the distinctive style of the new subject.

The mathematical basis of our algorithm is a statistical numerical technique known as *n-mode analysis*. The two-mode analysis algorithm that we adapt to our purposes was described for scalar observations by Magnus and Neudecker in their book *Matrix Differential Calculus* (Wiley, 1999).

## Experiments

We begin by collecting a corpus of motion data spanning 10 different subjects using a Vicon motion capture system. Applying smoothing, interpolation, and IK motion-processing steps, the data are reduced to time-varying joint angles for complete cycles of three types of motions: walking, ascending stairs, and descending stairs. In a "leave-one-person-out" validation experiment, we verified that our algorithm is able to extract motion signatures and accurately synthesize all three types of motions.

Figure 1 shows a stair-ascending motion synthesized for one of the individuals. Our algorithm extracted the motion signature from a sample walk of this individual. The extracted motion signature was combined with general stair-ascending parameters to synthesize the stair-ascending motion that exhibits the characteristic signature.

Figure 2 shows frames from a short animation that was created with synthesized data. For the clown, the motion signature is that of a strutting male, and the action parameters are those for a walk. The other character was animated using the motion signature of a female and the action parameters of a walk.

## Conclusion

We have introduced the concept of decomposing human motion data into motion-signature and action elements. These elements are useful in the synthesis of novel motions for animation of articulated characters.

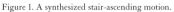

Figure 1. A synthesized stair-ascending motion.

Figure 2. A short animation created using motion data synthesized by our algorithm.

*200*

# Hybrid Ink-Line Rendering in a Production Environment

*Contact*
Rasmus Tamstorf
Walt Disney Feature Animation
500 South Buena Vista Street
Burbank, California 91521 USA
Rasmus.Tamstorf@disney.com

Ramón Montoya-Vozmediano
Daniel Teece
Patrick Dalton
Walt Disney Feature Animation

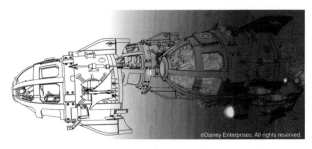

A frame from Walt Disney's "Atlantis." Left: ink-line rendering produced by Inka; right: final composite with paint layers, effects, and background.

Walt Disney Feature Animation has used a number of in-house ink-line rendering solutions in the past, all of which have been image-based. Used in the production of sequences such as the Hydra in "Hercules," these post-processors were slow and had high memory demands. Inka was developed as a robust long-term alternative, and has been employed on "The Emperor's New Groove" as well as in several hundred shots on "Atlantis."

Inka takes a hybrid approach. While it is primarily geometry-based, with information from the 3D model driving placement of 2D ink lines, it also uses some image-processing methods and employs a z-buffer to perform hidden-line removal. Rendering speed is typically an order of magnitude faster than previous image-based techniques, and ink lines found during the geometry processing stage can be rendered without the artifacts inherent in pixel-based methods.

To ensure consistent, high-quality renders, the user can set attributes for specific NURBS patches or meshes in a text file. This allows the appearance of the ink-line image to be tailored to particular needs and settings to be tweaked for complex shots. These attributes may affect not only the appearance of a line (width, color, opacity) but also visibility determination and surface tessellation parameters. In this way, the user has a great deal of low-level control over each part of each individual line, which has proved invaluable in a production environment.

In addition, custom shaders allow users to control how a line is drawn based on the underlying geometry or screen position. They are currently being used extensively on upcoming features to create more stylized strokes. Another feature that has turned out to be valuable, despite its simplicity, is attenuation of opacity and line width as a function of depth. This allows a smooth transition of objects as they recede into the background.

Geometry-based ink-line rendering is very sensitive to its input geometry. In production use, models that work flawlessly with a shaded renderer can cause imperfect ink lines. Some problems can be fixed by setting attributes, whereas others require re-modeling. However, modeling for Inka also provides new opportunities. As an example, curves defined on the surface of a patch can be used to substitute for texture or to better convey the shape of an object, as if the modeler were drawing on the geometry.

As Inka has matured, its approach has proven to be scalable and flexible enough to accommodate increasing scene complexity as well as models that range from rigid and mechanical to animated and organic. It is now being used in production on "Treasure Planet" and "Lilo and Stitch."

*Special thanks to Joe Lohmar, Yun-Chen Sung, and Mike King.*

201

# Image-Based Rendering and Illumination Using Spherical Mosaics

*Contact*
Chen Shen
EECS, Computer Science Division
University of California, Berkeley
Berkeley, California 94720-1776
USA
+1.510.642.3631
csh@cs.berkeley.edu

Heung-Yeung Shum
Microsoft Research, China

James F. O'Brien
University of California, Berkeley

## Introduction

Rather than rendering using geometric primitives, image-based rendering techniques synthesize novel views directly from a collection of sample images. This approach has proven to be a powerful alternative to traditional geometry-based methods, making it possible to interactively render views of complex scenes.

The work described here extends the concentric mosaic representation developed by Shum and He[1] to spherical mosaics that allow the viewer greater freedom of movement. Additionally, by precomputing maps for diffuse and specular lighting terms, we use high-dynamic-range image data to compute realistic illumination for objects that can be interactively manipulated within the scene.

## Spherical Mosaics

Concentric mosaics represent a scene using a series of sample images captured along a circular path looking outward. Spherical mosaics simply extend this approach by using a set of sample images that are taken from locations distributed over the surface of a sphere. Within an inner sphere, whose radius is determined by the sample camera's field of view, any exiting ray can be mapped to a location in one of the sample images.

The mapping is accomplished by intersecting the exiting ray with the capture sphere to determine the nearest sample cameras. A point along the ray at a constant depth is then projected back to the center of projection for each camera to determine the closest pixels within each image. Linear interpolation of the resulting values yields the value for the exiting ray. If depth estimates are available, they may be used to improve the accuracy of the projection into the sample images. Because the sample images form a 4D representation of the external light field, the virtual camera is afforded a full six degrees of freedom within the inner sphere.

## Diffuse and Specular Maps

Once a scene has been sampled, adding additional objects into the environment requires realistically replicating environmental illumination when shading the new object. If the sample images have high dynamic range with pixel values that record incident radiance, then the illumination at any point within the inner sphere can be determined from the sampled data. Unfortunately, shading calculations at a point on the surface of the new object require expensive summations over all the incoming ray directions.

To achieve interactive rendering speeds, we move the summations to a preprocessing step and implement them by filtering the sampled data to form diffuse and specular maps. Both of these maps are stored as spherical mosaics. A mipmap-like structure holds multiple versions of the specular map computed with different-sized kernels that can be used for different specular falloff parameters. The diffuse map is indexed according to surface position and normal, while the specular map is indexed by surface position and the reflected viewing direction. Simple ray tracing provides a unified way to render both the spherical mosaic environment and the added objects.

## Results and Future Work

We do not currently have a physical device for capturing spherical mosaics of real environments, so we have tested our methods using synthetic images generated using the RADIANCE rendering package.[2] The figures on this page (and the accompanying video) show images that were synthesized from a data set consisting of 9172 small (256 x 256) sample images acquired with a 90° field of view. The user is able to interactively change the view, add new objects, move the new objects, and modify their surface properties. A 256 x 256 anti-aliased image with exposure compensation can be re-synthesized in 1.05 seconds on an SGI 350MHz R12000. Without anti-aliasing, only .35 seconds are required.

The primary future extension of this work would be to build a physical capture device. Another area for further investigation is allowing the added objects to affect the environment lighting by casting shadows or creating reflections.

*References*
1. Shum, H.-Y. & He, H.-W. (1999). Rendering with concentric mosaics. *Proceedings of SIGGRAPH 99,* 299-306.
2. Ward, G. (1994). The RADIANCE lighting simulation and rendering system. *Proceedings of SIGGRAPH 94,* 459-472.

Image-based renderings showing inserted objects with different surface properties.

# IMAGE-BASED PHOTOMETRIC RECONSTRUCTION FOR MIXED REALITY

*Contact*
S. GIBSON
Advanced Interfaces Group
Department of Computer Science
Manchester, United Kingdom
sg@cs.man.ac.uk
aig.cs.man.ac.uk

T.L.J. HOWARD
R.J. HUBBOLD
Advanced Interfaces Group

Image-based photometric reconstruction is the process of estimating the illumination and surface reflectance properties of an environment from a set of photographs. For mixed-reality applications, such a reconstruction is required if synthetic objects are to be correctly illuminated or if synthetic light sources are to be used to re-illuminate the scene.

Current approaches to photometric reconstruction[1,2] are limited in the situation they can be applied. The user must often provide a complete geometric model of the environment, and in some cases, the position and intensity of the light sources that are illuminating the scene. Additionally, current reconstruction algorithms are limited by the fact that they cannot be applied when a mixture of artificial and natural illumination lights the scene. This sketch shows results from applying a new reconstruction algorithm[3] to the problem of estimating the photometric properties of real scenes.

## A NEW APPROACH

We use a combination of computer vision and photogrammetry algorithms to calibrate cameras and build a partial geometric model of a scene. A small number of high-dynamic-range images are then captured, and registered to the geometric model. Radiance values from these images are associated with each visible surface. A number of virtual light sources are then automatically positioned around the scene. These light sources are used to mimic the effects of unknown luminaries in the parts of the environment that have not been modelled, as well as the effect of light reflected indirectly off unknown geometry. An iterative refinement algorithm is used to estimate the intensity distributions of these virtual light sources, as well as the diffuse and specular properties of surfaces. At each stage of refinement, an optimisation process chooses light source intensities so that the illumination they cast on each surface matches the radiance values in the high-dynamic-range photographs. Further details are available in Gibson, Howard & Hubbold.[3]

## RESULTS

Figures 2 and 3 show synthetic renderings using materials and virtual light source intensities estimated for a scene containing artificial and natural light (Figure 1). These data were then used as input to a global illumination algorithm, allowing photo-realistic renderings to be obtained from novel viewpoints (Figure 4), and where the images have been augmented with synthetic light sources and artificial objects (Figures 4 and 5).

*References*
1. Yu, Debevec, P., Malik, J., & Hawkins, T. (1999). Inverse global illumination: Recovering reflectance models of real scenes from photographs. *Proceedings of SIGGRAPH 99.*
2. Loscos, C., Drettakis, G., & Robert, L. (2000). Interactive virtual relighting of real scenes. *IEEE Transactions on Visualization and Computer Graphics, 6* (4).
3. Gibson, S., Howard, T.L.J., & Hubbold, R.J. (2001). Flexible image-based photometric reconstruction using virtual light-sources. *Computer Graphics Forum (Proceedings of Eurographics 2001), 19* (3).

Figure 1. Original high-dynamic-range images for artificial and natural light.

Figure 2; Synthetic renderings using the reconstructed illumination data (without texture).

Figure 3. Synthetic renderings using the reconstructed illumination data (with texture).

Figure 4. Renderings from a novel viewpoint and with synthetic light sources.

Figure 5. Rendering the scene with synthetic objects.

*203*

# Image-Based Reconstruction of Shift-Variant Materials

*Contact*
Hendrik P. A. Lensch
Max-Planck-Institut für
Informatik
lensch@mpi-sb.mpg.de

Jan Kautz
Michael Goesele
Hans-Peter Seidel
Max-Planck-Institut für
Informatik

Wolfgang Heidrich
University of British Columbia

The use of realistic models for all components of image synthesis is a fundamental prerequisite for photo-realistic rendering. Manually generating these models often becomes infeasible as the demand for visual complexity steadily increases. In this sketch, we concentrate on acquisition of realistic materials. In particular, we describe an acquisition method for shift-variant BRDFs: acquiring a specific BRDF for each surface point.

## Data Acquisition

We acquire the geometry of the object with a 3D scanner (for example, a structured light or computer tomography scanner) which yields a triangular mesh. In order to capture the reflection properties, we take a relatively small number (around 20) of high-dynamic-range (HDR) images of the object, lit by a point light source. We recover the camera position and orientation as well as the light-source position relative to the geometric model for all images.

For every point on the object's surface, we collect all available data from the different views in a data structure called lumitexel. It contains the position of the surface point, its normal, and a list of radiance samples together with their viewing and lighting directions.

## Clustering of Materials

Since a single lumitexel does not carry enough information to reliably fit a BRDF model to the radiance samples, we first determine clusters of lumitexels belonging to similar materials. Starting with a single cluster containing all lumitexels, the parameters of an average BRDF are fitted using the Levenberg-Marquardt algorithm. From this, two new sets of parameters are generated by varying the fitted parameters along the direction of maximum variance, yielding two slightly separated BRDFs. The lumitexels of the original cluster are then assigned to the nearest of these BRDFs, forming two new clusters. A stable separation of the materials in the clusters is obtained by repeatedly fitting BRDFs to the two clusters and redistributing the original lumitexels. Further splitting isolates the different materials until the number of clusters matches the number of materials of the object as illustrated in Figure 1.

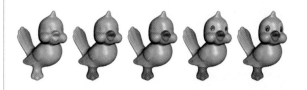

Figure 1. The clustering process at work. In every image, a new cluster was created.

## Shift-Variant Behavior

After the clustering, we still have the same reflection behavior assigned to all lumitexels in one cluster. However, small features on the surface and smooth transition between materials can only be represented if every lumitexel is assigned its own BRDF. In our algorithm, this BRDF is a linear combination of the BRDFs recovered by the clustering procedure. This can be represented by a set of basis BRDFs for the entire model plus a set of weighting coefficients for each lumitexel. An optimal set of weighting coefficients minimizes the error between the measured radiance and the weighted radiance values obtained by evaluating the basis BRDFs for the specific viewing and lighting directions. To recover the coefficients we compute the least-square solution of the corresponding system of equations using singular-value decomposition. This method allows for accurately shaded, photo-realistic rendering of complex solid objects from new viewpoints under arbitrary lighting conditions with relatively small acquisition effort.

Figure 2. Two models rendered with shift-variant BRDFs acquired with our reconstruction method.

*Related Work*
1. Debevec, P., Hawkins, T., Tchou, C. Duiker, H.P., Sarokin, W., & Sagar, M. (2000). Acquiring the reflectance field of a human face. *Proceedings of SIGGRAPH 2000*, 145-156.
2. Wood, D., Azuma, D., Aldinger, K., Curless, B., Duchamp, T., Salesin, D., & Stuetzle, W. (2000). Surface light fields for 3D photography. *Proceedings of SIGGRAPH 2000*, 287-296.

# Image-Based Rendering for Animated Deforming Objects

*Contact*
Hiroshi Kawasaki
Institute of Industrial Science
University of Tokyo
4--6--1 Komaba, Meguro-ku
Tokyo 153-8505 Japan
h-kawa@sak.iis.u-tokyo.ac.jp

Hiroyuki Aritaki
Takeshi Ooishi
Katsushi Ikeuchi
Masao Sakauchi
Institute of Industrial Science

This technical sketch presents a description of how an image-based rendering (IBR) technique can be used to produce photo-realistic animation of real-world objects that usually have non-rigid-surface effects (for example, animal fur and velvet).

In recent years, principles and various kinds of implementation and theoretical analyses of IBR have been proposed and published one after another. However, for practical use of IBR (for example, for animation production), little research has been done, and few actual applications have been developed. Although there may be many reasons for this, the following two reasons are significant:

1. Huge data size.
2. Lack of interactivity among objects and illumination.

IBR data volumes are very large. This is a crucial issue for actual implementation, and there have been many attempts to reduce the data volumes. On the other hand, little research has been devoted to realizing interactivity for IBR. Therefore, we leave the data-volume problem for future research and concentrate on the interactivity problem encountered in the process of making photo-realistic animations.

Our method is based on the surface-light-field technique, a term coined by Miller et al.[1] Our research is also inspired by the work done by Nishino et al.[2] and Daniel N.Wood et al.[3]

## Interactivity and Animation

Basically, we assume that the interaction of the objects can be defined by three aspects: the arbitrary position of the object, including deformation of the object; the arbitrary illumination change that usually causes shadow changes; and real-time rendering.

The purpose of our system, to achieve interactivity for IBR, can be translated as rendering arbitrarily positioned objects with arbitrary deformation and illumination in real time.[*] However, real-time rendering is not necessary for animation, and we are not currently interested in real time.

## System

To synthesize an object whose position and pose change arbitrarily, we re-use the actual ray derived from the object's surface. To achieve photo-realistic rendering, we developed a mesh-based rendering algorithm that selects the appropriate ray from the whole ray based on the BRDF (bidirectional reflectance distribution function) for the individual mesh. Also, because the data acquisition process is very important for this system, we configured an original data-acquisition system: "light dome," shown in the following figure. The light dome can automatically acquire the 4D data that is necessary for image synthesis.

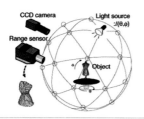

## Results

We performed several experiments to show the effectiveness of our method. The following figure shows the result that was achieved by using a Tatami block.[**] The image on the left is the actual captured image, while the image on the right is the synthesized image after deformation.

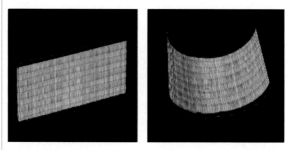

The next figure shows another result using a paper-wrapped can; the left image is the image synthesized with our method; the right image is a texture-mapped image.

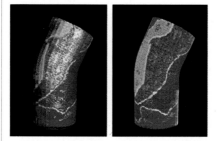

These results demonstrate the effectiveness of our proposed method to render photo-realistic images of the deformed objects with non-rigid surface effects. In the future, we will synthesize the object under arbitrary illumination changes.

*References*
1. Miller, G., Rubin, S., & Ponceleon, D. (1998). Lazy decompression of surface light fields for precomputed global illumination. *Rendering Techniques (Eurographics Proceedings)*, June 1998.
2. Nishino, K., Sato, Y., & Ikeuchi, K. (1999). Appearance compression and synthesis based on 3D model for mixed reality. *Proceedings of Seventh International Conference on Computer Vision*.
3. Wood, D., Azuma D., Aldinger, W., Curless, B., Duchamp, T., Salesin, D., & Steutzle, W. (2000) Surface light fields for 3D photography. *Proceedings of SIGGRAPH 2000*.

[*] Rendering such a deformed object with consistent illumination and geometry is always difficult.

[**] A 3D block made of tightly bound straw. This material also has non-rigid effects on the surface.

*205*

# Imaging the Living Computer: Neuroscience Methods in Visualizing the Performance of Parallel Programs

*Contact*
Daniel L. Herman
DigitalFish Films
dh@digitalfish.com
www.digitalfish.com

## Introduction

Neuros is a testbed system for graphical visualization of program executions on large parallel computers. It consists of an extensible, configurable toolkit that provides still-frame and animated views of parallel tracefiles. The system has several unusual strengths that set it apart from most other execution visualizers, including its ability to manipulate and display networks that have high dimensionality or that contain large numbers of processors. Neuros takes a scalable, summarizing approach to viewing trace data, which makes it suitable for work with both small-scale and large, highly complex executions.

Neuros is built on the OpenDX (formerly IBM Data Explorer) visualization system, so users familiar with this popular environment can extend the built-in views and add their own. Input is an MPICL trace file. Publicly available converters allow use of other data formats.

## Neuroimaging Techniques

We focused on massively parallel (MP) programs because the problems in visualizing such programs tend to be more severe than those faced in small-scale parallelism. Numerous similarities exist between the obstacles in MP execution visualization and those faced in neurological diagnosis of brain disorders, including the large number of nodes (processors/neurons) involved, high aggregate bandwidth, difficulty in obtaining execution data without perturbing the system under study, difficulty in abstracting high-level information from single-node statistics, and difficulty in performing hardware monitoring on large numbers of individual nodes.

A number of elegant and powerful visualization solutions have been developed to aid in neurological diagnosis. Four that we focus on particularly are electroencephalography (EEG), evoked potential (EP), positron emission tomography (PET), and the magnetoencephalogram (MEG).

There are a number of ideas we can borrow from these techniques. The first is an emphasis on high-level characterizations that employ summary statistics. While it is possible for neurologists to make single-cell recordings, summary information tends to be more useful for practical diagnostics. Further, neurologists rely on visualization to study large sets of measured data. They use topographical mappings of data to some notion of the problem domain. In neuroimaging, the mappings usually reflect the physical layout of the system. In our application, such mappings could be to the logical topology of the processor network or to some abstract representation of the problem domain.

## Neuros Visualization Techniques

Neuros provides tools to assist in visualizing topologies with high dimensionality and large numbers of nodes. It supports mapping data to topologies of arbitrary dimensionality, while providing various means of projecting an $n$-dimensional space onto a three-dimensional space for display. *Nesting* supports the representation of four-dimensional hypercubes, for example, as two nested three-dimensional cubes, one within the other. A similar projection is *staggering*, in which the second 3-cube is displaced laterally (in 3-space) from the first. A *shadow cast* computes the shadow that the $n$-dimensional object would make on a $k < n$ dimensional volume. When dealing with large numbers of nodes, rather than strictly representing individual processors and interconnections (for example, spheres and lines), Neuros can display summarizing abstractions for groups of nodes as clouds or isosurfaces through the machine topology. This gives an amorphous view of activity that mandates abstract reading and interpretation.

Time is represented in various ways. It may be spread out along some spatial dimension, as is done frequently for EP and EEG, or the entire visualization may be presented as distinct time slices or a time-dilated animation, typical of PET and MEG.

Any data values in the execution (including statistical observations such as average load at a node or messaging rate along an edge) can be encoded into the visualization. They may directly affect glyph properties (for example, color or scale), or they may cause more abstract effects such as general warpings of space. This allows, for instance, load to be represented by causing an $n$-ary mesh to bulge outward in high-load regions. Other visualizations include lighting effects and volumetric fog density.

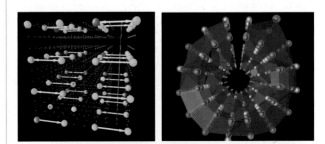

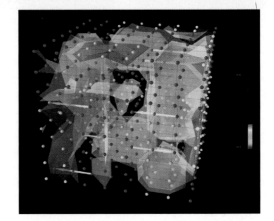

Figure 1. Top left: processor load (node color) and messaging (arrows) during an FFT on a 1,024-processor machine. The data have been downsampled so that only statistics at 64 "virtual" nodes are displayed. Top right: a 16-processor machine performing an FFT. The processor nodes at a given time-slice are arranged in a circle, and successive time-slices are layered to produce a tube. Event type at a given processor is shown by node color, and latency is shown by the diameter of the surrounding clouds. Distortions in the cylinder surface indicate load. Bottom: a complex visualization of a computation on a 512-processor machine. Isosurfaces provide a statistical overview of machine state and algorithm performance.

# Immersive Visualization of a Very-Large-Scale Seismic Model

*Contact*
Prashant Chopra
Mississippi State University
NSF Engineering Research
Center for
Computational Systems
2 Research Boulevard
Starkville, Mississippi 39759 USA
prash@erc.msstate.edu

Joerg Meyer
Michael L. Stokes
Mississippi State University
NSF Engineering Research
Center for
Computational Systems

This application portrays our ongoing efforts to interactively and immersively visualize the results of very-large-scale earthquake simulations.

## Origin of the Dataset

The original dataset is a result of a collaborative effort among the University of California, Berkley; Carnegie Mellon University; and Mississippi State University. The basic geometry consists of 11,800,639 nodes with their tetrahedral connectivity. In addition, each node has a velocity-vector attribute spanning over 120 time steps. Each simulation run generates structural responses for buildings with varying physical properties. The building locations are associated with selected nodes on the top surface of the structure, which represents a layered, block-shaped soil model.

## Challenges

Our visualization team faced two immediate challenges: a large number of files in the raw dataset and numerous generated and derived attributes (for example, velocity, acceleration, ground motion, structural response for buildings, etc.).

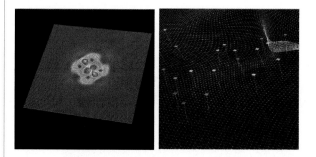

## Preprocessing

The first essential step to reduce this large-scale dataset was extraction of the geometry of the topmost layer as a triangulated surface, followed by an efficient loss-less encoding scheme for the whole dataset based on wavelet compression.

## Visualization Paradigms

The first paradigm that was implemented was an interactive 3D time-varying visualization of the ground motion on a desktop. Though it was not very immersive, it gave us our first insight into the temporal behavior of the model. The next step led to an interactive simulation and visualization Web portal that generated the structural response data for selected parameters. The back-end rendering engine was made flexible enough to move the user to a prespecified location around the model with results presented in the form of an animated GIF or MPEG movie.

## The Model

Initially, the buildings were modeled as simple sticktop structures, where the top of the buildings moved in response to the shaking ground. Now, fully textured translucent buildings have replaced this simple model. We decided on four visual cues for better insight: the color of the surface nodes (velocity), the color of the buildings' roofs (structural response), the shaky ground motion, and the shaking buildings in response to the ground displacement.

## Immersion: Feel the Tremors

The above paradigms, though useful in their own ways, turned out to not fully exploit the immersive capabilities of a four walled CAVE. Currently, a pre-computed simulation can be viewed from different angles. Future versions will allow us to interactively manipulate the scene and control the simulations. Imagine moving around when the earthquake is "actually" happening around you. You can "see" the buildings shaking and the tremors spread out, while the ground below your feet is sliding and moving!

## What's next in this project?

Adding an additional cue for sound, exploring below the surface as the tremor spreads out, modeling buildings with different structural properties in the same scene, and adding more photo-realism.

## Acknowledgements

Contributors: Gregory L. Fenves, Bozidar Stojadinovic (University of California, Berkeley), Jacobo Bielak et al. (Carnegie Mellon University), Tomasz Haupt, Purushotham Bangalore (Mississippi State University). Supported by the National Science Foundation.

*Contact*
JOHN HADDON
NCCA
Bournemouth University
United Kingdom
theboyhaddon@hotmail.com

IAN STEPHENSON
NCCA
Bournemouth University
United Kingdom

The predominant method of texturing for production is using bitmap image files in conjunction with procedural shading. However, the storage demands of bitmap images increase greatly with resolution, and procedural techniques are typically unsuitable for generation and fine control of complex figures.

Vector graphics provide resolution-independent, scaleable images, typically with low file sizes, and are easily designed using available software. This makes them ideal for use in some texturing situations, particularly where it is necessary to incorporate imagery in a graphic style. This sketch presents the implementation of vector-based texturing in a RenderMan renderer.

## API
As implemented, vector graphics lookups appear to the shader writer much as the built-in texture() calls do. A family of new shadeops of the general form vtexture (uniform string filename, float u, float v, string filtertype) return texture color and alpha information. Beyond this, the shader writer requires no knowledge of the system's internals.

## IMPLEMENTATION
vtexture() is implemented as two DSO shadeop calls. The first, called once per grid with uniform parameters, ensures that the required texture is loaded into a texture cache and marked as being current. At this point, the texture is in its idealised, resolution-free form.

A second shadeop call, executed once per micro-polygon, receives areas to be filtered as arbitrary quads in texture space and returns texture color and alpha information. This is achieved by generating and maintaining a cache of tiles (rasterised sections of texture) and filtering them appropriately. Tiles are rasterised at resolutions adapted to the lookups requested, and a new tile typically includes a reasonable area surrounding the current lookup area. This means that there is a fair chance of a tile that is suitable for the following lookups being already present in the cache. Rasterisation is a computationally significant process, so the effectiveness of this caching is essential to performance.

## EXAMPLE USAGE
vtexture() was employed in rendering a sequence that shows a track into a globe, starting at a point where the whole earth is visible and ending on a small high-resolution section, specifically the Isle of Wight. For comparison, the same sequence was textured using an 8,000 x 8,000-pixel bitmap.

Both sequences were net-rendered with PRMan 3.9. The vector version required approximately three times the computing time of the bitmap. The vector texture was approximately 800K in size, whereas the bitmap was significantly larger (almost 250 MB of uncompressed data). However, most significantly, the vector texture provides resolution several orders of magnitude greater than that achievable with a bitmap of this size (Figure 1).

## CONSIDERATIONS
vtexture() has been implemented and tested with PRMan. The

Reyes algorithm typically generates successive texture lookups that are adjacent in texture space, as they are generated from adjacent grid points. Other rendering algorithms, particularly ray tracing, are unlikely to generate such adjacent lookups, resulting in much less effective caching of tiled data. Presumably, this would significantly limit performance.

Currently, rendering with the system is significantly slower than with substitute bitmaps. Although this is likely to always be the case, it is believed that optimisations, particularly at the rasterising and filtering stages, could significantly increase performance.

Vector texturing is by no means a panacea. Textures of a photographic nature are simply not representable in a vector form. Text and graphic shapes are among those most suitable for vector description, and these could be augmented with procedural techniques in situations that demand greater photo-realism.

## CONCLUSION
It has been shown that vector-based texturing can be successfully implemented under RenderMan as an extension to the shading language. The system described operates with viable performance and over a significant range of resolution. This demonstrates the potential value of vector textures in production.

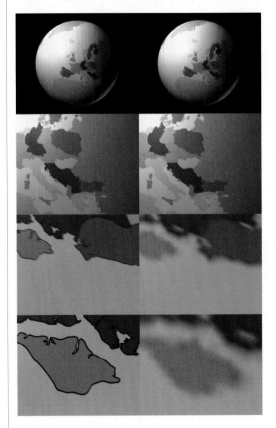

Figure 1: The vector texture (left) provides significantly increased resolution in comparison with the test bitmap texture (right).

*Contact*
MATHEW LAMB
Digital Domain
lamb@d2.com

Over the last few years, pre-visualization has become an essential tool in development of visual effects work. Quite often at this stage, it is easy to have close directorial interaction and, as a result, produce work of fundamental significance to the project. When camera moves are being designed for stage, pre-visualization is doubly important, for not only is the director involved in an otherwise lengthy and tedious process, but also it is important that the integrity of the move that the director designs is not compromised by motion-control operators on stage, who may be trying to fix unforeseen problems, in a costly manner, on the day of the shoot.

To maintain the integrity of this previsualization work, Digital Domain developed a technique for transforming data from an animation package to a motion-control stage in an instantaneous and pixel-accurate manner. The system was first employed in production of "Supernova," and, over the following two years, it was refined to the extent that it has become the de facto solution for both designing and driving motion-control camera moves.

The solution was recently employed in development of a sequence of intricate camera moves for the notable commercial "Brobeck." The difficult challenge in this project was a requirement for a number of hook-ups among live, CG, and motion-control elements. Integral to this was the acute timing among all elements, so pre-visualization rapidly became a low-resolution proxy for development of the whole show. All the pre-visualization files included a kinematically accurate model of the motion-control rig and a complete model of the stage on which it was being shot.

Our current model of the rig contains a huge amount of flexibility. Essentially, it is a double-ended kinematic chain in which the track on which the rig rides, as well as the camera mounted at the other end of the chain, may be positioned independently of one another. In addition, since the rig has more degrees of freedom than are needed to solve for any given camera goal, redundant configurations exist. We capitalize on this and provide them as alternate solutions, which allows for greater flexibility in overcoming obstructions or space constraints on stage. The entire system is modeled in Houdini, our software of choice for integration and effects work, with the result that the director is, in real-time, able to repeat a proposed move until it works.

The range of achievable moves is significantly enhanced because the system includes interaction of the model being shot in the simulation. In this manner, degrees of freedom unobtainable by the camera can be handed off to the model mover (or vice-versa). A good example is the "boomerang," in which a camera move that pushes up to a model and then way past it is converted into a push toward a model, combined rotations of the model and camera, and then a pull away that is visually identical but requires half the length of the stage.

Accuracy is of utmost importance, so the solution includes a triangulation step in which the camera rig and model are precisely localized in space. This process, which only takes a few minutes, results in construction of a transform that allows the pre-visualization camera to align perfectly with stage. Throughout the process, the shoot is augmented by a video tap from the camera that is overlaid on the view of the model in Houdini. From this vantage point, it is trivial to verify that intended and actual moves remain aligned.

This system has proven hugely successful from the very first time it was rolled out, when it saved some 50 percent of our time on stage, to the "Brobeck" commercial, in which the director and animator barely noticed the underlying solution. Instead, they could concentrate on producing high-quality animations, secure in the knowledge that nothing would be compromised anywhere else in the process.

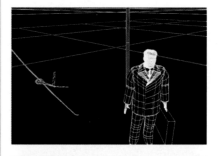

Figure 1. Three stages of the motion-control shoot: a wireframe camera view in Houdini; the green-screen plate on the day of the shoot; and the final composited image in the commercial.

209

# AN INTERACTIVE SYSTEM FOR ROBUST TOPOLOGICAL MODELING OF MESHES

*Contact*
ERGUN AKLEMAN
Visualization Laboratory
216 Langford Center
Texas A&M University
College Station, Texas 77843
USA
+1.979.845.6599
+1.979.845.4491 fax
ergun@viz.tamu.edu

JIANER CHEN
Department of Computer Science
Texas A&M University

VINOD SRINIVASAN
Visualization Sciences
Department of Architecture
Texas A&M University

Current computer graphics practice is almost exclusively based on polygonal meshes. To avoid artifacts such as wrongly oriented or missing polygons, and T-junctions, the polygonal mesh must satisfy a mathematical property called 2-manifold. 2-manifolds are essential for most computer graphics applications. For instance, initial control mesh for subdivision schemes must satisfy 2-manifold property. A polygonal mesh that has a missing polygon can ruin the radiosity computation. In ray tracing, a transparent shape with a wrongly oriented polygon can cause undesirable artifacts in the resulting image.

Topological modeling of 2-manifold polygonal meshes has always been a difficult challenge in computer graphics. Our Doubly Linked Face List (DLFL)[1,2] provides an effective solution to this challenge. It always corresponds to a valid, orientable 2-manifold polygonal mesh and provides a minimal set of operations to change the topology of 2-manifold meshes.

This sketch presents a prototype system to demonstrate the power of DLFL for development of interactive polygonal mesh modelers. Users of our system can easily change topology: create and delete holes and handles, connect and disconnect surfaces. Our system also provides subdivision schemes to create smooth surfaces. Moreover, the system provides automatic texture mapping during topology and smoothing operations. It is topologically robust in the sense that users will never create invalid 2-manifold mesh.

To demonstrate the effectiveness of the system, we have created various polygonal meshes that would be extremely difficult to model interactively without our system. The nested shapes shown here represent an example of models that can be interactively constructed using our system. The inspiration for this shape came from Chinese sculptures consisting of a set of nested, rotatable balls. The actual sculptures can have up to 16 nested balls. Our version consists of three surfaces with genera 31, 31, and 41, respectively.

Creating holes and handles is not only useful for aesthetic purposes. In fact, holes and handles are essential to construction of functional models. The teapot shown here represents an example of a functional model. As can be seen from an X-ray image, this teapot has a real (not just a "look-like") hole to let the water pour from the spout. Because of the hole in the spout, this teapot can be used in physical simulations. The hole and the handle are designed in our system starting from a few rectangular prisms.

## ACKNOWLEDGMENTS
We are thankful to Sajan Skaria, P. David Romei, Glen Vigus, Christina Haaser, Mark Clayton, and Derya Guven Akleman for their help and suggestions.

*References*
1. Akleman, E. & Chen, J. Guaranteeing the 2-manifold property for meshes with Doubly Linked Face List. *International Journal of Shape Modeling*, 5 (2), 149-177.
2. 1. Akleman, E., Chen, J., & Srinivasan, V. (2000). *A new paradigm for changing topology during subdivision modeling*, 192-201. Pacific Graphics, 2000.

Nested manifold surfaces that are interactively constructed using our system.

A teapot created by using our system (top) and its X-ray image (bottom).

# Interactive Virtual Clay Using Implicit Surfaces and Particle Systems

*Contact*
Masatoshi Matsumiya
Nara Institute of Science
and Technology
masato-m@is.aist-nara.ac.jp
yokoya.aist-nara.ac.jp/

Naokazu Yokoya
Haruo Takemura
Nara Institute of Science
and Technology

This sketch presents a virtual clay model developed for interactive virtual clay works that require real-time computation and rendering. Ordinary modeling software for 3D free-form objects has a lot of parameters to tune and a number of limitations on the object's topology and geometry due to underlying mathematical descriptions. Therefore, users must have enough mathematical knowledge and flexible spatial recognition to apply geometric and topological operations to free-form objects. Such problems in free-form modeling can be solved by regarding the objects as clay that can be deformed freely. When users can deal with objects in the same way they would deal with real clay, handling of free-form objects becomes very easy and user-friendly. To realize this modeling concept, virtual clay model must deform in real time.

## Virtual Clay Model

Because it is a plastic fluid, clay has a yield point, a shear stress that has to be overcome so the fluid can start to flow. When a shear stress is below the yield point, clay has a solid structure that prevents plastic flow. Once the yield point is exceeded, the plastic flow allows clay to deform as its volume is preserved. We represent clay using particle systems and implicit surfaces.

In implementing particle systems, spatially interacting particles are used to approximate models for clay. In Figure 1, spatial interaction forces (attraction and repulsion) that act on any pair of particles, are defined depending on their positions. The motion of a particle is governed by:

$$F_i = m_i \frac{d^2 x_i}{dt^2}$$

where Fi denotes a spatial interaction force applied to the i-th particle, which has mass mi and position xi. Particles that receive force below a threshold Fth (particle moving threshold) are not governed and stay where they are. We use Euler's method in calculating a numerial solution of this derivative function.

An implicit surface based on skeletons (skeletal implicit surfaces)[1] is employed to represent smooth surfaces. A skeletal implicit surface is defined by:

$$\{P \in R^3 | f(P) = c\}, f(P) = \sum_{i=1}^{n} F_i(d(P, S_i)),$$

where P is a point in space, and f(P) is the value of a scalar field (implicit value) at the point P. An iso-surface surrounds a solid whose points satisfy f(P) = c. In skeletal implicit surfaces, the implicit value f(P) is generated by a set of skeletal elements Si(i = 1... n) with a set of associated field functions Fi as shown in Figure 1.

We combine particle systems and implicit surfaces into a virtual clay model. First, particles are evenly arranged with a stable distance as shown in Figure 2(a). In the interactive deformation process, each particle moves, preserving the stable distance as shown in Figure 2(b). Therefore, the deformation can preserve the volume like real clay. The particle-moving threshold Fth corresponds to the yield point of plastic fluid. The surface shape of clay

is generated by regarding these particles as skeletal elements of skeletal implicit surfaces as shown in Figure 2(c).

To achieve interactive deformation of the virtual clay model, an image of the deformation must be renderd in real time. To reduce the time required for rendering for interactive modeling, we have developed an efficient algorithm for polygonizing skeletal implicit surfaces based on Bloomenthal's algorithm,[2] because polygons can be quickly rendered by using conventional graphics hardware. In our polygonization algorithm, real-time processing is realized by limiting the area of polygonization to the area around the moving particles.

## Result

Figure 3 shows an image sequence of a deforming virtual clay model that consists of 343 particles. The model is deformed by pushing a part of the model. The computation time during the deformation is measured on a SGI Onyx2 (six MIPS R10000 195MHz CPUs). In the polygonization process, 0.65 seconds are required for one cycle at the maximum load. In particle systems, 0.044 seconds are required for one cycle of calculation of Euler's method. The frame rate of 30 fps is accomplished by carrying out these processes using multiple threads. These results show that a virtual clay model exhibits clay-like deformation and can be calculated and rendered in real time.

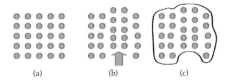

Figure 1. Spatial interaction forces (left) and field function (right).

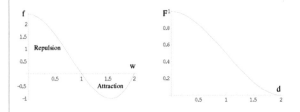

Figure 2. Virtual clay model using particle systems and implicit surfaces.

Figure 3. Image sequence of model deformation.

*References*
1. Cani-Gascuel, M.P. & Desbrun, M. (1997). Animation of deformable models using implicit surfaces. IEEE Trans. on Visualization and Computer Graphics, 3 (1), 39-50.
2. Bloomenthal, J. (1984). An implicit surface polygonizer. In P. Heckbert, Ed., *Graphics Gems IV*, 324-349. Academic Press, 1994.

*211*

# Intuitive Multiple Viewpoints Control using Interlocked Motion of Coordinate Pairs

*Contact*
Shinji Fukatsu
Osaka University
fukatsu@eie.eng.osaka-u.ac.jp

Yoshifumi Kitamura
Toshihiro Masaki
Fumio Kishino
Osaka University

Adequate presentation of multiple views from different positions and directions, as well as in different scales, enables a user to acquire much information about an environment and recognize the environment in detail. In considering effective use of multiple views, the control method for multiple viewpoints (specifically, a primary viewpoint and additional viewpoints) must be clear to the user. A lot of existing viewpoint manipulation methods originally deal with a single viewpoint;[1] however, a method for effectively controlling multiple viewpoints has not yet been discussed. In this sketch, we propose the "interlocked motion of coordinate pairs" as a manipulation technique for intuitively controlling additional viewpoints and the primary viewpoint.

## Interlocked Motion of Coordinate Pairs

Figure 1 shows the coordinate system used in the proposed technique. Three coordinate systems (world coordinates, primary-view coordinate, and additional-view coordinates) are used to present primary and additional view. In addition to these three fundamental coordinate systems, we introduce a secondary coordinate system to determine the additional viewpoints and then interlock the motion of the additional viewpoint with the relative motion of the primary viewpoint and the secondary coordinate system. The secondary coordinate system differs from a world coordinate system for the environment in the geometric relationship (scale, origin, and coordinate system axes). The generated additional view is displayed in the window on the projection plane of the primary view (Figure 2). Therefore, the original data size of the geometry of the environment does not increase even if the number of additional view images (viewpoints) does.

## Intuitive Control of Multiple Viewpoints

There is some variation in the implementation of our proposed technique. Humans intuitively perceive the position and orientation of their own bodies by the sense called proprioception. Therefore, we couple the primary viewpoint and the secondary coordinate system with the user's natural movements. For example, the primary viewpoint is coupled with the user's head motion, and the secondary coordinate is coupled with the user's hand motion (Figure 3). Figure 4 shows the change of the user's view from initial condition (Figure 2) by the user's movements in this implementation example. The user's head rotation changes the orientation of both primary viewpoint and additional viewpoint – Figure 4(a) – and the user's hand rotation changes the orientation of the additional viewpoint – Fig. 4(b). This enables the user to intuitively understand the correspondence between the additional view and the primary view based on proprioception. Also, users can feel that they hold and manipulate a miniature of the environment in their hands and observe it through the window of their primary view.

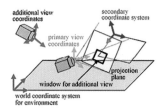

Figure 1. Coordinate systems of proposed technique.

Figure 2. User's view.

Figure 3. System overview.

Figure 4. Change of user's view: (a) rotation of user's head; (b) rotation of user's hand.

*Reference*
1. Ware, C. & Osborne, S. (1990). Exploration and virtual camera control in virtual three-dimensional environment. *Computer Graphics of the ACM, 24* (4) , 175-183.

212

# K-DOPs as Tighter Bounding Volumes for Better Occlusion Performance

*Contact*
Dirk Bartz
Dirk Staneker
WSI/GRIS
Universität Tübingen
bartz@gris.uni-tuebingen.de

James T. Klosowski
IBM T. J. Watson Research
Center

Bounding volumes are used in computer graphics to approximate the actual geometric shape of an object in a scene. The main objective is to reduce the costs associated with interference tests such as intersection tests in ray tracing and collision detection, and to determine the visibility of an object. The bounding volumes most commonly used for these purposes are axis-aligned bounding boxes (AABB). However, in many cases this approximation fills a much larger volume in object space and a much larger screen area (once rasterized into screen space) than the actual geometry. This results in false-positive interference results that can increase the computational load significantly.

Alternatively, oriented bounding boxes (OBB) were proposed, where the spanning axes of the bounding box are oriented according to the shape of the object, thus generating a tighter approximation of the original shape than AABBs. While OBBs perform better for collision detection than AABBs, the benefits for occlusion culling are significantly smaller. This is mainly due to the fact that the rasterized screen area of an OBB is almost the same as for an AABB, and that the corners of an OBB still protrude through exterior hull elements, which occlude the actual geometry.

Another commonly used bounding volume primitive is spheres, which have also been used for ray tracing and collision detection, since intersection with a sphere is very easy to compute. However, a sufficiently tessellated sphere requires many polygons, which increase the costs for an image-space occlusion culling interference test. Furthermore, spheres tend only to approximate compact objects well.

Convex hulls are also good bounding primitives, but they are significantly more expensive to compute than other bounding volumes,[1] and they quickly become impractical in design tasks, where model objects are modified frequently.

In 1996, Klosowski et al.[1] proposed a collision-detection scheme using discrete orientation polytopes (k-dops), which enabled faster collision tests than OBBs. Essentially, k-dops are an approximation of an object by computing bounding planes of an object along k/2 directions.[2] An AABB is one example of a 6-dop, whose bounding planes correspond to the coordinate axes. Another common k-dop is the 26-dop, which is an AABB with the 12 edges and eight corners cut to the object's surface (6 + 12 + 8 = 26 bounding planes).

## Experiments

In our experiments, we employed an image-space occlusion-culling test using the Hewlett-Packard occlusion-culling flag, implemented on the HP fx-series of graphics subsystems. This flag determines if geometry rendered during a special occlusion mode will modify the depth buffer, which indicates potential visibility. In other words, if a bounding volume is rendered, but the HP occlusion-culling flag indicates that the depth buffer would not have changed, then we need not render any of the geometry contained within that bounding volume. We use this flag on a depth-sorted list of objects of the tested models, which are located in the view frustum.

We tested a variety of "real-world" MCAD datasets using AABBs and k-dops. On average, we achieved a 50-percent improvement in the culling rate using k-dops instead of AABBs. The interior objects of MCAD datasets are frequently occluded by exterior hood or cover objects, like the hull of the servo screwdriver in Figure 1. However, AABBs do not provide a very tight approximation for rounded shapes. Hence, they frequently extend through the hull objects and generate false-positive visibility test results. In contrast, k-dops provide a much tighter approximation, where corners of the respective AABB have been cut off.

The polygonal complexity of a k-dop is naturally larger than the complexity of an AABB; if k = 26, up to 26 polygons are used for a kdop, while only six polygons are needed for an AABB. However, an occlusion-culling query requires an update or synchronization of the visibility information, which is a pipeline flush for HP occlusion-culling flag-based approaches. The latency of the pipeline flush is equivalent to rendering approximately 190 triangles of an average size.[3] If the graphics subsystem does not provide hardware support for such queries, this latency is even larger. Experiments with specific polygonal models where k-dops do not facilitate a higher culling rate provide evidence for this statement, since the higher overhead of rendering three times more polygons for the occlusion test is not reflected in a lower frame rate. In fact, the frame rate did not change much beyond the limits of measurement noise.

Overall, k-dops provide tight bounding volumes for polygonal objects. Compared to AABBs, they significantly reduce false-positive visibility queries. The increased rendering costs due to the higher polygonal complexity of the k-dops are overshadowed by the latency of the required synchronization step of state-of-the-art graphics subsystems.

*References*
1. Held, M., Klosowski, J., & Mitchell, J. (1996). Real-time collision detection for motion simulation within complex environments. *Visual Proceedings of SIGGRAPH 96*, 151.
2. Kay, T. & Kajiya, J. Ray tracing complex scenes. *Proceedings of SIGGRAPH 86*, 269-278.
3. Severson, K. (1999). VISUALIZE fx graphics accelerator hardware. Hewlett-Packard Company Whitepaper, 1999.

Figure 1. Servo screwdriver: (top left) motor part and AABB; (top right) motor part and 26-dop; (bottom) AABB of motor part is visible through hull, while 26-dop is completely occluded by hull.

# LIFE-SIZED PROJECTOR-BASED DIORAMAS: SPATIALLY REAL AND VISUALLY VIRTUAL

*Contact*

KOK-LIM LOW
Department of Computer Science
University of North Carolina at
Chapel Hill
lowk@cs.unc.edu

GREG WELCH
ANSELMO LASTRA
HENRY FUCHS
Department of Computer Science
University of North Carolina at
Chapel Hill

In this sketch, we present work in progress on a new projector-based approach to visualizing re-creations of real or virtual places. The major difference between our approach and previous ones is that we use a set of life-sized display surfaces that closely approximate the scene geometry. The effect is a virtual environment that is both visually and spatially realistic, which gives the user a strong sense of immersion.

Our long-term goal is to re-create real remote places, providing users with a realistic sense of presence in the real places. We are interested in allowing people to experience re-creations of famous places such as Monticello, President Thomas Jefferson's home. For now we are working in a research laboratory, but we envision museum spaces with changing exhibits of far-away locations.

Raskar et al. have explored the use of projectors to illuminate real-world objects by projecting images of computer models that closely approximate the objects' geometry.[1] Here, we extend their ideas to life-sized virtual environments, using life-sized display surfaces that closely approximate the actual scene geometry.

## ADVANTAGES AND LIMITATIONS

Using physical display surfaces that closely match the actual scene geometry has many advantages over traditional approaches, such as HMD VR and CAVE.[2] Like a CAVE, our approach offers a wide-field-of-view experience that fills the user's peripheral vision. Such peripheral vision is necessary for maintaining spatial awareness during navigation in virtual environments[3] and provides a better sense of immersion.

The physical arrangement of display surfaces allows the user to really walk around in the virtual scene. Real walking gives a stronger sense of presence than walking in place and virtual flying[4] but at the expense of much larger physical space.

In general, different degrees of approximation of the scene geometry produce a spectrum of display surfaces that range from single flat screens to display surfaces that exactly match the scene geometry. When the display surfaces are significantly different from the scene geometry (which is typically the case in a CAVE), sensitivity to viewing errors (caused by system latency, errors in projector and tracker calibration, etc.) is significant. However, when the display surfaces closely match the scene geometry, sensitivity to such errors is minimized. In the best case, the approach effectively offers auto-stereovision that can support multiple untracked users who simultaneously explore the same virtual scene.

Unfortunately, building an exact detailed physical replica of the scene is usually infeasible. This has forced us to use a simplified set of display surfaces that approximate the scene geometry. For example, primary structures of building interiors and mid-sized architectural objects (walls, columns, cupboards, tables, etc.) can usually be approximated with simple shapes (boxes, cylinders, etc.). The trade-offs include re-introduction of some latency in visual feedback and partial loss of auto-stereovision. The user's eyes now need to be tracked.

Another significant limitation of our approach is that it requires a large physical space to faithfully re-create a large scene. Our approach is also not suitable for dynamic scenes that have large moving objects (cars, for example). Finally, while we have ideas for projector placement that would minimize viewer occlusions, we find it natural to want to approach and touch the display surfaces. In our envisioned museum setting, one might actually have to "rope off" areas near the display surfaces.

## STATUS

We have performed some preliminary experiments in which the scene geometry is approximated by styrofoam blocks, and a two-pass rendering approach is used to generate the correct images as viewed from the user's tracked eye (see figures). The results are encouraging. While we currently only demonstrate our ideas with a synthetic scene, we have collected and are in the process of preparing very high-quality image-based models of the Monticello library. We acquired the models using a 3rdTech laser scanner during a multi-day trip to Monticello.

## CHALLENGES

The need to model and build non-trivial physical display surfaces is a challenge not seen in other projector-based approaches. The other problems of our approach are common to most multi-projector display systems. These problems include shadows, inter-reflections, overlapping projections, non-ideal display-surface properties, projector placement and calibration, multiple views, and rendering resource management. Moreover, to re-create real places, efficient and effective methods are needed to acquire the data, process them, store them, and make them suitable for interactive rendering.

### References

1. Raskar, R., Welch, G., & Low, K. (2000). Shader lamps: Animating real objects with imaged-based illumination. Technical Report TR00-027, Department of Computer Science, UNC-Chapel Hill, January 2000.
2. Cruz-Neira, C. et al. (1993). Surround-screen projection-based virtual reality: The design and implementation of the CAVE. *Proceedings of SIGGRAPH 93.*
3. Leibowitz, H.W. (1986). Recent advances in our understanding of peripheral vision and implications. In the 30th Annual Meeting of the Human Factors Society, 1986.
4. Usoh, M. et al. (1999). Walking > walking-in-place > flying, in virtual environments. *Proceedings of SIGGRAPH 99.*

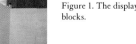

Figure 1. The display surfaces are built from styrofoam blocks.

Figure 2. Perspectively correct imagery of the scene is generated in real time and projected onto the blocks.

Figure 3. A user is virtually spray painting from a tracked "spray gun."

# LIFTING DETAIL FROM DARKNESS

*Contact*
J.P. LEWIS
Disney TSL
3100 Thornton Avenue
Burbank, California 91505 USA
zilla@computer.org

This application describes a high-quality method for separating detail from overall image region intensity, an intensity-detail decomposition. The method can be used to automate some specialized image alteration tasks.

Our work was motivated by the movie "102 Dalmatians," which featured a dalmatian puppy without spots. Animal handlers determined that the obvious idea of applying makeup to the dog was not possible. There was no suitable makeup that was both safe to the dogs and that would stay in place during normal dog activity (including licking). This left Disney TSL with the task of painting out all the spots on the dog every few frames (the paintings were carried for a few frames with a simple scheme).

The spot-removal task was larger than anyone guessed, and ultimately required a large number of artists (up to 40) working for eight months. The problem also proved to be more difficult than expected from an algorithmic point of view. As the spots often had visible fur texture, we initially believed that there must be some simple compositing technique that could lighten the spots.

To get a feel for the problem, consider one representative approach inspired by unsharp masking: blur the dog and then subtract the blurred version from the original, giving a high-pass texture containing the fur. Then correct the intensity of the blurred dog to remove the spots (without saying how this is done). Lastly, add the high-pass texture to the lightened, blurred dog, resulting (we hoped) in a dalmatian without spots but with fur derived from the original texture. The problem with this approach is suggested in Figure 1: the scale of the blur must be exactly matched to the spot profile or there will be an overshoot/undershoot around the spot edge. This is not achievable, since the spot transition regions have markedly different widths even on opposite sides of a single spot. Some more adaptive technique was required.

## ADAPTIVE FILTERING

The intensity-detail decomposition problem is reminiscent of the problem addressed by Wiener filtering: separating signal from noise. Making use of this observation, by casting detail in the role of "noise" and intensity in the role of "signal," we were able to apply a Wiener separation approach; a simple spatial-domain adaptive Wiener filtering algorithm described by Lim[1] works quite well.

## INTENSITY MODIFICATION

Once the detail is successfully separated, we need a means of altering the image region intensity in a simple and controllable fashion. The membrane (Laplace) equation $\nabla 2u = 0$ produces an interpolation of specified boundary conditions that minimizes $\int (\nabla u)2dA$ (the integrated gradient); as such, it provides an adequate way of interpolating intensity specified on a boundary curve (for example, a rough spot boundary). The Laplace equation is a linear system $Au = b$ with $A$ being a sparse square matrix whose dimension is the number of pixels in the region. The intensity-detail decomposition was initially prototyped in MATLAB, which took less than a day and used that package's sparse matrix routines. Our algorithm was later reimplemented in Java, which took about three months.

Approximately half of that time was devoted to the membrane solution. The first implementation was a direct (non-sparse) matrix solution, programmed by Yi-Xiong Zhou. This was adequate for very small regions but was too inefficient for larger regions. Areas of $150^2$ pixels were requiring several minutes and 0.5G of memory! Fortunately, the Laplace equation can be solved with the multigrid technique[2] (and in fact is the model problem for this approach). A multigrid implementation of the membrane reduced the solution time to several seconds even for large regions.

## APPLICATIONS

In addition to the spot-removal application, intensity-detail decomposition has other specialized applications such as altering or removing shadows and reducing wrinkles (Figure 3). It should be emphasized that although the effects shown here are routine work for a photoshop artist:

- Each image alteration shown here was produced with no artistic skill from a crude outline for the desired region in a few seconds. Consider Figure 3: the altered regions have luminance gradients as well as recovered original texture, so the effects could not be produced with a simple cloning operation but would require careful airbrushing followed by detail painting.
- Unlike manual retouching, the detail decomposition can be keyframed and produces consistent effects across frames.

*References*
1.  Lim, J.S. (1990). *Two-dimensional signal and image processing*. Prentice-Hall, 1990.
2.  Press, W.H., Teukolsky, S.A., Vetterling, W.T., & Flannery, B.P. (1993). *Numerical recipes.* Cambridge, 1993.

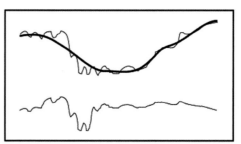

Figure 1. Hypothetical spot luminance profile, blurred luminance (heavy), and unsharp mask (bottom). When the blur size is too large, the texture overshoots; when it is too small, the blurred curve follows the texture, and texture amplitude is reduced.

Figure 2. Demi-dalmatian.

Figure 3. Altered regions include shadows under nose and eyes, and other changes.

*215*

# Light Field Rendering with Triangular Viewpoint Mesh

**Contact**

**Dongho Kim**
Department of Computer Science
The George Washington
University
dkim@seas.gwu.edu

**James K. Hahn**
Department of Computer Science
The George Washington
University

Light field rendering[1] is a representative image-based rendering system using two-plane parameterization. The dataset in this scheme is a set of rays passing through regular grids sampled on two parallel planes. And this 4D dataset in (s,t,u,v) space can be thought of as a set of 2D images that have their viewpoints located at rectangular grids on a plane. We use (s,t) coordinates to parameterize the viewpoints and (u,v) coordinates to parameterize pixels in the images.

Rendering from this dataset is a process of reconstruction of rays. Due to the nature of digital sampling with limited resolution, we cannot avoid rendering error. In this work, we propose a new triangular sampling scheme of (s,t) plane. And we compare this scheme with rectangular sampling.

Figure 1(a) shows rectangular sampling in the original light field rendering. The viewpoints are sampled regularly at rectangular grids in (s,t) space. Figure 1(b) shows new parameterization of (s,t) based on triangular sampling. Here, the viewpoints are located at the vertices of a triangular mesh. This sampling can be obtained by moving the sample points in alternate rows of the original sampling by half the distance between the samples, and we can know that the sampling density is the same in both cases. In other words, the cost for the sampling does not change in new parameterization.

Since a light field is a set of discrete samples, we have to consider the aliasing problem. Figure 2(a) shows the frequency domain spectrum after the sampling in Figure 1(a). Due to the digital sampling, the spectrum of the original signal is repeated along two dimensions of the frequency domain. The spacing between the repetitions is determined by the sampling intervals. Here, we assume that the original signal is band-limited within a circle. This assumption makes sense if the original signal does not have any directional strength. Because of the overlapping spectrums, we get aliasing error from the overlapping spectrums. Figure 2(b) shows the frequency domain spectrum after the sampling in Figure 1(b). In this case, due to the characteristics of interlaced sampling, the amount of aliasing is reduced because the distances between spectrums are increased. In other words, for the same amount of aliasing, we need a smaller number of sampling points with new parameterization.

For reconstruction in original light field rendering, quadrilinear interpolation is used in (s,t,u,v) space. This is bilinear interpolation in (s,t) viewpoint sampling space. For new triangular parameterization, we interpolate with the barycentric coordinates of the reconstructed rays. So barycentric weights determine the interpolation in (s,t) space. Since we still use bilinear interpolation in (u,v), 12 samples are involved in the reconstruction, while original light field rendering uses 16 samples. Obtaining barycentric coordinates for reconstructed rays can be done quickly by calculating the distance to the parallel lines of the triangular mesh. Or hardware-based rendering presented in Isaksen et al.[3] can be used. Figure 3 is a rendering example from the DRAGON dataset in the Stanford light field archive.[4]

In order to compare two parameterizations, the images are reconstructed using the same viewpoints. From the original 32 x 32 images in the DRAGON dataset, we use 16 x 16 images for both parameterizations so that the samplings are performed as in Figure 1. And we reconstruct at the viewpoints along the blue lines in Figure 1, where the correct images are known from the DRAGON dataset but are not used in both samplings. From a rendering of 225 viewpoints, triangular sampling showed 2.1 percent less error on average, while using fewer samples for reconstruction. Moreover, the maximum error is smaller than original light field rendering. This is due to the enhanced sampling with less aliasing.

In future work, we need more concrete verification of the suggested parameterization. One method could be rendering a lot of images from randomly sampled viewpoints and performing statistical comparison. Or it is possible that spectral analysis like that suggested by Chai et al.[2] will be desirable.

*References*
1. Levoy, M. & Hanrahan, P. (1996). Light field rendering. *Proceedings of SIGGRAPH 96*, 31-42.
2. Chai, J., Chan, S., Shum, H., & Tong, X. (2000). Plenoptic sampling. *Proceedings of SIGGRAPH 2000*, 307-318.
3. Isaksen, A., McMillan, L., & Gortler, S.J. (2000). Dynamically reparameterized light fields. *Proceedings of SIGGRAPH 2000*, 297-306.
4. URL: www-graphics.stanford.edu/software/lightpack/lifs.html

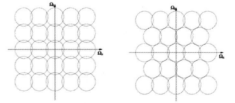

Figure 1. Sampling grids: (a) rectangular sampling, (b) triangular sampling.

Figure 2. Frequency spectrum: (a) rectangular sampling, (b) triangular sampling.

Figure 3. Reconstructed image.

*216*

*Contact*
TIM HAWKINS
Institute for Creative
Technologies
University of Southern California
timh@ict.usc.edu

JONATHAN COHEN
CHRIS TCHOU
PAUL DEBEVEC
Institute for Creative
Technologies
University of Southern California

At SIGGRAPH 2000, we presented an apparatus for capturing the appearance of a person's face under all possible directions of illumination. The captured data can be directly used to render the person into any imaginable lighting environment, and can also be used to build photo-real computer graphics models that capture the unique texture and reflectance of the face. We have recently been developing the next generation of this lighting apparatus, which we call Light Stage 2.0.

Light Stage 2.0 is a much faster and more precise version of its predecessor[1]. The original device allowed a single light to be spun around on a spherical path so that a subject could be illuminated from all directions, and regular video cameras were used to record the subject's appearance as the light moved. This system had two major problems. First, since the light was moved around by pulling on various ropes, it was hard to be sure what the precise location of the light was at any given time. Second, because the device could not be spun very fast, and because of the limit of 30 frames per second imposed by the video cameras, it took over a minute to do a data capture. Since the subject must remain still during the data capture, this meant we could only capture people in very passive expressions, and even then multiple trials were often needed.

With Light Stage 2.0 (shown in Figure 1), we can capture all of the different lighting directions much more rapidly, with only a single rotation of a semicircular arm, and with greater accuracy. Thirty strobe lights arrayed along the length of the arm flash repeatedly in rapid sequence as the arm rotates. High-speed digital cameras capture the subject's appearance. This allows all directions of illumination to be provided in about four seconds, a period of time for which a person can easily remain still. It is also much easier to capture facial expressions that would be very difficult to maintain for an extended period of time (smiling, frowning, wincing, etc.).

We are currently working on integrating geometry capture to provide a complete model of the subject. For this, we use digital LCD projectors to project different structured patterns onto the subject, quickly recording the appearance of the subject under each of the patterns with our high-speed cameras. From these structured-light data, the geometry of the subject is easily recovered. These data together with the reflectance data may provide more complete and photo-real models of faces than ever before.

In the next few months, we will be researching new ways of analyzing the large amount of reflectance field information captured in a Light Stage 2.0 scan and adapting the datasets for use in facial animation. We would also like to make our capture process even faster, with the goal of being able to capture both geometry and reflectance information in about five seconds. Our future plans include new prototype lighting devices that will allow similar datasets to be captured many times a second. This will allow an actor's performance to be recorded and then rendered photo-realistically into virtual environments with arbitrary lighting, where the performance can be viewed from arbitrary angles.

Another approach is to directly illuminate an actor with light sources aimed from all directions whose intensity and color is controlled by the computer. In this case, if the incident illumination necessary to realistically composite the actor into a particular scene is known in advance, the actor can be filmed directly under this illumination.

*Reference*
1. Debevec, P., Hawkins, T., Tchou, C., Duiker,H.-P., Sarokin, W., & Sagar, M. (2000). Acquiring the reflectance field of a human face. In *Proceedings of SIGGRAPH 2000*.

Light Stage 2.0, with seated subject.

A 10-second-exposure photograph of Light Stage 2.0 acquiring a 4D reflectance field dataset of the subject's face.

*217*

# LIGHTING-SENSITIVE DISPLAYS

*Contact*
**SHREE K. NAYAR**
Computer Science
Columbia University
New York, New York 10027
USA
nayar@cs.columbia.edu

**PETER N. BELHUMEUR**
Electrical Engineering and
Computer Science
Yale University

**TERRY BOULT**
Electrical Engineering and
Computer Science
Lehigh University

Displays have become a vital part of our everyday lives. They are used to convey information in a wide range of products including televisions, computers, PDAs, and cellular phones. Recently, high-quality digital displays have also emerged as possible replacements for physical media such as photographs, paintings, and sculptures.

Research on display technology has made great strides in improving the resolution, brightness, and color characteristics of displays. However, all display technologies suffer from a serious drawback: they are unable to respond to the wide spectrum of illumination conditions to which they are exposed. We introduce new technologies that enable a display to sense the illumination of its environment and render the appearance of its content accordingly.

## SENSING A DISPLAY'S ILLUMINATION FIELD

Today, the only lighting-related controls that the user has on a display are global brightness and color adjustments. These can be varied manually by the user, or automatically, using one or a few photodetectors.[1,2,3] Such adjustments are crude, as they only enable global brightness and color changes. The light field around a display (or for that matter, any object) is rather complex, and true compensation for environmental illumination requires a dense sampling and representation of the light field (see figure below) incident upon the display. To this end, we have developed a suite of sensing technologies that permit dense estimation of the illumination field in real time. These technologies include the arrangement of compact photosensitive arrays over and around the display device, the distribution of optical fibers around the device, and the placement of wide-angle imaging systems close to the device. In all cases, we obtain a dense spatial and/or directional sampling of the illumination field. In the system shown on the right, a very compact imaging system with a hemispherical field of view is embedded within the frame of the display device. The directional illumination distribution captured at the location of the imaging system is extrapolated over the surface of the display.

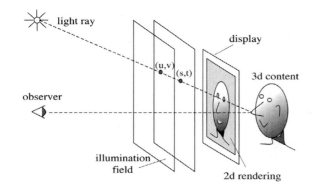

## RENDERING ILLUMINATION-CONSISTENT CONTENT

Once the illumination field as been measured, this information can be used to modify the visual content in several ways. The visual content can be either 2D images or 3D models of objects with arbitrary shapes and reflectance properties. These images and objects can be either purely synthetic, or data obtained by photographing/scanning real scenes, or some combination of the two. In the case of 2D images, the goal may be to spatially adapt the brightness of the image so that it appears to be lit by the environmental illumination. In the case of 3D scenes, the displayed image is rendered so that the scene is lit by the illumination of the environment. In both cases, a high degree of photo-realism is achieved. In the pictures shown below, the face is rendered based on the illumination field measured by the wide-angle camera attached to the display. As can be seen, the shadings and shadows in the image are consistent with the location of the light source. Since the illumination field is measured by the camera at video rate, the displayed content adapts to changing illumination conditions in real time.

## ACKNOWLEDGEMENTS

This work was supported in part by an NSF ITR Award under Grant No. IIS-0085864. The authors thank Rahul Swaminathan at Columbia University and Melissa Koudelka at Yale University for their help in acquiring data related to this project.

*References*
1. Biggs, A.J. (1995). Compensator for color television receivers for chromacity variations in ambient light. United States Patent 3,200,193, August 1965.
2. Constable, D.W. (1978). Ambient light contrast and color control circuit. United States Patent 4,090,216, May 1978.
3. Heijligers, H. (1962). Circuit arrangement for automatically adjusting the brightness and the contrast in a television receiver. United States Patent 3,027,421, March 1962.

218

*Contact*
JEFFREY WIKE
Software Development Manager
DreamWorks Feature Animation
jwike@anim.dreamworks.com

## OVERVIEW

The technology group at DreamWorks was given the task of lowering its capital budget, while at the same time providing increased computing power to address the ever-increasing creative appetite of our filmmakers. The decision was made to commit all new productions, beginning with a production that started in March 2001, to the all-Intel/Linux pipeline. The next question was: When would Linux be ready for prime time at the scale required to produce a full feature-length animated film? This technical sketch examines the challenges that we faced as the first major studio to successfully deploy an all-Intel/Linux production pipeline.

Most animation and visual effects production facilities have experimented with Intel/Linux solutions on some scale. Some have even successfully deployed departmental workstations and/or render-farm solutions. DreamWorks has, however, successfully deployed a complete Intel/Linux production pipeline consisting of hundreds of desktop and render-farm machines for all aspects of its traditional and CG pipelines. The challenges of early adoption on this scale included making the right hardware and software choices, effectively utilizing the open-source community, porting a large in-house code base, aligning third-party application support, and addressing support and training for our production users.

## THE CHALLENGES

A significant challenge was aligning our hardware and software choices to get the OpenGL performance necessary for our demanding applications and users. It would not be good enough to simply meet the current performance expectations (most artists were working on high-end graphics workstations). We had to raise the bar. Selecting a graphics card that met our 3D rendering benchmarks provided several options. However, finding a card that could also support our image-playback requirement and provide support for hardware overlay planes (required for our internal code base) proved to be a challenge. Most vendors claimed to have Linux support but we quickly found that most of this support was shallow, and we were really in uncharted territory. We ultimately found support in a handful of key vendors who partnered with us to find our way through the maze of hardware, Linux kernels, OpenGL, X-Server, window managers, widget sets, desktops, and applications. Testing included rendering tens of thousands of frames on both our current and Linux platforms. The resultant images were compared, pixel-by-pixel, to access the impact of numerical-precision and compiler-optimization issues when differences occurred.

Our software and systems group also had various issues to deal with in making the transition. Configuration management, automated-machine building, and component installation became critical in order to keep pace with machine-deployment schedules. Core components of our infrastructure also had to be addressed to support Intel/Linux. Finding an adequate set of software development tools and solutions for source-code management, debugging, and optimization for our internal development staff also presented significant challenges.

## THE RESULTS

We benchmarked our Linux against current platforms for interactive hardware renders, exercising moderate-to-heavy processor and graphics loads. We found that, on average, we could achieve nearly twice the performance at a fraction of the hardware cost. Based upon our success and results in driving toward the goal of our March 2001 production start, we were able to deploy into earlier productions to realize the benefit of the Intel/Linux solution almost a year ahead of our anticipated dates.

Intel/Linux is real for entertainment and will have a dramatic impact on studios small and large. We hope that this technical sketch can provide some insight into our journey and encourage others to follow and realize the potential of Intel/Linux for entertainment.

219

# THE LIVING FOREST:
## THE STORY OF A 3D FEATURE FILM IN EUROPE

*Contact*
JUAN NOUCHE
DYGRA Films
Linares Riva S9
La Coruña 15005 Spain
cristobal@filloa.com

In this animation sketch, we explain the production process of "The Living Forest," a 3D animated feature film based on Wenceslao Fernández Florez' novel about life in the forests of Galicia. The movie was made in Spain by DYGRA Films, a 3D animation studio based in La Coruña. Buena Vista International Spain released the film in Spain in the summer of 2001. Other participants included MEGATRIX, Antena 3TV, Vía Digital, and TVG, and the production was supported by the European Union Media Programme, the Spanish Ministry of Culture, and the regional government of Galicia.

## THE WORK PROCESS

DYGRA Films created this film using Maya 2.5 and 3.0 from Alias|Wavefront. It also devoted considerable effort to research and development. After the character designer drew the characters, instead of immediately modelling them in a computer, we sculpted them in paste, so that each one had a distinct personality. Only then did the computer work start.

After the character was modelled, we added a skeleton and movement controls. The next stage was character texturization, in which the materials and colours were chosen. This task is all the more complicated because each character had to be handled separately. Insects cannot be texturized as trees are, and trees cannot be texturized as humans are. We had to make the characters credible and, at the same time, harmonize them with their surroundings.

We set two goals for this film:

1. To recreate the atmosphere of the Atlantic Galician forest.
2. To make the characters as expressive as possible.

The animation phase began when the programming engineer prepared the character interface to support the animator's work. This required building the controls that the animator used to move arms, hands, and other body parts without having to learn computer programming.

All the animation work was handled by a team of traditional animators who were able to use computers thanks to an exclusive animation interface, designed by the DYGRA Films R&D department, that lets the characters move like classic cartoon characters.

DYGRA has a multidisciplinary team of animators, writers, computer and telematics experts, physicists, sculptors, painters, and software engineers. Teamwork, in which each member's contribution is required to make the feature movie project a success, and computing combined to join the worlds of art and technology.

## THE TECHNOLOGY

The standard computer used for this production had a 550-MHz dual processor with double monitor and Tornado 3000 Open GL accelerators from Evans & Sutherland. The software in addtion to, Maya 2.5 and 3.0 from Alias|Wavefront, included Maya Fusion, Jaleo for post-production, and Real Flow and Real Wave from Next Limit for particles. Additional support was obtained from Videalab at Universidade da Coruña for R+D and CESGA for the render process.

See also: www.thelivingforest.com

# Locally Reparameterized Light Fields

Xin Tong
Heung-Yeung Shum
Tao Feng
Microsoft Research China

Sing Bing Kang
Richard Szeliski
Microsoft Research

IBR techniques that have the most potential for photo-realism tend to be those that make use of densely sampled images. While using geometry helps reduce the database size, there is the problem of nonrigid effects such as reflection, transparency, and highlights. Without explicitly accounting for these effects, the light field sampling rate requirement would be even higher.

In this sketch, we propose a novel IBR representation to handle non-diffuse effects compactly, which we call locally reparameterized light field (LRLF). LRLF is based on the use of local and separate diffuse and non-diffuse geometries. The diffuse geometry is associated with true depth while the non-diffuse geometry has virtual depth that provides local photo-consistency with respect to its neighbors.

## The Concept

The concept of LRLF can be explained using the Epipolar Plane Image (EPI).[1] An EPI is a 3D representation *(u,v,t)* of a stacked sequence of camera images taken along a path, with *(u,v)* being the image coordinates and *t* being the frame index. For a diffuse point on a scene with a linear camera path – Figure 1(a) – its trail within the *(u,t)* cross-section of the EPI is straight. The slope $k$ of this trail is proportional to the depth $z$ of this point. A non-diffuse point will also generate a trail: Figure 1(b). This non-diffuse point has an associated local virtual depth, which is often different from the actual object surface depth. In order to account for both diffuse and non-diffuse components, it is then necessary to provide separate depth compensations. The main idea of LRLF is to provide such local depth compensations in the form of local geometries.

## Rendering

Our renderer is similar to the one described for the Lumigraph.[2] It uses the two-slab, 4D parameterization of light rays. As with the Lumigraph, each rendering ray is computed based on quadrilinear interpolation of rays from the nearest four sampling cameras using the local geometry for depth compensation. After each layer is separately rendered, the results are directly added to produce the output view.

## Results and Future Work

Figures 2 and 3 show rendering results for a real scene involving strong reflective components. This scene consists of a picture frame with a toy dog placed at an angle to it on the same side as the camera. The input images are acquired using a camera attached to a vertical precision X-Y table that can accurately translate the camera to programmed positions. A grid of 9 x 9 images, each of resolution 384 x 288, was captured. The rendering resolution is also 384 x 288. The reflective component is extracted using the dominant motion-estimation technique.[3] As can be seen, the rendering results using the LRLF representation look markedly better than those obtained using just a single geometry. Each local geometry is approximated using a single plane.

Future extensions of this work include automatically computing all the non-diffuse effects and estimating separate geometries for different types of non-diffuse effects in the same scene.

*References*
1. Bolles, R.C., Baker, H.H., & Marimont, D.H. (1987). Epipolar-plane image analysis: An approach to determining structure from motion. *International Journal of Computer Vision, 1,* 7-55.
2. Gortler, S.J., Grzeszczuk, R., Szeliski, R., & Cohen, M.F. (1996). The lumigraph. *Proceedings of SIGGRAPH 96,* 43-54.
3. Szeliski, R., Avidan, S., & Anandan, R. (2000). Layer extraction from multiple images containing reflections and transparency. In *Conference on Computer Vision and Pattern Recognition,* I, 246-253.

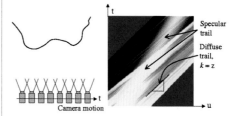

Figure 1. (left) Camera path, (right) EPI slice with highlight one-layer-middle.

Figure 2. Two views rendered with a single local depth.

Figure 3. The same two views rendered using LRLF.

221

# The Magic Behind the Magic: "Pearl Harbor"

Marshall Krasser
Compositing Supervisor
Industrial Light + Magic

For every spectacular shot that appears in a movie, there are untold scores of dedicated people who helped achieve its (hopefully) flawless execution.

At times, people have made the assumption that the computer has automatically created these visual wonders. I would like to take a moment and look at all of the phases of shot creation, not just the technical aspects.

Disciplines: model building, viewpainting, animating, matchmoving, lighting and rendering, plate photography, practical element photography, paint and rotoscoping, digital matte painting, and compositing.

This sketch presents video versions of "Pearl Harbor" shots that highlight how each discipline contributed to its creation. My goal is to step beyond the purely technical aspects of VFX creation and reveal more of the artistic and creative aspects. For example, in the case of compositing, we show a version of the shot that includes all of the elements prior to their integration into the plate. This reveals how artistic and visual talent is critical to the success of a shot.

# Manipulate the Unreachable: Through-The-Lens Remote Object Manipulation in Virtual Environments

*Contact*
Stanislav L. Stoev
Universität Tübingen
sstoev@gris.uni-tuebingen.de

Dieter Schmalstieg
Technische Universität Wien

Wolfgang Strasser
Universität Tübingen

We have found that even though is does not have a counterpart in real life, remote object manipulation is both useful and intuitive. Our approach provides a solution to the problem of changing and examining the scene from the current viewpoint, while manipulating objects in distant locations of the virtual world. We achieve this with the aid of though-the-lens tools.

## Through-the-Lens Concept

Through-the-lens (TTL) tools provide an additional viewpoint and display the scene in a dedicated viewing window. In this way, a preview window to a remote location is provided. In our semi-immersive setup, this window can be mapped onto a hand-held pad tracked with six degrees of freedom for convenient placement.[7] The pad becomes a magic lens[1,10] into a remote location.

Previous remote object manipulation technologies such as Voodoo Dolls,[5] scaled-world grab,[2] or go-go,[6] allow viewing and manipulation either in the remote or the local environment, but not spontaneous combination of both. TTL remote object manipulation improves upon that by allowing both modes to be arbitrarily combined.

We have discussed elsewhere how the lens can be adjusted to show the desired remote location.[9] Once this is done, the user can manipulate remote objects that are visible through the lens, usually with the lens frozen in space rather than coupled to the hand-held pad. A tracked stylus is used for interaction with the remote objects. Similar to image-plane interaction methods,[4] the user can manipulate remote objects by reaching with the stylus into the frustum volume defined by the lens and the current viewpoint (see figure 1). If the stylus is outside this volume, it acts on the local environment in the normal way. Moving the stylus from the remote volume to the local volume and vice versa instantly changes the context of interaction, similar to the point-to-focus approach popular in some 2D windowing systems.

Moreover, this change of context can be exploited to teleport objects between locations by drag-and-drop operations between volumes. In a slightly more complex scenario, objects can be transferred between multiple remote locations with drag-and-drop operations. This application resembles some aspects of ToolSpaces.[3]

We have found TTL manipulations to be intuitive and efficient. The user is not required to navigate to the remote location in order to manipulate objects, but can stay at the current location and examine the result of the remotely performed actions. The proposed scenario is useful even if the "remote" location is within reach of the user, since scale and position of the remote view can be arbitrarily chosen. For example, a magnifying lens allows precise manipulation of details, while a minifying lens allows manipulation similar to using a world-in-miniature approach.[8]

*References*
1. Bier, E.A., Stone, M.C., Pier, K., Buxton, W., & DeRose, T.D. (1993). Toolglass and magic lenses: The see-through interface. In *Proceedings of SIGGRAPH 93*, 73-80.
2. Mine, M.R., Brooks, F.P., Jr., & Carlo H. Séquin. (1997). Moving objects in space: Exploiting proprioception in virtual-environment interaction. In *Proceedings of SIGGRAPH 97*, 19-26.
3. Pierce, J.S. (1999). Toolspaces and glances: Storing, accessing and retrieving objects in 3D desktop applications. In *Proceedings of the 1999 Symposium on Interactive 3D Graphics*.
4. Pierce, J.S., Forsberg, A.S., Conway, M.J., Hong, S., Zeleznik, R.S., & Mine, M.R. (1997). Image plane interaction techniques in 3D immersive environments. In *1997 Symposium on Interactive 3D Graphics*.
5. Pierce, J.S., Stearns, B.C., & Pausch, R. (1999). Voodoo dolls: Seamless interaction at multiple scales in virtual environments. In *Proceedings of the 1999 Symposium on Interactive 3D Graphics*, 141-146.
6. Poupyrev, I., Billinghurst, M. Weghorst, S., & Ichikawa, T. (1996). The go-go interaction technique: Non-linear mapping for direct manipulation in VR. In *Proceedings of the ACM Symposium on User Interface Software and Technology*, 79-80.
7. Schmalstieg, D., Encarnação, L.M., & Szalavári, Z. (1999). Using transparent props for interaction with the virtual table (color plate p. 232). In *Proceedings of the 1999 Symposium on Interactive 3D Graphics*, 147-154.
8. Stoakley, R., Conway, M.J., & Pausch, R. (1995). Virtual reality on a WIM: Interactive worlds in miniature. In *Proceedings of ACM CHI'95 Conference on Human Factors in Computing Systems*, 265-272.
9. Stoev, S.L., Schmalstieg, D., & Strasser, W. (2001). Two-handed through-the-lens-techniques for navigation in virtual environments. In *Proceedings of the Eurographics Workshop on Virtual Environments*, 16-18 May 2001.
10. Viega, J., Conway, M.J., Williams, G., & Pausch, R. (1996). 3D magic lenses. In *Proceedings of the ACM Symposium on User Interface Software and Technology*, 51-58.

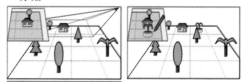

Figure 1: Schamatic drawing of the remote manipulation process. After defining the additional viewing window (left picture), one can manipulate the remote location through the window shown in the right picture.

First, a window (mapped on the pad) is defined through which the remote location is viewed.

After freezing the viewing window in space, two-handed manipulation is performed at the remote location.

*Contact*
MARCO ATTENE
IMA-CNR
Via De Marini 6
Genova, Italy
attene@ima.ge.cnr.it

GEOFF WYVILL
University of Otago

Triangulation of parametric surfaces is important for visualization and finite element analysis. The wrong choice of parameterization can spoil a triangulation or even cause the algorithm to fail. We present a new method that uses a local inverse mapping for almost uniformly sampling and triangulating a surface, so that its parameterization becomes irrelevant; differential geometry provides almost all we need.[1]

## THE INVERSE METRIC TENSOR

The metric tensor, G, is a symmetrical 2 x 2 matrix whose elements are the coefficients of the first fundamental form. G transforms vectors, at a given point in parameter space, to the tangent plane at the corresponding point on the surface. The inverse, $G^{-1}$ reverses this transformation. Given that $G^{-1}$ exists, how can we sample the parameter domain so that the surface triangulation is as uniform as possible?

## THE "NORMAL UMBRELLA"

Given a point $p_p$ in the parameter domain whose image in the surface is p, let $H = \{p_1, p_2 ..., p_6\}$ be a regular hexagon centered on p and lying in the tangent plane at p, $Tp(p)$. For each $p_i$, draw a curve of arc length r on the surface from p to a point $q_i$ so that its projection on $Tp(p)$ is a straight line parallel to $v_i = p_i - p$. Connect each end-point, $q_i$, with its neighbor, $q_{i+1}$. This process defines the normal umbrella of radius r and center p which will be triangulated by the star $\{(p,q_1,q_2), (p,q_2,q_3), ...,(p,q_6,q_1)\}$.

To construct these curves we start at the point $p_p$ and crawl in the direction $G^{-1}J^Tv_i$, where $J = [\mathbf{x_u} \ \mathbf{x_v}]$ is the Jacobian matrix of the surface's first derivatives. Notice that G and J vary as we proceed. Effectively, we are solving a differential equation defined by G and J at each point.

By definition, given a center point and a radius, the normal umbrella is independent of the parameterization, provided that the surface is smooth and regularly parameterized.

## THE ALGORITHM

1. Choose a random starting point, $p_p \in$ parameter domain.
2. The user chooses a radius, r, the expected average edge length in the final mesh.
3. Build the normal umbrella at p with radius r.
4. While there exists a vertex on the boundary of the mesh whose image in parameter space belongs to the required domain, complete its approximate normal umbrella.

To complete an approximate normal umbrella, centered on $q_i$, treat the triangles meeting at $q_i$ as if they were already part of a normal umbrella about $q_i$. Project this part onto the tangent plane, compute the remaining angle, $\alpha$, to be triangulated and divide it by an integer, n, so that $\alpha/n$ is as close as possible to 60 degrees. Finally, trace n-1 curves as described above to complete a set of triangles meeting at $q_i$ with angle $\alpha/n$.

E. Hartmann[2] proposed a similar marching method for implicit surfaces and it can also be used for parametric surfaces. However, it does not guarantee the desired edge length and requires two more numerical approximation steps (implicitization and point location) which can increase the error. Our method of computing lengths on the surface, rather than on the tangent plane, improves the accuracy of the mesh in regions of high curvature.

## WORK IN PROGRESS

Even if a uniform triangulation is suitable for some applications, it is not the best choice for interactive visualization. A mesh in which triangle size and shape varies depending on local surface behavior is preferable. We are working on the definition of a "distorted tensor" by which we can achieve a stretching and twisting of the local coordinate system; in particular we want the triangles to be stretched in proportion to the two principal curvature radii.[3]

*References*
1. Lipshutz, S. (1983). *Shaum's outline of differential geometry*. McGraw Hill, 1983.
2. Hartman, E. (1998). A marching method for triangulation of surfaces. *The Visual Computer* 14: 95-108.
3. Seibold, W. & Wyvill, G. (1999). Near-optimal adaptive polygonization. In *Proceedings CGI'99 IEEE Computer Society*, 206-213.

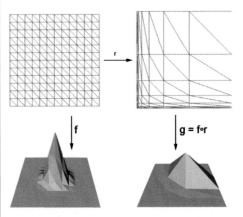

Figure 1. Example of "bad" parameterization. Uniform sampling of the parameter space does not imply uniform sampling in real space.

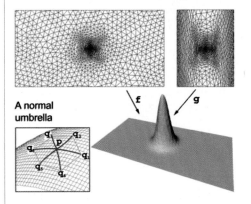

Figure 2. As the mapping changes, so does the triangulation in parameter space. The real-space mesh does not vary.

# Mayhem: A New Trend for Virtual Environments (and Online Games)

*Contact*
MANUEL OLIVEIRA
University College London
Department Computer Science
Gower Street WC1E 6BT
London, United Kingdom
m.oliveira@cs.ucl.ac.uk

JON CROWCROFT
MEL SLATER
University College London
Department Computer Science

## MOTIVATION

The ultimate aim of virtual environment (VE) research is to build a global networked infrastructure with high-resolution 3D graphics. However, current VE are confined to laboratory experiments, military simulations or are customized to carry out a specific task. In every case, the VEs are session based so user identity is short-lived. Online games and multi-user dungeons (MUDs) include social interaction as part of the core system design. This promotes the emergence of cybercommunities.

However, all the systems experience serious problems that prevent the achievement of the aforementioned goal. Two examples are: monolithic implementations -- this makes upgrades, adaptation, and evolution difficult; and scalability is limited which results in rudimentary mechanisms that compromise the maximum number of simultaneous users.

## DESCRIPTION

We believe that most of the problems are related to how the problem domain has been addressed so far. Therefore we created the Mayhem project to test and develop new concepts and approaches in building VE and online games. At present, the project consists of a massive online role playing game (MORPG) that has adopted similar aims as the Internet:

- Heterogeneity. It should be possible to support different applications (either client or server, or both), each with their own particular set of quality of service (QoS) demands and capabilities.
- Scalability. The system should be able to scale independently of the content size, the number of players or the network infrastructure.
- Evolutionary. Any application should be connected to the infrastructure without requiring a restart. An existing application should not require to shutdown every time an upgrade is available or modification is required.

## SYSTEM OVERVIEW

The current system built for the Mayhem project uses hybrid architecture based on client/server, which is used to support persistency and non-realtime services to users, such as character creation, locating worlds, and configuring their client application.

The location of worlds resembles a naming service of downloadable components associated to each VE, so when a user chooses a particular world then their client downloads the specific code and necessary resources. This means the client application is built at runtime.

After the customized configuration has finalised, the client is ready for real-time interaction with the system. As a result, the system architecture shifts to being distributed, with occasional remote connections to a remote server whenever resources (content or code) are necessary.

As the client plays the game, various mechanisms are in place to assure scalability in terms of computational and network resources. At the heart of it all is the AOIModule, which is responsible for coping with one or more area of interest management (AOIM) policies.

## COMPONENT DESIGN

The cornerstone of our approach is a strong component oriented design, along with an application framework that is flexible enough to be partially or fully adopted.

We have built the Java Adaptive Dynamic Environment (JADE),[1] which is itself a component framework. The module represents the main building block of the framework, which defines the necessary interface for JADE to manage a component. A microkernel is responsible for the management of modules enforcing the chosen security policies.

With JADE, it is possible for a system to load a module at runtime, replace an existing one, or just use one of the operations available: activate, deactivate, reload, initialise, and shutdown. Thus an application may evolve over time. To aid the system development, a set of extension modules are provided, such as TreacleWell (TW),[2] which is responsible for providing any network connectivity and protocol composition.

## CONCLUSIONS

VE and online games seem to bear little resemblance to each other when in fact the underlying objectives are similar. Unfortunately, the knowledge and experience garnered is hard to reuse in existing or new systems. The Mayhem project provides a new approach to VE, and consequently, games. Its goal is to provide a system with heterogeneity, scalability, and evolutionary properties to demonstrate our new trend. Our approach addresses the existing problems of current VE and online games.

*References*
1. Oliveira, M., Crowcroft, J. & Slater, M.. (2000). Component framework infrastructure for distributed virtual environments. In *Proceedings ACM CVE'00*.
2. Oliveira, M., Crowcroft, J. & Slater, M.(2000). Treaclewell: unraveling the magic "black box" of the network. Submitted for publication.

225

*Contact*
Ronald N. Perry
Mitsubishi Electric
Research Laboratories
perry@merl.com

## Introduction

Numerical constrained optimization is an important tool with extensive applications in computer graphics[3] and many other diverse fields.[1] In computer animation, for example, constrained optimization has been used for finding initial conditions, smoothing or finishing motion paths, interpolating orientations, animating flexible bodies, self-assembly of objects, and finding boundaries.[3]

An ideal problem for constrained optimization is one that has a single measure defining the quality of a solution plus some requirements upon that solution that must not be violated. The quality measure is called the *objective function* (denoted as F below); the requirements are called *constraints* (denoted as $C_i$ below). A constrained optimization solver maximizes (or minimizes) the objective function while satisfying the constraints. In this sketch, we propose a new method for constraint handling that can be applied to established optimization algorithms and which significantly improves their ability to traverse through constrained space. To make the presentation concrete, we apply the new constraint method to the Nelder and Mead polytope algorithm.[2] The resulting technique, called SPIDER, has shown great initial promise for solving difficult (e.g., nonlinear, nondifferentiable, noisy) constrained problems.

## The Idea

Many constrained problems have optima that lie near constraint boundaries. Consequently, avoidance of constraints can hinder an algorithm's path to the answer. By allowing (and even encouraging) an optimization algorithm to move its vertices into constrained space, a more efficient and robust algorithm emerges. In the new method, constraints are partitioned into multiple levels. A constrained performance, independent of the objective function, is defined for each level. A set of rules, based on these partitioned performances, specify the ordering and movement of vertices as they straddle constraint boundaries; these rules (employing the insight stated above) have been shown to significantly aid motion along constraints toward an optimum. Note that the new approach uses no penalty function and thus does not warp the performance surface, thereby avoiding the possible ill-conditioning of the objective function typical in penalty methods.

## Problem Statement

Maximize $F(\mathbf{x})$ for all $\mathbf{x} \in R^N$ such that $C_i(\mathbf{x}) \geq 0$ where $F:R^N \to R$, $C_i:R^N \to R$, and $i = [1...M]$. F or any $C_i$ may be highly nonlinear, nondifferentiable, and/or *noisy*. A function (e.g., F) is considered noisy when repeated evaluation of that function with identical input yields different values. Figure 1 contains a detailed description of the SPIDER algorithm.

## Notes and Extensions

*1.* One effective classification of constraints is to place simple limits on **x** that are independent of F into level 1, all other constraints into level 2, and the objective function F into level 3. Many different strategies for classification are being explored. *2.* SPIDER permits dynamic classification of constraints at anytime. This classification can be specified by a user (through observation of how SPIDER is moving) or by a classification algorithm which, for example, categorizes constraints into "active" and "inactive" levels. *3.* Other non-polytope optimization methods[2] can be modified to use the dynamic partitioned performances and corresponding rules introduced above, thereby improving their ability to traverse constrained space.

## Summary

Partitioned performances permit many optimization algorithms, including SPIDER, to better traverse constrained space. The dynamic classification of constraints, either by a user or a classification algorithm, further enhances navigation through difficult terrain. Finally, the SPIDER algorithm, including the centroid computation, leg flipping when shrinking, and cycling through all legs before resorting, is a robust method for solving difficult constrained problems.

*References*
See www.merl.com/reports/TR2001-14

### SPIDER Algorithm

1. Pick a starting location $\mathbf{x}_s \in R^N$
2. Partition F and the constraints $C_i$ into W levels $[L_1...L_w]$ with $L_w = \{ F \}$. We define the **performance** of a location $\mathbf{x} \in R^N$ as a 2-tuple $<P,L>$ consisting of a floating point scalar P and an integer level indicator L. P represents the "goodness" of **x** at level L. P and L are computed as follows:
    a. $P_1 \leftarrow \sum \min(C_k(\mathbf{x}), 0)$, for all $C_k$ in $L_1$
    b. If ($P_1$ is nonzero) $P \leftarrow P_1$, $L \leftarrow 1$, Stop
    c. $P_2 \leftarrow \sum \min(C_k(\mathbf{x}), 0)$, for all $C_k$ in $L_2$
    d. If ($P_2$ is nonzero) $P \leftarrow P_2$, $L \leftarrow 2$, Stop
    e. ...
    f. ...
    g. $P_W \leftarrow F(\mathbf{x})$, $P \leftarrow P_W$, $L \leftarrow W$, Stop

    The performances of two locations $\mathbf{x}_1$ ($<P_1,L_1>$) and $\mathbf{x}_2$ ($<P_2,L_2>$) are compared as follows:
    a. If ($L_1 == L_2$) if ($P_1 > P_2$) $\mathbf{x}_1$ is better else $\mathbf{x}_2$ is better, Stop
    b. If ($L_1 > L_2$) $\mathbf{x}_1$ is better else $\mathbf{x}_2$ is better
3. Determine the performance of the starting location $\mathbf{x}_s$ to form the starting vertex $\mathbf{v}_s = <\mathbf{x}_s,P_s,L_s>$
4. Pick the scale of each dimension to form the **size of space** vector $\mathbf{s} \in R^N$
5. Generate an initial set of N+1 vertices $[\mathbf{v}_1...\mathbf{v}_{n+1}]$ using $\mathbf{v}_s$ and $\mathbf{s}$. For example (where N = 2 and vector indices begin at 1),

    $\mathbf{v}_1, \mathbf{v}_2, \mathbf{v}_3 \leftarrow \mathbf{v}_s$
    $\mathbf{v}_2.\mathbf{x}[1] \leftarrow \mathbf{v}_2.\mathbf{x}[1] + \text{random}() * \mathbf{s}[1]$
    $\mathbf{v}_3.\mathbf{x}[2] \leftarrow \mathbf{v}_3.\mathbf{x}[2] + \text{random}() * \mathbf{s}[2]$
6. Determine the performance of each vertex $[\mathbf{v}_1...\mathbf{v}_{n+1}]$
7. Sort the vertices $[\mathbf{v}_1...\mathbf{v}_{n+1}]$ from worst to best. Label the overall best vertex $\mathbf{B}_{all}$ and the overall worst vector $\mathbf{W}_{all}$.
8. For each vertex **v** in the set $[\mathbf{v}_1...\mathbf{v}_{n+1}]$ from worst to best:
    a. Determine the centroid **c** of $[\mathbf{v}_1...\mathbf{v}_{n+1}]$, excluding **v** and other vertices at a lower level than **v**. If there are insufficient vertices to compute a valid centroid (e.g., < 2), incrementally include other vertices at lower levels until there are a sufficient number.
    b. If **v** is not the best vertex:
        b1. $\mathbf{x}_t \leftarrow \mathbf{c} + (\mathbf{c} - \mathbf{v}.\mathbf{x}) * \text{expansionFactor}$ (e.g., 1.1)
        b2. $<P_t,L_t> \leftarrow \text{ComputePerf}(\mathbf{x}_t)$
        b3. Form trial vertex $\mathbf{v}_t$: $\mathbf{v}_t.\mathbf{x} \leftarrow \mathbf{x}_t$, $\mathbf{v}_t.P \leftarrow P_t$, $\mathbf{v}_t.L \leftarrow L_t$
        b4. Either accept $\mathbf{v}_t$ or reject $\mathbf{v}_t$ (where accept **means** replace **v** with $\mathbf{v}_t$) using the following criteria: if $\mathbf{v}_t.L == \mathbf{v}.L$, accept $\mathbf{v}_t$ if $\mathbf{v}_t.P > \mathbf{v}.P$; if $\mathbf{v}_t.L > \mathbf{v}.L$, accept $\mathbf{v}_t$ if Perf($\mathbf{v}_t$) > Perf($\mathbf{B}_{all}$); if $\mathbf{v}_t.L < \mathbf{v}.L$, accept $\mathbf{v}_t$ if Perf($\mathbf{v}_t$) > Perf($\mathbf{W}_{all}$)
    c. If **v** is the best vertex:
        c1. $\mathbf{x}_t \leftarrow \mathbf{c} - (\mathbf{c} - \mathbf{v}.\mathbf{x}) * \text{expansionFactor}$ (e.g., 1.1)
        c2. $<P_t,L_t> \leftarrow \text{ComputePerf}(\mathbf{x}_t)$
        c3. Form trial vertex $\mathbf{v}_t$: $\mathbf{v}_t.\mathbf{x} \leftarrow \mathbf{x}_t$, $\mathbf{v}_t.P \leftarrow P_t$, $\mathbf{v}_t.L \leftarrow L_t$
        c4. Accept $\mathbf{v}_t$ if Perf($\mathbf{v}_t$) > Perf($\mathbf{v}$)
    d. Relabel $\mathbf{B}_{all}$ and $\mathbf{W}_{all}$ if either has changed
9. If Perf($\mathbf{B}_{all}$) has not improved, shrink the vertices at the same level as $\mathbf{B}_{all}$ toward $\mathbf{B}_{all}$, and flip (as well as shrink) vertices at lower levels over $\mathbf{B}_{all}$. The later rule helps to move legs (vertices) across a constraint boundary towards feasibility.
10. If the number of successive shrinks exceeds some threshold, rebuild the vertex set using $\mathbf{B}_{all}$ as $\mathbf{v}_s$ and the current size in each dimension as $\mathbf{s}$ (see step 5)
11. If there are more iterations to perform, repeat from step 7

Figure 1. The SPIDER algorithm.

226

*Contact*
TATSUYA SAITO
Keio University
tatsu@wem.sfc.keio.ac.jp

The experience provided by this technology will allow a visitor to visualize and interact with microscopic structures that cannot be seen with the naked eye, but that commonly exist in our everyday surroundings. Through the combination of Micro Archiving technology and Virtual Reality technology, we present immersive virtual environments in which people will be able to observe these microscopic structures in a private or collaborative workspace.

Micro-Presence is our term to describe the ability to experience these hidden realities. There are many terms that describe experiences of presence other than the real world in which we feel something through our sense organs directly. For example, Tele-Presence is a term to describe the technology that enables people to feel as if they are actually present in a different place or time. We define Micro-Presence as the environment in which people can feel as if they became minute and can observe and interact naturally with things in the Microcosmic world.

With the Micro Archiving technology, it is possible to create the high definition virtual 3D models. And these models can be fit for the academic research in such fields as biology and zoology that requires the actual things to observe. In addition, for educational use, this technology will create the high definition multimedia space in which visitors can freely participate and interact with the exhibit.

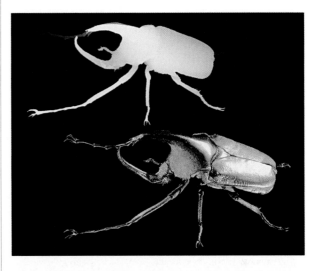

227

# Model-Based Analysis and Synthesis of Human Body Images

*Contact*
Junichi Hoshino
University of Tsukuba
PRESTO, JST Science and
Technology Corporation
jhoshino@esys.tsukuba.ac.jp

Generating digital actors is important for many applications such as special effects in movies, games, and virtual reality. In this sketch, we present a mode-based analysis and synthesis of human body images. First, we estimate the current 3D pose of the human figure by using the spatio-temporal analysis with kinematic constraints. Then, we store the intensity images of the human body as textures of the 3D body model. Such a human model can be used to generate multiple views, merge virtual objects, and change motion characteristics of human figures in video.

## Generation of the Texture-Mapped Body Model

First, we need to register the 3D body model onto input images to collect the human body texture. We represent a human body by an articulated structure consisting of 10 rigid parts corresponding to body, head, upper arms, under arms, upper legs, under legs. The motion parameters between the image frames are estimated using the spatial and temporal gradient method.[1] One of the drawbacks in the previous method[1] is that the operator needs to give the initial position of the human body model. In our new method, the system estimates the initial position from the center line of each body part extracted from the silhouette. Personal variations in the 3D body model can be also adjusted by searching the size parameters that minimize the difference between the silhouette boundary and the body model. Such new extensions are also useful for video motion capture applications.

## Interpolation of Missing Texture

The 3D body model supplements the whole-body textures that cannot be collected from a single camera view:

- Texture collection from multiple frames. The missing texture at one frame may be visible in other frames. When new intensity regions appear in the input image, we update the stored texture of the 3D body model.

- Supplementing missing textures. The missing textures cannot be identified until they become visible. However, convincing results may be obtained by using the texture of the other body parts. One simple method is to use the symmetry of the body parts and mirror the texure of the opposite side. Another alternative is to generate missing textures by CG objects. Body parts such as hair can be generated by using CG hairstyles. The color and the texture of the hairstyle can be extracted from the visible regions.

## Model-Based Editing of Human Body Images

The texture-mapped 3D human model can be used for virtual view generation and model-based video editing:

- Merging virtual objects. Virtual objects (for example, CG cloth and hairstyle) are added to the texture-mapped 3D model of the human body. We render the texture-mapped body model and CG objects together to obtain a synthesized image.

- Converting motion characteristics. Because the body pose can be obtained at each frame, we can change the behavior by replacing the pose values. For example, we can change the mass and inertia of the body model and simulate the motion by using standard computer graphics techniques. We can also replace the pose parameters with motioncapture data of a different person.

## Example

Figure1 illustrates model-based analysis and synthesis of human body images: (a) is the typical input image; (b) is the result of the automatic registration; (c) is the side view with the human body texture from the input image.

Because we can obtain partial texture in (a), we cannot recover the whole view. We estimate the missing texture by assuming that the intensity distribution is symmetric around the body axis.

Hairstyle was generated by CG; (d) shows interpolation of missing texture (when the textures within body parts are uniform, these simple techniques can generate a realistic view); (e) is the result of merging CG cloth from the side view; (f) is an example of changing motion characteristics by replacing the pose parameters of the body model.

*Reference*
1. Hoshino, J., Saito, H., & Yamamoto, M. (2000). Match moving technique for human body images. *SIGGRAPH 2000 Conference Abstracts and Applications*.

(a) Input image.      (b) Tracking result.      (c) Generate different view.

(d) After estimating missing texture.      (e) Merging CG cloth.      (f) Changing pose.

Figure 1. Result of model-based synthesis of human body images.

# Modeling and Dynamics of Clouds Using a Coupled Map Lattice

*Contact*
Yoshinori Dobashi
Hokkaido University
doba@nis-ei.eng.hokudai.ac.jp

Tomoyuki Nishtia
Ryo Miyazaki
Satoru Yoshida
The University of Tokyo

## Introduction

Clouds play an important role in creating images of outdoor scenes. This abstract proposes a new method for modeling various kinds of clouds. The shape of clouds is determined by atmospheric fluid dynamics. This implies that various types of clouds can be modeled by a physically based simulation of cloud formation. Our method simulates cloud formation by using a method called the coupled map lattice (CML). The proposed method can create various types of clouds and can also realize the animation of these clouds.

## Classification of Clouds

Clouds can be classified roughly into two types based on their formation processes. Clouds in the first type are known as cumuliform (cumulus and cumulonimbus), and they are formed by ascending air currents. These air currents are generated by various mechanisms such as temperature rising on the ground. Clouds in the second category are generated by the cooling down of vapor that flows upward from the ground. In particular, the patterns observed in the cell-like shapes of stratocumulus, altocumulus, and cirrocumulus are generated by the Bénard convection.[1]

## Overview of Our Method

Our method simulates cloud formation using a simplified numerical model, called CML. The advantages of using CML are that it is easy to implement and the computational cost is small. Figure 1 shows our system for cloud modeling-rendering. Firstly, the user specifies the types of clouds desired and the conditions for the simulation, i.e. the parameters for the atmospheric properties such as the viscosity and diffusion coefficient. The cloud formation is simulated based on the specified conditions. During the simulation, the distribution of the state values such as temperature, velocity and density of the clouds are visualized at every time step. The user can change the simulation parameters interactively to control the shape of the clouds.

## Simulation of Cloud Formation Using CML

CML is an extension of cellular automaton, and the simulation space is subdivided into lattices. Each lattice has several state variables, and their status is updated depending on the variables on the adjacent lattices. The cloud formation processes are summarized as follows: clouds are formed as a bubble of air is heated by the underlying terrain, causing the bubble to rise into regions of lower temperature; the phenomenon known as phase transition then occurs, when water vapor in the bubble becomes water droplets, or clouds. Therefore, our method takes into account the following factors: viscosity and pressure effects, the advection by the fluid flow, diffusion of water vapor, thermal diffusion, thermal buoyancy, and the phase transition. For generating cumulus or cumulonimbus clouds, the distribution of the ascending current is specified, and then the velocity distribution is calculated by using CML method. We also input the humidity distribution and the humid air moves upward due to the ascending air currents. Then, clouds are formed by the phase transition. If we want to generate the cell-like cloud formations we simulate the Bénard convection by inputting the difference in the temperature in the vertical direction and, clouds are generated by using the calculated velocity field.

## Result

Figure 2 shows images of clouds generated by our method. Figures (a) and (b) are the cumulonimbus and the altocumulus, respectively. In Figure (a), the tower-like cloud is generated by the strong ascendant current. In Figure (b), the sky is dotted with relatively small clouds. The numbers of lattices for Figures (a) and (b) are 178 x 178 x 98 and 256 x 256 x 10, respectively. The computation times per time step of the simulation are five and two seconds, respectively, for Figs. (a) and (b). Rendering times are less than one minute by using the method developed by Dobashi et al.[2]

*References*
1. Houze, R.A. (1993). Cloud dynamics. *International Geophysics Series* Vol. 53, Academic Press, New York, 1993.
2. Dobashi, Y., Kaneda, K., Yamashita, H., Okita, T., Nishita, T. et al.(2000). A simple, efficient method for realistic animation of clouds. In *Proceedings SIGGRAPH 2000,* 19-28.

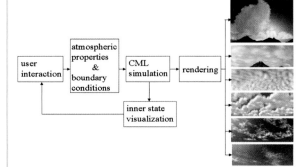

Figure 1. Our system for modeling and rendering clouds.

Figure 2. Simulation of clouds: (a) cumulonimbus, (b) altocumulus.

229

# THE MOUTHESIZER: A FACIAL GESTURE MUSICAL INTERFACE

*Contact*
MICHAEL J. LYONS
ATR Media Integration &
Communication Research Labs
2-2-2 Hikaridai, Seika-cho
Kyoto 619-0288 Japan
http://www.mic.atr.co.jp/~mlyons

*Contributors*
MICHAEL HAEHNEL
NOBUJI TETSUTANI

## INTRODUCTION

In this technical sketch we introduce a new interaction paradigm: using facial gestures and expressions to control musical sound. The mouthesizer, a prototype of this general concept, consists of a miniature head mounted camera which acquires video input from the region of the mouth, extracts the mouth shape using a simple computer vision algorithm, and converts shape parameters to MIDI commands to control a synthesizer or musical effects device.

## FACE AND GESTURE MUSICAL INTERFACES

Leading the edge of musical technology innovation are the efforts to interface expressive gestures to sound synthesis and modulation.[1,2] The face is a salient source of non-verbal communication conveying information about attention, intention, and emotion through facial expressions and gestures. The lower face is also critical to speech production through the action of the lips, tongue, and jaw. It therefore seems natural to us to link expressive action of the face to the control of musical sound.

## TECHNOLOGY OF THE MOUTHESIZER

Our system consists of a wearable, lightweight, head mounted camera (Figure 1). The open area of the mouth is segmented by intensity and color thresholding and the largest blob is selected. The mouth opening is not a surface so the segmentation algorithm is robust over a wide range of illumination conditions. Statistical shape analysis is used to extract parameters proportional to the width and height of the mouth opening, which are normalized and output in MIDI format to a synthesizer-effects unit. The system runs at 30 fps on a notebook computer. Experimentation has revealed several intuitive shapesound mappings. The video demo at the site below implemented mouth-controlled guitar effects of wahwah and distortion (Figure 2). Performers report that the mouth controller is more intuitive and versatile than a foot pedal and that it feels good to use. Another example uses mouth aspect ratio to audio morph between three formant filters corresponding to vowel sounds [i], [a], and [o]. These audio effects can be applied to synthesizer patches or analog signals. Future work will consider other regions of the face and further explore the rich space of gesture-sound mappings. The research is targeted both at musical performers, who have their hands busy playing an instrument, and the handicapped, who may lack control of their limbs due to spinal damage, but who retain control of their facial muscles.

A short video is available at:
http://www.mic.atr.co.jp/~mlyons/mouthesizer.html

*References*
1. Wanderley, M. & Baffier, M., eds. (2000). Trends in gestural control of music, CD-ROM. IRCAM, Paris, 2000.
2. Cutler, M., Robair, G., & Bean. (2000). The outer limits: a survey of unconventional musical input devices. *Electronic Musician*, August 2000: 50 - 72.

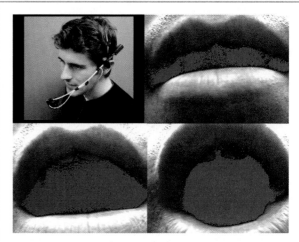

Figure 1. The head mounted video camera with views of the vowels [i], [a], and [o].The segmented area is shown in red.

Figure 2. Guitarist Ichiro Umata using the Mouthesizer.

# Multi-Modal Translation System by Using Automatic Facial Image Tracking and Model-Based Lip Synchronization

Shin Ogata
Takafumi Misawa
Faculty of Engineering
Seikei University

Kazumasa Murai
Satoshi Nakamura
Shigeo Morishima
ATR Spoken Language
Translation Research Labs

This sketch introduces a multi-modal English-to-Japanese and Japanese-to-English translation system that also translates the speaker's physical speech motion by synchronizing it to the translated speech.

Current speech translation systems transmit verbal information, but they cannot translate and transmit articulation and intonation. Although verbal information is a key element of human communication, facial expression also plays an important role in face-to-face communication. If we could develop a technology that is able to translate facial motions synchronized to translated speech, we could construct a multi-lingual tool that would be much more natural than existing systems.

## Overview of System

Figure 1 shows an overview of the system developed in this research. The system is divided broadly into two parts: speech translation and image translation. The speech-translation part is composed of ATR-MATRIX,[1] which was developed at ATR-ITL. In the speech-translation process, the two parameters of phoneme notation and duration information are applied to facial image translation. These two parameters are outputs from CHATR[2] that generate synthesized speech.

The first step of the image-translation process is to make a 3D model of the mouth region for each speaker by fitting a standard facial wireframe model to an input image. The second step is face-tracking processing by template matching. Tracking motions of the face from video images is one of the key technologies required for translating images. The third step in image translation is to generate lip movements for the corresponding utterance. The 3D model is transformed by controlling the acquired lip-shape parameters so that they correspond to the phoneme notations from the database used in the speech-synthesis stage. Duration information is also applied and interpolated by linear interpolation for smooth lip movement. In the final step of image translation, the translated synthetic mouth region's 3D model is embedded in input images. In this step, the 3D model's color is adjusted to the input images. Even if an input video image is moving during an utterance, we can acquire natural synthetic images because the 3D model has geometry information. Consequently, the system outputs a face movie lip-synchronized to the translated synthetic speech and image sequence at 30 frames/second.

## Automatic Face Tracking

Tracking by template matching can be divided into three steps. First, texture mapping of one of the video-frame images is carried out on the individual 3D face-shape model. Here, a frontal face image is chosen from the video-frame images for the texture mapping, since the video images used in this experiment are mainly frontal in movement and rotation. Next, we make a 2D template image for each movement and rotation by using a 3D model. Here, in order to reduce matching errors, the mouth region is excluded from the template images. Consequently, even while the person in a video image is speaking, tracking can be carried out more stably. Finally, we carry out template matching between the template images and an input video-frame image, and estimate movement and rotation values so that the matching error becomes minimum.

## Generation of Lip Shape and Movement

To prepare a lip-shape database, we used reference lip-shape images from the front and side. Then, we transformed the wireframe model to approximate the reference images. In this process, we acquired momentum vectors of lattice points on the wireframe model. Then, we stored these momentum vectors in the lip-shape database. This database is normalized by the mouth region's size, so we do not need speaker adaptation. We classified English and Japanese phonemes into 28 types based on visemes (a viseme is the smallest linguistic visual sound unit). Lip shapes composed of visemes are decided by the phonemic notation outputs from CHATR. And lip movement is generated by linear interpolation of momentum vectors located on keyframes according to phoneme duration time, also from CHATR.

## Summary

As a result of this research, the proposed system can create any lip shape with an extremely small database, and it is also speaker-independent. Furthermore, the system retains the speaker's original facial expression by using input images other than those of the mouth region.

For further improvement of this system, we need to design a model that expresses images more precisely. At the same time, we must improve the method for linear interpolation of the li shape. Furthermore, higher speed is needed to operate the system online.

*References*
1. Takezawa, T., Morimoto, T., Sagisaka, Y., Campbell, N., Iida, H., Sugaya, F., Yokoo, A., & Yamamoto, S. A. (1998). Japanese-to-English speech translation system ATR-MATRIX. *Proceedings International Conference of Spoken Language Processing, ICSLP*, 957-960.
2. Campbell, N. & Black, A.W. (1995). CHATR : a multi-lingual speech re-sequencing synthesis system. *IEICE Technical Report, sp96-7*, 45.
3. Ogata, S., Nakamura, S., & Morishima, S. (2001). Multi-modal translation system - model based lip synchronization with automatically translated synthetic voice. *IPSJ Interaction 2001*, 203.

(a) Input image.    (b) Mouth-region model.    (c) Translated image.

# A MULTIPURPOSE ARRAY OF TACTILE RODS FOR INTERACTIVE eXPRESSION

*Contact*
DAN OVERHOLT
Media Laboratory
Massachusetts Institute
of Technology
dano@media.mit.edu

EGON PASZTOR
ALI MAZALEK
Massachusetts Institute
of Technology

## INTRODUCTION

The MATRIX (Multipurpose Array of Tactile Rods for Interactive eXpression) is a device that offers real-time control of a deformable surface, enabling the manipulation of a wide range of audiovisual effects. The interface functions as a versatile controller that can be adapted to many different tasks in a variety of application domains. It was first used as a new type of musical instrument in the Emonator project.[1] New domains are now being explored in areas such as real-time graphics animation, sculptural design and rendering, still and moving image modification, and the control of physical simulations.

## THE INTERFACE AND TECHNOLOGY

The human hand has shaped and produced many amazing things over the centuries. It is one of the most nimble and dexterous tools at our disposal. One of the goals of the MATRIX project was to create an interface that would make the most of our skill with our hands. The result was a human-computer interface that can extract useful information from a gesture, exploiting the senses of touch and kinesthesia. It allows a computer to respond in real time to the form of a 3D surface, and captures the shape and movement of the hand at high resolution, taking advantage of the skills we have developed through a lifetime of interaction with the physical world.

The MATRIX interface consists of 144 rods which move vertically in a 12 by 12 grid, and are held up by springs at rest. The device uses this bed of rods to provide a large number of continuous control points, thereby improving the communication bandwidth with the computer. The deformation of the surface is determined using opto-electronics, and a FPGA (Field Programmable Gate Array). A technique called quadrature encoding is used to derive the current rod positions. All resulting positions are sent to the computer at a frame rate of 30 Hz, letting the system respond quickly and smoothly to a users input.

## VISUAL APPLICATIONS

The surface of the MATRIX can be used as a controller for any real-time graphics application where dynamic user input is required. Its responsive model of the hand provides a much richer method of control than a mouse, joystick, or keyboard. For example, the animation of ocean waves is traditionally done using a combination of physical simulation and careful positioning of isolated control points. Using the MATRIX, the motion of a user's hand can be mapped directly to the underlying forces in a wave simulation. The user would then have the experience of interactively creating the simulated ocean swells. This technique can also be applied to many other physical simulations for things that behave as particle systems, such as wind flow or the rippling of cloth.

Currently the MATRIX is being used as an input device for real-time graphics animation, image manipulation, and physical simulation. Figure 2 shows several examples of different tasks using the MATRIX. The upper left shows the rods of the device as perceived by the computer. These rods are interpreted as a shaded surface, which is shown on the upper right. This same surface can be used to deform virtual objects or images, such as the picture of the dog on the lower left. The surface can also be interpreted as an array of wind forces in a simulation of a grassy plain, as shown in the final image. As the user moves their hand, the blades of grass bend back and forth in response to the virtual winds.

In addition to these applications, the MATRIX is being used for the dynamic control of colored lights. The transparent acrylic rods serve as light guides for four computer controlled ColorKinetics C-30 lights[2] placed beneath the device. Colors and patterns of light are synchronized to the movement of the rods based on different mappings. For example, the average value and rate information of each quadrant of rods can be used to determine the color and intensity of each light.

## FUTURE EXTENSIONS

We are beginning to use the MATRIX for real-time processing of an incoming video stream using effects such as stretching, morphing, and other visual deformations. In the future, we plan to investigate using the interface to sculpt complete 3D objects by allowing users to change the orientation of the object in space and shape each of its sides individually.

## ACKNOWLEDGEMENTS

We would like to thank Professors Tod Machover, Glorianna Davenport, and Joe Paradiso, as well as our colleagues in the Hyperinstruments and Interactive Cinema groups.

See also: www.media.mit.edu/~dano/matrix/

*References*
1.  Overholt, D. (2000). The Emonator: a novel musical instrument. MIT Media Laboratory master's thesis, 2000.
2.  ColorKinetics lights: URL: www.colorkinetics.com/

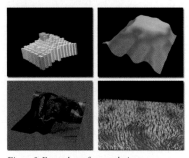

Figure 1. User interacting with the MATRIX interface.

Figure 2. Example surface renderings generated by the MATRIX interface.

*Contact*
EUGENE LAPIDOUS
ViewSpace Technologies Inc.
eugene@viewspace.com

JIANBO ZHANG
TIMOTHY WILSON
Trident Microsystems Inc.

One of the important factors affecting design of 3D applications is what depth precision is available across the view volume. Currently, the common denominator is a 24-bit screen Z buffer, which loses roughly $\log2(Zf/Zn)$ bits close to the far plane ($Zf/Zn$ is a ratio of the distances to the far and near planes). More precise depth buffer algorithms[1,3], even when available, remain unused by the applications optimized for screen Z. To make high-precision depth buffers more popular, and therefore more widely supported, they have to benefit the majority of 3D applications.

We present new type of the multi-resolution depth buffer that allows applications optimized for screen Z to take advantage of the hardware support for high-precision depth buffer algorithms. It provides a flexible trade-off between precision and performance, easily adjustable in software.

Our observation is that in the open environments, or when camera is close to the ground, precision of the 24-bit screen Z-buffer at the far plane is often lower than precision of 16-bit depth buffers that remain linear or quasi-linear across the view volume. One such example is W-buffer, where stored depth is proportional to the distance from the camera. Figure 1 compares renderings of the human face using 24-bit screen Z buffer (Figure 1a) and 16-bit W- buffer (Figure 1b). The model is positioned close to the far plane at $Zf/Zn = 4000$; 24-bit screen Z-buffer fails to resolve objects behind the face mask (eyes, teeth), while 16-bit W-buffer renders them correctly.

Obviously, the 16-bit W-buffer cannot be used instead of 24-bit screen Z: when the object is close to the near plane, screen Z precision can be equal or larger than 24-bit; 3D applications can use it by keeping ratios $Zf/Zn$ relatively low or by rendering complex objects close to the near plane. On the other hand, 3D applications cannot count on the depth precision higher than 24 bits, because the 24-bit W-buffer is currently a quality standard for 3D accelerators with 24-bit depth buffers.

We propose to leverage advantages of linear and quasi-linear depth buffers by dynamically switching resolution from 24 to 16 bits, so that the resulting precision is always kept at or above screen Z level (as long as it does not exceed 24 bits). As shown in Figure 2 for the dynamic ratio $Zf/Zn = 1000$, a switch from 24-bit to 16-bit W-buffer at half of the distance between far and near planes will be enough to support any application optimized for 24-bit Z. The share of the view volume where a 16-bit W-buffer can be used grows roughly as a cube of the distance between the switching point and the far plane, providing significant bandwidth savings.

It is important to note that a decision to use 16 or 24 bits can be based solely on the newly computed depth value and before the old one is read from the depth buffer. If the new distance from the camera is farther than the threshold, we'll read and write 16 bits of the corresponding depth value per pixel; otherwise we'll read and write 24 bits/pixel. This allows for a true multi-resolution depth buffer: no flags are necessary to define per-pixel resolution, because it is defined by the data itself.

The resolution switch threshold depends on the ratio $Zf/Zn$ and can be set at the same time as a view matrix. Figure 3 shows how this threshold changes for three different types of depth buffers: fixed-point W (24->16); floating-point complementary Z with 4-bit exponent (4.20 -> 4.12); and floating-point 1/W with 4-bit exponent (4.20 -> 4.12). While multi-resolution 1/W is useful only if $Zf/Zn > 5000$, the resolution switch for complementary Z and fixed-point W may provide bandwidth savings for $Zf/Zn > 500..1000$. Complementary Z is significantly easier to implement than fixed-point W: it is a (1 - screen Z) value stored in the floating-point format.[1]

In conclusion, the proposed multi-resolution depth buffer allows 3D applications to improve performance by relaxing depth precision requirements with an increase of the distance from the camera. This optimization, already useful for legacy 3D hardware, does not have to be abandoned for the next generation of depth buffers. A tradeoff between precision and performance can be finely tuned by changing the resolution switch threshold.

*References*
1. Lapidous, E. & Jiao, G. (1999). Optimal depth buffer for low-cost graphics hardware. In *Proceedings. of SIGGRAPH 99/Eurographics Workshop on Graphics Hardware*, 67-73.
2. Deering, M.F.. US Patent 6046746: Method and apparatus implementing high resolution rendition of Z-buffered primitives.
3. Microsoft Corp. (2000). What are depth buffers? DirectX8 SDK, 2000. URL: msdn.microsoft.com/library/psdk/directx/DX8_C/hh/directx8_c/_dx_what_are _depth_buffers_graphics.htm

233

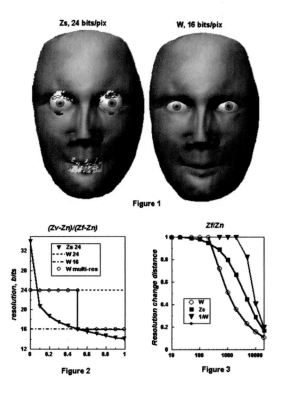

Zs, 24 bits/pix    W, 16 bits/pix

**Figure 1**

(Zv-Zn)/(Zf-Zn)    Zf/Zn

**Figure 2**    **Figure 3**

# Multi-Resolution Light Field Rendering with the Wavelet Stream

*Contact*
Ingmar Peter
WSI/GRIS
Universität Tübingen
peter@gris.uni-tuebingen.de

Wolfgang Strasser
WSI/GRIS
UniversitätTübingen

## Introduction

In this sketch we describe the wavelet stream, a new data structure for progressive transmission, storage, and rendering of compressed light field data. It employs non-standard 4D wavelet decomposition to make use of the coherence in all of the four dimensions of a light field data set. Compression ratios of up to 1:200 were obtained still providing visually pleasing results. Furthermore our data structure allows for an adaptive multi-resolution representation of the data. In contrast to similar approaches, the wavelet stream can be decompressed in real time for rendering and thus allows for use in interactive graphic applications.

## Light Field Rendering

Image based rendering (IBR) tries to overcome the limitations of traditional geometry based computer graphics by replacing geometrical with pictorial information. One of the most general image based scene representations is the light field,[1,2] which can be used to represent arbitrary real or synthetic objects. It is independent as well from the objects geometry as from its material properties.

A light field is formed by a 2D array of images of an arbitrary object where all images share the same image plane. Using a parameterization as proposed in,[1,2] all light field samples can be addressed by a 4D coordinate (s,t,u,v). Unfortunately a large number of samples is required to create a light field which allows for a visually pleasing reconstruction of new views of arbitrary objects, overlaid with cross hairs after program.

## Wavelet-Based Light field Compression

During compression the light field data is decomposed into one scaling coefficient and a number of detail coefficients employing non-standard 4D wavelet decomposition with the Haar-basis. Detail coefficients with very low values are discarded. The positions of the surviving coefficients are encoded using significance maps.

To support progressive storage, transmission, and rendering of light field data, the detail coefficients are stored together with the significance maps and some meta information for navigation in a byte stream. The data is ordered in a way, that the most important (i.e. with a high impact on the result) coefficients are encoded first. In this way an approximation of the light field can be rendered even if only a small fraction of the wavelet stream is transmitted.

## Silhouette Encoding

Usually solitary objects are encoded in light fields. Unfortunately, due to the border's high frequency it causes the generation of a large number of detail coefficients during wavelet decomposition. This can be avoided by encoding the silhouette of the object. In this way the number of coefficients sufficient to encode the objects appearance is bounded by the number of samples with values belonging to the object.

Our silhouette encoding is fully embedded into the wavelet stream. By exploiting coherence, for typical data sets about 10 percent of the entire data have to be used to encode the silhouette information. On the other hand, the utilization of silhouette information reduces the number of coefficients about 20-30 percent while obtaining the same compression error compared to data sets compressed without using silhouette information.

## Rendering

During light field rendering a texture map showing the new light field view is created and displayed using Open GL. The reconstruction algorithm is completed by supplementary image based caching schemes. Three different cache levels allow for reconstruction and rendering of 10-15 frames/second on standard PC-hardware.

## Results

Our approach improves on existing wavelet-based compression schemes since it allows for:
- interactive reconstruction times;
- high compression ratios while preserving image quality;
- additional silhouette encoding to reduce the number of coefficients significantly.

Some results are given showing the Dragon light field and respective error measurements.

*References*
1. Gortler, S., Grzeszczuk, R., Szeliski, R., & Cohen, M. (1996). The lumigraph. In *Proceedings SIGGRAPH 96*.
2. Levoy, M. & Hanrahan, P. (1996). Light field rendering. In *Proceedings SIGGRAPH 96*.
3. Peter, I. & Strasser, W. (1999). The wavelet stream: progressive transmission of compressed light field data. In *IEEE Visualization 1999 Late Breaking Hot Topics*.

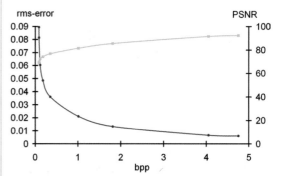

PSNR and rms-error measured for different compression ratios of Dragon light- field.

Comparison of Dragon Light Field from The Stanfords Light Field Archive for different compression ratios.

# My Finger's Getting Tired: Interactive Installations for the Mind and Body

*Contact*
Don Ritter
Pratt Institute
Computer Graphics and
Interactive Media
Brooklyn, New York 11205 USA
ritter@aesthetic-machinery.com
http://aesthetic-machinery.com

## Introduction

This sketch presents an overview of Ritter's large scale interactive video and sound installations which use interactivity as content, and require viewers to use their entire bodies to control unencumbered interactive experiences for multiple users simultaneously.

## Unencumbered Interactivity for the Entire Body

When experiencing interactive art as a cultural medium, the goal is to create an overall aesthetic experience. The use of any encumbered device, such as a mouse, can detract from this experience because the physical motions required by an encumbered input device rarely provide a pleasant physical experience. In the interactive video-sound installation "Fit,"[1] viewers use their entire bodies to interact with a video projection of an aerobics instructor. In response to a viewer's own exercising, the aerobics instructor begins exercising in synchronization with music. Within "Fit," viewers interact with their entire body without the use of an encumbered input device.

## Interactivity as Content

Many interactive computer based works incorporate designs that are functionally similar to light switches: a button is pressed and a light turns on, a mouse is clicked and an image is displayed. Although this capability provides a convenience when coordinating events over time, the physical gestures expressed by viewers are not conceptually related to the responses. The experience of interactive media may be more satisfying aesthetically if a conceptual relationship exists between the human gesture and the interactive response: interactivity can be used as content. In the interactive video-sound installation "TV Guides,"[2] viewers encounter a living room environment containing a television which plays live programs overlaid with cross hairs. In response to any form of movement by the viewers, the television sound fades out and the cross hairs recede into a small circle, followed by text on the screen which requests viewers to remain still. The television imagery and sound will resume only when viewers remain motionless. The inactivity required by the viewers reflects the intended content: TV as medium of control.

## Multiple Users Simultaneously

Because most people enjoy and apparently prefer group experiences -- especially during cultural events -- it seems appropriate that exhibitions of interactive art provide simultaneous interactive experiences to groups rather than single users. In the interactive sound installation "Intersection"[3] viewers encounter the sounds of cars speeding across a dark 40 x 50 foot exhibition space. In response to a viewer's presence in a lane, the cars screech, idle, accelerate and crash. This installation exists as a four or eight lane version and can accommodate more than 100 users simultaneously.

## Multiple Users as Content

The accommodation of many viewers simultaneously by an interactive work is an efficient use of technology and provides a social environment for viewers. This form of design also has the potential to use the multiple-user design as an element within the content. The 50 x 50 foot interactive video-sound installation "Skies"[4] presents people with the experience of cooperation between themselves and cooperation with nature. As viewers walk onto video projected imagery, they discover black paths under their feet. According to the combination of paths discovered, different video sequences of nature are projected onto the wall and floor. The installation can accommodate and be controlled by an unlimited number of viewers simultaneously, although at least five must cooperate with each other to experience the work completely.

## Conclusion

Although the experience of screen based interactive art may be satisfying visually and audibly, the experience of mouse clicking is not a satisfying physical experience. If interactive art is going to become an influential and cultural medium, the entire body and mind should be involved in the interactive and aesthetic experience. This can be accomplished by using human interfaces which are conceptually related to a project's content and require participation by the entire body.

*References*
1. aesthetic-machinery.com/fit.html
2. aesthetic-machinery.com/tvguides.html
3. aesthetic-machinery.com/intersection.html
4. aesthetic-machinery.com/skies.html

235

Don Ritter, "Skies" interactive video-sound installation, 50 x 50 feet.

Don Ritter, "TV Guides" detail of interactive video-sound installation, 15 x 25 feet.

# NATO.0+55+3D.Modular – A New real-Time and Non-Real-Time Multimedia Authoring and DSP Environment

*Contact*
Netochka Nezvanova
0f0003 Maschinenkunst
Stichting STEIM
Achtergracht 19
1017 WL Amsterdam
The Netherlands
ecdysone@eusocial.com

The vectors are meant to converge through morphogenesis. They chart a fundamental shift away from the millennia, from old, worn, and static rational discourse toward the pleasure of the transient and momentary, toward the allure of a brevity of meaning, the spectral wall of impossibilities, toward the thermophilic envelope of desire that most elegantly unveils the dynamic core of a lifeform's functional cluster. Suspended in the undecided and wavering viscosity of reality, this sketch discusses a new authoring and DSP evironment distributed by 0f0003 Maschinenkunst and Ircam.

The NATO.0+55/DEAF2000 festival literature reads: "NATO.0+55 is a new software that is set to revolutionize the realtime manipulation of video and sound." Arie van Schutterhoef, artistic director of the Schreck Ensemble writes: "I think that Nato Modular is the most interesting software for Max, since Max... consider the contradiction... and offers possibilities for live manipulation of images, that can only be rivaled in the audio domain by SuperCollider."

NATO.0+55+3D. Modular is an advanced real-time and non-real-time, component driven visual authoring environment for creative construction of audio-visual networks in Ircam Max. It is a non-linear, vastly expressive and syntactic, modular infrastructure for live video and graphics, specifically 2D and 3D graphics, VR (virtual reality), DV (digital video), live video, Firewire, QuickTime, Flash, MP3, OpenGL, and real-time Internet streaming. It may be used for research, image analysis and editing, video conferencing, real-time 3D/VR viewing and modeling, real-time word processing, installations, and stand-alone multimedia applications.

NATO.0+55+3D. Modular has been deployed at Prix-Ars Electronica, DEAF, Interferences, ISEA, ICMC, the Guggenheim Museum, SIGGRAPH 2000, the US. Open, FCMM, VIPER Festival, Momentum, Expo 2000, Sonar, Not Still Art Festival, Mouse on Mars, Junge Hunde Festival, etc. It is used globally by hundreds of institutes, organizations, and individuals. NATO.0+55 workshops and seminars have been hosted by BEK, IAMAS, SALON/JAPAN, Ircam, V2/DEAF, etc.

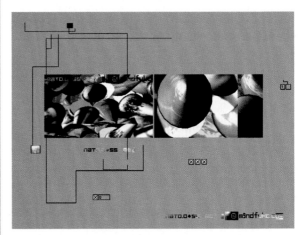

Figure 1. NATO+0+55+3d real-time 3D texture mapping.

Figure 2. NATO+0+55+3d real-time 2D alphabet.

# Non-Graphical Application of Hardware Accelerated Voxelization

*Contact*
**Steffi Beckhaus**
GMD - Media Communication Institute
Sankt Augustin, Germany
steffi.beckhaus@gmd.de

**Jürgen Wind**
GMD - Media
Communication Institute

## Introduction

Voxelization is used in a number of applications, mainly in the field of volume graphics. We require it for a non-graphical application, the dynamic generation of animations for automatic presentation of models or scenes according to a user specified interest.[1] In this sketch we present the utilization of hardware accelerated voxelization to generate voxelized object data keeping a reference to the unique, single objects. With this voxelization approach we are now able to employ our animation system in highly dynamic environments and with increased resolutions.

## Application

With our camera data generating approach based on potential fields, we can deal with rapidly changing user interest in objects of a scene, as well as with dynamic models and changes of the camera position introduced interactively by the user.[1] For this purpose the space is discretized into a regular 3D grid, or voxel space (see Figure 3), with object IDs assigned to each occupied voxel. According to queries to an underlying information space, user requests are mapped to objects, which in turn are set attractively in the voxel space. As a result, the camera will be attracted by these voxels and will visit all attractive objects consecutively.

In static environments the voxelization process has to be performed only once. In dynamic interactive environments the voxelization speed becomes crucial, as every dynamic object has to be mapped immediately to the voxel space when moved. Software based voxelization techniques soon become too slow to provide interactive response. With hardware based voxelization we are able to work with increased resolutions of the voxel space and with larger scenes.

## Implementation

The system is implemented in AVANGO, our Performer-based framework for virtual environment development.[3] The voxelization process uses the Performer scene graph, which is at the same time used to render the scene. A custom node that handles switching between the normal rendering mode and the voxelization mode replaces the top node of each object of interest. An ID is assigned to this custom node to identify the object. In the voxelization mode this ID is mapped to an RGB color, which is then applied as an emissive material to the object's geometry. All other materials and textures for this object are disabled in this mode to ensure that the object is rendered only in the color of the ID. Objects that are not assigned a custom node are rendered in a single color. For the hardware accelerated voxelization we take advantage of the clipping capabilities of the graphics engine.[2] To voxelize the scene in a given resolution x, y, z of the voxel data set, we render the scene slice by slice in voxelization mode, thereby producing z slices of resolution x*y. The near and far clipping planes of the viewport are set to bound each slice to be as wide as the current z voxel. The hardware clips the geometry, and an image of the geometry in this slice is rendered (see Figures 1 and 2). The result is written into memory. It could now be directly rendered as a texture. For our purpose we analyze the colors in memory, obtaining for each position of the voxel space the information about whether, and by which object, it is occupied.

The voxelization time increases linearly with the resolution, but the influence of the number of slices to be rendered – the z resolution – is in our case four to five times larger than the influence of enlarging the image size by x or y (we used an Onyx2 IR2). Therefore, for efficient voxelization, the scene has to be transformed in a way that the smallest resolution of the voxel space maps to the z direction. Analyzing only sub-regions of the voxel space when only parts of the scene have changed also increases efficiency.

*References*
1. Beckhaus, S., Ritter, F., & Strothotte, T. (2000). Cubical path – dynamic potential fields for guided exploration in virtual environments. In *Proceedings of Pacific Graphics*, 387-395, October 2000.
2. Fang, S. & Chen, H. (2000). Hardware accelerated voxelization. In *Computers and Graphics*, 24(3): 433 - 442, June 2000.
3. Tramberend, H. (1999). Avocado: A distributed virtual reality framework. In *Proceedings of IEEE Virtual Reality*, L. Rosenblum & P. A. & Detlef Teichmann, editors, 14 - 21, March 1999.

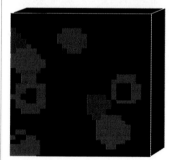

Figure 1. One slice is rendered for each z.

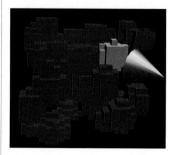

Figure 2. Slice with color-coded objects rendered in a resolution of 20 x 20 x 1.

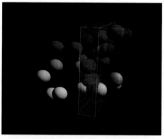

Figure 3. Bounding box in raster space.

*237*

*Contact*
ANDREAS GENZ
Universität Bremen
genzo@informatik.uni-bremen.de

We present a method integrating occlusion-culling[3] into the Catmull recursive-subdivision algorithm.[2] The Catmull recursive-subdivision algorithm is the ancestor of the REYES architecture, implemented in Pixar's renderer PRMan. It is capable of producing pictures from geometrically complex scenes. PRMan performs occlusion culling through sorting objects in a bucket (a rectangular pixel region) from front to back.[1]

In contrast, our method is optimized for scenes of very high depth complexity containing procedurally described geometry. The raster image is not split into buckets, instead the viewing volume is split into layers along the z-axis. Any sorting of objects is avoided. In a case study[6] the method is used to render scenes containing 100,000 trees with geometrically different features (Figure 1).

Here is an outline of the Catmull recursive-subdivision algorithm:
Given: camera, geometric objects
Requested: raster image of the scene

For every geometric object:
1. Compute camera-space axis-aligned bounding box.
2. If bounding box is entirely outside viewing volume, drop object.
3. Else: project bounding box into raster space.
4. If bounding box covers more than one pixel, subdivide object.
5. Else: rasterize object, z-buffer visibility test.

## OUR METHOD

- Split scene into layers along the z-axis (Figure 2).
- Render the front most layer with the Catmull recursive subdivision algorithm.
- Build a summed-area table $T(x,y)$ of the function $f(x,y)$, where $f(x,y) = 1$, if element $(x,y)$ is covered by some geometric object, otherwise $f(x,y) = 0$.
- Render the next layer with a modified Catmull recursive-subdivision algorithm:

4. If bounding box covers more than one pixel:
4.1. If bounding box is occluded: drop object.
4.2. Else: subdivide object.

Return to step c, until the image has totally been covered or the last layer is reached.

## THE OCCLUSION TEST IN DETAIL (FIGURE 3)
Number of raster elements covered by a bounding box $b = (x_1-x_0)(y_1-y_0)$
Number of raster elements covered by some object in this bounding box $a = T(x_1,y_1) + T(x_0,y_0) - T(x_1,y_0) - T(x_0,y_1)$
Error tolerance $t \geq 0$
Drop object, if $a \geq b - t$

## FURTHER WORK
For which kind of scenes and visible features is this method advantageous? Does it make sense to integrate it into, or combine with, the REYES architecture?

*References*
1. Apodaca, A.A. & Gritz, L. (2000). Advanced renderman. Creating CGI for Motion Pictures, Morgan Kaufmann.
2. Catmull, E.E. (1974). A subdivision algorithm for computer display of curved surfaces. Ph.D. thesis, Department of Computer Science, University of Utah.
3. Cohen-Or, D. et al. (2000). Visibility, problems, techniques and applications, *SIGGRAPH 2000 Course Notes.*
4. Crow, F.C. (1984). Summed-area tables for texture mapping. *Proceedings of SIGGRAPH '84* , 207-212.
5. Foley, J. et al. (1990). *Computer Graphics, Principles and Practice*, 2nd ed. Reading, MA: Addison-Wesley.
6. Genz, A. (1998). Baum & Wald – Modellierung & bildsynthese. Dimplomarbeit, Informatik, Universität Bremen.

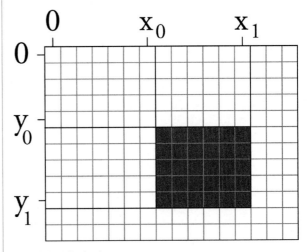

Figure 1: Trees.

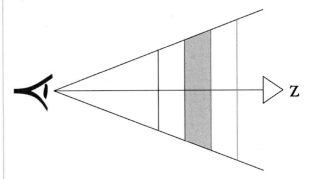

Figure 2: Split viewing volume.

Figure 3. Bounding box in raster space.

238

# OPEN PROCESSES CREATE OPEN PRODUCTS: "INTERFACE ECOLOGY" AS A METADISCIPLINARY BASE FOR COLLAGEMACHINE

*Contact*
ANDRUID KERNE
Creating Media
380 Lafayette Street, Suite 202
New York, New York 10003
USA
andruid@creatingmedia.com

## INTRODUCTION

Most interactive artifacts are very finite state machines. They represent determinate solutions to closed form problems. However, life is an open-ended series of situations which are not very well formed at all. The more that computational artifacts are integrated with everyday life, the more culturally significant this gap becomes. Equal value in interface ecology traverses this gap – in the process of the developer – by opening the range of methodologies that are invoked. Collage dynamically creates new meanings by combining found objects. Indeterminacy opens the set of possible states in an interactive automata. The decisions to use collage and indeterminacy in CollageMachine followed directly from an equal value, interface ecology process.

## EQUAL VALUE IN INTERFACE ECOLOGY

Interface ecology brings the perspectives of diverse disciplines to bear on the form and function of interfaces. It does this in a non-hierarchical way, according to the principle of equal value. Gertrude Stein developed equal value in consideration of the paintings of Cézanne, as a way of writing in which all words and aspects of what is represented are assigned the same rights, responsibilities, and weights. This conception of value comes from painting, where it refers to the magnitude of brightness.

Likewise, with interface ecology, no discipline dominates; none are considered subordinate. Rather, they are interdependent components, connected by flows of interaction. This "meshwork" ecosystem form supports open-ended inquiry. It enables the development of artifacts, like CollageMachine, that support open-ended processes.

## COLLAGE

Collage is work created by combining found objects. In collage, pasted objects function semiotically to introduce new meaning to the work. As with Duchamp's readymades – such as *Fountain* – the new presentation environment of the collage creates a new context for the interpretation of its elements. Additionally, the juxtaposition of elements within a collage further alters their context, and thus their meaning. It forms semiotic relationships between them. Disciplines are a form of information age readymade; a discipline is a urinal. In interface ecology, disciplines are among the found objects which are recombined.

## INDETERMINACY

Indeterminacy is a means for structuring decision-making during collage-making. It has a long history as a cultural method, predating collage by many millennia. Indeterminacy refers to the utilization of chance procedures, such as random selection operations and random factors that influence the values of parameters. That is, certain creative decisions are expressed in an algorithmic form that relies partially on randomness.

## COLLAGEMACHINE

CollageMachine is a creative Web visualization tool that affords browsing through streaming collage. The program deconstructs Web sites into media elements – images and chunks of text. These media elements continuously stream into a collage. A point and click, drag and drop interface enables the user to rearrange the elements. From this interaction, an agent learns about users' interests. It acts to shape the ongoing development of the collage. The agent model structures the use of indeterminacy in collage making decisions.

## OPEN ENDED BROWSING

CollageMachine supports an open-ended process of Web browsing, in which the user may start only with a sense of direction. Clear advance goals are not required. On-going feedback with actual media elements enables direction to emerge. Some of the burden for clicking through hypermedia to find interesting material is relieved. This open process is an essential part of browsing. Open-ended browsing is an essential part of what makes up life. Inasmuch as interactive artifacts are integrated with everyday life, they must be conceived in terms of the full range of activities that life encompasses. Through interface ecology, the methods of collage, creative cognition, machine learning, usability, and software engineering are blended in CollageMachine with equal value.

www.mrl.nyu.edu/andruid

239

One state of a CollageMachine (mrl.nyu.edu/collagemachine): news collage session.

One state of a search's collage session with Greenham Common, Marcel Duchamp.

# Organic Textures with Controlled Anisotropy and Directionality

*Contact*
Kazunori Miyata
Department of Media Art
Tokyo Institute of Polytechnics
1583 Iiyama, Atsugi-shi
Kanagawa 243-0297 Japan
+81.46.242.9634
+81.46.242.9634 fax
miyatak@acm.org

Takayuki Itoh
IBM Research
Tokyo Research Lab

Kenji Shimada
Mechanical Engineering
Carnegie Mellon University

## Introduction

We propose a computational method for generating organic textures with controlled anisotropy and directionality. The method first tessellates a region into a set of pseudo Voronoi polygons (cells) using a particle model, and then generates the detailed geometry of each of the polygons using a subdivision surface method with fractal noises.

A user can create various types of realistic looking organic textures with ease by simply choosing a cell arrangement type, anisotropy, and directionality, along with the geometry control parameters.

## Pseudo Voronoi Tessellation via Anisotropic Meshing

Our tessellation technique to represent organic texture consists of three steps: (1) elliptic or rectangular particle packing;[1] (2) anisotropic meshing by connecting the centers of the particles; and (3) Voronoi tessellation as a dual of the anisotropic mesh. Given preferred cell sizes and directionality within a geometric domain, the technique outputs Voronoi polygons compatible with the specified cell sizes, directionality, and anisotropy.

## Organic Texture Generation

An organic texture is obtained by generating a skin texture for each of the pseudo Voronoi cells created by the method described in the previous section. Each skin texture is generated in the following three steps:

- generation of an initial skin mesh for each polygon.
- smoothing of the initial skin mesh by a subdivision surface method.
- addition of small bump features with fractal noises.

First, an initial skin mesh is generated according to the geometry of each cell. A 3D prism shape is obtained by sweeping each cell by a given skin height in the skin's normal vector direction. The initial skin mesh is then generated by deforming this prism by displacing each of the top corners randomly, skewing each of the top corners in a specified flow vector, and tapering the prism.

After initial skin meshes have been generated, they are subdivided and refined by using Loop's subdivision method.[2] Finally, small bump features are added to the skin meshes with fractal noises.

## Results

The processing time depends on the number of the cells, but it is much faster than previous methods. On an Intel Pentium III 650MHz processor it takes only 10 seconds on average for the packing process and only 10 seconds on average for the skin texture generation for a texture size of 512 x 512. Figures 2 and 3 show organic textures with controlled anisotropy and directionality created by the proposed method.

*References*
1. Shimada, K., Liao, L., & Itoh, T. (1998). Quadrilateral meshing with directionality control through the packing of square cells. Seventh International Meshing Roundtable, 61-76, 1998.
2. Loop, C. (1994). Smooth spline surfaces over irregular meshes. In *Proceedings of SIGGRAPH '94*, 303-310, 1994.

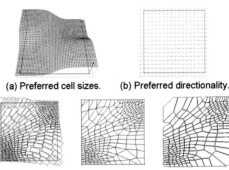

(a) Preferred cell sizes.    (b) Preferred directionality.

(c) Packed particles.    (d) Anisotropic mesh.    (e) Voronoi tessellation

Figure 1. Three sub-steps of packing pattern generation.

Figure 2. Example of organic textures.

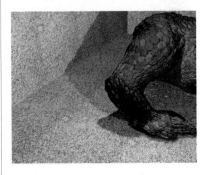

Figure 3. Textured leg.

## Paint the Town Red: Recreating Stalingrad for "Enemy at the Gates"

*Contact*
Paul Franklin
Double Negative Ltd
paul@dneg.com

Jim Bowers
Matte Painting Supervisor
Double Negative Ltd

Åsa Svedberg
Technical Director
Double Negative Ltd

Martin Preston
Senior Programmer
Double Negative Ltd

"Enemy at the Gates" seeks to recreate the savagery and enormity of the Battle of Stalingrad. For Double Negative, one of the more challenging moments in the film was the sequence depicting a German air raid on the heart of Stalingrad. This called for a travelling aerial view of the ruined city stretching for twenty miles. All buildings would be seen in full 3D, revealing battle damage in great detail.

A previsualisation animation of camera movement and timing gained directorial approval, but it did not highlight the real star of the shot, Stalingrad itself. The model of the city's layout would be crucial to balance the need for historical accuracy with the drama of the story, but the question remained: how to quickly and simply design something as complex as the war torn city? Direct modelling was deemed too cumbersome. Instead, using Maya, a perspective grid of the city was created as seen from the animated camera. Selected frames, printed as hardcopy, became the basis for pencil sketches allowing the city plan to be rapidly approved. The sketches were then scanned back into the system, projected onto simple geometry, and tested with the animated camera as proof of concept.

Working from the layouts a team of two modellers set about creating the buildings. All structures were built intact with interior walls and floors, later to be revealed by bomb damage. Fortunately, Stalingrad was a model Soviet development constructed in the 1930s along modular lines; extensive research revealed that many forms were repeated throughout the city. Eventually a base library of approximately 50 buildings was settled on, capturing Stalingrad's essential architectural themes. Each building had a corresponding simple proxy version, which were used to recreate the sketched layout in 3D.

By this point it became impossible to avoid dealing with large amounts of geometry. Somewhere in the region of 2000 proxies had been created, and each would need to be replaced with its high-resolution version and dressed with individualised damage. Using the Maya Embedded Language (MEL) a database of the models was created allowing the team to quickly call up any city component and work on it in isolation. Additional tools enabled efficient substitution and detailing.

For the final texturing phase, the team returned to the ideas that had informed initial layout. High resolution frames of the unshaded city model were rendered from the animated camera at intervals along the timeline. These became the basis for detailed Photoshop paintings which were applied directly to the model as texture projections using custom-written RenderMan shaders. By effectively baking all lighting information into the textures, render times were minimised.

Despite the scene's complexity, a high degree of artistic control was achieved through a hand drawn and painted approach to layout. The flexible database toolset enabled a core team of only four people to manage a large number of assets. As a bonus, the efficiency of this approach allowed the team to deliver a second shot of the city seen from a different viewpoint within the original deadline.

241

## PERMANENT SHUTDOWN: EXPERIMENTS IN INTERACTIVITY

*Contact*
JUSTIN KENT
Massachusetts Institute
of Technology
Center for Advanced
Visual Studies
www.justinkent.com

Artificial intelligence finds assisted suicide, online trust accesses ownership and consumption, and interaction becomes anti-interaction, as art moves towards its own inevitable permanent shutdown.

"Permanent Shutdown" is an interactive installation in which a computer has the ability to initiate its own destruction. In the initial versions of the project, this control is accomplished via serial port radio communication with an electromagnet, which suspends a cinder block over the computer. The system stands posed on the brink of self-destruction, with only a click of a button by the user to consume and complete the work.

Future versions will incorporate Web access into the piece, giving users the potential to initiate the destruction sequence from a Web terminal in any location. The site will have live video confirmation and will be password protected. Other versions will utilize other means of destruction, such as a gunshot.

In an age where the ideas of artificial intelligence and neural networks have become highly refined, and where computing power gives such programs the ability to approximate the size and complexity of the human brain, at what point does the termination of such a system become more than mere property damage? At what point will such devices be seen as more than slavish automatons, and their termination seen as murder or assisted suicide?

In experiencing any piece of art, the viewer almost always has the option of destroying it; this interaction is rarely exploited, however. It has been addressed, such as in Robert Rauschenberg's erasure of a Willem de Kooning drawing. But when a work instigates its own obliteration, does the work require that eventual destruction for it to be complete? If a work of art is created totally from commercially available stock components, does it become disposable or renewable? How does decentralized access to a work of art affect its experience?

By limiting the user's choice of interaction to one sole possibility, one single instance of that interaction, that interaction becomes exclusive and off limits to the majority of its viewers. What does it mean to have an interactive piece that cannot be interacted with? Does an interactive work require the interaction to be experienced fully? Who feels justified in completely experiencing the work themselves, thereby rendering it unusable to anyone else? Does the artist, by offering the interaction, share the responsibility with the viewer in exercising it? And how does the idea of interaction change when the cost or consequence of that interaction is greatly increased?

In an environment where art has been totally commodified and electronic trust is auctioned online, the two must inevitably intermingle. Ownership of such a work is multileveled – while only one person can possess the actual sculptural element, an unlimited number of people can be given the right to destroy (and complete) it. Furthermore, the person that initiates the piece's eventual destruction has possessed it in a unique way. This brings up issues of trust, security, and privacy, and questions the idea of art ownership.

"Permanent Shutdown" is one work in a series that explores interactivity by minimizing it through various means. Another work, "Webwheel," trivializes user interaction by using it as input into a chaotic system, thereby divorcing any specific output from a user's actions, which become noise to the system. The upcoming "Digital Gas Mask" wards off user interaction by associating with it the potential for severe physical illness.

By treating interactivity as an axis along which an artist and his or her audience must negotiate, then carefully restricting this territory, one can elucidate and differentiate interaction as art.

# PlaceWorld: An Integration of Shared Virtual Worlds

*Contact*
Jon Cook
Advanced Interfaces Group
University of Manchester
United Kingdom
cookj@cs.man.ac.uk

Steve Pettifer
Advanced Interfaces Group
University of Manchester
United Kingdom

PlaceWorld is the result of collaboration between artists, social and computer scientists undertaken as part of the eSCAPE Project (ESPRIT 25377, 1997-2000), the aim of which was to inform the development of future large scale shared and social virtual environments. Realized as a distributed multi-user VE capable of running over wide-area networks, PlaceWorld has three goals: first, to act as a coherent metaphor for browsing and experiencing disparate electronic art installations and virtual artefacts; second, to be an evolving social environment in its own right; and third, to provide a persistent software architecture in which non-trivial virtual artefacts may be dynamically created and integrated.

Borrowing from previous multimedia installations "Place - a user's manual" and "The Virtual Museum,"[1] PlaceWorld combines a familiar planar city-like layout with unusual virtual content. Cylindrical "buildings" act as portals leading to the more extensive electronic art works, while self-contained artefacts are situated on the main landscape itself.

As well as being a container for dynamically created content, the PlaceWorld environment itself gradually evolves a structure based on its usage by its inhabitants. Artefacts and environments of interest slowly become larger, drawing attention to their popularity. Users each leave behind glowing translucent trails as they pass through the environment; these can be utilised by other inhabitants to chart the movement of companions, but also contribute automatically to the network of pathways that connect areas of the worlds. User trails following similar routes reinforce one another to become concrete "highways" allowing rapid transport from region to region, whilst trails leading to unpopular areas of the world fade over time. A user's personal trial can be used as a transport mechanism allowing multiple users to gather and interact through a text-based chat facility. Users are encouraged to personalize and contribute to the environment – from creating links to favourite areas, to using personalized objects to mark territory, and for advanced users, creating new art pieces.

The initial implementation of PlaceWorld contained two existing electronic artworks each with a number of sub-environments: The Legible City representing a 3D textural journey through three distinct virtual cityscapes; and Memory Theatre VR, in which four separate environments chart an artist's view of the development of Virtual Reality. To further populate PlaceWorld, two other applications were also embedded for the purposes of demonstration: a radiosity model of the Advanced Interfaces Group lab; and a detailed CAD model of a chemical plant.

These four works (shown in image 2) were pre-existing, stand alone single-user applications that had been developed independently on different projects. The data structures and rendering techniques required to efficiently store and display each work are radically different.

The AIG's MAVERIK system[2] was used to unite these disparate works. MAVERIK employs a callback mechanism to encapsulate the data structures and rendering techniques specific to each work. This common interface to the works allows them to coexist within a single virtual environment. The AIG's complementary Deva system[3] provided the distribution layer on top of MAVERIK that was used to implement PlaceWorld. Deva utilizes a client-server architecture with a customisable high-level language to describe schemes for synchronization. Furthermore, customisable smoothing techniques are employed to reduce the effect of network lag.

The PlaceWorld architecture, contents, and a purpose-built walk-in panoramic navigation display device with cylindrical projection screen and touch sensitive display were publicly exhibited at the ESPRIT i3NET conference in Jonkoping, Sweden, and at The Doors of Perception conference, Amsterdam, both in Q4 2000.

Further information about the architecture and future exhibitions can be found at www.placeworld.org. Contributors include: James Marsh, Simon Gibson, Andreas Kratky, Jeffrey Shaw, and Gideon May.

*References*
1. Dugeuet, A.M. et al. (1997). *Jeffrey Shaw - a user's manual*. Cantz Verglag, 1997.
2. Hubbold, R. et al. (1999). GNU/MAVERIK: a micro-kernel for large-scale virtual environments. In *Proceedings VRST'99*.
3. Pettifer, S. et al. (2000) DEVA3: architecture for a large scale virtual reality system. In *Proceedings VRST '00*.

243

1. An overview of PlaceWorld.

2. The four sub-environments of PlaceWorld.

3. PlaceWorld in use at ESPRIT i3NET conference.

*Contact*
DEBORAH CARLSON
Sony Pictures Imageworks
dcarlson@imageworks.com

NICKSON FONG
Centropolis Effects, LLC

## INTRODUCTION

This sketch describes the image-based lighting pipeline developed at Centropolis Effects. The project was inspired by recent high-dynamic range photography and image-based lighting research by Paul Debevec.[1,2] The goal of our system is to collect accurate lighting information from the set and use that data to directly light the computer graphics scene. Because the long rendering times of a physically based global illumination renderer are not yet practical in a visual effects production environment, we created a technique that could easily fit into our existing CG pipeline using photorealistic RenderMan. Our system was developed during production on "Arac Attack," which features giant furry spiders, so it was designed to handle lighting fur as well as surfaces.

## LIGHTING FROM FISHEYE PHOTOGRAPHS

The basic idea we are referencing is that the incoming radiance can be captured at a given point on the set by taking fisheye photographs from that point with a range of exposures. The technique for creating high-dynamic range (HDR) radiance maps from photographs taken at multiple exposures is described in a 1997 SIGGRAPH presentation.[1] For each position on the set we wish to sample, we take two sets of 180-degree fisheye photographs to cover the entire sphere of incoming light.

## DIFFUSE MAPS

Once we have the HDR fisheye environment map, we process it to create a HDR diffuse normal map, essentially rendering a map of the surface of a small diffuse white sphere as if lit by the environment. This map is ideal for capturing the color variation of the diffuse lighting in outdoor shots. The normal map is used in a renderman diffuse light shader which returns a color given the surface normal at the point being shaded. If necessary, a variation of this light shader can be used that interpolates among several diffuse maps sampled from multiple points on the set, much like the irradiance volume technique used for synthetic scenes.[3]

## SPECULAR LIGHT AND SHADOWS

In order to add specular highlights and shadows to the scene, we need to know the approximate positions, color, and intensities of the main light sources in the environment. The incoming light directions as well as the colors and intensities can be calculated directly from the HDR environment map. The distances of the lights from the sampled position can be guessed at, or they can be more accurately approximated by triangulation if the light from more than one position is sampled on the set. Extra lights that only add specular highlights and lights that only subtract diffuse shadows can be added to the scene using this information. Also, the HDR environment map itself can be used as a reflection map for shiny surfaces.

## EXTENDING THE TECHNIQUE TO FUR

The method described above works well for standard surface shaders that use a diffuse function based on the surface normal. However, the diffuse component of a typical fur shader uses the tangent to the curve at the point being shaded, not a normal.

Therefore, to extend our technique to work for fur, we create a diffuse tangent map from the HDR environment just for fur lighting, analogous to the diffuse normal map for surface lighting. The tangent maps are used in a separate light shader for fur, and our fur shaders were extended to add the diffuse illumination from the image-based fur light. The additional specular-only and shadow-only lights work as well for fur as for surfaces.

*References*
1. Debevec, P. & Malik, J. (1997). Recovering high dynamic range radiance maps from photographs. In *Proceeding of SIGGRAPH 97,* August 1997.
2. Debevec, P. (1998). Rendering synthetic objects into real scenes: bridging traditional and image-based graphics with global illumination and dynamic range photography. In *Proceedings of SIGGRAPH 98.*
3. Greger, G., Shirley, P., Hubbard, P., & Greenberg, D. (1998). The irradiance volume. In *IEEE Computer Graphics and Applications,* 18, (2), March/April 1998.

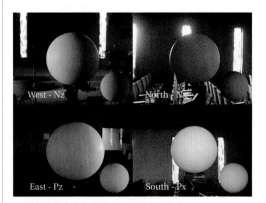

Comparison test with rendered diffuse ball from HDR fisheye environment maps composited over photographs of matte-painted beach ball.

Objects rendered using image-based lighting with additional specular lights and no shadows composited over background plate.

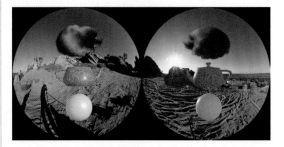

Objects rendered using image-based lighting with additional specular lights and no shadows composited over fisheye environment images.

*Contact*
MARKUS KURTZ
Digital Domain
300 Rose Avenue
Venice, California 90291 USA
markusk@d2.com

When Ron Howard approached Digital Domain with the idea of creating a computer graphics sleigh to be used in over 50 shots of "Dr. Seuss' How the Grinch Stole Christmas," we knew that we would have to develop a system that looked realistic enough to match a set piece but was also fast and flexible enough to match the creative vision of the director in shots where the actual prop was not an option. To achieve this goal, a procedural dynamics system was written that depended solely on the sleigh's motion and its interaction with the ground surface to compute the animation of the sleigh and all of its parts.

Because our sleigh had to be able to match the physical sleigh in back to back cuts, we had to ensure that we not only captured the look of the sleigh in terms of color and lighting but also captured the behavior and dynamics of the sleigh, including its precarious payload. Traditional key frame animation was not an option due to the number of animating parts on the sleigh. Employing animators to hand animate more than 60 moving pieces on the sleigh would have been too costly and time-consuming. Additionally, standard simulation techniques are typically a very time-consuming and serial process that do not allow for much creative direction. Our sleigh needed to look realistic while still allowing for fast use of "creative license,"

Thus, a pseudo-simulation technique was developed that combined the flexibility of key frame animation with the accuracy of a simulation technique. Because of its open structure and procedural workflow, Houdini (Side Effects Software, Inc.) was chosen to build a new dynamics system, which was able to control the animation of all objects on the sleigh in a very realistic and dynamically correct way. Instead of using simulation on the entire behavior, the system was designed to be a computation of a series of individual steps based on basic physics and mathematics. Every step could be controlled and approved before moving on to the next layer of calculation. This idea developed into one single procedural flow of data, but with the option of adjusting the result after every step. Once the system was developed, workflow was pretty simple. Starting out with a given terrain and a simple key frame animation to define the rough path of the sleigh in the shot, Houdini's CHOPs (Channel Operators) were used to compute the force, acceleration, velocity, and speed of the sleigh. With that information, combined with a basic model of the underlying terrain, animation was computed so that the sleigh rode correctly on the surface, banking in curves, shifting weight, and even occasionally becoming airborne over jumps. The resulting animation could be controlled by either adjusting the original path animation or by tuning parameters in the computation.

After locking the primary animation, further procedural compution steps calculated the animation of the sleigh's runners, the six shock absorbers, the sleigh-bag, and all the little packages, bags, and other paraphernalia that dangled off it. Every object mounted on the bag was driven not only by the sleigh's motion but also by the bag's animation based on that motion.

In the end, artists were able to set up the sleigh animation for each shot within a couple hours and the turnaround times of iterations

were minimal. The procedural dynamics system returned accurate, sometimes purposely exaggerated, but always dynamically realistic animation. Because this system proved so useful on "Grinch," it has been generalized and used successfully in a number of other projects at Digital Domain. Animation of objects over any kind of terrain can be derived from this setup with only minor adjustment.

Figure 1. A simple key frame animation defines the rough path.

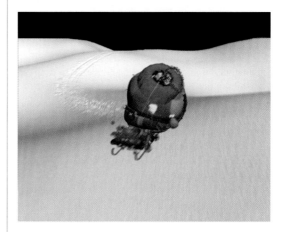

Figure 2. The procedural dynamics system computes the animation of the entire sleigh.

# RainMan: Fluid Pseudodynamics with Probabilistic Control for Stylized Raindrops

*Contact*
Daniel L. Herman
Pixar Animation Studios
dh@digitalfish.com
www.digitalfish.com

## Introduction

Simulation and production have traditionally had an uneasy relationship. Film production particularly demands that images and motion be highly directable, while simulation is generally associated with poor directability and opaque relationships between user-level control and the resulting imagery. Still there are some effects that are difficult or impossible to achieve without procedural means. This is a domain in which pseudodynamics, that is, dynamics employing a mix of theoretical and empirical bases, applies greatly.

Presented with the problem of portraying highly stylized falling rain for Pixar and Disney's film "A Bug's Life," we applied a pseudodynamic technique incorporating probabilistic control to achieve a specific look.

This control occurs via shapable Probability Distribution Functions (PDFs) that guide stochastic processes in the simulator. For fine control, the user can specify the location, timing, and precise shape of splashes produced by raindrop impacts, as well as tug on the flow to guide it in a particular direction. Alternatively, the user can allow RainMan to create falling raindrops stochastically while maintaining statistical control over the shape and timing of impacts. Finally, the overall character of flow can be broadly manipulated, providing a range of realistic or cartoon-like behavior. These multiple levels of control are a natural byproduct of the PDF representation we use.

The resulting system is fast and stable, giving intuitive and reproducible results. This stability is essential in allowing animation design iteration. These traits make RainMan well suited for use in film production.

## The RainMan Particle Simulator

RainMan employs a variable mass, spatially coupled particle system. An implicit surface is rendered over the particles. Individual raindrops are composed of single large particles that may fragment on a hard impact with the ground, producing a "splat" composed of many small particles. Particles interact with each other and collision surfaces in ways that mimic the effects of surface tension and viscosity. Large streams of particles may coalesce and flow downhill, twisting, splashing, and ultimately soaking into the ground as would rainwater runoff.

Forces in the particle system include gravity, external viscous drag of particles in flight, internal viscous drag of particles in-contact moving past one another, and attractive-repulsive forces between neighboring particles (Lennard-Jones forces). Mass flows between particles of differing size in contact, equalizing surface energies between neighboring droplets, allowing particles of varying mass to interact without producing a lumpy isosurface.

## Splat Generation

The characteristic shapes formed by splats are predicted by the Navier-Stokes equations. These equations are notoriously expensive to solve in 3D and result in highly realistic motion, which we do not seek. Instead, we control splat shape indirectly by specifying how water exits from the impact. To do this, we envision a PDF that maps from the 7-dimensional particle state space (position $\mathbf{x}$, velocity $\mathbf{v}$, and mass $m$) to the scalar probability $P((\mathbf{x}, \mathbf{v}, m))$ that a water particle is created with a given state vector. To generate particles under this distribution $P$, we establish a deformation $\mathbf{W}_P$ that maps a uniform distribution to $P$. We may then pass a uniform random distribution of vectors through $\mathbf{W}_P$ and initialize particles with these deformed vectors.

The user-level controls in RainMan generally manipulate this $\mathbf{W}_P$. This provides a particle-independent means of controlling splat shape while providing a convenient level-of-detail mechanism: we may create more or fewer particles as appropriate to screen-projection size, yet the splat will statistically retain its shape. This *probabilistic control* further allows us to stochastically generate the $\mathbf{W}_P$'s themselves. We may populate a large area with many splats that vary in shape pseudorandomly while retaining control over broad aspects, such as to what extent they conserve energy, whether they tend to splash upwards or lay flat, or whether they are generally neat or very noisy. This higher-order control was essential on large shots containing hundreds of impacting drops.

## Results

RainMan was used by a small team of technical animators in two weeks to produce the foreground rain that falls throughout most of Act 3 of "A Bug's Life." In all, nearly 10,000 RainMan raindrops fall on Ant Island by the end of the film. Simulation was a natural choice for this project, but it involves procedural and control limitations to which few directors or producers are used. The association between physical parameters and visual behavior of a simulation is often obscure, even to the simulation authors. Providing controls that corresponded to visual behavior of the simulation rather than the underlying physics enabled us to communicate more meaningfully with the directors and allowed users to become proficient with the system very quickly. This intuitive control was made possible by the use of probabilistic methods in guiding the simulation and the willingness to adopt non-physical representations. Had we employed a purely CFD technique, such high-level direction would have been impossible.

# A Real-Time High Dynamic Range Light Probe

*Contact*
Jamie Waese
USC Institute for
Creative Technologies
13274 Fiji Way, 5th Floor
Marina del Rey, California 90292
USA
waese@ict.usc.edu

Paul Debevec
USC Institute for
Creative Technologies

In order to successfully composite computer graphics elements into live action scenes it is important that the lighting of the CG object match the lighting of the scene into which it is being composited. One technique that has been used to reproduce the incident illumination in a live-action scene is to acquire a high-dynamic-range photograph of a mirrored ball placed in the scene and then use this light-probe image as a source of illumination for image-based lighting.[1]

## Previous Work

Currently, in order to create a high dynamic range image of a mirrored ball one must take an iterative series of photographs with the exposure value of each image being stopped down by a given increment from the exposure value of the one before. Later, each of the images are assembled into a single high dynamic range image using a program such as HDR Shop[3]. If an artist wished to accurately illuminate a CG object traveling through a complex lighting environment, it would be necessary to capture these iterative photographs at numerous locations (ideally at every frame) along the object's path. Clearly, this would be an ambitious task.

## Technique

One solution for creating a real-time high-dynamic range light probe is to develop a system in which multiple exposures of the same image can be captured within a single video frame. We did this by modifying a five point multi-image filter (a faceted lens that is commonly used to create photographic kaleidoscope effects), and applying successively increasing values of neutral density gel to four of the five facets of the filter (3, 6, 10 and 13 stops). This modified filter effectively produces a single image that is divided into five identical regions, with the center region capturing a "direct" view and the four outer regions stopped down to their respective exposure values. This modified filter is placed on a video camera that is mounted along with a mirrored ball on a span of angle iron (see Figure 1).

Assuming the relation between the camera and the ball never changes, the light probe only needs to be calibrated once. To compensate for the angle shift introduced by parallax effects from the facets of the multi-image filter, one can compute the arctangent of the distance between facets divided by the distance between the lens and the silver ball. By determining the number of degrees each facet is offset from the center, we are able to warp each region of the filter according to the direction space of its view of the ball. In our case, each facet's view of the ball was computed to be 2.7 degrees off from center.

More accurate calibration can be done with the help of a light stage,[2] which provides a "master key" for factoring out lens distortion and imperfections in the mirrored ball. However, we found that simply computing the pixel shift and then overlapping each region of the filter was sufficient for assembling a usable image.

In order to capture high dynamic range light probe data at every frame along a path, one presses "record" on the video camera and carries the light probe along the desired path. A computer program then imports each recorded frame, isolates the five distinct images in the frame, aligns them according to predetermined calibration data, and then assembles the aligned images into a high dynamic range omnidirectional measurement of incident illumination.

## Results

Figure 2 shows a raw, unprocessed image from the light probe.

Figure 3 shows several exposures of a high dynamic range image that were assembled from a single light probe frame.

Figure 4 shows a CG object, lit with captured light from the real time high dynamic range light probe.

## Conclusion

This new technique will permit artists to composite CG objects into dynamic complex lighting environments, accurately reproducing high dynamic range lighting parameters for each frame. In the future, this technique would benefit from greater precision in applying the neutral density gels to the multi-image filter, a smaller camera rig, and higher resolution video cameras.

*References*
1. Debevec, P. (1998). Rendering synthetic objects into real scenes: bridging traditional and image-based graphics with global illumination and high dynamic range photography. In *Proceedings SIGGRAPH 98*.
2. Debevec, P., Hawkins, T., Tchou, C., Duiker, H.P., Sarokin, W., & Sagar, M. Acquiring the reflectance field of a human face. In *Proceedings SIGGRAPH 2000*.
3. Tchou, C. & Debevec, P. (2001). HDR shop. *SIGGRAPH 2001 Conference Abstracts and Applications*.

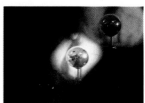

Figure 1. A real time high dynamic range light probe.

Figure 2. Five exposures of a mirrored ball in a single image.

Figure 3. Five exposures of a high dynamic range image captured in a single frame.

Figure 4. A CG model that is synthetically illuminated with light captured with the real time light probe.

# Real-Time Rendering of Populated Urban Environments

*Contact*
Franco Tecchia
University College London
Gower Street
WC1E 6BT London
United Kingdom
hrysanthou/crowds/sketch/

Celine Loscos
Yiorgos Chrysanthou
University College London

## Introduction

The wide use of computer graphics in games, entertainment, medical, architectural, and cultural applications, has led it to becoming a prevalent area of research. At the current stage of technology, users can interactively navigate through complex, polygon-based scenes rendered with sophisticated lighting effects and high quality antialiasing techniques. Animated characters (or agents) with whom the users can interact, are also becoming more and more common. However, the rendering of crowded scenes with thousands of different animated avatars has still not been addressed sufficiently for real-time use. In this paper we propose new methods for the rendering and culling of these highly populated scenes.

The system makes use of a subdivision of space into a 2D grid. This data structure is used to perform efficient occlusion culling on the environment and on the avatars, as well as for the agents' navigation and shadowing.

### Rendering Thousands of Walking People in Real Time

Part of our work is based on the approach of Tecchia et al.[1] In order to minimize geometrical complexity, each human is represented with a single adaptive impostor. Appropriate images for the impostors are selected depending on the viewpoint position and the frame of animation. Current graphics hardware architectures often limit the maximum amount of texture memory that can be used in interactive visualizations, introducing a trade-off between memory usage and quality/variety of the rendering for image based techniques. Our current work boosts the quality of rendering using aggressive optimizations and adding important environmental effects such as shadows. We optimize the in-memory organization of the impostor images, reducing in this way the memory requirements by about three-quarters. The use of hardware-accelerated texture compression introduces an additional 1:4 compression factor. Because of this reorganization, each impostor's image can have an arbitrary size, which depends on the view direction and the frame of animation. At rendering time, the appropriate size and displacement of the impostor are computed on the fly, so as to match those of the sample image.

To enhance the crowd variety without increasing the memory usage, we use a combination of multi-pass rendering and alpha testing. In this way we can selectively address and modulate the base color of different regions on each impostor image using multiple rendering passes. Using the same impostor approach, we compute and display the shadows of the moving humans, by projecting a shadow texture of the human impostor onto the ground plane, with regard to the light direction. Shadow maps need not be regenerated, as they are simply warped versions of the existing impostors; so no additional memory is needed. Finally, a 2D environment shadow discretization is used to determine if humans are in the shade of the buildings. When a human occupies an in-shade cell, its impostor is gradually darkened. This greatly improves the visual realism of the scene.

### Dynamic Culling

When the viewpoint gets closer to the ground, the buildings become very effective occluders. We employ a new occlusion algorithm based on binary tree merging, which uses the discretization and the properties of urban scenes to quickly cull away not only the nonvisible static geometry but also the avatars.

First we build a KD-tree of the scene geometry, using as partitions only planes that coincide with tile edges (given by the 2D grid). Then for each frame we build an occlusion tree from the current viewpoint and merge it with the KD-tree, marking its leaves, and indirectly the tiles, as visible or hidden. Finally, for each avatar, we check the state of the occupied cell before processing the avatar any further.

### Results and Future Work

The system was tested on a PC Pentium 833Mhz with an NVIDIA GeForce GTS2 64 Mb. We populated our environment with a total of 10,000 different humans, walking around a village modeled with 41,260 polygons and performing collision avoidance against the building and between the avatars themselves. At a video resolution of 1152 x 864 pixels, the display is updated on average at 17 frames per second. The results show that the use of impostors produces interactive frame rates for crowded scenes, even on low cost hardware.
www.cs.ucl.ac.uk/staff/Y.Chrysanthou/crowds/sketch/

*References*
1. Tecchia, F. & Chrysanthou, Y. (2000). Real time rendering of densely populated urban environments. In *Rendering Techniques '00* (10th Eurographics Workshop on Rendering), Péroche and Rushmeier, eds., 45-56.

Crowd rendering in real time.

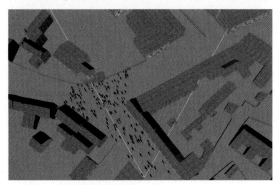

Occlusion culling performed on the crowd.

# Real vs. Approximate Collisions: When Can We Tell the Difference?

*Contact*
**Carol O'Sullivan**
Image Synthesis Group
Trinity College
Dublin, Ireland
Carol.OSullivan@cs.tcd.ie

**John Dingliana**
Image Synthesis Group
Trinity College Dublin

The behaviour of objects in the physical world is described by Newtonian mechanics, using dynamic concepts such as force and mass. However, it has been reported that many people have intuitive preconceptions concerning mechanical events that, although incorrect according to Newtonian mechanics, are highly stable and widespread.[3] Profitt and Gilden showed that people use only one dimension of information when making dynamical judgements.[6] Therefore, when a dynamic event involves more than one dimension of information such as velocity and rotation (i.e. an extended body motion as opposed to a particle which has only one dimension of information), humans are less able to correctly identify anomalous physical behaviour. They also discovered that judgements about collisions were made based on heuristics and that people are influenced by kinematic data, such as velocity after impact and the way that the colliding objects ricochet.[4]

Can we exploit this imprecision of the human brain for the purpose of producing plausible real-time simulations of colliding objects? Earlier work has exploited the plausibility of certain types of approximations for simulation.[1,2] In particular, if less time is spent on processing a collision, under what circumstances will this degradation in accuracy be imperceptible? In this sketch we will present several robust factors that can significantly affect a viewer's perception of a collision and may be used to prioritise collision processing in a perceptually-adaptive system. The effect of these factors was examined in a series of psychophysical experiments.

Causality refers to the ability to detect whether one event causes another.[5] For example, a collision of a moving object with a stationary one will cause the second object to move, whereas a stationary object that starts to move by itself is perceived to be autonomous. We ran an experiment similar to Michotte's famous causality tests and found that adding a time delay between object contact and collision response reduced the perception of causality and thereby the plausibility of the collision event itself. Therefore, we can conclude that constant frame rates are imperative in any real-time collision handling system and hence interruptible collision detection is the only feasible solution for large numbers of complex objects.

Interrupting collision detection before it is complete either leads to interpenetrations, which are usually unacceptable, or more frequently to objects which bounce off each other at a distance. We found that the separation of objects when they collide provides a strong visual impression of an erroneous collision, but that this effect may be ameliorated by factors such as occlusion of the collision points, eccentricity (i.e. peripheral events) and the presence, number, and type of distractors (e.g. visually similar distractors have a stronger masking effect).

We also found that, despite reduced collision detection resolution, it is possible to produce a random collision response that is as believable as the more accurate ones, thus further masking collision anomalies. As Profitt and Gilden found, we conclude that people seem to be capable of correctly perceiving errors in collision response only when there is one salient feature (such as gap size), whereas when the simulation becomes more complex, they rely on their own naïve or common-sense judgements of dynamics, which

are more often than not inaccurate. We are now conducting further experiments, using an eyetracker as shown in Figure 1, to identify the effect of these factors in more complex scenarios with large numbers of colliding entities. We will discuss the results of these experiments also.

*References*
1. Barzel, R., Hughes, J.F., & Wood, D.N. (1996). Plausible motion simulation for computer graphics animation. *Computer Animation and Simulation '96*, 183-197.
2. Chenney, S. & Forsythe, D.A. (2000) Sampling plausible solutions to multi-body constraint problems. In *Proceedings of SIGGRAPH 2000*, 219-228.
3. Clement, J. (1982). Students' preconceptions in introductory mechanics. *American Journal of Physics*, 50. (1), 66-71.
4. Gilden, D. & Profitt, D. (1989). Understanding collision dynamics. *Journal of Experimental Psychology: Human Perception and Performance*, 5. (2), 372-383.
5. Michotte, A. (1963). *The perception of causality*. New York: Basic Books, 1963.
6. Profitt, D. and D. Gilden. (1989). Understanding natural dynamics. *Journal of Experimental Psychology: Human Perception and Performance*, 15. (2), 384-393.

Figure 1. New Experiments using an eye-tracker.

# Real-time Cloth Simulation with Sparse Particles

*Contact*
Masaki Oshita
Kyushu University, Japan
moshita@db.is.kyushu-u.ac.jp

Akifumi Makinouchi
Kyushu University

Physically-based dynamic simulation is a common technique for cloth animation. The clothes are modeled as a combination of mass-distributed particles and elastic forces that work between the particles. Typically between a few thousand and a hundred thousand particles are required to simulate cloth movement. Although many techniques have been developed for fast and robust simulation,[1] dynamic simulation requires too much computational time to animate clothes in real-time.

In this sketch, a novel technique for real-time cloth simulation is presented. The method combines dynamic simulation and geometric techniques. Only a small number of particles (a few hundred) are controlled using dynamic simulation to simulate global cloth behaviors such as waving and bending. The cloth surface is then smoothed based on elastic forces applied to each particle and the distance between each pair of adjacent particles. Using this geometric smoothing, local cloth behaviors such as twists and wrinkles are efficiently simulated (Figure 1).

## Proposed Method

In the proposed method, PN triangles[2] is used to smooth a cloth mesh. This is a smoothing technique that substitutes a three-sided cubic Bézier patch for each triangular face of a mesh. It facilitates control of the smoothing mesh using the normal of the vertices, while other smoothing techniques such as subdivision (e.g. Catmull-Clark) and parametric (e.g. NURBS) surfaces generate a smoothed mesh from the vertices of a simple mesh. In addition, PN triangles ensures that the generated surface matches the original mesh on each vertex.

The cloth surface is smoothed by controlling particle normals and edge length using the PN triangles. Figure 2 illustrates the smoothing method. Figure 2 (a) is the original mesh and (b) is the smoothed surface using PN triangles without normal control. The normal of each particle is computed from the elastic forces that are applied to the particle from the adjacent faces. The elastic forces work so as to make the tangent of the cloth surface parallel with the elastic forces. Therefore we compute the normal direction by balancing the vectors that are orthogonal to the elastic forces – Figure 2 (c). In addition, when the length of an edge is shorter than its original length, the midpoint of the curve is moved so as to maintain the original edge length – Figure 2 (d). As a result, the smoothed surface reflects the elastic forces and maintains surface dimensions.

## Implementation and Results

A particle-based dynamic simulation using the proposed method has been implemented. The proposed method is very simple and is easy to implement and integrate with an existing particle-based system. In terms of dynamic simulation, existing techniques[1] could be used. However, the proposed method efficiently smoothes the cloth surface in response to the distance between adjacent particles by setting low stiffness of the cloth, while standard systems maintain the shape of the cloth by setting high stiffness.

Figure 3 shows a snapshot of the resulting animation. Forty particles of the skirt were controlled using dynamic simulation – Figure 3 (a), and 4,096 triangles used for the smoothed surface – Figure 3 (b). The computational time was approximately 30 milliseconds for each frame of the 30 Hz simulation. As a result, the skirt was animated in real-time. The proposed method has potential for use in computer games, virtual studios, and virtual fashion shows.

*References*
1. Baraff, D. & Witkin, A. (1998). Large steps in cloth simulation. *In Proceedings of SIGGRAPH 98*, 43-54.
2. Vlachos, A., Peters, J., Boyd, C., & Mitchell, J. (2001). Curved PN triangles. *Proceedings of the 2001 ACM Symposium on Interactive 3D Graphics*.

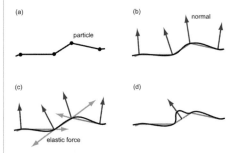

Figure 1. An example of the proposed approach: (a) a small number of particles (25 particles in this case) are controlled using dynamic simulation; (b) the cloth surface is then smoothed using geometrical techniques (2,048 triangles were rendered).

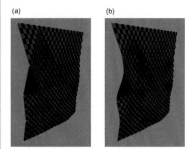

Figure 2. Smoothing method: (a) a section of an original mesh – the middle edge is shortened and the elastic forces are working so as to part the two vertices; (b) the smoothed surface by PN triangles; (c) with normal control; and (d) edge length control.

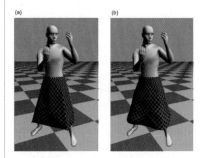

Figure 3. A snapshot from an animation of a skirt: (a) the controlled mesh (40 particles); and (b) the smoothed surface (4,096 triangles).

# Real-Time Computer Graphics for On-Set Visualization: "A.I." and "The Mummy Returns"

Seth Rosenthal
Motion Capture Supervisor

Doug Griffin
Mike Sanders
Motion Capture Engineer
Industrial Light + Magic

One of the basic challenges of directing visual effects shots is imagining the result. The skill of directors can be undermined when they cannot see the elements of a shot on which they typically base their decisions. As a result, effects shots often require extensive iterations during post-production to address aesthetic issues that directors can otherwise handle instinctively and immediately when shooting non-effects shots. For "A.I." and "The Mummy Returns," we used real-time computer graphics and 3D tracking techniques to give the directors the ability to see some of the effects they were directing.

For "A.I.", we assembled a virtual set system on a large blue-screen stage to give Steven Spielberg the ability to compose shots of actors walking and dancing through a futuristic city. For "The Mummy Returns", we used real-time motion capture combined with camera match-moves to visualize Arnold Vosloo's computerized counterpart performs live over clean background plates. Although these projects required different tools, they were motivated by the same basic desire to move key artistic decisions about effects shots back into the realm of live production.

## Artist Application
The Rouge City sequence in "A.I" required actors to perform in a large blue screen stage while the camera framed their action against a nonexistent skyline. The storyboards called for complex compositions of the actors and the synthetic city. For example, in one shot, after a long walking conversation, two characters step up onto a fountain and pause while the camera swings around to frame them alongside action taking place high up on a building façade. They then step off the fountain and stroll off down the boulevard while the camera pulls back to frame them against another dramatic structure. In order to visualize these shots, we assembled a virtual-set system consisting of a real-time camera tracker capable of working over an area approximately 60 feet by 120 feet with a 35 foot ceiling, a real-time blue-screen keyer/compositor, and a computer and software capable of rendering the computer model of our city directly to a video signal. In addition, we integrated this system with the film camera package in use by the "A.I." production, and devised a method for calibrating the virtual camera parameters to match the film lenses.

Our visualization system was used on the "A.I." set for three weeks of principal photography. The remarkable power of this tool was immediately apparent on set. As soon as the system generated a live image, everyone on set who usually relies on the image from the camera to guide his or her work was at home with the system; in spite of its technical complexity, it required no explanation. The system allowed the director to compose elaborate camera moves, make subtle adjustments to the timing and framing of the shots, and to play spontaneously off of the changing composition of the actors and the virtual environments exactly as he would do on a traditional live-action shoot.

## Real-time motion capture for "The Mummy Returns."
As in "The Mummy," a number of shots in this sequel required that the title character, played menacingly by Arnold Vosloo, be represented by a computer generated character. Our work on the first project gave us an appreciation of some of the subtle challenges of directing dramatic performances for motion capture. In particular, we found that with conventional offline motion capture it is difficult to direct dramatic close-up shots in which small variations in posture or attitude can completely alter the composition and feel of a performance. "The Mummy Returns" provided us with the opportunity to address these challenges with a new generation of technology. We used a new real-time optical motion system, the Vicon 8, to track Arnold Vosloo's performance. We composited a low-resolution CG character driven by the real-time data over clean background plates that had been shot earlier in the production. By rendering the CG character through a match-moved camera, we maintained a perspective correct match between the live character and the pre-existing plate.

As in the case of the visualization system for "A.I.," the usefulness of this technique was immediately apparent. The ability to see a live composite of the shot made it possible to direct Arnold Vosloo's performances according to fine decisions about timing and composition and dramatic quality. In post-production, we found that these performances, for the most part, fit neatly into the final shots with little need for adjustments to the structure of the performance, thus allowing animators to concentrate on facial and hand animation.

## Conclusion
We have made a concerted effort to apply real-time tracking, computer graphics, and video technology to the feature film production. Although these projects used different tools to visualize different aspects of the desired shots – the synthetic city for "A.I." and the CG performer for "The Mummy Returns" – they both illustrated the same basic advantages of real-time visualization for feature-film visual effects production: the director gains artistic control over the shot and the post-production artists get an unambiguous representation of the director's vision as a starting point for their work.

*251*

*Contact*
Bert Freudenberg
Institut für Simulation
und Graphik
Otto-von-Guericke-Universität
Magdeburg
Universitätsplatz 2, 39106
Magdeburg, Germany
bert@isg.cs.uni-magdeburg.de

Shading in line drawings is expressed by varying the stroke width or density of strokes covering an object's surface. In their pioneering work, Winkenbach and Salesin introduced the concept of "prioritized stroke textures" to the emerging field of non-photorealistic rendering.[1] Despite the advances in processing power in the years since then, the sheer number of lines to draw prevents this method from running in real time. A real-time approach for hatching was presented by Lake et al,[2] which chooses from a set of textures based on the brightness at vertices, subdividing polygons if necessary. However, the method is very CPU-heavy and requires many polygons.

Our new technique uses per-pixel shading graphics hardware to implement non-photorealistic shading. The texture-combining facilities accessible via OpenGL on NVIDIA GeForce and ATI Radeon cards provide the flexibility necessary to vary the line width or number of strokes per area.

To indicate shading by variable-width hatching, a 3D halftone pattern is created as texture $T$ and compared at every pixel with the target intensity $I$, creating black or white pixels.[3] Halftoning, however, yields unsatisfying results for interactive applications because of the computer screen's limited resolution. To smooth the harsh transition from white to black we instead take the inverted sum of $T$ and $I$ and scale it by some constant $c > 1$. After clamping the result to the range $(0\ldots1)$ we get a mostly black and white output while still preserving a few gray levels (see Figure 1).

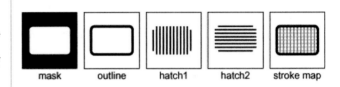

Figure 2. Stroke map construction.

Figure 3. Real-time stroke textures.

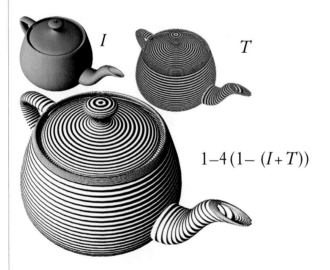

$$1-4\left(1-\left(I+T\right)\right)$$

Figure 1. Lighting-dependend stroke width.

We follow a similar approach with stroke textures. Strokes are drawn on different layers. To facilitate one-pass rendering, all stroke layers are composited into the texture $T$ in a pre-processing step, using a different gray level for each layer (Figure 2). At runtime, all layers needed to visually approximate the intensity $I$ are selected for drawing, employing the same combiner operations as introduced above (see Figure 3).

There are many ways to extend the basic idea of stroke map shading. Lightmaps can be used to vary the amount of detail drawn on a surface. With bump maps, individual strokes can be made sensitive to lighting. Shadows can be rendered in additional passes. We are working on integrating all these into our interactive line drawings.

Our method does not require any additional CPU work at runtime. The configurability or even programmability of recent graphics hardware is a very powerful device to achieve non-standard looks. We are looking forward to seeing more visually rich interactive rendering styles emerge in the future.

*References*
1. Winkenbach, G. & Salesin, D.H. (1994). Computer-generated pen-and-ink illustration. In *Proceedings. SIGGRAPH 94*, 91-100.
2. Lake, A., Marshall, C., Harris, M., & Blackstein, M. (2000). Stylized rendering techniques for scalable real-time 3D animation. In *Proceedings NPAR 2000*, 13-20.
3. Haeberli, P. & Segal, M. (1993). Texture mapping as a fundamental drawing primitive. In *Fourth Eurographics Workshop on Rendering*, 259-266.

*252*

# Rendering by Manifold Hopping

*Contact*
HEUNG-YEUNG SHUM
Microsoft Research, China
hshum@microsoft.com

LIFENG WANG
Microsoft Research, China

JIN-XIANG CHAI
Carnegie Mellon University

## Introduction

IBR in general simulates a continuous range of camera viewpoints from a discrete set of input images. Much of the work on IBR has depended on view interpolation, which is however a difficult task because feature correspondence needs to be known. Many IBR techniques are therefore proposed to make use of a large collection of images to avoid the correspondence. The minimum number of images needed was studied recently.[1] In this sketch, we propose a novel IBR rendering technique called manifold hopping, which breaks the Nyquist limit for perfect light field reconstruction[1] by taking human perception into account. Specifically, our technique provides users with perceptually continuous navigation by using a small number of strategically sampled manifold mosaics or multi-perspective panoramas.

## Basic Ideas

Manifold hopping has two modes of navigation: moving continuously along any manifold, and discretely across manifolds. Figures (a) and (b) show these two modes of navigation using concentric mosaics.[3] A user can move continuously along any of the circles as shown in Figure (a), while the arrows in (b) indicate that the user can only hop to the viewpoints on the circle, but not stop anywhere in between. To render a novel view, we locally warp[2] the concentric mosaic where the viewpoint is located. Because we do not know the accurate scene depth and use the constant depth assumption for warping, the rendering error is inevitable. However, local warping does not introduce any structural errors such as double images, which are common for view interpolation without accurate correspondence. Moreover, the geometric distortion introduced by warping can be tolerated by human visual perception when the field of view of the rendered image is small (e.g., below 40°).

Moving discretely along the radial direction can be made perceptually smooth if the interval can be set reasonably small. A key observation is that there exists a critical hopping interval for users to perceive a smooth navigation. In other words, manifold hopping provides users with perceived continuous camera movement, without continuously rendering viewpoints using infinitesimal steps. As a result, manifold hopping significantly reduces the input data size without accurate depth information or correspondence.

Using the signed Hough ray space, we carried out the detailed analysis of manifold hopping to address two important questions: First, what is the largest field of view that still produces acceptable local warping error? Second, how large can the hopping interval be so that continuous motion can be perceived?

## Results and Future Work

Using a Sony DV camera, a total of 5726 frames of resolution 720 x 576 are captured for a full circle. Instead of using 720 rebinned concentric mosaics of size 5726 x 576, we select only a small subset of resampled concentric mosaics. To further reduce the amount of data used in manifold hopping, we can resize the original concentric mosaics. As shown in Figures (c) and (d), two images with low resolution 184 x 144 are rendered from 11 resized smaller concentric mosaics which are compressed with a predictive coding compression algorithm. All the 11 concentric mosaics are com-

pressed to only 88k with a compression ratio 78. An important future direction would be to conduct a more comprehensive study on the psychophysics of visualization for our technique. We also plan to extend manifold hopping to other kinds of manifold mosaics than concentric mosaics.

*References*
1. Chai, J.-X., Tong, X., Chan, S.-C. & Shum, H.-Y. (2000). Plenotpic sampling. In *Proceedings SIGGRAPH 2000*, 307-318.
2. Mark, W., McMillan, L., & Bishop, G. (1997). Post-rendering 3D warping. In *Proceedings Symposium I3D*, 7-16.
3. Shum, H.-Y. & He, L.-W. (1999). Rendering with concentric mosaics. In *Proceedings SIGGRAPH 99*, 299-306.

(a)

(b)

(c)

(d)

253

# Rendering "Pepe" with Global Illumination

*Contact*
Marcos Fajardo
Institute for Creative
Technologies
University of Southern California
13274 Fiji Way
Marina del Rey, California 90292
USA
fajardo@ict.usc.edu

This animation sketch focuses on lighting and rendering aspects of the animation short by Daniel Martinez Lara, featuring his Pepe digital puppet and rendered using an early version of our custom Monte Carlo ray tracing system, code-named Arnold. The short is 100-percent CG and achieves a realistic hand-held-video-camera look through the use of believable camera motion and zoom, scanned textures, exquisite character animation, and high-quality soft shadows and inter-reflections in a daylight setting.

With a traditional scanline-based renderer, the artist would have to painfully and skillfully position fill lights to mimic the soft effects of sky and bounce light. Our Monte Carlo-based renderer offers a much simpler approach. By specifying a direction and intensity for the sun (a standard CG directional light), and the color and intensity of the sky (uniform background radiance), we let the renderer automatically compute the subtle bounce light and soft shadow effects. Since the characters walk, jump, and interact with the environment, the illumination cannot be stored in advance and is in fact calculated for every pixel, for every frame. Thus, we get extraordinarily high-quality dynamic lighting effects with subpixel accuracy, at the expense of slower rendering times. We are in effect trading manual scene set-up time, which requires valuable human resources and skills, for CPU rendering time, which requires comparatively cheaper hardware resources, while achieving a unique, natural look. In particular, moving soft shadows and contact shadows are extremely accurate and contribute greatly to the overall sense of realism.

It is important for the artist to have quick feedback from the renderer, where it responds immediately to arbitrary changes in geometry, materials, or lighting. We achieved acceptable feedback by rendering in two stages. In the first stage, the renderer uses a single sample per pixel, providing a useful rough (noisy) version of the image in a small fraction of the total render time. In a second stage, each pixel is super-sampled and the image is progressively "cleaned." There is no meshing or radiosity pre-processing. The user can also interactively select a small region in the image and quickly render those pixels only. This immediate access to any pixel in the image proved invaluable in production of the animation.

Another important factor was the ability to render very dense triangle meshes with little increase in rendering time, thus letting the artist use very finely subdivided characters, on the order of 100,000 triangles each. Finite-element global illumination renderers would have a very hard time in this character animation environment. Any gathering Monte Carlo renderer will have some difficulty with concentrated sources of illumination due to occlusion, like a room with a small window to the sky. In order to further reduce rendering times, a favorable scene setup was created, where we removed the roof of the room and also the back walls. This helped sky light fill in the scene. Final render times were around 10 minutes per frame on a dual Pentium III 500MHz machine with 256 MB of RAM, at a resolution of 320 x 240 pixels. The scene contains over 600,000 triangles in total. Around 3,000 frames were distributed across a network of machines.

## Key Credits

*Animation*
Daniel Martinez Lara, Carlos Fernandez Puertolas

*Additional animation*
Kike Oliva

*Custom programming*
Gonzalo Rueda

*Core rendering software*
Marcos Fajardo

See also: www.pepeland.com

254

*Contact*
SCOTT SINGER
Visual Effects Animator
PDI/DreamWorks

PDI/DreamWorks' computer graphics animated film, "Shrek," required that a technique be developed to create realistic tubes that appeared to be made of mud. This sketch describes the approach used to render the deforming semi-solid mud objects without making them look like stretchy rubber sacks.

The shot called for several mud tubes to be pushed out of a hollow log and appear to be very gross; the effect was ultimately referred to as "mud poop." The direction called for each mud tube to deform and stretch for comedic effect. Early tests using traditional texture mapping always made the tubes look like stretchy, painted rubber sacks, and the approach was abandoned early on. What was clear was that in order to make the effect work, we would need a way of rendering surface detail which would not stretch with surface area changes. Instead, the surface detail needed to appear to separate, combine, and shift in response to changes in the underlying geometry.

We needed to find the right kind of renderable primitive and a method for applying it to the surface of the poop geometry. We also had to figure out how to handle surface detail that would necessarily be revealed as the surface details separated. After experimenting with instanced geometry, we settled on particles. They provided us the right level of directability with the right level of spatial ambiguity. Particles brought with them their own set of difficulties, chief among them being motion blur and specularity.

Separation was handled by having a sub-strata of particles below the rendered surface which would be revealed by the surface particles as they were moved apart by the stretching parent geometry.

255

# RitSens - Computer Aided System for Studying Rhythmic Abilities in Bimanual Coordination

*Contact*

**Artemis Moroni**
Instituto Nacional de Tecnologia
da Informação
Rod. D. Pedro I, km 143,6
13089-500, Campinas, Brazil
Artemis.Moroni@iti.br

**Alaide P. Mammana**
Instituto Nacional de Tecnologia
da Informação

**Luis Teixeira**
Escola de Educação Física e
Esportes
Universidade de São Paulo

## Introduction

The integration of several sources of sensorial information (stimuli) and the production of motor responses involving coordination is a necessary function in several daily situations. Nowadays, a great effort is devoted to understanding which mechanisms are responsible for driving the movements and which processes occur in their learning. In particular, the study of rhythmic ability in bimanual coordination is becoming the object of intense research, in order to determine the space and time patterns that characterize the movement, and to understand the basic principles and mechanisms that are guiding the system to present specific coordination patterns. But, these investigations require the development of special methods and techniques. Computer systems are very attractive for this usage due to their capabilities for the processing, storage, and exhibition of information, if they can be used with special devices that detect the response of both hands in real time. To be largely accessible for institutions and individuals, these peripherals must be simple, dispensing previous training; versatile, for using with different computers and programs; comfortable, safe, and cheap.

Since these peripherals are not available, we developed a transparent and resistive tablet[1] that can operate with two pointers, one for each hand. The tablet can be fixed directly on the computer video screen or can be operated on a common table. It can also be used with one pointer, as a precision digital table, a light-pen, a mouse, or a special keyboard. In short, the tablet architecture was conceived so that it may be connected to any equipment with an RS232 serial interface, which makes the software development very easy. Many applications were demonstrated as an alternative and augmentative communication with patients with language limitations, and in literacy and pre-literacy of children with brain paralysis.

Besides the device driver software, the development included the software for the specific application in the rhythmic ability investigation in bimanual coordination. In this sketch, we present RitSens, an improved application specially designed for investigation of rhythmic abilities in bimanual coordination.

## RitSens

RitSens produces static and dynamic, visual and aural stimuli, allowing the determination of the spatial and temporal right and left hand responses. The screen must be touched by the individual in response to these visual or aural stimuli.

Figure 1. Tablet with two pointers being used with a head mounted display.

Four signals, two aural and two visual, may be independently produced, with programmed duration and frequency. These stimuli may also be produced in a synchronized way, with relations among them, i.e., two for one, etc., between an aural and a visual signal. The visual stimuli consist of targets with shape, size, distance, orientation, and colors that can be defined at each test and presented in the video screen. The use of a head mounted display to present the visual and aural stimuli has the advantage of producing a complete immersion in the sensorial environment.

The preliminary version worked with the common sound library available in the computer,[2] but in this last version a MIDI driver was added so that any MIDI file can be read and played. The system allows the determination of the initial and final time for the visual and aural stimuli as well as the user response time. For each response, the time and the x and y coordinates of the touch are registered, both for the right and the left hand. In this way, the temporal and spatial patterns produced by the user may be analyzed.

In order to study the rhythmic learning and memorizing, the stimuli may be presented and removed, but continue to serve as a temporal reference to the user response pattern. The system operates with a set of commands that allows a great flexibility in the creation of the essay's storyboard without previous programming language. The operation with a MIDI library opens the possibility that the transparent tablet be used as a musical keyboard, applied on the video screen. More than that, it can be used with Vox Populi,[3] which is a composition system that uses line drawings as fitness functions in an evolutionary computation approach for algorithmic composition.

## Acknowledgements

The results obtained with the transparent tablet were due to the great engagement and dedication of M. A. Schreiner and M. R. R. M. Gobbo in its development. The programming and presentation of the visual and aural stimuli were founded in the extensive research which Professor A. M. Pellegrini developed in motor coordination studies, with C. Y. Hiraga. RitSens' functions were programmed by C. K. Moritani. M. A. Schreiner, M. R. R. M. Gobbo and C. K. Moritani are members of Laboratório de Mostradores de Informação, Instituto Nacional de Tecnologia da Informação. Prof. A. M. Pellegrini and C. Y. Hiraga are members of LABORDAM, Departamento de Educação Física, Instituto de Biociências, Universidade Estadual Paulista.

*References*
1. Schreiner, M.A., Sánchez, C.A., Gobbo, M.R.R.M. & Mammana, A.P. (2000). *with Tablete inteligente a filme fino transparente-Iberdiscap 2000*, Madrid, 353.
2. Mammana, A.P., Schreiner, M.A., Ferreira, D.V,. Bohorqueze, J.C., & Garcia, A. (1999). In *Mobilidade e Comunicação - Desafios à Tecnologia e à Inclusão Social*, A.A.F. Quevedo, J.R. Oliveira, M.T.E. Mantoan, eds. Unicamp, 1999, 255.
3. Teixeira, L.A., Pellegrini, A.N, Hiraga, C.Y., Schreiner, M.A., Sánchez, C.A., Gobbo, M.R.R.M. & Mammana, A.P. *Actas del 3er de Comunicación Alternativa y aumentativa y 1er de Tecnologias de Apoyo para la Discapacidad - Iberdiscap 2000*, Madrid, October, 2000, 77.
4. Moroni, A., Manzolli, J., Von Zuben, F., and Gudwin, R. (2000). Vox Populi. *Leonardo Music Journal*, Vol. 10, 49-54.

# Shadermaps: A Method for Accelerating Procedural Shading

Thouis R. Jones
Ronald N. Perry
Michael Callahan
MERL

## Introduction

Procedural shading[1] has proven to be an indispensable tool in computer generated animations. Procedural shading's primary benefit is its flexibility, since shaders can be arbitrarily complex in their actions. This flexibility has its price: it can take hours or days to render a single frame for a studio animation.

Shadermaps are a new method for accelerating procedural shading, driven by two observations. First, objects tend to have intrinsic appearances (e.g., the grain in a wooden figurine) that are static from frame to frame. Second, the intrinsic appearance of an object is usually responsible for most of its complexity and rendering cost. Shadermaps accelerate shaders by exploiting this static complexity. Shaders are separated into static and dynamic phases, and the former's output is stored and reused from frame to frame.

## Algorithm

We define the static phase of a shader as the part depending only on static appearance parameters, and the dynamic phase as everything else. Since the static phase's computations depend only on static parameters, one can reuse those computations between frames. In our algorithm, the static phase's output is generated at multiple resolutions and stored in a shadermap, a mipmap of intermediate computations. These intermediate computations are a "snapshot" of the interface between the static and dynamic phases at points on the surface. For each frame, it is possible to reconstruct the intermediate computation on the surface from the shadermap. This reconstruction warps the shadermap to screen space, analogous to texture mapping, using a high quality anisotropic filter.[2] The dynamic phase uses this reconstruction to complete the shader calculation and produce the final color. Since the warp is usually much less expensive than an evaluation of the static phase, the reuse of static computations results in a significant acceleration of the shading calculation.

A benefit of procedural shading is resolution independence; a shader can have detail at a wide range of scales. Generating shadermap data at all scales would be wasteful, since in any single frame the dynamic phase requires only part of the shadermap. To avoid unnecessary computation, the shadermap is generated on demand. If the anisotropic filter operation requires data that has not been created, the static phase is invoked to produce the needed data, and the result stored in the shadermap. To reduce overhead, shadermaps are stored in a sparse mipmap made up of tiles, and an entire tile is generated when that tile is first accessed. Since a shadermap is stored at several resolutions, it is similar to a mipmap. Unlike mipmaps, however, the data is generated by a procedure, rather than by filtering a high-resolution image.

## Results

One of the factors controlling the acceleration from shadermaps is reuse of shadermap data, which we measure as the ratio of the number dynamic phase evaluations to the number of static phase evaluations. A ratio of 10:1 means that for every ten evaluations of the dynamic phase, the static phase is evaluated only once. This ratio does not depend on the particular shader applied to a surface, but rather on the geometry and parameterization of the surface and the directions from which it is rendered. We have tested several animations and found good ratios, usually around 15:1, or about 95% reuse.

See www.merl.com/reports/TR2000-25

### References

1. Apodaca, Anthony A., & Gritz, L. (2000). *Advanced RenderMan*. Morgan Kaufmann, 2000.
2. McCormack, J., Perry, R., Farkas, K., & Jouppi, N. Feline: fast elliptical lines for anisotropic texture mapping. In *Proceedings of SIGGRAPH 99*, 243-250.

Two images generated with shadermaps.

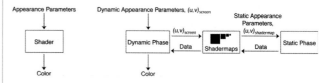

Figure 1. Dataflow diagrams for a traditional shader and a shader using shadermaps. On the right, the shader has been separated into its dynamic and static phases. The shadermap is similar to a cache between the two phases.

# Simulation Fidelity Metrics for Virtual Environments Based on Memory Semantics

*Contact*

Katerina Mania
School of Engineering and
Information Technology
University of Sussex
United Kingdom
k.mania@sussex.ac.uk

Alan Chalmers
University of Bristol
United Kingdom

Tom Troscianko
University of Sussex
United Kingdom

Rycharde Hawkes
Hewlett Packard Laboratories
Bristol, United Kingdom

A photorealistic, computer-generated interactive environment strives to achieve the same sense of space as in the real world. Subjective measures based on human spatial perception supplementary to accurate geometry, illumination, and task performance, reveal the actual cognitive mechanisms in the perception of a virtual environment that are not otherwise apparent.[2] In this sketch, we present a methodology for the assessment of simulation fidelity of virtual environments (VEs), centred on a validated theory of memory awareness states.[1] It is challenging to identify whether VE simulations, displayed on head mounted displays (HMDs) and related interaction interfaces have an effect on the actual mental processes participants employ in order to achieve a spatial memory task in a VE, compared to reality and more traditional displays.

One-hundred-and-five participants were involved in a study which investigates participants' accurate memory recall and awareness states of elements and objects in a VE replica of a real-world room displayed on a typical desktop monitor or on a HMD (mono, stereo, head-tracked, or non-head tracked). Each memory recall question included a choice between four awareness states for each object recall. Traditional memory research has established that "remember" and "know" are two subjective states of awareness linked with memory recollections. Some elements of a visual space may be "remembered" if they are linked to a specific mental image; alternatively, the information could be semantically (non-visually) recalled – in this case, it is said to be "known." Remembering refers to experiences of the past that are recreated with the awareness of re-living them mentally. Knowing refers to those in which there is no awareness of re-living any experiences. What has been experienced recently, although this recent occurrence can not be recalled, could feel "familiar." Also, recall could be reported as a "guess."

The radiosity rendering of the room was based on photometry data acquired in the real space. The resultant space memory recall and cognitive states as well as participants sense of presence is compared with that obtained from an analogous experiment in the actual physical space. The extent to which judgements of memory recall, memory awareness states and presence in the physical and VE are similar provides a measure for the fidelity of the simulation in question.

Overall, the level of presence was higher for the real condition compared to the HMD and desktop conditions. Across the technological conditions, presence and memory recall were, due to the high quality of the rendering, similar. Results show that the navigation method (head movements vs mouse) has an effect on the cognitive strategy adopted and therefore on the type of mental representation of the scene. In particular, the proportion of accurate responses under the "remember" state was significantly higher for the HMD-monocular-mouse condition compared with the HMD, mono and stereo head-tacked conditions. These responses revealed a weaker mnemonics strategy based on recollections of words for this particular condition, expressed by the lower proportion of correct responses under the "know" awareness state.

A VE system is likely to involve navigation in a synthetic space. Does the higher proportion of correct "remember" responses for the HMD-mono-mouse make this condition more "realistic?" The cognitive strategy is proven to be affected by the degree of realism of the motor response. The utilisation of a novel viewing method (HMD) plus a unreal motor response, such as the mouse, stopped the participants using this mnemonic – "unreal" – strategy and resulted in a more natural distribution of remember-know responses than even the real scene. By decreasing the degree of "reality" of the motor response, participants paradoxically adopt a more natural strategy. Something less "real," thus, but more demanding because of its novelty, may restore a more naturalistic cognitive strategy. By employing methodologies that have been examined and validated through decades of experimentation as the memory awareness states methodology, computer graphics research and VE technologies get closer to actually exploiting the human perceptual mechanisms towards successful applications.

## Acknowledgements
This research is funded by Hewlett Packard Laboratories External Research Program.

*References*
1. Gardiner, J.M. (2000). Remembering and knowing. In *Oxford Handbook on Memory*, E. Tulving and F .I. M. Craik, eds. Oxford: Oxford University Press, 2000.
2. Mania, K. & Chalmers, A. (2001). The effects of levels of immersion on presence and memory. *Cyberpsychology and Behavior Journal*, issue 4.2.

Figure 1. Real and VE.

# Simulation of Deforming Elastic Solids in Contact

*Contact*
Gentaro Hirota
Department of Computer Science
University of North Carolina at Chapel Hill
hirota@cs.unc.edu

Susan Fisher
Andrei State
Henry Fuchs
Department of Computer Science
University of North Carolina at Chapel Hill

Chris Lee
Health Sciences Center
University of Colorado

In the simulation of human and animal bodies, complicated mechanical contact between nonlinearly viscoelastic tissues imposes a challenging numerical problem. The definition of the reaction forces that act on the interface (contact forces) is the key for designing a reliable contact handling algorithm. Traditional methods pay little attention to the continuity of contact forces as a function of deformation, which leads to a poor convergence characteristic. This convergence problem becomes especially serious in simulation scenarios that involve complicated self-contacting surfaces such as folding skin.

We introduce a novel penalty finite element formulation based on the concept of material depth, the distance between a particle inside an object and the object's boundary in a reference configuration. By linearly interpolating pre-computed material depths at node points of a finite element mesh, contact forces can be analytically integrated over contacting regions without raising computational cost. The continuity achieved by this formulation enables an efficient and reliable solution of the nonlinear system. This algorithm is implemented as a part of our implicit finite element program for dynamic, quasistatic, and static analysis of nonlinear viscoelastic solids. High nonlinearity and anisotropy, typically observed in biological materials, are also supported.

## Toward Automatic, Realistic Human Motion from 3D Scans

To demonstrate the effectiveness of our method, we simulated flexion of a human knee joint. A finite element leg model with 40,000 tetrahedral elements was built based on the visible human male (Figure 1). Most of the boundaries between the various components are treated as frictionless interfaces. Various material parameters are assigned to tetrahedral elements in order to approximate the mechanical properties of different tissues. The femur is fixed in space. The cross section of the thigh is constrained on the cutting plane. The tibia is rotated 150-degree around an axis in the knee joint.

As shown in Figures 2 through 5, realistic effects such as skin fold and sliding contacts of tissues were obtained. To our knowledge, this is the first demonstrated simulation of large-scale motion of a complex model derived from the widely used visible human dataset and encompassing multiple tissue types including bone, muscle, tendons, and skin.

For more information: www.cs.unc.edu/~us/fem/

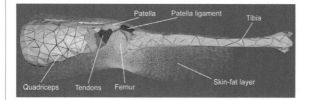

Figure 1. Constituent parts of the leg model derived from the Visible Human dataset.

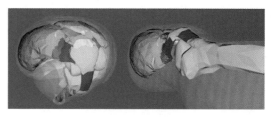

Figure 2. Knee in bent position (left) and stretched (initial) position (right). Note that the patella slides over the head of the femur.

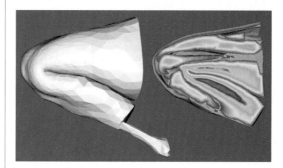

Figure 3. Skin surface of highly flexed knee (left), cut-away view of the same flexed knee (right). Only parts of the tibia and femur are visible in the cut-away since they are partly in front or behind the cutting plane. Note natural looking sliding contact between skin areas, skin and bones/muscles, patella and femur. The complex self-contact of folding skin was handled without revealing visible penetration. Pseudocolor encodes the value of material depth.

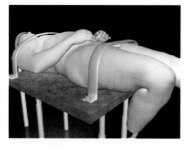

Figure 4. Visible Human dataset with flexed knee.

Figure 5. Close-up of the knee, illustrating the shape of skin folds.

# SIMULTANEOUS MODEL ASSEMBLY IN REAL AND VIRTUAL SPACES

*Contact*
ECKHARD MEIER
GMD - German National
Research Center for Information
Technology
Schloss Birlinghoven
D-53754 Sankt Augustin
Germany
eckhard.meier@gmd.de

This sketch presents an application for the assembly of complex static models by using elements of a construction kit. Based on the Real Reality approach,[1] models are created in physical and virtual space simultaneously. By tracking the user's hand movements, the system generates a virtual reproduction of the original construction. In addition to the management of discrete model components, the system performs an analysis of the existing scenery. The spatial layout of individual building blocks is interpreted in such a way that adjacent elements are combined to interconnected units. The application's primary objective is to transfer the substantial behavior of physical building blocks to their virtual counterpart and to ensure extensive conformity of the real and virtual scene.

## CONNECTIVITY

A construction kit is a set of building blocks following a consistent combinational principle. An application that aims at the reproduction of a physical construction kit's methodology has to reproduce the connecting behavior of each building block in order to prevent restrictions of the element's connecting properties on a structural level. The prototype specifically is designed to handle construction kits that are based on plug connections. For this purpose, the basic geometrical representation of physical building blocks is extended by joint structures. Joints dynamically establish links of building blocks during the term of assembly and store this information internally.

In addition, a joint structure defines a set-up for valid building block connections. The determination of valid links fundamentally relies on the path of movement of building blocks, since only this real world information is tracked by the application. To validate potential links, the system compares correlations among joints of adjacent elements and the direction of movement (DoM). Joints only become linked if their predefined direction of connection vectors (DoC) point in opposite directions and essentially lie in parallel to the DoM vector. Robustness is added to this approach by a tolerance vector perpendicular to the DoC vector. Its purpose is to eliminate discrepancies due to tracking data inaccuracies. A cone spanned by the tolerance and DoC vector is used to validate deviations of the DoC and DoM vectors to make a joint become connectable. Furthermore, the tolerance and DoC vectors dimension a cylindrical region, which is used to determine connectable target joints.

## ASSEMBLY

Model assembly is an interactive and dynamic process that has to be reproduced by the application in real time. The application's main task within that process is to recognize modifications of the physical model and to map each alteration to its virtual counterpart. For this task, the in-betweens of each model state are of vital importance, since these time-frames decide about structural alterations of a model. Consequently, it requires the system to perform a precise analysis of each modification period in order to reproduce physical model iterations correctly. Each iteration can be subdivided into three sub-phases:

The first phase is the grasping phase that marks the beginning of a model alteration. A user automatically initiates it by grasping a building block. This action notifies the system that the block is taken off the model and will be rearranged. The system starts tracking the user's hand movements and revokes each disconnectable joint in dependency on the brick's motion. This separation process will subdivide the original model into a number of autonomous model subsets. The grasping phase directly terminates with model disassembly completion.

The second phase is the moving phase that lasts as long as the user keeps holding the grabbed model. Within this period the grabbed model's position continuously changes. The system's main task is to constantly track the user's hand movements, to determine the actual DoM vector and to update the spatial arrangement of the virtual models. In a following step all potentially connectable joints of the grabbed model and corresponding targets of immobile models are determined in dependency on the DoM vector. Performing this preselection is of vital importance, since the termination of the moving phase by releasing the grabbed model is in the total control of the user, and in consequence cannot be predicted by the system. Thus it is important to predetermine all relevant information for the subsequent assembly operation that depends on the grabbed model's motion.

The third phase is the release phase that realizes the reconnection of the grabbed model to the stationary models of the scene. This process does not have a real world complement due to the fact that the physical model is immediately in a valid static configuration. In contrast, this situation has to be accomplished explicitly in the simulation. Since the formerly grabbed model is still is an independent entity, it has to be integrated into the topological structure of the overall construction by linking all connectable joints. The completion of the release phase results in a consistent model scenario that graphically and structurally represents the physical model set-up adequately.

*Reference*
1.  Brauer, V. & Bruns, W. Bridging the gap between real and virtual modeling: a new approach to human-computer interaction. In *Proceedings of IFIP 5.10 Workshop on Virtual Prototyping,* May 1996.

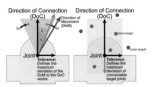

Figure 1. Graphical represenation of a joint structure.

Figures 2 and 3. Synchronized real and virtual model.

BILL BRODY
Arctic Region
Supercomputing Center
University of Alaska, Fairbanks

CHRIS HARTMAN
GLENN G. CHAPPELL
Arctic Region
Supercomputing Center

We have developed a method for turning our gestures into tangible reality. Eventually we hope for an interaction with computers unmediated by wires and clunky hardware, an interaction where the user can focus on the task at hand rather than the tool being used. One step on the path toward achieving this vision is our development of a way to create artistic forms in space. When we sketch, we energize space as we turn the moving position of our hand and the dynamics of our body as recorded by a wand into fields of potential. Then we go from potential energy to the creation of a mesh that meets the rigorous demands of the stereo lithography file format in order to produce an object that can be built into a tangible form.

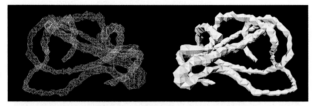

Example of an object created in BLUI and realized with rapid prototyping.

Our interface is BLUI, the Body Language User Interface. BLUI is a work in progress, a virtual reality 3D object creation and editing application that runs in the CAVE environment. One component of BLUI is our implementation of volume sketching that divides space into a cubical grid of cells. These cells are filled with potential energy dependent on the locus and dynamic character of how an artist draws in space. A surface is generated from this set of potential energy loci, translated into a stereo lithography file, and is then passed to a 3D printer for output as a solid object.

A video of an artist at work in our environment will show the body language that is a significant determinant to the character of the generated forms. The dynamic history of each developing form is reflected in the thickness, smoothness, and color of the virtual reality display. Our discussion will include the technical details involved in painting with potentials and creating isosurface meshes. We will also show a flyby of the scene; the viewpoint path and look at path are drawn using BLUI.

An elaboration of our development and implementation of a virtual reality drawing application on the way toward a body-centered user interface will explain and provide a context for the following items:

- Video of the artist at work. The relationship between the artist's body language and the scene will become apparent.

- Video recording of one channel (right-eye view) of the display.
  This will show the creation-editing history of an object.

- Tangible 3D objects sketched in BLUI and built in a rapid prototyping printer will complete the demonstration.

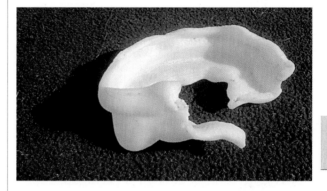

261

Example of a mesh suitable for rapid prototyping that was drawn in space.

# Skinning Cats and Dogs Using Muscle Deformations

*Contact*
Hans Rijpkema
Rhythm & Hues Studios
Los Angeles, California
hans@rhythm.com

Brian J. Green
Rhythm & Hues Studios

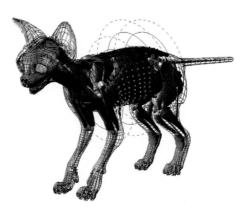

## Introduction

This sketch describes the techniques used for deforming animal models of cats and dogs. The process is anatomical in nature, using a rigid skeleton upon which muscles are placed. The deformations of the muscles are driven by the animation of the skeleton and in turn used to drive the deformation of a skin model. The process is entirely interactive, and the artist is given numerous controls to alter the output of the simulation.

## Muscle Attachment

Since the skeleton motion is the driving force for the muscle motion, extra attention is paid during the character setup phase to ensure that the skeleton will behave in a physiologically sound manner. Muscles are then attached to the bones of the skeleton. When the skeleton is moved, attachment points may change position relative to each other. This motion causes the muscles to either stretch or bulge in order to maintain volume. The artist is given various controls to shape the muscles, such as tendon lengths and muscle volume. Since volume preservation plays a key role in muscle deformation, the artist is given controls to specify the total volume and the volume distribution of each muscle.

## Muscle Models

To more accurately simulate the diverse behavior of real muscles, our software provides several muscle models. A ball muscle is ellipsoidal in shape and is useful for modeling such muscles as the biceps. A tube muscle is a surface created by interpolating two elliptical discs normal to a spline. By defining interior points for the spline, the artist can freely shape the muscle around the skeleton. The tube muscle is useful for modeling such muscles as the pectorals. In addition to ball and tube muscle, we have several other muscle models with more specialized purposes.

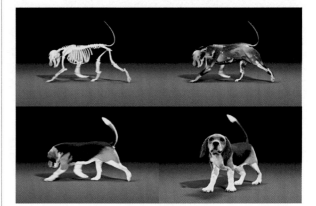

## Skin Binding and Relaxation

Once we have placed the appropriate muscles on the skeleton, we use them to deform the skin model. The essential concept is to associate each vertex of the skin with surface points of nearby muscles. The primary factor to determine the amount of influence a muscle has on a skin vertex is distance: the closer the muscle the greater the effect. The binding process need only be performed once, at a neutral pose.

We allow multiple muscles to affect a single vertex. The resulting deformation is a weighted average of each contributing muscle's deformation. This reduces hard edges at muscle influence boundaries at the cost of increased computational complexity. The artist is given various controls to alter distance weighting and attenuation. In practice we found the use of such controls reduced the need to model large numbers of muscles and also allowed us to move the animal into extreme poses.

After the skin has been deformed by the muscles we must "relax" the skin. Distances between vertices need to remain similar between the neutral pose and the deformed positions. A dynamic relaxation algorithm is applied to the skin for this purpose. During the relaxation, we also perform collision detection with simplified bone geometry to simulate the rolling of skin over bone. As with the deformation process, the artist is provided with controls that can fine tune this process.

# Solving a 3D Cube Puzzle in a Collaborative Virtual Environment: As Good as Really Being There Together?

*Contact*

**Anthony Steed**
Department of Computer Science
University College London
London, United Kingdom
A.Steed@cs.ucl.ac.uk

**Ralph Schroeder**
**Ann-Sofie Axelsson**
**Alexander Nilsson**
**Ilona Heldal**
Department of Technology
and Society
Chalmers University
Göteburg, Sweden

**Josef Wideström**
Chalmers Medialab
Chalmers University
Göteborg, Sweden

**Åsa Abelin**
Department of Linguistics
Göteborg University
Göteburg, Sweden

Immersive projection technology (IPT) installations are proliferating around the world and increasingly they are being used in networked situations where users collaborate in a shared virtual environment. In these preliminary studies we investigated the ability of pairs of users to collaborate on a simple puzzle-solving task. We found that pairs of users who are both immersed in IPTs can perform almost as well as when they do the same task in the real world. But we also found that collaboration can be problematic when participants are using very different systems such as an IPT and a desktop.

## Trial Settings

We compared performance and experience in solving a 3D cube puzzle between three conditions: two participants in real space (R condition), two participants in different IPTs (C2C condition), and one participant in an IPT and one on a desktop system (C2D condition). The participants in the R condition performed the task with real blocks. In the C2C condition we used a Tan VR-CUBE at Chalmers University and a Trimension ReaCToR at University College London. In the C2D condition we used the Chalmers Tan VR-CUBE and a SGI O2 workstation. The non-immersed participant used a mouse and keyboard to move and interact with the cube puzzle. The participants did not know what type of system their partner was using. The C2D condition was implemented in dVISE (now renamed DIVISION, www.ptc.com/products/division). For the C2C condition the environment was precisely replicated on the DIVE platform (www.sics.se/dive). Figure 1 shows a pair of immersed participants in the C2C condition at various stages of the task.

## Performance and Findings

The R condition is a standard that we did not expect to be bettered in a simple collaborative virtual environment. Figure 2 shows the percentage of pairs that completed the task for each condition. Twenty-two pairs did each condition. Note that users were stopped after 20 minutes if they had not completed the task. The mean completion times were: R condition 5.75 minutes; C2C 8.82 minutes; and C2D 15 minutes.

In the C2C condition interaction between the two participants was very fluid, and in our opinion collaboration was much more successful than any of our previous experiences with similar systems or applications. In the C2D condition confusion seemed to arise between the participants because they did not comprehend how the other participant interacted with the world and the limitations that the other's interface might impose. Consequently we observed IPT users becoming frustrated with the slow performance of the non-immersed user and in post-trial questionnaires and interviews they rated the desktop user as contributing considerably less to the task or even being uncooperative.

## Conclusions

Performance on the puzzle-solving task using IPTs was almost as good as performance on the task in real space. However collaboration and performance were very poor when one user was immersed and one user was not. We hypothesize, based on our observation and participant feedback, that this is not simply due to the effect of the non-immersed participant's poorer interface, but that a secondary factor is the confusion between the users about what the other is capable of. Further study is required to understand how to better support collaboration between virtual environment systems with such dissimilar interfaces.

Figure 1. Two participants completing the 3D cube puzzle.

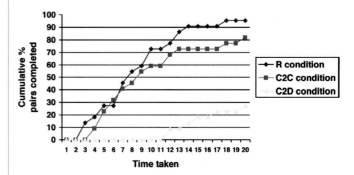

Figure 2. Cumulative percentage of pairs of participants that had completed the task by the given time for each of the three conditions. Note that not all pairs complete the task within 20 minutes.

*263*

# Spatial Resolution in Haptic Rendering

*Contact*
Juli Yamashita
National Institute of Advanced
Industrial Science and
Technology
Tsukuba Central 6
1-1-1, Higashi, Tsukuba-City
Ibaraki 305-8566 Japan
yamashita-juli@aist.go.jp

Yukio Fukui
University of Tsukuba
National Institute of Advanced
Industrial Science and
Technology

Osamu Morikawa
Shigeru Sato
National Institute of Advanced
Industrial Science and
Technology

## Introduction

The effect of spatial resolution in haptic rendering[1] remains to be well understood or studied. How much resolution is actually required? How sensitive are human beings? To answer such questions, we conducted psychophysical experiments to measure absolute thresholds of haptic smoothness in perceiving curved surfaces presented by two point-contact type force feedback devices with different spatial resolutions.

## Experiments

Apparatus: The stimulus (Figure 1) was a polygonal approximation of a cylindrical surface by tangent planes. It was displayed haptically using PHANToM 1.0 T (nominal positional res.: 0.07mm) and A (0.03mm) (SensAble Technologies, Inc.). Subjects touched the stimulus and responded "yes" if they felt it to be a smooth cylindrical surface and "no" if not. Resolution angle $\alpha$ was varied in 1-degree increments and threshold angles of surface smoothness were measured by the method of limits. To avoid the effect of haptic bump mapping, the direction of feedback force was force shaded.[2]

Parameters: radius of stimulus: {30 60, 90, 120} (mm); surface stiffness: 0.5 (N/mm); force shading: {cylindrical, linear}. In the "cylindrical" condition, the feedback force vector magnitude was the surface stiffness (0.5 N/mm) times penetration depth of the cursor into the stimulus (mm), and its direction was that of an actual cylinder. In the "linear" condition, the feedback force vector was a linear interpolation of two vectors to the first and second tangent planes nearest to the cursor (Figure 1). Force applied by subjects was also recorded at several points on the stimulus.

## Results

Figure 2 shows that the threshold angle is positively proportional to the curvature (1/radius) (R=0.7-0.9). The analysis of covariance on their regression lines showed that (1) inclinations do not differ statistically ($p<0.4$); (2) two lines for the linear condition do not differ ($p<0.9$); and (3) line pairs {T-Cyl., A-Cyl.} and {T-Cyl., T-Linear} are different statistically at 1% level. The magnitude of applied force was almost constant over the surface (about 0.7-1.0 N), but depended strongly on the individual subject. It is weakly positively proportional to the radius.

## Discussion

Since the applied force has a constant magnitude, the shape that the subject actually touches should be a "contour surface" for force magnitude F (Figure 3). Let "$d$" be the maximum difference between the contour surface and a cylindrical surface inscribed in it. Figure 4 shows "$d$" calculated for measured threshold angles and their force magnitude. In conditions other than T-Cyl., "$d$" is independent of curvature and nearly equal to 0.1mm. Interestingly, their distribution shown by SD seems to be "digitized" by the spatial resolution of equipment.

## Conclusion and Future Work

When the direction of feedback force is $C^1$ or more continuous, perception of haptic smoothness of a cylindrical surface is defined by the height of "bumps" on the surface, and its absolute threshold is about 0.1 mm. The value is useful for haptic display design and shape simplification. Our future work includes experiments on perceiving doubly curved surfaces and human sensitivity in the time-domain.

*References*
1. Salisbury, K. et al. (1995). Haptic rendering: programming touch interaction with virtual objects. In *ACM Symposium on Interactive 3D Graphics*, 1995.
2. Morgenbesser, H.B. & Srinivasan, M.A. (1996). Force shading for haptic shape perception. In *ASME Dynamics Systems and Control Division*, 1996.

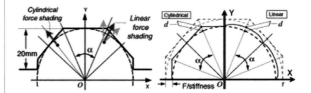

Figure 1. Sectional image of the stimulus. Angle $\alpha$ defines the size of each tangent plane that approximates the cylindrical surface. Black dotes denote cursor positions and dark gray arrows show feedback force directions for Cylindrical (left) and Linear (right) conditions.

Figure 3. Contour surface for a constant force. When the subject touches teh stimulus shape with constant force F, the locus of the cursor follows the surface shown in solid lines.

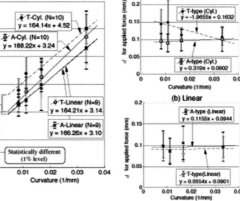

Figure 2. Results (Error bar: SD).

Figure 4. *d* calculated for threshold angle and applied force.

# A Suggestive Interface for 3D Drawing

*Contact*
Takeo Igarashi
Brown University
CS Department, Box 1910
Providence, Rhode Island 02912
USA
takeo@acm.org

John F. Hughes
Brown University

We have designed an interface where users can construct 3D scenes as if they are sketching on paper without searching for editing commands in menus and buttons. Other gestural interfaces[3] have met this goal and have shown that carefully designed gestures can support fluent interaction. What we present here is a new type of interface that enhances gestural interfaces in several ways, using hinting and suggestions.

In the proposed suggestive interface, users give the system hints about the desired operation by highlighting related components in the scene, and the system suggests subsequent operations in an array of small thumbnails derived from the hints and the overall scene configuration (Figure 1). Users can complete an operation by choosing one of these suggestions, or ignore them and continue constructing and/or hinting.

A suggestive interface can be viewed as a mediated version of a gestural interface. Instead of responding to the user's input by updating the scene immediately, the system asks for the user's confirmation after showing multiple suggestions. This approach has several advantages over earlier gestural interfaces. First, the hinting mechanism lets us use existing components as input. This naturally helps in specification of geometric relations among components in the scene. Second, because suggestions are merely offered, a single collection of hints can serve both as a gesture and as a subset of a more complex gesture. Third, the suggestive interface helps the learning process because users can progressively refine their hints until the desired result appears among the suggestions.

## The Chateau System

We have implemented a simple proof-of-concept 3D modeling tool (called Chateau) to explore the suggestive interface idea. Users construct 3D scenes by drawing 2D lines on the screen. The system converts 2D lines on the screen into 3D lines by projecting them onto 3D elements in the scene. Prediction[1] and suggestion facilitate this drawing process by offering possible subsequent operations. Highlighting plays an essential role throughout; highlighted lines guide the snapping during line drawing and provide hints for prediction and suggestions.

Figure 1 shows an example operation sequence. Users first highlight two lines, and the system presents three suggestions (a). Then they choose the first suggestion, which creates a new drawing plane (b). They draw two new lines on the drawing plane, unhighlight the vertical line, and highlight a horizontal line. The system presents three new suggestions based on the three highlighted lines (c). They choose the second suggestion and see the scene shown in (d). In this way, users can construct various 3D scenes by drawing, highlighting, and choosing suggestions with no explicit editing commands.

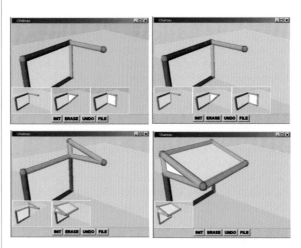

Figure 1. Example operation sequence: (a) highlight two lines; (b) choose the first candidate; (c) after a few drawing and highlighting; (d) choose the second candidate.

Candidates are generated by a set of suggestion engines. Each engine observes the scene, and when the current scene configuration matches its input test pattern, it returns the updated scene as a candidate. The behavior of an individual suggestion engine can be seen as a variation of the constraint-based search-and-replace operation in Chimera,[2] but our engines focus only on the highlighted lines instead of pattern-matching against the entire scene. The current implementation contains 21 suggestion engines, and Figure 2 shows a few examples.

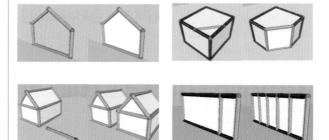

Figure 2. Example of suggestion engines (left: hints, right: result):
(a) highlight two lines; (b) choose the first candidate; (c) after a few drawing and highlighting; (d) choose the second candidate.
(a) polygon in a closed loop; (b) chamfering; (c) block copy; (d) equal division.

*References*
1. Igarashi, T., Matsuoka, S., Kawachiya, S., & Tanaka, H. (1998). Pegasus: A drawing system for rapid geometric design. *CHI'98 Summary*, 24-2.
2. Kurlander, D. & Feiner, S. (1992). Interactive constraint-based search and replace. *Proceedings of CHI'92*, 609-618.
3. Zeleznik, R.C., Herndon, K.P., & Hughes, J.F. (1996). SKETCH: An Interface for Sketching 3D Scenes. *Proceedings of SIGGRAPH 96*, 163-170.

*265*

# "Summer Breeze:" Creating a High-End 3D Movie Using Limited Resources

*Contact*
Yaron Canetti
Sheng-Fang Chen
School of Visual Arts
133 West 21st Street, 10F
New York, New York 10010
USA
yaron@sva.edu

*Cloth Simulations*
Jimmy Chim

*Vegetation*
Anthony Patti

*Collaborators*
Tami Zori, Alen Lai,
Charlotte M. Griffin

Until recently, only a handful of studios could attain a certain degree of complexity in CGI. Working in a high-profile studio with a highly budgeted project has obvious advantages. However, this environment can be limiting, especially in regard to content. We believe that CGI technologies are quickly acquiring a degree of accessibility that will enable individuals to intuitively create sophisticated moving imagery that is competitive with major studios.

The purpose of this sketch is to demonstrate some of the techniques developed during production of "Summer Breeze" (working title), a short animation that is still in production by a group of students at the School of Visual Arts MFA Computer Art Department. These solutions are distinctive in that they were developed by art students, rather than programmers, using only off-the-shelf tools, so the solutions were "artist-friendly" and did not require extensive computer science knowledge.

## The Movie

Our seven minute movie tells the story of a young woman's evolution into an independent person during the course of 24 dramatic hours. The story takes place in a Tuscan village in the 1970s. The visuals re-create the sensual beauty of a place we experienced and bring a warm atmosphere to life, setting the stage for expressive characters to live and unfold their story. Our story is subtle and aimed at adults. Our sources of inspiration are rooted in traditional art and movie-making history. They range from Miyazaki to Degas and Monet, from European comics art to the great tradition of American animation.

The challenges in achieving our artistic vision are many. Most of the past two years were spent on research and development. The School of Visual Arts gave us the space and resources we needed to start realizing this vision and the opportunity to build a versatile and committed team of people who are working without budget and free of commercial constraints.

## The Tools

Technology is becoming more accessible to artists on two fronts: affordability and ease of use. This project cannot be realized without the latest technology available to the artist, and it is dependent on new tools that are yet to be released. However, none of us is a computer engineer. Our technical skills were acquired in conjunction with our artistic goals. We have tried to establish a unique, yet coherent, visual style for both characters and environments while keeping our files efficient and manageable within the limited resources available.

The characters are built to be free-moving and capable of expressing the wide range of feelings that our story evokes. They are fully modeled and textured nude, and their clothing doesn't serve as skin. Instead, clothing is a separate layer, caressing and complementing the body beneath. The environments are modeled and textured with the highest sensitivity to details, but at the same time our files are kept as light as possible.

# Symplectic Ray Tracing: Ray Tracing with Hamiltonian Dynamics in Black-Hole Spacetime

*Contact*
Tetsu Satoh
JST/CREST
tetu-s@is.aist-nara.ac.jp

Haruo Takemura
Naokazu Yokoya
Nara Institute of Science
and Technology

This technical sketch presents symplectic ray tracing, a novel approach to extend ray tracing in curved spacetime with black-holes. In conventional studies of visualizing black-hole spacetime, the path of light is computed by solving geodesic equations numerically. However, ray tracing based on the geodesic equation suffers from some problems concerning computational cost and accuracy of results. In order to overcome such problems, we have developed symplectic ray tracing based on Hamilton's canonical equation instead of the geodesic equation. Hamilton's canonical equation can be numerically solved by a symplectic process suited to long-time computation in black-hole spacetime.

## Symplectic Ray Tracing

Original ray tracing technique[1] traces the light projected from light sources (or a viewpoint), assuming that the path of light draws a straight line. An equation of this straight line is given by:

$$\frac{d^2 x^i}{ds^2} = 0, \qquad (1)$$

where $x^i$ indicates the component of three-dimensional coordinates and $s$ is a parameter of the straight line. In gravitational ray tracing,[2] extended from original raytracing, the following geodesic equation is employed to compute a path of light:

$$\frac{d^2 x^i}{ds^2} + \Gamma^i_{kl} \frac{dx^k}{ds} \frac{dx^l}{ds} = 0, \qquad (2)$$

where $\Gamma^i_{kl}$, called Christoffel's symbol, a function to calculate curvature of space and other variables, is the same as in Eq. (1). By adding the term of $\Gamma^i_{kl}$ to Eq. (1), Eq. (2) have some difficulties as follows. First, Eq. (2) is a second-order nonlinear differential equation of parameter s. Secondly, a suitable numerical method for solving Eq. (2) has been not proposed. Thirdly, it is not easy to concretely derive the geodesic equation of black-hole spacetime. From the above considerations, we propose symplectic ray tracing, is a new ray-tracing method using the following Hamilton's canonical equation instead of the geodesic equation:

$$\begin{cases} \dfrac{dp_i}{ds} = -\dfrac{\partial H}{\partial q_i} \\ \dfrac{dq_i}{ds} = \dfrac{\partial H}{\partial p_i} \end{cases}, \qquad (3)$$

where $q^i$ indicates the component of 4D coordinates, the same as $x^i$ in Eqs. (1) and (2), $p^i$ indicates the momentum of $q^i$, and H (Hamiltonian) is a function of $q^i$ and $p^i$. Note that symplectic ray tracing needs eight-dimensional phase-space constructed of four coordinate components and four momentum components. Compared with Eq. (2), Eq. (3) is a first-order linear differential equation so that the suitable numerical method, symplectic numerical analysis[3] is applicable, and the concrete derivation of Hamilton's canonical equation for the black-hole spacetime is simple. It is especially important to introduce symplectic numerical analysis. Because non-symplectic numerical analyses such as classical Runge-Kutta methods and Euler methods are known to break the energy conservation law, they are not suitable for long-term calculation to trace the light in the universe. The main difference between the proposed and conventional methods for ray tracing in curved spacetime is whether symplectic numerical analysis is applicable or not.

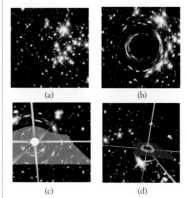

Figure 1. Visualization of a spherically symmetric blackhole: (a) no blackhole; (b) blackhole in the center; (c) superimposing x-y-z axes and x-y plane; (d) volume rendering of scalar curvature as well as three axes.

## Visualization of Black-Hole Spacetime

We assume the universe can be modeled by a sphere and that a black hole is located at the center of the sphere. An image of galaxies[1] (credit: Don Figer and NASA) is mapped on the inside surface of the sphere. An observer is in the celestial sphere. Images perceived by the observer are generated with the proposed method as shown in Figure 1.

Figure 2. Immersive environment for observing a black-hole spacetime.

Because symplectic ray tracing is specialized for the Hamilton system, precise, fast computation is more possible than in conventional ray tracing with the geodesic equation. All images in Figure 1 are rendered on the SGI Onyx2 and Origin2000 with parallel computation by OpenMP. Each rendering took 30-60 minutes using 13 MIPS R10000 CPUs. We have also implemented the method on the cylindrical immersive projection display CYLINDRA( See Figure 2).

*References*
1. Goldstein, R.A. & Nagel, R. (1971). 3-d visual simulation. *Simulation, 23* (6), 25-31.
2. Yamashita, Y. (1989). Computer graphics of black holes: The extension of ray-tracings to 4-dimensional curved space-time. *Trans. Information Processing Society of Japan, 30* (5), 642-651, (in Japanese).
3. Yoshida, H. (1993). Recent progress in the theory and application of symplectic integrators. *Celestial Mechanics and Dynamical Astronomy, 56,* 27-43.

# TANGIBLE COMMUNICATION

*Contact*
KEN-ICHI KAMEYAMA
Toshiba Corporate R&D Center
1, Komukai-toshiba-cho
Saiwai-ku, Kawasaki 212-8582
Japan
+81.44.5492286
kenichi.kameyama@toshiba.co.jp

YASUNOBU YAMAUCHI
Toshiba Corporate R&D Center

In face-to-face communication, we establish mutual understanding and intimate friendship easily and naturally. However, it is not so easy to do the same thing in networked environments. For example, phones or email systems sometimes cause mutual misunderstanding. This is because current systems focus on transmitting only verbal or semantic messages. This sketch shows how to achieve more realistic communication over a narrow network with limited hardware resources like mobile computers. It focuses on developing a virtual handshake and interactive facial image deformation because these are simple but effective techniques for influencing affection.[1]

To produce a virtual handshake, we use small vibrators that represent the grasping motion of another human being. Bend sensors are used to detect handshake action. Figure 1 shows a rear view of the prototype system. About half of its surface is covered by black film backed with sponge, which simulates human skin. The vibrators stimulate hand locations (Figure 1) with very low frequencies. The bend sensors are attached to a soft plastic board at the front of the terminal (Figure 2).

The facial-image deformation algorithm is very simple. It applies the fact that we receive multiple impressions from only a single-fold facial image on paper if we look at it from different angles (Figure 3). Because its deformation can be realized by shearing and changing the ratio of only four stripe sections of the facial image (only four quad polygons), the facial animation can be smoothly updated without a powerful computational environment. The deformation is mapped into a tilt motion in the device. The facial image turns downward if another user tilts the device to the side; it turns right if the user tilts the device to the left, and so on. The image can also be shrunk by the user's handshake motion. To exaggerate the situation, funny paintings are imposed on the image (Figure 2). Sound effects are also added to the image deformation. The quality of the images is not high, but they are sufficient to make communication rich and interesting.

Related works include inTouch,[2] HandJive,[3] and Vibrobod.[4] But our approach is different because we employ multiple modalities. The prototype system is based on a small PC (Pentium II 266MHz), and all the data transmitted among terminal devices are managed by a server PC. Its data transfer rate is only 10KBps even when the facial images are updated every 30 ms.

*References*
1. Basics of Physiology, Vol.1, K. Fujisawa, et. al., Eds. ISBN4-7628-2114, 1998 (in Japanese).
2. Brave, S. & Dahley. A. (1997). inTouch: A medium for haptic interpersonal communication. *CHI'97 Extended Abstracts*, 363-364.
3. Fogg, B., Culter, L., Arnold, P., & Eisbach, C. (1998). HandJive: A device for interpersonal haptic entertainment. *Proceedings CHI'98*, 57-64.
4. Dobson, K., Boyd, D., Ju,W., Donath, J., & Ishii, H. (2001). Creating visceral personal and social interactions in mediated spaces. *CHI'2001 Extended Abstracts*, 151-152.

Figure 1. Rear view of the terminal device.

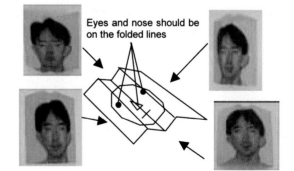

Figure 2. Front view of the terminal device.

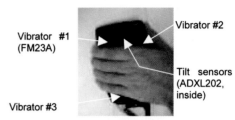

Figure 3. The principle.

268

# Texture and Shape Synthesis on Surfaces

*Contact*
Lexing Ying
NYU Media Research Lab
719 Broadway, 12th Floor
New York, New York 10002
USA
+1.212.998.3389
lexing@mrl.nyu.edu

Aaron Hertzmann
Henning Biermann
Denis Zorin
New York University
www.mrl.nyu.edu/publications
/synthsurf

This sketch presents a novel method for synthesizing functions on surfaces from examples, including various types of textures and displacement maps. Our method synthesizes the function directly on the surface, avoiding many problems of traditional texture mapping. The synthesized results have the same qualitative visual appearance as a texture example provided by the user, without simply tiling the example, and without producing seams or distortion. The method is independent of the surface representation and works on meshes as well as smooth surfaces.

## Synthesis Procedures

Our method generalizes recent image texture synthesis techniques[1,2,4] to surfaces. These algorithms generate each new pixel by matching its texel neighborhoods with the neighborhoods in the example. The center of the closest matching neighborhood is then copied to the target image. We have developed two synthesis procedures:

1. Multiscale synthesis,[4] in which textures are generated from coarse to fine
2. Coherent synthesis,[1] which greedily copies coherent patches from the example image.

We find that the algorithm synthesizes surface textures that are perceptually similar to those produced by their 2D counterparts.

## Neighborhood Sampling

Unlike images, most surfaces of interest lack global parameterization or orientation. We establish orientation on the surface by computing a vector field in advance.[3] This field specifies the correspondence between orientation on the surface and orientation in the example texture. In order to compare surface neighborhoods with image neighborhoods, we first resample the function values on a regular sampling pattern near the surface point. This neighborhood can then be compared to an image neighborhood.

One approach to sampling a regular pattern is to march directly on the surface. However, this method is slow and sensitive to noisy surface features. Our implementation uses predistorted sampling in the parametric domain, which is much faster than surface marching. We synthesize directly to texture or displacement maps, allowing for efficient rendering without extra resampling steps.

## Results

The images shown here demonstrate synthesis of texture, transparency, and displacement maps. They took between one to three minutes each to generate. The source textures are shown next to the resulting surfaces. For more results and details of the algorithm, see: www.mrl.nyu.edu/publications/synthsurf

*References*
1. Ashikhmin, M. (2001). Synthesizing natural textures. I3D 2001.
2. Efros, A. & Leung, T. (1999). Texture synthesis by non-parametric sampling. *ICCV 99*.
3. Hertzmann, A. & Zorin, D. (2000). Illustrating smooth surfaces. *Proceedings of SIGGRAPH 2000*.
4. Wei, L.Y. & Levoy, M. (2000). Fast texture synthesis using tree-structured vector quantization. *Proceedings of SIGGRAPH 2000*.

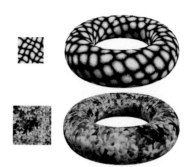

Top: multiscale synthesis; bottom: coherent synthesis.

Synthesis of texture/displacement map.

Sea horse. Synthesis on complex geometry.

Wicker cow: transparency map synthesis.

*269*

*Contact*
**HAN-WEI SHEN**
Department of Computer and
Information Science
The Ohio State University
Columbus, Ohio 43210 USA
hwshen@cis.ohio-state.edu

**XINYUE LI**
Department of Computer and
Information Science
The Ohio State University

Although the speed of volume rendering has significantly increased in the past decade, the size of the average volumetric dataset also continues to grow. The amount of data from a large-scale volume can easily overload underlying computational resources such as CPU speed or texture-memory capacity, which makes interactive volume rendering very difficult. To overcome this challenge, researchers have proposed to use hierarchical rendering algorithms to trade image quality for speed. While effective, most of the existing hierarchical methods rely on the user to make run-time decisions to select appropriate levels of detail. As the speed of volume rendering is a combination effect of 3D projection, transfer function, and visibility, it is a non-trivial task to predict the rendering speed for an arbitrary level of detail in the volume hierarchy. As a result, the quality/speed tradeoff is often done on a trial-and-error basis. For real-time applications such as virtual reality or computer-assisted medical surgery, relying on trial and error to tune the performance is impractical, as these applications require immediate responses, and performance requirements can change very frequently.

In this technical sketch, we present a time-critical volume rendering algorithm to tackle the aforementioned problem. The goal of our algorithm is to alleviate the user's burden of searching the levels of detail that can meet the performance requirement. With our algorithm, the user only needs to specify a desired wall clock time for each frame, and the algorithm will adaptively render data of appropriate resolutions from the volume hierarchy to complete the computation just in time. In addition, our algorithm allows the user to specify regions of interest (ROI) in the underlying volume. This ROI information is taken into account when allocating the computation time budget required to render the volume, so that overall image quality can be maximized.

In general, the run-time performance of hierarchical volume rendering is controlled by an error tolerance. A low error tolerance produces better quality, while a high error tolerance allows a faster rendering speed. We tackle the problem of time-critical volume rendering by designing an automatic error tolerance specification algorithm to guarantee the frame time. To achieve the goal, a feedback control system is constructed to monitor the rendering speed and adjust the error tolerance whenever necessary. We use a divide-and-conquer algorithm to implement the feedback control system. The algorithm starts by subdividing the underlying volume into several subdomains, hereafter called sub-volumes, and splitting the total computation time budget into smaller shares. Each sub-volume is assigned a share of the time budget. Given the subdivision, we feed each sub-volume into a feedback-control loop in a front-to-back depth order and perform a hierarchical rendering for each sub-volume using the corresponding branch in the volume hierarchy. For the first sub-volume, as there is no error tolerance given by the user, an initial guess is used for the rendering. At the end of this rendering, the actual rendering time is fed back to the control unit. With the feedback information, the control unit updates the available computation time and revises a new time budget for each of the remaining sub-volumes. In addition, the control unit estimates a rendering time for the next sub-volume based on the previous rendering result. This estimated rendering time will be compared with the sub-volume's allocated time budget, and the difference is then used to calculate a new error tolerance. This feedback control loop continues until all sub-volumes are rendered.

The key component in our feedback control system is a fuzzy controller that can choose an appropriate error tolerance based on past experience so that the next sub-volume can be rendered at the expected speed. The fuzzy controller adjusts the error tolerance at the end of each feedback iteration based on the difference between the estimated rendering time and the budgeted time for the next sub-volume. Intuitively, if the difference is high, a larger change to the error tolerance will be needed. Otherwise, the control unit will make a small or no change. Exactly how much change is needed is determined by our fuzzy inference rules.

A unique feature of our time-critical algorithm is that it is possible to take into account the importance of the sub-volumes and spend different fractions of the time budget on different sub-volumes. This is done by defining an importance function for the subvolumes and using the importance function to calculate the computation time budget for each sub-volume. We have designed a flexible time-budget allocation algorithm that can take into account multiple factors such as opacities, data errors, or gaze direction to control the rendering algorithm's interactivity.

We have conducted preliminary experiments for the proposed time-critical volume rendering algorithm and received very promising results. We integrated both the software-based ray casting algorithm and 3D texture mapping hardware volume rendering method into our control system. We are able to guarantee a five percent difference between the actual and the desired rendering time. In addition, we are able to accelerate both software and hardware volume rendering and receive high-quality rendering results by allocating more computation time to render important regions. Figure 1 shows two images generated by our time-critical volume rendering algorithm.

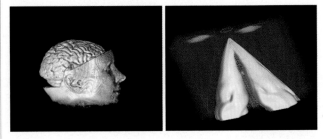

Figure 1.

*Reference*
1. Li, X. & Shen, H.W. (2001) Adaptive volume rendering using fuzzy logic control. Joint Eurographics-IEEE TCVG Symposium on Visualization. May, 2001.

# TREES IN "HOW THE GRINCH STOLE CHRISTMAS:" AUTOMATING THE TASK OF CREATING AND RENDERING LARGE NUMBERS OF COMPLEX OBJECTS

*Contact*
CHARLOTTE MANNING
Digital Domain
300 Rose Avenue
Venice, California 90291 USA
charo@d2.com

Many of the shots in "Dr. Seuss' How the Grinch Stole Christmas" involved partial or entire views of the terrain surrounding Whoville. Since none of the surroundings were built as a set, an entire CG environment had to be constructed so the director could roam through it freely with the camera. This environment had to be highly detailed, it had to be stylized yet photo-realistic, and the pipeline behind it had to be robust enough to handle a large volume of shots. The mountainous terrain had to be populated with tens of thousands of coniferous trees, complete with Seussian curlicues and sprinkled with snow. The trees represented a huge task, because there were so many of them, and they were present in nearly all the outdoor shots. As much as possible, we had to automate and streamline the tree-placement task in all these shots. This was accomplished at three different points in the pipeline: modeling, placement, and rendering.

Automation at the modeling stage was done through procedural modeling with Houdini SOPs. A template network of SOPs was set up for a basic tree, and generating new tree variants was just a matter of making a few adjustments at different points in the SOP network. This was also useful for quickly increasing or decreasing the overall polygonal count of a tree without altering the look. Fifteen different tree types were modeled, each in different resolutions. This may not seem like enough for a whole population of trees, but it turned out to be sufficient when combined with our placement methods.

Placement of the trees was done with an object-instancing system constructed using the SOP network and particle system within Houdini. Each of the various tree models was randomly assigned to a particle-holding random scaling-and-rotation information that would later be translated as a transformation matrix for each tree instance. Although only 15 tree variants were modeled, the random transformations made it look as if all trees were individual and different in some way. Object instancing also greatly reduced the size of the .rib file (only the source models are geometrically defined; each instance then refers back to the original model definition and then applies its own unique transformation). The tree positions were also derived from the particles. Using a copy of the terrain geometry, the particles were manipulated to stick to the surface of the terrain and point upward (within an allowed range of deviation). In nature, trees tend to grow together in clumping patterns. Certain rules were established to cause the particles to stick to the terrain in clumps. Once an initial template system was set up, all the various control parameters could be adjusted for different shots: density, global size, clumpiness, randomness, etc. Setting up a new shot was then only a matter of loading new terrain or swapping out tree models if necessary, adjusting parameters and re-running the simulation.

When the trees were rendered, if the camera was static, regions of trees were classified for low-, medium-, or high-resolution models based on proximity to the camera. However, many of the shots involved a moving camera, so this step had to be automated. This

was accomplished with RenderMan's Level of Detail feature, which involves specifying multiple resolutions of a model ranging from coarse to detailed, and a pixel-projection range for each resolution. The renderer automatically loads the appropriately sized model based on its screen projection. This greatly reducd geometric complexity, and the best performance gain (speed-up factor of 69.4! with 100 MB shaved off the memory consumption) occurred in the worst-case scenario, in which up to 40,000 trees were in frame at one time, many of them with a minute projection area on the image.

Completing the massive task of tree generation in a timely manner required taking these steps to make the pipeline fast, flexible, and user-friendly, so the artists could quickly and efficiently incorporate trees into their assigned shots.

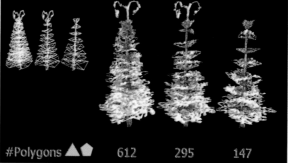

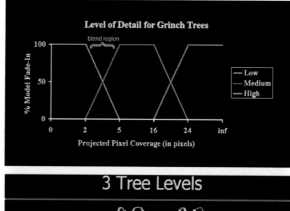

# Using Color-Changing Textiles as a Computer Graphics Display

*Contact*
Lars Erik Holmquist
PLAY research studio
Interactive Institute
Box 620, SE-405 30
Göteborg, Sweden
leh@interactiveinstitute.se
www.playresearch.com/

Linda Melin
PLAY research studio
Interactive Institute

The connection between textiles and computer graphics goes as far back as the early 19th century, when Joseph Jacquard developed punch cards to store textile patterns for weaving on automatic looms (the first digital image format). Surprisingly little has happened in the textile industry since then (punch cards are still widely used), but through the introduction of affordable computer-controlled looms and knitting machines, it is now becoming possible to weave or knit textiles with an ease approaching that of printing computer graphics on paper.

We are using these facilities of modern textile production in conjunction with another development: photochromically treated materials. Companies such as SolarActive (www.solaractiveintl.com) have created threads that change color when subjected to ultraviolet (UV) light (for example, from the rays of the sun or from a special lamp). For instance, a thread might be white in its original state, but change color to an intense blue or red when subjected to UV light. When the UV light is removed, the new color fades away after five to 20 minutes, depending on the material.

In our first experiment, we wove a fabric out of threads with different photochromic properties to create a curtain that would appear white during at night but become colorfully striped when subjected to the rays of the sun.[1] We are now developing ways to selectively turn portions of a fabric's color "on" and "off," much as if they were pixels, to create a dynamic display made entirely of textile. We believe it would be appropriate to use this material to construct displays that are more "calm" or "ambient" than traditional computer displays,[2] (for instance, by creating displays in the form of draperies or tapestries).

Figure 1 shows our first attempt at constructing such a device, where a UV lamp is mounted in a rack so that it can be raised and lowered by a computer-controlled motor. A piece of fabric is attached to the rack, and by moving the lamp, we expose different areas of the fabric to the UV light, thus revealing the "hidden" patterns. The fabric was created from two threads to get a red pattern on a blue background, and to demonstrate how it is now possible to incorporate digital images into textiles, we based the pattern on a version of the Utah teapot downloaded from the Web. This arrangement might be used as a simple ambient information display. For instance, if each teapot is associated with a person in a workgroup, the pots could indicate if the person is online (or perhaps even if the person is having a cup of tea, if that information could be made digitally available using some appropriate sensor technology!). Figure 2 shows another experiment, where we created a pattern that reveals new information when subjected to UV light. First, the textile is shown in its normal state; when it has been subjected to UV light, an additional piece of text becomes visible.

In the future, we intend to extend control over our display, either by adding a second motor, or by introducing a system of several lamps in parallel. We will also experiment with custom-made textile patterns for different types of information. Although these are early steps, we think they indicate one possibility for computer graphics to go beyond current screens and projectors to find new materials and modalities to display computer-generated information and images.

*References*
1. Melin, L. (2001). The information curtain: Creating digital patterns with dynamic textiles. *Extended Abstracts of CHI 2001*, ACM Press, 2001.
2. Wisneski, C., et al. (1998). Ambient displays: Turning architectural space into an interface between people and digital information. In *Proceedings of CoBuild '98*, 22-32, Springer.

Figure 1. A textile is mounted in a wooden rack, and a computer-controlled motor moves a UV lamp over the fabric to create different patterns. The color changes remain visible for 5-10 minutes after the last UV exposure.

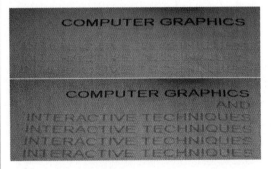

Figure 2. The top image shows another custom-created textile in its initial state; the bottom image shows it after it has been subjected to UV light, revealing additional text woven into the fabric. (The background has also changed color.) The new text remains visible for 5-10 minutes after the UV light has been removed.

# Using Precomputed Cloth Simulations for Interactive Applications

*Contact*
Daniel L. Herman
Pixar Animation Studios
dh@digitalfish.com
www.digitalfish.com

This sketch presents a method for reconstructing the form of cloth dynamically draped on an animated body without the need to run a simulator during animation iteration. The reconstruction is interpolation-based and does not display hysteresis. Because the simulation is run off-line, the technique is suitable for use as a real-time preview mechanism to see roughly how clothing falls on a body while an animator manipulates the body interactively. It would also be useful in other contexts such as games.

## Simulation Sampling

This technique is a hybrid of physically based simulation and kinematic pose-based animation. A computer model (to be used as input to a simulator) is automatically animated through a range of animation control values that fully explore the configuration space through which fast reconstruction is desired. The animation is "paused" (the rate of change in control values is held at zero) at discrete *sample points* that fall on a regular grid in the configuration space. The simulator is run on this animated motion sequence. Simulator output is extracted as a number of *poses*, one at each sample point, indexed with the animation-control values corresponding to that sample point. This yields a lattice of poses embedded in a space whose dimensionality equals the number of exercised animation controls (the dimensionality of the configuration space through which the model was exercised).

Rather than storing cloth poses directly, we compute a difference vector $\mathbf{D}_P$ between the simulated pose and some predictor pose that is easily computed from the animation-control values. $\mathbf{D}_P$ is expressed as per-point offsets relative to the predictor surface, and we store the lattice of $\mathbf{D}_P$'s. A good predictor algorithm is to feed the cloth mesh through the same sequence of deformations that affects the underlying body.

## Pose Reconstruction

Reconstruction involves the synthesis of an output form given a particular setting of animation controls. Each animation control corresponds to an axis in the lattice space. For a lattice of dimension $d$, reconstruction involves multilinear interpolation among the $2^d$ nearest difference vectors, corresponding to the corners of the enclosing $d$-cube in pose space. Thus, reconstruction time depends only on the dimensionality of the space and is $O(2^d)$, which is constant-time relative to the total number of sampled poses $n$ (given that the poses are gridded; ungridded sampling is discussed below). We use the predictor algorithm to generate a predicted form for the current animation control values, then apply the interpolated difference vector to obtain our final cloth geometry. This output exactly recovers the simulated cloth pose at sample points and interpolates nearby poses between sample points.

## Data Representation

Systematic exploration of the pose space can lead to an enormous amount of data. We can take either or both of two strategies to combat this data explosion. The description above assumes we are sampling the space on a rectangular grid, but we could extend this to ungridded sampling, allowing us to selectively add samples wherever in the pose space we need more detail while throwing out samples in areas of the space that won't often be used. Ungridded sampling complicates the reconstruction process, however, as interpolating nearest points involves inserting a new site into the Delauney triangulation of the pose points, which is $O(\sqrt{n})$. However, ungridded sampling potentially allows a dramatic reduction in the total sample points $n$.

Alternatively, we can apply multi-resolution techniques in representing the sample lattice. The difference vectors generally vary by small amounts across local surface regions. We can exploit this to simultaneously reduce our data storage needs while reducing reconstruction cost by representing the pose data with wavelets. We can selectively throw away subtle surface irregularities while retaining major features such as pronounced creases and the general form of the cloth. In fact, this technique gives us a continuous level-of-detail control that trades off reconstruction accuracy for speed and storage.

## Results

The images below show this technique applied to pants on animated legs. Both legs were considered together as a 6-dof articulated figure (2-dof in the hip + 1-dof in the knee, for two legs). Each dof was sampled at three values, giving a total of $3^6 = 729$ sampled poses. The predicted poses were computed by feeding the cloth mesh points through the body deformer network.

On this dataset, the results are very good. However, the rejection of hysteresis is both a strength and a limitation of the system. On a looser-fitting garment that displayed marked hysteresis, it is likely that our reconstruction would significantly misrepresent the actual motion of the simulated cloth.

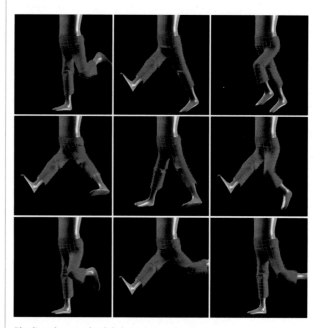

Blue lines show simulated cloth. Magenta surface shows real-time reconstruction. Top row: exact recovery of simulated pose at sample points. Lower rows: approximate recovery via interpolation between sampled poses.

# Variational Classification for Visualization of 3D Ultrasound Data

*Contact*
**Raanan Fattal**
The Hebrew University of
Jerusalem, Israel
raananf@cs.huji.ac.il

**Dani Lischinski**
The Hebrew University
of Jerusalem

Three-dimensional ultrasound (3DUS) is a relatively new technology for imaging distribution of ultrasonic echo information throughout a 3D volume of interest inside a patient. The main advantages of 3DUS over other imaging technologies is that the acquisition procedure is fast, non-invasive, non-radiative, and relatively inexpensive, which enables acquisition to be performed in clinicians' offices.

Unfortunately, compared to other volumetric medical imaging technologies, such as CT and MRI, high-quality visualization of 3DUS datasets is an extremely challenging task, since such datasets typically suffer from considerable noise and speckle, low dynamic range, fuzzy boundaries, and several other problems. These properties make extraction of smooth, or even continuous, surfaces extremely difficult.

In this sketch, we present a new method for opacity classification of 3DUS datasets, which is an essential step for displaying smooth surfaces of interest from volumetric data. Our method is based on the Variational Principle, a mathematical framework for optimization over function spaces. More specifically, we design a functional that imposes several simultaneous requirements on the opacity function. An optimal opacity function that minimizes the integral of the functional over the entire volume is then computed by solving the Euler-Lagrange equation, which in our method gives rise to a large but sparse system of linear equations.

The functional is defined as a weighted sum of three terms. The first term allows the function to attain non-zero values only in areas where the original volume has values near a user-specified isovalue. The second term forces the opacity function gradients to point in the same directions as the gradients of a smoothed version of the original volume. The third term requires the function to have a user-specified non-zero value, whenever possible. In particular, it pulls the function toward this value in areas in which the original volume exhibits high gradients. The resulting optimal opacity function essentially defines soft shells of finite, approximately constant thickness around isosurfaces in the volume. At the same time, the function is smooth and insensitive to noise and speckle in the data. It is also quite sparse (typically over 80 percent of the voxels are zero).

Once the opacity function has been computed, it becomes possible to visualize the corresponding surfaces at interactive rates, using existing techniques, such as Marching Cubes surface extraction or shear-warp volume rendering. Utilizing the sparsity of our opacity function, we also propose a new visualization method, oriented splatting, which associates a single splat polygon (oriented perpendicular to the opacity gradient) with each non-zero opacity voxel. The rasterization and texture mapping hardware is then used to compute the corresponding footprints on the image plane.

Figure 1 shows a visualization of a fetal 3DUS dataset before (left) and after (right) variational classification. Figure 2 shows images of four different 3DUS datasets produced using variational classification and oriented splatting. Such images are generated at interactive rates on today's commodity 3D graphics accelerators.

Additional information can be found at:
www.cs.huji.ac.il/~danix/research/3dus

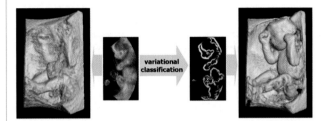

Figure 1. A surface extracted from 3D ultrasound data (left) vs. a surface displayed after variational opacity classification (right).

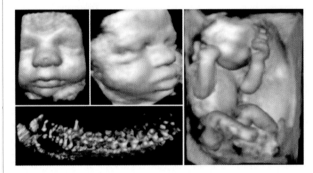

Figure 2. Examples: two different fetal faces (top); a spine (bottom); and an entire fetus (right).

*274*

# VideoFOCUS and VideoFOCUSWire: Transforming Moving Images to Stills

*Contact*
LAURA TEODOSIO
Salient Stills Inc.
268 Summer Street, Sixth Floor
Boston, Massachusetts 02210
USA
teo@salientstills.com

JOANNA BERZOWSKA
Salient Stills Inc.

In the pervasive discussion of media convergence, there is one type that is rarely hyped: the convergence between moving images and still images. Certainly, capture devices are beginning to blur the lines between these types of imagery. The latest video cameras include a still-capture mode, and many still cameras can produce a small digital movie. Editors looking for still images for print or electronic publications are also crossing the boundaries. Still frames from video footage, in particular, are often the only timely source for newsworthy still images.

We present a new model for image acquisition and distribution that uses video and other moving imagery as input. VideoFOCUS is a software environment that allows easy creation of high-quality still imagery from low-resolution moving imagery for use in print or online. And we introduce VideoFOCUSWire, a distributed version for still image creation and dissemination online. The vision is to make high-quality, timely images of all broadcast and video events generally available.

## PROBLEM

When images of a particular event are not yet available or do not exist in photograph form, publications turn to video. But there are many problems with using video for still imagery. The low resolution of video is inappropriate for print publications. Furthermore, there is no efficient method for finding a frame from a moving image sequence that can stand on its own as a still image.

Our goal was to create a system that is simple enough to make high-quality stills from video in the time-critical environment of a newsroom but is also robust and versatile enough to be used by a sophisticated imaging professional.

The result is the VideoFOCUS software. Image quality is addressed by using algorithms to take advantage of the great redundancy in moving-image frames. Images are aligned by sub-pixel optical flow and then statistically combined. By combining the data over frames, we can produce an image with less noise and higher overall resolution than any individual frame.[1]

The software allows monitoring and digitization of video. When capturing to disk, it records every single frame. This large body of data can be browsed in a movie player or as a storyboard of frames at eight different temporal resolutions, providing context from the surrounding frame content. This allows editors to easily find the frame that conveys editorial intent.

The created images can be exported at resolutions appropriate to print media, and they incorporate metadata in the news-industry standard IPTC headers.

## VideoFOCUSWire

To take advantage of the large volume of existing video and film content and to address the issues of rights management and timely distribution, VideoFOCUSWire, a new model for still acquisition, is predicated on archiving, indexing, and dissemination of digital video in near-real time. It will give users access to a previously inaccessible body of video and images made from live broadcast events. By working directly with owners of news, sports, and entertainment video content, VideoFOCUSWire will provide a stream of time-critical still images and video clips to print and online media customers.

VideoFOCUSWire will continuously capture, index, and process licensed content. From a video server, editors can mark interesting video and images. Users then can either select from a pre-edited selection of stills or view a video stream of a live event. While viewing the stream, they can select frames to process using VideoFOCUS algorithms. Services such as user notification of new content, editorial decision-making, and transactions can all be delivered online or via a wireless device. VideoFOCUSWire will also incorporate security features and rights management.

## FUTURE WORK

One can imagine recording devices that would capture enough metadata to make the still extraction process more rapid and automatic. Additionally, we are exploring uses of the system for repurposing film and video content to create still products such as picture books from movies and photo-novelas from soap operas.

## CONTRIBUTORS

Thanks to the many contributors, including: Walter Bender, Matt Antone, George Kierstein, and Jeff Hunter.

*References*
1. Teodosio, L. (1992). Masters thesis, Massachusetts Institute of Technology, September 1992.
2. Teodosio, L. & Bender, W. (1993). Salient video stills: Content and context preserved. *Proceedings of ACM Multimedia*, 1993.
3. Massey, M., & Bender, W. (1996). Salient stills: Process and practice. *IBM Systems Journal*, 1996.

By combining the data over frames, VideoFOCUS can produce an image with less noise and higher overall resolution than any individual frame.

VideoFOCUSWire will allow users to select any frame from a video stream of a live event.

# View-Dependent Texture Mapping of Video for Realistic Avatars in Collaborative Virtual Environments

*Contact*
Vivek Rajan
Electronic Visualization
Laboratory
The University of Illinois
at Chicago
Chicago, Illinois 60607 USA
vrajan@evl.uic.edu

Damin M. Keenan
Daniel J. Sandin
Thomas A. DeFanti
Electronic Visualization
Laboratory
The University of Illinois
at Chicago

Satheesh G. Subramanian
Intel Corporation

Representing human users in virtual environments has always been a challenging problem in collaborative virtual reality applications. Earlier avatar representations use various techniques such as real-time animation of users' facial features, or green/blue screen chroma-keying, or stereo-based methods to retrieve users' video cutouts. The effort required to obtain a good degree of realism was enormous and was dependent on constrained lighting and background to extract the cutout of the user. So these methods were not applicable for situations outside of controlled studio environments or in virtual environments like the CAVE[1] that are inherently dark.

This sketch presents how view-dependent texture mapping[2] can be used to produce realistic avatars and, in the process, eliminate constraints posed by background and lighting requirements. A two-step approach is taken to achieve realistic 3D video avatars using projective texture mapping of video.

## Approach

As a first step, an accurate 3D model of the user's head is obtained using a Cyberware laser scanner. This model is used as the head of the avatar, and the head tracking in the CAVE controls its motion. The coordinate system of the model and the tracker sensor element are aligned manually.

The camera that captures the video of the user is calibrated in the CAVE/tracker space using the method suggested by Tsai.[3] The tracking in the CAVE is exploited to calibrate the camera. Hence the accuracy of the calibration is dependent on the accuracy of the tracking system. With the hybrid tracking systems from Intersense, the accuracy of the tracking and the calibration is very good. Registration of the video image with the head model controls the realism of the final 3D avatar. The registration is not perfect when the user's lips move, since the head model is static. This error in registration is not very noticeable.

The camera is calibrated by tracking an LED in the tracker's coordinate system with its corresponding location on the image. Tracking the LED on the image is easily done using simple computer vision techniques to locate the point of high saturation and hue in the red region. The intrinsic and extrinsic properties of the camera obtained from the camera calibration are used to fix the camera in virtual space as a virtual projector. Since the head model is a reasonably accurate geometric model of the user's head, we can project the video (obtained from the camera) through the virtual projector to obtain a realistic avatar. The need for segmentation of the head from the background is eliminated, since the video is projected only onto the head model. This can be implemented efficiently in real time, as projective texture mapping is a commonly available feature in most polygon graphics hardware.[4]

Transferring whole frames of video can be extremely network-intensive. By sending only the rectangular portion corresponding to a bounding box of video containing the user's head, bandwidth requirements are reduced considerably. The coordinates of this portion can be computed by projecting the corners of the bounding box of the user's head model onto the video image using the camera parameters obtained. Compressing this rectangular portion reduces the bandwidth further.

Using a single camera, the portion of the head facing away from the camera is not texture mapped. To overcome this problem we use another camera that captures the video of the person from another angle, and the video is projected onto the head model from the viewpoint corresponding to the second camera.

The result of the aforementioned method is a realistic video avatar that can be easily used in virtual environments like the CAVE.

*References*
1. Cruz-Neira, C., Sandin, D.J., DeFanti, T.A., Kenyon, R.V., & Hart, J.C. (1992). The CAVE: Audio visual experience automatic virtual environment. *Communications of the ACM, 35* (6), 65-72.
2. Debevec, P.E., Taylor, C.J., & Malik, J. (1996). Modeling and rendering architecture from photographs: A hybrid geometry and imagebased approach. *Proceedings of SIGGRAPH 96*, 11-20.
3. Tsai, R. (1986). An efficient and accurate camera calibration technique for 3D machine vision. In *IEEE CVPR 1986*.
4. Haeberli, P. (1992). Fast shadows and lighting effects using texture mapping. *Proceedings of SIGGRAPH 92*.

3D model of the user's head with the projected video texture.

Closer view of a video avatar.

*Contact*
OLIVER BIMBER
Fraunhofer Institute for
Computer Graphics
obimber@rostock.igd.fhg.de

L. MIGUEL ENCARNAÇÃO
Fraunhofer Center for Research
in Computer Graphics

BERND FRÖHLICH
German National Research
Center for Information
Technology

DIETER SCHMALSTIEG
Vienna University of Technology

## INTRODUCTION AND MOTIVATION

Intuitive access to information in habitual environments is a grand challenge for information technology. An important question is how established and well-functioning everyday environments can be enhanced by rather than replaced with virtual environments. Augmented reality (AR) technology has a lot of potential in this respect, since it allows augmentation of real world environments with computer-generated imagery. Traditional (even see-through) head-mounted AR displays, however, present many shortcomings with respect to unencumbered use, which prohibits them from being seamlessly integrated with habitual environments. In this technical sketch, we describe a new AR display system – the Virtual Showcase (see Figure 1) – and introduce developed real-time rendering and image transformation techniques.

## CONCEPTUAL DESIGN

The Virtual Showcase has the same form factor as a real showcase, so it is compatible with traditional museum displays. Physical scientific and cultural artifacts can be placed inside the Virtual Showcase, where they can share the same space with virtual representations. The showcase's visuals can respond in various ways to a visitor's input. These interactive showcases are an important step in the direction of ambient intelligent landscapes, where the computer acts as an intelligent server in the background and visitors can focus on exploring the exhibited content rather than on operating computers.

## TECHNOLOGICAL SETUP

The Virtual Showcase consists of two main parts: a convex assembly of half-silvered mirrors[1] and a graphics display.[2] So far, we have built two different mirror configurations. Our first prototype consists of four half-silvered mirrors assembled as a truncated pyramid. Our second prototype uses a single mirror sheet to form a truncated cone. These mirror assemblies are placed on top of a projection screen[2] in both setups. Through the half-silvered mirrors, multiple users can see real objects merged with the graphics displayed on the projection screen. The showcase contents are illuminated using a controllable light source,[3] while view-dependent stereoscopic graphics are presented to the observer(s). For our current prototypes, stereo separation and graphics synchronization are achieved using active shutter glasses[5] in combination with infrared emitters,[4] and headtracking is realized using an electro-magnetic tracking device.[6] The cone-shaped prototype is particularly intriguing because it provides a seamless surround view onto the displayed artifact.

This work is supported by the European Union: IST-2001-28610.

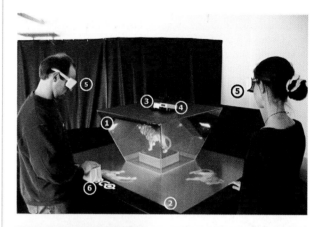

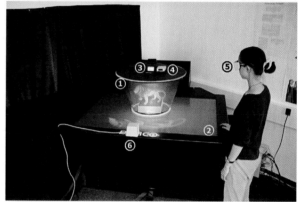

Figure 1. Two different Virtual Showcase configurations: a truncated pyramid (top) and a cone-shaped device (middle/bottom).

# Visual Attention Driven Progressive Rendering for Interactive Walkthroughs

*Contact*
Jörg Haber
Max-Planck-Institut für
Informatik
Saarbrücken, Germany
haberj@mpi-sb.mpg.de

Karol Myszkowski
Hitoshi Yamauchi
Hans-Peter Seidel
Max-Planck-Institut für
Informatik

## Introduction and Overview

Despite of the progress in (graphics) hardware development, interactive walkthroughs in photometrically complex scenes are still a challenging application, if high-quality rendering is required. Since full ray tracing at interactive rates is usually impossible, we render a pre-computed global illumination solution using graphics hardware and use remaining computational power to correct the appearance of non-diffuse objects on the fly. To obtain the best image quality as perceived by a human observer within a limited amount of time for each frame, we control corrective computation of non-diffuse objects according to a computational model of visual attention.

Our multi-threaded implementation consists of one *rendering thread* $T_R$, one *analyzer thread* $T_A$, and one or more *ray tracing threads* $T_{RT_i}$. $T_R$ renders the scene using OpenGL hardware. Non-diffuse objects are rendered simultaneously into the stencil buffer with a unique ID code. The frame buffer is analyzed by $T_A$, and the resulting order of corrections is passed to the $T_{RT_i}$ via a priority queue. Every sample that is computed by one of the $T_{RT_i}$ is sent back to $T_R$, where it is splatted into the frame buffer using a stencil test to ensure that only the corresponding (non-diffuse) object will be affected by this correction.

## Visual Attention Processing

To select and order the non-diffuse objects that need to be corrected, we extend the state-of-the-art model of attention developed by Itti et al.[1] This bottom-up model performs very well for static images and has been soundly validated by its developers in many demanding applications. Every input image is decomposed into a set of channels (intensity, color components), which are further decomposed into eight frequency scales each using Gaussian pyramids. By applying center-surround differences and across-scale normalization, a *saliency map* is generated, which encodes the saliency of objects into grey levels. To take into account the user's volitional focus of attention during interactive walkthroughs, we additionally consider task-driven factors such as distance from image center and pixel coverage for non-diffuse objects. Weighted blending between these top-down components and the saliency obtained from the Itti model results in a *visual-importance priority* assigned to each non-diffuse object.

## Sampling and Splatting

We use a hierarchical image-space sampling scheme to control ray tracing and splat the generated point samples with a square footprint. Due to the layout of the sampling scheme, which is adapted from,[2] the resulting image converges progressively to a ray-traced solution if the viewing parameters remain unchanged. Moreover, a sample cache is used to enhance visual appearance if the time budget for correction has been too low for some frame. We measure the validity of the cached samples based on the deviation of the dot product between the surface normal in the hit point and the current viewing direction with respect to the value of the dot product during sample generation. Valid samples are then reprojected into the current view.

## Results

In our current implementation, we obtain frame rates of about 10 fps on an sgi Onyx3 for interactive walkthroughs in scenes with up to 100,000 primitives of various photometrical complexity such as mirrors, glasses, and glossy objects. We found the predictions of our visual attention model to be usually in good agreement with the user's fixations. We would like to extend our approach using some level-of-detail and occlusion culling techniques to speed up rendering for scenes of higher geometric complexity.

*References*
1. Itti, L., Koch, C., & Niebur, E. (1998). A model of saliency-based visual attention for rapid scene analysis. *Pattern Analysis and Machine Intelligence, 20* (11), 1254-1259.
2. Stamminger, M. & Drettakis, G. (2001). Interactive sampling and rendering for complex and procedural geometry. *Rendering Techniques 2001 (Proceedings 12th EG Workshop on Rendering),* in press.

Different stages of our correction process. Top: An input image showing a view-independent global illumination solution computed in a pre-processing step. Middle: The saliency map resulting from visual-attention processing of the input image. Grey levels encode the saliency of objects. Bottom: A fully converged solution is obtained after corrections have been splatted according to the results of our attention model for about five seconds.

278

WHIPPIN' UP A STORM

*Contact*
ALEX SEIDEN
Cyclotron VFX Studios
220 East 42nd Street
New York, New York 10017
USA
alexs@cyclotronNYC.com

What happens when two crusty old cowboys get hit by a tornado? A furious frenzy of visual effects work, especially when confronted by a looming Super Bowl air date and a dangerously delayed shoot. In only 14 days of CG animation, the team at Cyclotron's VFX studios whipped up a storm.

The rush began with principal photography in late December. Since the schedule didn't permit waiting until the spot was fully edited to start animation, selections for the backgrounds for CG shots were made before the final edit was completed. More than ever, carefully choosing which shots could be accomplished practically, which would need 3D CG, and which could be done with composites was critical.

The effects challenge began in early January. Our tools were Houdini for motion, RenderMan for rendering, and Inferno for compositing. We decided against building a complicated simulation or using any kind of volumetric approach. Our motion systems were relatively coarse (on the order of hundreds of particles, rather than hundreds of thousands); procedural shading filled in fine details.

Our usual procedure is to have our CG technical directors composite their own shots, since they are most familiar with the technical and aesthetic details. Also, the interplay between issues of rendering and compositing is often too tight to make splitting up the different pieces sensible. However, because of the tight time constraints, we had the CG team do rough comps and used our Inferno for the finals.

We deliberately kept the crew small. Although the tendency when deadlines loom is to throw bodies at the problem, we felt that this would only make things slower and more complicated (the "mythical man-month" fallacy).

Cyclotron's team for this project:

*Visual Effects Supervisor*
ALEX SEIDEN

*Visual Effects Producer*
ALICIANE SMYTHE

*Senior Technical Director*
SCOTT PETILL

*Technical Director*
KEVIN GILLEN

*Digital Compositing Artist*
JOANNE UNGAR

*Modeller*
SCOTT FINK

A montage of in-progress images.

279

*Contact*
Don Brutzman
brutzman@nps.navy.mil

Mike Kass
Nicholas Polys

Extensible 3D (X3D) graphics is the XML version of the next-generation VRML 200x specification. X3D-Edit is a free graphics file editor for X3D that enables simple error-free editing, authoring, and validation of X3D or VRML scene- graph files. In this sketch, we show how X3D-Edit has been used to create hundreds of example scenes, including all examples from the VRML 2.0 Sourcebook. We also show how to install and use X3D-Edit. Validation of content before it is published is immensely powerful. Reducing content bugs and eliminating the syntax idiosyncrasies of VRML really helps! Context-sensitive tooltips for every node and attribute in a scene graph have made X3D-Edit an excellent tool for teaching beginning and intermediate 3D graphics.

The Web3D VRML and X3D Conformance Test Suite combine a body of work that originated from the NIST VRML97 Conformance Suite. Those tests are now available in XML format, allowing the tests to evolve with the VRML and X3D specifications. This suite has been developed primarily by the U.S. National Institute for Standards and Technology (NIST) and is now maintained by the nonprofit Web3D Consortium.

The test suite, consisting of approximately 800 tests, allows viewers to evaluate their VRML97 and (in the future) X3D browsers online, by simply browsing through an online directory of documented tests. Tests are broken down by node-group functionality (for example geometry, lights, sounds) and include tests of browser state, field-range testing, audio/graphical rendering, scene-graph state, generated events, and minimum conformance requirements. Each test consists of an XML (X3D) file, its VRML97 equivalent file, and an HTML "pretty print" version of its XML content for inspection. Also included with each test is a complete description of initial conditions of the test and expected results. In addition, "sample results" in the form of JPG or MPG video are also provided via hyperlink to give the tester a complete "picture" of a successful test result.

Because of its simple design and usability, the Web3D VRML/X3D Conformance Test Suite lends itself to easy test submission as well. The future of Web3D testing lies in public, Web-based submission of XML files with a simple test design structure Web-based test reporting is another feature that will be added to this suite in the near future, further empowering people to participate in the evolution of 3D on the Web.

Finally, we present the Web3D X3D Software Development Kit (SDK) CDs (sdk.web3d.org). The kit provides a huge range of content, tools, applications, viewers, and source code. The primary purpose of the SDK is to enable further development of X3D-aware applications and content. The SDK CDs support each of the other X3D presentations at SIGGRAPH 2001. Primary contributions are demonstrated, and free CDs are given to attendees.